→ **Use the Learning Calendar to track your progress through each chapter. Easily see the work you have left to do to master the material and prepare for quizzes and exams.**

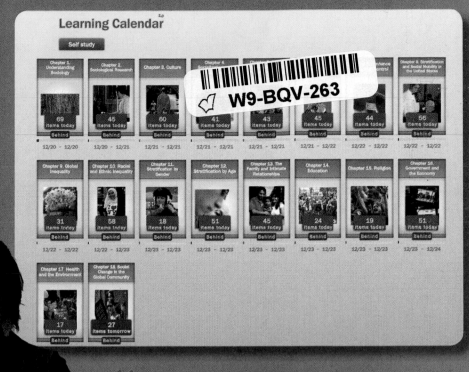

" The LearnSmart modules ask you the same questions in multiple ways so you can understand and actually *learn* the material. "

—*California State University, Dominguez Hills*

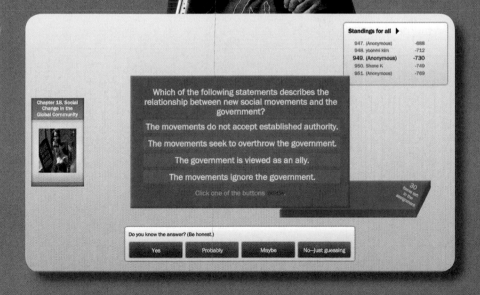

← **Intelligent questioning that adapts to your specific needs, providing a study plan JUST FOR YOU.**

" LearnSmart is an amazing study tool. I wish all of my courses had this online material. "

— *University of Colorado, Denver*

sociology

in modules

sociology
in modules

second edition

Richard T. Schaefer

DEPAUL UNIVERSITY

Mc
Graw
Hill

Connect
Learn
Succeed™

SOCIOLOGY IN MODULES, SECOND EDITION
Published by McGraw-Hill, a business unit of The McGraw-Hill Companies, Inc., 1221 Avenue of the
Americas, New York, NY 10020. Copyright © 2013 by The McGraw-Hill Companies, Inc. All rights reserved.
Printed in the United States of America. Previous edition © 2011. No part of this publication may be reproduced
or distributed in any form or by any means, or stored in a database or retrieval system, without the prior written
consent of The McGraw-Hill Companies, Inc., including, but not limited to, in any network or other electronic
storage or transmission, or broadcast for distance learning.

Some ancillaries, including electronic and print components, may not be available to customers outside the
United States.

This book is printed on acid-free paper.

1 2 3 4 5 6 7 8 9 0 DOW/DOW 1 0 9 8 7 6 5 4 3 2

ISBN 978-0-07-131841-9
MHID 0-07-131841-0

All credits appearing on page or at the end of the book are considered to be an extension of the copyright page.

about the author

Richard T. Schaefer: Professor, DePaul University

B.A. Northwestern University M.A., Ph.D. University of Chicago

Growing up in Chicago at a time when neighborhoods were going through transitions in ethnic and racial composition, Richard T. Schaefer found himself increasingly intrigued by what was happening, how people were reacting, and how these changes were affecting neighborhoods and people's jobs. His interest in social issues caused him to gravitate to sociology courses at Northwestern University, where he eventually received a BA in sociology.

"Originally as an undergraduate I thought I would go on to law school and become a lawyer. But after taking a few sociology courses, I found myself wanting to learn more about what sociologists studied, and fascinated by the kinds of questions they raised." This fascination led him to obtain his MA and PhD in sociology from the University of Chicago. Dr. Schaefer's continuing interest in race relations led him to write his master's thesis on the membership of the Ku Klux Klan and his doctoral thesis on racial prejudice and race relations in Great Britain.

Dr. Schaefer went on to become a professor of sociology, and now teaches at DePaul University in Chicago. In 2004 he was named to the Vincent DePaul professorship in recognition of his undergraduate teaching and scholarship. He has taught introductory sociology for over 35 years to students in colleges, adult education programs, nursing programs, and even a maximum-security prison. Dr. Schaefer's love of teaching is apparent in his interaction with his students. "I find myself constantly learning from the students who are in my classes and from reading what they write. Their insights into the material we read or current events that we discuss often become part of future course material and sometimes even find their way into my writing."

Dr. Schaefer is the author of the thirteenth edition of *Sociology* (McGraw-Hill, 2012), the tenth edition of *Sociology: A Brief Introduction* (McGraw-Hill, 2013), and the sixth edition of *Sociology Matters* (McGraw-Hill, 2013). He is also the author of *Racial and Ethnic Groups,* now in its thirteenth edition (2012), and *Race and Ethnicity in the United States,* seventh edition (2013), both published by Pearson. Together with William Zellner, he coauthored the ninth edition of *Extraordinary Groups,* published by Worth in 2011. Dr. Schaefer served as the general editor of the three-volume *Encyclopedia of Race, Ethnicity, and Society,* published by Sage in 2008. His articles and book reviews have appeared in many journals, including *American Journal of Sociology; Phylon: A Review of Race and Culture; Contemporary Sociology; Sociology and Social Research; Sociological Quarterly;* and *Teaching Sociology.* He served as president of the Midwest Sociological Society in 1994–1995.

Dr. Schaefer's advice to students is to "look at the material and make connections to your own life and experiences. Sociology will make you a more attentive observer of how people in groups interact and function. It will also make you more aware of people's different needs and interests—and perhaps more ready to work for the common good, while still recognizing the individuality of each person."

brief contents

contents

chapter opening excerpts

Every chapter in this textbook begins with an excerpt from one of the works listed here. These excerpts convey the excitement and relevance of sociological inquiry and draw readers into the subject matter from each chapter.

boxed features

Research Today

Sociology in the Global Community

Sociology on Campus

Taking Sociology to Work

trend spotting

social policy sections

maps

Tracking Sociological Perspectives

summing up tables

Modules Work for Instructors & Students

Modules allow you to assign the content you want in the order you prefer and the format promotes student learning and success by presenting content in small, manageable chunks.

Modules Work for **you**

3 Culture

MODULE 9   What Is Culture? 61

MODULE 10   Elements of Culture 64

MODULE 11   Development of Culture around the World 73

MODULE 12   Cultural Variation 77

McGraw Hill create   *Create,* Because Customization Matters.

Finally you have the ability to customize your introductory Sociology course materials to align with your course goals.

- Prefer to cover Deviance in the first few weeks of class? No problem. Just click and rearrange the modules.
- Want additional coverage on Family Relationships? **Easy.** Just search our database to find the best content for your students.
- Don't cover Research Methods in your course? **Simple.** Just omit those modules.

You can also upload your syllabus or any other content you have written to tailor your McGraw-Hill Sociology materials just how you want them, in a snap. Register today at **www.mcgrawhillcreate.com** and craft your course resources to match the way you teach!

| SOCIOLOGY

Sociology in Modules is available to instructors and students in traditional print format as well as online within McGraw-Hill's Connect Sociology, an integrated assignment and assessment platform. Connect Sociology's online tools make managing assignments easier for instructors—and make learning and studying more motivating and efficient for students.

- **LearnSmart** This powerful learning system helps students assess their knowledge of course content through a series of adaptive questions, intelligently pinpointing concepts the student does not understand and mapping out a personalized study plan for success.

- *Investigate Sociology* These engaging, interactive, story-based online activities challenge students to delve deeply into issues of race, class, gender, and culture, giving them the experience of *doing* sociology.

- **Integrated eBook** A fully loaded eBook allows students to review *Sociology in Modules* anytime and anywhere. They can highlight, take notes, and quickly search for key terms and phrases.

- **Real-time Reports** These printable, exportable reports show how well each student (or section) is performing on each course segment. Instructors can use this feature to spot problem areas before they crop up on an exam.

- **Assignable and Assessable Activities** Instructors can easily deliver assignments and tests online, and students can practice skills that fulfill learning objectives at their own pace and on their own schedule.

Experience a new classroom dynamic with *LearnSmart*.

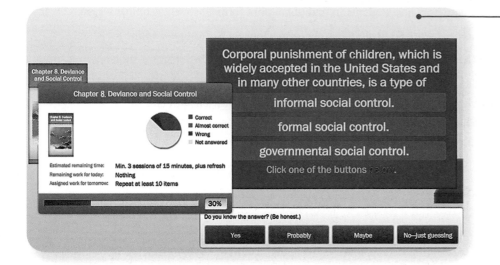

LearnSmart is an adaptive learning system that helps students study efficiently and effectively for greater success. *LearnSmart* intelligently pinpoints concepts students do not understand and maps out personalized study plans that ground students in the fundamentals of sociology, allowing instructors to focus valuable class time on higher-level concepts.

Give students the experience of doing sociology with *Investigate Sociology*.

The engaging, interactive, story-based scenarios in *Investigate Sociology* help students develop their sociological imagination, challenging them to use the lenses of culture, race, class, and gender to delve deeply into significant and timely issues. To complete these scenarios, students study background information, analyze data, conduct interviews, and write up and support their conclusions.

Taking Sociology with You

Sociology in Modules highlights the distinctive way in which sociologists examine human social behavior and how their research findings can be used to understand the broader principles that guide our lives. In doing so, it helps students to begin to think like sociologists and to become capable of using sociological theories and concepts to evaluate human interactions and institutions. In other words, *Sociology in Modules* gives students the tools they need to take sociology with them when they graduate from college, pursue careers, and get involved in their communities and the world at large.

 Use Your Sociological Imagination These short, thought-provoking reflection prompts encourage students to apply the sociological concepts they have learned to the world around them.

 Sociology in the Global Community These segments provide a global perspective on topics such as inequality, marriage, technology use, and the women's movement.

 Sociology on Campus These sections apply a sociological perspective to issues of immediate interest to students, such as impression management on campus, social class, and financial aid.

 Trendspotting These boxes alert students to trends on their campuses and in their communities, viewed through a sociological lens.

Thinking about Movies Two films that underscore chapter themes are featured at the end of each chapter, along with a set of questions that encourage students to use their sociological imagination when viewing movies.

 Taking Sociology to Work These segments underscore the value of an undergraduate degree in sociology by profiling individuals who majored in sociology and now use its principles in their work.

 Research Today These sections present new sociological findings on topics such as online socializing, reality television, and Islam in the United States.

 Social Policy Sections The Social Policy sections play a critical role in helping students to think like sociologists. These sections apply sociological principles and theories to important social and political issues currently being debated by policymakers and the general public. "Take the Issue with You" questions prompt students to consider their own experiences and thoughts regarding the issue.

Take *Sociology in Modules* with you . . . wherever you go

Teaching and Learning with *Sociology in Modules*

Teaching Resources

Instructor's Manual written by Susan Cody-Rydzewski, *Georgia Perimeter College.*

The Instructor's Manual incorporates tips for both new and experienced instructors.

PowerPoint Slides written by Gerry William.

The selections can be used as is or modified to meet the needs of individual instructors.

Test Bank written by Jonathan M. Bullinger.

This resource offers multiple-choice, true or false, and essay questions for each chapter. McGraw-Hill's computerized EZ Test allows the instructor to create customized exams using the publisher's supplied test items or the instructor's own questions. A version of the test bank is also provided in Microsoft Word files for instructors who prefer that format. Additional questions are available for use with in-class clicker systems through the Classroom Performance System (CPS), a wireless polling system that provides immediate feedback from every student in the class. A CPS tutorial is available at www.einstruction.com.

🄣egrity campus

Tegrity Campus is a service that makes class time available all the time by automatically capturing every lecture in a searchable format for students to review when they study and complete assignments.

With a simple one-click start-and-stop process, you capture all computer screens and corresponding audio. Students replay any part of any class with easy-to-use browser-based viewing on a PC or Mac.

With Tegrity Campus, students quickly recall key moments by using Tegrity Campus's unique search feature. This search helps students efficiently find what they need, when they need it across an entire semester of class recordings.

Help turn all your students' study time into learning moments immediately supported by your lecture.

To learn more about Tegrity watch a two-minute Flash demo at **http://tegritycampus.mhhe.com**

Visit **coursesmart.com** to purchase registration codes for this exciting new product.

CourseSmart offers thousands of the most commonly adopted textbooks across hundreds of courses from a wide variety of higher education publishers. It is the only place for faculty to review and compare the full text of a textbook online, providing immediate access without the environmental impact of requesting a printed exam copy. At CourseSmart, students can save up to 50% off the cost of a printed book, reduce their impact on the environment, and gain access to powerful Web tools for learning, including full text search, notes and highlighting, and e-mail tools for sharing notes among classmates. Learn more at **www.coursesmart.com**

● What's New

Module 1: What is Sociology

- Discussion of how different social scientists would study the impact of the global recession that began in 2008
- Discussion of the common misconception that the area bordering Mexico in the southwestern United States is a high-crime area

Module 3: Major Theoretical Perspectives

- Trendspotting box, "The Changing Third Place"
- Research Today box, "Looking at the Gulf Coast Oil Spill from Four Sociological Perspectives"

Module 4: Taking Sociology with You

- Emphasis on the theme "Taking Sociology with You" in the last two sections, Applied and Clinical Sociology and Developing a Sociological Imagination
- Discussion of the Northeast Florida Center for Community Initiatives (CCI), based at the University of North Florida, and its Magnolia Project as examples of applied sociology

Module 5: What Is the Scientific Method?

- Chapter-opening excerpt from *The Tender Cut: Inside the Hidden World of Self-Injury* by Patricia A. Adler and Peter Adler
- Discussion of nonrespondents to the Current Population Survey

Module 6: Major Research Designs

- Discussion of the need to adjust survey questions in response to changes in society
- Coverage of ethnography as a major research design, and observation as one component of ethnography, with cartoon
- Research Today box, "Gender Messages in Scouting"
- Coverage of content analysis of gender stereotyping in children's coloring books, and of television coverage of men's versus women's sports

Module 8: Developments of Methodology

- Discussion of feminist research on self-injury
- Discussion of epidemiologists' use of Google topic searches in tracking the spread of the H1N1 virus
- Discussion of the vastly increased amount of data now available to sociologists and its ethical implications

Module 10: Role of Language

- Sociology in the Global Community box, "Symbolizing 9/11," with photo
- Discussion of value differences in different cultures' views of cram schools
- Figure, "Valuing Ethnicity by Country"

Module 11: Development of Culture around the World

- Use of official responses to the invention of electronic cigarettes as an illustration of culture lag

Module 12: Cultural Variation

- Coverage of countercultural patriot militia groups

Module 13: The Role of Socialization

- Trendspotting on multiple births updated with latest data

Module 15: Agents of Socialization

- New cartoon on social networking

Module 16: Social Interaction and Social Structure

- Taking Sociology to Work box, "Danielle Taylor, Account Manager, Cash Cycle Solutions"
- Research Today box, "Social Networks and Obesity," with figure
- Trendspotting box, "The Growth of Online Societies"
- Case study, "Second Life Virtual World," with Use Your Sociological Imagination exercise

Module 19: Understanding Organizations

- Social Policy section, "Media Concentration"

Module 20: Sociological Perspectives on the Media

- Chapter-opening excerpt from *Alone Together: Why We Expect More from Technology and Less from Each Other,* by Sherry Turkle
- Taking Sociology to Work box, "Lindsey Wallen, Social Media Coordinator, Northwestern University"
- Research Today box, "Inside the Bubble: Internet Search Filters"
- Discussion of the use of the Internet and social media to fuel anti-government protests during the 2011 upheavals in Egypt, Tunisia, Libya, Bahrain, and Syria, with cartoon
- Discussion of the differential impact of online gaming on male and female adolescents

Module 21: The Audience

- Sociology in the Global Community box, "Charity Begins at Home Online"
- Trendspotting box, "Who's on the Internet?"
- Discussion of audience segmentation in the two major political parties' placement of television advertisements during the 2010 midterm elections

Module 22: The Media's Global Reach

- Discussion of how the arrival of television in Brazil's Amazon region created a new social norm, with photo
- Social Policy section on the right to privacy, including discussions of online tracking, the compilation and sale of personal profiles, and the use of such information to deny insurance or employment (called *Weblining*)

Module 25: Crime

- Subsection on hate crime, with figure, "Categorization of Reported Hate Crimes"
- Reorganized section on crime statistics, with subsections on (a) index crimes and victimization surveys, (b) crime trends, and (c) international crime rates.
- Social Policy section on the death penalty, with Mapping Life Worldwide map, "Death Penalty Status by Country"

Module 26: Systems of Stratification

- Chapter-opening excerpt from *What Is Occupy? Inside the Global Movement,* by Rana Foroohar

- Discussion of the crime of trafficking in humans in the subsection on slavery, with table, "Human Trafficking Report"
- Subsection on the supposed existence of class warfare in the United States
- Key term treatment of "conspicuous consumption"

Module 28: Poverty and Social Mobility

- Discussion of the possibility that the recent economic recession may swell the underclass
- Social Policy section, "Executive Compensation," with cartoon

Module 29: Stratification in the World System

- Chapter-opening excerpt from *Portfolios of the Poor: How the World's Poor Live on $2 a Day,* by Daryl Collins
- Trendspotting box, "Feeding the World"
- Revised definition of the key term *world systems analysis*
- Sociology in the Global Community box, "Income Inequality: A Global Perspective"

Module 30: Stratification with Nations: A Comparative Perspective

- In the Social Policy section, discussion of (a) the personal toll of the Greek economic collapse and financial bailout and (b) Europe's shrinking social safety net

Module 31: Minority, Racial, and Ethnic Groups

- Opening excerpt from A Country for All: An Immigrant Manifesto by Jorge Ramos
- Taking Sociology to Work box, "Prudence Hannis, Associate Director, First Nations Post-Secondary Institution, Odanak, Québec"
- Discussion of new state laws requiring voters to show a photo ID as an example of institutional discrimination, with Mapping Life Nationwide map, "Voter ID Requirements"
- Discussion of the 2010 census finding that the majority of all children ages three and under are now either Hispanic or non-White
- Discussion of the finding that in 2009, Asian American men earned slightly more income than White men

Module 32: Sociological Perspectives on Race and Ethnicity

- Discussion of France's expulsion of the ethnic Roma (Gypsies) beginning in 2009
- Coverage of secession as a pattern of intergroup relations
- Figure, "Spectrum of Intergroup Relations"
- Discussion of recent census data on the segregation of U.S. cities, and its implications for Black and Latino households
- Discussion of a study comparing the assimilation of immigrant groups in the United States, Canada, and Europe

Module 33: Race and Ethnicity in the United States

- Research Today box, "Asian Americans: A Model Minority?"
- Subsection on Filipino Americans
- Discussion of recent census findings that from 2000 to 2010, Mexican Americans accounted for 42 percent of the nation's

population growth, and that those who were born in the United States far outnumbered those who immigrated

Module 34: Social Construction of Gender

- Opening excerpt from "Skating Femininity: Gender Maneuvering in Women's Roller Derby," by Nancy J. Finley
- Discussion of the social construction of gender roles and women's rights in Afghanistan

Module 35: Women: The Oppressed Majority

- Discussion of a new World Bank report on the status of the world's women
- Discussion of gender inequality in housework among (a) the rich and the poor, with figure, "Gender Inequality in Housework" and (b) unemployed men and women
- Discussion of research showing small-investor bias against female members of corporate boards of directors
- In the Social Policy section, updated information on (a) U.S. public opinion on abortion, (b) new state restrictions on abortion, and (c) abortion laws in foreign countries

Module 36: Aging and Society

- New opening excerpt from "Shock of Gray" by Ted Fishman

Module 37: Aging Worldwide

- Figure 37-1, "World's Oldest Countries," updated
- New Figure 37-2, "Baby Boomers Eyeing Retirement"
- Up-to-date info on trends such as GLBT elders, working in retirement

Module 38: Age Stratification in the United States

- New figure 38-1, "Percentage of U.S. Population in Selected Age Groups, 1970-2050"
- New movie listing

Module 39: Global View of the Family

- Chapter-opening excerpt from *The Accordion Family: Boomerang Kids, Anxious Parents, and the Private Toll of Global Competition,* by Katherine S. Newman

Module 40: Marriage and Family

- Statistics on interracial and interethnic marriages in the United States
- Discussion of the impact of new media technologies, including the Internet, on the practice of polygyny in Turkey and Morocco
- Discussion of how accordion families differ depending on their social class
- Research Today box, "Transracial Adoption: The Experience of Children from Korea"

Module 42: Human Sexuality

- New module, "Human Sexuality," with subsection, "Labeling and Human Sexuality"
- Research Today box, "Adolescent Sexual Networks," with network diagram

- Mapping Life Nationwide map, "Same-Sex Couples per 1,000 Households"
- Two Use Your Sociological Imagination exercises

Module 43: Sociological Perspectives on Education
- Discussion of a new study showing that the number of years of formal schooling a person receives outweighs race, ethnicity, and gender as a determinant of lifetime earnings, with figure, "Lifetime Earnings by Race, Gender, and Degree Level"
- Trendspotting box, "Rising College Enrollment among Racial and Ethnic Minorities, Women"
- Discussion of the ways in which increased spending on college women's sports since the passage of Title IX has benefited men

Module 44: Schools as Formal Organizations
- Taking Sociology to Work box, "Diane Belcher, Assistant Director of Volunteer Services, New River Community College"
- Social Policy section on charter schools, with (a) Mapping Life Nationwide map, "Charter Schools," and (b) discussion of the failure rate among charter schools

Module 45: The Sociological Approach to Religion
- Discussion of how religious organizations use social media to provide social support to those who identify themselves as religious

Module 46: World Religions
- Figure, "Test Your Religious Knowledge"
- Use Your Sociological Imagination exercise

Module 47: Religious Organization
- Research Today box, "Wicca: Religion or Quasi-Religion?"

Module 48: Government, Power, and Authority
- Chapter-opening excerpt from *The Fair Trade Revolution*, edited by John Bowes, with key term treatment of *fair trade*
- Sociology in the Global Community box, "Sovereignty in the Aloha State"
- Trendspotting box, "Democracy on the Rise?"
- Discussion of the nation-state perspective on the supposed socioeconomic benefits of war
- Taking Sociology to Work box, "Joseph W. Drummond, Management Analyst, U.S. Army Space and Missile Defense Command"
- Updated coverage of terrorism, including cyberattacks
- new key term, "sovereignty movement"

Module 50: Economic Systems
- Discussion of the Cuban government's decision to allow citizens to own small businesses

Module 51: Changing Economies
- Discussion of Apple Computer's use of outsourcing to build its products
- Table, "Occupations Most Vulnerable to Offshoring"
- Social Policy section, "Microfinancing"

Module 53: Social Epidemiology and Health
- Trendspotting box, "Longer Life Spans, More Social Change"
- Mapping Life Nationwide map, "Percentage of Children without Health Insurance"

Module 54: Health Care in the United States
- Research Today box, "Women as Physicians and Surgeons"

Module 55: Sociological Perspectives on the Environment
- Subsection on ecological modernization, with key term treatment
- Expanded discussion of the health costs of unsafe water
- Key term treatment of "environmental refugee"
- Figure, "The Environment versus Energy Production"
- Updated discussion of the conflict perspective on environmentalism

Module 56: Social Movements
- Chapter-opening excerpt from *I Live in the Future and Here's How It Works: Why Your World, Work, and Brain Are Being Creatively Disrupted,* by Nick Bilton
- Discussion of the mobilization of social movements by institutional insiders
- Sociology in the Global Community box, "Women's Social Movements in South Korea and India"
- Key term coverage of "computer-mediated communication"
- Research Today box, "Organizing for Controversy via Computer-Mediated Communication"

Module 57: Social Change
- Trendspotting box, "Social Change and Travel to the United States after 9/11"

Module 58: Global Social Change
- Discussion of the use of cell phones to improve agriculture in developing countries, as an alternative to biotechnology
- New Thinking Critically questions
- Discussion of the role of migrants in facilitating global trade and development in the Social Policy section on transnationals

Acknowledgments

As with the first edition, Elaine Silverstein has played a significant role in the development of my sociology book in the module format.

I deeply appreciate the contributions to this book made by my editors. Development editor Joni Fraser assisted me to make this edition even better than its predecessor. I have received strong support and encouragement from Gina Boedeker, managing director of products and markets and Mary E. Powers, production manager. Additional guidance and support were provided by Toni Michaels, photo researcher; Judy Brody, text permissions editor; Barbara Heinssen, development manager; Matt Busbridge, director; Mutiara Stillman and Emily Moore, editorial coordinators; Trevor Goodman, design manager; and Carey Lange, copy-editor. At DePaul University, assistance was provided by student workers Jessica Chiarella and Kathleen Tallmadge. This edition continues to reflect many insightful suggestions made by reviewers of the thirteen hardcover editions and the ten paperback brief editions. I also continue to benefit from the creative ideas of Rhona Robbin, Director of Development.

I would also like to acknowledge the contributions of the following individuals: Lyn Newhart on the Online Learning Center, John Bullinger for his work on the student study guide and the test bank, Susan Cody-Rydzewski for her work on the instructor's guide, and Gerry Williams for his work on the PowerPoint slides and CPS questions. Kate Scheinman coordinated the development of all supplementary materials. Finally, I would like to thank Peter D. Schaefer, Marymount Manhattan College, for developing the end-of-chapter sections, "Thinking about Movies."

As is evident from these acknowledgments, the preparation of a textbook is truly a collaborative effort. The most valuable member of this effort continues to be my wife, Sandy. She provides the support so necessary in my creative and scholarly activities.

I have had the good fortune to introduce students to sociology for many years. These students have been enormously helpful in spurring on my sociological imagination. In ways I can fully appreciate but cannot fully acknowledge, their questions in class and queries in the hallway have found their way into this work.

Richard T. Schaefer
www.schaefersociology.net
schaeferrt@aol.com

Academic Reviewers

This project has benefited from constructive and thorough evaluations provided by sociologists from both two-year and four-year institutions.

Jennifer Altman, *Middlesex County College*
Michelle Bentz, *Central Community College, Columbus*
Cathy Blair, *Minnesota West Community and Technical College*
Marshall Botkin, *Frederick Community College*
Richard Deutsch, *John A Logan College*
Rose Hunte, *Metro Community College, Fort Omaha*
Bethany Johnson, *Gordon College*
Keith Kerr, *Quinnipiac University*
Joan Luxenburg, *University of Central Oklahoma*
Carla Newman, *El Paso Community College, Valle Verde*
Douglas O'Neill, *South Dakota State University*
Trish Ramirez, *El Paso Community College, Valle Verde*
Lucia Rodriguez, *El Paso Community College, Valle Verde*
David Schjott, *Northwest Florida State College*
Denise Shuster, *Owens Community College*
Monica Sosa, *Tarrant County College, Southeast*
Frank Stanford, *Blinn College, Bryan*
Glen Tolle, *Blinn College, Bryan*
Jonathan Treas, *Wichita State University*
Brent Ur, *Blinn College, Bryan*
Jay Vargas, *Minnesota West Community and Technical College*
Shonda Whetstone, *Blinn College, Bryan*

Connect Consultants

The creation of *Connect Sociology* has been a highly collaborative effort. Thank you to the following for their guidance, insight, and innovative suggestions.

Douglas Adams, *University of Arkansas*
Paul Calarco, *Hudson Valley Community College*
Susan Ciriello, *Northern Virginia Community College*
Susan Cody-Rydzewski, *Georgia Perimeter College*
Lisa Coole, *Bridgewater College*
Gianna Durso Finley, *Mercer County Community College*
Ike Eberstein, *Florida State University*
Erica Hunter, *University at Albany*
Terina Lathe, *Central Piedmont Community College*
Royal Loresco, *South Texas College*
Michael Loukinen, *Northern Michigan University*
Melinda Messineo, *Ball State University*
Narayan Persaud, *Florida A&M University*
Olga Rowe, *Oregon State University*
Alan Rudy, *Central Michigan University*
Megan Seely, *Sierra College*
Tomecia Sobers, *Fayetteville Tech Community College*
Karrie A. Snyder, *Northwestern University*
Margaret Taylor, *Greenville Technical College*

Connect Contributors

These instructors contributed their time, thought, and creativity to make our vision for *Connect Sociology* a reality. Thank you to the following content authors.

Russell Davis, *University of West Alabama*
Shelly Dutchin, *Western Technical College*
Lois Easterday, *Onondaga Community College*
Samuel Echevarria-Cruz, *Austin Community College*
Tammie Foltz, *Des Moines Area Community College*
Kimberly K. Hennessee, *Ball State University*
Thomas Kersen, *Jackson State University*
Laura Johnson, *Southeast Missouri State University*
David Locher, *Missouri Southern State University*
Linda Lombard, *Embry-Riddle Aeronautical University*
Kevin Parent, *Point Park University*
Tommy Sadler, *Union University*
Denise Shuster, *Owens Community College*
Rachel Stehle, *Cuyahoga Community College*
John C. Tenuto, *College of Lake County*
Marie Wallace, *Pima Community College*
Sally Vyain, *Ivy Tech Community College*

Symposia Attendees

Every year McGraw-Hill conducts several Introductory Sociology symposia for instructors from across the country.

These events offer a forum for instructors to exchange ideas and experiences with colleagues they might not have the chance to meet otherwise. They also provide an opportunity for members of the McGraw-Hill team to learn about the needs and challenges of the Introductory Sociology course for both instructors and students. The feedback we have received has been invaluable and contributed—directly and indirectly—to *Sociology in Modules*.

Douglas Adams, *University of Arkansas*
Isaac Addai, *Lansing Community College*
Robert Aponte, *Purdue University*
Sergio Banda, *Fullerton College*
John Batsie, *Parkland College*
Janice Bending, *University of Cincinnati*
Elaine Cannon, *El Camino College*
Nina Chapman, *Golden West College*
Margaret Choka, *Pellissippi State Tech College*
Susan Cody-Rydzewski, *Georgia Perimeter College*
Charles Combs, *Sinclair Community College*
Lisa Coole, *Bridgewater College*
Carolyn Corrado, *University of Albany*
Larry Curiel, *Cypress College*
Scott Davis, *Treasure Valley Community College*
Aimee Dickinson, *Lorain County Community College*
Joe Donnermeyer, *Ohio State University*
Brian Donovan, *University of Kansas*
Gianna Durso-Finley, *Mercer County Community College*
Shelly Dutchin, *Western Technical College*
Ike Eberstein, *Florida State University*
Samuel Echevarria-Cruz, *Austin Community College*
John Ehle, *Northern Virginia Community College*
David Embrick, *Loyola University*
Kathryn Feltey, *University of Akron*
Tammie Foltz, *Des Moines Area Community College*
Sergio Gomez, *Chaffey College*
Kyra Greene, *San Diego State University*
Mike Greenhouse, *Middlesex County College*
Bram Hamovitch, *Lakeland Community College*
Carl Hand, *Valdosta State University*
Garrison Henderson, *Tarrant County College*
Paul Ketchum, *University of Oklahoma*
Steve Keto, *Kent State University*
Brian Klocke, *State University of New York Plattsburgh*
Laura Jamison, *Parkland College*
Jodie Lawston, *DePaul University*
Jason Leiker, *Utah State University*
Joe Lengermann, *University of Maryland*

sociology

in modules

1 Understanding Sociology

No matter where you're going—to work, to study abroad, or just on vacation—you can take sociology and its insights with you.

Today you may have thought about what to wear. But did you ask yourself where those garments came from, or who made them?

Journalist Kelsey Timmerman offers some answers to these questions. His book speaks to the way we see ourselves, not only in the mirror when we're getting dressed, but in the world at large.

❝ I was made in America. My *Jingle These* Christmas boxers were made in Bangladesh.

I had an all-American childhood in rural Ohio. My all-American blue jeans were made in Cambodia.

I wore flip-flops every day for a year when I worked as a SCUBA diving instructor in Key West. They were made in China.

One day while staring at a pile of clothes on the floor, I noticed the tag of my favorite T-shirt: "Made in Honduras."

I read the tag. My mind wandered. A quest was born.

Where am I wearing? It seems like a simple question with a simple answer. It's not.

The question inspired the quest that took me around the globe. It cost me a lot of things, not the least of which was my consumer innocence. Before the quest, I could put on a piece of clothing without reading its tag and thinking about Arifa in Bangladesh or Dewan in China, about their children, their hopes and dreams, and the challenges they face.

Where am I wearing? This isn't so much a question related to geography and clothes, but about the people who make our clothes and the texture of their lives. This quest is about the way *we* live and the way *they* live; because when it comes to clothing, others make it, and we have it made. And there's a big, big difference. . . .

Workers flood the narrow alley beside the Delta Apparel Factory in San Pedro Sula, Honduras. They rush to catch one of the many waiting buses at the highway. Merchants hoping to part them from a portion of their daily earnings—$4 to $5—fight for their attention. Vehicles push through the crowd. A minivan knocks over a girl in her midtwenties and then runs over her foot. She curses, is helped to her feet, and limps onto a waiting bus.

The buildings behind the fence are shaded in Bahamian pastels and very well kept. The shrubs have been recently shaped, and the grass trimmed. In the bright Honduran sun, they seem as pleasant as a factory can get.

The lady at Delta Apparel, based in Georgia, giggled at me on the phone when I told her my plans. She was happy to tell me that their Honduran factory was located in the city of Villanueva just south of San Pedro Sula. She even wished me good luck.

Now that I'm in Honduras, the company doesn't think it's very funny.

I stand among the chaos overwhelmed. A thousand sets of eyes stare at me; perhaps they recognize my T-shirt. The irony that this is Tattoo's tropical paradise wore off long ago—somewhere between the confrontation with the big-bellied guards at the factory gate who had guns shoved down their pants like little boys playing cowboy and the conversation with the tight-lipped company representative who failed to reveal much of anything about my T-shirt or the people who assembled it. There was no way I was getting onto the factory floor. All I learned was that eight humans of indiscriminate age and sex stitched my shirt together in less than five minutes. ❞

Where am I wearing? This isn't so much a question related to geography and clothes, but about the people who make our clothes and the texture of their lives.

(Timmerman 2009:xiii–xiv, 14) Additional information about this excerpt can be found on the Online Learning Center at www.mhhe.com/schaefermod2e.

In his book *Where Am I Wearing? A Global Tour to the Countries, Factories, and People that Make Our Clothes,* Timmerman recounts his travels to the countries where his jeans, T-shirts, and flip-flops—the uniform of today's young adult—were made. From Honduras to Bangladesh, from Cambodia to the United States, he tracked down the factories and befriended the seamstresses who labored there. Timmerman found that garment workers lived in what would be considered substandard conditions in the United States. He argues that global apparel companies should take responsibility for conditions at their suppliers' factories (Fairtrade Foundation 2010).

Timmerman's book focuses on an unequal global economy, which is a central topic in sociology. His investigative work is informed by sociological research that documents the existence and extent of inequality around the world. Social inequality has a pervasive influence on human interactions and institutions.

Although it might be interesting to know how one individual, like Kelsey Timmerman or a foreign factory worker, is affected by social inequality, sociologists consider how entire groups of people and society itself are affected. Sociologists are concerned with what people do as members of a group or in interaction with one another, and what that means for individuals and for society as a whole. For example, sociologists have considered how college students have taken sociology with them, organizing to confront the sportswear companies that underpay the overseas workers who create their team uniforms and T-shirts proclaiming their school pride (Esbenshade 2008; Silverstein 2010).

As a field of study, sociology is extremely broad. You will see throughout this book the range of topics sociologists investigate—from suicide to TV viewing habits, from Amish society to global economic patterns, from peer pressure to genetic engineering. Sociology looks at how others influence our behavior; how major social institutions like the government, religion, and the economy affect us; and how we ourselves affect other individuals, groups, and even organizations.

How did sociology develop? In what ways does it differ from other social sciences? This chapter will explore the nature of sociology as both a field of inquiry and an exercise of the "sociological imagination." We'll look at the discipline as a science and consider its relationship to other social sciences. We'll meet four pioneering thinkers—and examine the theoretical perspectives that grew out of their work. We'll note some of the practical applications for sociological theory and research. Finally, we'll see how sociology helps us to develop a sociological imagination.

MODULE 1   What Is Sociology?

"What has sociology got to do with me or with my life?" As a student, you might well have asked this question when you signed up for your introductory sociology course. To answer it, consider these points: Are you influenced by what you see on television? Do you use the Internet? Did you vote in the last election? Are you familiar with binge drinking on campus? Do you use alternative medicine? These are just a few of the everyday life situations described in this book that sociology can shed light on. But as the opening excerpt indicates, sociology also looks at large social issues. We use sociology to investigate why thousands of jobs have moved from the United States to developing nations, what social forces promote prejudice, what leads someone to join a social movement and work for social change, how access to computer technology can reduce social inequality, and why relationships between men and women in Seattle differ from those in Singapore.

Sociology is, simply, the scientific study of social behavior and human groups. It focuses on social relationships; how those relationships influence people's behavior; and how societies, the sum total of those relationships, develop and change.

● The Sociological Imagination

In attempting to understand social behavior, sociologists rely on a particular type of critical thinking. A leading sociologist, C. Wright Mills, described such thinking as the **sociological imagination**—an awareness of the relationship between an individual and the wider society, both today and in the past (Mills [1959] 2000a). This awareness allows all of us (not just sociologists) to comprehend the links between our immediate, personal social settings and the remote, impersonal social world that surrounds and helps to shape us. Kelsey Timmerman certainly used a sociological imagination when he studied foreign garment workers.

A key element in the sociological imagination is the ability to view one's own society as an outsider would, rather than only from the perspective of personal experiences and cultural biases. Consider something as simple as sporting events. On college campuses in the United States, thousands of students cheer well-trained football players. In Bali, Indonesia, dozens of spectators gather around a ring to cheer on roosters trained in cockfighting. In both instances, the spectators debate the merits of their favorites and bet on the outcome of the events. Yet what is considered a normal sporting event in one part of the world is considered unusual in another part.

The sociological imagination allows us to go beyond personal experiences and observations to understand broader public issues. Divorce, for example, is unquestionably a personal hardship for a husband and wife who split apart. However, C. Wright Mills advocated using the sociological imagination to view divorce not as simply an individual's personal problem but rather as a societal concern. Using this perspective, we can see that an increase in the divorce rate actually redefines a major social institution—the family. Today's households frequently include stepparents and half-siblings whose parents have divorced and remarried. Through the complexities of the blended family, this private concern becomes a public issue that affects schools, government agencies, businesses, and religious institutions.

The sociological imagination is an empowering tool. It allows us to look beyond a limited understanding of human behavior to see the world and its people in a new way and through a broader lens than we might otherwise use. It may be as simple as understanding why a roommate prefers country music to hip-hop, or it may open up a whole different way of understanding other populations in the world. For example, in the aftermath of the terrorist attacks on the United States on September 11, 2001, many citizens wanted to understand how Muslims throughout the world perceived their country, and why. From time to time this textbook will offer you the chance to exercise your sociological imagination in a variety of situations.

Sociology is the scientific study of social behavior and human groups.

🔆 use your **sociological imagination**

You are walking down the street in your city or hometown. In looking around you, you can't help noticing that half or more of the people you see are overweight. How do you explain your observation? If you were C. Wright Mills, how do you think you would explain it?

● Sociology and the Social Sciences

Is sociology a science? The term **science** refers to the body of knowledge obtained by methods based on systematic observation. Just like other scientific disciplines, sociology involves the organized, systematic study of phenomena (in this case, human behavior) in order to enhance understanding. All scientists, whether studying mushrooms or murderers, attempt to collect precise information through methods of study that are as objective as possible. They rely on careful recording of observations and accumulation of data.

Of course, there is a great difference between sociology and physics, between psychology and astronomy. For this reason, the sciences are commonly divided into natural and social sciences. **Natural science** is the study of the physical features of nature and the ways in which they interact and change. Astronomy, biology, chemistry, geology, and physics are all natural sciences. **Social science** is the study of the social features of humans and the ways in which they interact and change. The social sciences include sociology, anthropology, economics, history, psychology, and political science.

These social science disciplines have a common focus on the social behavior of people, yet each has a particular orientation. Anthropologists usually study past cultures and preindustrial societies that continue today, as well as the origins of humans. Economists explore the ways in which people produce and exchange goods and services, along with money and other resources. Historians are concerned with the peoples and events of the past and their significance for us today. Political scientists study international relations, the workings of government, and the exercise of power and authority. Psychologists investigate personality and individual behavior. So what do *sociologists* focus on? They study the influence that society has on people's attitudes and behavior and the ways in which people interact and shape society. Because humans are social animals, sociologists examine our social relationships scientifically. The range of the relationships they investigate is vast, as the current list of sections in the American Sociological Association suggests (Table 1-1).

Let's consider how different social scientists might study the impact of the global recession that began in 2008. Historians would stress the pattern of long-term fluctuations in world markets. Economists would discuss the roles played by government, the private sector, and the world monetary system. Psychologists would study individual cases of emotional stress among workers, investors, and business owners. And political scientists would study the degree of cooperation among nations—or lack of it—in seeking economic solutions.

What approach would sociologists take? They might note a change in marital patterns in the United States. Since the recession began, the median age of first marriage has risen to 28.7 years for men and 26.7 years for women. Sociologists might also observe that today, fewer people are making that trip to the altar than in the past. If the U.S. marriage rate had remained the same as it was in 2006, about 4 million more Americans would have married by 2010.

Similarly, sociologists might evaluate the recession's impact on education. In the United States, private school enrollment from elementary through high school declined from 13.6 percent in 2006 to 12.8 percent in 2010 as families cut back on nonessential expenditures. Sociologists might even consider the recession's effect on environmental actions, such as carpooling. In all but 1 of the 50 largest metropolitan areas in the United States (New Orleans), the percentage of working people aged 16 to 64 dropped significantly during the recession. When friends and co-workers are laid off, carpools shrink and more people end up driving to work alone (El Nasser and Overberg 2011).

Sociologists would take a similar approach to studying episodes of extreme violence. In April 2007, just as college students were beginning to focus on the impending end of the semester,

Table 1-1 Sections of the American Sociological Association

Aging and the Life Course	Environment and Technology	Peace, War, and Social Conflict
Alcohol, Drugs, and Tobacco	Ethnomethodology and Conversation Analysis	Political Economy of the World-System
Altruism, Morality and Social Solidarity	Evolution, Biology, and Sociology	Political Sociology
Animals and Society	Family	Population
Asia and Asian America	Global and Transnational Sociology	Race, Gender, and Class
Body and Embodiment	History of Sociology	Racial and Ethnic Minorities
Children and Youth	Human Rights	Rationality and Society
Collective Behavior and Social Movements	International Migration	Religion
Communication and Information Technologies	Labor and Labor Movements	Science, Knowledge, and Technology
Community and Urban Sociology	Latino/a Sociology	Sex and Gender
Comparative and Historical Sociology	Law	Sexualities
Consumers and Consumption	Marxist Sociology	Social Psychology
Crime, Law, and Deviance	Mathematical Sociology	Sociological Practice and Public Sociology
Culture	Medical Sociology	Teaching and Learning
Development	Mental Health	Theory
Disability and Society	Methodology	
Economic Sociology	Organizations, Occupations, and Work	
Education		
Emotions		

The range of sociological issues is very broad. For example, sociologists who belong to the Animals and Society section of the ASA may study the animal rights movement; those who belong to the Sexualities section may study global sex workers or the gay, bisexual, and transgendered movements. Economic sociologists may investigate globalization or consumerism, among many other topics.

Source: American Sociological Association 2012.

Think about It

Which of these topics do you think would interest you the most? Why?

tragedy struck on the campus of Virginia Tech. In a two-hour shooting spree, a mentally disturbed senior armed with semi-automatic weapons killed a total of 32 students and faculty at Virginia's largest university. Observers struggled to describe the events and place them in some social context. For sociologists in particular, the event raised numerous issues and topics for study, including the media's role in describing the attacks, the presence of violence in our educational institutions, the gun control debate, the inadequacy of the nation's mental health care system, and the stereotyping and stigmatization of people who suffer from mental illness.

Besides doing research, sociologists have a long history of advising government agencies on how to respond to disasters. Certainly the poverty of the Gulf Coast region complicated the huge challenge of evacuation in 2005. With

Katrina bearing down on the Gulf Coast, thousands of poor inner-city residents had no automobiles or other available means of escaping the storm. Added to that difficulty was the high incidence of disability in the area. New Orleans ranked second among the nation's 70 largest cities in the proportion of people

As the nation struggled to recover from a deep and lengthy recession, recently laid-off workers jostled the long-term unemployed at a crowded job fair in San Francisco. Sociologists use a variety of approaches to assess the full impact of economic change on society.

over age 65 who are disabled—56 percent. Moving wheelchair-bound residents to safety requires specially equipped vehicles, to say nothing of handicap-accessible accommodations in public shelters. Clearly, officials must consider these factors in developing evacuation plans (Bureau of the Census 2005b).

Sociological analysis of the disaster did not end when the floodwaters receded. Long before residents of New Orleans staged a massive anticrime rally at City Hall in 2007, researchers were analyzing resettlement patterns in the city. They noted that returning residents often faced bleak job prospects. Yet families who had stayed away for that reason often had trouble enrolling their children in schools unprepared for an influx of evacuees. Faced with a choice between the need to work and the need to return their children to school, some displaced families risked sending their older children home alone. Meanwhile, opportunists had arrived to victimize unsuspecting homeowners. And the city's overtaxed judicial and criminal justice systems, which had been understaffed before Katrina struck, had been only partially restored. All these social factors led sociologists and others to anticipate the unparalleled rise in reported crime the city experienced in 2006 and 2007 (Jervis 2008; Sarah Kaufman 2006).

Throughout this textbook, you will see how sociologists develop theories and conduct research to study and better understand societies. And you will be encouraged to use your sociological imagination to examine the United States (and other societies) from the viewpoint of a respectful but questioning outsider.

Sociology and Common Sense

Sociology focuses on the study of human behavior. Yet we all have experience with human behavior and at least some knowledge of it. All of us might well have theories about why people become homeless, for example. Our theories and opinions typically come from common sense—that is, from our experiences and conversations, from what we read, from what we see on television, and so forth.

In our daily lives, we rely on common sense to get us through many unfamiliar situations. However, this commonsense knowledge, while sometimes accurate, is not always reliable, because it rests on commonly held beliefs rather than on systematic analysis of facts. It was once considered common sense to accept that the earth was flat—a view rightly questioned by Pythagoras and Aristotle. Incorrect commonsense notions are not just a part of the distant past; they remain with us today.

Contrary to the common notion that women tend to be chatty compared to men, for instance, researchers have found little difference between the sexes in terms of their talkativeness. Over a five-year period they placed unobtrusive microphones on 396 college students in various fields, at campuses in Mexico as well as the United States. They found that both men and women spoke about 16,000 words per day (Mehl et al. 2007).

Similarly, common sense tells us that today, violent crime holds communities on the border between the United States and Mexico in a kind of death grip, creating an atmosphere of lawlessness reminiscent of the old Wild West. Based on televised news stories and on concerns expressed by elected officials throughout the southwestern United States, this assertion may sound reasonable;

however, it is not true. Although some communities in Mexico have fallen under the control of drug cartels, the story is different on the U.S. side of the border. All available crime data—including murder, extortion, robbery, and kidnapping rates, whether reported or documented in victim surveys—show that in the hundred-mile-deep border area stretching from San Diego to Brownsville, Texas, crime rates are significantly lower than in similar U.S. cities outside the area. Furthermore, the crime rate has been dropping faster near the border than in other similar-size U.S. communities for at least the last 15 years (Gillon 2011; Gomez et al. 2011).

Like other social scientists, sociologists do not accept something as a fact because "everyone knows it." Instead, each piece of information must be tested and recorded, then analyzed in relation to other data. Sociologists rely on scientific studies in order to describe and understand a social environment. At times, the findings of sociologists may seem like common sense, because they deal with familiar facets of everyday life. The difference is that such findings have been *tested* by researchers. Common sense now tells us that the earth is round, but this particular commonsense notion is based on centuries of scientific work that began with the breakthroughs made by Pythagoras and Aristotle.

◼ What Is Sociological Theory?

Why do people commit suicide? One traditional common-sense answer is that people inherit the desire to kill themselves. Another view is that sunspots drive people to take their lives. These explanations may not seem especially convincing to contemporary researchers, but they represent beliefs widely held as recently as 1900.

Sociologists are not particularly interested in why any one individual commits suicide; they are more concerned with identifying the social forces that systematically cause some people to take their own lives. In order to undertake this research, sociologists develop a theory that offers a general explanation of suicidal behavior.

We can think of theories as attempts to explain events, forces, materials, ideas, or behavior in a comprehensive manner. In sociology, a **theory** is a set of statements that seeks to explain problems, actions, or behavior. An effective theory may have both explanatory and predictive power. That is, it can help us to see the relationships among seemingly isolated phenomena, as well as to understand how one type of change in an environment leads to other changes.

The World Health Organization (2010) estimates that almost a million people die from suicide every year. More than a hundred years ago, a sociologist tried to look at suicide data scientifically. Émile Durkheim ([1897] 1951) developed a highly original theory about the relationship between suicide and social factors. Durkheim was primarily concerned not with the personalities of individual suicide victims, but rather with suicide rates and how they varied from country to country. As a result, when he looked at the number of reported suicides in France, England, and Denmark in 1869, he also noted the total population of each country in order to determine the rate of suicide in each nation. He found that whereas England had only

67 reported suicides per million inhabitants, France had 135 per million and Denmark had 277 per million. The question then became "Why did Denmark have a comparatively high rate of reported suicide?"

Durkheim went much deeper into his investigation of suicide rates. The result was his landmark work *Suicide,* published in 1897. Durkheim refused to accept unproved explanations regarding suicide, including the beliefs that inherited tendencies or cosmic forces caused such deaths. Instead, he focused on social factors, such as the cohesiveness or lack of cohesiveness of religious, social, and occupational groups.

Durkheim's research suggested that suicide, although it is a solitary act, is related to group life. He found that people without religious affiliations had a higher suicide rate than those who were affiliated; the unmarried had much higher rates than married people; and soldiers had a higher rate than civilians. In addition, there seemed to be higher rates of suicide in times of peace than in times of war and revolution, and in times of economic instability and recession rather than in times of prosperity. Durkheim concluded that the suicide rates of a society reflected the extent to which people were or were not integrated into the group life of the society.

Émile Durkheim, like many other social scientists, developed a theory to explain how individual behavior can be understood within a social context. He pointed out the influence of groups and societal forces on what had always been viewed as a highly personal act. Clearly, Durkheim offered a more *scientific* explanation for the causes of suicide than that of inherited tendencies or sunspots. His theory has predictive power, since it suggests that suicide rates will rise or fall in conjunction with certain social and economic changes.

Of course, a theory—even the best of theories—is not a final statement about human behavior. Durkheim's theory of suicide is no exception. Sociologists continue to examine factors that contribute to differences in suicide rates around the world and to a particular society's rate of suicide. In Las Vegas, for example, sociologists have observed that the chances of dying by suicide are strikingly high—twice as high as in the United States as a whole.

Noting Durkheim's emphasis on the relationship between suicide and social isolation, researchers have suggested that Las Vegas's rapid growth and constant influx of tourists have undermined the community's sense of permanence, even among longtime residents. Although gambling—or more accurately, losing while gambling—may seem a likely precipitating factor in suicides there, careful study of the data has allowed researchers to dismiss that explanation. What happens in Vegas may stay in Vegas, but the sense of community cohesiveness that the rest of the country enjoys may be lacking (Wray et al. 2008, 2011).

MODULE 1 Recap and Review

Summary

Sociology is the scientific study of social behavior and human groups. In this module, we examine the nature of sociological theory and the work of some of the founders of the discipline.

1. The **sociological imagination** is an awareness of the relationship between an individual and the wider society. It is based on the ability to view our own society as an outsider might, rather than from the perspective of our limited experiences and cultural biases.

2. In contrast to other **social sciences,** sociology emphasizes the influence that groups can have on people's behavior and attitudes and the ways in which people shape society.

3. Knowledge that relies on common sense is not always reliable. Sociologists must test and analyze each piece of information they use.

4. Sociologists employ **theories** to examine relationships between observations or data that may seem completely unrelated.

Thinking Critically

1. What aspects of the social and work environment in a fast-food restaurant would be of particular interest to a sociologist? How would the sociological imagination help in analyzing the topic?

2. Can you think of any explanation, other than lack of community, for the high suicide rate in Las Vegas? Does that explanation agree with Durkheim's theory?

3. Think about the sociologists profiled in this module, Mills and Durkheim. Whose work seems most relevant to today's social problems? Why did you choose that thinker, and which social problems were you thinking of?

Key Terms

Natural science 6
Science 6
Social science 6
Sociological imagination 5
Sociology 5
Theory 5

People have always been curious about sociological matters—how we get along with others, what we do for a living, whom we select as our leaders. Philosophers and religious authorities of ancient and medieval societies made countless observations about human behavior. They did not test or verify those observations scientifically; nevertheless, their observations often became the foundation for moral codes. Several of these early social philosophers correctly predicted that a systematic study of human behavior would emerge one day. Beginning in the 19th century, European theorists made pioneering contributions to the development of a science of human behavior.

Early Thinkers

Auguste Comte

The 19th century was an unsettling time in France. The French monarchy had been deposed in the revolution of 1789, and Napoleon had suffered defeat in his effort to conquer Europe. Amid this chaos, philosophers considered how society might be improved. Auguste Comte (1798–1857), credited with being the most influential of the philosophers of the early 1800s, believed that a theoretical science of society and a systematic investigation of behavior were needed to improve society. He coined the term *sociology* to apply to the science of human behavior.

Writing in the 1800s, Comte feared that the excesses of the French Revolution had permanently impaired France's stability. Yet he hoped that the systematic study of social behavior would eventually lead to more rational human interactions. In Comte's hierarchy of the sciences, sociology was at the top. He called it the "queen," and its practitioners "scientist-priests." This French theorist did not simply give sociology its name; he presented a rather ambitious challenge to the fledgling discipline.

Harriet Martineau

Scholars learned of Comte's works largely through translations by the English sociologist Harriet Martineau (1802–1876). But Martineau was a pathbreaker in her own right: she offered insightful observations of the customs and social practices of both her native Britain and the United States. Martineau's book *Society in America* ([1837] 1962) examined religion, politics, child rearing, and immigration in the young nation. It gave special attention to social class distinctions and to such factors as gender and race. Martineau ([1838] 1989) also wrote the first book on sociological methods.

Martineau's writings emphasized the impact that the economy, law, trade, health, and population could have on social problems. She spoke out in favor of the rights of women, the emancipation of slaves, and religious tolerance. Later in life, deafness did not keep her from being an activist. In Martineau's ([1837] 1962) view, intellectuals and scholars should not simply offer observations of social conditions; they should *act* on their convictions in a manner that will benefit society. That is why Martineau conducted research on the nature of female employment and pointed to the need for further investigation of the issue (Deegan 2003; Hill and Hoecker-Drysdale 2001).

Herbert Spencer

Another important early contributor to the discipline of sociology was Herbert Spencer (1820–1903). A relatively prosperous Victorian Englishman, Spencer (unlike Martineau) did not feel compelled to correct or improve society; instead, he merely hoped to understand it better. Drawing on Charles Darwin's study *On the Origin of Species,* Spencer applied the concept of evolution of the species to societies in order to explain how they change, or

Harriet Martineau, an early pioneer of sociology who studied social behavior both in her native England and in the United States, proposed some of the methods still used by sociologists.

evolve, over time. Similarly, he adapted Darwin's evolutionary view of the "survival of the fittest" by arguing that it is "natural" that some people are rich while others are poor.

Spencer's approach to societal change was extremely popular in his lifetime. Unlike Comte, Spencer suggested that since societies are bound to change eventually, one need not be highly critical of present social arrangements or work actively for social change. This viewpoint appealed to many influential people in England and the United States who had a vested interest in the status quo and were suspicious of social thinkers who endorsed change.

Émile Durkheim

Émile Durkheim made many pioneering contributions to sociology, including his important theoretical work on suicide. The son of a rabbi, Durkheim (1858–1917) was educated in both France and Germany. He established an impressive academic reputation and was appointed one of the first professors of sociology in France. Above all, Durkheim will be remembered for his insistence that behavior must be understood within a larger social context, not just in individualistic terms.

To give one example of this emphasis, Durkheim ([1912] 2001) developed a fundamental thesis to help explain all forms of society. Through intensive study of the Arunta, an Australian tribe, he focused on the functions that religion performed and underscored the role of group life in defining what we consider to be religion. Durkheim concluded that like other forms of group behavior, religion reinforces a group's solidarity.

Another of Durkheim's main interests was the consequences of work in modern societies. In his view, the growing division of labor in industrial societies, as workers became much more specialized in their tasks, led to what he called "anomie." **Anomie** refers to the loss of direction felt in a society when social control of individual behavior has become ineffective. Often, the state of anomie occurs during a time of profound social change, when people have lost their sense of purpose or direction. In a period of anomie, people are so confused and unable to cope with the new social environment that they may resort to suicide.

Durkheim was concerned about the dangers that alienation, loneliness, and isolation might pose for modern industrial societies. He shared Comte's belief that sociology should provide direction for social change. As a result, he advocated the creation of new social groups—mediators between the individual's family and the state—that would provide a sense of belonging for members of huge, impersonal societies. Unions would be an example of such groups.

Like many other sociologists, Durkheim did not limit his interests to one aspect of social behavior. Later in this book we will consider his thinking on crime and punishment, religion, and the workplace. Few sociologists have had such a dramatic impact on so many different areas within the discipline.

Max Weber

Another important early theorist was Max Weber (pronounced VAY-ber). Born in Germany, Weber (1864–1920) studied legal and economic history, but gradually developed an interest in sociology. Eventually, he became a professor at various German universities. Weber taught his students that they should employ **verstehen** (pronounced fair-SHTAY-en), the German word for "understanding" or "insight," in their intellectual work. He pointed out that we cannot analyze our social behavior by the same type of objective criteria we use to measure weight or temperature. To fully comprehend behavior, we must learn the subjective meanings people attach to their actions—how they themselves view and explain their behavior.

For example, suppose that a sociologist was studying the social ranking of individuals in a fraternity. Weber would expect the researcher to employ *verstehen* to determine the significance of the fraternity's social hierarchy for its members. The researcher might examine the effects of athleticism or grades or social skills or seniority on standing within the fraternity. He or she would seek to learn how the fraternity members relate to other members of higher or lower status. While investigating these questions, the researcher would take into account people's emotions, thoughts, beliefs, and attitudes (L. Coser 1977).

We also owe credit to Weber for a key conceptual tool: the ideal type. An **ideal type** is a construct or model for evaluating specific cases. In his works, Weber identified various characteristics of bureaucracy as an ideal type (discussed in detail in Module 19). In presenting this model of bureaucracy, Weber was not describing any particular organization, nor was he using the term *ideal* in a way that suggested a positive evaluation. Instead, his purpose was to provide a useful standard for measuring how bureaucratic an actual organization is (Gerth and Mills 1958). Later in this book, we will the concept of *ideal type* to study the family, religion, authority, and economic systems, as well as to analyze bureaucracy.

Although their professional careers coincided, Émile Durkheim and Max Weber never met and probably were unaware of each other's existence, let alone ideas. Such was not true of the work of Karl Marx. Durkheim's thinking about the impact of the division of labor in industrial societies was related to Marx's writings, while Weber's concern

FIGURE 2-1 **Contributors to Sociology**

	Émile Durkheim 1858–1917	Max Weber 1864–1920	Karl Marx 1818–1883	W. E. B. DuBois 1868–1963
Academic training	Philosophy	Law, economics, history, philosophy	Philosophy, law	Sociology
Key works	1893—*The Division of Labor in Society* 1897—*Suicide: A Study in Sociology* 1912—*Elementary Forms of Religious Life*	1904–1905—*The Protestant Ethic and the Spirit of Capitalism* 1921—*Economy and Society*	1848—*The Communist Manifesto* 1867—*Das Kapital*	1899—*The Philadelphia Negro* 1903—*The Negro Church* 1903—*Souls of Black Folk*

for a value-free, objective sociology was a direct response to Marx's deeply held convictions. Thus, it is not surprising that Karl Marx is viewed as a major figure in the development of sociology, as well as several other social sciences (Figure 2-1).

Karl Marx

Karl Marx (1818–1883) shared with Durkheim and Weber a dual interest in abstract philosophical issues and the concrete reality of everyday life. Unlike them, however, Marx was so critical of existing institutions that a conventional academic career was impossible. He spent most of his life in exile from his native Germany.

Marx's personal life was a difficult struggle. When a paper he had written was suppressed, he fled to France. In Paris, he met Friedrich Engels (1820–1895), with whom he formed a lifelong friendship. The two lived at a time when European and North American economic life was increasingly dominated by the factory rather than the farm.

While in London in 1847, Marx and Engels attended secret meetings of an illegal coalition of labor unions known as the Communist League. The following year they prepared a platform called *The Communist Manifesto,* in which they argued that the masses of people with no resources other than their labor (whom they referred to as the *proletariat*) should unite to fight for the overthrow of capitalist societies. In the words of Marx and Engels:

> The history of all hitherto existing society is the history of class struggles. . . . The proletarians have nothing to lose but their chains. They have a world to win. WORKING MEN OF ALL COUNTRIES, UNITE! (Tucker 1978:473, 500).

After completing *The Communist Manifesto,* Marx returned to Germany, only to be expelled. He then moved to England, where he continued to write books and essays. Marx lived there

in extreme poverty; he pawned most of his possessions, and several of his children died of malnutrition and disease. Marx clearly was an outsider in British society, a fact that may well have influenced his view of Western cultures.

In Marx's analysis, society was fundamentally divided between two classes that clashed in pursuit of their own interests. When he examined the industrial societies of his time, such as Germany, England, and the United States, he saw the factory as the center of conflict between the exploiters (the owners of the means of production) and the exploited (the workers). Marx viewed these relationships in systematic terms; that is, he believed that a system of economic, social, and political relationships maintained the power and dominance of the owners over the workers. Consequently, Marx and Engels argued that the working class should overthrow the existing class system. Marx's influence on contemporary thinking has been dramatic. His writings inspired those who would later lead communist revolutions in Russia, China, Cuba, Vietnam, and elsewhere.

Even apart from the political revolutions that his work fostered, Marx's significance is profound. Marx emphasized the *group* identifications and associations that influence an *individual's* place in society. This area of study is the major focus of contemporary sociology. Throughout this textbook, we will consider how membership in a particular gender classification, age group, racial group, or economic class affects a person's attitudes and behavior. In an important sense, we can trace this way of understanding society back to the pioneering work of Karl Marx.

W. E. B. DuBois

Marx's work encouraged sociologists to view society through the eyes of those segments of the population that rarely influence decision making. In the United States, some early Black sociologists, including W. E. B. DuBois (1868–1963), conducted research that they hoped would assist in the struggle for a racially egalitarian society. DuBois (pronounced doo-BOYSS) believed that knowledge was essential in combating prejudice and achieving tolerance and justice. Sociologists, he contended, needed to draw on scientific principles to study social problems such as those experienced by Blacks in the United States. To separate opinion from fact, he advocated basic research on the lives of Blacks. Through his in-depth studies of urban life, both White and Black, in cities such as Philadelphia and Atlanta, DuBois ([1899] 1995) made a major contribution to sociology.

Like Durkheim and Weber, DuBois saw the importance of religion to society. However, he tended to focus on religion at the community level and the role of the church in the lives of its members ([1903] 2003). DuBois had little patience with theorists such as Herbert Spencer, who seemed content with the status quo. He believed that the granting of full political rights to Blacks was essential to their social and economic progress.

Because many of his ideas challenged the status quo, DuBois did not find a receptive audience within either the government or the academic world. As a result, he became increasingly involved with organizations whose members questioned the established social order. In 1909 he helped to found the National Association for the Advancement of Colored People, better known today as the NAACP (Wortham 2008).

DuBois's insights have been lasting. In 1897 he coined the term **double consciousness** to refer to the division of an individual's identity into two or more social realities. He used the term to describe the experience of being Black in White America. Today, an African American holds the most powerful office in the nation, president of the United States. Yet for millions of African Americans, the reality of being Black in the United States typically is not one of power (DuBois [1903] 1961).

◉ Twentieth-Century Developments

Sociology today builds on the firm foundation developed by Émile Durkheim, Max Weber, Karl Marx, and W. E. B. DuBois. However, the field certainly has not remained stagnant over the past hundred years. While Europeans have continued to make contributions to the discipline, sociologists from throughout the world and especially the United States have advanced sociological theory and research. Their new insights have helped us to better understand the workings of society.

Charles Horton Cooley

Charles Horton Cooley (1864–1929) was typical of the sociologists who came to prominence in the early 1900s. Born in Ann Arbor, Michigan, Cooley received his graduate training in economics but later became a sociology professor at the University of Michigan. Like other early sociologists, he had become interested in this new discipline while pursuing a related area of study.

Cooley shared the desire of Durkheim, Weber, and Marx to learn more about society. But to do so effectively, he preferred to use the sociological perspective to look first at smaller units—intimate, face-to-face groups such as families, gangs, and

friendship networks. He saw these groups as the seedbeds of society, in the sense that they shape people's ideals, beliefs, values, and social nature. Cooley's work increased our understanding of groups of relatively small size.

Jane Addams

In the early 1900s, many leading sociologists in the United States saw themselves as social reformers dedicated to systematically studying and then improving a corrupt society. They were genuinely concerned about the lives of immigrants in the nation's growing cities, whether those immigrants came from Europe or from the rural American South. Early female sociologists, in particular, often took active roles in poor urban areas as leaders of community centers known as *settlement houses.* For example, Jane Addams (1860–1935), a member of the American Sociological Society, cofounded the famous Chicago settlement called Hull House.

Addams and other pioneering female sociologists commonly combined intellectual inquiry, social service work, and political activism—all with the goal of assisting the underprivileged and creating a more egalitarian society. For example, working with the Black journalist and educator Ida Wells-Barnett, Addams successfully prevented racial segregation in the Chicago public schools. Addams's efforts to establish a juvenile court

Jane Addams (right) was an early pioneer both in sociology and in the settlement house movement. She was also an activist for many causes, including the worldwide campaign for peace.

system and a women's trade union reveal the practical focus of her work (Addams 1910, 1930; Deegan 1991; Lengermann and Niebrugge-Brantley 1998).

By the middle of the 20th century, however, the focus of the discipline had shifted. Sociologists for the most part restricted themselves to theorizing and gathering information; the aim of transforming society was left to social workers and activists. This shift away from social reform was accompanied by a growing commitment to scientific methods of research and to value-free interpretation of data. Not all sociologists were happy with this emphasis. A new organization, the Society for the Study of Social Problems, was created in 1950 to deal more directly with social inequality and other social problems.

Robert Merton

Sociologist Robert Merton (1910–2003) made an important contribution to the discipline by successfully combining theory and research. Born to Slavic immigrant parents in Philadelphia, Merton won a scholarship to Temple University. He continued his studies at Harvard, where he acquired his lifelong interest in sociology. Merton's teaching career was based at Columbia University.

Merton (1968) produced a theory that is one of the most frequently cited explanations of deviant behavior. He noted different ways in which people attempt to achieve success in life. In his view, some may deviate from the socially approved goal of accumulating material goods or the socially accepted means of achieving that goal. For example, in Merton's classification scheme, *innovators* are people who accept the goal of pursuing material wealth but use illegal means to do so, including robbery, burglary, and extortion. Although Merton based his explanation of crime on individual behavior that has been influenced by society's approved goals and means, it has wider applications. His theory helps to account for the high crime rates among the nation's poor, who may see no hope of advancing themselves through traditional modes of success. Module 24 discusses Merton's theory in greater detail.

Merton also emphasized that sociology should strive to bring together the *macro-level* and *micro-level* approaches to the study of society. **Macrosociology** concentrates on large-scale phenomena or entire civilizations. Émile Durkheim's cross-cultural study of suicide is an example of macro-level research. More recently, macrosociologists have examined international crime rates (see Module 25) and the stereotype of Asian Americans as a "model minority" (see Module 33). In contrast, **microsociology** stresses the study of small groups, often through experimental means.

Sociological research on the micro level has included studies of how divorced men and women disengage from significant social roles (see Module 10) and of how a teacher's expectations can affect a student's academic performance (see Module 42).

Pierre Bourdieu

Increasingly, scholars in the United States have been drawing on the insights of sociologists in other countries. The ideas of the French sociologist Pierre Bourdieu (1930–2002) have found a broad following in North America and elsewhere. As a young man, Bourdieu did fieldwork in Algeria during its struggle for independence from France. Today, scholars study Bourdieu's research techniques as well as his conclusions.

Bourdieu wrote about how capital in its many forms sustains individuals and families from one generation to the next. To Bourdieu, *capital* included not just material goods, but cultural and social assets. **Cultural capital** refers to noneconomic goods, such as family background and education, which are reflected in a knowledge of language and the arts. Not necessarily book knowledge, cultural capital refers to the kind of education that is valued by the socially elite. Though a knowledge of Chinese cuisine is culture, for example, it is not the prestigious kind of culture that is valued by the elite. In the United States, immigrants—especially those who arrived in large numbers and settled in ethnic enclaves—have generally taken two or three generations to develop the same level of cultural capital enjoyed by more established groups. In comparison, **social capital** refers to the collective benefit of social networks, which are built on reciprocal trust. Much has been written about the importance of family and friendship networks in providing people with an opportunity to advance. In his emphasis on cultural and social capital, Bourdieu's work extends the insights of early social thinkers such as Marx and Weber (Bourdieu and Passerson 1990; Field 2008).

Today sociology reflects the diverse contributions of earlier theorists. As sociologists approach such topics as divorce, drug addiction, and religious cults, they can draw on the theoretical insights of the discipline's pioneers. A careful reader can hear Comte, Durkheim, Weber, Marx, DuBois, Cooley, Addams, and many others speaking through the pages of current research. Sociology has also broadened beyond the intellectual confines of North America and Europe. Contributions to the discipline now come from sociologists studying and researching human behavior in other parts of the world. In describing the work of these sociologists, it is helpful to examine a number of influential *theoretical perspectives,* also known as *approaches* or *views*.

MODULE 2 | Recap and Review

Summary

The thinkers who founded the discipline of sociology and developed it in the 19th and 20th centuries were reacting to the social world in which they lived.

1. Nineteenth-century thinkers who contributed sociological insights included Auguste Comte, a French philosopher; Harriet Martineau, an English sociologist; and Herbert Spencer, an English scholar.

2. Other important figures in the development of sociology were Émile Durkheim, who pioneered work on suicide; Max Weber, who taught the need for insight in intellectual work; Karl Marx, who emphasized the importance of the economy and social conflict; and W. E. B. DuBois, who advocated for the usefulness of basic research in combating prejudice and fostering racial tolerance and justice.

3. In the 20th century, the discipline of sociology was indebted to the U.S. sociologists Charles Horton Cooley and Robert Merton, as well as to the French sociologist Pierre Bourdieu.

4. **Macrosociology** concentrates on large-scale phenomena or entire civilizations; **microsociology** stresses the study of small groups.

Thinking Critically

1. Consider the work of early sociologists such as Comte and Martineau. What social problems were they reacting to? To what extent have those problems been rectified today?

2. How is 19th-century industrialization related to the development of sociological thought?

3. What are some examples of social and cultural capital that you possess?

Key Terms

Anomie 11

Cultural capital 14

Double consciousness 13

Ideal type 11

Macrosociology 14

Microsociology 14

Social capital 14

Verstehen 11

MODULE 3 | Major Theoretical Perspectives

Sociologists view society in different ways. Some see the world basically as a stable and ongoing entity. They are impressed with the endurance of the family, organized religion, and other social institutions. Other sociologists see society as composed of many groups in conflict, competing for scarce resources. To still other sociologists, the most fascinating aspects of the social world are the everyday, routine interactions among individuals that we sometimes take for granted. These three views, the ones most widely used by sociologists, are the functionalist, conflict, and interactionist perspectives. Together, these approaches will provide an introductory look at the discipline.

Functionalist Perspective

Think of society as a living organism in which each part of the organism contributes to its survival. This view is the **functionalist perspective,** which emphasizes the way in which the parts of a society are structured to maintain its stability.

Talcott Parsons (1902–1979), a Harvard University sociologist, was a key figure in the development of functionalist theory. Parsons was greatly influenced by the work of Émile Durkheim, Max Weber, and other European sociologists. For more than four decades, he dominated sociology in the United States with his advocacy of functionalism. Parsons saw any society as a vast network of connected parts, each of which helps to maintain the system as a whole. His approach, carried forward by German sociologist Niklas Luhmann (1927–1998), holds that if an aspect of social life does not contribute to a society's stability or survival—if it does not serve some identifiably useful function or promote value consensus among members of society—it will not be passed on from one generation to the next (Joas and Knöbl 2009; Knudsen 2010).

Let's examine an example of the functionalist perspective. Many Americans have difficulty understanding the Hindu prohibition against slaughtering cows (specifically, zebu). Cattle browse unhindered through Indian street markets, helping themselves to oranges and mangoes while people bargain for the little food they can afford. What explains this devotion to the cow in the face of human deprivation—a devotion that appears to be dysfunctional?

The simple explanation is that cow worship is highly functional in Indian society, according to economists, agronomists, and social scientists who have studied the matter. Cows perform two essential tasks: plowing the fields and producing milk. If eating beef were permitted, hungry families might be tempted to slaughter their cows for immediate consumption, leaving themselves without a means of cultivation. Cows also produce dung, which doubles as a fertilizer and a fuel for cooking. Finally, cow meat sustains the neediest group in society, the *Dalit*, or untouchables, who sometimes resort to eating beef in secrecy. If eating beef were socially acceptable, higher-status Indians would no doubt bid up its price, placing it beyond the reach of the hungriest.

Manifest and Latent Functions

A college catalog typically states various functions of the institution. It may inform you, for example, that the university intends to "offer each student a broad education in classical and contemporary thought, in the humanities, in the sciences, and in the arts." However, it would be quite a surprise to find a catalog that declared, "This university was founded in 1895 to assist people in finding a marriage partner." No college catalog will declare this as the purpose of the university. Yet societal institutions serve many functions, some of them quite subtle. The university, in fact, *does* facilitate mate selection.

Robert Merton (1968) made an important distinction between manifest and latent functions. **Manifest functions** of institutions are open, stated, and conscious functions. They involve the intended, recognized consequences of an aspect of society, such as the university's role in certifying academic competence and excellence. In contrast, **latent functions** are unconscious or unintended functions that may reflect hidden purposes of an institution. One latent function of universities is to hold down unemployment. Another is to serve as a meeting ground for people seeking marital partners.

Dysfunctions

Functionalists acknowledge that not all parts of a society contribute to its stability all the time. A **dysfunction** refers to an element or process of a society that may actually disrupt the social system or reduce its stability.

Cows (zebu), considered sacred in India, wander freely through this city, respected by all who encounter them. The sanctity of the cow is functional in India, where plowing, milking, and fertilizing are far more important to subsistence farmers than a diet that includes beef.

We view many dysfunctional behavior patterns, such as homicide, as undesirable. Yet we should not automatically interpret them in this way. The evaluation of a dysfunction depends on one's own values, or as the saying goes, on "where you sit." For example, the official view in prisons in the United States is that inmate gangs should be eradicated because they are dysfunctional to smooth operations. Yet some guards have come to view prison gangs as a functional part of their jobs. The danger posed by gangs creates a "threat to security," requiring increased surveillance and more overtime work for guards, as well as requests for special staffing to address gang problems (G. Scott 2001).

▊ Conflict Perspective

Where functionalists see stability and consensus, conflict sociologists see a social world in continual struggle. The **conflict perspective** assumes that social behavior is best understood in terms of tension between groups over power or the allocation of resources, including housing, money, access to services, and political representation. The tension between competing groups need not be violent; it can take the form of labor negotiations, party politics, competition between religious groups for new members, or disputes over the federal budget.

Throughout most of the 1900s, the functionalist perspective had the upper hand in sociology in the United States. However, the conflict approach has become increasingly pervasive since the late 1960s. The widespread social unrest resulting from battles over civil rights, bitter divisions over the war in Vietnam, the rise of the feminist and gay liberation movements, the Watergate political scandal, urban riots, confrontations at abortion clinics, and shrinking economic prospects for the middle class have offered support for the conflict approach—the view that our social world is characterized by continual struggle between competing groups. Currently, the discipline of sociology accepts conflict theory as one valid way to gain insight into a society.

The Marxist View

As we saw earlier, Karl Marx viewed struggle between social classes as inevitable, given the exploitation of workers that he perceived under capitalism. Expanding on Marx's work, sociologists and other social scientists have come to see conflict not merely as a class phenomenon but as a part of everyday life in all societies. In studying any culture, organization, or social group, sociologists want to know who benefits, who suffers, and who dominates at the expense of others. They are concerned with the conflicts between women and men, parents and children, cities and suburbs, Whites and Blacks, to name only a few. Conflict theorists are interested in how society's institutions—including the family, government, religion, education, and the media—may help to maintain the privileges of some groups and keep others in a subservient position. Their emphasis on social change and the redistribution of resources makes conflict theorists more radical and activist than functionalists (Dahrendorf 1959).

The Feminist Perspective

Sociologists began embracing the feminist perspective only in the 1970s, although it has a long tradition in many other disciplines. The **feminist perspective** sees inequity in gender as central to all behavior and organization. Because it focuses clearly on one aspect of inequality, it is often allied with the conflict perspective. Proponents of the feminist view tend to focus on the macro level, just as conflict theorists do. Drawing on the work of Marx and Engels, contemporary feminist theorists often view women's subordination as inherent in capitalist societies. Some radical feminist theorists, however, view the oppression of women as inevitable in *all* male-dominated societies, whether capitalist, socialist, or communist.

An early example of this perspective (long before the label came into use by sociologists) can be seen in the life and writings of Ida Wells-Barnett (1862–1931). Following her groundbreaking publications in the 1890s on the practice of lynching Black Americans, she became an advocate in the women's rights campaign, especially the struggle to win the vote for women. Like feminist theorists who succeeded her, Wells-Barnett used her analysis of society as a means of resisting oppression. In her case, she researched what it meant to be Black, a woman in the United States, and a Black woman in the United States (Giddings 2008; Wells-Barnett 1970).

Those who take the Marxist view ask "Who benefits, who suffers, and who dominates?" How would a Marxist analyze the situation at this homeless encampment in Reno, Nevada?

Ida Wells-Barnett explored what it meant to be female and Black in the United States. Her work established her as one of the earliest feminist theorists.

Feminist scholarship has broadened our understanding of social behavior by extending the analysis beyond the male point of view. Consider sports, for example. Feminist theorists consider how watching or participating in sports reinforces the roles that men and women play in the larger society:

- Although sports generally promote fitness and health, they may also have an adverse effect on participants' health. Men are more likely to resort to illegal steroid use (among bodybuilders and baseball players, for example); women, to excessive dieting (among gymnasts and figure skaters, for example).

- Gender expectations encourage female athletes to be passive and gentle, qualities that do not support the emphasis on competitiveness in sports. As a result, women find it difficult to enter sports traditionally dominated by men, such as Indy or NASCAR.

- Although professional women athletes' earnings are increasing, they typically trail those of male athletes.

 use your **sociological imagination**

You are a sociologist who takes the conflict perspective. How would you interpret the practice of prostitution? How would your view of prostitution differ if you took the functionalist perspective? The feminist perspective?

Interactionist Perspective

Workers interacting on the job, encounters in public places like bus stops and parks, behavior in small groups—all these aspects of microsociology catch the attention of interactionists. Whereas functionalist and conflict theorists both analyze large-scale, society-wide patterns of behavior, theorists who take the **interactionist perspective** generalize about everyday forms of social interaction in order to explain society as a whole. Today, given rising concern over the cost and availability of gas, interactionists have begun to study a form of commuter behavior called "slugging." To avoid driving to work, commuters gather at certain preappointed places to seek rides from complete strangers. When a driver pulls into the parking area or vacant lot and announces his destination, the first slug in line who is headed for that destination jumps in. Rules of etiquette have emerged to smooth the social interaction between driver and passenger: neither the driver nor the passenger may eat or smoke; the slug may not adjust the windows or radio or talk on a cell phone. The presence of the slugs, who get a free ride, may allow the driver to use special lanes reserved for high-occupancy vehicles (Slug-Lines.com 2011).

Interactionism (also referred to as *symbolic interactionism*) is a sociological framework in which human beings are viewed as living in a world of meaningful objects. Those "objects" may include material things, actions, other people, relationships, and even symbols. Interactionists see symbols as an especially important part of human communication (thus the term *symbolic* interactionism). Symbols have a shared social meaning that is understood by all members of a society. In the United States, for example, a salute symbolizes respect, while a clenched fist signifies defiance. Another culture might use different gestures to convey a feeling of respect or defiance. These types of symbolic interaction are classified as forms of **nonverbal communication,** which can include many other gestures, facial expressions, and postures (Masuda et al. 2008).

Manipulation of symbols can be seen in dress codes. Schools frown on students who wear clothes displaying messages that appear to endorse violence or drug and alcohol consumption. Businesses stipulate the attire employees are allowed to wear on the job in order to impress their customers or clients. In 2005, the National Basketball Association (NBA) adopted a new dress code for the athletes who play professional basketball—one that involved not the uniforms they wear on court, but the clothes they wear off court on league business. The code requires "business casual attire" when players are representing the league. Indoor sunglasses, chains, and sleeveless shirts are specifically banned (Crowe and Herman 2005:A23).

While the functionalist and conflict approaches were initiated in Europe, interactionism developed first in the United States. George Herbert Mead (1863–1931) is widely regarded as the founder of the interactionist perspective. Mead taught at the University of Chicago from 1893 until his death. As his teachings have become better known, sociologists have expressed greater interest in the interactionist perspective. Many have moved away from what may have been an excessive preoccupation with the macro (large-scale) level of social behavior and have redirected their attention toward behavior that occurs on the micro (small-scale) level.

Erving Goffman (1922–1982) popularized a particular type of interactionist method known as the **dramaturgical approach,** in which people are seen as theatrical performers. The dramaturgist compares everyday life to the setting of the theater and stage. Just as actors project certain images, all of us seek to present particular features of our personalities while we hide other features. Thus, in a class, we may feel the need to project a serious image; at a party, we may want to look relaxed and friendly.

The Sociological Approach

Which perspective should a sociologist use in studying human behavior? Functionalist? Conflict? Interactionist? Feminist? We simply cannot squeeze all sociological thinking into three or four theoretical categories—or even ten, if we include several other productive approaches. However, by studying the three major frameworks, we can better grasp how sociologists seek to explore social behavior. Table 3-1 summarizes these three broad approaches to sociological study.

Although no one approach is correct by itself, and sociologists draw on all of them for various purposes, many sociologists tend to favor one particular perspective over others. A sociologist's theoretical orientation influences his or her approach to a research problem in important ways—including the choice of what to study, how to study it, and what questions to pose (or not to pose). Box 3-1 (page 19) shows how researchers would study the 2010 Gulf Coast oil spill from different sociological perspectives.

Whatever the purpose of sociologists' work, their research will always be guided by their theoretical viewpoints. For example, sociologist Elijah Anderson (1990) embraces both the interactionist perspective and the groundbreaking work of

trend spotting

The Changing Third Place

For a generation, sociologists have spoken of the "third place," a social setting between the "first place" of home and the "second place" of work. People gather routinely in the third place, typically a coffeehouse or fast-food restaurant, to see familiar faces or make new friends.

Will this social pattern persist? Sociologists have identified forces that both encourage and discourage it. The availability of free Wi-Fi definitely encourages people to seek out such establishments, but do laptops truly enhance social interactions there? And though talking among friends may be easy in the living-room settings that coffeehouses provide, proprietors don't always welcome these social gatherings. Some enforce anti-loitering regulations or require patrons to make purchases at regular time intervals. Still, as the second place (the workplace) becomes less relevant to growing numbers of telecommuters, the third place may well grow in social significance.

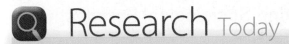
Looking at the Gulf Coast Oil Spill from Four Sociological Perspectives

The Gulf Coast oil spill, which began on April 20, 2010, dominated the national news in the United States for much of that year. Like other disasters, the huge spill had social effects that can be analyzed from the four major sociological perspectives.

Functionalist Perspective

In evaluating the effects of the Gulf Coast oil spill, functionalists would stress society's supportive function. For example:

- Functionalists might expect a revitalization of the environmental movement, as happened in the early 1900s after the damming of the Hetch Hetchy Valley just outside Yosemite, and later in the 1990s, after massive wildfires swept through the Everglades.
- Functionalists might note full employment in selected occupations, such as the manufacture of containment booms, even when jobs in other industries were scarce.
- Functionalists would observe that churches and other charities along the Gulf Coast provided both spiritual and material support to households affected by the spill.
- Functionalists would not be surprised that because offshore oil drilling is an integral part of the Gulf Coast economy, the governor of Louisiana strongly opposed a moratorium on deep-sea drilling, despite questions about its safety.

Conflict Perspective

Because conflict theorists see the social order in terms of conflict or tension between competing groups, they would emphasize the coercion and exploitation that underlies relations between the oil companies and Gulf Coast communities:

- The oil industry, conflict theorists would note, is a form of big business, in which profits are more important than workers' health and safety.
- Conflict theorists would emphasize the often-overlooked effect of the spill on minority groups living in inland communities, including Vietnamese Americans, Native American tribal groups, and African Americans. These groups, which were living a marginal existence before the spill, endured particularly significant economic setbacks after the spill.
- Conflict theorists would note that although news outlets tend to focus on oil spills that affect wealthy industrial countries, often the worst spills afflict communities in disadvantaged developing nations, such as Nigeria.

SWIMMING WATER QUALITY STATUS

HEALTH ADVISORY:

THE PUBLIC IS ADVISED NOT TO SWIM IN THESE WATERS DUE TO THE PRESENCE OF OIL-RELATED CHEMICALS

> Feminists would note that during times of economic upheaval and dislocation, women bear a disproportionate share of the burden in their role as caregivers.

Feminist Perspective

Feminists would note that during times of economic upheaval and dislocation, such as the Gulf Coast oil crisis, women bear a disproportionate share of the burden in their role as caregivers:

- As family wage earners leave home to seek work elsewhere, women with children or elderly dependents are left to cope as best they can.
- With time, the physical separation these families experience may turn into marital separation.

Interactionist Perspective

Interactionists would examine the Gulf Coast oil spill on the micro level, by focusing on how it shaped personal relations and day-to-day social behavior:

- Interactionists would note that difficult times often strengthen ties among neighbors and family members.

- At the same time, stressful events can contribute to social breakdowns, including divorce or even suicide—a pattern researchers observed in the aftermath of the *Exxon Valdez* oil spill in 1989.

Despite their differences, functionalists, conflict theorists, feminists, and interactionists would all agree that disasters like the Gulf Coast oil spill are a worthy subject for sociological study.

LET'S DISCUSS

1. Which of the four sociological perspectives seems most useful to you in analyzing the Gulf Coast oil crisis? Why?
2. For many people, the worldwide economic crisis that began in 2008 had disastrous personal consequences. Use the four sociological perspectives to analyze what happened to you, your family, and your community during the Great Recession.

Sources: Capriccioso 2010; Freudenburg and Gramling 2010; Greenemeier 2010; Jopling and Morse 2010; Liptak 2010; Molotch 1970; Samuels 2010; N. Wallace 2010.

Table 3-1 Major Sociological Perspectives

Tracking Sociological Perspectives

	Functionalist	Conflict	Interactionist
View of Society	Stable, well integrated	Characterized by tension and struggle between groups	Active in influencing and affecting everyday social interaction
Level of Analysis Emphasized	Macro	Macro	Micro, as a way of understanding the larger macro phenomena
Key Concepts	Manifest functions Latent functions Dysfunctions	Inequality Capitalism Stratification	Symbols Nonverbal communication Face-to-face interaction
View of the Individual	People are socialized to perform societal functions	People are shaped by power, coercion, and authority	People manipulate symbols and create their social worlds through interaction
View of the Social Order	Maintained through cooperation and consensus	Maintained through force and coercion	Maintained by shared understanding of everyday behavior
View of Social Change	Predictable, reinforcing	Change takes place all the time and may have positive consequences	Reflected in people's social positions and their communications with others
Example	Public punishments reinforce the social order	Laws reinforce the positions of those in power	People respect laws or disobey them based on their own past experience
Proponents	Émile Durkheim Talcott Parsons Robert Merton	Karl Marx W. E. B. DuBois Ida Wells-Barnett	George Herbert Mead Charles Horton Cooley Erving Goffman

W. E. B. DuBois. For 14 years Anderson conducted fieldwork in Philadelphia, where he studied the interactions of Black and White residents who lived in adjoining neighborhoods. In particular, he was interested in their public behavior, including their eye contact—or lack of it—as they passed one another on the street. Anderson's research tells us much about the everyday social interactions of Blacks and Whites in the United States, but it does not explain the larger issues behind those interactions. Like theories, research results illuminate one part of the stage, leaving other parts in relative darkness.

MODULE 3 | Recap and Review

Summary

Sociologists make use of four major perspectives, all of which offer unique insights into the same issues.

1. The **functionalist perspective** emphasizes the way in which the parts of a society are structured to maintain its stability.

2. The **conflict perspective** assumes that social behavior is best understood in terms of conflict or tension between competing groups.

3. The **interactionist perspective** is concerned primarily with fundamental or everyday forms of interaction, including symbols and other types of **nonverbal communication**.

4. The **feminist** perspective which is often allied with the conflict perspective, sees inequity in gender as central to all behavior and organization.

Thinking Critically

1. Describe an aspect of contemporary society that you consider to be a dysfunction.

2. Describe a symbol or object that has particular meaning on your campus.

3. Relate the toys on display in your local store to issues of race, class, and gender.

Key Terms

Conflict perspective 16

Dramaturgical approach 18

Dysfunction 16

Feminist perspective 17

Functionalist perspective 15

Interactionist perspective 18

Latent function 16

Manifest function 16

Nonverbal communication 18

You've seen how sociologists employ the major sociological perspectives in their research. How does sociology relate to *you,* your own studies, and your own career? In this section you'll learn about *applied* and *clinical sociology,* two growing fields that allow sociology majors and those with advanced degrees in sociology to apply what they have learned to real-world settings. You'll also see how to develop your sociological imagination, one of the keys to thinking like a sociologist. See the appendix at the end of this chapter for more information on careers in sociology.

Applied and Clinical Sociology

Many early sociologists—notably, Jane Addams, W. E. B. DuBois, and George Herbert Mead—were strong advocates for social reform. They wanted their theories and findings to be relevant to policymakers and to people's lives in general. For instance, Mead was the treasurer of Hull House, where he applied his theory to improving the lives of those who were powerless (especially immigrants). He also served on committees dealing with Chicago's labor problems and public education. Today, **applied sociology** is the use of the discipline of sociology with the specific intent of yielding practical applications for human behavior and organizations. By extension, Michael Burawoy (2005), in his presidential address to the American Sociological Association, endorsed what he called *public sociology,* encouraging scholars to engage a broader audience in bringing about positive outcomes. In effect, the applied sociologist reaches out to others and joins them in their efforts to better society.

Often, the goal of such work is to assist in resolving a social problem. For example, in the past 50 years, eight presidents of the United States have established commissions to delve into major societal concerns facing our nation. Sociologists are often asked to apply their expertise to studying such issues as violence, pornography, crime, immigration, and population. In Europe, both academic and government research departments are offering increasing financial support for applied studies.

One example of applied sociology is the growing interest in learning more about local communities. Since its founding in 1994, the Northeast Florida Center for Community Initiatives (CCI), based at the University of North Florida in Jacksonville, has conducted several community studies, including a homeless census and survey, an analysis of the economic impact of the arts in Jacksonville, and a long-term survey of the effects of

Hurricane Katrina. Typical of applied sociology, these outreach efforts are collaborative, involving faculty, undergraduate and graduate students, volunteers, and community residents (Center for Community Initiatives 2012a).

Another of CCI's applications of sociology, the Magnolia Project, is based in a storefront clinic in an underprivileged area of Jacksonville. Part of the federal Healthy Start initiative, which aims to decrease high infant mortality rates, the project serves

The Center for Community Initiatives' Magnolia Project, an example of applied sociology, aims to decrease high rates of infant mortality.

women of childbearing age who have little or no regular access to health care. CCI's responsibilities include (1) interviewing and surveying key community participants, (2) coordinating data collection by the project's staff, (3) analyzing data, and (4) preparing progress reports for funding agencies and community partners. Through March 2012, not a single infant death had occurred among the 293 participants in the program (Center for Community Initiatives 2012b).

Growing interest in applied sociology has led to such specializations as *medical sociology* and *environmental sociology*. The former includes research on how health care professionals and patients deal with disease. To give one example, medical sociologists have studied the social impact of the AIDS crisis on families, friends, and communities (see Module 53). Environmental sociologists examine the relationship between human societies and the physical environment. One focus of their work is the issue of "environmental justice" (see Module 55), raised when researchers and community activists found that hazardous waste dumps are especially likely to be situated in poor and minority neighborhoods (M. Martin 1996).

The growing popularity of applied sociology has led to the rise of the specialty of clinical sociology. Louis Wirth (1931) wrote about clinical sociology more than 75 years ago, but the term itself has become popular only in recent years. While applied sociology may simply evaluate social issues, **clinical sociology** is dedicated to facilitating change by altering social relationships (as in family therapy) or restructuring social institutions (as in the reorganization of a medical center).

Applied sociologists generally leave it to policymakers to act on their evaluations. In contrast, clinical sociologists take direct responsibility for implementation and view those with whom they work as their clients. This specialty has become increasingly attractive to graduate students in sociology because it offers an opportunity to apply intellectual learning in a practical way. A shrinking job market in the academic world has made such alternative career routes appealing.

Applied and clinical sociology can be contrasted with **basic sociology** (also called *pure sociology*) which seeks a more profound knowledge of the fundamental aspects of social phenomena. This type of research is not necessarily meant to generate specific applications, although such ideas may result once findings are analyzed. When Durkheim studied suicide rates, he was not primarily interested in discovering a way to eliminate suicide. In this sense, his research was an example of basic rather than applied sociology.

⬛ Developing a Sociological Imagination

In this book, we will be illustrating the sociological imagination in several different ways—by showing theory in practice and in current research; by thinking globally; by exploring the significance of social inequality; by speaking across race, gender, and religious boundaries; and by highlighting social policy throughout the world.

Theory in Practice

We will illustrate how the major sociological perspectives can be helpful in understanding today's issues, from capital punishment to abortion. Sociologists do not necessarily declare, "Here I am using functionalism," but their research and approaches do tend to draw on one or more theoretical frameworks, as will become clear in the pages to follow.

Research Today

Sociologists actively investigate a variety of issues and social behavior. We have already seen that research can shed light on the social factors that affect suicide rates. Sociological research often plays a direct role in improving people's lives, as in the case of increasing the participation of African Americans in diabetes testing. Throughout the rest of the book, the research performed by sociologists and other social scientists will shed light on group behavior of all types.

Thinking Globally

Whatever their theoretical perspective or research techniques, sociologists recognize that social behavior must be viewed in a global context. **Globalization** is the worldwide integration of government policies, cultures, social movements, and financial markets through trade and the exchange of ideas. Although public discussion of globalization is relatively recent, intellectuals have been pondering both its negative and positive social consequences for a long time. Karl Marx and Friedrich Engels warned in *The Communist Manifesto* (written in 1848) of a world market that would lead to production in distant lands, sweeping away existing working relationships.

Today, developments outside a country are as likely to influence people's lives as changes at home. For example, though much of the world was already in recession by September 2001, the terrorist attacks on New York and Washington, D.C., caused an immediate economic decline, not just in the United States, but throughout the world. One example of the massive global impact was the downturn in international tourism, which lasted for at least two years. The effects have been felt by people far removed from the United States, including African game wardens and Asian taxi drivers. Some observers see globalization and its effects as the natural result of advances in communications technology, particularly the Internet and satellite transmission of the mass media. Others view it more critically, as a process that allows multinational corporations to expand unchecked. We examine the impact of globalization on our daily lives and on societies throughout the world in Box 4-1 and throughout this book (Fiss and Hirsch 2005).

The Significance of Social Inequality

Who holds power? Who doesn't? Who has prestige? Who lacks it? Perhaps the major theme of analysis in sociology today is **social inequality,** a condition in which members of society have differing amounts of wealth, prestige, or power.

Today, both the positive and negative aspects of globalization are receiving increased scrutiny from sociologists.

Sociologists have noted, for example, that the huge tsunami that hit South Asia in 2004 affected men and women differently. When the waves hit, mothers and grandmothers were at home with the children; men were outside working, where they were more likely to become aware of the impending disaster. Moreover, most of the men knew how to swim, a survival skill that women in these traditional societies usually do not learn. As a result, many more men than women survived the catastrophe—about 10 men for every 1 woman. In one Indonesian village typical of the disaster area, 97 of 1,300 people survived; only 4 were women. The impact of this gender imbalance will be felt for some time, given women's primary role as caregivers for children and the elderly (BBC News 2005).

For example, the disparity between what coffee bean pickers in developing nations are paid and the price you pay for a cup of coffee underscores global inequality (see Box 4-1). Kelsey Timmerman's research among foreign garment workers uncovered some other aspects of global inequality. And the impact of Hurricane Katrina on residents of the Gulf Coast drew attention to social inequality in the United States. Predictably, the people who were hit the hardest by the massive storm were the poor, who had the greatest difficulty evacuating before the storm and have had the most difficulty recovering from it.

Some sociologists, in seeking to understand the effects of inequality, have made the case for social justice. W. E. B. DuBois ([1940] 1968:418) noted that the greatest power in the land is not "thought or ethics, but wealth." As we have seen, the contributions of Karl Marx, Jane Addams, and Ida Wells-Barnett also stressed this belief in the overarching significance of social inequality, and by extension, social justice. In this book, social inequality will be the central focus of Chapters 8 and 9, and sociologists' work on inequality will be highlighted throughout.

Speaking across Race, Gender, and Religious Boundaries

Sociologists include both men and women, who come from a variety of ethnic, national, and religious origins. In their work, sociologists seek to draw conclusions that speak to all people—not just the affluent or powerful. Doing so is not always easy. Insights into how a corporation can increase its profits tend to attract more attention and financial support than do, say, the merits of a needle exchange program for low-income inner-city residents. Yet today more than ever, sociology seeks to better understand the experiences of all people.

Social Policy throughout the World

One important way we can use a sociological imagination is to enhance our understanding of current social issues throughout the world. Approximately one-third of the modules in this book include a discussion of a contemporary social policy issue. In some cases, we will examine a specific issue facing national governments. For example, government funding of child care centers will be discussed in Module 15, Agents of Socialization; global immigration in Module 33, Race and Ethnicity in the United States; and religion in the schools in Module 46, Religious Organizations. These Social Policy sections will demonstrate how fundamental sociological concepts can enhance our critical thinking skills and help us to better understand current public policy debates taking place around the world.

In addition, sociology has been used to evaluate the success of programs or the impact of changes brought about by policymakers and political activists. For example, Module 28, Poverty and Social Mobility, includes a discussion of research on the effectiveness of welfare programs. Such discussions underscore the many practical applications of sociological theory and research.

Sociologists expect the next quarter of a century to be perhaps the most exciting and critical period in the history of the discipline. That is because of a growing recognition—both in the United States and around the world—that current social problems must be addressed before their magnitude overwhelms human societies. We can expect sociologists to play an increasing role in government by researching and developing public policy alternatives. It seems only natural for this textbook to focus on the connection between the work of sociologists and the difficult questions confronting policymakers and people in the United States and around the world.

Your Morning Cup of Coffee

When you drink a cup of coffee, do you give much thought to where the coffee beans came from, or do you think more about the pleasure you get from the popular beverage? Coffee certainly is popular—as an import, it is second only to petroleum, the most traded commodity in the world.

Although the coffee trade has been globalized, the customs of coffee drinking still vary from place to place. Starbucks, which now has 4,500 locations outside the United States, has over 1,000 locations in Europe. Managers find that in European countries, where the coffeehouse culture originated, 80 percent of their customers sit down to drink their coffee. In the United States, 80 percent of Starbucks' customers leave the store immediately, taking their coffee with them.

Today, the coffee trade relies on the exploitation of cheap labor. Coffee is a labor-intensive crop: there is little that technology can do to ease the coffee picker's burden. The typical coffee picker works in a developing nation near the equator, receiving for a day's wages an amount that matches the price of a single cup of coffee in North America. In the 1940s, advocacy groups began to promote the sale of certified *fair trade coffee,* which gives a living wage to those who harvest the crop, allowing them to become economically self-sufficient. But as of late 2009, fair trade coffee accounted for only 2.5 percent of the coffee that was bought and sold in the United States. Recently, a similar movement has begun to promote fair trade in the global clothing industry, reported on by Kelsey Timmerman in his book *Where Am I Wearing?*

Ecological activists have drawn attention to what they see as the coffee industry's contribution to the trend toward global warming.

The need to make room for more coffee fields, they charge, has encouraged the destruction of rain forests. The same criticism can be aimed at much of the consumption in industrial nations. Of all the products that emerge from developing nations, however, few have as singular a place in many people's daily ritual as that morning cup of joe. The drink in your hand is your tangible link to rural workers in some of the poorest areas of the world.

LET'S DISCUSS

1. Do you enjoy coffee? Would you willingly pay more for a cup of coffee if you knew that the worker who picked the beans would benefit from the higher price?

2. The coffee trade has been blamed for perpetuating social inequality and global warming. Can you think of any positive effects of the coffee trade? Who benefits most from this economic activity?

Sources: Adamy 2008; Fieser 2009; Jaffee 2007; Luttinger and Dicum 2006; E. Marx 2009; Pendergrast 1999; Ritzer 2011:218–227.

> The typical coffee picker works in a developing nation near the equator, receiving for a day's wages an amount that matches the price of a single cup of coffee in North America.

MODULE 4 | Recap and Review

Summary

Studying sociology allows you many ways to exercise your sociological imagination.

1. **Applied** and **clinical sociology** use the discipline of sociology to solve practical problems in human behavior and organizations. In contrast, **basic sociology** is sociological inquiry that seeks only a deeper knowledge of the fundamental aspects of human phenomena.

2. This textbook makes use of the sociological imagination by showing theory in practice and in current research: by thinking globally; by focusing on the significance of **social inequality;** by speaking across racial, gender, and religious boundaries; and by highlighting social policy around the world.

Thinking Critically

1. What issues facing your local community would you like to address with applied sociological research? Do you see any global connections to these issues?

2. In what specific ways does globalization affect your everyday life? Do you think the impact of globalization is primarily positive or negative?

Key Terms

Applied sociology 21

Basic sociology 22

Clinical sociology 22

Globalization 22

Social inequality 22

For the past two decades the number of U.S. college students who have graduated with a degree in sociology has risen steadily (Figure A-1). In this appendix we'll consider some of the options these students have after completing their undergraduate education.

How do students first learn about the sociological perspective on society? Some may take a sociology course in high school. Others may study sociology at community college, where 40 percent of all college students in the United States are enrolled. Indeed, many future sociology majors first develop their sociological imaginations at a community college.

An undergraduate degree in sociology doesn't just serve as excellent preparation for future graduate work in sociology. It also provides a strong liberal arts background for entry-level positions in business, social services, foundations, community organizations, not-for-profit groups, law enforcement, and many government jobs. A number of fields—among them marketing, public relations, and broadcasting—now require investigative skills and an understanding of the diverse groups found in today's multiethnic and multinational environment. Moreover, a sociology degree requires accomplishment in oral and written communication, interpersonal skills, problem solving, and critical thinking—all job-related skills that may give sociology graduates an advantage over those who pursue more technical degrees.

Consequently, while few occupations specifically require an undergraduate degree in sociology, such academic training can be an important asset in entering a wide range of occupations. To emphasize this point, a number of chapters in this book highlight a real-life professional who describes how the study of sociology has helped in his or her career. For example, in Module 20 a Taking Sociology to Work box explains how a college graduate uses her training in sociology as a social media manager for nonprofit organizations. And in Module 48, another Taking Sociology to Work box shows how a recent graduate uses the skill set he acquired as a sociology major in his role as a government analyst.

Figure A-2 summarizes the sources of employment for those with BA or BS degrees in sociology. It shows that the areas of nonprofit organizations, education, business, and government offer major career opportunities for sociology graduates. Undergraduates who know where their career interests lie are well advised to enroll in sociology courses and specialties best suited to those interests. For example, students hoping to become health planners would take a class in medical sociology; students seeking employment as social science research assistants

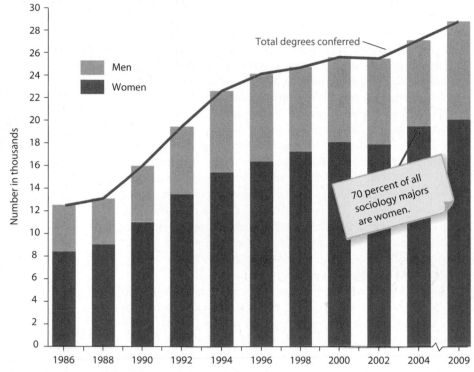

FIGURE A-1 **Sociology Degrees Conferred in the United States by Gender**

Total degrees conferred

Men
Women

70 percent of all sociology majors are women.

Number in thousands

1986 1988 1990 1992 1994 1996 1998 2000 2002 2004 2009

Source: National Center for Education Statistics 2011:Table 286 on p. 429.

would focus on courses in statistics and methods. Internships, such as placements at city planning agencies and survey research organizations, afford another way for sociology students to prepare for careers. Studies show that students who choose an internship placement have less trouble finding jobs, obtain better jobs, and enjoy greater job satisfaction than students without internship placements.

Finally, students should expect to change fields during their first five years of employment after graduation—for example, from sales and marketing to management (American Sociological Association 2009; Salem and Grabarek 1986; Spalter-Roth and Van Vooren 2010).

Many college students view social work as the field most closely associated with sociology. Traditionally, social workers received their undergraduate training in sociology and allied fields such as psychology and counseling. After some practical experience, social workers would generally seek a master's degree in social work (MSW) to be considered for supervisory or administrative positions. Today, however, some students choose (where it is available) to pursue a bachelor's

Did you know that as a student at Princeton University, Michelle Obama majored in sociology? She used that degree as a stepping-stone to Harvard Law School. Read her senior thesis at www.politico.com/news/stories/0208/8642.html.

degree in social work (BSW). This degree prepares graduates for direct service positions, such as caseworker or group worker.

Many students continue their sociological training beyond the bachelor's degree. More than 250 universities in the United States have graduate programs in sociology that offer PhD and/or master's degrees. These programs differ greatly in their areas of specialization, course requirements, costs, and the research and teaching opportunities available to graduate students. About 71 percent of the graduates are women (American Sociological Association 2005, 2010a).

Higher education is an important source of employment for sociologists with graduate degrees. About 83 percent of recent PhD recipients in sociology seek employment in colleges and universities. These sociologists teach not only majors who are committed to the discipline but also students hoping to become doctors, nurses, lawyers, police officers, and so forth (American Sociological Association 2005).

Sociologists who teach in colleges and universities may use their knowledge and training to influence public policy. For example, sociologist Andrew Cherlin (2003) has commented on the debate over proposed federal funding to promote marriage among welfare recipients. Citing the results of two of his studies, Cherlin questioned the potential effectiveness of such a policy in strengthening low-income families. Because many single mothers choose to marry someone other than the father of their children—sometimes for good reason— their children often grow up in stepfamilies. Cherlin's research shows that children who are raised in stepfamilies are no better off than those in single-parent families. He sees government efforts to promote marriage as a politically motivated attempt to foster traditional social values in a society that has become increasingly diverse.

For sociology graduates who are interested in academic careers, the road to a PhD (or doctorate) can be long and difficult. This degree symbolizes competence in original research; each candidate must prepare a book-length study known as a dissertation. Typically, a doctoral student in sociology will engage in four to seven years of intensive work, including the time required to complete the dissertation. Yet even this effort is no guarantee of a job as a sociology professor.

The good news is that over the next 10 years, the demand for instructors is expected to increase because of high rates of retirement among faculty from the baby boom generation, as well as the anticipated slow but steady growth in the college student population in the United States. Nonetheless, anyone who launches an academic career must be prepared for considerable uncertainty and competition in the college job market (American Sociological Association 2009).

Of course, not all people who work as sociologists teach or hold doctoral degrees. Take government, for example. The Census Bureau relies on people with sociological training to interpret data for other government agencies and the general public. Virtually every agency depends on survey research—a field in which sociology students can specialize—in order to assess everything from community needs to the morale of the agency's workers. In addition, people with sociological training can put their academic knowledge to effective use in probation and parole, health sciences, community development, and recreational services. Some people working in government or

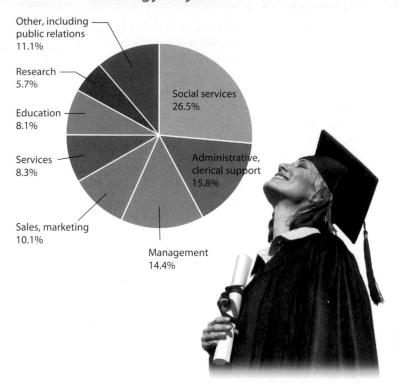

FIGURE A-2 **Occupations of Graduating Sociology Majors**

Other, including public relations 11.1%

Research 5.7%

Education 8.1%

Services 8.3%

Sales, marketing 10.1%

Social services 26.5%

Administrative, clerical support 15.8%

Management 14.4%

Note: Based on a national survey conducted in early 2007 of 1,800 sociology majors who graduated in 2005.
Source: Spalter-Roth and Van Vooren 2008a, p. 3.

private industry have a master's degree (MA or MS) in sociology; others have a bachelor's degree (BA or BS).

Currently, about 15 percent of the members of the American Sociological Association use their sociological skills outside the academic world, whether in social service agencies or in marketing positions for business firms. Increasing numbers of sociologists with graduate degrees are employed by businesses, industry, hospitals, and nonprofit organizations. Studies show that many sociology graduates are making career changes from social service areas to business and commerce. For an undergraduate major, sociology is excellent preparation for employment in many parts of the business world (Spalter-Roth and Van Vooren 2008b).

Whether you take a few courses in sociology or complete a degree, you will benefit from the critical thinking skills developed in this discipline. Sociologists emphasize the value of being able to analyze, interpret, and function within a variety of working situations—an asset in virtually any career. Moreover, given rapid technological change and the expanding global economy, all of us will need to adapt to substantial social change, even in our own careers. Sociology provides a rich conceptual framework that can serve as a foundation for flexible career development and assist you in taking advantage of new employment opportunities.

For more information on career opportunities for individuals with a background in sociology, visit the Online Learning Center at **www.mhhe.com/schaefermod2e**. Go to "Student Edition," and in the section titled "Course-wide Content," click on "Web Resources." Then click on "Career Opportunities," which will provide you with numerous links to sites offering career advice and information.

Mastering This Chapter

taking sociology with you

1 Research! Find out who makes the sports apparel sold at your school's bookstore. What can you learn (perhaps from a company website) about where such products are manufactured and what the working conditions are?

2 In what ways have you been affected by the recent spate of home mortgage foreclosures? Has the widespread loss of home ownership made you and others more aware of the problem of homelessness, or has it pushed the issue out of sight?

3 Consider some group or organization that you participate in. Using Robert Merton's concepts, list its manifest and latent functions.

key terms

Anomie The loss of direction felt in a society when social control of individual behavior has become ineffective. (page 11)

Applied sociology The use of the discipline of sociology with the specific intent of yielding practical applications for human behavior and organizations. (21)

Basic sociology Sociological inquiry conducted with the objective of gaining a more profound knowledge of the fundamental aspects of social phenomena. Also known as *pure sociology*. (22)

Clinical sociology The use of the discipline of sociology with the specific intent of altering social relationships or restructuring social institutions. (22)

Conflict perspective A sociological approach that assumes that social behavior is best understood in terms of tension between groups over power or the allocation of resources, including housing, money, access to services, and political representation. (16)

Cultural capital Noneconomic goods, such as family background and education, which are reflected in a knowledge of language and the arts. (14)

Double consciousness The division of an individual's identity into two or more social realities. (13)

Dramaturgical approach A view of social interaction in which people are seen as theatrical performers. (18)

Dysfunction An element or process of a society that may disrupt the social system or reduce its stability. (16)

Feminist perspective A sociological approach that views inequity in gender as central to all behavior and organization. (17)

Functionalist perspective A sociological approach that emphasizes the way in which the parts of a society are structured to maintain its stability. (15)

Globalization The worldwide integration of government policies, cultures, social movements, and financial markets through trade and the exchange of ideas. (22)

Ideal type A construct or model for evaluating specific cases. (11)

Interactionist perspective A sociological approach that generalizes about everyday forms of social interaction in order to explain society as a whole. (18)

Latent function An unconscious or unintended function that may reflect hidden purposes. (16)

Macrosociology Sociological investigation that concentrates on large-scale phenomena or entire civilizations. (14)

Manifest function An open, stated, and conscious function. (16)

Microsociology Sociological investigation that stresses the study of small groups, often through experimental means. (14)

Natural science The study of the physical features of nature and the ways in which they interact and change. (6)

Nonverbal communication The sending of messages through the use of gestures, facial expressions, and postures. (18)

Science The body of knowledge obtained by methods based on systematic observation. (6)

Social capital The collective benefit of social networks, which are built on reciprocal trust. (14)

Social inequality A condition in which members of society have differing amounts of wealth, prestige, or power. (22)

Social science The study of the social features of humans and the ways in which they interact and change. (6)

Sociological imagination An awareness of the relationship between an individual and the wider society, both today and in the past. (5)

Sociology The scientific study of social behavior and human groups. (5)

Theory In sociology, a set of statements that seeks to explain problems, actions, or behavior. (8)

Verstehen The German word for "understanding" or "insight"; used to stress the need for sociologists to take into account the subjective meanings people attach to their actions. (11)

Read each question carefully and then select the best answer.

1. Sociology is
   a. very narrow in scope.
   b. concerned with what one individual does or does not do.
   c. the systematic study of social behavior and human groups.
   d. an awareness of the relationship between an individual and the wider society.

2. Which of the following thinkers introduced the concept of the sociological imagination?
   a. Émile Durkheim
   b. Max Weber
   c. Karl Marx
   d. C. Wright Mills

3. Émile Durkheim's research on suicide suggested that
   a. people with religious affiliations had a higher suicide rate than those who were unaffiliated.
   b. suicide rates seemed to be higher in times of peace than in times of war and revolution.
   c. civilians were more likely to take their lives than soldiers.
   d. suicide is a solitary act, unrelated to group life.

4. Max Weber taught his students that they should employ which of the following in their intellectual work?
   a. anomie
   b. verstehen
   c. the sociological imagination
   d. microsociology

5. Robert Merton's contributions to sociology include
   a. successfully combining theory and research.
   b. producing a theory that is one of the most frequently cited explanations of deviant behavior.
   c. an attempt to bring macro-level and micro-level analyses together.
   d. all of the above

6. Which sociologist made a major contribution to society through his in-depth studies of urban life, including both Blacks and Whites?
   a. W. E. B. DuBois
   b. Robert Merton
   c. Auguste Comte
   d. Charles Horton Cooley

7. In the late 19th century, before the term *feminist perspective* was even coined, the ideas behind this major theoretical approach appeared in the writings of
   a. Karl Marx.
   b. Ida Wells-Barnett.
   c. Charles Horton Cooley.
   d. Pierre Bourdieu.

8. Thinking of society as a living organism in which each part of the organism contributes to its survival is a reflection of which theoretical perspective?
   a. the functionalist perspective
   b. the conflict perspective
   c. the feminist perspective
   d. the interactionist perspective

9. Karl Marx's view of the struggle between social classes inspired the contemporary
   a. functionalist perspective.
   b. conflict perspective.
   c. interactionist perspective.
   d. dramaturgical approach.

10. Erving Goffman's dramaturgical approach, which postulates that people present certain aspects of their personalities while obscuring other aspects, is a derivative of what major theoretical perspective?
    a. the functionalist perspective
    b. the conflict perspective
    c. the feminist perspective
    d. the interactionist perspective

11. While the findings of sociologists may at times seem like common sense, they differ because they rest on _____ analysis of facts.

12. Within sociology, a(n) _____ is a set of statements that seeks to explain problems, actions, or behavior.

13. In _____ _____ 's hierarchy of the sciences, sociology was the "queen," and its practitioners were "scientist-priests."

14. In *Society in America,* originally published in 1837, English scholar _____ _____ examined religion, politics, child rearing, and immigration in the young nation.

15. _____ _____ adapted Charles Darwin's evolutionary view of the "survival of the fittest" by arguing that it is "natural" that some people are rich while others are poor.

16. Sociologist Max Weber coined the term _____ _____ in referring to a construct or model that serves as a measuring rod against which actual cases can be evaluated.

17. In *The Communist Manifesto,* _____ _____ and _____ _____ argued that the masses of people who have no resources other than their labor (the proletariat) should unite to fight for the overthrow of capitalist societies.

18. _____ _____, an early female sociologist, cofounded the famous Chicago settlement house called Hull House and also tried to establish a juvenile court system.

19. The university's role in certifying academic competence and excellence is an example of a(n) _____ function.

20. The _____ _____ draws on the work of Karl Marx and Friedrich Engels in that it often views women's subordination as inherent in capitalist societies.

We Were Here

In the 1980s, in response to the onset of the AIDS crisis, people came together to ameliorate suffering and strengthen a community.

When the Levees Broke

Spike Lee directs this documentary about the social costs of Hurricane Katrina.

Frozen River

Two working-class women overcome racial prejudice to form an unlikely friendship.

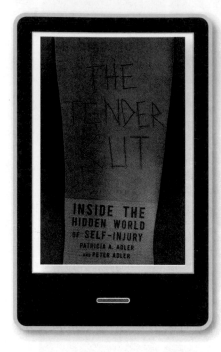

Did you ever wonder how researchers study behaviors that are private and personal?

Sociologists Patricia Adler and Peter Adler went on the Internet to study people who injure themselves. Read on to see what they learned.

" Self-injury has existed for nearly all of recorded history. Although it has been defined and regarded in various ways over time, its rise in the 1990s and early 2000s has taken a specific, although contested, form and meaning. We focus in this book on the deliberate, nonsuicidal destruction of one's own body tissue, incorporating practices such as self-cutting, burning, branding, scratching, picking at skin. . . . Our goal here is to discuss the form of this latest incarnation of self-injury, now often regarded as a typical behavior among adolescents, describing and analyzing it through the voices and from the perspective of those who practice it. . . .

Many self-injurers were driven to this behavior by nothing more serious than the minor stresses typically associated with normal adolescence. . . . People cited upsets with their friends, romantic relationships, and family members as having led them to self-injury. Mike was a scruffy-looking college student who always wore a stocking cap. He started cutting and burning himself between the ages of 12 and 14. When he was in high school Mike's girlfriend broke up with him, leaving him devastated. He reflected, "Yeah, I thought every relationship was the end of the world. I kept getting further and further depressed, and I just needed something to where I could vent and rage without having any outward signs so that anybody could tell

Mike was a scruffy-looking college student who always wore a stocking cap. He started cutting and burning himself between the ages of 12 and 14.

anything was wrong." He turned to cutting to assuage his feelings of sadness. . . .

Over the years that we were actively involved in the self-injury cyber world, it took several twists and turns. The earliest of the sites we discovered probably originated during the late 1990s. At that time, most sites were privately owned and unmonitored. Participants often used the term *self-mutilation*, and it was not uncommon to find graphic details and pictures of injuries. Sites had names such as "bleed me," "ruin your life," "bioetchings," "bleeding to ease the pain," "cut it out," and "gallery of pain." Their main purpose, it appeared, was to offer fellowship to self-harmers so they would know they were not alone. . . .

Over the course of our research we also collected tens of thousands (in the range of 30,000–40,000) of Internet messages and emails, including those posted publicly and those written to and by us. In 2006 we enlisted the aid of three student coders to help us sort and analyze the emails and postings from the Internet groups. At this time we were working on one paper, and the students helped us find posts and emails pertinent to our specific focus. We repeated this process again in 2008 with ten more student coders, expanding the project greatly. Each student took one set of emails we had collected from a group, board, or chat room and poured[sic] through the years of postings we had assembled. We divided the students into groups of five and met with each group biweekly. At each session the students submitted notes and memos about the material they had scanned, and we brainstormed for sociological codes, categories, concepts, trends, and patterns. "

(P. Adler and P. Adler 2011:1, 43, 44, 54–55) Additional information about this excerpt can be found on the Online Learning Center at www.mhhe.com/schaefermod2e.

I n this excerpt from Patricia A. Adler and Peter Adler's book *The Tender Cut: Inside the Hidden World of Self-Injury,* the authors describe their extensive research on a little-known behavior and its social underpinnings. The Adlers conducted lengthy, emotionally intense interviews with self-injurers, becoming friends with many. They met others through Internet-based support groups and web postings. "Rather than remaining strictly detached from our subjects, we became involved in their lives, helping them and giving voice to their experiences and beliefs" (2007:542; 2011).

Though many people would like to ignore the phenomenon of self-injury, believing that those who practice it will eventually "grow out of it," the Adlers' research allows us to consider it intelligently and scientifically, within the social context. Self-injurers,

the Adlers found, are a diverse group, whose behavior is carefully planned and considered. Surprisingly, members often begin to injure themselves in the company of others. They have recently begun to coalesce as a subculture (2007:559–560).

This chapter will examine the research process used in conducting sociological studies. How do sociologists go about setting up a research project? How do they ensure that the results of the research are reliable and accurate? Can they carry out their research without violating the rights of those they study?

We will look first at the steps that make up the scientific method. Then we will look at various techniques used in sociological research, such as experiments, observations, and surveys. We will pay particular attention to the ethical challenges sociologists face in studying human behavior, and to the debate raised by Max

Weber's call for "value neutrality" in research. We will also examine feminist methodology and the role technology plays in research today. The Social Policy section that closes this chapter describes the difficulties and challenges of researching closely guarded sexual behaviors.

Whatever the area of sociological inquiry and whatever the perspective of the sociologist—whether functionalist, conflict, feminist, interactionist, or any other—there is one crucial requirement: imaginative, responsible research that meets the highest scientific and ethical standards.

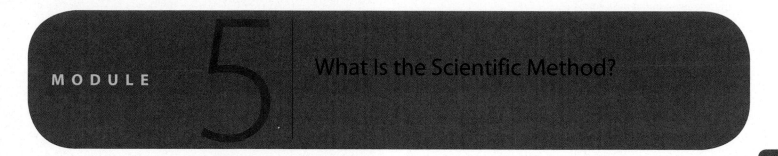

MODULE 5 | What Is the Scientific Method?

Like all of us, sociologists are interested in the central questions of our time: Is the family falling apart? Why is there so much crime in the United States? Can the world feed a growing population? Such issues concern most people, whether or not they have academic training. However, unlike the typical citizen, the sociologist has a commitment to use the **scientific method** in studying society. The scientific method is a systematic, organized series of steps that ensures maximum objectivity and consistency in researching a problem.

Many of us will never actually conduct scientific research. Why, then, is it important that we understand the scientific method? The answer is that it plays a major role in the workings of our society. Residents of the United States are constantly bombarded with "facts" or "data." A television news report informs us that "one in every two marriages in this country now ends in divorce," yet Module 41 will show that this assertion is based on misleading statistics. Almost daily, advertisers cite supposedly scientific studies to prove that their products are superior. Such claims may be accurate or exaggerated. We can better evaluate such information—and will not be fooled so easily—if we are familiar with the standards of scientific research.

These standards are quite stringent, and they demand as strict adherence as possible. The scientific method requires precise preparation in developing research. Otherwise, the research data collected may not prove accurate. Sociologists and other researchers follow five basic steps in the scientific method: (1) defining the problem, (2) reviewing the literature, (3) formulating the hypothesis, (4) selecting the research design and then collecting and analyzing data, and (5) developing the conclusion (Figure 5-1). We'll use an actual example to illustrate the scientific method.

● Defining the Problem

Does it "pay" to go to college? Some people make great sacrifices and work hard to get a college education. Parents borrow money for their children's tuition. Students work part-time jobs or even take full-time positions while attending evening or weekend classes. Does it pay off? Are there monetary returns for getting that degree?

FIGURE 5-1 **The Scientific Method**

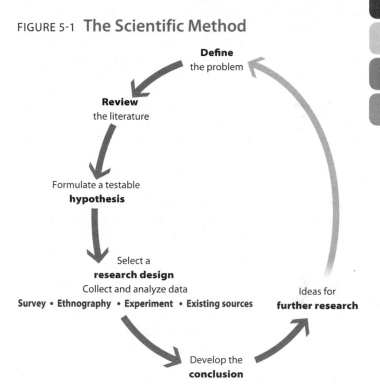

The scientific method allows sociologists to objectively and logically evaluate the data they collect. Their findings can suggest ideas for further sociological research.

The first step in any research project is to state as clearly as possible what you hope to investigate—that is, *define the problem.* In this instance, we are interested in knowing how schooling relates to income. We want to find out the earnings of people with different levels of formal schooling.

Early on, any social science researcher must develop an operational definition of each concept being studied. An **operational definition** is an explanation of an abstract concept that is specific enough to allow a researcher to assess the concept. For example, a sociologist interested in status might use membership in exclusive social clubs as an operational definition of status. Someone studying prejudice might consider a person's unwillingness to hire or work with members of minority groups as an operational definition of prejudice. In our example, we need to develop two operational definitions—education and earnings—in order to study whether it pays to get an advanced educational degree. We'll define *education* as the number of years of schooling a person has achieved and *earnings* as the income a person reports having received in the past year.

Initially, we will take a functionalist perspective (although we may end up incorporating other perspectives). We will argue that opportunities for more earning power are related to level of schooling, and that schools prepare students for employment.

◉ Reviewing the Literature

By conducting a *review of the literature*—relevant scholarly studies and information—researchers refine the problem under study, clarify possible techniques to be used in collecting data, and eliminate or reduce avoidable mistakes. In our example, we would examine information about the salaries for different occupations. We would see if jobs that require more academic training are better rewarded. It would also be appropriate to review other studies on the relationship between education and income.

The review of the literature would soon tell us that many factors besides years of schooling influence earning potential. For example, we would learn that the children of rich parents are more likely to go to college than those of poor parents, so we might consider the possibility that rich parents may later help their children to secure better-paying jobs.

We might also look at macro-level data, such as state-by-state comparisons of income and educational levels. In one macrolevel study based on census data, researchers found that in states whose residents have a relatively high level of education, household income levels are high as well (Figure 5-2). This finding suggests that schooling may well be related to income, though it does not speak to the micro-level relationship we are interested in. That is, we want to know whether *individuals* who are well educated are also well paid.

◉ Formulating the Hypothesis

After reviewing earlier research and drawing on the contributions of sociological theorists, the researchers may then *formulate the hypothesis*. A **hypothesis** is a speculative statement about the relationship between two or more factors known as variables. Income, religion, occupation, and gender can all serve as variables in a study. We can define a **variable** as a measurable trait or characteristic that is subject to change under different conditions.

Researchers who formulate a hypothesis generally must suggest how one aspect of human behavior influences or affects another. The variable hypothesized to cause or influence another is called the **independent variable.** The other variable is termed the **dependent variable** because its action *depends* on the influence of the independent variable. In other words, the researcher believes that the independent variable predicts or causes change in the dependent variable. For example, a researcher in sociology might anticipate that the availability of affordable housing

It seems reasonable that these graduates of Fort Bethold Community College on the Fort Bethold Reservation, North Dakota, will earn more income than high school graduates. How would you go about testing that hypothesis?

(the independent variable, x) affects the level of homelessness in a community (the dependent variable, y).

Our hypothesis is that the higher one's educational degree, the more money one will earn. The independent variable that is to be measured is the level of education. The variable that is thought to depend on it—income—must also be measured.

Identifying independent and dependent variables is a critical step in clarifying cause-and-effect relationships. As shown in Figure 5-3 on page 36, **causal logic** involves the relationship between a condition or variable and a particular consequence, with one leading to the other. For instance, being less integrated into society may be directly related to, or produce a greater likelihood of, suicide. Similarly, the time students spend reviewing material for a quiz may be directly related to, or produce a greater likelihood of, getting a high score on the quiz.

A **correlation** exists when a change in one variable coincides with a change in the other. Correlations are an indication that causality *may* be present; they do not necessarily indicate causation. For example, data indicate that people who prefer to watch televised news programs are less knowledgeable than those who read newspapers and newsmagazines. This correlation between people's relative knowledge and their choice of news media seems to make sense, because it agrees with the common belief that television dumbs down information. But the correlation between the two variables is actually caused by a third variable, people's relative ability to comprehend large amounts of information. People with poor reading skills are much more likely than others to get their news from television, while those who are more educated or skilled turn more often to the print media. Though television viewing is *correlated* with lower news comprehension, then, it does not *cause* it. Sociologists seek to identify the *causal* link between variables; the suspected causal link is generally described in the hypothesis (Neuman 2009).

FIGURE 5-2 **Educational Level and Household Income In the United States**

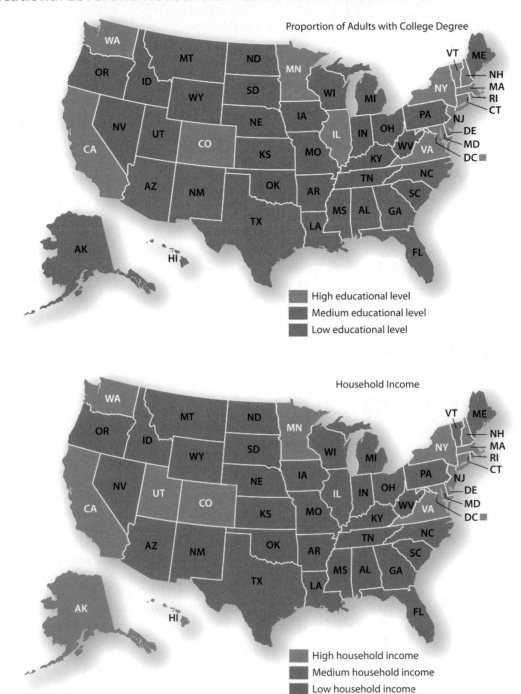

Proportion of Adults with College Degree

High educational level
Medium educational level
Low educational level

Household Income

High household income
Medium household income
Low household income

Notes: Cutoffs for high/medium and medium/low educational levels in 2009 were 29.7 percent and 24.5 percent of the population with a college degree, respectively; median for the entire nation was 27.9 percent. Cutoffs for high/medium and medium/low household income levels in 2010 were $53,900 and $43,000, respectively; national median household income was $50,046 in 2010.
Source: 2010 American Community Survey in Bureau of the Census 2011b:Table S1903; 2011a:Table 233.

● Collecting and Analyzing Data

How do you test a hypothesis to determine if it is supported or refuted? You need to collect information, using one of the research designs described later in the chapter. The research design guides the researcher in collecting and analyzing data.

Selecting the Sample

In most studies, social scientists must carefully select what is known as a sample. A **sample** is a selection from a larger population that is statistically representative of that population. There are many kinds of samples, but the one social scientists use most frequently is the random sample. In a **random sample,** every

FIGURE 5-3 Causal Logic

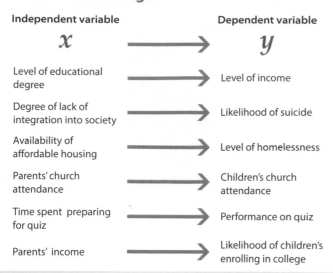

Independent variable		Dependent variable
x	$\longrightarrow$	y
Level of educational degree	$\longrightarrow$	Level of income
Degree of lack of integration into society	$\longrightarrow$	Likelihood of suicide
Availability of affordable housing	$\longrightarrow$	Level of homelessness
Parents' church attendance	$\longrightarrow$	Children's church attendance
Time spent preparing for quiz	$\longrightarrow$	Performance on quiz
Parents' income	$\longrightarrow$	Likelihood of children's enrolling in college

Think about It

Identify two or three dependent variables that might be influenced by this independent variable: number of alcoholic drinks ingested.

member of an entire population being studied has the same chance of being selected. Thus, if researchers want to examine the opinions of people listed in a city directory (a book that, unlike the telephone directory, lists all households), they might use a computer to randomly select names from the directory. The results would constitute a random sample. The advantage of using specialized sampling techniques is that sociologists do not need to question everyone in a population (Igo 2007).

In some cases, the subjects researchers want to study are hard to identify, either because their activities are clandestine or because lists of such people are not readily available. How do researchers create a sample of illegal drug users, for instance, or of women whose husbands are at least 10 years younger than they are? In such cases, researchers employ what are called *snowball* or *convenience samples*—that is, they recruit participants through word of mouth or by posting notices on the Internet. With the help of special statistical techniques, researchers can draw conclusions from such nonrandom samples.

It is all too easy to confuse the careful scientific techniques used in representative sampling with the many *nonscientific* polls that receive much more media attention. For example, website viewers are often encouraged to register their views on headline news or political contests. Such polls reflect nothing more than the views of those who happened to visit the website and took the time, perhaps at some cost, to register their opinions. These data do not necessarily reflect (and indeed may distort) the views of the broader population. Not everyone has access to a computer on a regular basis, or the means and/or inclination to register their opinions. Even when these techniques include answers from tens of thousands of people, they will be far less accurate than a carefully selected representative sample of 1,500 respondents.

For the purposes of our research example, we will use information collected in the Current Population Survey conducted by the Bureau of the Census. Each year, the Census Bureau surveys approximately 77,000 households across the United States. Technicians at the bureau then use the data to estimate the nation's entire population.

Ensuring Validity and Reliability

The scientific method requires that research results be both valid and reliable. **Validity** refers to the degree to which a measure or scale truly reflects the phenomenon under study. A valid measure of income depends on the gathering of accurate data. Various studies show that people are reasonably accurate in reporting how much money they earned in the most recent year. If a question is written unclearly, however, the resulting data might not be accurate. For example, respondents to an unclear question about income might report their parents' or spouse's income instead of their own.

Reliability refers to the extent to which a measure produces consistent results. Some people may not disclose accurate information, but most do. In the Current Population Survey, some people refuse to give their income, or even to participate. Periodically, the Census Bureau follows up with a personal visit to nonrespondents, to ensure that their data do not differ significantly from data obtained from those who do cooperate (Bureau of the Census 2004b).

◼ Developing the Conclusion

Scientific studies, including those conducted by sociologists, do not aim to answer all the questions that can be raised about a particular subject. Therefore, the conclusion of a research study represents both an end and a beginning. Although it terminates a specific phase of the investigation, it should also generate ideas for future study.

Supporting Hypotheses

In our example, we find that the data support our hypothesis: people with more formal schooling *do* earn more money than others. Those with a high school diploma earn more than those who failed to complete high school, but those with an associate's degree earn more than high school graduates. The relationship continues through more advanced levels of schooling, so that those with graduate degrees earn the most.

The relationship is not perfect, however. Some people who drop out of high school end up with high incomes, and some with advanced degrees earn modest incomes, as shown in Figure 5-4. A successful entrepreneur, for example, might not have much formal schooling, while the holder of a doctorate may choose to work for a low-paying nonprofit institution. Sociologists are interested in both the general pattern that emerges from their data and exceptions to the pattern.

Sociological studies do not always generate data that support the original hypothesis. Many times, a hypothesis is refuted, and researchers must reformulate their conclusions. Unexpected results may also lead sociologists to reexamine their methodology and make changes in the research design.

Controlling for Other Factors

A **control variable** is a factor that is held constant to test the relative impact of an independent variable. For example, if researchers wanted to know how adults in the United States feel about restrictions on smoking in public places, they would probably

FIGURE 5-4 **Impact of a College Education on Income**

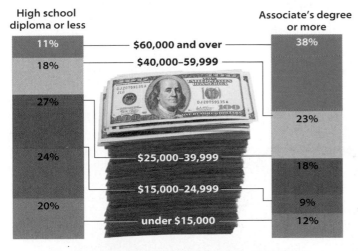

Source: Author's analysis of DeNavas-Walt et al. 2011, Detailed Table PINC-03. Forty-four percent of people with a high school diploma or less (left) earn under $25,000 a year, while only 29 percent earn $40,000 or more. In contrast, only 21 percent of those with an associate's degree or higher (right) earn less than $25,000, while 61 percent earn $40,000 or more.

Think about It

What kinds of knowledge and skills do people with an associate's degree or higher possess, compared to those with a high school education or less? Why would employers value those kinds of knowledge and skills?

trend|spotting

Overcounting and Undercounting in the U.S. Census

Every 10 years, as required by the Constitution, the U.S. government conducts a census to determine how many congressional representatives each state is allowed. Besides determining the states' political power, these data are used for a myriad of other purposes, from distributing federal aid to education to researching the market for breakfast cereal.

Despite concerns about government intrusion into people's private lives, U.S. citizens are relatively compliant with the head count. About three-quarters of households fill out and return the form or answer face-to-face questions from a census worker. Other industrial countries have much less success than the United States. Because of strong concerns about privacy, for example, the Netherlands has not had a door-to-door census since 1971.

With detailed knowledge of three out of every four households in the United States, census workers can use statistical techniques to estimate data for the other quarter. Still, officials have long recognized that the count is more likely to miss certain groups of people than others. This tendency, called *undercounting*, applies especially to low-income people, non-English speakers, and the homeless. Those who have good reason to avoid census workers, such as illegal immigrants and families who crowd together in inadequate housing, also swell the ranks of the undercounted.

Recently, however, concern has been growing about *overcounting*, or the tendency to count some people twice. College students who live at school rather than at home with their parents, "snowbirds" (retirees who move to warmer climes during the winter), active military personnel, and children whose parents share their custody all are likely to be overcounted.

Census officials estimate that the 2000 Census overcounted the nation's population by 11.6 million people. To correct the problem, the Bureau sought to identify people who had been listed twice, and by 2010 had reduced the overcount to just 36,000. In the 2010 Census, the undercount—that is, people who were not counted—was about 16 million, similar to the proportion of the population that was missed in 2000. Blacks, Hispanics, young children, and renters were more likely than others to be overlooked. Given the importance of accuracy in the nation's population count, officials will continue to address these issues in the 2020 Census.

attempt to use a respondent's smoking behavior as a control variable. That is, how do smokers versus nonsmokers feel about smoking in public places? The researchers would compile separate statistics on how smokers and nonsmokers feel about antismoking regulations.

Our study of the influence of education on income suggests that not everyone enjoys equal educational opportunities, a disparity that is one of the causes of social inequality. Since education affects a person's income, we may wish to call on the conflict perspective to explore this topic further. What impact does a person's race or gender have? Is a woman with a college degree likely to earn as much as a man with similar schooling? Later in this textbook we will consider these other factors and variables. That is, we will examine the impact that education has on income while controlling for variables such as gender and race.

In Summary: The Scientific Method

Let us briefly summarize the process of the scientific method through a review of the example. We *defined a problem* (the question of whether it pays to get a higher educational degree). We *reviewed the literature* (other studies of the relationship between education and income) and *formulated a hypothesis* (the higher one's educational degree, the more money one will earn). We *collected and analyzed the data,* making sure the sample was representative and the data were valid and reliable. Finally, we *developed the conclusion:* the data do support our hypothesis about the influence of education on income.

MODULE 5 | Recap and Review

Summary

Sociologists are committed to the use of the **scientific method** in their research efforts. In this module we examine the basic principles of the scientific method.

1. There are five basic steps in the scientific method: define the problem, review the literature, formulate a hypothesis, collect and analyze data, and develop the conclusion.

2. Whenever researchers wish to study abstract concepts, such as intelligence or prejudice, they must develop workable **operational definitions.**

3. A **hypothesis** states a possible relationship between two or more **variables.**

4. By using a **sample,** sociologists avoid having to test everyone in a population.

5. According to the scientific method, research results must possess both **validity** and **reliability.**

Thinking Critically

1. What might be the effects of a college education on society as a whole? Think of some potential effects on the family, government, and the economy.

2. Suppose that two researchers used different operational definitions for the same term. Could both researchers' results be reliable and valid? Explain your answer.

Key Terms

Causal logic 34

Control variable 37

Correlation 34

Dependent variable 34

Hypothesis 34

Independent variable 34

Operational definition 33

Random sample 35

Reliability 36

Sample 35

Scientific method 33

Validity 36

Variable 34

MODULE 6 | Major Research Designs

An important aspect of sociological research is deciding *how* to collect the data. A **research design** is a detailed plan or method for obtaining data scientifically. Selection of a research design is often based on the theories and hypotheses the researcher starts with (Merton 1948). The choice requires creativity and ingenuity, because it directly influences both the cost of the project and the amount of time needed to collect the data. Research designs that sociologists regularly use to generate data include surveys, ethnography, experiments, and existing sources.

Surveys

Almost all of us have responded to surveys of one kind or another. We may have been asked what kind of detergent we use, which presidential candidate we intend to vote for, or what our

Doonesbury

Think about It

> What would constitute a less biased question for a survey on smoking?

favorite television program is. A **survey** is a study, generally in the form of an interview or questionnaire, that provides researchers with information about how people think and act. As anyone who watches the news during presidential campaigns knows, surveys have become a staple of political life.

When you think of surveys, you may recall seeing online polls that offer instant results. Although such polls can be highly interesting, they reflect only the opinions of those who visit the website and choose to respond online. As we have seen, a survey must be based on precise, representative sampling if it is to genuinely reflect a broad range of the population. Box 6-1 describes the challenges of conducting a public opinion survey over the telephone.

In preparing to conduct a survey, sociologists must not only develop representative samples; they must also exercise great care in the wording of questions. An effective survey question must be simple and clear enough for people to understand. It must also be specific enough so that there are no problems in interpreting the results. Open-ended questions ("What do you think of the programming on educational television?") must be carefully phrased to solicit the type of information desired. Surveys can be indispensable sources of information, but only if the sampling is done properly and the questions are worded accurately and without bias.

In wording questions, researchers must also pay careful attention to changes in society. In December 2010, officials at the Bureau of Labor Statistics recognized the effects of an extended recession by changing a decades-old practice. In the past, multiple-choice questions about how long a respondent had been unemployed had ended with a maximum of "99 weeks or over." By the end of 2010, joblessness had become so chronic that the bureau increased the number of choices, ending with "290 weeks or longer."

There are two main forms of the survey: the **interview,** in which a researcher obtains information through face-to-face, telephone, or online questioning, and the **questionnaire,** in which the researcher uses a printed or written form to obtain information from a respondent. Each of these has its own advantages. An interviewer can obtain a higher response rate, because people find it more difficult to turn down a personal request for an interview than to throw away a written questionnaire. In addition, a skillful interviewer can go beyond written questions and probe for a subject's underlying feelings and reasons. On the other hand, questionnaires have the advantage of being cheaper, especially in large samples.

Why do people have sex? A straightforward question, but until recently it was rarely investigated scientifically, despite its significance to public health, marital counseling, and criminology. In a study published in 2007, researchers interviewed nearly 2,000 undergraduates at the University of Texas at Austin. To develop the question for the interview, they first asked a random sample of 400 students to list all the reasons why they had ever had sex. The explanations were highly diverse, ranging from "I was drunk" to "I wanted to feel closer to God." The team then asked another sample of 1,500 students to rate the importance of each of the 287 reasons given by the first group. Table 6-1 ranks the results. Nearly every reason was rated most important by at least some respondents. Though there were some gender differences in the replies, there was significant consensus between men and women on the top 10 reasons (Meston and Buss 2007).

Studies have shown that the characteristics of the interviewer have an impact on survey data. For example, female interviewers tend to receive more feminist responses from female subjects than do male interviewers, and Black interviewers tend to receive more detailed responses about race-related issues from Black subjects than do White interviewers. The possible impact of gender and race indicates again how much care social research requires (D. W. Davis and Silver 2003).

The survey is an example of **quantitative research,** which collects and reports data primarily in numerical form. Most of the survey research

Surveying Cell Phone Users

"Can you hear me now?" This question, familiar to cell phone callers everywhere, could be used to characterize a debate among researchers in sociology. Until recently, calling people on the telephone was a common way for survey takers to reach a broad range of people. Though not everyone owns a telephone—particularly not low-income people—researchers managed to account for that relatively small portion of the population in other ways.

However, the fact that many people now have a cell phone but no landline presents a serious methodological problem to scholars who depend on surveys and public opinion polling. As of 2012, 32 percent of households in the United States could be reached only by cell phone, and the proportion was rising. Among those under 30, the abandonment of landlines was nearly three times as common. These cell phone subscribers are more likely than others to be male and to earn a modest income.

Scholars are reluctant to rely only on landline-based surveys. They are concerned about the potential for misleading results, such as underestimates of the prevalence of health problems. For example, 38 percent of cell phone–only households have a binge drinker, compared to only 17 percent of landline households. And 28 percent of cell phone–only households do not have health insurance, compared to 14 percent of landline households.

> As of 2012, 32 percent of households in the United States could be reached only by cell phone, and the proportion was rising.

Unfortunately, surveying cell phone users has its own problems. In general, cell phone users are more likely than landline users to screen incoming calls or ignore them. And studies show that because cell phone users often take calls while they are involved in other activities, they are much more likely to break off a call midsurvey than someone who is speaking on a landline. Thus, it takes an average of nine calls to a working cell phone number to complete one survey, compared to five calls to a working landline number. Furthermore, federal law requires that calls to cell phones be hand-dialed; the use of automatic dialers, a standard tool of survey firms, is illegal. Survey takers have also found that calling cell phone numbers means they will reach a higher proportion of nonadults than when calling landline numbers. Finally, there are some ethical issues involved in randomly dialing cell phone users, who may be driving a motor vehicle or operating dangerous machinery when they answer.

Researchers are taking steps to stay abreast of technological change. For example, they are making allowances for people who communicate without any kind of telephone, using their personal computers and the Internet. And by drawing on historical data that suggest what kinds of people tend to adopt other wireless technologies, researchers are projecting which people are likely to abandon their landlines in the near future.

LET'S DISCUSS

1. Are you a cell phone–only user? If so, do you generally accept calls from unknown numbers? Aside from underestimating certain health problems and distorting the degree of support for certain politicians, what other problems might result from excluding cell phone–only users from survey research?

2. Apply what you have just learned to the task of surveying Internet users. Which of the problems that arise during telephone surveys might also arise during Internet surveys? Might Internet surveys involve some unique problems?

Sources: Blumberg and Luke 2007; David Brown 2009; Goldman 2012; Harrisinteractive 2008; Keeter and Kennedy 2006; Lavrakas et al. 2007.

---

discussed so far in this book has been quantitative. While this type of research can make use of large samples, it can't offer great depth and detail on a topic. That is why researchers also make use of **qualitative research,** which relies on what is seen in field and naturalistic settings, and often focuses on small groups and communities rather than on large groups or whole nations. The most common form of qualitative research is ethnography, or observation, which we consider next. Throughout this book you will find examples of both quantitative and qualitative research, since both are used widely. Some sociologists prefer one type of research to the other, but we learn most when we draw on many different research designs and do not limit ourselves to a particular type of research.

Ethnography

Investigators often collect information or test hypotheses through firsthand studies. **Ethnography** is the study of an entire social setting through extended systematic fieldwork. **Observation,** or direct participation in closely watching a group or organization, is the basic

Table **6-1** Top Reasons Why Men and Women Had Sex

Reason	Men	Women
I was attracted to the person	1	1
It feels good	2	3
I wanted to experience the physical pleasure	3	2
It's fun	4	8
I wanted to show my affection to the person	5	4
I was sexually aroused and wanted the release	6	6
I was "horny"	7	7
I wanted to express my love for the person	8	5
I wanted to achieve an orgasm	9	14
I wanted to please my partner	10	11
I realized I was in love	17	9
I was "in the heat of the moment"	13	10

Source: Meston and Buss 2007:506.

HEY GUYS, I THINK THE RESEARCHERS ARE LEAVING IF YOU WANT TO PUT YOUR CLOTHES BACK ON.

© 2007 CARRILLO, DIST. BY UFS, INC.

technique of ethnography. However, ethnographic research also includes the collection of historical information and the conduct of in-person interviews. Although ethnography may seem a relatively informal method compared to surveys or experiments, ethnographic researchers are careful to take detailed notes while observing their subjects.

In some cases, the sociologist actually joins a group for a period, to get an accurate sense of how it operates. This approach is called *participant observation*. In Barbara Ehrenreich's widely read book *Nickel and Dimed: On (Not) Getting By in America*, the author was a participant observer. Disguising herself as a divorced, middle-aged housewife without a college degree,

Sergeant Britt Damon, a social scientist on the U.S. Army Human Terrain Team, chats with Afghani children during a search operation. The participation of social scientists in the Army program, which some see as a violation of scholarly detachment, has proved controversial.

Ehrenreich set out to see what life was like for low-wage workers. Her book chronicles her own and others' experiences trying to make ends meet on a minimum wage (Ehrenreich 2001).

During the late 1930s, in a classic example of participant-observation research, William F. Whyte moved into a low-income Italian neighborhood in Boston. For nearly four years he was a member of the social circle of "corner boys" that he describes in *Street Corner Society*. Whyte revealed his identity to these men and joined in their conversations, bowling, and other leisure-time activities. His goal was to gain greater insight into the community that these men had established. As Whyte (1981:303) listened to Doc, the leader of the group, he "learned the answers to questions I would not even have had the sense to ask if I had been getting my information solely on an interviewing basis." Whyte's work was especially valuable, since at the time the academic world had little direct knowledge of the poor, and tended to rely for information on the records of social service agencies, hospitals, and courts (P. Adler et al. 1992).

The initial challenge that Whyte faced—and that every participant observer encounters—was to gain acceptance into an unfamiliar group. It is no simple matter for a college-trained sociologist to win the trust of a religious cult, a youth gang, a poor Appalachian community, or a circle of skid row residents. It requires a great deal of patience and an accepting, nonthreatening type of personality on the part of the observer.

Ethnographic research poses other complex challenges for the investigator. Sociologists must be able to fully understand what they are observing. In a sense, then, researchers must learn

Carnegie Mellon University's Data Truck lets researchers go where their subjects are—from nightclubs to marathon races. Equipped with the latest technology, the truck allows social scientists to enter the responses to their community surveys into their databases on site. It also gives them access to online social networks in the area, and even lets them videotape street activity.

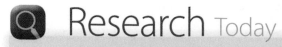
Gender Messages in Scouting

Nearly 5 million children in the United States participate in scouting. What gender messages do these young people receive during their time as Scouts?

A key form of guidance not just for Scouts but for their leaders is the Scout's handbook. Sociologist Kathleen Denny did a content analysis of the Boy Scouts' *Webelos Handbook* and the *Junior Girl Scout Handbook*. Focusing specifically on material for Scouts in the fourth and fifth grades, she found that both handbooks delivered traditional gender messages. Girl Scout activities were more likely than Boy Scout activities to be communal or other-oriented; Boy Scout activities were more likely to be solo undertakings.

Denny found that the names of merit badges also conveyed traditional gender messages. Girl Scout badge names often include

> The most gender-specific aspect of the Girl Scout handbook is the subjects of the badges themselves. Many refer to stereotypically feminine activities.

puns or other forms of word play; Boy Scout badges do not. For example, the Boy Scout badge for studying rocks and geology is called simply the Geologist badge; the comparable Girl Scout badge is called the Rocks Rock badge. Boy Scout badges more often have career-oriented names—Engineer, Craftsman, Scientist; Girl Scout badge names have less of a career orientation—Sky Search instead of Astronomer, Car Care instead of Mechanic.

The most gender-specific aspect of the Girl Scout handbook is the subjects of the badges themselves. Many refer to stereotypically feminine activities: Caring for Children, Looking Your Best, Sew Simple. Besides personal hygiene and healthy eating, the Looking Your Best badge includes an "Accessory Party," which

requires Scouts to "experiment to see how accessories highlight your features and your outfit." Needless to say, such badges are not offered in the Boy Scouts. The most nearly comparable one in the Boy Scout handbook is the Fitness badge, which includes activities such as keeping a food diary and warning a relative about the dangers of drugs and alcohol.

Denny acknowledges that Scout handbooks are not the only influence on gender roles in scouting. How are gender messages communicated in person during troop or pack meetings and ceremonies, for example? How do parents reinforce or mediate the gender themes in scouting? And how do children adjust to, accept, or rebel against the gender messages they receive as Scouts? Denny's research suggests the need for further research on gender socialization in the Boy Scouts and Girl Scouts.

LET'S DISCUSS

1. Did you participate in scouting as a child? If so, were you aware of the gender messages you were receiving as part of the scouting experience? How did you react?

2. If you were a Scout leader yourself, what kind of gender model would you attempt to be? How would you become that kind of model?

Sources: Boy Scouts of America 2010; K. Denny 2011; Girl Scouts of the USA 2001:39; World Association of Girl Guides and Girl Scouts 2011.

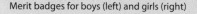

Merit badges for boys (left) and girls (right)

---

to see the world as the group sees it in order to fully comprehend the events taking place around them. This raises a delicate issue. If the research is to be successful, the observer cannot allow the close associations or even friendships that inevitably develop to influence the subjects' behavior or the conclusions of the study. Even while working hard to gain acceptance from the group being studied, the participant observer *must* maintain some degree of detachment.

Recently, the issue of detachment became a controversial one for social scientists embedded with the U.S. military in Afghanistan and Iraq. Among other studies, the academicians participated in the creation of the Army's Human Terrain System, a $4 million effort to identify the customs, kinship structures, and internal social conflicts in the two countries. The intention was to provide military leaders with information that would help them to make better decisions. Although the idea of

scholars cooperating in any way with soldiers struck many people as inappropriate, others countered that the information they developed would help the military to avoid needless violence and might even facilitate the withdrawal of troops from the region (Glenn 2007; Human Terrain System 2011).

⬤ Experiments

When sociologists want to study a possible cause-and-effect relationship, they may conduct experiments. An **experiment** is an artificially created situation that allows a researcher to manipulate variables.

In the classic method of conducting an experiment, two groups of people are selected and matched for similar characteristics, such as age or education. The researchers then assign the subjects to one of two groups: the experimental or the control group. The **experimental group** is exposed to an independent variable; the **control group** is not. Thus, if scientists were testing a new type of antibiotic, they would administer the drug to an experimental group but not to a control group.

In some experiments, just as in observation research, the presence of a social scientist or other observer may affect the behavior of the people being studied. Sociologists have used the term **Hawthorne effect** to refer to the unintended influence that observers of experiments can have on their subjects. The term originated as the result of an experiment conducted at the Hawthorne plant of the Western Electric Company during the 1920s and 1930s. Researchers found that *every* change they made in working conditions—even reduced lighting—seemed to have a positive effect on workers' productivity. They concluded that workers had made a special effort to impress their observers. Though the carefully constructed study did identify some causes for changes in the workers' behavior that did not have to do with their being observed, the term *Hawthorne effect* has become synonymous with a placebo or guinea pig effect (Franke and Kaul 1978).

◼ Use of Existing Sources

Sociologists do not necessarily need to collect new data in order to conduct research and test hypotheses. The term **secondary analysis** refers to a variety of research techniques that make use of previously collected and publicly accessible information and data. Generally, in conducting secondary analysis, researchers use data in ways that were unintended by the initial collectors of information. For example, census data are compiled for specific uses by the federal government but are also valuable to marketing specialists in locating everything from bicycle stores to nursing homes. Box 6-2 describes a content study of gender differences in the way Boy Scouts and Girl Scouts earn merit badges.

Sociologists consider secondary analysis to be *nonreactive*—that is, it does not influence people's behavior. For example, Émile Durkheim's statistical analysis of suicide neither increased nor decreased human self-destruction. Researchers, then, can avoid the Hawthorne effect by using secondary analysis.

There is one inherent problem, however: the researcher who relies on data collected by someone else may not find exactly what is needed. Social scientists who are studying family violence can use statistics from police and social service agencies on *reported* cases of spouse abuse and child abuse, but how many cases are not reported? Government bodies have no precise data on *all* cases of abuse.

Many social scientists find it useful to study cultural, economic, and political documents, including newspapers, periodicals, radio and television tapes, the Internet, scripts, diaries, songs, folklore, and legal papers (Table 6-2). In examining these sources, researchers employ a technique known as **content analysis,** which is the systematic coding and objective recording of data, guided by some rationale.

Content analysis can be revealing. We might think that in the 21st century, blatant favoritism in media representations of men versus women is a thing of the past. However, research suggests

Table **6-2** **Existing Sources Used in Sociological Research**

Most Frequently Used Sources
Census data
Crime statistics
Birth, death, marriage, divorce, and health statistics

Other Sources
Newspapers and periodicals
Personal journals, diaries, e-mail, and letters
Records and archival material of religious organizations, corporations, and other organizations
Transcripts of radio programs
Videotapes of motion pictures and television programs
Web pages, blogs, and chat rooms
Song lyrics
Scientific records (such as patent applications)
Speeches of public figures (such as politicians)
Votes cast in elections or by elected officials on specific legislative proposals
Attendance records for public events
Videos of social protests and rallies
Literature, including folklore

Think about It

Which of these sources do you access to collect information?

otherwise. An analysis of hundreds of characters in children's coloring books shows that males are more likely than females to be shown taking an active role. Gender-stereotyped behavior dominates, with only 3 percent of males engaged in stereotypically female behavior, and only 6 percent of females engaged in stereotypically male behavior (Fitzpatrick and McPherson 2010).

Similarly, despite women's participation in all sports, content analysis of televised sports coverage shows that even when a men's sport is out of season (for example, men's basketball in late summer), it gets more coverage than women's sports in season (for example, women's basketball in July). Furthermore, coverage of female cheerleaders and athletes' wives exceeds coverage of the female athletes who compete in sports (Messner and Cooky 2010).

Table 6-3 summarizes the major research designs, along with their advantages and limitations.

 use your **sociological imagination**

Imagine you are a legislator or government policymaker working on a complex social problem. What might happen if you were to base your decision on faulty research?

Table **6-3**   Major Research Designs   **summingup**

Method	Examples	Advantages	Limitations
Survey	Questionnaires, interviews	Yields information about specific issues	Can be expensive and time-consuming
Ethnography	Observation	Yields detailed information about specific groups or organizations	Involves months if not years of labor-intensive data
Experiment	Deliberate manipulation of people's social behavior	Yields direct measures of people's behavior	Ethical limitations on the degree to which subjects' behavior can be manipulated
Existing sources/ Secondary analysis	Analysis of census or health data Analysis of films or TV commercials	Cost-efficiency	Limited to data collected for some other purpose

MODULE 6 | **Recap and Review**

Summary

In this module we focus on **research designs**, or the types of plans sociologists use to collect data.

1. Sociologists use four major research designs: surveys, **observation,** experiments, and existing sources.

2. The two principal forms of **survey** research are the **interview** and the **questionnaire**.

3. **Ethnography** allows sociologists to study certain behaviors and communities that cannot be investigated through other research methods.

4. When sociologists wish to study a cause-and-effect relationship, they may conduct an **experiment**.

5. Sociologists may also make use of existing sources in **secondary analysis** and **content analysis**.

Thinking Critically

1. How would you set up an experiment to measure the effect of TV watching on school-age children's grades?

2. Suppose your sociology instructor has asked you to study homelessness in your community. Which research technique would you find most useful? How would you use that technique?

Key Terms

Content analysis 43

Control group 43

Ethnography 40

Experiment 42

Experimental group 43

Hawthorne effect 43

Interview 39

Observation 40

Qualitative research 40

Quantitative research 39

Questionnaire 39

Research design 38

Secondary analysis 43

Survey 39

A biochemist cannot inject a drug into a human being unless it has been thoroughly tested and the subject agrees to the shot. To do otherwise would be both unethical and illegal. Sociologists, too, must abide by certain specific standards in conducting research, called a **code of ethics.** The professional society of the discipline, the American Sociological Association (ASA), first published the society's *Code of Ethics* in 1971 and revised it most recently in 1997. It puts forth the following basic principles:

1. Maintain objectivity and integrity in research.
2. Respect the subject's right to privacy and dignity.
3. Protect subjects from personal harm.
4. Preserve confidentiality.
5. Seek informed consent when data are collected from research participants or when behavior occurs in a private context.
6. Acknowledge research collaboration and assistance.
7. Disclose all sources of financial support (American Sociological Association 1999).

These basic principles probably seem clear-cut. How could they lead to any disagreement or controversy? Yet many delicate ethical questions cannot be resolved simply by reading these seven principles. For example, should a sociologist who is engaged in participant-observation research always protect the confidentiality of subjects? What if the subjects are members of a religious cult allegedly involved in unethical and possibly illegal activities? What if the sociologist is interviewing political activists and is questioned by government authorities about the research?

Because most sociological research uses *people* as sources of information—as respondents to survey questions, subjects of ethnography, or participants in experiments—these sorts of questions are important. In all cases, sociologists need to be certain they are not invading their subjects' privacy. Generally, they do so by assuring subjects of anonymity and by guaranteeing the confidentiality of personal information. In addition, research proposals that involve human subjects must now be overseen by a review board, whose members seek to ensure that subjects are not placed at an unreasonable level of risk. If necessary, the board may ask researchers to revise their research designs to conform to the code of ethics.

We can appreciate the seriousness of the ethical problems researchers confront by considering the experience of sociologist Rik Scarce, described in the next section. Scarce's vow to protect his subjects' confidentiality got him into considerable trouble with the law.

Confidentiality

Like journalists, sociologists occasionally find themselves subject to questions from law enforcement authorities because of knowledge they have gained in the course of their work. This uncomfortable situation raises profound ethical questions.

In May 1993, Rik Scarce, a doctoral candidate in sociology at Washington State University, was jailed for contempt of court. Scarce had declined to tell a federal grand jury what he knew—or even whether he knew anything—about a 1991 raid on a university research laboratory by animal rights activists. At the time, Scarce was conducting research for a book about environmental protesters and knew at least one suspect in the break-in. Curiously, although he was chastised by a federal judge, Scarce won respect from fellow prison inmates, who regarded him as a man who "wouldn't snitch" (Monaghan 1993:A8).

The American Sociological Association supported Scarce's position when he appealed his sentence. Scarce maintained his silence. Ultimately the judge ruled that nothing would be gained by further incarceration, and Scarce was released after serving 159 days in jail. In January 1994, the U.S. Supreme Court declined to hear Scarce's case on appeal. The Court's failure to consider his case led Scarce (2005) to argue that federal legislation is needed to clarify the right of scholars and members of the press to preserve the confidentiality of those they interview.

Conflict of Interest

Sometimes disclosing all the sources of funding for a study, as required in principle 7 of the ASA's *Code of Ethics,* is not a sufficient guarantee of ethical conduct. Especially in the case of both corporate and government funding, money given ostensibly for the support of basic research may come with strings attached. Accepting funds from a private organization or even a government agency that stands to benefit from a study's results can call into question a researcher's objectivity and integrity (principle 1). The controversy surrounding the involvement of social scientists in the U.S. Army's Human Terrain System is one example of this conflict of interest.

Another example is the Exxon Corporation's support for research on jury verdicts. In 1989, the Exxon oil tanker *Valdez* hit a reef off the coast of Alaska, spilling more than 11 million gallons of oil into Prince William Sound. Five years later a federal court ordered Exxon to pay $5.3 billion in damages for the accident. Exxon appealed the verdict and began approaching

A floating containment barrier (or boom) encircles the Exxon oil tanker *Valdez* after its grounding on a reef off the coast of Alaska. Exxon was found negligent in the environmental disaster and was ordered to pay $5.3 billion for the cleanup. On appeal, the company managed to reduce the damages to $500 million based on academic research that it had funded—research that some scholars believe involved a conflict of interest.

legal scholars, sociologists, and psychologists who might be willing to study jury deliberations. The corporation's objective was to develop academic support for its lawyers' contention that the punitive judgments in such cases result from faulty deliberations and do not have a deterrent effect.

Some scholars have questioned the propriety of accepting funds under these circumstances, even if the source is disclosed. In at least one case, an Exxon employee explicitly told a sociologist that the corporation offers financial support to scholars who have shown the tendency to express views similar to its own. An argument can also be made that Exxon was attempting to set scholars' research agendas with its huge war chest. Rather than funding studies on the improvement of cleanup technologies or the assignment of long-term environmental costs, Exxon chose to shift scientists' attention to the validity of the legal awards in environmental cases.

The scholars who accepted Exxon's support deny that it influenced their work or changed their conclusions. Some received support from other sources as well, such as the National Science Foundation and Harvard University's Olin Center for Law, Economics, and Business. Many of their findings were published in respected academic journals after review by a jury of peers. Still, at least one researcher who participated in the studies refused monetary support from Exxon to avoid even the suggestion of a conflict of interest.

Exxon has spent roughly $1 million on the research, and at least one compilation of studies congenial to the corporation's point of view has been published. As ethical considerations require,

the academics who conducted the studies disclosed Exxon's role in funding them. Nevertheless, the investment appears to have paid off. In 2006, drawing on these studies, Exxon's lawyers succeeded in persuading an appeals court to reduce the corporation's legal damages from $5.3 to $2.5 billion. In 2008 Exxon appealed that judgment to the Supreme Court, which further reduced the damages to $500 million. The final award, which is to be shared by about 32,000 plaintiffs, will result in payments of about $15,000 to each person (Freudenburg 2005; Liptak 2008).

● Value Neutrality

The ethical considerations of sociologists lie not only in the methods they use and the funding they accept, but also in the way they interpret their results. Max Weber ([1904] 1949) recognized that personal values would influence the questions that sociologists select for research. In his view, that was perfectly acceptable, but under no conditions could a researcher allow his or her personal feelings to influence the *interpretation* of data. In Weber's phrase, sociologists must practice **value neutrality** in their research.

As part of this neutrality, investigators have an ethical obligation to accept research findings even when the data run counter to their personal views, to theoretically based explanations, or to widely accepted beliefs. For example, Émile Durkheim challenged popular conceptions when he reported that social (rather than supernatural) forces were an important factor in suicide.

Although some sociologists believe that neutrality is impossible, ignoring the issue would be irresponsible. Let's consider what might happen if researchers brought their own biases to the investigation. A person investigating the impact of intercollegiate sports on alumni contributions, for example, might focus only on the highly visible revenue-generating sports of football and basketball and neglect the so-called minor sports, such as tennis or soccer, which are more likely to involve women athletes. Despite the early work of W. E. B. DuBois and Jane Addams, sociologists still need to be reminded that the discipline often fails to adequately consider all people's social behavior.

In her book *The Death of White Sociology* (1973), Joyce Ladner called attention to the tendency of mainstream sociology to treat the lives of African Americans as a social problem. More recently, feminist sociologist Shulamit Reinharz (1992) has argued that sociological research should be not only inclusive but also open to bringing about social change and to drawing on relevant research by nonsociologists. Both Ladner and Reinharz maintain that researchers should always analyze whether women's unequal social status has affected their studies in any way. For example, one might broaden the study of the impact of education on income to consider the implications of the unequal pay status of men and women. The issue of value neutrality does not mean that sociologists can't have opinions, but it does mean that they must work to overcome any biases, however unintentional, that they may bring to their analysis of research.

Sociologist Peter Rossi (1987) admits to having liberal inclinations that direct him to certain fields of study. Yet in line with Weber's view of value neutrality, Rossi's commitment to rigorous research methods and objective interpretation of data has sometimes led him to controversial findings that are not necessarily supportive of his liberal values. For example, his measure of the extent of homelessness in Chicago in the mid-1980s fell far below the estimates of the Chicago Coalition for the Homeless.

Coalition members bitterly attacked Rossi for hampering their social reform efforts by minimizing the extent of homelessness. Rossi (1987:79) concluded that "in the short term, good social research will often be greeted as a betrayal of one or another side to a particular controversy."

MODULE 7 | Recap and Review

Summary

Sociologists must abide by certain ethical principles when conducting research.

1. The *Code of Ethics* of the American Sociological Association calls for objectivity and integrity in research, confidentiality, and disclosure of all sources of financial support.

2. Max Weber urged sociologists to practice value neutrality in their research by ensuring that their personal feelings do not influence their interpretation of data.

Thinking Critically

1. If you were planning to do research on human sexuality, which of the seven principles in the ASA's *Code of Ethics* would particularly concern you? What ethical problems might arise in such a study, and how would you attempt to prevent them?

2. Why did Max Weber specify the need for neutrality in the interpretation of data? Is complete value neutrality possible in sociological research? To what extent should researchers try to overcome their own biases?

Key Terms

Code of ethics 45

Value neutrality 46

MODULE 8 | Development of Methodology

● Feminist Methodology

Of the four theoretical approaches to sociology introduced in Chapter 1, the feminist perspective has had the greatest impact on the current generation of social researchers. How might this perspective influence research? Although researchers must be objective, their theoretical orientation may influence the questions they ask—or just as important, the questions they fail to ask. Until recently, for example, researchers frequently studied work and the family separately. Yet feminist theorists see the two spheres of activity as being closely integrated. Similarly, work and leisure, paid and unpaid domestic work may be seen not as two separate spheres, but as two sides of the same coin.

Recently, feminist scholars have become interested in self-injury, a practice described at the beginning of this chapter. Research shows that 85 percent of self-injurers are female; feminist researchers seek to explain why women predominate in this population. Rather than treat the behavior as a medical disorder, they note that society encourages women much more than men to attend to their bodies through hair removal, skin treatments, and depigmentation. Given this heightened attention to the female body, feminists suggest that specific instances of victimization can lead women to self-injure. They also seek to better understand male self-injurers, and are testing the hypothesis that among men, self-injury is a manifestation of hypermasculinity in the tolerance of pain (P. Adler and P. Adler 2011:25–27, 35–36).

Feminist theorists see the global trafficking of sex workers as a sign of the close relationship between the supposedly separate worlds of industrial nations and dependent developing nations.

The feminist perspective has also had an impact on global research. To feminist theorists, the traditional distinction between industrial nations and developing nations overlooks the close relationship between these two supposedly separate worlds. Feminist theorists have called for more research on the special role that immigrant women play in maintaining their households; on the use of domestic workers from less developed nations by households in industrial nations; and on the global trafficking of sex workers (Cheng 2003; Cooper et al. 2007; Sprague 2005).

Feminist researchers tend to involve and consult their subjects more than other researchers, and they are more oriented toward seeking change, raising the public consciousness, and influencing policy. They are particularly open to a multidisciplinary approach, such as making use of historical evidence or legal studies (T. Baker 1999; L. Lofland 1975; Reinharz 1992).

The Data-Rich Future

Advances in technology have affected all aspects of our lives, and sociological research is no exception. Massive increases in available data have allowed sociologists to undertake research that was virtually impossible just a decade ago. In the recent past, only people with grants or major institutional support could work easily with large amounts of data. Now anyone with a computer can access huge amounts of data and learn more about social behavior. Moreover, data from foreign countries are sometimes as available as information from the United States.

In the latter part of 2009, the world experienced an intense burst of influenza initially referred to as "swine flu," but later identified as the H1N1 flu strain. How did medical researchers track the virus's spread across a nation, much less the world? Epidemiologists typically rely on reports that originate in doctors' offices and are funneled through government agencies. Data collection is a time-consuming process, with many days passing between the detection of symptoms and the publication of official statistics. However, public health researchers found a way to track contagious diseases using Google. By monitoring

Taking Sociology to Work

Dave Eberbach, *Associate Director, Iowa Institute for Community Alliances*

Dave Eberbach is a people person who has been working with computers most of his career. In 1994 he was hired as a research coordinator by the United Way of Central Iowa. In that position he helped to create and implement Iowa's Homeless Management Information System (HMIS), which coordinates data on housing and homeless service providers. Eberbach also collaborated with the Human Service Planning Alliance to create and maintain a "data warehouse" of social statistics from diverse sources. As a research coordinator, he found that the data helped him to identify small pockets of poverty that were generally hidden in state and county statistics.

Today, Eberbach works at the Iowa Institute for Community Alliances, a small nonprofit organization that offers computerized client management and on-site program monitoring to homeless and housing service providers. As

Associate Director, Eberbach oversees a staff of seven and meets with clients who are working to improve service delivery to vulnerable people. "As fewer resources are being spent on social programs, it has been imperative to make sure that the focus of programs is on client success, not maintaining systems," he explains.

Eberbach went to Grinnell College, where he took a variety of social sciences courses before settling on sociology as a major. While there, he benefited from the presence of several visiting professors, who exposed him to a variety of racial and cultural perspectives. He found that his personal acquaintance with them complemented the concepts he was learning in his sociology classes. Today, Eberbach draws on his college experiences in his work, which brings him into contact with a diverse group of people.

As a student, Eberbach recalls, he never thought he would use statistics in his career, and didn't work very hard in the course. "As it turned out," he says, "I use it nearly every day.

Understanding data and statistics and being able to explain numbers to others has been very important in my job." The reverse has also been true, however: having a background in sociology has been helpful to him in systems design. "Understanding that systems need to work for a variety of groups of people, not just folks that grew up like I did," he explains, has been very helpful. "The world is not a computer problem or a math problem to be solved," he continues, "but rather a complex environment where groups of people continually bump into one another."

LET'S DISCUSS

1. Do you know what you want to be doing 10 years from now? If so, how might a knowledge of statistics help you in your future occupation?

2. What kinds of statistics, specifically, might you find in the Human Service Planning Alliance's data warehouse? Where would they come from?

the topics people search for and compensating for the relative access to computers in different countries (high in Sweden and low in Nigeria, for example), they can monitor the spread of disease almost in real time (Dukić et al. 2011).

Similarly, in the past sociologists had to rely on victims' complaints or police reports to understand crime patterns. Now they are beginning to access real-time, geocoded (that is, location-specific) incident reports. These new data will offer sociologists much more information, which they can interpret and relate to other aspects of the social environment (G. King 2011). Box 8-1 describes some new opportunities the Internet offers to researchers who study dating and mate selection (and who once were confined to surveying undergraduates).

One ethical concern raised by all these data involves individual privacy. Sociologists now have access to information about people's real estate transactions, campaign contributions, online product purchases, and even travel along tollways. What steps should they take to protect the privacy of the individuals whose data they are using? This is not an academic question. Today, 87 percent of the people in the United States can be personally identified given only their gender, date of birth, and ZIP code (G. King 2011).

We have seen that researchers rely on a number of tools, from time-tested observational research and use of existing sources to the latest in computer technologies. The Social Policy section that follows will describe researchers' efforts to survey the general population about a controversial aspect of social behavior: human sexuality. (For more on human sexuality, see Chapter 12, The Family and Intimate Relationships.) This investigation was complicated by its potential social policy implications. Because in the real world, sociological research can have far-reaching consequences for public policy and public welfare, many of the modules in this book will close with a Social Policy section.

 # Research Today

BOX 8-1

Lying for Love Online

Today, about 40 million people seek love online, and according to one estimate, 21 percent of heterosexual couples and 61 percent of same-sex couples meet online. But do these people tell the truth in their online postings? Not always, and not often.

Data gathered from online dating sites like Match.com, OkCupid, and Yahoo reveals both truthfulness and deception in people's online postings:

- In their profiles, people often describe an idealized self—for example, "I rock climb."

> Men are more likely than women to say they are younger, taller, and wealthier than they really are.

- Women typically describe themselves as 8.5 pounds heavier than they really are; men, as 2 pounds lighter.
- Men are more likely than women to say they are younger, taller, and wealthier than they really are.
- Less attractive people often post enhanced or retouched photos.
- Women post photos that are an average of 1.5 years old; men post photos that are 6 months old.

- Men are more likely than women to lie about their occupation, education, and marginally, their relationship status.

Although much of the time these deceptions may be small, their widespread nature has made them an almost expected part of the game. In one study, a man who posted a five-year-old photograph said he looked the "same" now except that he had a beard. In another case, a woman saw no problem in listing her occupation as "marketing" rather than retail sales. After all, she explained, "it's not like me saying I'm a janitor, and then lying and saying that I'm a CEO." That, she concluded, would be unacceptable.

Little wonder that research shows daters like the personalities they meet online better than the ones they meet in person.

LET'S DISCUSS

1. Have you tried using an online dating service? If so, were you truthful in describing yourself online? Did the people you were matched with turn out to be truthful?

2. Why do you think online daters engage in deception if they are hoping eventually to meet someone face-to-face?

Sources: N. Ellison et al. 2012; R. Epstein 2009; Gelles 2011; Rosenbloom 2011; Toma et al. 2008; Toma and Hancock 2010.

MODULE 8 Development of Methodology ▪ **49**

How can researchers study human sexual behavior? Neuroscientists Ogi Ogas and Sai Gaddam (2011) studied millions of web searches, websites, and videos related to sex. They found that women and men differ decidedly in their preferences, but very little (if any) distinction between heterosexuals and homosexuals, other than their sexual orientation. This type of research has significant limitations, however. Ogas and Gaddam could not distinguish between online fantasies and rational desires, or between a single search and one of many repeated searches by the same person. Nevertheless, this cyber study is a step forward in the effort to understand human sexual behavior, the subject of this policy section (Bartlett 2011).

Looking at the Issue

In this age of devastating sexually transmitted diseases, there is no time more important to increase our scientific understanding of human sexuality. As we will see, however, this is a difficult topic to research, not only because of privacy concerns but because of all the preconceptions, myths, and beliefs people bring to the subject of sexuality. Many people actively oppose research on human sexuality. How does one carry out scientific research on such a controversial and personal topic?

Applying Sociology

Sociologists have little reliable national data on patterns of sexual behavior in the United States. Until the 1990s, the only comprehensive study of sexual behavior was the famous two-volume *Kinsey Report,* prepared in the 1940s (Kinsey et al. 1948, 1953; see also Igo 2007). Although the *Kinsey Report* is still widely quoted, the volunteers interviewed for the report were not representative of the nation's adult population.

In part, we lack reliable data on patterns of sexual behavior because it is difficult for researchers to obtain accurate information about this sensitive subject. Moreover, until AIDS emerged in the 1980s, there was little scientific demand for data on sexual behavior, except for specific concerns such as contraception. And even though the AIDS crisis has reached dramatic proportions (as will be discussed in Module 53), government funding for studies of sexual behavior is still controversial and therefore difficult to obtain.

The controversy surrounding research on human sexual behavior raises the issue of value neutrality (see page 46), which becomes especially delicate when one considers the relationship of sociology to the government. The federal government has become the major source of funding for sociological research. Yet Max Weber urged that sociology remain an autonomous discipline and not become unduly influenced by any one segment of society. According to Weber's ideal of value neutrality, sociologists must remain free to reveal information that is embarrassing to the government, or for that matter, supportive of government institutions.

Initiating Policy

In 1987 the National Institute of Child Health and Human Development sought proposals for a national survey of sexual behavior. Sociologists responded with various plans that a review panel of scientists approved for funding. However, in 1991, the U.S. Senate voted to forbid funding any survey of adult sexual practices. Despite the vote, sociologists developed the National Health and Social Life Survey (NHSLS) to better understand the sexual practices of adults in the United States. The researchers raised $1.6 million of *private* funding to make their study possible (Laumann et al. 1994a, 1994b).

The authors of the NHSLS believe that their research is important. They argue that data from their survey allow interest groups to more easily address public policy issues such as AIDS, sexual harassment, welfare reform, sex discrimination, abortion, teenage pregnancy, and family planning. Moreover, the research findings help to counter some commonsense notions. For instance, contrary to the popular beliefs that

FIGURE 8-1 **Median Age of First Sex**

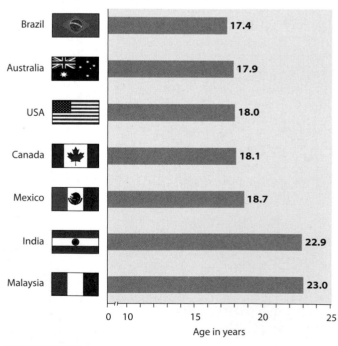

Country	Age in years
Brazil	17.4
Australia	17.9
USA	18.0
Canada	18.1
Mexico	18.7
India	22.9
Malaysia	23.0

Source: Durex 2007.

Sex may sell, but persuading legislators to fund research on human sexual behavior is still a challenge.

women regularly use abortion for birth control and that poor teens are the most likely socioeconomic group to have abortions, researchers found that three-fourths of all abortions are the first for the woman, and that well-educated and affluent women are more likely to have abortions than poor teens (Sweet 2001).

The usefulness of the NHSLS in addressing public policy issues has proved influential. As Figure 8-1 shows, scholars around the world are now studying human sexual behavior, in an effort to reduce the occurrence of HIV/AIDS.

TAKE THE ISSUE WITH YOU

1. Do you see any merit in the position of those who oppose government funding for research on sexual behavior? Explain your reasoning.

2. Exactly how could the results of research on human sexual behavior be used to control sexually transmitted diseases?

3. Compare the issue of value neutrality in government-funded research to the same issue in corporate-funded research. Are concerns about conflict of interest more or less serious in regard to government funding?

MODULE 8 | Recap and Review

Summary

Feminist theory and technological change have had important impacts on sociological research.

1. The feminist perspective has affected the questions sociologists ask, what groups they choose to study, the methods they use, and how globalization influences research.

2. Technology plays an important role in sociological research, whether it be a computer database or information obtained from the Internet.

3. Despite failure to obtain government funding, researchers developed the National Health and Social Life Survey (NHSLS) to better understand the sexual practices of adults in the United States.

Thinking Critically

1. Even if women are represented in a study, could the researcher's gender influence the data that are collected? If so, how? How might the problem be prevented?

2. Male sociologists once overlooked women in their studies of city life. What other groups could easily be overlooked in today's research, and why?

3. Suppose that you are a sociologist. You are trying to obtain funding for a study of adult sexual behavior from a government source. What arguments would you make to convince the government to fund your study?

In their effort to better understand social behavior, sociologists rely heavily on numbers and statistics. How have attitudes toward the legalization of marijuana changed over the past 40 years? A quick look at the results of 12 national surveys shows that while support for legalization of the drug has increased, it remains relatively weak (Figure A-3).

Using Statistics

The most common summary measures used by sociologists are percentages, means, modes, and medians. A **percentage** is a portion of 100. Use of percentages allows us to compare groups of different sizes. For example, if we were comparing financial contributors to a town's Baptist and Roman Catholic churches, the absolute numbers of contributors in each group could be misleading if there were many more Baptists than Catholics in the town. By using percentages, we could obtain a more meaningful comparison, showing the proportion of persons in each group who contribute to churches.

The **mean**, or *average,* is a number calculated by adding a series of values and then dividing by the number of values. For example, to find the mean of the numbers 5, 19, and 27, we would add them together (for a total of 51), divide by the number of values (3), and discover that the mean is 17.

The **mode** is the single most common value in a series of scores. Suppose we were looking at the following scores on a 10-point quiz:

10 10 9 9 8 8 7 7 7 6 5

The mode—the most frequent score on the quiz—is 7. While the mode is easier to identify than other summary measures, it tells sociologists little about all the other values. Hence, you will find much less use of the mode in this book than of the mean and the median.

The **median** is the midpoint or number that divides a series of values into two groups of equal numbers of values. For the quiz just discussed, the median, or central value, is 8. The mean, or average, would be 86 (the sum of all scores) divided by 11 (the total number of scores), or 7.8.

Some of these statistics may seem confusing at first. But think how difficult it is to comb through an endless list of numbers to identify a pattern or central tendency. Percentages, means, modes, and medians are essential time-savers in sociological research and analysis.

Reading Graphs

Tables and figures (that is, graphs) allow social scientists to display data and develop their conclusions more easily. In 2010, the Gallup poll interviewed 1,025 people in the United States, age 18 and over.

FIGURE A-3 **Changing Attitudes toward the Legalization of Marijuana**

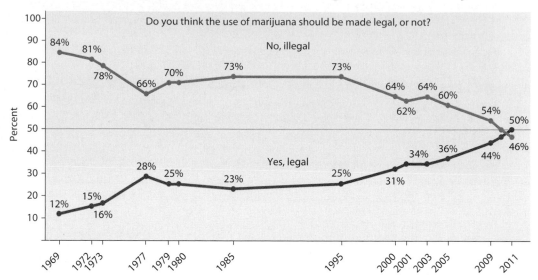

Source: Gallup 2011; see Newport 2011b in references.

Each respondent was asked, "Do you think the use of marijuana should be made legal, or not?" Without some type of summary, there is no way that analysts could examine the hundreds of individual responses to this question and reach firm conclusions. One type of summary sociologists use, a **cross-tabulation**, shows the relationship between two or more variables. Through the cross-tabulations presented graphically in Figure A-4, we can quickly see that older people are less likely to favor the legalization of marijuana than younger people, and that women are less supportive of legalization than men.

Graphs, like tables, can be quite useful to sociologists. And illustrations are often easier for the general public to understand, whether in newspapers or in PowerPoint presentations. Still, as with all data, we need to be careful how they are presented.

FIGURE A-4 **People Who Favor Legalization of Marijuana by Gender and Age, 2011**

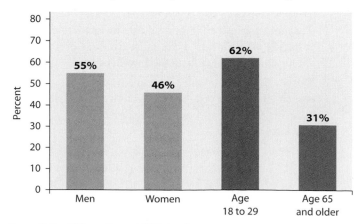

Source: Gallup 2011; see Newport 2011b in references.

Let's say you have decided to write a report on cohabitation (unmarried couples living together). How do you go about doing the necessary library research? Students must follow procedures similar to those used by sociologists in conducting original research. For your first step you must define the problem that you wish to study—perhaps in this case, how much cohabitation occurs and what its impact is on later marital happiness. The next step is to review the literature, which generally requires library research.

Finding Information

The following steps will be helpful in finding information:

1. Check this textbook and other textbooks that you own. Don't forget to begin with the materials closest at hand, including the website associated with this textbook, www.mhhe.com/schaefer10e.

2. Use the library's online catalog. Computerized library systems now access not only the college library's collection but also books and magazines from other libraries, available through interlibrary loans. These systems allow you to search for books by author or title. You can use title searches to locate books by subject as well. For example, if you search the title base for the keyword *cohabitation,* you will learn where books with that word in the title are located in the library's stacks. Near those books will be other works on cohabitation, which may not happen to have that word in the title. You may also want to search other, related keywords, such as *unmarried couples.*

3. Investigate using computerized periodical indexes, if they are available in your library. *Sociological Abstracts* online covers most sociological writing since 1963. In 2012, a search of just this one database found more than 2,233 documents having either *cohabitation* or *unmarried couples* as keywords. Some dealt with laws about cohabitation, while others focused on trends in other countries. If you limited your topic to same-sex couples, you would find 2,039 citations. Other electronic databases cover general-interest periodicals (*Time, Ms., National Review, Atlantic Monthly,* and so forth), reference materials, or newspapers. These electronic systems may be connected to a printer, allowing you to produce a printout complete with bibliographic information, and sometimes even complete copies of articles.

4. Examine government documents. The U.S. government, states and cities, and the United Nations publish information on virtually every subject of interest to social science researchers. Publications of the Census Bureau, for example, include tables showing the number of unmarried couples living together and some social characteristics of those households.

5. Use newspapers. Major newspapers publish annual or even weekly indexes that are useful in locating information about specific events or issues. Lexis-Nexis is an electronic index to U.S. and international newspapers.

6. Ask people, organizations, and agencies concerned with the topic for information and assistance. Be as specific as possible in making requests. You might receive very different information on the issue of cohabitation from talking with marriage counselors and with clergy from different religions.

7. If you run into difficulties, consult the instructor or the reference librarian at your college library.

A word of caution: be extremely careful in using the Internet to do research. Much of the information on the Internet is simply incorrect—even if it looks authoritative, is accompanied by impressive graphics, or has been widely circulated. Unlike the information in a library, which must be screened by a highly qualified librarian, "information" on the Internet can be created and posted by anyone with a computer. Check the sources for the information and note the Web page sponsor. Is the author qualified to write on the subject? Is the author even identified? Is the Web page sponsor likely to be biased? Whenever possible, try to confirm what you have read on the Internet through a well-known, reputable source or organization. If the accuracy of the information could be affected by how old it is, check the date on which the page or article was created or updated. Used intelligently, the Internet is a wonderful tool that offers students access to many of the reliable print sources noted earlier, including government documents and newspaper archives extending back over a century.

Writing the Report

Once you have completed all your research, you can begin writing the report. Here are a few tips:

- Be sure the topic you have chosen is not too broad. You must be able to cover it adequately in a reasonable amount of time and a reasonable number of pages.

- Develop an outline for your report. You should have an introduction and a conclusion that relate to each other, and the discussion should proceed logically throughout the paper. Use headings within the paper if they will improve clarity and organization.

- Do not leave all the writing until the last minute. It is best to write a rough draft, let it sit for a few days, and then take a fresh look before beginning revisions.

- If possible, read your paper aloud. Doing so may be helpful in locating sections or phrases that don't make sense.

Remember that you *must* cite all information you have obtained from other sources, including the Internet. Plagiarism is a serious academic offense, for which the penalties are severe. If you use an author's exact words, it is essential that you place them in quotation marks. Even if you reworked someone else's ideas, you must indicate the source of those ideas.

11. Unlike the typical citizen, the sociologist has a commitment to use the _____ method in studying society.

12. A(n) _____ is a speculative statement about the relationship between two or more factors known as variables.

13. _____ refers to the degree to which a measure or scale truly reflects the phenomenon under study.

14. In order to obtain data scientifically, researchers need to select a research _____.

15. If scientists were testing a new type of toothpaste in an experimental setting, they would administer the toothpaste to a(n) _____ group, but not to a(n) _____ group.

16. The term _____ _____ refers to the unintended influence that observers of experiments can have on their subjects.

17. Using census data in a way unintended by its initial collectors would be an example of _____ _____.

18. Using _____ _____, researchers conducted a study of gender-stereotyped behavior in children's coloring books.

19. The American Sociological Association's *Code of* _____ requires sociologists to maintain objectivity and integrity and to preserve the confidentiality of their subjects.

20. As part of their commitment to _____ neutrality, investigators have an ethical obligation to accept research findings even when the data run counter to their personal views or to widely accepted beliefs.

thinking about movies

Gasland

This documentary investigates the possible health effects of a new technique for drilling natural gas, called *hydraulic fracturing* ("fracking").

An Inconvenient Truth

In this documentary about global warming, Al Gore makes the case that certain social groups are already paying the price for climate change.

Kinsey

Researchers confront the ethical challenges of studying human behavior in this film about the *Kinsey Report*.

What do you think of the society described here by anthropologist Horace Miner?

Could you live in such a culture?

❝ Nacirema culture is characterized by a highly developed market economy which has evolved in a rich natural habitat. While much of the people's time is devoted to economic pursuits, a large part of the fruits of these labors and a considerable portion of the day are spent in ritual activity. The focus of this activity is the human body, the appearance and health of which loom as a dominant concern in the ethos of the people. While such a concern is certainly not unusual, its ceremonial aspects and associated philosophy are unique.

The fundamental belief underlying the whole system appears to be that the human body is ugly and that its natural tendency is to debility and disease. Incarcerated in such a body, man's only hope is to avert these characteristics through the use of the powerful influences of ritual and ceremony. Every household has one or more shrines devoted to this purpose. The more powerful individuals in the society have several shrines in their houses and, in fact, the opulence of a house is often referred to in terms of the number of such ritual centers it possesses. Most houses are of wattle and daub construction, but the shrine rooms of the more wealthy are walled with stone. Poorer families imitate the rich by applying pottery plaques to their shrine walls.

While each family has at least one such shrine, the rituals associated with it are not family ceremonies but are private

The focal point of the shrine is a box or chest which is built into the wall. In this chest are kept the many charms and magical potions without which no native believes he could live.

and secret. The rites are normally only discussed with children, and then only during the period when they are being initiated into these mysteries. I was able, however, to establish sufficient rapport with the natives to examine these shrines and to have the rituals described to me.

The focal point of the shrine is a box or chest which is built into the wall. In this chest are kept the many charms and magical potions without which no native believes he could live. These preparations are secured from a variety of specialized practitioners. The most powerful of these are the medicine men, whose assistance must be rewarded with substantial gifts. However, the medicine men do not provide the curative potions for their clients, but decide what the ingredients should be and then write them down in an ancient and secret language. This writing is understood only by the medicine men and by the herbalists who, for another gift, provide the required charm.

The charm is not disposed of after it has served its purpose, but is placed in the charm-box of the household shrine. As these magical materials are specific for certain ills, and the real or imagined maladies of the people are many, the charm-box is usually full to overflowing. The magical packets are so numerous that people forget what their purposes were and fear to use them again. While the natives are very vague on this point, we can only assume that the idea in retaining all the old magical materials is that their presence in the charm-box, before which the body rituals are conducted, will in some way protect the worshipper. ❞

(Miner 1956:503–504) Additional information about this excerpt can be found on the Online Learning Center at www.mhhe.com/schaefermod2e.

In this excerpt from his journal article "Body Ritual among the Nacirema," Horace Miner casts an anthropologist's observant eye on the intriguing rituals of an exotic culture. If some aspects of this culture seem familiar to you, you are right, for what Miner is describing is actually the culture of the United States ("Nacirema" is "American" spelled backward). The "shrine" Miner writes of is the bathroom; he correctly informs us that in this culture, one measure of wealth is how many bathrooms one's home has. In their bathroom rituals, he goes on, the Nacirema use charms and magical potions (beauty products and prescription drugs) obtained from specialized practitioners (such as hair stylists), herbalists (pharmacists), and medicine

men (physicians). Using our sociological imaginations, we could update Miner's description of the Nacirema's charms, written in 1956, by adding tooth whiteners, anti-aging creams, Waterpiks, and hair gel.

When we step back and examine a culture thoughtfully and objectively, whether it is our own culture in disguise or another less familiar to us, we learn something new about society. Take Fiji, an island in the Pacific where a robust, nicely rounded body has always been the ideal for both men and women. This is a society in which traditionally, "You've gained weight" has been considered a compliment, and "Your legs are skinny," an insult. Yet a recent study shows that for the first time, eating disorders have been showing up among young people in Fiji. What has happened to change their body image? Since the introduction of cable television in 1995, many Fiji islanders, especially young women, have begun to emulate not their mothers and aunts, but the small-waisted stars of television programs currently airing there, like *Gossip Girl* and *Modern Family*. Studying culture in places like Fiji, then, sheds light on our society as well (A. Becker 2007; Fiji TV 2012).

In these four modules we will study the development of culture around the world, including the cultural effects of the worldwide trend toward globalization. We will see just how

basic the study of culture is to sociology. Our discussion will focus both on general cultural practices found in all societies and on the wide variations that can distinguish one society from another. We will define and explore the major aspects of culture, including language, norms, sanctions, and values. We will see how cultures develop a dominant ideology, and how functionalist and conflict theorists view culture. We'll also see what can happen when a major corporation ignores cultural variations. Then, in the Social Policy section, we will look at the conflicts in cultural values that underlie current debates over bilingualism.

MODULE 9 | What Is Culture?

Culture is the totality of learned, socially transmitted customs, knowledge, material objects, and behavior. It includes the ideas, values, and artifacts (for example, DVDs, comic books, and birth control devices) of groups of people. Patriotic attachment to the flag of the United States is an aspect of culture, as is a national passion for the tango in Argentina.

Sometimes people refer to a particular person as "very cultured" or to a city as having "lots of culture." That use of the term *culture* is different from our use in this textbook. In sociological terms, culture

does not refer solely to the fine arts and refined intellectual taste. It consists of *all* objects and ideas within a society, including slang words, ice-cream cones, and rock music. Sociologists consider both a portrait by Rembrandt and the work of graffiti spray painters to be aspects of culture. A tribe that cultivates soil by hand has just as much culture as a people that relies on computer-operated machinery. Each people has a distinctive culture with its own characteristic ways of gathering and preparing food, constructing homes, structuring the family, and promoting standards of right and wrong.

Navigating cultural differences can be a challenge. During a visit to Tokyo, President Obama was criticized for his deep bow to Emperor Akihito. And at the 2010 Winter Olympics, Russian ice dancers Domnina and Shabalin were criticized for their interpretation of Aboriginal dress. Favored to win, they took third place.

The fact that you share a similar culture with others helps to define the group or society to which you belong. A fairly large number of people are said to constitute a **society** when they live in the same territory, are relatively independent of people outside their area, and participate in a common culture. Metropolitan Los Angeles is more populous than at least 150 nations, yet sociologists do not consider it a society in its own right. Rather, they see it as part of—and dependent on—the larger society of the United States.

A society is the largest form of human group. It consists of people who share a common heritage and culture. Members of the society learn this culture and transmit it from one generation to the next. They even preserve their distinctive culture through literature, art, video recordings, and other means of expression.

Sociologists have long recognized the many ways in which culture influences human behavior. Through what has been termed a tool kit of habits, skills, and styles, people of a common culture construct their acquisition of knowledge, their interactions with kinfolk, their entrance into the job market—in short, the way in which they live. If it were not for the social transmission of culture, each generation would have to reinvent television, not to mention the wheel (Swidler 1986).

Having a common culture also simplifies many day-to-day interactions. For example, when you buy an airline ticket, you know you don't have to bring along hundreds of dollars in cash. You can pay with a credit card. When you are part of a society, you take for granted many small (as well as more important) cultural patterns. You assume that theaters will provide seats for the audience, that physicians will not disclose confidential information, and that parents will be careful when crossing the street with young children. All these assumptions reflect basic values, beliefs, and customs of the culture of the United States.

Today, when text, sound, and video can be transmitted around the world instantaneously, some aspects of culture transcend national borders. The German philosopher Theodor Adorno and others have spoken of the worldwide **culture industry** that standardizes the goods and services demanded by consumers. Adorno contends that globally, the primary effect of popular culture is to limit people's choices. Yet others have shown that the culture industry's influence does not always permeate international borders. Sometimes the culture industry is embraced; at other times, soundly rejected (Adorno [1971] 1991:98–106; Horkheimer and Adorno [1944] 2002).

● Cultural Universals

All societies have developed certain common practices and beliefs, known as **cultural universals.** Many cultural universals are, in fact, adaptations to meet essential human needs, such as the need for food, shelter, and clothing. Anthropologist George Murdock (1945:124) compiled a list of cultural universals, including athletic sports, cooking, dancing, visiting, personal names, marriage, medicine, religious ritual, funeral ceremonies, sexual restrictions, and trade.

The cultural practices Murdock listed may be universal, but the manner in which they are expressed varies from culture to culture. For example, one society may let its members choose their marriage partners; another may encourage marriages arranged by the parents.

Not only does the expression of cultural universals vary from one society to another; within a society, it may also change dramatically over time. Each generation, and each year for that matter, most human cultures change and expand.

● Ethnocentrism

Many everyday statements reflect our attitude that our culture is best. We use terms such as *underdeveloped, backward,* and *primitive* to refer to other societies. What "we" believe is a religion; what "they" believe is superstition and mythology.

It is tempting to evaluate the practices of other cultures on the basis of our perspectives. Sociologist William Graham Sumner (1906) coined the term **ethnocentrism** to refer to the tendency to assume that one's own culture and way of life represent the norm or are superior to all others. The ethnocentric person sees his or her group as the center or defining point of culture and views all other cultures as deviations from what is "normal." Westerners who think cattle are to be used for food might look down on India's Hindu religion and culture, which view the cow as sacred. Or people in one culture may dismiss as unthinkable the mate selection or child-rearing practices of another culture. In sum, our view of the world is dramatically influenced by the society in which we were raised.

Ethnocentrism is hardly limited to citizens of the United States. Visitors from many African cultures are surprised at the disrespect that children in the United States show their parents. People from India may be repelled by our practice of living in the same household with dogs and cats. Many Islamic fundamentalists in the Arab world and Asia view the United States as corrupt, decadent, and doomed to destruction. All these people may feel comforted by membership in cultures that in their view are superior to ours.

● Cultural Relativism

While ethnocentrism means evaluating foreign cultures using the familiar culture of the observer as a standard of correct behavior, **cultural relativism** means viewing people's behavior from the perspective of their own culture. It places a priority on understanding other cultures, rather than dismissing them as "strange" or "exotic." Unlike ethnocentrists, cultural relativists employ the kind of value neutrality in scientific study that Max Weber saw as so important.

Cultural relativism stresses that different social contexts give rise to different norms and values. Thus, we must examine practices such as polygamy, bullfighting, and monarchy within the particular contexts of the cultures in which they are found. Although cultural relativism does not suggest that we must unquestioningly accept every cultural variation, it does require a serious and unbiased effort to evaluate norms, values, and customs in light of their distinctive culture.

Consider the practice of children marrying adults. Most people in North America cannot fathom the idea of a 12-year-old girl marrying. The custom, which is illegal in the United States,

FIGURE 9-1 **Countries with High Child Marriage Rates**

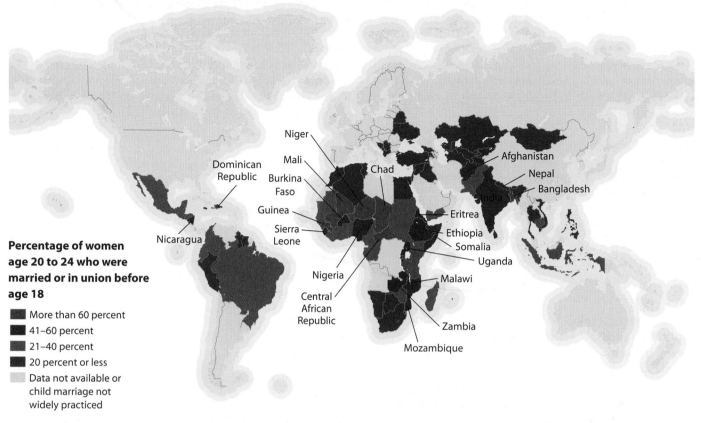

Niger
Mali
Dominican
Republic
Chad
Afghanistan
Burkina
Faso
Nepal
Bangladesh
Guinea
India
Eritrea
Sierra
Leone
Nicaragua
Ethiopia
Somalia
Uganda
Nigeria
Malawi
Central
African
Republic
Zambia
Mozambique

**Percentage of women
age 20 to 24 who were
married or in union before
age 18**

- More than 60 percent
- 41–60 percent
- 21–40 percent
- 20 percent or less
- Data not available or
  child marriage not
  widely practiced

Note: Data are the most recent available, ranging from 1987 to 2006.
Source: UNICEF 2010.

In 21 countries, 40 percent or more of the women under 18 are married.

is common in West Africa and South Asia. Should the United States respect such marriages? The apparent answer is no. In 2006 the U.S. government spent $623 million to discourage the practice in many of the countries with the highest child-marriage rates (Figure 9-1).

From the perspective of cultural relativism, we might ask whether one society should spend its resources to dictate the norms of another. However, federal officials have defended the government's actions. They contend that child marriage deprives girls of education, threatens their health, and weakens public health efforts to combat HIV/AIDS (Jain and Kurz 2007; B. Slavin 2007).

Sociobiology and Culture

While sociology emphasizes diversity and change in the expression of culture, another school of thought, sociobiology, stresses the universal aspects of culture. **Sociobiology** is the systematic study of how biology affects human social behavior. Sociobiologists assert that many of the cultural traits humans display, such as the almost universal expectation that women will be nurturers and men will be providers, are not learned but are rooted in our genetic makeup.

Sociobiology is founded on the naturalist Charles Darwin's (1859) theory of evolution. In traveling the world, Darwin had noted small variations in species—in the shape of a bird's beak, for example—from one location to another. He theorized that over hundreds of generations, random variations in genetic makeup had helped certain members of a species to survive in a particular environment. A bird with a differently shaped beak might have been better at gathering seeds than other birds, for instance. In reproducing, these lucky individuals had passed on their advantageous genes to succeeding generations. Eventually, given their advantage in survival, individuals with the variation began to outnumber other members of the species. The species was slowly adapting to its environment. Darwin called this process of adaptation to the environment through random genetic variation *natural selection.*

Sociobiologists apply Darwin's principle of natural selection to the study of social behavior. They assume that particular forms of behavior become genetically linked to a species if they contribute to its fitness to survive (van den Berghe 1978). In its extreme form, sociobiology suggests that *all* behavior is the result of genetic or biological factors, and that social interactions play no role in shaping people's conduct.

Sociobiologists do not seek to describe individual behavior on the level of "Why is Fred more aggressive than Jim?" Rather, they focus on how human nature is affected by the genetic composition of a *group* of people who share certain characteristics (such as men or women, or members of isolated tribal bands). In general, sociobiologists have stressed the basic genetic heritage that *all* humans share and have shown little interest in speculating about alleged differences between racial groups or nationalities. A few researchers have tried to trace specific behaviors, like criminal activity, to certain genetic markers, but those markers are not deterministic. Family cohesiveness, peer group behavior, and other social factors can override genetic influences on behavior (Guo et al. 2008; E. Wilson 1975, 1978).

Certainly most social scientists would agree that there is a biological basis for social behavior. But there is less support for the extreme positions taken by certain advocates of sociobiology. Like interactionists, conflict theorists and functionalists believe that people's behavior rather than their genetic structure defines social reality. Conflict theorists fear that the sociobiological approach could be used as an argument against efforts to assist disadvantaged people, such as schoolchildren who are not competing successfully (Freese 2008; Machalek and Martin 2010; E. Wilson 2000).

MODULE 9 | Recap and Review

Summary

Culture is the totality of learned, socially transmitted customs, knowledge, material objects, and behavior. This module examines the social practices common to all cultures.

1. A shared culture helps to define the group or **society** to which we belong.

2. Anthropologist George Murdock compiled a list of **cultural universals,** or common practices found in every culture, including marriage, sports, cooking, medicine, and sexual restrictions.

3. People who assume their own culture is superior to other cultures engage in **ethnocentrism.** In contrast, **cultural relativism** is the practice of viewing other people's behavior from the perspective of their own culture.

Thinking Critically

1. Select three cultural universals from George Murdock's list (page 62) and analyze them from a functionalist perspective. Why are these practices found in every culture? What functions do they serve?

2. What are some problems with looking at social behavior from a sociobiological point of view? What are some benefits? How useful do you find this perspective?

Key Terms

Cultural relativism 62

Cultural universal 62

Culture 61

Culture industry 62

Ethnocentrism 62

Society 62

Sociobiology 63

MODULE 10 | Elements of Culture

Role of Language

Language is one of the major elements of culture that underlie cultural variations. It is also an important component of cultural capital. Recall from Module 2 that Pierre Bourdieu used the term *cultural capital* to describe noneconomic assets, such as family background and past educational investments, which are reflected in a person's knowledge of language and the arts.

Members of a society generally share a common language, which facilitates day-to-day exchanges with others. When you ask a hardware store clerk for a flashlight, you don't need to draw a picture of the instrument. You share the same cultural term for a small,

A native speaker trains instructors from the Oneida Nation of New York in the Berlitz method of language teaching. As of 2012, there were 527 speakers of the Oneida language. Many Native American tribes are taking similar steps to recover their seldom used languages, realizing that language is the essential foundation of any culture.

portable, battery-operated light. However, if you were in England and needed this item, you would have to ask for an electric torch. Of course, even within the same society, a term can have a number of different meanings. In the United States, *pot* signifies both a container that is used for cooking and an intoxicating drug. In this section we will examine the cultural influence of language, which includes both the written and spoken word and nonverbal communication.

Language: Written and Spoken

Seven thousand languages are spoken in the world today—many more than the number of countries. For the speakers of each one, whether they number 2,000 or 200 million, language is fundamental to their shared culture.

The English language, for example, makes extensive use of words dealing with war. We speak of "conquering" space, "fighting" the "battle" of the budget, "waging war" on drugs, making a "killing" on the stock market, and "bombing" an examination; something monumental or great is "the bomb." An observer from

an entirely different and warless culture could gauge the importance that war and the military have had in our lives simply by recognizing the prominence that militaristic terms have in our language. Similarly, the Sami people of northern Norway and Sweden have a rich diversity of terms for snow, ice, and reindeer (Haviland et al. 2008; Magga 2006).

Language is, in fact, the foundation of every culture. **Language** is an abstract system of word meanings and symbols for all aspects of culture. It includes speech, written characters, numerals, symbols, and nonverbal gestures and expressions. Because language is the foundation of every culture, the ability to speak other languages is crucial to intercultural relations. Throughout the Cold War era, beginning in the 1950s and continuing well into the 1970s, the U.S. government encouraged the study of Russian by developing special language schools for diplomats and military advisers who dealt with the Soviet Union. And following September 11, 2001, the nation recognized how few skilled translators it had for Arabic and other languages spoken in Muslim countries. Language quickly became a key not only to tracking potential terrorists, but also to building diplomatic bridges with Muslim countries willing to help in the war against terrorism.

Language does more than simply describe reality; it also serves to *shape* the reality of a culture. For example, most people in the United States cannot easily make the verbal distinctions concerning snow and ice that are possible in the Sami culture. As a result, they are less likely to notice such differences.

The **Sapir-Whorf hypothesis,** named for two linguists, describes the role of language in shaping our interpretation of reality. According to Sapir and Whorf, because people can conceptualize the world only through language, language *precedes* thought. Thus, the word symbols and grammar of a language organize the world for us. The Sapir-Whorf hypothesis also holds that language

Using American Sign Language, a form of nonverbal communication, a football coach discusses a play with his team. The Silent Warriors, four-time national champions and the pride of the Alabama School for the Deaf, have defeated both hearing and nonhearing teams.

is not a given. Rather, it is culturally determined, and it encourages a distinctive interpretation of reality by focusing our attention on certain phenomena (Sapir 1929).

For decades, the Navajo have referred to cancer as *lood doo na'dziihii.* Now, through a project funded by the National Cancer Institute, the tribal college is seeking to change the phrase. Why? Literally, the phrase means "the sore that does not heal," and health educators are concerned that tribal members who have been diagnosed with cancer view it as a death sentence. Their effort to change the Navajo language, not easy in itself, is complicated by the Navajo belief that to talk about the disease is to bring it on one's people (Fonseca 2008).

Similarly, feminists have noted that gender-related language can reflect—although in itself it does not determine—the traditional acceptance of men and women in certain occupations. Each time we use a term such as *mailman, policeman,* or *fireman,* we are implying (especially to young children) that these occupations can be filled only by males. Yet many women work as *mail carriers, police officers,* and *firefighters*—a fact that is being increasingly recognized and legitimized through the use of such nonsexist language.

Language can shape how we see, taste, smell, feel, and hear. It also influences the way we think about the people, ideas, and objects around us. Language communicates a culture's most important norms, values, and sanctions. That's why the decline of an old language or the introduction of a new one is such a sensitive issue in many parts of the world (see the Social Policy section at the end of Module 12).

trend|spotting

Linguistic Isolation

In 2006, a severe winter storm hit the northwest United States, knocking out electrical power in many communities. Residents turned on their generators, some without heeding warnings about the risk of carbon monoxide poisoning. Although local media ran public service announcements about the need for adequate ventilation of the generators, six people died and several others fell ill from exposure to carbon monoxide. Investigators later determined that the victims had been unable to understand the English-only warnings. In response to the discovery, the *Seattle Times* took the unprecedented step of publishing the front-page story in six languages: English, Vietnamese, Chinese, Spanish, Russian, and Somali.

Although most immigrants can communicate effectively in English, language does isolate a small percentage of them. In the United States, social scientists use the term *linguistic isolation* to refer to households in which all members age 14 and older speak a non-English language and at the same time do not speak English very well. They have found that the proportion of the U.S. population that is linguistically isolated has been increasing steadily, from 3.2 percent in 2000 to 4.7 percent in 2009.

Studies show that those who are linguistically isolated are cut off from many public services. For example, public health professionals find that even after controlling for education and income, members of linguistically isolated households are less likely than others to receive adequate health care, or even to participate in basic health screening. And as the 2006 power outage in the Northwest showed, in some cases linguistic isolation can be deadly.

Nonverbal Communication

If you don't like the way a meeting is going, you might suddenly sit back, fold your arms, and turn down the corners of your mouth. When you see a friend in tears, you may give a quick hug. After winning a big game, you probably high-five your teammates. These are all examples of *nonverbal communication,* the use of gestures, facial expressions, and other visual images to communicate.

We are not born with these expressions. We learn them, just as we learn other forms of language, from people who share our same culture. This statement is as true for the basic expressions of happiness and sadness as it is for more complex emotions, such as shame or distress (Fridlund et al. 1987).

Like other forms of language, nonverbal communication is not the same in all cultures. For example, sociological research done at the micro level documents that people from various cultures differ in the degree to which they touch others during the course of normal social interactions. Even experienced travelers are sometimes caught off guard by these differences. In Saudi Arabia, a middle-aged man may want to hold hands with a partner after closing a business deal. In Egypt, men walk hand in hand in the street; in cafés, they fall asleep while lounging in each other's arms. These gestures, which would shock an American businessman, are considered compliments in those cultures. The meaning of hand signals is another form of nonverbal communication that can differ from one culture to the next. In Australia, the thumbs-up sign is considered rude (Passero 2002; Vaughan 2007).

A related form of communication is the use of symbols to convey meaning to others. **Symbols** are the gestures, objects, and words that form the basis of human communication. The thumbs-up gesture, a gold star sticker, and the smiley face in an e-mail are all symbols. Often deceptively simple, many symbols are rich in meaning and may not convey the same meaning in all social contexts. Around someone's neck, for example, a cross can symbolize religious reverence; over a grave site, a belief in everlasting life; or set in flames, racial hatred. Box 10-1 describes the delicate task of designing an appropriate symbol for the 9/11 memorial at New York's former World Trade Center—one that would have meaning for everyone who lost loved ones there, regardless of nationality or religious faith.

● Norms and Values

"Wash your hands before dinner." "Thou shalt not kill." "Respect your elders." All societies have ways of encouraging and enforcing what they view as appropriate behavior while discouraging and punishing what they consider to be inappropriate behavior. They also have a collective idea of what is good and desirable in life—or not. In this section we will learn to distinguish between the closely related concepts of norms and values.

Norms

Norms are the established standards of behavior maintained by a society. For a norm to become significant, it must be widely shared and understood. For example, in movie theaters in the

BOX 10-1

Sociology in the Global Community

Symbolizing 9/11

On September 11, 2001, the World Trade Center's twin towers took only minutes to collapse. Nearly a decade later, the creator of the memorial to those lost that day was still perfecting the site plan. Thirty-four-year-old architect Michael Arad, the man who submitted the winning design, had drawn two sunken squares, measuring an acre each, in the footprints left by the collapsed towers. His design, "Reflecting Absence," places each empty square in a reflecting pool surrounded by cascading water. Today, as visitors to the massive memorial stand at the edge of the site, they are struck by both the sound of the thundering water and the absence of life.

The memorial does not encompass the entire area destroyed in the attack, as some had wanted. In one of the great commercial capitals of the world, economic forces demanded that some part of the property produce income. Others had argued against constructing a memorial of any kind on what they regarded as hallowed ground. "Don't build on my sister's grave," one of them pleaded. They

too had to compromise. On all sides of the eight-acre memorial site, new high rises have been and continue to be built. When construction is finished, the site will also accommodate a new underground transit hub.

Originally, the architect's plans called for the 2,982 victims of the attack to be listed elsewhere on the site. Today, in a revised plan, the names are displayed prominently along the sides of the reflecting pool. Arad had suggested that they be placed randomly, to symbolize the "haphazard brutality of life." Survivors objected, perhaps because they worried about locating their loved ones' names. In a compromise, the names were chiseled into the bronze walls of the memorial in groups that Arad calls "meaningful adjacencies": friends and co-workers; fellow passengers on the two downed aircraft, arranged by seat number; and first responders, grouped by their agencies or fire companies. Suggestions that would give first responders special recognition were set aside. The list includes victims of the simultaneous attack on the Pentagon in Washington,

D.C., and passengers on the flight headed for the White House, who were attempting to thwart the attack when the plane crashed in a field in Pennsylvania. The six people who perished in the 1993 truck bombing at the World Trade Center are also memorialized.

Away from Ground Zero, symbols of 9/11 abound. Numerous small monuments and simple plaques grace intersections throughout metropolitan New York, particularly those that had a direct line of sight to the twin towers. In hundreds of cities worldwide, scraps of steel from the twisted buildings and remnants of destroyed emergency vehicles have been incorporated into memorials. And the USS *New York*, whose bow was forged from seven and a half tons of steel debris salvaged from the towers, has served as a working symbol of 9/11 since its commissioning in 2009.

LET'S DISCUSS

1. What does the 9/11 memorial symbolize to you? Explain the meaning of the cascading water, the reflecting pools, and the empty footprints. What does the placement of the victims' names suggest?

2. If you were designing a 9/11 memorial, what symbol or symbols would you incorporate? Use your sociological imagination to predict how various groups would respond to your design.

Sources: Blais and Rasic 2011; Kennicott 2011; Needham 2011.

> Numerous small monuments and simple plaques grace intersections throughout metropolitan New York, particularly those that had a direct line of sight to the twin towers.

United States, we typically expect that people will be quiet while the film is shown. Of course, the application of this norm can vary, depending on the particular film and type of audience. People who are viewing a serious artistic film will be more likely to insist on the norm of silence than those who are watching a slapstick comedy or horror movie.

One persistent social norm in contemporary society is that of heterosexuality. Children are socialized to accept this norm from a very young age. Overwhelmingly, parents describe adult romantic relationships to their children exclusively as heterosexual

relationships. That is not necessarily because they consider same-sex relationships unacceptable, but more likely because they see heterosexuality as the norm in marital partnerships. According to a national survey of mothers of three- to six-year-olds, one in five mothers teaches her young children that homosexuality is wrong. The same survey showed that parenting reflects the dominant ideology, in which homosexuality is treated as a rare exception. Most parents assume that their children are heterosexual; only one in four has even considered whether his or her child might grow up to be gay or lesbian (K. Martin 2009).

When a society's nonmaterial culture (its values and laws) does not keep pace with rapid changes in its material culture, people experience an awkward period of maladjustment called *culture lag*. The transition to nuclear power generation that began in the second half of the 20th century brought widespread protests against the new technology, as well as serious accidents that government officials were poorly prepared to deal with. Tensions over the controversial technology have not run as high in some countries as in others, however. France, where this nuclear power plant is situated, generates 78 percent of all its electricity through nuclear power. The technology is not as controversial there as in the United States and Canada, which generate less than 20 percent of their electricity through nuclear reaction.

and desires" (Nolan and Lenski 2009:357). Today's technological developments no longer await publication in journals with limited circulation. Press conferences, often carried simultaneously on the Internet, trumpet the new developments.

Technology not only accelerates the diffusion of scientific innovations but also transmits culture. The English language and North American culture dominate the Internet and World Wide Web. Such control, or at least dominance, of technology influences the direction of cultural diffusion. For example, websites cover even the most superficial aspects of U.S. culture but offer little information about the pressing issues faced by citizens of other nations. People all over the world find it easier to visit electronic chat rooms about the latest reality TV shows than to learn about their own governments' policies on day care or infant nutrition.

Sociologist William F. Ogburn (1922) made a useful distinction between the elements of *material* and *nonmaterial culture*. **Material culture** refers to the physical or technological aspects of our daily lives, including food, houses, factories, and raw materials. **Nonmaterial culture** refers to ways of using material objects, as well as to customs, beliefs, philosophies, governments, and patterns of communication. Generally, the nonmaterial culture is more resistant to change than the material culture. Consequently, Ogburn introduced the term **culture lag** to refer to the period of maladjustment when the nonmaterial culture is still struggling to adapt to new material conditions. For example, in 2010, manufacturers introduced electronic cigarettes, battery-powered tubes that turn nicotine-laced liquid into a vapor mist. The innovation soon had officials at airlines (which ban smoking) and the Food and Drug Administration scrambling to respond to the latest technology (Kesmodel and Yadron 2010; Swidler 1986).

Resistance to technological change can lead not only to culture lag, but to some real questions of cultural survival (Box 11-2).

⊕ Sociology in the Global Community

BOX 11-2

Cultural Survival in Brazil

When the first Portuguese ships landed on the coast of what we now know as Brazil, more than 2 million people inhabited the vast, mineral-rich land. The natives lived in small, isolated settlements, spoke a variety of languages, and embraced many different cultural traditions.

Today, over five centuries later, Brazil's population has grown to more than 192 million, only about 650,000 of whom are indigenous peoples descended from the original inhabitants. Over 200 different indigenous groups

In Mato Grosso, a heavily forested state near the Amazon River, loggers have been clear-cutting the land at a rate that alarms the Bororo.

have survived, living a life tied closely to the land and the rivers, just as their ancestors did. But over the past two generations, their numbers have dwindled as booms in mining, logging, oil drilling, and agriculture have encroached on their land and their settlements.

Many indigenous groups were once nomads, moving around from one hunting or fishing ground to another. Now they are hemmed in on the reservations the government confined them to, surrounded by huge farms or ranches whose owners deny their right to live off the land. State officials may insist that laws restrict the development of indigenous lands, but indigenous peoples tell a different story. In Mato Grosso, a heavily forested state near the Amazon River, loggers have been clear-cutting the land at a rate that alarms the Bororo, an indigenous group that has lived in the area for centuries. According to one elder, the Bororo are now confined to six small reservations of about 500 square miles—much less than the area officially granted them in the 19th century.

In the face of dwindling resources, indigenous groups like the Bororo struggle to maintain their culture. Though the tribe still observes the traditional initiation rites for adolescent boys, members are finding it difficult to continue their hunting and fishing rituals, given the scarcity of game and fish in the area. Pesticides in the runoff from nearby farms have poisoned the water they fish and bathe in, threatening both their health and their culture's survival.

LET'S DISCUSS

1. Compare the frontier in Brazil today to the American West in the 1800s. What similarities do you see?

2. What does society lose when indigenous cultures die?

Sources: Brazier and Hamed 2007; H. Chu 2005; Survival International 2012.

Summary

In this module we examine the ways in which culture changes and spreads.

1. Human culture is constantly expanding through the process of **innovation**, which includes both **discovery** and **invention**.

2. **Diffusion**—the spread of cultural items from one place to another—has fostered globalization. Still, people resist ideas that seem too foreign, as well as those they perceive as threatening to their own values and beliefs.

Thinking Critically

1. Name one culturally significant discovery and one culturally significant invention that occurred in your lifetime. Explain how these innovations have changed your culture.

2. Describe one positive example and one negative of McDonaldization that you have experienced.

Key Terms

Culture lag 76

Diffusion 74

Discovery 73

Innovation 73

Invention 73

Material culture 76

Nonmaterial culture 76

Technology 75

MODULE **12** | Cultural Variation

Each culture has a unique character. Inuit tribes in northern Canada, wrapped in furs and dieting on whale blubber, have little in common with farmers in Southeast Asia, who dress for the heat and subsist mainly on the rice they grow in their paddies. Cultures adapt to meet specific sets of circumstances, such as climate, level of technology, population, and geography. Thus, despite the presence of cultural universals such as courtship and religion, great diversity exists among the world's many cultures. Moreover, even *within* a single nation, certain segments of the populace develop cultural patterns that differ from the patterns of the dominant society.

● Subcultures

Rodeo riders, residents of a retirement community, workers on an offshore oil rig—all are examples of what sociologists refer to as *subcultures*. A **subculture** is a segment of society that shares a distinctive pattern of customs, rules, and traditions that differs from the pattern of the larger society. In a sense, a subculture can be thought of as a culture existing within a larger, dominant culture. The existence of many subcultures is characteristic of complex societies such as the United States.

Members of a subculture participate in the dominant culture while engaging in unique and distinctive forms of behavior. Frequently, a subculture will develop an **argot,** or specialized language, that distinguishes it from the wider society. Athletes who play *parkour,* an extreme sport that combines forward running with fence leaping and the vaulting of walls, water barriers, and even moving cars, speak an argot they devised especially to describe their feats. Parkour runners talk about doing *King Kong vaults*—diving arms first over a wall or grocery cart and landing in a standing position. They may follow this maneuver with a *tic tac*—kicking off a wall to overcome some kind of obstacle (Tschorn 2010).

Such argot allows insiders—the members of the subculture— to understand words with special meanings. It also establishes patterns of communication that outsiders can't understand. Sociologists associated with the interactionist perspective emphasize that language and symbols offer a powerful way for a subculture to feel cohesive and maintain its identity.

Employees of an international call center in India socialize after their shift has ended. Call center employees, whose odd working hours isolate them from others, tend to form tight-knit subcultures.

In India, a new subculture has developed among employees at the international call centers established by multinational corporations. To serve customers in the United States and Europe, the young men and women who work there must be fluent speakers of English. But the corporations that employ them demand more than proficiency in a foreign language; they expect their Indian employees to adopt Western values and work habits, including the grueling pace U.S. workers take for granted. In return they offer perks such as Western-style dinners, dances, and coveted consumer goods. Significantly, they allow employees to take the day off only on U.S. holidays, like Labor Day and Thanksgiving—not on Indian holidays like Diwali, the Hindu festival of lights. While most Indian families are home celebrating, call center employees see only each other; when they have the day off, no one else is free to socialize with them. As a result, these employees have formed a tight-knit subculture based on hard work and a taste for Western luxury goods and leisure-time pursuits.

Another shared characteristic among some employees at Indian call centers is their contempt for the callers they serve. In performing their monotonous, repetitive job day after day, hundreds of thousands of these workers have come to see the faceless Americans they deal with as slow, often rude customers. Such shared understandings underpin this emerging subculture (Bhagat 2007; Gentleman 2006; Patel 2010).

Functionalist and conflict theorists agree that variation exists within cultures. Functionalists view subcultures as variations of particular social environments and as evidence that differences can exist within a common culture. However, conflict theorists suggest that variations often reflect the inequality of social arrangements within a society. A conflict theorist would view the challenges to dominant social norms by African American activists, the feminist movement, and the gay rights movement as reflections of inequity based on race, gender, and sexual orientation. Conflict theorists also argue that subcultures sometimes emerge when the dominant society unsuccessfully tries to suppress a practice, such as the use of illegal drugs.

● Countercultures

By the end of the 1960s, an extensive subculture had emerged in the United States, composed of young people turned off by a society they believed was too materialistic and technological. The group included primarily political radicals and hippies who had dropped out of mainstream social institutions. These young men and women rejected the pressure to accumulate cars, homes, and an endless array of material goods. Instead, they expressed a desire to live in a culture based on more humanistic values, such as sharing, love, and coexistence with the environment. As a political force, this subculture opposed the United States' involvement in the war in Vietnam and encouraged draft resistance (Flacks 1971; Roszak 1969).

When a subculture conspicuously and deliberately opposes certain aspects of the larger culture, it is known as a **counterculture.** Countercultures typically thrive among the young, who have the least investment in the existing culture. In most cases, a 20-year-old can adjust to new cultural standards more easily than someone who has spent 60 years following the patterns of the dominant culture (Zellner 1995).

In the last decade, counterterrorism experts have become concerned about the growth of ultraconservative militia groups in the United States. Secretive and well armed, members of these

Members of the militia group Ohio Defense Force engage in paramilitary exercises, imagining they are destroying a threatening Muslim stronghold in the United States.

Culture Shock

Anyone who feels disoriented, uncertain, out of place, or even fearful when immersed in an unfamiliar culture may be experiencing **culture shock.** For example, a resident of the United States who visits certain areas in China and wants local meat for dinner may be stunned to learn that the specialty is dog meat. Similarly, someone from a strict Islamic culture may be shocked by the comparatively provocative dress styles and open displays of affection common in the United States and various European cultures.

All of us, to some extent, take for granted the cultural practices of our society. As a result, it can be surprising and even disturbing to realize that other cultures do not follow our way of life. The fact is, customs that seem strange to us may be considered normal and proper in other cultures, which may see our social practices as odd.

countercultural groups tend to be antigovernment, and they often tolerate racism in their midst. Watchdogs estimate that 127 militias are operating in the United States today (Southern Poverty Law Center 2010).

use your **sociological imagination**

You arrive in a developing African country as a Peace Corps volunteer. What aspects of a very different culture do you think would be the hardest to adjust to? What might the citizens of that country find shocking about your culture?

social policy and Culture | Bilingualism

Looking at the Issue

All over the world, nations face the challenge of how to deal with minorities who speak a different language from that of mainstream culture. Because languages know no political boundaries, minority languages are common. In India, for example, Hindi is the most widely spoken language, while English is used widely for official purposes. Yet 18 other languages are officially recognized in this nation of about 1 billion people.

Throughout the world, then, schools must deal with incoming students who speak many languages. **Bilingualism** refers to the use of two languages in a particular setting, such as the workplace or schoolroom, treating each language as equally legitimate. Thus, a teacher of bilingual education may instruct children in their native language while gradually introducing them to the language of the host society. If the curriculum is also bicultural, children will learn about the mores and folkways of both the dominant culture and the subculture.

To what degree should schools in the United States present the curriculum in a language other than English? This issue has prompted a great deal of debate among educators and policymakers. According to the Bureau of the Census, 59 million U.S. residents over age five—that's about 20 percent of the population—spoke a language other than English as their primary language at home in 2009 (Figure 12-1). Indeed, 23 other languages are each spoken by at least 200,000 U.S. residents (Shin and Kominski 2010).

Do bilingual programs help the children of these families to learn English? It is difficult to reach firm conclusions, because bilingual programs in general vary so widely in their quality and approach. They differ in the length of the transition to English and in how long they allow students to remain in bilingual classrooms. Moreover, results have been mixed.

—Continued

MAPPING LIFE NATIONWIDE

FIGURE 12-1 **Comparing Percentage of People Who Speak a Language Other Than English at Home, by State**

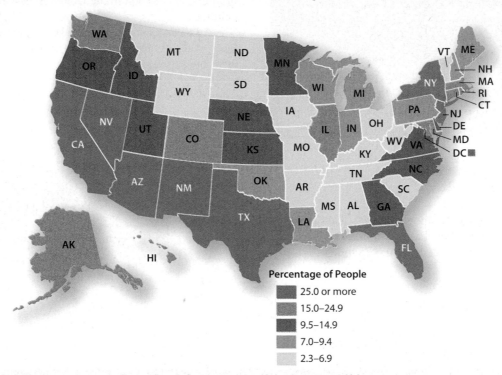

Percentage of People

- 25.0 or more
- 15.0–24.9
- 9.5–14.9
- 7.0–9.4
- 2.3–6.9

Note: Data drawn from the 2009 American Community Survey of people five years and over. National average was 20.0 percent.
Source: American Community Survey 2010:Table R1601.

In the years since California effectively dismantled its bilingual education program, reading and math scores of students with limited English proficiency rose dramatically, especially in the lower grades. Yet a major overview of 17 studies, done at Johns Hopkins University, found that students who are offered lessons in both English and their home languages make better progress than similar students who are taught only in English (R. Slavin and Cheung 2003).

Applying Sociology

For a long time, people in the United States demanded conformity to a single language. This demand coincided with the functionalist view that language serves to unify members of a society. Little respect was granted to immigrants' cultural traditions.

Recent decades have seen challenges to this pattern of forced obedience to the dominant ideology. Beginning in the 1960s, active movements for Black pride and ethnic pride insisted that people regard the traditions of all racial and ethnic subcultures as legitimate and important. Conflict theorists explain this development as a case of subordinated language minorities seeking opportunities for self-expression. Partly as a result of these challenges, people began to view bilingualism as an asset. It seemed to provide a sensitive way of assisting millions of non-English-speaking people in the United States to *learn* English in order to function more effectively within the society.

The perspective of conflict theory also helps us to understand some of the attacks on bilingual programs. Many of them stem from an ethnocentric point of view, which holds that any deviation from the majority is bad. This attitude tends to be expressed by those who wish to stamp out foreign influence wherever it occurs, especially in our schools. It does not take into account that success in bilingual education may actually have beneficial results, such as decreasing the number of high school dropouts and increasing the number of Hispanics in colleges and universities.

Initiating Policy

Bilingualism has policy implications largely in two areas: efforts to maintain language purity and programs to enhance bilingual education. Nations vary dramatically in their tolerance for a variety of languages. China continues to tighten its cultural control over Tibet by extending instruction of Mandarin, a Chinese dialect, from high school into the elementary schools there, which will now be bilingual along with Tibetan. In contrast, nearby Singapore establishes English as the medium of instruction but allows students to take their mother tongue as a second language, be it Chinese, Malay, or Tamil.

One bilingual hot spot is Québec, the French-speaking province of Canada. The Québécois, as they are known, represent 83 percent of the province's population, but only 25 percent of Canada's total population. A law implemented in 1978 mandated education in French for all Québec's children except those whose parents or siblings had learned English elsewhere in Canada. While special laws like this one have advanced French in the province, dissatisfied Québécois have tried to form their own separate country. In 1995, the people of Québec indicated their preference of remaining united with Canada by only the narrowest of margins (50.5 percent). Language and language-related cultural areas both unify and divide this nation of 33 million people (*The Economist* 2005b; R. Schaefer 2011).

Policymakers in the United States have been somewhat ambivalent in dealing with the issue of bilingualism. In 1965, the Elementary and Secondary Education Act (ESEA) provided for bilingual, bicultural education. In the 1970s, the federal government took an active role in establishing the proper form for bilingual programs. However, more recently, federal policy has been less supportive of bilingualism, and local school districts have been forced to provide an increased share of funding for their bilingual programs. Yet bilingual programs are an expense that many communities and states are unwilling to pay for and are quick to cut back.

In 1998, voters in California approved a proposition that all but eliminated bilingual education: it requires instruction in English for 1.4 million children who are not fluent in the language.

In the United States, repeated efforts have been made to introduce a constitutional amendment declaring English as the nation's official language. As of 2012, 31 states had declared English their official language—an action that is now more symbolic than legislative in its significance.

Public concern over a potential decline in the use of English appears to be overblown. In reality, most immigrants and their offspring quickly become fluent in English and abandon their mother tongue. Nevertheless, many people are impatient with those immigrants who continue to use their mother tongue. The release in 2006 of *"Nuestro Himno,"* the Spanish-language version of the "Star-Spangled Banner," produced a strong public reaction: 69 percent of those who were surveyed on the topic said the anthem should be sung only in English. In reaction against the Spanish version, at least one congressman defiantly sang the national anthem in English—with incorrect lyrics. And the proprietor of a restaurant in Philadelphia posted signs advising patrons that he would accept orders for his famous steak sandwiches only in English. Throughout the year, passions ran high as policymakers debated how much support to afford people who speak other languages (J. Carroll 2006; U.S. English 2012).

In the end, the immigrant's experience is not only about learning a new language. It is about learning a whole new culture—a new totality of socially transmitted customs, knowledge, material objects, and behavior (Viramontes 2007).

TAKE THE ISSUE WITH YOU

1. Have you attended a school with students for whom English is a second language? If so, did the school set up a special bilingual program? Was it effective? What is your opinion of such programs?

2. The ultimate goal of both English-only and bilingual programs is for foreign-born students to become proficient in English. Why should the type of program students attend matter so much to so many people? List all the reasons you can think of for supporting or opposing such programs. What do you see as the primary reason?

3. Besides bilingualism, can you think of another issue that has become controversial recently because of a clash of cultures? If so, analyze the issue from a sociological point of view.

Summary

Each human culture has unique characteristics that evolve to meet specific circumstances of climate, geography, technological development, and population.

1. A **subculture** is a small culture that exists within a larger, dominant culture. **Countercultures** are subcultures that deliberately oppose aspects of the larger culture.

2. A person who becomes immersed in an unfamiliar culture may experience **culture shock**.

3. The social policy of **bilingualism** calls for the use of two or more languages, treating each as equally legitimate. It is supported by those who want to ease the transition of non-native-language speakers into a host society, but opposed by those who adhere to a single cultural tradition and language.

Thinking Critically

1. To what subcultures do you belong? How do they function in relation to the larger society?

2. Why do people experience culture shock? What does this phenomenon reveal about the role of culture and of everyday customs?

Key Terms

Argot 77

Bilingualism 79

Counterculture 78

Culture shock 79

Subculture 77

Mastering This Chapter

taking sociology with you

1 Locate ethnocentrism. For two days, bearing in mind what sociologists mean by *ethnocentrism*, systematically record the places where you see or hear evidence of it.

2 Document a subculture. For two days, record the norms, values, sanctions, and argot evident in a subculture you are familiar with.

3 Study popular culture. For two days, record whatever evidence of the dominant culture you see on the Internet or in literature, music, movies, theater, television programs, and sporting events.

Argot Specialized language used by members of a group or subculture. (page 77)

Bilingualism The use of two languages in a particular setting, such as the workplace or schoolroom, treating each language as equally legitimate. (79)

Counterculture A subculture that deliberately opposes certain aspects of the larger culture. (78)

Cultural relativism The viewing of people's behavior from the perspective of their own culture. (62)

Cultural universal A common practice or belief found in every culture. (62)

Culture The totality of learned, socially transmitted customs, knowledge, material objects, and behavior. (61)

Culture industry The worldwide media industry that standardizes the goods and services demanded by consumers. (62)

Culture lag A period of maladjustment when the nonmaterial culture is still struggling to adapt to new material conditions. (76)

Culture shock The feeling of surprise and disorientation that people experience when they encounter cultural practices that are different from their own. (79)

Culture war The polarization of society over controversial cultural elements. (71)

Diffusion The process by which a cultural item spreads from group to group or society to society. (74)

Discovery The process of making known or sharing the existence of an aspect of reality. (73)

Dominant ideology A set of cultural beliefs and practices that helps to maintain powerful social, economic, and political interests. (72)

Ethnocentrism The tendency to assume that one's own culture and way of life represent the norm or are superior to all others. (62)

Folkway A norm governing everyday behavior whose violation raises comparatively little concern. (68)

Formal norm A norm that has been written down and that specifies strict punishments for violators. (68)

Informal norm A norm that is generally understood but not precisely recorded. (68)

Innovation The process of introducing a new idea or object to a culture through discovery or invention. (73)

Invention The combination of existing cultural items into a form that did not exist before. (73)

Language An abstract system of word meanings and symbols for all aspects of culture; includes gestures and other nonverbal communication. (65)

Law Governmental social control. (68)

Material culture The physical or technological aspects of our daily lives. (76)

Mores Norms deemed highly necessary to the welfare of a society. (68)

Nonmaterial culture Ways of using material objects, as well as customs, beliefs, philosophies, governments, and patterns of communication. (76)

Norm An established standard of behavior maintained by a society. (66)

Sanction A penalty or reward for conduct concerning a social norm. (69)

Sapir-Whorf hypothesis A hypothesis concerning the role of language in shaping our interpretation of reality. It holds that language is culturally determined. (65)

Society A fairly large number of people who live in the same territory, are relatively independent of people outside their area, and participate in a common culture. (62)

Sociobiology The systematic study of how biology affects human social behavior. (63)

Subculture A segment of society that shares a distinctive pattern of customs, rules, and traditions that differs from the pattern of the larger society. (77)

Symbol A gesture, object, or word that forms the basis of human communication. (66)

Technology Cultural information about the ways in which the material resources of the environment may be used to satisfy human needs and desires. (75)

Value A collective conception of what is considered good, desirable, and proper—or bad, undesirable, and improper—in a culture. (69)

Read each question carefully and then select the best answer.

1. Which of the following is an aspect of culture?
   a. a comic book
   b. patriotic attachment to the flag of the United States
   c. slang words
   d. all of the above

2. People's adaptations to meet the needs for food, shelter, and clothing are examples of what George Murdock referred to as
   a. norms.
   b. folkways.
   c. cultural universals.
   d. cultural practices.

3. What term do sociologists use to refer to the process by which a cultural item spreads from group to group or society to society?
   a. diffusion
   b. globalization
   c. innovation
   d. cultural relativism

4. The appearance of Starbucks coffeehouses in China is a sign of what aspect of culture?
   a. innovation
   b. globalization
   c. diffusion
   d. cultural relativism

5. Which of the following statements is true according to the Sapir-Whorf hypothesis?
   a. Language simply describes reality.
   b. Language does not transmit stereotypes related to race.
   c. Language precedes thought.
   d. Language is not an example of a cultural universal.

6. Which of the following statements about norms is correct?
   a. People do not follow norms in all situations. In some cases, they evade a norm because they know it is weakly enforced.
   b. In some instances, behavior that appears to violate society's norms may actually represent adherence to the norms of a particular group.
   c. Norms are violated in some instances because one norm conflicts with another.
   d. all of the above

7. Which of the following statements about values is correct?
   a. Values never change.
   b. The values of a culture may change, but most remain relatively stable during any one person's lifetime.
   c. Values are constantly changing; sociologists view them as being very unstable.
   d. all of the above

8. Which of the following terms describes the set of cultural beliefs and practices that help to maintain powerful social, economic, and political interests?
   a. mores
   b. dominant ideology
   c. consensus
   d. values

9. Terrorist groups are examples of
   a. cultural universals.
   b. subcultures.
   c. countercultures.
   d. dominant ideologies.

10. What is the term used when one places a priority on understanding other cultures, rather than dismissing them as "strange" or "exotic"?
    a. ethnocentrism
    b. culture shock
    c. cultural relativism
    d. cultural value

11. _____ are gestures, objects, and/or words that form the basis of human communication.

12. _____ is the process of introducing a new idea or object to a culture.

13. The bow and arrow, the automobile, and the television are all examples of _____.

14. Sociologists associated with the _____ perspective emphasize that language and symbols offer a powerful way for a subculture to maintain its identity.

15. "Put on some clean clothes for dinner" and "Thou shalt not kill" are both examples of _____ found in U.S. culture.

16. The United States has strong _____ against murder, treason, and other forms of abuse that have been institutionalized into formal norms.

17. From a(n) _____ perspective, the dominant ideology has major social significance. Not only do a society's most powerful groups and institutions control wealth and property—more important, they control the means of production.

18. Countercultures (e.g., hippies) are typically popular among the _____, who have the least investment in the existing culture.

19. A person experiences _____ when he or she feels disoriented, uncertain, out of place, even fearful when immersed in an unfamiliar culture.

20. From the _____ perspective, subcultures are evidence that differences can exist within a common culture.

thinking about movies

Attack the Block

A subculture's values are put to the test in this sophisticated science fiction film, which takes place in a low-income housing project in London.

Smoke Signals

Members of the Coeur d'Alene Indian tribe hold to their own norms and values.

Sugar

A baseball player from the Dominican Republic copes with culture shock after being drafted into the U.S. Major Leagues.

Who introduced you to your culture? Who made you feel that you belong?

In Groveland, a Chicago neighborhood, the list includes parents and relatives, friends and neighbors, teachers and church members.

" Charisse...is six-teen and lives with her mother and younger sister, Deanne, across the street from St. Mary's Catholic Church and School. Charisse's mother is a personnel assistant at a Chicago university, and is taking classes there to get her bachelor's degree. Mr. Baker is a Chicago fire-fighter. While her father and mother are sepa-rated, Charisse sees her father many times a week at the after-school basketball hour that he supervises at St. Mary's gym. He and Charisse's mother are on very good terms, and Charisse has a loving relationship with both parents. Mr. Baker is as active as any parent could be, attending the father/daughter dances at Charisse's high school, never missing a big performance, and visiting his daughters often.

Charisse and her sister are being raised by the neighborhood family in addition to their biological parents. "We [are] real close. Like all our neighbors know us because my dad grew up over here. Since the '60s." Charisse is a third-generation Grovelandite just like Neisha Morris. Her grandparents moved into Groveland with Charisse's then-teenage father when the neighborhood first opened to African Americans.... Now Charisse is benefit-ing from the friends her family has made over their years of resi-dence in Groveland, especially the members of St. Mary's church, who play the role of surrogate parents. When Charisse was in elementary school at St. Mary's, her late paternal grandmother was the school secretary, and so the Baker girls were always under the watchful eye of their grandmother as well as the staff, who were their grandmother's friends. And in the evenings Cha-risse's mother would bring her and her sister to choir practice, where they accumulated an ensemble of mothers and fathers.

After St. Mary's elementary school, Charisse went on to St. Agnes Catholic High School for girls, her father's choice. St. Agnes is located in a suburb of Chicago and is a solid, inte-grated Catholic school where 100 percent of the girls graduate and over 95 percent go on to college....

Most of Charisse's close friends went to St. Mary's and now go to St. Agnes with her, but her choice of boyfriends shows modest signs of rebellion.... Many of Charisse's male interests are older than she, and irregularly employed—although some are in and out of school. She meets many of them hanging out at the mall. One evening, members of the church's youth choir sat around talking about their relationships. Charisse cooed while talking about her present boy-friend, who had just graduated from high school but did not have a job and was uncertain about his future. But in the middle of that thought, Charisse spontaneously changed her attentions to a new young man that she had just met. "Charisse changes boyfriends like she changes her clothes," her sister joked, indicating the impetuous nature of adolescent relationships.

Charisse is a third-generation Grovelandite just like Neisha Morris. Her grandparents moved into Groveland with Charisse's then-teenage father when the neighborhood first opened to African Americans.

While these young men are not in gangs or selling drugs, many of them do not seem to share Charisse's strong career goals and diligence in attaining them. Some of them would not gain the approval of her parents. However, this full list of boyfriends has not clouded Charisse's focus. "

(Pattillo-McCoy 1999:100–102) Additional information about this excerpt can be found on the Online Learning Center at www. mhhe.com/schaefermod2e.

This excerpt from *Black Picket Fences: Privilege and Peril among the Black Middle Class* describes the upbringing of a young resident of Groveland, a close-knit African American community in Chicago. The author, sociologist Mary Pattillo-McCoy, became acquainted with Charisse while living in the Groveland neigh-borhood, where she was doing ethnographic research. Charisse's childhood is similar to that of other youths in many respects. Regardless of race or social class, a young person's development involves a host of influences, from parents, grandparents, and siblings to friends and classmates, teachers and school adminis-trators, neighbors and churchgoers—even youths who frequent the local mall. Yet in some ways, Charisse's development is spe-cifically influenced by her race and social class. Contact with family and community members, for instance, has undoubt-edly prepared her to deal with prejudice and the scarcity of positive images of African Americans in the media (W. Wilson et al. 2006).

Sociologists are interested in the patterns of behavior and attitudes that emerge *throughout* the life course, from infancy to old age. These patterns are part of the lifelong process of *socialization,* in which people learn the attitudes, values, and behaviors appropriate for members of a particular culture. In these three modules we will examine the role of socialization in human development. We will begin by analyzing the interaction of heredity with environmental factors. We will pay particular attention to how people develop perceptions, feelings, and beliefs about themselves. We will also explore the lifelong nature of the socialization process, as well as important agents of socialization, among them the family, schools, peers, the media, and technology. Finally, the Social Policy section will focus on the socialization experience of group child care for young children.

Sociologists are interested in the process of **socialization,** through which people learn the attitudes, values, and behaviors appropriate for members of their culture. Socialization occurs through human interactions that begin in infancy and continue throughout life. We learn a great deal from those people who are most important in our lives—immediate family members, best friends, and teachers. But we also learn from people we see on the street, on television, on the Internet, and in films and magazines. From a microsociological perspective, socialization helps us discover how to behave "properly" and what to expect from others if we follow (or challenge) society's norms and values. From a macrosociological perspective, socialization provides for the transmission of a culture from one generation to the next and thereby for the long-term continuance of society. Socialization also shapes our self-images. For example, in the United States, a person who is viewed as "too heavy" or "too short" does not conform to the ideal cultural standard of physical attractiveness.

This kind of unfavorable evaluation can significantly influence the person's self-esteem. In this sense, socialization experiences can help shape our personalities. In everyday speech, the term **personality** refers to a person's typical patterns of attitudes, needs, characteristics, and behavior.

How much of a person's personality is shaped by culture, as opposed to inborn traits? In other words, what makes us who we are? Is it the genes we are born with, or the environment in which we grow up? Researchers have traditionally clashed over the relative importance of biological inheritance and environmental factors in human development—a conflict called the *nature versus nurture* (or *heredity versus environment*) debate. Today, most social scientists have moved beyond this debate, acknowledging instead the *interaction* of these variables in shaping human development. We can best appreciate how heredity and environmental factors interact and influence the socialization process if we first examine situations in which one factor operates almost entirely without the other (Homans 1979).

Social Environment: The Impact of Isolation

In the 1994 movie *Nell,* Jodie Foster played a young woman hidden from birth by her mother in a backwoods cabin. Raised without normal human contact, Nell crouches like an animal, screams wildly, and speaks or sings in a language all her own. This movie was drawn from the actual account of an emaciated 16-year-old boy who appeared mysteriously in 1828 in the town square of Nuremberg, Germany (Lipson 1994).

Isabelle: A Case Study

Some viewers may have found the story of Nell difficult to believe, but the painful childhood of Isabelle was all too real. For the first six years of her life, Isabelle lived in almost total seclusion in a darkened room. She had little contact with other people, with the exception of her mother, who could neither speak nor hear. Isabelle's mother's parents had been so deeply ashamed of Isabelle's illegitimate birth that they kept her hidden away from the world. Ohio authorities finally discovered the child in 1938, when Isabelle's mother escaped from her parents' home, taking her daughter with her.

When she was discovered at age six, Isabelle could not speak; she could merely make various croaking sounds. Her only communications with her mother were simple gestures. Isabelle had been largely deprived of the typical interactions and socialization experiences of childhood. Since she had seen few people, she showed a strong fear of strangers and reacted almost like a wild animal when confronted with an unfamiliar person. As she became accustomed to seeing certain individuals, her reaction changed to one of extreme apathy. At first, observers believed that Isabelle was deaf, but she soon began to react to nearby sounds. On tests of maturity, she scored at the level of an infant rather than a six-year-old.

Specialists developed a systematic training program to help Isabelle adapt to human relationships and socialization. They sought to overcome the several years when Isabelle has been left in seclusion in a dark room shut off from family members. She did come in contact with her mother but she was unable to speak or hear so nobody interacted or played with her in a way most young children experience. Lack of exposure to the outdoors and an inadequate diet had left her in poor health as well.

After a week of intensive effort, she made her first attempt to verbalize. Although she started slowly, Isabelle quickly passed through six years of development. In a little over two months she was speaking in complete sentences. Nine months later she could identify both words and sentences in books. Before Isabelle reached age nine, she was ready to attend school with other children. By age 14 she was in sixth grade, doing well in school, and emotionally well adjusted.

Yet without an opportunity to experience socialization in her first six years, Isabelle had been hardly human in the social sense when she was first discovered. Her inability to communicate at the time of her discovery—despite her physical and cognitive potential to learn—and her remarkable progress over the next few years underscore the impact of socialization on human development (K. Davis 1940, 1947).

The conclusion of this case study is that human children need socialization in the form of love, care, and affection. Absent of that, humans cannot learn to speak and interact in a manner that is expected. Of course, this need for positive social interaction does not end with childhood but continues throughout our lives. Unfortunately, other children who have been locked away or severely neglected have not fared so well as Isabelle. In many instances, the consequences of social isolation have proved much more damaging.

Isabelle's experience is important to researchers because there are only a few cases of children reared in total isolation. Unfortunately, however, there are many cases of children raised in extremely neglectful social circumstances. In the 1990s, public attention focused on infants and young

Can you become human if you have had little human contact? Jodie Foster directed the motion picture Nell in which she played the title role of a girl discovered in a remote North Carolina backwoods cottage by a local doctor. While not based on a true story, it did draw upon cases of children raised in isolation like Isabelle. With significant intervention, Nell shows great progress in the several years covered in the movie, but still displays behavior reflective of her lack of childhood socialization.

children from orphanages in the formerly communist countries of Eastern Europe. In Romanian orphanages, babies once lay in their cribs for 18 to 20 hours a day, curled against their feeding bottles and receiving little adult care. Such minimal attention continued for the first five years of their lives. Many of them were fearful of human contact and prone to unpredictable antisocial behavior.

This situation came to light as families in North America and Europe began adopting thousands of the children. The adjustment problems for about 20 percent of them were often so dramatic that the adopting families suffered guilty fears of being ill-fit adoptive parents. Many of them have asked for assistance in dealing with the children. Slowly, efforts are being made to introduce the deprived youngsters to feelings of attachment that they have never experienced before (Groza et al. 1999; Craig Smith 2006).

Increasingly, researchers are emphasizing the importance of the earliest socialization experiences for children who grow up in more normal environments. We now know that it is not enough to care for an infant's physical needs; parents must also concern themselves with children's social development. If, for example, children are discouraged from having friends even as toddlers, they will miss out on social interactions with peers that are critical for emotional growth.

Despite the striking physical resemblance between these identical twins, there are undoubtedly many differences between them. Research points to some behavioral similarities between twins, but little beyond the likenesses found among nontwin siblings.

Primate Studies

Studies of animals raised in isolation also support the importance of socialization in development. Harry Harlow (1971), a researcher at the primate laboratory of the University of Wisconsin, conducted tests with rhesus monkeys that had been raised away from their mothers and away from contact with other monkeys. As was the case with Isabelle, the rhesus monkeys raised in isolation were fearful and easily frightened. They did not mate, and the females who were artificially inseminated became abusive mothers. Apparently, isolation had had a damaging effect on the monkeys.

A creative aspect of Harlow's experimentation was his use of "artificial mothers." In one such experiment, Harlow presented monkeys raised in isolation with two substitute mothers— one cloth-covered replica and one covered with wire that had the ability to offer milk. Monkey after monkey went to the wire mother for the life-giving milk, yet spent much more time clinging to the more motherlike cloth model. It appears that the infant monkeys developed greater social attachments from their need for warmth, comfort, and intimacy than from their need for milk.

While the isolation studies just discussed may seem to suggest that heredity can be dismissed as a factor in the social development of humans and animals, studies of twins provide insight into a fascinating interplay between hereditary and environmental factors.

 use your **sociological imagination**

What events in your life have had a strong influence on who you are?

● The Influence of Heredity

Identical twins Oskar Stohr and Jack Yufe were separated soon after their birth and raised on different continents, in very different cultural settings. Oskar was reared as a strict Catholic by his maternal grandmother in the Sudetenland of Czechoslovakia. As a member of the Hitler Youth movement in Nazi Germany, he learned to hate Jews. In contrast, his brother Jack was reared in Trinidad by the twins' Jewish father. Jack joined an Israeli kibbutz (a collective settlement) at age 17 and later served in the Israeli army. When the twins were reunited in middle age, however, some startling similarities emerged: They both wore wire-rimmed glasses and mustaches. They both liked spicy foods and sweet liqueurs, were absentminded, flushed the toilet before using it, stored rubber bands on their wrists, and dipped buttered toast in their coffee (Holden 1980).

The twins also differed in many important respects: Jack was a workaholic; Oskar enjoyed leisure-time activities. Oskar was a traditionalist who was domineering toward women; Jack was a political liberal who was much more accepting of feminism. Finally, Jack was extremely proud of being Jewish, whereas Oskar never mentioned his Jewish heritage (Holden 1987).

trend|spotting

in their tendency toward leadership or dominance, but significant differences in their need for intimacy, comfort, and assistance.

Researchers have also been impressed with the similar scores on intelligence tests of twins reared apart in *roughly similar* social settings. Most of the identical twins register scores even closer than those that would be expected if the same person took a test twice. At the same time, however, identical twins brought up in *dramatically different* social environments score quite differently on intelligence tests—a finding that supports the impact of socialization on human development (Joseph 2004; Kronstadt 2008a; McGue and Bouchard 1998; P. Miller 2012; Minnesota Center for Twin and Family Research 2012).

We need to be cautious in reviewing studies of twin pairs and other relevant research. Widely broadcast findings have often been based on preliminary analysis of extremely small samples. For example, one study (not involving twin pairs) was frequently cited as confirming genetic links with behavior. Yet the researchers had to retract their conclusions after they increased the sample and reclassified two of the original cases. After those changes, the initial findings were no longer valid.

Oskar and Jack are prime examples of the interplay of heredity and environment. For a number of years, the Minnesota Twin Family Study has been following 137 sets of identical twins reared apart to determine what similarities, if any, they show in personality traits, behavior, and intelligence. Preliminary results from the available twin studies indicate that *both* genetic factors *and* socialization experiences are influential in human development. Certain characteristics, such as temperaments, voice patterns, and nervous habits, appear to be strikingly similar even in twins reared apart, suggesting that these qualities may be linked to hereditary causes. However, identical twins reared apart differ far more in their attitudes, values, chosen mates, and even drinking habits; these qualities, it would seem, are influenced by environmental factors. In examining clusters of personality traits among such twins, researchers have found marked similarities

Critics add that studies of twin pairs have not provided satisfactory information concerning the extent to which separated identical twins may have had contact with each other, even though they were raised apart. Such interactions—especially if they were extensive—could call into question the validity of the twin studies. As this debate continues, we can certainly anticipate numerous efforts to replicate the research and clarify the interplay between heredity and environmental factors in human development (Horgan 1993; Plomin 1989).

MODULE 13 | Recap and Review

Summary

Socialization is the process through which people learn the attitudes, values, and actions appropriate for members of a particular culture.

1. Socialization affects the overall cultural practices of a society; it also shapes the images we hold of ourselves.

2. Heredity and environmental factors interact in influencing the socialization process.

Thinking Critically

1. What might be some ethical concerns regarding research on the influences of heredity and environment?

2. What are some social policy implications of research on the effects of early socialization experiences?

Key Terms

Personality   89

Socialization   89

We all have various perceptions, feelings, and beliefs about who we are and what we are like. How do we come to develop them? Do they change as we age?

We were not born with these understandings. Building on the work of George Herbert Mead (1964b), sociologists recognize that our concept of who we are, the *self,* emerges as we interact with others. The **self** is a distinct identity that sets us apart from others. It is not a static phenomenon, but continues to develop and change throughout our lives.

Sociologists and psychologists alike have expressed interest in how the individual develops and modifies the sense of self as a result of social interaction. The work of sociologists Charles Horton Cooley and George Herbert Mead, pioneers of the interactionist approach, has been especially useful in furthering our understanding of these important issues.

Sociological Approaches to the Self

Cooley: Looking-Glass Self

In the early 1900s, Charles Horton Cooley advanced the belief that we learn who we are by interacting with others. Our view of ourselves, then, comes not only from direct contemplation of our personal qualities but also from our impressions of how others perceive us. Cooley used the phrase **looking-glass self** to emphasize that the self is the product of our social interactions.

The process of developing a self-identity or self-concept has three phases. First, we imagine how we present ourselves to others—to relatives, friends, even strangers on the street. Then we imagine how others evaluate us (attractive, intelligent, shy, or strange). Finally, we develop some sort of feeling about ourselves, such as respect or shame, as a result of these impressions (Cooley 1902; M. Howard 1989).

A subtle but critical aspect of Cooley's looking-glass self is that the self results from an individual's "imagination" of how others view him or her. As a result, we can develop self-identities based on *incorrect* perceptions of how others see us. A student may react strongly to a teacher's criticism and decide (wrongly) that the instructor views the student as stupid. This misperception may be converted into a negative self-identity through the following process: (1) the teacher criticized me, (2) the teacher must think that I'm stupid, (3) I *am* stupid. Yet self-identities are also subject to change. If the student receives an A at the end of the course, he or she will probably no longer feel stupid.

Mead: Stages of the Self

George Herbert Mead continued Cooley's exploration of interactionist theory. Mead (1934, 1964a) developed a useful model of the process by which the self emerges, defined by three distinct stages: the preparatory stage, the play stage, and the game stage.

The Preparatory Stage During the *preparatory stage,* children merely imitate the people around them, especially family members with whom they continually interact. Thus, a small child will bang on a piece of wood while a parent is engaged in carpentry work, or will try to throw a ball if an older sibling is doing so nearby.

As they grow older, children become more adept at using symbols, including the gestures and words that form the basis of human communication. By interacting with relatives and friends, as well as by watching cartoons on television and looking at picture books, children in the preparatory stage begin to understand symbols. They will continue to use this form of communication throughout their lives.

The Play Stage Mead was among the first to analyze the relationship of symbols to socialization. As children develop skill in communicating through symbols, they gradually become more aware of social relationships.

Socialization can be negative as well as positive. When the very young come to view harmful behaviors like smoking or illegal drug use as "normal," socialization is negative. In Yemen, this child soldier has learned to use an automatic weapon.

As a result, during the play stage, they begin to pretend to be other people. Just as an actor "becomes" a character, a child becomes a doctor, parent, superhero, or ship captain.

Mead, in fact, noted that an important aspect of the play stage is role-playing. **Role taking** is the process of mentally assuming the perspective of another and responding from that imagined viewpoint. For example, through this process a young child will gradually learn when it is best to ask a parent for favors. If the parent usually comes home from work in a bad mood, the child will wait until after dinner, when the parent is more relaxed and approachable.

The Game Stage In Mead's third stage, the *game stage,* the child of about age eight or nine no longer just plays roles but begins to consider several tasks and relationships simultaneously. At this point in development, children grasp not only their own social positions but also those of others around them—just as in a football game the players must understand their own and everyone else's positions. Consider a girl or boy who is part of a Scout troop out on a weekend hike in the mountains. The child must understand what he or she is expected to do but must also recognize the responsibilities of other Scouts as well as the leaders. This is the final stage of development under Mead's model; the child can now respond to numerous members of the social environment.

Mead uses the term **generalized other** to refer to the attitudes, viewpoints, and expectations of society as a whole that a child takes into account in his or her behavior. Simply put, this concept suggests that when an individual acts, he or she takes into account an entire group of people. For example, a child will not act courteously merely to please a particular parent. Rather, the child comes to understand that courtesy is a widespread social value endorsed by parents, teachers, and religious leaders.

Table 14-1 summarizes the three stages of self outlined by George Herbert Mead.

Mead: Theory of the Self

Mead is best known for his theory of the self. According to Mead (1964b), the self begins at a privileged, central position in a person's world. Young children picture themselves as the focus of everything around them and find it difficult to consider the perspectives of others. For example, when shown a mountain scene and asked to describe what an observer on the opposite side of the mountain might see (such as a lake or hikers), young children describe only objects visible from their vantage point. This childhood tendency to place ourselves at the center of events never entirely disappears. Many people with a fear of flying automatically assume that if any plane goes down, it will be the one they are on. And who reads the horoscope section in the paper without looking at their own horoscope first? Why else do we buy lottery tickets, if we do not imagine ourselves winning?

Nonetheless, as people mature, the self changes and begins to reflect greater concern about the reactions of others. Parents, friends, co-workers, coaches, and teachers are often among those who play a major role in shaping a person's self. The term **significant others** is used to refer to those individuals who are most important in the development of the self. Many young people, for example, find themselves drawn to the same kind of work their parents engage in (H. Sullivan [1953] 1968).

 use your **sociological imagination**

How do you view yourself as you interact with others around you? How do you think you formed this view of yourself?

Goffman: Presentation of the Self

How do we manage our "self"? How do we display to others who we are? Erving Goffman, a sociologist associated with the interactionist perspective, suggested that many of our daily activities involve attempts to convey impressions of who we are. His observations help us to understand the sometimes subtle yet critical ways in which we learn to present ourselves socially. They also offer concrete examples of this aspect of socialization.

Early in life, the individual learns to slant his or her presentation of the self in order to create distinctive appearances and satisfy particular audiences. Goffman (1959) referred to this altering of the presentation of the self as **impression management.** Box 14-1 describes an everyday example of this concept—the way students behave after receiving their exam grades.

In analyzing such everyday social interactions, Goffman makes so many explicit parallels to the theater that his view has been termed the **dramaturgical approach.** According to this perspective, people resemble performers in action. For example, a clerk may try to appear busier than he or she actually is if a supervisor happens to be watching. A customer in a singles' bar may try to look as if he or she is waiting for a particular person to arrive.

Table **14-1** Mead's Stages of the Self **summingup**

Stage	Self Present?	Definition	Example
Preparation	No	Child imitates the actions of others.	When adults laugh and smile, child laughs and smiles.
Play	Developing	Child takes the role of a single other, as if he or she were the other.	Child first takes the role of doctor, then the role of patient.
Game	Yes	Child considers the roles of two or more others simultaneously.	In game of hide-and-seek, child takes into account the roles of both hider and seeker.

Sociology on Campus

BOX 14-1

Impression Management by Students

When you and fellow classmates get an exam back, you probably react differently depending on the grades that you and they earned. This distinction is part of *impression management*. Researchers have found that students' reactions differ depending on the grades that others received, compared to their own. These encounters can be divided into three categories: those in which all students earned high grades (Ace–Ace encounters); those between Aces and students who received low or failing grades (Ace–Bomber encounters); and those between students who all got low grades (Bomber–Bomber encounters).

Ace–Ace encounters occur in a rather open atmosphere, because there is comfort in sharing a high mark with another high achiever. It is even acceptable to violate the norm of modesty and brag when among other Aces, since as one student admitted, "It's much easier to admit a high mark to someone who has done better than you, or at least as well."

Ace–Bomber encounters are often sensitive. Bombers generally attempt to avoid such exchanges, because "you . . . emerge looking

> When forced into interactions with Aces, Bombers work to appear gracious and congratulatory.

like the dumb one" or "feel like you are lazy or unreliable." When forced into interactions with Aces, Bombers work to appear gracious and congratulatory. For their part, Aces offer sympathy and support to the dissatisfied Bombers and even rationalize their own "lucky" high scores. To help Bombers save face, Aces may emphasize the difficulty and unfairness of the examination.

Bomber–Bomber encounters tend to be closed, reflecting the group effort to wall off the feared disdain of others. Yet within the safety of these encounters, Bombers openly share their disappointment and engage in expressions of mutual self-pity that they themselves call "pity parties." They devise face-saving excuses for

their poor performance, such as "I wasn't feeling well all week" or "I had four exams and two papers due that week."

Of course, grade comparisons are not the only occasion when students engage in impression management. Another study has shown that students' perceptions of how often fellow students work out can also influence their social encounters. In athletic terms, a bomber would be someone who doesn't work out; an ace would be someone who works hard at physical fitness.

LET'S DISCUSS

1. How do you react to those who have received higher or lower grades than you? Do you engage in impression management? How would you like others to react to your grade?

2. What social norms govern students' impression management strategies?

Sources: Albas and Albas 1988, 1996; C. Austin 2009; M. Mack 2003.

Goffman (1959) also drew attention to another aspect of the self, **face-work.** How often do you initiate some kind of face-saving behavior when you feel embarrassed or rejected? In response to a rejection at the singles' bar, a person may engage in face-work by saying, "There really isn't an interesting person in this entire crowd." We feel the need to maintain a proper image of the self if we are to continue social interaction.

People judge us by our appearance, attire, body language, demeanor, and mannerisms. Knowing that they do, most of us alter the way we present ourselves to others, a strategy that Goffman called impression management.

Face-work is a necessity for those who are unemployed. In an economic downturn like the recent recession, unemployment affects people of all social classes, many of whom are unaccustomed to being jobless. A recent ethnographic study found the newly unemployed redefining what it means to be out of work. They were focusing more than in the past on what they were accomplishing, and had begun to value volunteer work more since they had become volunteers themselves. Participants in this study engaged in both impression management and face-work (Garrett-Peters 2009).

Goffman's work on the self represents a logical progression of sociological studies begun by Cooley and Mead on how personality is acquired through socialization and how we manage the presentation of the self to others. Cooley stressed the process by which we create a self; Mead focused on how the self develops as we learn to interact with others; Goffman emphasized the ways in which we consciously create images of ourselves for others.

Psychological Approaches to the Self

Psychologists have shared the interest of Cooley, Mead, and other sociologists in the development of the self. Early work in psychology, such as that of Sigmund Freud (1856–1939), stressed the role of inborn drives—among them the drive for sexual gratification—in channeling human behavior. More recently, psychologists such as Jean Piaget have emphasized the stages through which human beings progress as the self develops.

Like Charles Horton Cooley and George Herbert Mead, Freud believed that the self is a social product, and that aspects of one's personality are influenced by other people (especially one's parents). However, unlike Cooley and Mead, he suggested that the self has components that work in opposition to each other. According to Freud, our natural impulsive instincts are in constant conflict with societal constraints. Part of us seeks limitless pleasure, while another part favors rational behavior. By interacting with others, we learn the expectations of society and then select behavior most appropriate to our culture. (Of course, as Freud was well aware, we sometimes distort reality and behave irrationally.)

Research on newborn babies by the Swiss child psychologist Jean Piaget (1896–1980) has underscored the importance of social interactions in developing a sense of self. Piaget found that newborns have no self in the sense of a looking-glass image. Ironically, though, they are quite self-centered; they demand that all attention be directed toward them. Newborns have not yet separated themselves from the universe of which they are a part. For these babies, the phrase "you and me" has no meaning; they understand only "me." However, as they mature, children are gradually socialized into social relationships, even within their rather self-centered world.

In his well-known **cognitive theory of development,** Piaget (1954) identified four stages in the development of children's thought processes. In the first, or *sensorimotor,* stage, young children use their senses to make discoveries. For example, through touching they discover that their hands are actually a part of themselves. During the second, or *preoperational,* stage, children begin to use words and symbols to distinguish objects and ideas. The milestone in the third, or *concrete operational,* stage is that children engage in more logical thinking. They learn that even when a formless lump of clay is shaped into a snake, it is still the same clay. In the fourth, or *formal operational,* stage, adolescents become capable of sophisticated abstract thought and can deal with ideas and values in a logical manner.

According to Piaget, social interaction is the key to development. As children grow older, they pay increasing attention to how other people think and why they act in particular ways. In order to develop a distinct personality, each of us needs opportunities to interact with others. As we saw earlier, Isabelle was deprived of the chance for normal social interactions, and the consequences were severe (Kitchener 1991).

We have seen that a number of thinkers considered social interaction the key to the development of an individual's sense of self. As is generally true, we can best understand this topic by drawing on a variety of theory and research. Table 14-2 summarizes the rich literature, both sociological and psychological, on the development of the self.

◼ Socialization throughout the Life Course

The Life Course

Among the Kota people of the Congo in Africa, adolescents paint themselves blue. Mexican American girls go on a daylong religious retreat before dancing the night away. Egyptian mothers step over their newborn infants seven times, and graduating students at the Naval Academy throw their hats in the air. These are all ways of celebrating **rites of passage,** a means of dramatizing and validating changes in a person's status. Rites of passage can mark a separation, as in a graduation ceremony, or an incorporation, as in an initiation into an organization (Van Gennep [1909] 1960).

Rites of passage are a worldwide social phenomenon. The Kota rite marks the passage to adulthood. The color blue, viewed as the color of death, symbolizes the death of childhood. Hispanic girls celebrate reaching womanhood with a *quinceañera* ceremony at age 15. In the Cuban American community of Miami, the popularity of the *quinceañera* supports a network of party planners, caterers, dress designers, and the Miss Quinceañera Latina pageant. For thousands of years, Egyptian mothers have welcomed their newborns to the world in the Soboa ceremony by stepping over the seven-day-old infant seven times.

Table **14-2** **Theoretical Approaches to Development of the Self**

Tracking Sociological Perspectives

Scholar	Key Concepts and Contributions	Major Points of Theory
Charles Horton Cooley 1864–1929 sociologist (USA)	Looking-glass self	Stages of development not distinct; feelings toward ourselves developed through interaction with others
George Herbert Mead 1863–1931 sociologist (USA)	The self Generalized other	Three distinct stages of development; self develops as children grasp the roles of others in their lives
Erving Goffman 1922–1982 sociologist (USA)	Impression management Dramaturgical approach Face-work	Self developed through the impressions we convey to others and to groups
Sigmund Freud 1856–1939 psychotherapist (Austria)	Psychoanalysis	Self influenced by parents and by inborn drives, such as the drive for sexual gratification
Jean Piaget 1896–1980 child psychologist (Switzerland)	Cognitive theory of development	Four stages of cognitive development

These specific ceremonies mark stages of development in the life course. They indicate that the process of socialization continues through all stages of the life cycle. In fact, some researchers have chosen to concentrate on socialization as a lifelong process. Sociologists and other social scientists who take such a **life course approach** look closely at the social factors that influence people throughout their lives, from birth to death, including gender and income. They recognize that biological changes mold but do not dictate human behavior.

Several life events mark the passage to adulthood. Of course, these turning points vary from one society and even one generation to the next. In the United States, the key event seems to be the completion of formal schooling (Table 14-3). On average, Americans expect this milestone to occur by a person's 23rd birthday. Other major events in the life course, such as getting married or becoming a parent, are expected to follow three or four years later. Interestingly, comparatively few survey respondents identified marriage and parenthood as important milestones (Furstenberg, et al. 2004).

One result of these staggered steps to independence is that in the United States, unlike some other societies, there is no clear dividing line between adolescence and adulthood. Nowadays, few young people finish school, get married, and leave home at about the same age, clearly establishing their transition to adulthood. The terms *youthhood, emerging adulthood,* and *not quite adult* have been coined to describe the prolonged ambiguous status that young people in their 20s experience (Côté 2000; Settersten and Ray 2011; Christian Smith 2007).

Anticipatory Socialization and Resocialization

The development of a social self is literally a lifelong transformation that begins in the crib and continues as one prepares for death. Two types of socialization occur at many points throughout the life course: anticipatory socialization and resocialization.

Anticipatory socialization refers to processes of socialization in which a person rehearses for future positions, occupations, and social relationships. A culture can function more efficiently and smoothly if members become acquainted with the norms, values, and behavior associated with a social position before actually assuming that status. Preparation for many aspects of adult life begins with anticipatory socialization during childhood and adolescence, and continues throughout our lives as we prepare for new responsibilities.

You can see the process of anticipatory socialization take place when high school students start to consider what colleges they may attend. Traditionally, this task meant looking at

Table **14-3** **Milestones in the Transition to Adulthood**

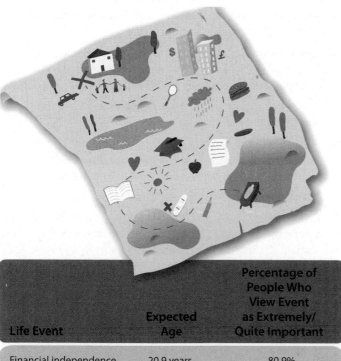

Life Event	Expected Age	Percentage of People Who View Event as Extremely/ Quite Important
Financial independence from parents/guardians	20.9 years	80.9%
Separate residence from parents	21.1	57.2
Full-time employment	21.2	83.8
Completion of formal schooling	22.3	90.2
Capability of supporting a family	24.5	82.3
Marriage	25.7	33.2
Parenthood	26.2	29.0

Note: Based on the 2002 General Social Survey of 1,398 people.
Source: T. Smith 2003.

Think about It

Why did so few respondents consider marriage and parenthood to be important milestones? Which milestones do you think are most important?

A young Apache woman undergoes a mudding ceremony traditionally used in rites of passage, such as puberty and in some cases weddings.

Socialization continues throughout the life course. When the Internet opened to commercial traffic, adults who are now in their 80s were over age 65. They were 75 when broadband became available.

publications received in the mail or making campus visits. However, with new technology, more and more students are using the web to begin their college experience. Colleges are investing more time and money in developing attractive websites through which students can take virtual campus tours and hear audio clips of everything from the college anthem to a sample zoology lecture.

Occasionally, assuming a new social or occupational position requires us to *unlearn* an established orientation. **Resocialization** refers to the process of discarding former behavior patterns and accepting new ones as part of a transition in one's life. Often resocialization occurs during an explicit effort to transform an individual, as happens in reform schools, therapy groups, prisons, religious conversion settings, and political indoctrination

camps. The process of resocialization typically involves considerable stress for the individual—much more so than socialization in general, or even anticipatory socialization (Gecas 2004).

Resocialization is particularly effective when it occurs within a total institution. Erving Goffman (1961) coined the term **total institution** to refer to an institution that regulates all aspects of a person's life under a single authority, such as a prison, the military, a mental hospital, or a convent. Because the total institution is generally cut off from the rest of society, it provides for all the needs of its members. Quite literally, the crew of a merchant vessel at sea becomes part of a total institution. So elaborate are its requirements, so all-encompassing its activities, a total institution often represents a miniature society.

Goffman (1961) identified four common traits of total institutions:

- All aspects of life are conducted in the same place under the control of a single authority.

- Any activities within the institution are conducted in the company of others in the same circumstances—for example, army recruits or novices in a convent.

- The authorities devise rules and schedule activities without consulting the participants.

- All aspects of life within a total institution are designed to fulfill the purpose of the organization. Thus, all activities in a monastery might be centered on prayer and communion with God (C. Davies 1989; P. Rose et al. 1979).

People often lose their individuality within total institutions. For example, a person entering prison may experience the humiliation of a **degradation ceremony** as he or she is stripped of clothing, jewelry, and other personal possessions. From this point on, scheduled daily routines allow for little or no personal initiative. The individual becomes secondary and rather invisible in the overbearing social environment (Garfinkel 1956).

MODULE 14 | Recap and Review

Summary

This module examines sociological and psychological views of the development of the **self.**

1. In the early 1900s, Charles Horton Cooley advanced the belief that we learn who we are by interacting with others, a phenomenon he called the **looking-glass self.**

2. George Herbert Mead, best known for his theory of the self, proposed that as people mature, their selves begin to reflect their concern about reactions from others, both **generalized others** and **significant others.**

3. Erving Goffman has shown that in many of our daily activities, we try to convey distinct impressions of who we are, a process he called **impression management.**

4. According to Jean Piaget's **cognitive theory of development,** social interaction is the key to psychological development.

5. Socialization proceeds throughout the life course. Some societies mark stages of development with formal **rites of passage.** In the culture of the United States, significant events such as marriage and parenthood serve to change a person's status.

Thinking Critically

1. Use Erving Goffman's dramaturgical approach to describe impression management among members of one of the following groups: athletes, college instructors, parents, physicians, or politicians.

2. What are some similarities between Mead's stages of the self and Piaget's cognitive development stages? What are some differences?

Key Terms

MODULE | 15 | Agents of Socialization

As we have seen, the culture of the United States is defined by rather gradual movements from one stage of socialization to the next. The continuing and lifelong socialization process involves many different social forces that influence our lives and alter our self-images.

The family is the most important agent of socialization in the United States, especially for children. In this chapter, we'll also discuss six other agents of socialization: the school, the peer group, the mass media and technology, the workplace, religion, and the state. We'll explore the role of religion in socializing young people into society's norms and values more fully in Chapter 15.

period of rebellion known as *rumspringa,* during which Amish children flirt with the adolescent subculture of mainstream American society.

In the United States, social development also includes exposure to cultural assumptions regarding gender and race. Black parents, for example, have learned that children as young as age two can absorb negative messages about Blacks in children's books, toys, and television shows—all of which are designed primarily for White consumers. At the same time, Black children are exposed more often than others to the inner-city youth gang culture. Because most Blacks, even those who are middle class, live near very poor neighborhoods, children such as Charisse

Family

The lifelong process of learning begins shortly after birth. Since newborns can hear, see, smell, taste, and feel heat, cold, and pain, they are constantly orienting themselves to the surrounding world. Human beings, especially family members, constitute an important part of their social environment. People minister to the baby's needs by feeding, cleaning, carrying, and comforting the baby.

All families engage in socialization, but the way that Amish families encourage their children to accept their community's subculture is particularly striking. Box 15-1 describes their tolerance for the

A daughter learns how to weave fabric from her mother in Guatemala. The family is the most important agent of socialization.

Rum Springa: Raising Children Amish Style

All families face challenges raising their children, but what if your parents expected you not to dance, listen to music, watch television, or access the Internet? This is the challenge faced by Amish teens and their parents, who embrace a lifestyle of the mid-1800s. Amish youths—boys in particular—often rebel against their parents' strict morals by getting drunk, behaving disrespectfully, and indulging in "worldly" activities, such as buying a car. At times even the girls may become involved, to

> All families face challenges raising their children, but what if your parents expected you not to dance, listen to music, watch television, or access the Internet?

their families' dismay. As one scholar puts it, "The rowdiness of Amish youth is an embarrassment to church leaders and a stigma in the larger community" (Kraybill 2001:138).

Yet the strong pull of mainstream American culture has led Amish parents to routinize, almost to accept, some of their children's worldly activities. They expect adolescents to test their subculture's boundaries during a period of discovery called *rum springa,* a German term meaning "running around." A common occurrence during which young people attend barn dances and break social norms

that forbid drinking, smoking, and driving cars, *rum springa* is definitely not supported by the Amish religion.

Parents often react to these escapades by looking the other way, sometimes literally. If they hear radio music coming from the barn, or a motorcycle driving onto their property in the middle of the night, they don't retaliate by punishing their offspring. Instead, they pretend not to notice, secure in the knowledge

that Amish children almost always return to the community's traditional values. Indeed, despite the flirtation with popular culture and modern technology that is common during the *rum springa,* the vast majority of Amish youths do return to the Amish community and become baptized. Scholars report that 85 to 90 percent of Amish children accept the faith as young adults.

To mainstream Americans, this little known and understood subculture became a source of entertainment when in 2004, UPN aired a 10-week reality program called *Amish in the City.* In the series, five Amish youths allegedly on *rum springa* moved in with six worldly wise young adults in Los Angeles. On behalf of the Amish community, some critics called the series exploitative, a sign of how vulnerable the Amish are. No similar series would be developed on the rebellion of Muslim or Orthodox Jewish youths, they charged.

LET'S DISCUSS

1. Do you or anyone you know come from a subculture that rejects mainstream American culture? If so, describe the community's norms and values. How do they resemble and how do they differ from Amish norms and values?

2. Why do you think so many Amish youths return to their families' way of life after rebelling against it?

Sources: Kraybill 2001; R. Schaefer and Zellner 2011; Shachtman 2006; Stevick 2007; Weinraub 2004.

(see the chapter-opening excerpt) are susceptible to these influences, despite their parents' strong family values (Linn and Poussaint 1999; Pattillo-McCoy 1999).

The term **gender role** refers to expectations regarding the proper behavior, attitudes, and activities of males and females. For example, we traditionally think of "toughness" as masculine—and desirable only in men—while we view "tenderness" as feminine. As we will see in Module 34, other cultures do not necessarily assign these qualities to each gender in the way that our culture does. The existence of gender roles does not imply that inevitably, males and females will assume certain roles, nor does it imply that those roles are quite distinct from one another. Rather, gender roles emphasize the fact that males and females are not genetically predetermined to occupy certain roles.

As the primary agents of childhood socialization, parents play a critical role in guiding children into those gender roles deemed appropriate in a society. Other adults, older siblings, the mass media, and religious and educational institutions also have

a noticeable impact on a child's socialization into feminine and masculine norms. A culture or subculture may require that one sex or the other take primary responsibility for the socialization of children, economic support of the family, or religious or intellectual leadership. In some societies, girls are socialized mainly by their mothers and boys by their fathers—an arrangement that may prevent girls from learning critical survival skills. In South Asia, fathers teach their sons to swim to prepare them for a life as fishermen; girls typically do not learn to swim. When a deadly tsunami hit the coast of South Asia in 2004, many more men survived than women.

◼ School

Like the family, schools have an explicit mandate to socialize people in the United States—especially children—into the norms and values of our culture.

Rakefet Avramovitz, *Program Administrator, Child Care Law Center*

Rakefet Avramovitz has been working at the Child Care Law Center in San Francisco since 2003. The center uses legal tools to foster the development of quality, affordable child care, with the goal of expanding child care options, particularly for low-income families. As a support person for the center's attorneys, she manages grants, oversees the center's publications, and sets up conferences and training sessions.

Avramovitz graduated from Dickinson College in 2000. She first became interested in sociology when she took a social analysis course. Though she enjoyed her qualitative courses most, she found her quantitative courses fun, "in that we got to do surveys of people on campus. I've always enjoyed fieldwork," she notes. Avramovitz's most memorable course was one that gave her the opportunity to interact with migrant farmworkers for an entire semester. "I learned ethnography and how to work with people of different cultures. It changed my life," she says.

Avramovitz finds that the skills she learned in her sociology courses are a great help to her on the job. "Sociology taught me how to work with people . . . and how to think critically. It taught me how to listen and find the stories that people are telling," she explains. Before joining the Child Care Law Center, Avramovitz worked as a counselor for women who were facing difficult issues. "My background in ethnography helped me to talk to these women and listen effectively," she notes. "I was able to help many women by understanding and

being able to express their needs to the attorneys we worked with."

Avramovitz is enthusiastic about her work and her ability to make a difference in other people's lives. Maybe that is why she looks forward to summer at the center, when the staff welcomes several law students as interns. "It is really neat to see people learn and get jazzed about child care issues," she says.

LET'S DISCUSS

1. What might be some of the broad, long-term effects of the center's work to expand child care options? Explain.

2. Besides the law, what other professions might benefit from the skills a sociology major has to offer?

As conflict theorists Samuel Bowles and Herbert Gintis (1976) have observed, schools in this country foster competition through built-in systems of reward and punishment, such as grades and evaluations by teachers. Consequently, a child who is experiencing difficulty trying to learn a new skill can sometimes come to feel stupid and unsuccessful. However, as the self matures, children become capable of increasingly realistic assessments of their intellectual, physical, and social abilities.

Functionalists point out that schools, as agents of socialization, fulfill the function of teaching children the values and customs of the larger society. Conflict theorists agree, but add that schools can reinforce the divisive aspects of society, especially those of social class. For example, higher education in the United States is costly despite the existence of financial aid programs. Students from affluent backgrounds therefore have an advantage in gaining access to universities and professional training. At the same time, less affluent young people may never receive the preparation that would qualify them for the best-paying and most prestigious jobs. The contrast between the functionalist and conflict views of education will be discussed in more detail in Module 43.

Peer Group

As a child grows older, the family becomes somewhat less important in social development. Instead, peer groups increasingly assume the role of Mead's significant others. Within the peer group, young people associate with others who are approximately their age, and who often enjoy a similar social status (Giordano 2003).

We can see how important peer groups are to young people when their social lives are strained by war or disaster. In Baghdad, the overthrow of Saddam Hussein has profoundly

changed teenagers' worlds, casting doubt on their future. Some young people have lost relatives or friends; others have become involved with fundamentalist groups or fled with their families to safer countries. Those youths who are left behind can suffer intense loneliness and boredom. Confined to their homes by crime and terrorism, those fortunate enough to have computers turn to Internet chat rooms or immerse themselves in their studies. Through e-mail, they struggle to maintain old friendships interrupted by wartime dislocation (Sanders 2004).

Gender differences are noteworthy among adolescents. Boys and girls are socialized by their parents, peers, and the media to identify many of the same paths to popularity, but to different degrees. Table 15-1 compares male and female college students' reports of how girls and boys they knew became popular in high school. The two groups named many of the same paths to popularity but gave them a different order of importance. While neither men nor women named sexual activity, drug use, or alcohol use as one of the top five paths, college men were much more likely than women to mention those behaviors as a means to becoming popular, for both boys and girls.

Mass Media and Technology

In the past 80 years, media innovations—radio, motion pictures, recorded music, television, and the Internet—have become important agents of socialization. Television, and increasingly the Internet, are critical forces in the socialization of children in the United States (Figure 15-1). The Internet has become so pervasive that 95 percent of all teens ages 12 to 17 were online by 2011, and 80 percent of them used social media sites. These sites echo and amplify much of teens' socialization (Lenhart et al. 2011).

Table 15-1 High School Popularity

What makes high school girls popular?		What makes high school boys popular?	
According to college men:	According to college women:	According to college men:	According to college women:
1. Physical attractiveness	1. Grades/intelligence	1. Participation in sports	1. Participation in sports
2. Grades/intelligence	2. Participation in sports	2. Grades/intelligence	2. Grades/intelligence
3. Participation in sports	3. General sociability	3. Popularity with girls	3. General sociability
4. General sociability	4. Physical attractiveness	4. General sociability	4. Physical attractiveness
5. Popularity with boys	5. Clothes	5. Car	5. School clubs/government

Note: Students at the following universities were asked in which ways adolescents in their high schools had gained prestige with their peers: Cornell University, Louisiana State University, Southeastern Louisiana University, State University of New York at Albany, State University of New York at Stony Brook, University of Georgia, and University of New Hampshire.

Source: Suitor et al. 2001:445.

These media, however, are not always a negative socializing influence. Television programs and even commercials can introduce young people to unfamiliar lifestyles and cultures. Not only do children in the United States learn about life in "faraway lands," but inner-city children learn about the lives of farm children, and vice versa. The same thing happens in other countries.

Sociologists and other social scientists have begun to consider the impact of technology on socialization. They are particularly interested in the online friendship networks, like Facebook. Does this way of communicating resemble face-to-face interaction, or does it represent a new form of social interaction? Box 15-2 explores the significance of this social phenomenon.

Not just in industrial nations, but in Africa and other developing areas, people have been socialized into relying on new communications technologies. Not long ago, if Zadhe Iyombe wanted to talk to his mother, he had to make an eight-day trip from the capital city of Kinshasa up the Congo River by boat to the rural town where he was born. Now both he and his mother have access to a cell phone, and they send text messages to each other daily. Iyombe and his mother are not atypical. Although cell phones aren't cheap, 1.4 billion owners in developing countries have come to consider them a necessity. Today, there are more cell phones in developing nations than in industrial nations—the first time in history that developing nations have outpaced the developed world in the adoption of a telecommunications technology (K. Sullivan 2006).

■ Workplace

Learning to behave appropriately in an occupation is a fundamental aspect of human socialization. It used to be that going to work began with the end of our formal schooling, but that is no longer the case, at least not in the United States. More and more young people work today, and not just for a parent or

relative. Adolescents generally seek jobs in order to make spending money; 80 percent of high school seniors say that little or none of what they earn goes to family expenses. These teens rarely look on their employment as a means of exploring vocational interests or getting on-the-job training.

Some observers feel that the increasing number of teenagers who are working earlier in life and for longer hours are finding the workplace almost as important an agent of socialization as school. In fact, a number of educators complain that student time at work is adversely affecting schoolwork. The level of teenage employment in the United States is the highest among industrial

FIGURE 15-1 The New Normal: Internet at Home

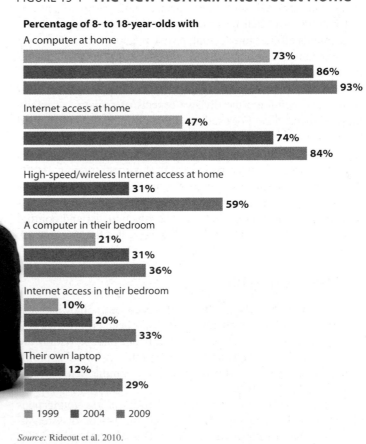

Percentage of 8- to 18-year-olds with

A computer at home
73%
86%
93%

Internet access at home
47%
74%
84%

High-speed/wireless Internet access at home
31%
59%

A computer in their bedroom
21%
31%
36%

Internet access in their bedroom
10%
20%
33%

Their own laptop
12%
29%

■ 1999   ■ 2004   ■ 2009

Source: Rideout et al. 2010.

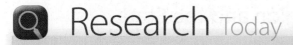
Online Socializing: A New Agent of Socialization

Membership in the online social networks Facebook and MySpace has grown exponentially in recent years. At first, young adults monopolized these social networks. Indeed, Facebook was created in 2004 as a way for students on a single campus to become acquainted with one another before actually meeting.

Even in the brief history of online networking, sociologists can see social trends. For example, older people are now creating profiles on these sites. As the accompanying figure shows, there is still a clear correlation between age and online profiles: in a national survey of community college students, younger people were much more likely than older people to be online. However, the fastest-growing age groups are now those over 30, including those who are much older. As a result, online socializing is becoming much less age-specific—more like socializing in the real world. Moreover, this new agent of socialization can continue to influence people throughout the life course. Twitter is largely the exception to this trend; it is still a very age-specific method of social interaction.

Online networks—especially those that indicate how many "friends" an individual has—can also be seen in terms of social capital. In fact, "friending" is one, if not *the,* main activity on some online sites. Often the number of friends a person socializes with becomes the subject of boasting. By extension, individuals may use these sites to search for "friends" who may prove helpful to them in future endeavors. Becoming aware of new opportunities, either social or economic, through friends is a significant benefit of social capital.

Researchers have looked at the relationship between the display of friends online and the number of real-world friends people socialize with, and have proposed two competing hypotheses. According to the social enhancement hypothesis ("the rich get richer"), those

> Online networks—especially those that indicate how many "friends" an individual has—can also be seen in terms of social capital.

who are popular offline further increase their popularity through online networking sites. According to the social compensation hypothesis ("the poor get richer"), however, social network users try to increase their popularity online to compensate for inadequate popularity offline. The social compensation hypothesis, if correct, would be an example of impression management. Research supports elements of both hypotheses; neither hypothesis fully defines the participants in online networking sites.

Viewed from a societal perspective, socializing online can have both positive and negative functions. For members of some marginalized populations, it is a way to socialize with like-minded people. For example, Muslims in Great Britain connect with friends online to learn how to navigate through a society in which they form a distinct minority. For other people, such as members of neo-Nazi groups in Germany

and the Mafia in Italy, online networking is a way to proclaim allegiance to socially objectionable organizations. Governments frown on such online organizing, seeing it as dysfunctional, and periodically monitor these sites to see whether any laws have been violated. Little wonder that during the Arab Spring of 2011, which was marked by popular revolts against the central governments of Tunisia, Egypt, and Libya, authorities cracked down on citizens' access to social media.

Staying Connected: Community College Students

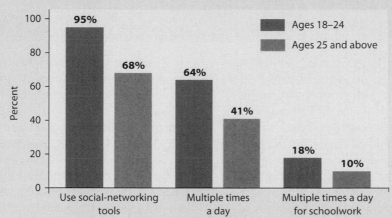

Note: Question asked was "How often do you use social networking tools, such as instant messaging, text messaging, MySpace and/or Facebook, Twitter, etc., for any purpose? (This does not include e-mail.)"
Source: Center for Community College Student Engagement 2009:8.

LET'S DISCUSS

1. Do you list your "friends" on an online social networking site? If so, what is your motivation for doing so? How much social capital do you think your list represents?

2. Do you think the advantages of online social networking outweigh the disadvantages?

Sources: Donadio 2009; N. Ellison et al. 2007; Facebook 2011; Gentile 2009; Hundley and Ramirez 2008; Lenhart 2009; Miyata and Kobayashi 2008; Zywica and Danowski 2008.

---

countries, which may provide one explanation for why U.S. high school students lag behind those in other countries on international achievement tests.

Socialization in the workplace changes when it involves a more permanent shift from an after-school job to full-time employment. Occupational socialization can be most intense during the transition from school to job, but it continues throughout one's work history. Technological advances may alter the requirements of the position and necessitate some degree of resocialization. Today, men and women change occupations,

DON'T GET ME WRONG, I'M A BIG FAN OF SOCIAL NETWORKING, BUT...

STAHLER
THE COLUMBUS DISPATCH. 2010.

employers, or places of work many times during their adult years. For example, the typical worker spends about four years with an employer. Occupational socialization continues, then, throughout a person's years in the labor market (Bialik 2010).

College students today recognize that occupational socialization is not socialization into one lifetime occupation. They anticipate going through a number of jobs. The Bureau of Labor Statistics (2010) has found that from ages 18 to 42, the typical person has held 11 jobs. This high rate of turnover in employment applies to both men and women, and to those with a college degree as well as those with a high school diploma.

Religion and the State

Increasingly, social scientists are recognizing the importance of both religion and government ("the state") as agents of socialization, because of their impact on the life course. Traditionally, family members have served as the primary caregivers in our culture, but in the 20th century, the family's protective function was steadily transferred to outside agencies such as hospitals, mental health clinics, and child care centers. Many of these agencies are run by groups affiliated with certain religions or by the state.

Both organized religion and government have impacted the life course by reinstituting some of the rites of passage once observed in agricultural communities and early industrial societies. For example, religious organizations stipulate certain traditional rites that may bring together all the members of an extended family, even if they never meet for any other reason. And government regulations stipulate the ages at which a person may drive a car, drink alcohol, vote in elections, marry without parental permission, work overtime, and retire. These regulations do not constitute strict rites of passage: most 18-year-olds choose not to vote, and most people choose their age of retirement without reference to government dictates.

In the Social Policy section at the end of this module, we will see that government is under pressure to become a provider of child care, which would give it a new and direct role in the socialization of infants and young children.

social
policy and Socialization | **Child Care around the World**

Child care programs are not just babysitting services; they have an enormous influence on the development of young children—an influence that has been growing with the movement of more and more women into the paid labor force. The rise in single-parent families, increased job opportunities for women, and the need for additional family income have all propelled mothers of young children into the working world. Who should care for the children of working mothers during working hours?

Looking at the Issue

Preschoolers typically are not cared for by their parents. Seventy-three percent of employed mothers depend on others to care for their children, and 30 percent of mothers who aren't employed have regular care arrangements. In fact, children under age five are more likely to be cared for on a daily basis by their grandparents than by their parents. Over a third of them are cared for by nonrelatives in nursery schools, Head Start programs, day care centers, family day care, and other arrangements (Bureau of the Census 2008c).

Researchers have found that high-quality child care centers do not adversely affect the socialization of children; in fact, good day care benefits children. The value of preschool programs was documented in a series of studies conducted in the United States. Researchers found no significant differences in infants who had received extensive nonmaternal care compared with those who had been cared for solely by their mothers. They also reported that more and more infants in the United States are being placed in child care outside the home, and that overall, the quality of those arrangements is better than has been found in previous studies. It is difficult, however, to generalize about child care, since there is so much variability among day care providers, and even among government policies from one state to another (Loeb et al. 2004; Ludwig and Sawhill 2007; NICHD 2007).

Few people in the United States or elsewhere can afford the luxury of having a parent stay at home, or of paying for high-quality live-in child care. For millions of mothers and fathers, finding the right kind of child care is a challenge both

—*Continued*

to parenting and to the pocketbook. At present, the federal government supports child care through subsidized programs, which target low-income families, and income tax credits, which benefit families with moderate incomes. The annual expenditure to assist low-income parents is about $12 billion; the expenditure to support parents with moderate incomes is $58 billion (Cushing-Daniels and Zedlewski 2008).

Applying Sociology

Studies that assess the quality of child care outside the home reflect the micro level of analysis and the interest of interactionists in the impact of face-to-face interaction. These studies also explore macro-level implications for the functioning of social institutions like the family. Some of the issues surrounding day care have also been of interest to those who take the conflict perspective.

Children play at the Communicare day care center in Perth, Australia. The Australian government subsidizes children's attendance at day care and afterschool programs from birth to age 12.

In the United States, high-quality day care is not equally available to all families. Parents in affluent communities have an easier time finding day care than those in poor or working-class communities. Finding *affordable* child care is also a problem. Viewed from a conflict perspective, child care costs are an especially serious burden for lower-class families. The poorest families spend 25 percent of their income for preschool child care, whereas families who are *not* poor pay only 6 percent or less of their income.

Feminist theorists echo the concern of conflict theorists that high-quality child care receives little government support because it is regarded as "merely a way to let women work." Nearly all child care workers (97 percent) are women; many find themselves in low-status, minimum-wage jobs. Typically, food servers, messengers, and gas station attendants make more money than the 23 million child care workers in the United States, whose average annual salary of $19,605 puts them right at the poverty level for a family of three (Bureau of the Census 2011a; Ruiz 2010).

Initiating Policy

Policies regarding child care outside the home vary throughout the world. Most developing nations do not have the economic base to provide subsidized child care. Thus, working mothers rely largely on relatives or take their children to work. In the comparatively wealthy industrialized countries of western Europe, government provides child care as a basic service, at little or no expense to parents. But even those countries with tax-subsidized programs occasionally fall short of the need for high-quality child care.

When policymakers decide that child care is desirable, they must determine the degree to which taxpayers should subsidize it. In Sweden and Denmark, one-half to two-thirds of preschoolers were in government-subsidized child care full-time in 2003. In the United States, annual fees for full-time child care of a four-year-old range from an average of $3,900 in Mississippi to an average of $11,678 in Massachusetts (Immervoll and Barber 2005; NACCRRA 2010).

We have a long way to go in making high-quality child care more affordable and accessible, not just in the United States but throughout the world as well. In an attempt to reduce government spending, France is considering cutting back the budgets of subsidized nurseries, even though waiting lists exist and the French public heartily disapproves of cutbacks. In Germany, reunification has reduced the options previously open to East German mothers, who had become accustomed to government-supported child care. Experts in child development view such reports as a vivid reminder of the need for greater government and private-sector support for child care (Hank 2001; L. King 1998).

TAKE THE ISSUE WITH YOU

1. Were you ever in a day care program? If so, do you recall the experience as good or bad? In general, do you think it is desirable to expose young children to the socializing influence of day care?

2. In the view of conflict theorists, child care receives little government support because it is "merely a way to let women work." Can you think of other explanations?

3. Should the costs of day care programs be paid by government, by the private sector, or entirely by parents?

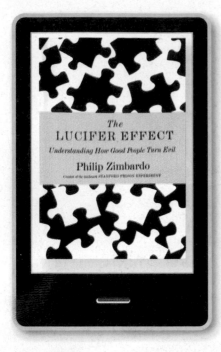

If you were a prison guard, would you mistreat the inmates?

To find the answer to this question, social psychologist Philip Zimbardo created a mock prison and enlisted college students to serve as the inmates and guards.

" As each of the blindfolded prisoners is escorted down the flight of steps in front of Jordan Hall into our little jail, our guards order them to strip and remain standing naked with their arms outstretched against the wall and legs spread apart. They hold that uncomfortable position for a long time as the guards ignore them because they are busy with last-minute chores, like packing away the prisoners' belongings for safekeeping, fixing up their guards quarters, and arranging beds in the three cells. Before being given his uniform, each prisoner is sprayed with powder, alleged to be a delouser, to rid him of lice that might be brought in to contaminate our jail. . . . The humiliation of being a prisoner has begun, much as it does in many institutions from military boot camps to prisons, hospitals, and low-level jobs. . . .

The morning shift comes on in the middle of the night, 2 a.m. . . .

The prisoners are sound asleep. Some are snoring in their dark, cramped cells. Suddenly the silence is shattered. Loud whistles shriek, voices yell, "Up and at 'em." "Wake up and get out here for the count!" "Okay, you sleeping beauties, it's time to see if you learned how to count." Dazed prisoners line up against the wall and count off mindlessly as the three guards alternate in coming up with new variations on count themes. The count and its attendant push-ups and jumping jacks for failures continue on and on for nearly a weary hour. Finally, the prisoners are ordered back to sleep—until reveille a few hours later. . . .

[By Tuesday] our prisoners are looking raggedy and bleary-eyed, and our little prison is beginning to smell like a men's toilet in a New York subway station. Seems that some guards have made toilet visits a privilege to be awarded infrequently and never after lights out. During the night, prisoners have to urinate and defecate in buckets in their cells, and some guards refuse to allow them to be emptied till morning. Complaints are coming fast and furiously from many of the prisoners. . . .

After less than three days into this bizarre situation, some of the students role-playing prison guards have moved far beyond mere playacting. They have internalized the hostility, negative affect, and mind-set characteristic of some real prison guards, as is evident from their shift reports, retrospective diaries, and personal reflections.

. . .

The depersonalization of the prisoners and the spreading extent of dehumanization are beginning to affect [one of the guards], too: "As I got angrier and angrier, I didn't question this behavior as much. I couldn't let it affect me, so I started hiding myself deeper behind my role. It was the only way of not hurting yourself. I was really lost on what was happening but didn't even think about quitting."

Blaming the victims for their sorry condition—created by our failure to provide adequate shower and sanitation facilities—became common among the staff. We see this victim blame in operation as [the guard] complains, "I got tired of seeing the prisoners in rags, smelling bad, and the prison stink. "

After less than three days into this bizarre situation, some of the students role-playing prison guards have moved far beyond mere playacting. They have internalized the hostility, negative affect, and mind-set characteristic of some real prison guards.

(Zimbardo 2007:40, 41, 52, 53, 80, 86) Additional information about this excerpt can be found on the Online Learning Center at www.mhhe.com/schaefermod2e.

I n this study, directed and described by social psychologist Philip Zimbardo, college students adopted the patterns of social interaction expected of guards and prisoners when they were placed in a mock prison. Sociologists use the term *social interaction* to refer to the ways in which people respond to one another. In the mock prison, social interactions between guards and prisoners were highly impersonal. The guards addressed the prisoners by number rather than name, and they wore reflective sunglasses that made eye contact impossible.

As in many real-life prisons, the simulated prison had a social structure in which guards held virtually total control over prisoners. The term *social structure* refers to the way in which

a society is organized into predictable relationships. The social structure of Zimbardo's mock prison influenced how the guards and prisoners interacted. Zimbardo and his colleagues (2009:516) note that it was a real prison "in the minds of the jailers and their captives." His simulated prison experiment, first conducted more than 30 years ago, has been repeated (with similar findings) both in the United States and in other countries.

In these modules we will study social structure and its effect on our social interactions. What determines a person's status in society? How do our social roles affect our social interactions? What is the place of social institutions such as the family, religion, and government in our social structure? How can we better understand and manage large organizations such as multinational corporations? We'll begin by considering how social interactions shape the way we view the world around us. Next, we'll focus on the six basic elements of social structure: statuses, social roles, groups, social networks, social institutions such as the family, religion, and government, and the mass media. We'll also touch on a new element of social network, *virtual worlds*. We'll see that functionalists, conflict theorists, and interactionists approach these institutions quite differently. We'll compare our modern social structure with simpler forms around the world. We'll note the differences between various types of groups, with particular attention to small groups. Next, we'll consider why formal organizations, such as corporations or the college you attend, came into existence, touching on Max Weber's model of the modern bureaucracy. The Social Policy section at the end of the chapter focuses on the recent concentration of the mass media in the hands of a few large corporations.

MODULE 16 | Social Interaction and Social Structure

The prison experiment described in *The Lucifer Effect* took on new relevance during the Iraq War, in the wake of shocking revelations of prisoner abuse at the U.S.-run Abu Ghraib military facility. Graphic photos showed U.S. soldiers humiliating naked Iraqi prisoners and threatening to attack them with police dogs. The structure of the wartime prison, coupled with intense pressure on military intelligence officers to get information about terrorist plots, contributed to the breakdown in the guards' behavior. But the guards' depraved behavior could have been predicted on the basis of Zimbardo's research.

The two concepts of social interaction and social structure are central to sociology. **Social interaction,** the ways people respond to one another, and **social structure,** the way society is organized into predictable relationships, work together. Both concepts are closely related to socialization (see Module 13), the process through which people learn the attitudes, values, and behaviors appropriate to their society. When the students in Zimbardo's experiment entered the mock prison, they began a process of resocialization. In that process, they adjusted to a new social structure and learned new rules for social interaction.

● Social Interaction and Reality

When someone in a crowd shoves you, do you automatically push back? Or do you consider the circumstances of the incident and the attitude of the instigator before you react? Chances are you do the latter. According to sociologist Herbert Blumer (1969:79), the distinctive characteristic of social interaction among people is that "human beings interpret or 'define' each other's actions instead of merely reacting to each other's actions." In other words, our response to someone's behavior is based on the *meaning* we attach to his or her actions. Reality is shaped by our perceptions, evaluations, and definitions.

These meanings typically reflect the norms and values of the dominant culture and our socialization experiences within that culture. As interactionists emphasize, the meanings that we attach to people's behavior are shaped by our interactions with them and with the larger society. Social reality is literally constructed from our social interactions (Berger and Luckmann 1966).

How do we define our social reality? Consider something as simple as how we regard tattoos. At one time, most of us in the United States considered tattoos weird or kooky. We associated them with fringe countercultural groups, such as punk rockers, biker gangs, and skinheads. Among many people, a tattoo elicited an automatic negative response. Now, however, so many people have tattoos—including society's trendsetters and major sports figures—and the ritual of getting a tattoo has become so legitimized, that mainstream culture regards tattoos differently. At this point, as a result of increased social interaction with tattooed people, tattoos look perfectly at home to us in a number of settings.

The nature of social interaction and what constitutes reality varies across cultures. In Western societies, with their emphasis on romantic love, couples see marriage as a relationship as well as a social status. From Valentine's Day flowers to more informal, everyday gestures, professions of love are an expected part of marriage. In Japan, however, marriage is considered more a social status than a relationship. Although many or most Japanese couples undoubtedly do love each other, saying "I love you" does not come easily to them, especially not to husbands. Nor do most husbands call their wives by name (they prefer "Mother") or look them in the eyes. In 2006, in an effort to change these restrictive customs, some Japanese men formed the Devoted Husband Organization, which has been sponsoring a new holiday, Beloved Wives Day. In 2008, this group organized an event called Shout Your Love from the Middle of a Cabbage Patch Day. Dozens of men stood in a cabbage patch north of Tokyo and shouted, "I love you!" to their wives, some of whom had never heard their husbands say those words. In another rare gesture, husbands pledged to be home by 8 p.m. that day (Japan Aisaika Organization 2012; Kambayashi 2008).

The ability to define social reality reflects a group's power within a society. In fact, one of the most crucial aspects of the relationship between dominant and subordinate groups is the ability of the dominant or majority group to define a society's values. Sociologist William I. Thomas (1923), an early critic of theories of racial and gender differences, recognized that the "definition of the situation" could mold the thinking and personality of the individual. Writing from an interactionist perspective, Thomas observed that people respond not only to the objective features of a person or situation but also to the *meaning* that person or situation has for them. For example, in Philip Zimbardo's mock prison experiment, student "guards" and "prisoners" accepted the definition of the situation (including the traditional roles and behavior associated with being a guard or prisoner) and acted accordingly.

As we have seen throughout the past 60 years—first in the civil rights movement of the 1950s and 1960s and since then among such groups as women, the elderly, gays and lesbians, and people with disabilities—an important aspect of the process of social change involves redefining or reconstructing social reality. Members of subordinate groups challenge traditional definitions and begin to perceive and experience reality in a new way.

Elements of Social Structure

All social interaction takes place within a social structure, including those interactions that redefine social reality. For purposes of study, we can break down any social structure into six elements: statuses, social roles, groups, social networks, virtual worlds, and social institutions. These elements make up social structure just as a foundation, walls, and ceilings make up a building's structure. The elements of social structure are developed through the lifelong process of socialization described in Module 14.

Statuses

We normally think of a person's *status* as having to do with influence, wealth, and fame. However, sociologists use the term **status** to refer to any of the full range of socially defined positions within a large group or society, from the lowest to the highest. Within our society, a person can occupy the status of president of the United States, fruit picker, son or daughter, violinist, teenager, resident of Minneapolis, dental technician, or neighbor. A person can hold a number of statuses at the same time.

Ascribed and Achieved Status   Sociologists view some statuses as *ascribed* and others as *achieved* (Figure 16-1). An **ascribed status** is assigned to a person by society without regard for the

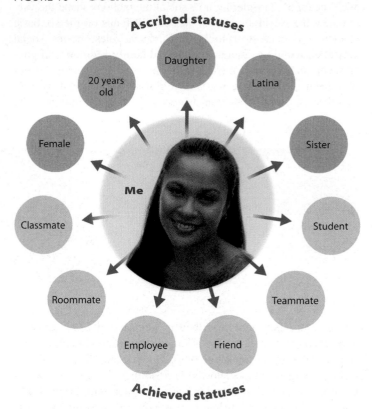

FIGURE 16-1 **Social Statuses**

Think about It

The young woman in this figure—"me"—occupies many positions in society, each of which involves distinct statuses. How would you define your statuses? Which have the most influence in your life?

person's unique talents or characteristics. Generally, the assignment takes place at birth; thus, a person's racial background, gender, and age are all considered ascribed statuses. Though these characteristics are biological in origin, they are significant mainly because of the *social* meanings they have in our culture. Conflict theorists are especially interested in ascribed statuses, since they often confer privileges or reflect a person's membership in a subordinate group. The social meanings of race, ethnicity, and gender will be analyzed more fully in Modules 32 and 34.

In most cases, we can do little to change an ascribed status, but we can attempt to change the traditional constraints associated with it. For example, the Gray Panthers—an activist political group founded in 1971 to work for the rights of older people—have tried to modify society's negative and confining stereotypes of the elderly. As a result of their work and that of other groups supporting older citizens, the ascribed status of "senior citizen" is no longer as difficult for millions of older people.

An ascribed status does not necessarily have the same social meaning in every society. In a cross-cultural study, sociologist Gary Huang (1988) confirmed the long-held view that respect for the elderly is an important cultural norm in China. In many

cases, the prefix "old" is used respectfully: calling some-one "old teacher" or "old person" is like calling a judge in the United States "your honor." Huang points out that positive age-seniority language distinctions are uncommon in the United States; consequently, we view the term *old man* as more of an insult than a celebration of seniority and wisdom.

Unlike ascribed statuses, an **achieved status** comes to us largely through our own efforts. Both "computer programmer" and "prison guard" are achieved statuses, as are "lawyer," "pianist," "sorority member," "convict," and "social worker." We must do something to acquire an achieved status—go to school, learn a skill, establish a friendship, invent a new product. But as we will see in the next section, our ascribed status heavily influences our achieved status. Being male, for example, would decrease the likelihood that we would consider child care as a career.

Ascribed status may intersect with a person's achieved status. This woman's achieved status as a low-income worker, combined with her minority ethnic status, contrast sharply with the high status of her customer.

Master Status   Each person holds many different and sometimes conflicting statuses; some may connote higher social position and some, lower position. How, then, do others view one's overall social position? According to sociologist Everett Hughes (1945), societies deal with inconsistencies by agreeing that certain statuses are more important than others. A **master status** is a status that dominates others and thereby determines a person's general position in society. For example, Arthur Ashe, who died of AIDS in 1993, had a remarkable career as a tennis star, but at the end of his life, his status as a well-known personality with AIDS may have outweighed his statuses as a retired athlete, author, and political activist. Throughout the world, many people with disabilities find that their status as disabled receives undue weight, overshadowing their actual ability to perform successfully in meaningful employment (Box 16-1).

Our society gives such importance to race and gender that they often dominate our lives. These ascribed statuses frequently influence our achieved status. The Black activist Malcolm X (1925–1965), an eloquent and controversial advocate of Black power and Black pride during the early 1960s, recalled that his feelings and perspectives changed dramatically in middle school. Elected class president and finishing near the top of his class academically, he had developed a positive outlook. However, his teachers, all of them White, discouraged him from taking more challenging courses, which they felt were not appropriate for Black students. When his eighth-grade English teacher, a White man, advised him that his goal of becoming a lawyer was not realistic, and encouraged him instead to become a carpenter, Malcolm X concluded that his being a Black man (ascribed status) was an obstacle to his dream of becoming a lawyer (achieved status). In the United States, the ascribed statuses of race and gender can function as master statuses that have an important impact on one's potential to achieve a desired professional and social status (Malcolm X [1964] 1999:37; Marable 2011:36–38).

Social Roles

What Are Social Roles?   Throughout our lives, we acquire what sociologists call social roles. A **social role** is a set of expectations for people who occupy a given social position or status. Thus, in the United States, we expect that cab drivers will know how to get around a city, that receptionists will be reliable in handling phone messages, and that police officers will take action if they see a citizen being threatened. With each distinctive social status—whether ascribed or achieved—come particular role expectations. However, actual performance varies from individual to individual. One secretary may assume extensive administrative responsibilities, while another may focus on clerical duties. Similarly, in Philip Zimbardo's mock prison experiment, some students were brutal and sadistic guards; others were not.

Roles are a significant component of social structure. Viewed from a functionalist perspective, roles contribute to a society's stability by enabling members to anticipate the behavior of others and to pattern their actions accordingly. Yet social roles can also be dysfunctional if they restrict people's interactions and relationships. If we view a person *only* as a "police officer" or "supervisor," it will be difficult to relate to him or her as a friend or neighbor.

Role Conflict   Imagine the delicate situation of a woman who has worked for a decade on an assembly line in an electrical plant, and has recently been named supervisor of her unit. How is this woman expected to relate to her longtime friends and co-workers? Should she still go out to lunch with them, as she has done almost daily for years? Is it her responsibility to recommend the firing of an old friend who cannot keep up with the demands of the assembly line?

Role conflict occurs when incompatible expectations arise from two or more social positions held by the same person. Fulfillment of the roles associated with one status may directly violate the roles linked to a second status. In the example just given, the newly promoted supervisor will most likely experience a sharp conflict between her social and occupational roles. Such role conflicts call for important ethical choices. The new supervisor will have to make a difficult decision about how much allegiance she owes her friend and how much she owes her employers, who have given her supervisory responsibilities.

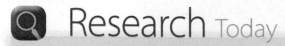
Disability as a Master Status

Throughout history and around the world, people with disabilities have been subjected to cruel and inhuman treatment. For example, in the 20th century, the disabled were frequently viewed as subhuman creatures who were a menace to society. In Japan more than 16,000 women with disabilities were involuntarily sterilized with government approval from 1945 to 1995. Sweden apologized for the same action taken against 62,000 of its citizens in the 1970s.

Such blatantly hostile treatment of people with disabilities has given way to a *medical model,* in which the disabled are viewed as chronic patients. Increasingly, however, people concerned with the rights of the disabled have criticized this model as well. In their view, it is the unnecessary and discriminatory barriers present in the environment—both physical and attitudinal—that stand in the way of people with disabilities, more than any biological limitations. Applying a *civil rights model,* activists emphasize that those with disabilities face widespread prejudice, discrimination, and segregation. For example, most voting places are inaccessible to wheelchair users and fail to provide ballots that can be used by those unable to read print.

Drawing on the earlier work of Erving Goffman, contemporary sociologists have

suggested that society attaches a stigma to many forms of disability, a stigma that leads to prejudicial treatment. People with disabilities frequently observe that the nondisabled see them only as blind, wheelchair users, and so forth, rather than as complex human beings with individual strengths and weaknesses, whose blindness or use of a wheelchair is merely one aspect of their lives.

Although discrimination against the disabled occurs around the world, attitudes are

> In Japan more than 16,000 women with disabilities were involuntarily sterilized with government approval from 1945 to 1995.

changing. The African nation of Botswana has plans to assist its disabled, most of whom live in rural areas and need special services for mobility and economic development. In many countries, disability rights activists are targeting issues essential to overcoming this master status and becoming a full citizen, including

employment, housing, education, and access to public buildings.

LET'S DISCUSS

1. Does your campus present barriers to disabled students? If so, what kinds of barriers—physical, attitudinal, or both? Describe some of them.

2. Why do you think nondisabled people see disability as the most important characteristic of a disabled person? What can be done to help people see beyond the wheelchair and the Seeing Eye dog?

Sources: Albrecht 2004; Goffman 1963; D. Murphy 1997; *Newsday* 1997; R. Schaefer 2012; J. Shapiro 1993.

---

use your **sociological imagination**

If you were a male nurse, what aspects of role conflict might you experience? Now imagine you are a professional boxer and a woman. What conflicting role expectations might that involve? In both cases, how well do you think you would handle role conflict?

Another type of role conflict occurs when individuals move into occupations that are not common among people with their ascribed status. Male preschool teachers and female police officers experience this type of role conflict. In the latter case, female officers must strive to reconcile their workplace role in law enforcement with the societal view of a woman's role, which does not embrace many skills needed in police work. And while female police officers encounter sexual harassment, as women do throughout the labor force, they must also deal with the "code of silence," an informal norm that precludes their implicating fellow officers in wrongdoing (Fletcher 1995; S. Martin 1994).

Role Strain Role conflict describes the situation of a person dealing with the challenge of occupying two social positions simultaneously. However, even a single position can cause problems. Sociologists use the term **role strain** to describe the

difficulty that arises when the same social position imposes conflicting demands and expectations.

People who belong to minority cultures may experience role strain while working in the mainstream culture. Criminologist Larry Gould (2002) interviewed officers of the Navajo Nation Police Department about their relations with conventional law enforcement officials, such as sheriffs and FBI agents. Besides enforcing the law, Navajo Nation officers practice an alternative form of justice known as Peacemaking, in which they seek reconciliation between the parties to a crime. The officers expressed great confidence in Peacemaking, but worried that if they did not make arrests, other law enforcement officials would think they were too soft, or "just taking care of their own." Regardless of the strength of their ties to traditional Navajo ways, all felt the strain of being considered "too Navajo" or "not Navajo enough."

Role Exit Often, when we think of assuming a social role, we focus on the preparation and anticipatory socialization a person undergoes for that role. Such is true if a person is about to become an attorney, a chef, a spouse, or a parent. Yet until recently, social scientists have given little attention to the adjustments involved in *leaving* social roles.

Sociologist Helen Rose Fuchs Ebaugh (1988) developed the term **role exit** to describe the process of disengagement from a role that is central to one's self-identity in order to establish a

Danielle Taylor, *Account Manager, Cash Cycle Solutions*

When Danielle Taylor entered Clemson University, she was planning to study medicine, but then she discovered that sociology was "ten times more interesting." Today she is an account manager with a company in Charlotte, North Carolina, that provides transaction processing services.

Taylor began her business career as a restaurant manager, a job that involved a good deal of interaction with the public. Sociology prepared her for a diverse work environment, she says, and helped her to handle customer complaints, allowing her to "defuse these often delicate situations more easily and with much less struggle" than managers without her background.

Taylor was managing a corporate restaurant when she made the connection that led to her present position as an account manager. "I was privy to meeting many people with lots of connections in other fields," she explains. "Networking is never as formal as it sounds and just simply conversing with my customers led to me finding a much better suited career."

Taylor thinks she is a more open and understanding person thanks to her sociological training. "I tend to judge less and analyze more," she says. She also sees the big picture that other people might miss. "Managing a restaurant with a degree in sociology was an eye-opening experience," she concludes.

LET'S DISCUSS

1. Before you read this box, would you have thought that a sociology major could be successful as a business manager? Why or why not?

2. Take the skills that Danielle Taylor gained from studying sociology and apply them to the job you hope to get when you graduate. Do they apply just as well to your chosen field?

According to sociologist Helen Rose Fuchs Ebaugh, role exit is a four-stage process. Is this transsexual in the first or the fourth stage of changing genders?

new role and identity. Drawing on interviews with 185 people—among them ex-convicts, divorced men and women, recovering alcoholics, ex-nuns, former doctors, retirees, and transexuals—Ebaugh (herself an ex-nun) studied the process of voluntarily exiting from significant social roles.

Ebaugh has offered a four-stage model of role exit. The first stage begins with *doubt.* The person experiences frustration, burnout, or simply unhappiness with an accustomed status and the roles associated with the social position. The second stage involves a *search for alternatives.* A person who is unhappy with his or her career may take a leave of absence; an unhappily married couple may begin what they see as a temporary separation.

The third stage of role exit is the *action stage* or *departure.* Ebaugh found that the vast majority of her respondents could identify a clear turning point that made them feel it was essential to take final action and leave their jobs, end their marriages, or engage in another type of role exit. Twenty percent of respondents saw their role exit as a gradual, evolutionary process that had no single turning point.

The fourth stage of role exit involves the *creation of a new identity.* Many of you participated in a role exit when you made the transition from high school to college. You left behind the role of offspring living at home and took on the role of a somewhat independent college student living with peers in a dorm. Sociologist Ira Silver (1996) has studied the central role that material objects play in this transition. The objects students choose to leave at home (like stuffed animals and dolls) are associated with their prior identities. They may remain deeply attached to those objects, but do not want them to be seen as part of their new identities at college. The objects they bring with them symbolize how they now see themselves and how they wish to be perceived. iPods and wall posters, for example, are calculated to say, "This is me."

Groups

In sociological terms, a **group** is any number of people with similar norms, values, and expectations who interact with one another on a regular basis. The members of a women's basketball team, a hospital's business office, a synagogue, or a symphony orchestra constitute a group. However, the residents of a suburb would not be considered a group, since they rarely interact with one another at one time.

Groups play a vital part in a society's social structure. Much of our social interaction takes place within groups and is influenced by their norms and sanctions. Being a teenager or a retired person takes on special meanings when we interact within groups designed for people with that particular status. The expectations associated with many social roles, including those accompanying the statuses of brother, sister, and student, become more clearly defined in the context of a group.

Social Networks

Groups do not merely serve to define other elements of the social structure, such as roles and statuses; they also link the individual with the larger society. We all belong to a number of different groups, and through our acquaintances make connections with people in different social circles. These connections are known as a **social network**—a series of social relationships that links a person directly to others, and through them indirectly to still more people. Social networks are one of the five basic elements of social structure.

Social networks can center on virtually any activity, from sharing job information to exchanging news and gossip, or even sharing sex. Much of network analysis serves as an example of applied research. Box 16-2 describes a long-term study in which public health officials used network analysis to curb obesity.

Involvement in social networks—commonly known as *networking*—is especially valuable in finding employment. Albert Einstein was successful in finding a job only when a classmate's father put him in touch with his future employer.

 Research Today

BOX 16-2

Social Networks and Obesity

Over the past two generations, obesity has become a public health problem in the United States. To explain the trend toward excess weight, researchers have focused on Americans' nutritional practices, as well as on their genetic tendencies. Another variable that contributes to obesity, less obvious than diet and heredity, is social networking.

Researchers identified this last variable in the course of a long-term heart health survey, during which they tracked the weight of

> Weight gain in one person is often associated with weight gain in his or her friends, siblings, spouse, and neighbors.

12,067 respondents. At the same time, they mapped the social networks that respondents belonged to (see the accompanying figure). Over the three decades since the survey began, they have noted that weight gain in one person is often associated with weight gain in his or her friends, siblings, spouse, and neighbors. In fact, a person's chances of becoming obese increased by 57 percent if a friend became overweight during the same period. This association, they found, was attributable solely to selectivity in the choice of friends—that is, to people of a certain weight seeking out others of roughly the same weight.

This study shows that social networks do influence the way people behave. More important, the results suggest that networking could be exploited to spread positive health behaviors—for example, by recruiting friends to participate in a person's weight-loss plan.

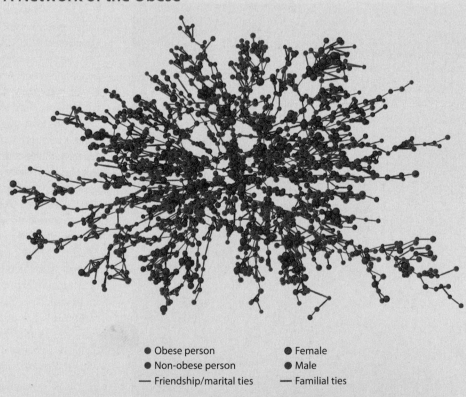

A Network of the Obese

- ● Obese person
- ● Non-obese person
- — Friendship/marital ties
- ● Female
- ● Male
- — Familial ties

Larger circles represent heavier people.

Through a similar approach, health practitioners could include social networking in efforts to control smoking, drinking, and drug abuse.

LET'S DISCUSS

1. Have you ever tried to lose weight, and if so, did your cluster of friends and family help or hinder you? In your experience, do people who are overweight tend to cluster in separate groups from those of normal weight?

2. Besides public health campaigns, what applications can you think of for research on social networking?

Sources: Christakis and Fowler 2007, 2009; Haas et al. 2010.

These kinds of contacts—even those that are weak and distant—can be crucial in establishing social networks and facilitating the transmission of information.

During the recent economic downturn, electronic social networks have served a new purpose, encouraging the jobless. Websites and chat rooms that cannot locate jobs for those who have been thrown out of work concentrate instead on helping them to stick together, support one another, and maintain a positive attitude. For the unemployed, online conversations with friends or even strangers in the same predicament can be an invaluable morale booster (Scherer 2010b).

Research indicates, however, that both in person and online, not everyone participates equally in social networks. Women and racial and ethnic minorities are at a disadvantage when seeking new and better job opportunities or social contacts (Trimble and Kmec 2011).

Virtual Worlds

Today, with recent advances in technology, people can maintain their social networks electronically; they don't need face-to-face contacts. Whether through text-messaging, handheld devices, or social networking sites like Facebook, a significant amount of

case study | The Second Life Virtual World

E-mail, webcams, and blogs are only the first stage in the creation of alternative forms of social reality. Recently a whole new society, the Second Life® world, has sprung up in virtual space. Web-based and three-dimensional, the Second Life virtual world included over 19 million networked "players" as of 2012. In this game, players assume avatars that may represent looking-glass selves very different from their actual identities. Once equipped with an avatar, they go about their lives in the virtual world, establishing businesses, even buying and decorating homes.

Just like real worlds, virtual worlds have become politicized and commercialized. In 2007, Sweden became the first real-world country to place an "embassy" in the Second Life world. Elsewhere in this virtual world, virtual protesters have paraded on behalf of a far-right French group in a confrontation with anti-Nazi protesters. The Second Life virtual world is now open to real-world corporations that want to "build" their stores in it. Some corporations have even purchased "islands" to use for training sessions or employee conferences. Employees who attend these exclusive functions may show up in their finest avatar attire. The commercialization of these spaces has been met with a good deal of antagonism: Reebok

has weathered a virtual nuclear bomb attack, and "customers" have been "shot" outside the American Apparel store.

A more positive side of the Second Life virtual world is evident in Al-Andalus, a democratically run nonprofit community dedicated to interfaith understanding. Begun after 9/11, Al-Andalus has equal numbers of Jewish, Muslim, Christian, and atheist avatars. It even boasts a library to provide objective information on religion, run by an avatar who in real life is a librarian at the Smithsonian Institution.

Sociologist Manuel Castells views these emerging electronic social networks as fundamental to new organizations, and to the growth of existing businesses and associations. With other scholars, sociologists are now scrambling to understand these environments and their social processes. The Second Life world went public in 2003—a millennium ago in the world of cyberspace. Scholars worry that after the current period of transition, given the absence of a historical record, reconstructing these worlds as they existed when they were populated by only a hundred avatars, much less tens of thousands, will be impossible (Boellstorff 2008; Borrelli 2010; Castells 2010a, 2010b, 2010c; Gilsdorf 2010; Malaby 2009; Second Life 2010).

Virtual worlds have just begun to test our imaginations. On the left, a group of avatars interacts in the Second Life® world. On the right, in the blockbuster film *Avatar,* the Na'vi people interact in the screen-based virtual world of Pandora.

Postindustrial and Postmodern Societies

When Lenski first proposed the sociocultural evolutionary approach in the 1960s, he paid relatively little attention to how maturing industrialized societies may change with the emergence of even more advanced forms of technology. More recently, he and other sociologists have studied the significant changes in the occupational structure of industrial societies as they shift from manufacturing to service economies. In the 1970s, sociologist Daniel Bell wrote about the technologically advanced **postindustrial society,** whose economic system is engaged primarily in the processing and control of information. The main output of a postindustrial society is services rather than manufactured goods. Large numbers of people become involved in occupations devoted to the teaching, generation, or dissemination of ideas. Jobs in fields such as advertising, public relations, human resources, and computer information systems would be typical of a postindustrial society (D. Bell [1973] 1999). The Social Policy section in Module 19 describes an important example of these postindustrial organizations—the media industry.

Bell views the transition from industrial to postindustrial society as a positive development. He sees a general decline in organized working-class groups and a rise in interest groups concerned with national issues such as health, education, and the environment. Bell's outlook is functionalist, because he portrays the postindustrial society as basically consensual. As organizations and interest groups engage in an open and competitive process of decision making, Bell believes, the level of conflict between diverse groups will diminish, strengthening social stability.

Conflict theorists take issue with Bell's functionalist analysis of the postindustrial society. For example, Michael Harrington (1980), who alerted the nation to the problems of the poor in his book *The Other America,* questioned the significance that Bell attached to the growing class of white-collar workers. Harrington conceded that scientists, engineers, and economists are involved in important political and economic decisions, but he disagreed with Bell's claim that they have a free hand in decision making, independent of the interests of the rich. Harrington followed in the tradition of Marx by arguing that conflict between social classes will continue in the postindustrial society.

Sociologists have gone beyond discussion of the postindustrial society to the ideal of the postmodern society. A **postmodern society** is a technologically sophisticated society that is preoccupied with consumer goods and media images (Brannigan 1992). Such societies consume goods and information on a mass scale. Postmodern theorists take a global perspective, noting the ways that culture crosses national boundaries. For example, residents of the United States may listen to reggae music from Jamaica, eat sushi and other Japanese foods, and wear clogs from Sweden. And online social networks know no national boundaries.

The emphasis of postmodern theorists is on observing and describing newly emerging cultural forms and patterns of social interaction. Within sociology, the postmodern view offers support for integrating the insights of various theoretical perspectives—functionalism, conflict theory, feminist theory, and interactionism—while incorporating other contemporary approaches. Feminist sociologists argue optimistically that with its indifference to hierarchies and distinctions, the postmodern society will discard traditional values of male dominance in favor of gender equality. Yet, others contend that despite new technologies, postindustrial and postmodern societies can be expected to display the same problems of inequality that plague industrial societies (Denzin 2004; Smart 1990; B. Turner 1990; van Vucht Tijssen 1990).

Durkheim, Tönnies, and Lenski present three visions of society's social structure. While they differ, each is useful, and this textbook will draw on all three. The sociocultural evolutionary approach emphasizes a historical perspective. It does not picture different types of social structure coexisting within the same society. Consequently, one would not expect a single society to include hunters and gatherers along with a postmodern culture. In contrast, Durkheim's and Tönnies's theories allow for the existence of different types of community—such as a *Gemeinschaft* and a *Gesellschaft*—in the same society. Thus, a rural New Hampshire community located 100 miles from Boston can be linked to the city by modern information technology. The main difference between these two theories is a matter of emphasis. While Tönnies emphasized the overriding concern in each type of community—one's own self-interest or the well-being of the larger society—Durkheim emphasized the division (or lack of division) of labor.

The work of these three thinkers reminds us that a major focus of sociology has been to identify changes in social structure and the consequences for human behavior. At the macro level, we see society shifting to more advanced forms of technology. The social structure becomes increasingly complex, and new social institutions emerge to assume some functions that once were performed by the family. On the micro level, these changes affect the nature of social interactions. Each individual takes on multiple social roles, and people come to rely more on social networks and less on kinship ties. As the social structure becomes more complex, people's relationships become more impersonal, transient, and fragmented.

MODULE 17 | Recap and Review

Summary

Sociologists have developed classification systems that help us contrast complex modern societies with simpler forms of social structure.

1. Émile Durkheim thought that social structure depends on the division of labor in a society. According to Durkheim, societies with minimal division of labor have a collective consciousness called **mechanical solidarity.**

Those with greater division of labor show an interdependence called **organic solidarity.**

2. Ferdinand Tönnies distinguished the close-knit community of *Gemeinschaft* from the impersonal mass society known as *Gesellschaft.*

3. Gerhard Lenski thinks that a society's social structure changes as its culture and technology become more sophisticated, a process he calls **sociocultural evolution.**

Thinking Critically

1. According to Lenski, technology is the key to sociocultural evolution. What social factors are most likely to influence whether a society's culture evolves to a new stage of sociocultural evolution?

2. How are Durkheim's and Tönnies's classifications similar? How are they different?

3. Describe any personal experiences you have had with a nonindustrial, or developing, society. If you have not had that kind of experience, how do you think you would prepare for it?

Key Terms

Agrarian society   125

Gemeinschaft   123

Gesellschaft   123

Horticultural society   125

Hunting-and-gathering society   124

Industrial society   125

Mechanical solidarity   123

Organic solidarity   123

Postindustrial society   126

Postmodern society   126

Sociocultural evolution   124

Technology   124

MODULE

18

Understanding Groups

Most of us use the term *group* loosely to describe any collection of individuals, whether three strangers sharing an elevator or hundreds attending a rock concert. However, in sociological terms a **group** is any number of people with similar norms, values, and expectations who interact with one another on a regular basis. College sororities and fraternities, dance companies, tenants' associations, and chess clubs are all considered groups. The important point is that members of a group share some sense of belonging. This characteristic distinguishes groups from mere *aggregates* of people, such as passengers who happen to be together on an airplane flight, or from *categories* of people, such as those who share a common feature (such as being retired) but otherwise do not act together.

Consider the case of a college singing group. It has agreed-on values and social norms. All members want to improve their singing skills and schedule lots of performances. In addition, like many groups, the singing ensemble has both a formal and an informal structure. The members meet regularly to rehearse; they choose leaders to run the rehearsals and manage their affairs. At the same time, some group members may take on unofficial leadership roles by coaching new members in singing techniques and performing skills.

The study of groups has become an important part of sociological investigation because they play such a key role in the transmission of culture. As we interact with others, we pass on our ways of thinking and acting—from language and values to ways of dressing and leisure activities.

A pizza delivery crew is an example of a *secondary group*—a formal, impersonal group in which there is little social intimacy or mutual understanding. While waiting for the next delivery, members of this crew in Surrey, England, will become well enough acquainted to distinguish those who see the job as temporary from those who view it as permanent. They will learn who looks forward to deliveries in perceived high-risk areas and who does not. They may even spend time together after work, joking or boasting about their exploits on the job, but their friendships typically will not develop beyond that point.

Types of Groups

Sociologists have made a number of useful distinctions between types of groups—primary and secondary groups, in-groups and out-groups, reference groups, and coalitions.

Primary and Secondary Groups

Charles Horton Cooley (1902) coined the term **primary group** to refer to a small group characterized by intimate, face-to-face association and cooperation. The members of a street gang constitute a primary group; so do members of a family living in the same household, as do a group of "sisters" in a college sorority.

Primary groups play a pivotal role both in the socialization process (see Module 13) and in the development of roles and statuses (see Module 16). Indeed, primary groups can be instrumental in a person's day-to-day existence. When we find ourselves identifying closely with a group, it is probably a primary group.

We also participate in many groups that are not characterized by close bonds of friendship, such as large college classes and business associations. The term **secondary group** refers to a formal, impersonal group in which there is little social intimacy or mutual understanding (Table 18-1). Secondary groups

often emerge in the workplace among those who share special understandings about their occupation. The distinction between primary and secondary groups is not always clear-cut, however. Some social clubs may become so large and impersonal that they no longer function as primary groups.

A considerable amount of sociological research has been done on people's behavior in groups. Box 18-1 describes the findings of one well-known but short-lived group: the jury.

summingup

Table **18-1** **Comparison of Primary and Secondary Groups**

Primary Group	Secondary Group
Generally small	Usually large
Relatively long period of interaction	Relatively short duration, often temporary
Intimate, face-to-face association	Little social intimacy or mutual understanding
Some emotional depth to relationships	Relationships generally superficial
Cooperative, friendly	More formal and impersonal

Research Today

BOX 18-1

The Drinking Rape Victim: Jury Decision Making

She was heavily intoxicated. He had drunk a few beers. They had sex. She said she was raped. He said it was consensual. The jury deliberated, and the verdict was....

This is not an actual case, but an experiment in group decision making. Few small groups have received as much attention from sociologists over the past decade and a half as juries. Scholars have used several research methods to investigate juries' decision making: interviews with jury members after they have reached a verdict; observation of jurors as they sit through and react to courtroom events; observation of actual jury deliberations, which presiding judges have permitted in a few instances; and experiments involving mock juries. The findings indicate that jurors do not always make decisions the way they are supposed to. How do jurors form impressions in rape cases, especially those that involve intoxication?

To find out, legal scholars Emily Finch and Vanessa

Munro simulated a rape trial in which intoxication was an issue. The two researchers varied the story to see what the effect might be on the verdict. In one version the alleged victim was drunk; in another she was drugged by a third person; in another she was drugged by the defendant.

Finch and Munro found that male or female, the mock jurors in their study followed a double standard. The more intoxicated the *defendant* was said to have been, the less likely jurors were to regard him as culpable. They were far more likely to regard a *victim* who had drunk too much as having contributed to her rape. This finding applied even in cases in which the victim's drink had been spiked. In short, before jurors could summon up much sympathy for the victim, the defendant had to engage in a great deal of bad behavior.

Today, research on juries is expanding to deal with generational changes in the experience of being a juror. Some jurors arrive at court expecting to see the kind of sophisticated DNA analysis or

> *Finch and Munro found that male or female, the mock jurors in their study followed a double standard.*

investigative methods featured on televised crime shows, such as *CSI*. Improved methods of documenting crime scenes, including the use of computer-generated re-creations, mean that today's jurors are more likely than past jurors to be exposed to images of graphic violence and gore.

LET'S DISCUSS

1. Have you ever served on a jury? If so, were you aware of jurors who made up their minds early in the trial, despite the judge's instructions? Did you experience stress from being exposed to graphic images of violence and bloodshed?

2. Is a jury a typical group? Why or why not?

Sources: S. Diamond and Rose 2005; Finch and Munro 2005, 2007, 2008; McGlynn and Munro 2010.

In-Groups and Out-Groups

A group can hold special meaning for members because of its relationship to other groups. For example, people in one group sometimes feel antagonistic toward or threatened by another group, especially if that group is perceived as being different, either culturally or racially. To identify these "we" and "they" feelings, sociologists use two terms first employed by William Graham Sumner (1906): *in-group* and *out-group*.

An **in-group** can be defined as any group or category to which people feel they belong. Simply put, it comprises everyone who is regarded as "we" or "us." The in-group may be as narrow as a teenage clique or as broad as an entire society. The very existence of an in-group implies that there is an out-group that is viewed as "they" or "them." An **out-group** is a group or category to which people feel they do *not* belong.

At a powwow, a drum circle breathes spirit into an ancient tribal tradition. These accomplished ceremonial musicians may serve as a reference group for onlookers who want to know more about drumming.

In-group members typically feel distinct and superior, seeing themselves as better than people in the out-group. Proper behavior for the in-group is simultaneously viewed as unacceptable behavior for the out-group. This double standard enhances the sense of superiority. Sociologist Robert Merton (1968) described this process as the conversion of "in-group virtues" into "out-group vices." We can see this differential standard operating in worldwide discussions of terrorism. When a group or a nation takes aggressive actions, it usually justifies them as necessary, even if civilians are hurt or killed. Opponents are quick to label such actions with the emotion-laden term of *terrorist* and appeal to the world community for condemnation. Yet these same people may themselves retaliate with actions that hurt civilians, which the first group will then condemn.

 use your **sociological imagination**

Try putting yourself in the shoes of an out-group member. What does your in-group look like from that perspective?

Conflict between in-groups and out-groups can turn violent on a personal as well as a political level. In 1999 two disaffected students at Columbine High School in Littleton, Colorado, launched an attack on the school that left 15 students and teachers dead, including themselves. The gunmen, members of an out-group that other students referred to as the Trenchcoat Mafia, apparently resented taunting by an in-group referred to as the Jocks. Similar episodes have occurred in schools across the nation, where rejected adolescents, overwhelmed by personal and family problems, peer group pressure, academic responsibilities, or media images of violence, have struck out against more popular classmates.

Reference Groups

Both primary groups and in-groups can dramatically influence the way an individual thinks and behaves. Sociologists call any group that individuals use as a standard for evaluating themselves and their own behavior a **reference group.** For example, a high school student who aspires to join a social circle of hip-hop music devotees will pattern his or her behavior after that of the group. The student will begin dressing like these peers, listening to the same downloads and DVDs, and hanging out at the same stores and clubs.

Reference groups have two basic purposes. They serve a normative function by setting and enforcing standards of conduct and belief. The high school student who wants the approval of the hip-hop crowd will have to follow the group's dictates, at least to some extent. Reference groups also perform a comparison function by serving as a standard against which people can measure themselves and others. An actor will evaluate himself or herself against a reference group composed of others in the acting profession (Merton and Kitt 1950).

Reference groups may help the process of anticipatory socialization. For example, a college student majoring in finance may read the *Wall Street Journal,* study the annual reports of corporations, and listen to midday stock market news on the radio. Such a student is using financial experts as a reference group to which he or she aspires.

Often, two or more reference groups influence us at the same time. Our family members, neighbors, and co-workers all shape different aspects of our self-evaluation. In addition, reference group attachments change during the life cycle. A corporate executive who quits the rat race at age 45 to become a social worker will find new reference groups to use as standards for evaluation. We shift reference groups as we take on different statuses during our lives.

Coalitions

As groups grow larger, coalitions begin to develop. A **coalition** is a temporary or permanent alliance geared toward a common goal. Coalitions can be broad-based or narrow and can take on many different objectives. Sociologist William Julius Wilson (1999) has described community-based organizations in Texas that include Whites and Latinos, working class and affluent, who have banded together to work for improved sidewalks, better drainage systems, and comprehensive street paving. Out of this type of coalition building, Wilson hopes, will emerge better interracial understanding.

Some coalitions are intentionally short-lived. For example, short-term coalition building is a key to success in popular TV programs like *Survivor*. In the program's first season, *Survivor: Borneo,* broadcast in 2000, the four members of the "Tagi alliance" banded together to vote fellow castaways off the island. The political world is also the scene of many temporary coalitions. For example, in 1997 big tobacco companies joined with antismoking groups to draw up a settlement for reimbursing states for tobacco-related medical costs. Soon after the settlement was announced the coalition members returned to their decades-long fight against each other (Pear 1997).

Can you outwit, outplay, outlast your competition? Maybe a coalition can help. In *Survivor: One World,* filmed on an island in Samoa, coalition building continued to be a key to success in the long-running television series, now in its 24th season.

 use your **sociological imagination**

Describe an experience you have had with coalition building, or one that you have read about—perhaps in politics. Was the coalition effective? What problems did the members need to overcome?

MODULE 18 | Recap and Review

Summary

Much of our social behavior takes place in groups.

1. When we find ourselves identifying closely with a group, it is probably a primary group. A secondary group is more formal and impersonal.

2. People tend to see the world in terms of in-groups and out-groups, a perception often fostered by the very groups to which they belong.

3. Reference groups set and enforce standards of conduct and serve as a source of comparison for people's evaluations of themselves and others.

4. Interactionist researchers have noted that groups allow coalitions to form and serve as links to social networks and their vast resources.

Thinking Critically

1. Describe an example of coalition building you have experienced or read about (perhaps in the political realm). Was the coalition effective? What problems had to be overcome?

2. Think of a primary and secondary group to which you belong. Under what circumstances might the primary group become a secondary group, or the secondary group become a primary group?

Key Terms

Coalition 130

Group 127

In-group 129

Out-group 129

Primary group 128

Reference group 129

Secondary group 128

Formal Organizations and Bureaucracies

As contemporary societies have shifted to more advanced forms of technology and their social structures have become more complex, our lives have become increasingly dominated by large secondary groups referred to as *formal organizations*. A **formal organization** is a group designed for a special purpose and structured for maximum efficiency. The U.S. Postal Service, McDonald's, and the Boston Pops orchestra are examples of formal organizations. Though organizations vary in their size, specificity of goals, and degree of efficiency, they are all structured to facilitate the management of large-scale operations. They also have a bureaucratic form of organization, described in the next section.

In our society, formal organizations fulfill an enormous variety of personal and societal needs, shaping the lives of every one of us. In fact, formal organizations have become such a dominant force that we must create organizations to supervise other organizations, such as the Securities and Exchange Commission (SEC) to regulate brokerage companies. Although it sounds more exciting to say that we live in the "computer age" than to say that we live in the "age of formal organization," the latter is probably a more accurate description (Azumi and Hage 1972; Etzioni 1964).

Ascribed statuses such as gender, race, and ethnicity can influence how we see ourselves within formal organizations. For example, a study of female lawyers in the nation's largest law firms found significant differences in the women's self-images, depending on the relative presence or absence of women in positions of power. In firms in which less than 15 percent of partners were women, the female lawyers were likely to believe that "feminine" traits were strongly devalued and that "masculine" traits were equated with success. As one female attorney put it, "Let's face it: this is a man's environment, and it's sort of Jock City, especially at my firm." Women in firms where female lawyers were better represented in positions of power had a stronger desire for and higher expectations of promotion (Ely 1995:619).

Characteristics of a Bureaucracy

A **bureaucracy** is a component of formal organization that uses rules and hierarchical ranking to achieve efficiency. Rows of desks staffed by seemingly faceless people, endless lines and forms, impossibly complex language, and frustrating encounters with red tape—all these unpleasant images have combined to make *bureaucracy* a dirty word and an easy target in political campaigns. As a result, few people want to identify their occupation as "bureaucrat," despite the fact that all of us perform various bureaucratic tasks. In an industrial society, elements of bureaucracy enter into almost every occupation.

Max Weber ([1913–1922] 1947) first directed researchers to the significance of bureaucratic structure. In an important sociological advance, Weber emphasized the basic similarity of structure and process found in the otherwise dissimilar enterprises of religion, government, education, and business. Weber saw bureaucracy as a form of organization quite different from the family-run business. For analytical purposes, he developed an ideal type of bureaucracy that would reflect the most characteristic aspects of all human organizations. By **ideal type** Weber meant a construct or model for evaluating specific cases. In actuality, perfect bureaucracies do not exist; no real-world organization corresponds exactly to Weber's ideal type.

Weber proposed that whether the purpose is to run a church, a corporation, or an army, the ideal bureaucracy displays five basic characteristics. A discussion of those characteristics, as well as the dysfunctions of a bureaucracy, follows.

Being an accountant in a large corporation may be a relatively high-paying occupation. In Marxist terms, however, accountants are vulnerable to alienation, since they are far removed from the product or service that the corporation creates.

1. **Division of labor.** Specialized experts perform specific tasks. In your college bureaucracy, the admissions officer does not do the job of registrar; the guidance counselor does not see to the maintenance of buildings. By working at a specific task, people are more likely to become highly skilled and carry out a job with maximum efficiency. This emphasis on specialization is so basic a part of our lives that we may not realize it is a fairly recent development in Western culture.

The downside of division of labor is that the fragmentation of work into smaller and smaller tasks can divide workers and remove any connection they might feel to the overall objective of the bureaucracy. In *The Communist Manifesto* (written in 1848), Karl Marx and Friedrich Engels charged that the capitalist system reduces workers to a mere "appendage of the machine" (Tucker 1978). Such a work arrangement, they wrote, produces extreme **alienation**—a condition of estrangement or dissociation from the surrounding society. According to both Marx and conflict theorists, restricting workers to very small tasks also weakens their job security, since new employees can easily be trained to replace them.

Although division of labor has certainly enhanced the performance of many complex bureaucracies, in some cases it can lead to **trained incapacity;** that is, workers become so specialized that they develop blind spots and fail to notice obvious problems. Even worse, they may not care about what is happening in the next department. Some observers believe that such developments have caused workers in the United States to become less productive on the job.

In some cases, the bureaucratic division of labor can have tragic results. In the wake of the coordinated attacks on the World Trade Center and the Pentagon on September 11, 2001, Americans wondered aloud how the FBI and CIA could have failed to detect the terrorists' elaborately planned operation. The problem, in part, turned out to be the division of labor between the FBI, which focuses on domestic matters, and the CIA, which operates overseas. Officials at these intelligence-gathering organizations, both of which are huge bureaucracies, are well known for jealously guarding information from one another. Subsequent investigations revealed that they knew about Osama bin Laden and his Al-Qaeda terrorist network in the early 1990s. Unfortunately, five federal agencies—the CIA, FBI, National Security Agency, Defense Intelligence Agency, and National Reconnaissance Office—failed to share their leads on the network. Although the hijacking of the four commercial airliners used in the massive attacks may not have been preventable, the bureaucratic division of labor definitely hindered efforts to defend against terrorism, undermining U.S. national security.

2. **Hierarchy of authority.** Bureaucracies follow the principle of hierarchy; that is, each position is under the supervision of a higher authority. A president heads a college bureaucracy; he or she selects members of the administration, who in turn hire their own staff. In the Roman Catholic Church, the pope is the supreme authority; under him are cardinals, bishops, and so forth.

3. **Written rules and regulations.** What if your sociology professor gave your classmate an A for having such a friendly smile? You might think that wasn't fair, that it was against the rules. Through written rules and regulations, bureaucracies generally offer employees clear standards for an adequate (or exceptional) performance. In addition, procedures provide a valuable sense of continuity in a bureaucracy. Individual workers will come and go, but the structure and past records of the organization give it a life of its own that outlives the services of any one bureaucrat.

Of course, rules and regulations can overshadow the larger goals of an organization to the point that they become dysfunctional. What if a hospital emergency room physician failed to treat a seriously injured person because he or she had no valid proof of U.S. citizenship? If blindly applied, rules no longer serve as a means to achieving an objective, but instead become important (and perhaps too important) in their own right. Robert Merton (1968) used the term **goal displacement** to refer to overzealous conformity to official regulations.

4. **Impersonality.** Max Weber wrote that in a bureaucracy, work is carried out *sine ira et studio,* "without hatred or passion." Bureaucratic norms dictate that officials perform their duties without giving personal consideration to people as individuals. Although this norm is intended to guarantee equal treatment for each person, it also contributes to the often cold and uncaring feeling associated with modern organizations. We typically think of big government and big business when we think of impersonal bureaucracies. In some cases, the impersonality that is associated with a bureaucracy can have tragic results. More frequently, bureaucratic impersonality produces frustration and disaffection. Today, even small firms filter callers with electronic menus.

5. **Employment based on technical qualifications.** Within the ideal bureaucracy, hiring is based on technical qualifications rather than on favoritism, and performance is measured against specific standards. Written personnel policies dictate who gets promoted, and people often have a right to appeal if they believe that particular rules have been violated. Such procedures protect bureaucrats against arbitrary dismissal, provide a measure of security, and encourage loyalty to the organization.

Although ideally, any bureaucracy will value technical and professional competence, personnel decisions do not always follow that ideal pattern. Dysfunctions within bureaucracy have become well publicized, particularly because of the work of Laurence J. Peter. According to the **Peter principle,** every employee within a hierarchy tends to rise to his or her level of incompetence (Peter and Hull 1969). This hypothesis, which has not been directly or systematically tested, reflects a possible dysfunctional outcome of advancement on the basis of merit. Talented people receive promotion after promotion, until sadly, some of them finally achieve positions that they cannot handle with their usual competence.

Table 19-1 summarizes the five characteristics of bureaucracy. These characteristics, developed by Max Weber more than 80 years ago, describe an ideal type rather than an actual

Table **19-1** Characteristics of a Bureaucracy

summingup

	Positive Consequence	Negative Consequence	
		For the Individual	For the Organization
Division of labor	Produces efficiency in a large-scale corporation	Produces trained incapacity	Produces a narrow perspective
Hierarchy of authority	Clarifies who is in command	Deprives employees of a voice in decision making	Permits concealment of mistakes
Written rules and regulations	Let workers know what is expected of them	Stifle initiative and imagination	Lead to goal displacement
Impersonality	Reduces bias	Contributes to feelings of alienation	Discourages loyalty to company
Employment based on technical qualifications	Discourages favoritism and reduces petty rivalries	Discourages ambition to improve oneself elsewhere	Fosters Peter principle

bureaucracy. Not every formal organization will possess all five of Weber's characteristics. In fact, wide variation exists among actual bureaucratic organizations.

Bureaucracy pervades modern life; through McDonaldization, it has reached new heights. As Box 19-1 on page 134 shows, the McDonald's organization provides an excellent illustration of Weber's concept of bureaucracy (Ritzer 2011).

 use your sociological imagination

Your school or workplace suddenly ceases to exhibit one of the five characteristics of bureaucracy. Which characteristic is it, and what are the consequences?

Bureaucratization as a Process

Have you ever had to speak to 10 or 12 individuals in a corporation or government agency just to find out which official has jurisdiction over a particular problem? Ever been transferred from one department to another until you finally hung up in disgust? Sociologists have used the term **bureaucratization** to refer to the process by which a group, organization, or social movement becomes increasingly bureaucratic.

Normally, we think of bureaucratization in terms of large organizations. But bureaucratization also takes place within small-group settings. Sociologist Jennifer Bickman Mendez (1998) studied domestic houseworkers employed in central California by a nationwide franchise. She found that housekeeping tasks were minutely defined, to the point that employees had to follow 22 written steps for cleaning a bathroom. Complaints and special requests went not to the workers, but to an office-based manager.

Oligarchy: Rule by a Few

Conflict theorists have examined the bureaucratization of social movements. The German sociologist Robert Michels (1915) studied socialist parties and labor unions in Europe before World War I and found that such organizations were becoming increasingly bureaucratic. The emerging leaders of the organizations—even some of the most radical—had a vested interest in clinging to power. If they lost their leadership posts, they would have to return to full-time work as manual laborers.

Through his research, Michels originated the idea of the **iron law of oligarchy,** which describes how even a democratic organization will eventually develop into a bureaucracy ruled by a few, called an oligarchy. Why do oligarchies emerge? People who achieve leadership roles usually have the skills, knowledge, or charismatic appeal (as Weber noted) to direct, if not control, others. Michels argued that the rank and file of a movement or organization look to leaders for direction and thereby reinforce

the process of rule by a few. In addition, members of an oligarchy are strongly motivated to maintain their leadership roles, privileges, and power.

Bureaucracy and Organizational Culture

How does bureaucratization affect the average individual who works in an organization? The early theorists of formal organizations tended to neglect this question. Max Weber, for example,

focused on the management personnel in bureaucracies, but had little to say about workers in industry or clerks in government agencies.

According to the **classical theory** of formal organizations, or **scientific management approach,** workers are motivated almost entirely by economic rewards. This theory stresses that only the physical constraints on workers limit their productivity. Therefore, workers may be treated as a resource, much like the machines that began to replace them in the 20th century. Under the scientific management approach, management attempts to achieve maximum work efficiency through scientific planning,

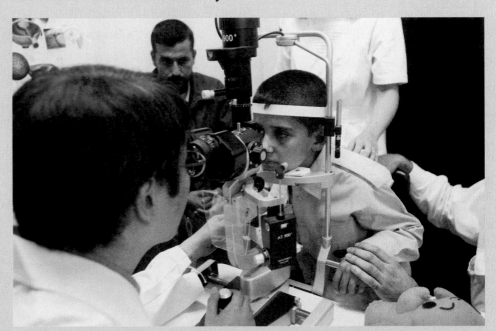

established performance standards, and careful supervision of workers and production. Planning involves efficiency studies but not studies of workers' attitudes or job satisfaction.

Not until workers organized unions—and forced management to recognize that they were not objects—did theorists of formal organizations begin to revise the classical approach. Social scientists became aware that along with management and administrators, informal groups of workers have an important impact on organizations. An alternative way of considering bureaucratic dynamics, the **human relations approach,** emphasizes the role of people, communication, and participation in a bureaucracy. This type of analysis reflects the interest of interactionist theorists in small-group behavior. Unlike planning under the scientific management approach, planning based on the human relations approach focuses on workers' feelings, frustrations, and emotional need for job satisfaction.

The gradual move away from a sole focus on the physical aspects of getting the job done—and toward the concerns and needs of workers—led advocates of the human relations approach to stress the less formal aspects of bureaucratic structure. Informal

groups and social networks within organizations develop partly as a result of people's ability to create more direct forms of communication than under the formal structure. Charles Page (1946) used the term *bureaucracy's other face* to refer to the unofficial activities and interactions that are such a basic part of daily organizational life.

Today, research on formal organizations is following new avenues. Among them are

- The recent arrival of a small number of women and minority group members in high-level management;
- In large corporations, the decision-making role of groups that lie outside the top ranks of leadership;
- The loss of fixed boundaries in organizations that have outsourced key functions; and
- The role of the Internet and virtual worlds in influencing business and consumer preferences.

Though research on organizations still embraces Max Weber's insights, then, it has gone well beyond them (Hamm 2007; Kleiner 2003; W. Scott and Davis 2007).

social policy and Social Structure | Media Concentration

One of the most pervasive social institutions in our society, the mass media encompass information outlets ranging from printed leaflets to online virtual worlds. Perhaps more than any other institution, they exemplify our postmodern society. According to Lenski's theory of sociocultural evolution, all societies undergo continual change, whether rapid or slow. In today's postmodern world, one of the more noticeable changes—and a potentially undesirable one—is the trend toward control of the media by fewer and fewer corporations.

Looking at the Issue

Who owns the media production and distribution process? Increasingly, the answer is a small number of very large corporations. The social consequence of this trend toward the concentration of media ownership is a reduction in the number of information outlets.

True, the United States still has thousands of independent media outlets—small-town newspapers, radio stations, and television broadcasters—but the clear trend in the media industry is toward the consolidation of ownership. The fact is, a few multinational corporations dominate the publishing, broadcasting, and film industries, although their influence may be hard

to identify, since global conglomerates manage many different product names. Consider Time Warner (HBO, CNN, AOL, *Time* and *People* magazines); Rupert Murdoch's News Corporation, founded in Australia (Fox Network Television, several book publishers, numerous newspapers and magazines, Dow Jones, and 20th Century Fox); Sony of Japan (Columbia Pictures, IMAX, CBS Records, and Columbia

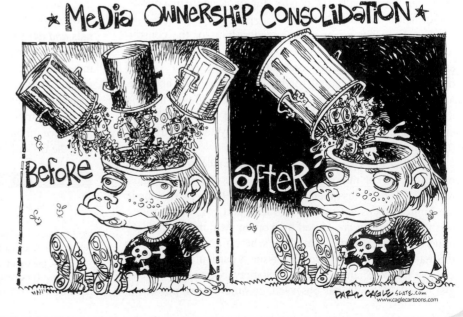

Records); and Viacom/CBS (Paramount, DreamWorks SKG, MTV, and Black Entertainment Television), and the extent of their power becomes clear.

Similar concerns have been raised about the situation in countries such as China, Cuba, Iraq, and North Korea, where the ruling party owns and controls the media. The difference, which is considerable, is that in the United States the gatekeeping process lies in the hands of private individuals, whose main desire is to maximize profits. In totalitarian countries, the gatekeeping process belongs to political leaders, whose desire is to maintain control of the government.

We should note one significant exception to the centralization and concentration of the media: the Internet. Today, more and more people receive their media content through the Internet. The World Wide Web is now accessible to millions of producers of media content, through independent outlets. Obviously, the producer must be technologically proficient and must have access to a computer, but compared to other media outlets, the Internet is much more readily available. Media conglomerates, well aware of the Internet's potential, are already delivering their material via the web. But for now, the Internet is the only medium that allows the average individual to become a media entrepreneur with a potential audience of millions. Some media scholars warn, however, that it is only a matter of time before corporate giants like AT&T and Comcast begin to dominate the Internet (Noam 2009; Wu 2010).

Applying Sociology

Concentration of ownership is not unique to the media (think about aircraft and automobile manufacturers). However, the media deserve special attention given the way they filter our view of reality. New media technologies also form the basis for group membership and networking, making them a powerful influence on today's society.

Functionalists see media concentration—or the consolidation of any business—as a step toward greater economic efficiency. In their view, consolidation reduces the cost of operations, freeing capital for the development of new creative outlets. Furthermore, they believe that global trade in the media facilitates the free exchange of intellectual property, which is often hampered by arbitrary local restrictions (Croteau and Hoynes 2006).

Conflict theorists believe that media concentration stifles opportunities for minority ownership. According to the most recent FCC data, less than 4 percent of television stations in the United States are owned by racial and ethnic minorities; less than 5 percent are owned by women. Minority owners are underrepresented even in markets where minorities make up the majority of the audience. This issue is particularly troubling not just to politicians but to all of society, because as sociologist Manuel Castells has observed, communicative power can shape human behavior. As such, it lies at the heart of the social structure (Castells 2009; S. Turner and Cooper 2006).

Interactionists see a change in the way people get their news, although not in their interest in it. In the past people may have met or called one another to discuss the latest episode of *Survivor;* now they share the latest Internet news via e-mail or buddy list. Why wait for the evening news when online sources are at your fingertips? Because savvy media users can seek out the media they consume, interactionists suggest that warnings about media concentration may be overdone (Bielby and Harrington 2008).

Initiating Policy

Any discussion of media regulation must begin with the Telecommunications Act of 1996, which marked the first overhaul of media policy since the early 1930s. The act, which covers everything from cable service to social issues such as obscenity and violence, made a significant distinction between information services, such as the Internet, and promoters of telecommunications service—that is, traditional telephone and wireless phone companies, as well as cable companies that offer phone service. Nevertheless, rapid technological development has rendered the act obsolete in many people's minds. With the convergence of telephone service, videocasting, and the Internet, not to mention the delivery of motion pictures online, such distinctions became archaic only a decade after the act was passed.

Significantly, the act eliminated most restrictions on media ownership; those that remain appear to be on their way out, as well. In 2007 the Federal Communications Commission went even further by allowing the consolidation of newspaper and television ownership in cities with only one local newspaper and one local television station. Critics worried that once the transition to digital television was completed in 2009, a single local media outlet could transmit a dozen signals *and* deliver the daily newspaper (Rice 2008).

The lack of governmental restraint of media concentration—indeed, the move toward deregulation of the media under several recent administrations—has been ascribed to the unique relationship politicians have with the media industry, compared to other industries. Elected leaders fear the impact that the media may have on their careers, given the control the media exercise over the flow of information to voters (McChesney 2008).

TAKE THE ISSUE WITH YOU

1. Are you aware of who owns or manages the media you watch or listen to? If not, find out.
2. Do concerns about media concentration differ from concerns over the monopoly of certain products or services? Explain.
3. Does the trend toward media concentration affect traditional media outlets (print, radio, and broadcast television) differently from the Internet? Why or why not?

Summary

As societies become larger and more complex, daily life is increasingly dominated by large **formal organizations.**

1. Max Weber argued that in its ideal form, a **bureaucracy** has five basic characteristics: division of labor, hierarchical authority, written rules and regulations, impersonality, and employment based on technical qualifications. Carefully constructed bureaucratic policies can be either undermined or redefined by an organization's informal structure.

2. The **scientific management approach** to management considers workers to be economic resources. In contrast, the **human relations approach** emphasizes the role of people, communications, and participation.

3. The Internet is the one significant exception to the trend toward media concentration, allowing millions of people to produce their own media content.

Thinking Critically

1. Select an organization that is familiar to you—for example, your college, workplace, religious institution, or civic association—and apply Weber's five characteristics of bureaucracy to it. To what degree does it correspond to Weber's ideal type of bureaucracy?

2. What are some of the benefits and drawbacks of large formal organizations?

Key Terms

Alienation   132

Bureaucracy   131

Bureaucratization   133

Classical theory   134

Formal organization   131

Goal displacement   132

Human relations approach   135

Ideal type   131

Iron law of oligarchy   133

Peter principle   132

Scientific management approach   134

Trained incapacity   132

Mastering This Chapter

taking sociology with you

1 Interview a professional in a field of your choice. What role conflicts does a professional in that field commonly experience? What guidance does the profession's code of conduct offer regarding such conflicts?

2 Enter the Second Life virtual world and create an avatar for yourself. Then take a look around. What evidence do you see of social status and social roles? What groups and networks reside in this virtual world? Do you recognize any formal organizations?

3 Talk with two or three business students or businesspeople about the bureaucratization of business. On balance, do they see bureaucratization as a positive or negative trend? What bureaucratic dysfunctions are common in business, and how do managers attempt to counteract them?

Achieved status A social position that a person attains largely through his or her own efforts. (page 115)

Agrarian society The most technologically advanced form of preindustrial society. Members engage primarily in the production of food, but increase their crop yields through technological innovations such as the plow. (125)

Alienation A condition of estrangement or dissociation from the surrounding society. (132)

Ascribed status A social position assigned to a person by society without regard for the person's unique talents or characteristics. (114)

Bureaucracy A component of formal organization that uses rules and hierarchical ranking to achieve efficiency. (131)

Bureaucratization The process by which a group, organization, or social movement becomes increasingly bureaucratic. (133)

Classical theory An approach to the study of formal organizations that views workers as being motivated almost entirely by economic rewards. (134)

Coalition A temporary or permanent alliance geared toward a common goal. (129)

Formal organization A group designed for a special purpose and structured for maximum efficiency. (131)

Gemeinschaft A close-knit community, often found in rural areas, in which strong personal bonds unite members. (123)

Gesellschaft A community, often urban, that is large and impersonal, with little commitment to the group or consensus on values. (123)

Goal displacement Overzealous conformity to official regulations of a bureaucracy. (132)

Group Any number of people with similar norms, values, and expectations who interact with one another on a regular basis. (117, 117)

Horticultural society A preindustrial society in which people plant seeds and crops rather than merely subsist on available foods. (125)

Human relations approach An approach to the study of formal organizations that emphasizes the role of people, communication, and participation in a bureaucracy and tends to focus on the informal structure of the organization. (135)

Hunting-and-gathering society A preindustrial society in which people rely on whatever foods and fibers are readily available in order to survive. (124)

Ideal type A construct or model for evaluating specific cases. (131)

Industrial society A society that depends on mechanization to produce its goods and services. (125)

In-group Any group or category to which people feel they belong. (129)

Iron law of oligarchy A principle of organizational life under which even a democratic organization will eventually develop into a bureaucracy ruled by a few individuals. (133)

Master status A status that dominates others and thereby determines a person's general position in society. (115)

Mechanical solidarity A collective consciousness that emphasizes group solidarity, characteristic of societies with minimal division of labor. (123)

Organic solidarity A collective consciousness that rests on mutual interdependence, characteristic of societies with a complex division of labor. (123)

Out-group A group or category to which people feel they do not belong. (129)

Peter principle A principle of organizational life according to which every employee within a hierarchy tends to rise to his or her level of incompetence. (132)

Postindustrial society A society whose economic system is engaged primarily in the processing and control of information. (126)

Postmodern society A technologically sophisticated society that is preoccupied with consumer goods and media images. (126)

Primary group A small group characterized by intimate, face-to-face association and cooperation. (128)

Reference group Any group that individuals use as a standard for evaluating themselves and their own behavior. (129)

Role conflict The situation that occurs when incompatible expectations arise from two or more social positions held by the same person. (115)

Role exit The process of disengagement from a role that is central to one's self-identity in order to establish a new role and identity. (116)

Role strain The difficulty that arises when the same social position imposes conflicting demands and expectations. (116)

Scientific management approach Another name for the classical theory of formal organizations. (134)

Secondary group A formal, impersonal group in which there is little social intimacy or mutual understanding. (128)

Social institution An organized pattern of beliefs and behavior centered on basic social needs. (120)

Social interaction The ways in which people respond to one another. (113)

Social network A series of social relationships that links a person directly to others, and through them indirectly to still more people. (118)

Social role A set of expectations for people who occupy a given social position or status. (115)

Social structure The way in which a society is organized into predictable relationships. (113)

Sociocultural evolution Long-term social trends resulting from the interplay of continuity, innovation, and selection. (124)

Status A term used by sociologists to refer to any of the full range of socially defined positions within a large group or society. (114)

Technology Cultural information about the ways in which the material resources of the environment may be used to satisfy human needs and desires. (124)

Trained incapacity The tendency of workers in a bureaucracy to become so specialized that they develop blind spots and fail to notice obvious problems. (132)

Read each question carefully and then select the best answer.

1. In the United States, we expect that cab drivers will know how to get around a city. This expectation is an example of which of the following?
   a. role conflict
   b. role strain
   c. social role
   d. master status

2. What occurs when incompatible expectations arise from two or more social positions held by the same person?
   a. role conflict
   b. role strain
   c. role exit
   d. both a and b

3. In sociological terms, what do we call any number of people with similar norms, values, and expectations who interact with one another on a regular basis?
   a. a category
   b. a group
   c. an aggregate
   d. a society

4. The Shakers, a religious sect that came to the United States in 1774, has seen their group's membership diminish significantly due to their inability to
   a. teach new recruits.
   b. preserve order.
   c. replace personnel.
   d. provide and maintain a sense of purpose.

5. Which sociological perspective argues that the present organization of social institutions is no accident?
   a. the functionalist perspective
   b. the conflict perspective
   c. the interactionist perspective
   d. the global perspective

6. The U.S. Postal Service, the Boston Pops orchestra, and the college or university in which you are currently enrolled as a student are all examples of
   a. primary groups.
   b. reference groups.
   c. formal organizations.
   d. triads.

7. One positive consequence of bureaucracy is that it reduces bias. Reduction of bias results from which characteristic of a bureaucracy?
   a. impersonality
   b. hierarchy of authority
   c. written rules and regulations
   d. employment based on technical qualifications

8. According to the Peter principle,
   a. all bureaucracies are notoriously inefficient.
   b. if something *can* go wrong, it *will.*
   c. every employee within a hierarchy tends to rise to his or her level of incompetence.
   d. all line workers get burned in the end.

9. Social control in what Ferdinand Tönnies termed a *Gemeinschaft* community is maintained through all but which of the following means?
   a. moral persuasion
   b. gossip
   c. legally defined punishment
   d. gestures

10. Sociologist Daniel Bell uses which of the following terms to refer to a society whose economic system is engaged primarily in the processing and control of information?
    a. postmodern
    b. horticultural
    c. industrial
    d. postindustrial

11. The term _____ refers to the way in which a society is organized into predictable relationships.

12. The African American activist Malcolm X wrote in his autobiography that his position as a Black man, a(n) _____ status, was an obstacle to his dream of becoming a lawyer, a(n) _____ status.

13. Sociologist Helen Rose Fuchs Ebaugh developed the term _____ to describe the process of disengagement from a role that is central to one's self-identity in order to establish a new role and identity.

14. _____ groups often emerge in the workplace among those who share special understandings about their occupation.

15. In many cases, people model their behavior after groups to which they may not belong. These groups are called _____ groups.

16. In studying the social behavior of word processors in a Chicago law firm, sociologist Mitchell Duneier drew on the _____ perspective.

17. Max Weber developed a(n) _____ of bureaucracy, which reflects the most characteristic aspects of all human organizations.

18. According to Émile Durkheim, societies with a minimal division of labor are characterized by _____ solidarity, while societies with a complex division of labor are characterized by _____ solidarity.

19. In Gerhard Lenski's theory of sociocultural evolution, a society's level of _____ is critical to the way it is organized.

20. A(n) _____ society is a technologically sophisticated society that is preoccupied with consumer goods and media images.

Answers

1 (c); 2 (a); 3 (b); 4 (c); 5 (b); 6 (c); 7 (a); 8 (c); 9 (c); 10 (d); 11 social structure; 12 ascribed, achieved; 13 role exit; 14 Secondary; 15 reference; 16 interactionist; 17 ideal type; 18 mechanical, organic; 19 technology; 20 postmodern

Restrepo

In this documentary, a U.S. Army platoon stationed in Afghanistan attempts to gain the trust of the local people as they clear the area of armed insurgents.

The Town

A career criminal tries to leave his life of crime, but his membership in a local gang complicates the attempt.

The Miners' Hymns

This documentary, set in the north of England, illustrates the difficulty of organizing coal miners into a union.

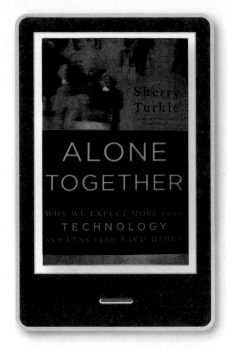

Did you ever suspect that you were hiding from people while you were online with them?

MIT psychologist Sherry Turkle thinks that the web may actually distance us from others.

66 Technology proposes itself as the architect of our intimacies. These days, it suggests substitutions that put the real on the run. The advertising for Second Life, a virtual world where you get to build an avatar, a house, a family, and a social life, basically says, "Finally, a place to love your body, love your friends, and love your life." In Second Life, a lot of people, as represented by their avatars, are richer than they are in first life and a lot younger, thinner, and better dressed. And we are smitten with the idea of sociable robots, which most people first meet in the guise of artificial pets. Zhu Zhu pet hamsters, the "it" toy of the 2009–2010 holiday season, are presented as "better" than any real pet could be. We are told they are lovable and responsive, don't require cleanup, and will never die.

Technology is seductive when what it offers meets our human vulnerabilities. And as it turns out, we are very vulnerable indeed. We are lonely but fearful of intimacy. Digital connections and the sociable robot may offer the illusion of companionship without the demands of friendship. Our networked life allows us to hide from each other, even as we are tethered to each other. We'd rather text than talk.

From the start, people used interactive and reactive computers to reflect on the self and think about the difference between machines and people. Were intelligent machines alive? If not, why not?

Digital connections and the sociable robot may offer the illusion of companionship without the demands of friendship.

Computers no longer wait for humans to project meaning onto them. Now, sociable robots meet our gaze, speak to us, and learn to recognize us. They ask us to take care of them; in response, we imagine that they might care for us in return. Indeed, among the most talked about robotic designs are in the area of care and companionship. In summer 2010, there are enthusiastic reports in the *New York Times* and the *Wall Street Journal* on robotic teachers, companions, and therapists. And Microsoft demonstrates a virtual human, Milo, that recognizes the people it interacts with and whose personality is sculpted by them. Tellingly, in the video that introduces Milo to the public, a young man begins by playing games with Milo in a virtual garden; by the end of the demonstration, things have heated up—he confides in Milo after being told off by his parents.

We are challenged to ask what such things augur. Some people are looking for robots to clean rugs and help with the laundry. Others hope for a mechanical bride. As sociable robots propose themselves as substitutes for people, new networked devices offer us machine-mediated relationships with each other, another kind of substitution. We romance the robot and become inseparable from our smartphones. As this happens, we remake ourselves and our relationships with each other through our new intimacy with machines. People talk about Web access on their BlackBerries as "the place for hope" in life, the place where loneliness can be defeated. A woman in her late sixties describes her new iPhone: "It's like having a little Times Square in my pocketbook. All lights. All the people I could meet." People are lonely. The network is seductive. But if we are always on, we may deny ourselves the rewards of solitude. 99

(*Turkle 2011:1–3*) Additional information about this excerpt can be found on the Online Learning Center at www.mhhe.com/schaefermod2e.

Think about your life before you owned a cell phone: How did you connect with others then? How do you connect with them now? In this excerpt from *Alone Together: Why We Expect More from Technology and Less from Each Other,* Sherry Turkle writes that modern technology is changing the way we relate to others. Today, our digital communications devices preoccupy us, often burying us in a deluge of information. Yet in the end, they cannot substitute for the face-to-face relationships that hold family and friends together. Ironically, in an effort to dig out from the communications overflow, we are constantly seeking new networking gadgets (Turkle 2011:280).

We've come a long way from the days when home entertainment meant black-and-white television, and "reaching out" involved a land-line telephone. Today, we not only carry the telephone with us; we use it to watch television and movies delivered over the Internet. Both television and the Internet are examples of the *mass media*, which embrace print and electronic means of communication and advertising.

Few aspects of society are as central as the mass media. Through the media we expand our understanding of people and events beyond what we experience in person. The media inform us about different cultures and lifestyles and about the latest forms of technology. For sociologists, the key questions are how the mass media affect our social institutions and how they influence our social behavior.

Why are the media so influential? Who benefits from media influence and why? How do we maintain cultural and ethical standards in the face of negative media images? In this chapter we will consider the ways sociology helps us to answer these questions. First we will look at how proponents of the various sociological perspectives view the media. Then we will examine who makes up the media's audience, not just at home but around the world. The chapter closes with a Social Policy section on the right to privacy in a digital age.

MODULE 20 | Sociological Perspectives on the Media

We have come a long way from the 1950s, when rabbit-ear antennas sat atop black-and-white television sets. Both television and the Net are forms of **mass media,** a term that refers to the print and electronic means of communication that carry messages to widespread audiences. Print media include newspapers, magazines, and books; electronic media include radio, satellite radio, television, motion pictures, and the Internet. Advertising, which falls into both categories, is also a form of mass media.

The social impact of the mass media is obvious. Consider a few examples. TV dinners were invented to accommodate the millions of couch potatoes who can't bear to miss their favorite television programs. Today, *screen time* encompasses not just television viewing but playing video games and surfing the Internet. Candidates for political office rely on their media consultants to project a winning image both in print and in the electronic media. World leaders use all forms of media for political advantage, whether to gain territory or to bid on hosting the Olympics. In parts of Africa and Asia, AIDS education projects owe much of their success to media campaigns. And during the second Iraq war, both the British and U.S. governments allowed journalists to be embedded with frontline troops as a means of "telling their story."

The social impact of the mass media has become so huge, in fact, that scholars have begun to speak of *cultural convergence.* The term **cultural convergence** refers to the flow of content across multiple media, and the accompanying migration of media audiences. As you watch a television program, for example, you wonder what the star of the show is doing at the moment, and turn to the Internet. Later, while texting your best friend, you tell her what you learned, accompanied by a Google Earth map showing the celebrity's location. Using Photoshop, you may even include the star's image next to your own, post the photo on your Facebook page, and then tweet your friends to create a caption. Media convergence is not orchestrated by the media, sophisticated though they may be. You initiate it, using techniques you likely learned by interacting with others, either face-to-face or through the media (H. Jenkins 2006).

In studying the impact of the mass media on socialization, sociologists must consider the wide variety of contact people have with communication outlets, from immersion in all types of media to relative isolation, especially from recent innovations. In 2007 the Pew Research Center released a report that sorted U.S. residents into 10 categories based on their use of information and communications technologies (ICTs; Table 20-1). According to the report, about 32 percent of the adult population falls into the top four categories, from the "Omnivores," who use these devices as a means of self-expression, to the "Productivity Enhancers," who use them to get the job done. Middle-of-the-road users, who represent about 19 percent of the population, take advantage of new technologies but aren't as excited about them. They range from the "Mobile Centrics," who are strongly attached to their cell phones, to the "Connected but Hassled." Close to half the people in the nation have few if any technology devices, or if they do, they are not wedded to them. Typically, younger people embrace technological change more than older people, who tend either to be indifferent toward new technologies or to find them annoying.

How do people's viewing and listening habits affect their social behavior? In the following sections we'll use the four major sociological perspectives to examine the impact of the mass media and changes in their usage patterns (Nelson 2004).

Functionalist Perspective

One obvious function of the mass media is to entertain. Except for clearly identified news or educational programming, we often think the explicit purpose of the mass media is to occupy our leisure time—from newspaper comics and crossword puzzles to the latest music releases on the Internet. While that is true, the media have other important functions. They also socialize us, enforce social norms, confer status, and promote consumption. An important dysfunction of the mass media is that they may act as a narcotic, desensitizing us to distressing events (Lazarsfeld and Merton 1948; C. Wright 1986).

Table **20-1**   Contours of Communication

Omnivores: 8% of American adults constitute the most active participants in the information society, consuming information goods and services at a high rate and using them as a platform for participation and self-expression.

The Connectors: 7% of the adult population surround themselves with technology and use it to connect with people and digital content. They get a lot out of their mobile devices and participate actively in online life.

Lackluster Veterans: 8% of American adults make up a group who are not at all passionate about their abundance of modern ICTs. Few like the intrusiveness their gadgets add to their lives and not many see ICTs adding to their personal productivity.

Productivity Enhancers: 9% of American adults happily get a lot of things done with information technology, both at home and at work.

Mobile Centrics: 10% of the general population are strongly attached to their cell phones and take advantage of a range of mobile applications.

Connected but Hassled: 9% of American adults fit into this group. They have invested in a lot of technology, but the connectivity is a hassle for them.

Inexperienced Experimenters: 8% of adults have less ICT on hand than others. They feel competent in dealing with technology, and might do more with it if they had more.

Light but Satisfied: 15% of adults have the basics of information technology but use it infrequently, so it does not register as an important part of their lives.

Indifferents: 11% of adults have a fair amount of technology on hand, but it does not play a central role in their daily lives.

Off the Net: 15% of the population, mainly older Americans, are off the modern information network.

Note: From a Pew Internet and American Life Project survey conducted in April 2006.
Source: Horrigan 2007:vii.

Think about It

What category would you place yourself in?

Agent of Socialization

The media increase social cohesion by presenting a common, more or less standardized view of culture through mass communication. Sociologist Robert Park (1922) studied how newspapers helped immigrants to the United States adjust to their environment by changing their customary habits and teaching them the opinions of people in their new home country. Unquestionably, the mass media play a significant role in providing a collective experience for members of society. Think about how the mass media bring together members of a community or even a nation by broadcasting important events and ceremonies (such as inaugurations, press conferences, parades, state funerals, and the Olympics) and by covering disasters.

Which media outlets did people turn to in the aftermath of the September 11, 2001, tragedy? Television, radio, and the telephone were the primary means by which people in the United States bonded. But the Internet also played a prominent role. About half of all Internet users—more than 5 million

people—received some kind of news about the attacks online (David L. Miller and Darlington 2002).

Today, the news media have moved further online. Afghans of all political persuasions now connect with the Muslim community overseas to gain both social and financial support. In the realm of popular culture, a spontaneous global sharing of reactions to Michael Jackson's sudden death in 2009 crashed the websites for Google, the *Los Angeles Times,* TMZ celebrity news, Perez Hilton's blog, and Twitter (Rawlinson and Hunt 2009; Shane 2010).

Some are concerned about the media's socialization function, however. For instance, many people worry about the effect of using television as a babysitter and the impact of violent programming on viewer behavior. Some people adopt a blame-the-media mentality, holding the media accountable for anything that goes wrong, especially with young people. Yet the media also have positive effects on young people. For young and even not-so-young adults, for example, a new sort of tribalism is emerging online, in which communities develop around common interests or shared identities (Adams and Smith 2008).

Enforcer of Social Norms

The media often reaffirm proper behavior by showing what happens to people who act in a way that violates societal expectations. These messages are conveyed when the bad guy gets clobbered in cartoons or is thrown in jail on *CSI.* Yet the media also sometimes glorify disapproved behavior, whether it is physical violence, disrespect to a teacher, or drug use.

The media play a critical role in human sexuality. Many people object to the widespread availability of pornography on the web; others are concerned about the way sexual predators use chat rooms to take advantage of children. Yet innovative uses of new media may also have positive consequences. On Valentine's Day 2007, New York City introduced the official "NYC Condom" on Facebook, in an attempt to make safer sex a social norm. Not only has New York's Department of Health and Mental Hygiene given away millions of condoms, but thousands of *e-condoms,* as they are called, have been distributed to Facebook users.

Programs have also been created to persuade teens not to send nude images of themselves to selected friends. Such images often go viral (that is, spread across the Internet) and may be used to harass teens and their parents. To define normative behavior regarding these images, one organization has launched a "That's not cool" campaign, complete with stalker messages that can be e-mailed to those who misuse such images. The widespread dissemination of compromising images that were meant to be shared only among close friends is just one aspect of the social phenomenon called *cyberbullying* (Chan 2009; Clifford 2009a; Gentile 2009).

Table 20-2 Status Conferred by Magazines

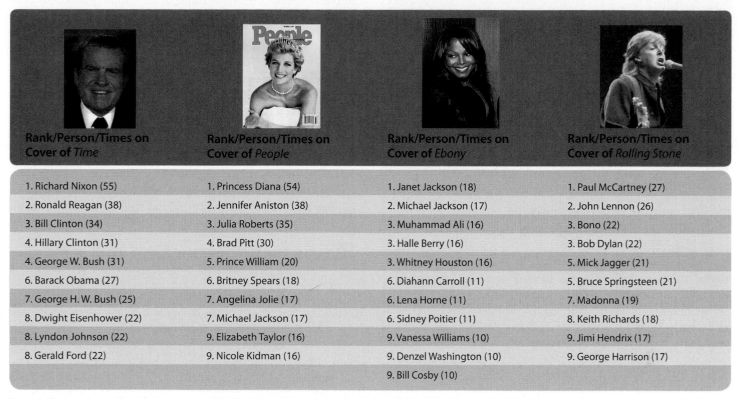

Rank/Person/Times on Cover of *Time*	Rank/Person/Times on Cover of *People*	Rank/Person/Times on Cover of *Ebony*	Rank/Person/Times on Cover of *Rolling Stone*
1. Richard Nixon (55)	1. Princess Diana (54)	1. Janet Jackson (18)	1. Paul McCartney (27)
2. Ronald Reagan (38)	2. Jennifer Aniston (38)	2. Michael Jackson (17)	2. John Lennon (26)
3. Bill Clinton (34)	3. Julia Roberts (35)	3. Muhammad Ali (16)	3. Bono (22)
4. Hillary Clinton (31)	4. Brad Pitt (30)	3. Halle Berry (16)	3. Bob Dylan (22)
4. George W. Bush (31)	5. Prince William (20)	3. Whitney Houston (16)	5. Mick Jagger (21)
6. Barack Obama (27)	6. Britney Spears (18)	6. Diahann Carroll (11)	5. Bruce Springsteen (21)
7. George H. W. Bush (25)	7. Angelina Jolie (17)	6. Lena Horne (11)	7. Madonna (19)
8. Dwight Eisenhower (22)	7. Michael Jackson (17)	6. Sidney Poitier (11)	8. Keith Richards (18)
8. Lyndon Johnson (22)	9. Elizabeth Taylor (16)	9. Vanessa Williams (10)	9. Jimi Hendrix (17)
8. Gerald Ford (22)	9. Nicole Kidman (16)	9. Denzel Washington (10)	9. George Harrison (17)
		9. Bill Cosby (10)	

Source: Author's content analysis of primary cover subject for full run of the periodicals beginning with *Time,* March 3, 1923; *People,* March 4, 1974; *Ebony,* November 1945; and *Rolling Stone,* September 1967 through January 1, 2012. When a periodical runs multiple covers, each version is counted. In case of ties, the more recent cover person is listed first.

Think about It

How do these magazines differ in the types of people they feature on their covers? Which type do you think enjoys the most status? Why?

Conferral of Status

The mass media confer status on people, organizations, and public issues. Whether it is an issue like the homeless or a celebrity like Cameron Diaz, they single out one from thousands of other similarly placed issues or people to become significant. Table 20-2 shows how often certain public figures are prominently featured on weekly magazine covers. Obviously, *People* magazine alone was not responsible for making Princess Diana into a worldwide figure, but collectively, all the media outlets created a notoriety that Princess Victoria of Sweden, for one, did not enjoy.

Another way the media confer celebrity status on individuals is by publishing information about the frequency of Internet searches. Some newspapers and websites carry regularly updated lists of the most heavily researched individuals and topics of the week. The means may have changed since the first issue of *Time* magazine hit the stands in 1923, but the media still confer status—often electronically.

Promotion of Consumption

Twenty thousand commercials a year—that is the number the average child in the United States watches on television, according to the American Academy of Pediatrics. Young people cannot escape commercial messages. They show up on high school scoreboards, at rock concerts, and as banners on web pages. They also surface in the form of *product placement*—for example, the Coca-Cola glasses that sit in front of the judges on *American Idol.* Product placement is nothing new. In 1951 *The African Queen* prominently displayed Gordon's Gin aboard the boat carrying Katharine Hepburn and Humphrey Bogart. However, commercial promotion has become far more common today: *American Idol* alone features over 4,600 product appearances each season. Moreover, advertisers are attempting to develop brand or logo loyalty at younger and younger ages (Buckingham 2007; Rodman 2011:395).

 use your **sociological imagination**

You are browsing through the magazines at a newsstand. Are you more likely than not to pick up a magazine because of the person on the cover? What kind of cover shot would attract you?

Product placement ("brand casting") is an increasingly important source of revenue for motion picture studios. The movie *The Hangover Part II* (2011) featured many brands, including Adidas, Foster's, Skype, Volvo, and as shown here, Hard Rock Cafe (Brandchannel.com 2012).

Using advertising to develop a brand name with global appeal is an especially powerful way to encourage consumption. U.S. corporations have been particularly successful in creating global brands. An analysis of the 100 most successful brands worldwide, each of which derives at least a third of its earnings outside the home country, shows that 51 of them originated in the United States; 49 others come from 14 different countries (Figure 20-1).

Media advertising has several clear functions: it supports the economy, provides information about products, and underwrites the cost of media. In some cases, advertising becomes part of the entertainment. A national survey showed that one-half of viewers watch the Super Bowl primarily for the commercials, and one-third of online conversations about the Super Bowl the day of and the day after the event are driven by Super Bowl advertising. Yet advertising's functions are related to dysfunctions. Media advertising contributes to a consumer culture that creates needs and raises unrealistic expectations of what is required to be happy or satisfied. Moreover, because the media depend heavily on advertising revenue, advertisers can influence media content (Carey and Gelles 2010; Nielsen Company 2009).

 use your **sociological imagination**

You are a news junkie. Where do you gather your facts or information—from newspapers, tabloids, magazines, TV newscasts, blogs, or the Internet? Why did you choose that medium?

Dysfunction: The Narcotizing Effect

In addition to the functions just noted, the media perform a *dysfunction*. Sociologists Paul Lazarsfeld and Robert Merton (1948) created the term **narcotizing dysfunction** to refer to the phenomenon in which the media provide such massive amounts of coverage that the audience becomes numb and fails to act on the information, regardless of how compelling the issue. Interested citizens may take in the information but make no decision or take no action.

Consider how often the media initiate a great outpouring of philanthropic support in response to natural disasters or family crises. But then what happens? Research shows that as time passes, viewer fatigue sets in. The mass media audience becomes numb, desensitized to the suffering, and may even conclude that a solution to the crisis has been found (S. Moeller 1999).

The media's narcotizing dysfunction was identified 70 years ago, when just a few homes had television—well before the advent of electronic media. At that time, the dysfunction went largely unnoticed, but today commentators often point out the ill effects of addiction to television or the Internet, especially among young people. Street crime, explicit sex, war, and HIV/AIDS apparently are such overwhelming topics that some in the audience may feel they have acted—or at the very least learned all they need to know—simply by watching the news.

● Conflict Perspective

Conflict theorists emphasize that the media reflect and even exacerbate many of the divisions in our society and world, including those based on gender, race, ethnicity, and social class. They point in particular to the media's ability to decide what is transmitted, through a process called *gatekeeping*. Conflict theorists also stress the way interest groups monitor media content; the way powerful groups transmit society's dominant ideology through the mass media; and the technological gap between the haves and have-nots, which limits people's access to the Internet.

Gatekeeping

What story appears on page 1 of the morning newspaper? What motion picture plays on three screens rather than one at the local cineplex? What picture isn't released at all? Behind these decisions are powerful figures—publishers, editors, and other media moguls.

The mass media constitute a form of big business in which profits are generally more important than the quality of the programming. Within the mass media, a relatively small number of people control what eventually reaches the audience through **gatekeeping.** This term describes how material must travel through a series of gates (or checkpoints) before reaching the public. Thus, a select few decide what images to bring to a broad audience. In many countries the government plays a gatekeeping role. Even the champions of Internet freedom, who pride themselves on allowing people to pass freely through the gate, may quickly channel them in certain directions (see Box 20-1).

Gatekeeping, which prevails in all kinds of media, is not a new concept. The term was coined by a journalism scholar in the 1940s to refer to the way that small-town newspaper editors control which events receive public attention. As sociologist C. Wright Mills ([1956] 2000b) observed, the real power of the media is that they can control what is being presented. In the recording industry, gatekeepers may reject a popular local band because it competes with a group already on their label. Even if the band is recorded, radio programmers may reject the music because it does not fit the station's sound. Television programmers may keep a pilot for a new TV series off the air because they

FIGURE 20-1 Branding The Globe

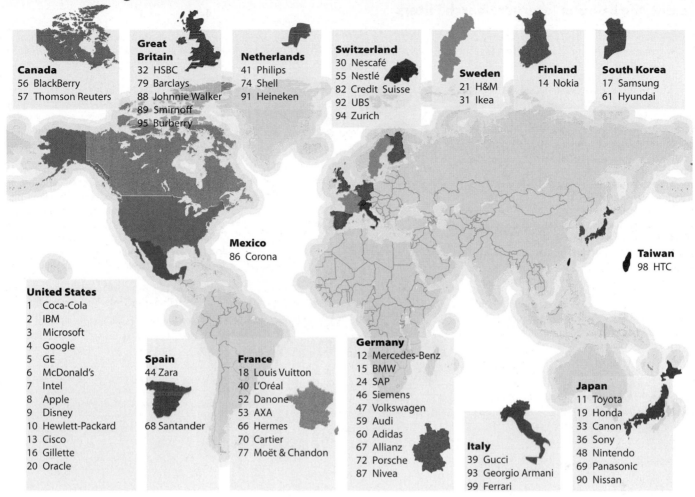

Canada
56 BlackBerry
57 Thomson Reuters

Great Britain
32 HSBC
79 Barclays
88 Johnnie Walker
89 Smirnoff
95 Burberry

Netherlands
41 Philips
74 Shell
91 Heineken

Switzerland
30 Nescafé
55 Nestlé
82 Credit Suisse
92 UBS
94 Zurich

Sweden
21 H&M
31 Ikea

Finland
14 Nokia

South Korea
17 Samsung
61 Hyundai

Mexico
86 Corona

Taiwan
98 HTC

United States
1 Coca-Cola
2 IBM
3 Microsoft
4 Google
5 GE
6 McDonald's
7 Intel
8 Apple
9 Disney
10 Hewlett-Packard
13 Cisco
16 Gillette
20 Oracle

Spain
44 Zara
68 Santander

France
18 Louis Vuitton
40 L'Oréal
52 Danone
53 AXA
66 Hermes
70 Cartier
77 Moët & Chandon

Germany
12 Mercedes-Benz
15 BMW
24 SAP
46 Siemens
47 Volkswagen
59 Audi
60 Adidas
67 Allianz
72 Porsche
87 Nivea

Italy
39 Gucci
93 Georgio Armani
99 Ferrari

Japan
11 Toyota
19 Honda
33 Canon
36 Sony
48 Nintendo
69 Panasonic
90 Nissan

Note: Map shows the top 100 brands in the world in 2011 by country of ownership, except for the United States, for which only brands in the top 20 are shown.
Source: Based on Interbrand 2012.

Based on revenue and name recognition, these are the brands that dominate the global marketplace. Just 15 nations account for all the top 100 brands.

Think about It

How many of these brands do you recognize?

believe it does not appeal to the target audience (which is sometimes determined by advertising sponsors). Similar decisions are made by gatekeepers in the publishing industry (Hanson 2005; White 1950).

Gatekeeping is not as dominant in at least one form of mass media, the Internet. You can send virtually any message to an electronic bulletin board, and create a web page or web log (blog) to advance any argument, including one that insists the earth is flat. The Internet is a means of quickly disseminating information (or misinformation) without going through any significant gatekeeping process.

Nevertheless, the Internet is not totally without restrictions. In many nations, laws regulate content on issues such as gambling, pornography, and even politics. And popular Internet service providers will terminate accounts for offensive behavior. After the terrorist attacks in 2001, eBay did not allow people to sell parts of the World Trade Center via its online auction. Despite such interference, growing numbers of people are actively involved in online communities. These **netizens** are committed to the free flow of information, with few outside controls.

Today, many countries try to control political dissent by restricting citizens' access to online comments unfavorable to the government. In 2011, online criticism fueled dissent in Arab countries like Egypt, Tunisia, Libya, Bahrain, and Syria. Using social media, activists in these countries encouraged their followers to demonstrate against the government at predetermined locales. To further encourage the opposition, they posted cell phone videos of the protests on the Internet. Even in China,

Research Today

BOX 20-1

Inside the Bubble: Internet Search Filters

Through Facebook, Classmates, and LinkedIn, the Internet allows us to reach out to those who are different from ourselves—or does it? Today, the search engines we use to navigate the Internet are personalized. Google, for example, uses as many as 57 sources of information, including a person's location and past searches, to make calculated guesses about the sites a person might like to visit. Its searches have been personalized in this way since 2009. In 2012 Google carried the process one step further by collecting information from the websites that people "friend" through social media, and then using it to direct their web searches. Google sees this personalization of its searches as a service, one that helps people to cut through irrelevant information and quickly find what they are looking for.

Although Google's approach may at first sound convenient, critics charge that it can trap users in their own worlds, by routing them ever more narrowly in the same direction. In his book *The Filter Bubble*, online political activist Eli Pariser complains that when a search engine filters our searches, it encloses us in a kind of invisible bubble that limits what we see to what we are already familiar with. Thus, we are not likely to discover people, places, and ideas that are outside our comfort zone. Secure in our online bubble, which we may not even realize is there, we visit only safe, predictable sites.

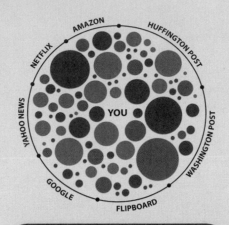

> Like network television and the major motion picture studios, Internet search engines may well limit the breadth of the material that people see.

What is wrong with that result? Given a choice, most of us go only to restaurants whose food we enjoy, read and listen to only those books and radio programs we know we like. Yet wasn't the Internet supposed to open new vistas to us? And if we are investigating a major

news event, shouldn't we all see the same information when we search for it? Pariser describes what happened when two friends searched for the term "BP" in the spring of 2010, during the Deepwater Horizon oil rig's accidental discharge of crude oil into the Gulf of Mexico. Using the same browser, the two friends got very different results. One saw links to information about the oil spill; the other saw links to information about BP's CEO, intended for investors.

Google's spokespeople deny that their search engine reduces people's exposure to new ideas. Its calculations, they say, "limit personalization and promote variety in the results page" (Weisberg 2011). Yet like network television and the major motion picture studios, Internet search engines may well limit the breadth of the material that people see.

LET'S DISCUSS

1. Have you ever been frustrated by the results of an Internet search? Describe what happened, or what didn't happen.

2. Choose a topic of interest to you and do an Internet search on it; ask several friends or classmates to do the same. Do your results differ? In what way?

Sources: Basulto 2011; Elgan 2011; Pariser 2011a, 2011b; Swartz 2012; Weisberg 2011.

---

where the government limits or even bans access to Google, Facebook, and Twitter, media-savvy Chinese have created local networks to share their dissatisfaction with the government. Surreptitiously, the U.S. government has distributed "shadow" Internet and mobile phone systems to dissidents around the world, to undermine their governments' censorship (Glanz and Markoff 2011; C. MacLeod 2010; Preston and Stelter 2011; Wasik 2012).

Media Monitoring

The term *media monitoring* is used most often to refer to interest groups' monitoring of media content. The public reaction to the shootings at Virginia Tech in April 2007 provides one example. People did not need to be constant news monitors to learn of the rampage. Ever since the mass shootings at Columbine High School near Littleton, Colorado, in 1999, news outlets of every type have descended on the sites of such school shootings, offering insight into the perpetrators and their families, covering the mass expressions of grief, and following the communities' efforts to recover. Once again, though media outlets provided valuable information and quickly reassured viewers, listeners, and readers that the shooters posed no further danger, many people criticized the reality that they constructed through their coverage.

The term *media monitoring* can also be applied to government monitoring of individuals' phone calls without their knowledge. For example, the federal government has been criticized for authorizing wiretaps of U.S. citizens' telephone conversations without judicial approval. Government officials argue that the wiretaps were undertaken in the interest of national security, to monitor contacts between U.S. citizens and known terrorist groups following the terrorist attacks of September 11, 2001. But critics who take the conflict perspective, among others, are concerned by the apparent invasion of people's privacy (Gertner 2005). We will examine the right to privacy in greater detail in the Social Policy section in Module 22.

What are the practical and ethical limits of media monitoring? In daily life, parents often oversee their children's online activities and scan the blogs they read—which are, of course, available for anyone to see. Most parents see such monitoring of children's media use and communications as an appropriate part of adult supervision. Yet their snooping sets an example for their children, who may use the technique for their own ends. Some media analysts have noted a growing trend among adolescents: the use of new media to learn not-so-public information about their parents (Delaney 2005).

Social media have facilitated both public criticism of government and government attempts to monitor dissent.

One unanticipated benefit of government monitoring of private communications has been expedited disaster relief. As in the aftermath of Hurricane Katrina in 2005, the U.S. government turned to media monitoring following the 2010 earthquake in Haiti. At the Department of Homeland Security, employees at the National Operations Center monitored 31 social media sites for information regarding the disaster. The intelligence they gathered helped responders to locate people in need of rescue and identify areas outside Port-au-Prince where relief was necessary (Department of Homeland Security 2010).

Dominant Ideology: Constructing Reality

Conflict theorists argue that the mass media maintain the privileges of certain groups. Moreover, powerful groups may limit the media's representation of others to protect their own interests. The term **dominant ideology** describes a set of cultural beliefs and practices that helps to maintain powerful social, economic, and political interests. The media transmit messages that essentially define what we regard as the real world, even though those images frequently vary from the ones that the larger society experiences.

Mass media decision makers are overwhelmingly White, male, and wealthy. It may come as no surprise, then, that the media tend to ignore the lives and ambitions of subordinate groups, among them working-class people, African Americans, Hispanics, gays and lesbians, people with disabilities, overweight people, and older people. Worse yet, media content may create false images or stereotypes of these groups that then become accepted as accurate portrayals of reality. **Stereotypes** are unreliable

generalizations about all members of a group that do not recognize individual differences within the group. Some broadcasters use stereotypes deliberately in a desperate bid for attention, with the winking approval of media executives. Shock radio host Don Imus may have been banned from the airwaves for his stereotyped description of Black female athletes, but within 10 months he was back on the air, earning a seven-figure income.

Television content is another example of this tendency to ignore reality. How many overweight TV characters can you name? Even though in real life 1 out of every 4 women is obese (30 or more pounds over a healthy body weight), only 3 out of 100 TV characters are portrayed as obese. Heavyset television characters have fewer romances, talk less about sex, eat more often, and are more often the object of ridicule than their thin counterparts (Hellmich 2001).

On the other hand, television news and other media outlets do alert people to the health implications of obesity. As with constructions of reality, whether some of this coverage is truly educational is debatable. Increasingly, the media have framed the problem not merely as an individual or personal one, but as a broad structural problem involving, for example, the manner in which food is processed and sold (Saguy and Almeling 2008).

As of 2011, 45 percent of all youths in the United States were children of color, yet few of the faces they saw on television reflected their race or cultural heritage. Using content analysis, sociologists have found that only 2 of the nearly 60 prime-time series aired in recent years—*Ugly Betty* and *George*

Despite the popularity of Hollywood entertainment, media that are produced abroad for local consumption also do well. The animated series *Freej* features Muslim grandmothers who stumble on a cursed book while tackling their culture's wedding traditions. Produced in Dubai, the United Arab Emirates, for adult viewers, the series was launched in 2006.

Lindsey Wallen, *Social Media Consultant*

Lindsey Wallen graduated from DePaul University with a major in sociology. She chose sociology because she wanted to help people, perhaps as a social worker for a nonprofit organization. Then, in her junior year, when her political science professor offered extra credit for work on a political campaign, Wallen's life took an unexpected turn. "I showed up at the Obama headquarters just as they were moving in to their downtown Chicago office," Wallen remembers. "I was assigned to the New Media department, using Facebook and MySpace to reach out to voters." At the time, the use of social media tools in a political campaign was groundbreaking. "It was an exciting place to be," she recalls. "I stayed on as a volunteer in New Media through the end of the campaign. When I graduated in 2008, I used that experience to pitch my social media services to nonprofits."

Today, Wallen is a social media manager for several nonprofit organizations in the Chicago area. She enjoys using her expertise in online organizing to help these worthy organizations grow. Wallen's work with a nonprofit that fights homelessness has been particularly satisfying to her. In 2010–11, her client joined a coalition of organizations dedicated to creating more affordable housing in the city. "My role was to attend city council meetings and 'live-tweet' the proceedings for supporters who couldn't be in the room," she explains. "On the day when a version of our legislation was passed, it was an exciting task indeed!"

Wallen also teaches an online course in social media to high school students, through the Gifted LearningLinks program at Northwestern University. In the first few weeks of the course, she draws from her old textbooks to give students a brief lesson in sociological theory. Then she asks them to apply the theory to Facebook and Twitter. "For the next generation, the Internet is the new frontier," she muses. "It's pretty amazing to see the perspectives of these 'digital natives' at work."

Wallen finds that her background in sociology is quite relevant to her career. "I spend much of my workweek interacting with communities on Facebook and Twitter, building a content schedule, and looking for content to share with my audience," she explains. To measure and track the success of her social media campaigns—a necessity in online organizing—Wallen relies on her training in statistics. "Metrics in social media is more than just counting the number of 'Likes' you have," she notes. "You need to look at the data and determine what kind of story it is telling you, what your audience is like and what they need from you." Wallen also applies what she learned in her senior capstone course, Visual Sociology, which taught her to use photography or video to tell a story about a sociological trend. "I use this tactic every day on Facebook and YouTube—visuals are what grab attention and add weight to the message you are trying to convey," she says.

LET'S DISCUSS

1. Have you ever used social media to participate in an online campaign? If so, how did you participate—by donating money, for example, or attending a fundraising event?

2. How might you use social media in your own career?

Lopez—focused on minority performers. What is more, programs that are shown earlier in the evening, when young people are most likely to watch television, are the least diverse (Grazian 2010:129; NAACP 2008; Wyatt 2009).

Another concern about the media, from the conflict perspective, is that television distorts the political process. Until the U.S. campaign finance system is truly reformed, the candidates with the most money (often backed by powerful lobbying groups) will be able to buy exposure to voters and saturate the air with commercials attacking their opponents.

Dominant Ideology: Whose Culture?

In the United States, on the popular television contest *The Apprentice,* the dreaded dismissal line is "You're fired." In Finland, on *Dilli (The Deal),* it's "*Olet vapautettu*" ("You're free to leave"); in Germany, on *Big Boss,* it's "*Sie haben frei*" ("You're off"). Although people throughout the world decry U.S. exports, from films to language to Bart Simpson, the U.S. media are still widely imitated. Sociologist Todd Gitlin describes American popular culture as something that "people love, and love to hate" (2002:177; Wentz and Atkinson 2005).

We risk being ethnocentric if we overstress U.S. dominance, however. For example, *Survivor, Who Wants to Be a Millionaire, Big Brother,* and *Iron Chef*—immensely popular TV programs in the United States—came from Sweden, Britain, the Netherlands, and Japan, respectively. Even *American Idol* originated in Britain as *Pop Idol,* featuring Simon Cowell. And the steamy telenovelas of Mexico and other Spanish-speaking countries owe very little of their origin to the soap operas on U.S. television. Unlike motion pictures, television is gradually moving away from U.S. domination and is now more likely to be locally produced. By 2003, all the top 50 British TV shows were locally produced. *Medium* may appear on television in London, but it is shown late at night. Even U.S.-owned TV ventures such as Disney, MTV, and CNN had dramatically increased their locally produced programming overseas. Still, *CSI: NY* was on top in France, where only sports programs had a higher rating (Bielby and Harrington 2008; Colucci 2008; *The Economist* 2003).

Nations that feel a loss of identity may try to defend against the cultural invasion from foreign countries, especially the economically dominant United States. Yet as sociologists know, audiences are not necessarily passive recipients of foreign cultural messages, either in developing nations or in industrial nations. Thus, research on consumers of cultural products like television, music, and film must be placed in social context. Although people may watch and even enjoy media content, that does not mean that they will accept values that are alien to their own (Bielby and Harrington 2008).

BOX 20-2

Sociology in the Global Community

The Global Disconnect

Bogdan Ghirda, a Romanian, is paid 50 cents an hour to participate in multiplayer Internet games like City of Heroes and Star Wars. He is sitting in for someone in an industrialized country who does not want to spend days ascending to the highest levels of competition in order to compete with players who are already "well armed." This arrangement is not unusual. U.S.-based services can earn hundreds of dollars for recruiting someone in a less developed country, like Ghirda, to represent a single player in an affluent industrial country.

Meanwhile, villagers in Arumugam, India, are beginning to benefit from their new Knowledge Centre. The facility, funded by a nonprofit organization, contains five computers that offer Internet access—an amenity unknown until now to thousands of villagers.

These two situations illustrate the technological disconnect between the developing and industrial nations. Around the world, developing nations lag far behind industrial nations in their access to and use of new technologies. The World Economic Forum's Networked Readiness Index (NRI), a ranking of 142 nations, shows the relative preparedness of individuals, businesses, and governments to benefit from information technologies. As the accompanying table shows, the haves of the world—countries like Singapore, the United States, and Denmark—are network ready; the have-nots—countries like Zimbabwe, Yemen, and Haiti—are not.

For developing nations, the consequences of the global disconnect are far more serious than an inability to surf the Net. Thanks to the Internet, multinational organizations can now function as a single global unit, responding instantly in real time, 24 hours a day. This new capability has fostered the emergence of what sociologist Manuel Castells calls a "global economy." But if large numbers of people—indeed, entire nations—are disconnected from the new global economy, their economic growth will remain slow and the well-being of their people will remain retarded. Those citizens who are educated and skilled will immigrate to other labor markets, deepening the impoverishment of nations on the periphery.

> For developing nations, the consequences of the global disconnect are far more serious than an inability to surf the Net.

Networked Readiness Index

Top 10 Countries	Bottom 10 Countries
1. Switzerland	133. Mozambique
2. Singapore	134. Swaziland
3. Sweden	135. Lesotho
4. Finland	136. Burkina Faso
5. United States	137. Mauritania
6. Germany	138. Yemen
7. Netherlands	139. Angola
8. Denmark	140. Burundi
9. Japan	141. Haiti
10. Great Britain	142. Chad

LET'S DISCUSS

1. For nations on the periphery, what might be some specific social and economic consequences of the global disconnect?
2. What factors might complicate efforts to remedy the global disconnect in developing nations?

Sources: Castells 2010a; Dutta and Mia 2010; *The Economist* 2005c; Lim 2007; Schwab 2011; T. Thompson 2005.

Many developing nations have long argued for a greatly improved two-way flow of news and information between industrial nations and developing nations. They complain that news from the Third World is scant, and what news there is reflects unfavorably on the developing nations. For example, what do you know about South America? Most people in the United States will mention the two topics that dominate the news from countries south of the border: revolution and drugs. Most know little else about the continent.

To remedy this imbalance, a resolution to monitor the news and content that cross the borders of developing nations was passed by the United Nations Educational, Scientific, and Cultural Organization (UNESCO) in the 1980s. The United States disagreed with the proposal, which became one factor in the U.S. decision to withdraw from UNESCO in the mid-1980s. In 2005, the United States opposed another UNESCO plan, meant to reduce the diminishment of cultural differences. Hailed as an important step toward protecting threatened cultures, particularly the media markets in developing nations, the measure passed the UN's General Assembly by a vote of 148–2. The United States, one of the two dissenters, objected officially to the measure's vague wording, but the real concern was clearly the measure's potential impact on a major U.S. export (Dominick 2009; Riding 2005).

The Digital Divide

Finally, as numerous studies have shown, advances in communications technology are not evenly distributed. Worldwide, low-income groups, racial and ethnic minorities, rural residents, and the citizens of developing countries have far less access than others to the latest technologies—a gap that is called the **digital divide.** People in low-income households and developing countries, for example, are less likely than others to have Internet access. When marginalized people do gain Internet access, they are still likely to trail the privileged. They may have dial-up service instead of broadband, or broadband instead of wireless Internet.

The implications of the digital divide go well beyond an inability to check sports results or celebrity comings and goings. The Internet and other new media are becoming essential to economic progress, whether it is finding a job or accessing information needed to improve one's skills.

The digital divide is most evident in developing countries. In Africa, 4 percent of the population has Internet access. These fortunate few typically pay the highest rates in the world—$250 to $300 a month—for the slowest connection speeds. Box 20-2 examines the global disconnect between the haves and have-nots of the information age (Robinson and Crenshaw 2010; P. Schaefer 2008).

use your **sociological imagination**

How do your favorite media reflect U.S. culture? How do they reflect the cultures of the rest of the world?

Feminist Perspective

Feminists share the view of conflict theorists that the mass media stereotype and misrepresent social reality. According to this view, the media powerfully influence how we look at men and women, communicating unrealistic, stereotypical, and limiting images of the sexes.

Educators and social scientists have long noted the stereotypical portrayal of women and men in the mass media. Women are often shown as being shallow and obsessed with beauty. They are more likely than men to be presented unclothed, in danger, or even physically victimized. When women achieve newsworthy feats in fields traditionally dominated by men, such as professional sports, the media are often slow to recognize their accomplishments.

Even when they are covered by the press, female athletes are not treated equally by television commentators. Communications researchers conducted a content analysis of over 200 hours of nationally televised coverage of professional golf events. The study showed that when female golfers are successful, they are more likely than male golfers to be called strong and intelligent. When they are not successful, they are more likely than men to be described as lacking in athletic ability. In contrast, male golfers receive more comments on their concentration and commitment. These findings suggest a subtle sexism, with women being portrayed as innately talented and men being portrayed as superior in mental or emotional makeup (T. Jacobs 2009).

Another aim of feminist research is to determine whether the media have a different impact on women than on men. Recently, researchers found that adolescent boys are almost three times as likely as adolescent girls to participate in online gaming. Young females who do participate are more likely than boy gamers to get into serious fights and report obesity. Clearly, this topic deserves further study (R. Desai et al. 2010).

A continuing, troubling issue for feminists and society as a whole is pornography. Feminists tend to be very supportive of freedom of expression and self-determination, rights that are denied to women more often than to men. Yet pornography presents women as sex objects and seems to make viewing women that way acceptable. Nor are concerns about pornography limited to this type of objectification and imagery, as well as their implicit endorsement of violence against women. The industry that creates risqué adult images for videos, DVDs, and the Internet is largely unregulated, even putting its performers at risk.

Feminist scholars are cautiously optimistic about new media. Although women are represented among bloggers, by some measures they are responsible for only about 10 percent of the most popular blogs. Still, in conservative cultures like Saudi Arabia, online media offer women the opportunity to explore lifestyles that traditional media outlets largely ignore (Jesella 2008; Worth 2008).

As in other areas of sociology, feminist researchers caution against assuming that what holds true for men's media use is true for everyone. Researchers, for example, have studied the different ways that women and men approach the Internet. Though men are only slightly more likely than women ever to have used the Internet, they are much more likely to use it daily. Yet according to a 2009 study, more women than men use the Internet. Not surprisingly, men account for 91 percent of the players in online sports fantasy leagues. Perhaps more socially significant, however, is the finding that women are more likely than men to maintain friendship networks through e-mail (Boase et al. 2006; Fallows 2006; Pew Internet Project 2009; Rainie 2005).

Interactionist Perspective

Interactionists are especially interested in shared understandings of everyday behavior. These scholars examine the media on the micro level to see how they shape day-to-day social behavior. Increasingly, researchers point to the mass media as the source of major daily activity; some argue that television serves essentially as a primary group for many individuals who share TV viewing. Other mass-media participation is not necessarily face-to-face. For example, we usually listen to the radio or read the newspaper as a solitary activity, although it is possible to share either with others (Cerulo et al. 1992; Waite 2000).

Online social networks, in fact, have become a new way of promoting consumption. As Figure 20-2 shows, advertisers have traditionally marketed

FIGURE 20-2 **Marketing Online through Social Networks**

Traditional Marketing

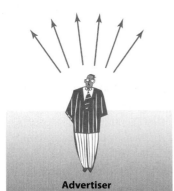

Advertiser

Online Marketing

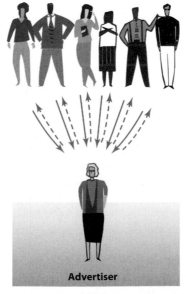

Advertiser

Traditional forms of advertising (left) allow only one-way communication, from the advertiser to the consumer. Online social networks (right) offer two-way communication, allowing advertisers to develop a relationship with consumers.

products and services through spot ads, mass mailings, or billboards, whether they are promoting flat-screen televisions or public service messages like "Don't drink and drive." Now, using social networks (see Box 15-2, page 101), they can find consumers online and attempt to develop a relationship with them there. Through Facebook, for example, Burger King awarded a free Whopper to anyone who would delete 10 friends. Facebook's staff was not happy with Burger King's promotion, which notified 239,906 Facebook users that they had been dropped for a burger—an action that violated the network's policy. Nevertheless, Burger King created a vast network of consumers who enjoy Whoppers. Similarly, Kraft Foods encouraged people to post images of the Wiener-mobile on the photo site Flickr (Bacon Lovers' Talk 2009; Burger King 2009; Gaudin 2009).

Interactionists note, too, that friendship networks can emerge from shared viewing habits or from recollection of a cherished television series from the past. Family members and friends often gather for parties centered on the broadcasting of popular events such as the Super Bowl or the Academy Awards. And as we've seen, television often serves as a babysitter or playmate for children and even infants.

The rise of the Internet has also facilitated new forms of communication and social interaction. Grandparents can now keep up with their grandchildren via e-mail, or even watch them on their laptops via Skype. Gay and lesbian teens have online resources for support and information. People can even find their lifetime partners through computer dating services.

Some troubling issues have been raised about day-to-day life on the Internet, however. What, if anything, should be done about terrorists and other extremist groups who use the Internet to exchange messages of hatred and even bomb-making recipes? What, if anything, should be done about the issue of sexual expression on the Internet? How can children be protected from it? Should "hot chat" and X-rated film clips be censored? Or should expression be completely free?

Though the Internet has created a new platform for extremists, hate groups, and pornographers, it has also given people greater control over what they see and hear. That is, the

Internet allows people to manage their media exposure so as to avoid sounds, images, and ideas they do not enjoy or approve of. The legal scholar Cass Sunstein (2002) has referred to this personalized approach to news information gathering as *egocasting*. One social consequence of this trend may be a less tolerant society. If we read, see, and hear only what we know and agree with, we may be much less prepared to meet people from different backgrounds or converse with those who express new viewpoints.

Furthermore, while many people in the United States embrace the Internet, we should note that information is not evenly distributed throughout the population. The same people, by and large, who experience poor health and have few job opportunities have been left off the information highway. Figure 20-3 breaks down Internet usage by gender, age, race,

FIGURE 20-3 **Who's on the Internet**

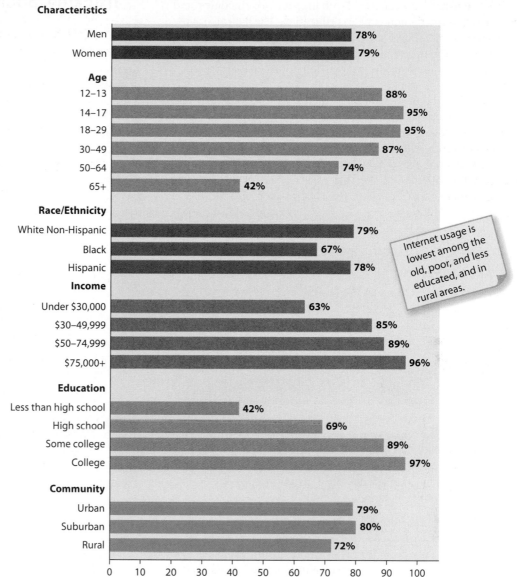

Note: Based on a national survey taken January–February 2012, except for community data taken June–September 2009. Hispanic data limited to English-speaking respondents.
Source: Pew Internet Project 2012a, 2012b.

income, education, and community type. Note the large disparities in usage between those with high and low incomes, and between those with more and less education. The data also show a significant racial disparity. Though educators and politicians have touted the potential benefits to the disadvantaged, Internet usage may be reinforcing existing social-class and racial barriers.

The interactionist perspective helps us to understand one important aspect of the entire mass media system—the audience. How do we actively participate in media events? How do we construct with others the meaning of media messages? We will explore these questions in the section that follows. (Table 20-3 summarizes the various sociological perspectives on the media.)

Tracking Sociological Perspectives

Table 20-3 Sociological Perspectives on the Mass Media

Theoretical Perspective	Emphasis
Functionalist	Socialization
	Enforcement of social norms
	Conferral of status
	Promotion of consumption
	Narcotizing effect (dysfunction)
Conflict	Gatekeeping
	Media monitoring
	Construction of reality
	Digital divide
Feminist	Misrepresentation of women
	Differential impact on women
Interactionist	Impact on social behavior
	Source of friendship networks

MODULE 20 | Recap and Review

Summary

The **mass media** are print and electronic instruments of communication that carry messages to often widespread audiences. They pervade all social institutions, from entertainment to education to politics.

1. From the functionalist perspective, the media entertain, socialize, enforce social norms, confer status, and promote consumption. They can be dysfunctional to the extent that they desensitize us to serious events and issues (the **narcotizing dysfunction**).

2. Conflict theorists think the media reflect and even deepen the division in society through **gatekeeping,** or control over which material reaches the public; media monitoring, the covert observation of people's media usage and choices; and support of the **dominant ideology,** which defines reality, overwhelming local cultures.

3. Feminist theorists point out that media images of the sexes communicate unrealistic, stereotypical, limiting, and sometimes violent perceptions of women.

4. Interactionists examine the media on the micro level to see how they shape day-to-day social behavior. Interactionists have studied shared TV viewing and staged public appearances intended to convey self-serving definitions of reality.

Thinking Critically

1. What do you think is the most important function of the mass media in our society? Why?

2. Which of the problems associated with the media troubles you most, and why?

3. Americans now get their news from many different cable news networks rather than from just three national networks. What is the effect of this trend on the media's tendency to promulgate a dominant ideology?

Key Terms

Cultural convergence   145

Digital divide   153

Dominant ideology   151

Gatekeeping   148

Mass media   145

Narcotizing dysfunction   148

Netizen 149

Stereotype   151

Ever feel like text-messaging everyone you know, to encourage them to vote for your favorite performer on a certain reality program? Ever looked over someone's shoulder as he watched last week's episode of *American Idol* on his iPhone—and been tempted to reveal the ending to him? Ever come across an old CD and tried to remember the last time you or a friend listened to one, or heard the songs in the order in which they were recorded? In this and many other ways, we are reminded that we are all part of a larger audience.

Who Is in the Audience?

The mass media are distinguished from other social institutions by the necessary presence of an audience. It can be an identifiable, finite group, such as an audience at a jazz club or a Broadway musical, or a much larger and undefined group, such as VH-1 viewers or readers of the same issue of *USA Today*. The audience may be a secondary group gathered in a large auditorium or a primary group, such as a family watching the latest Disney video at home.

We can look at the audience from the level of both *microsociology* and *macrosociology*. At the micro level, we might consider how audience members, interacting among themselves, respond to the media, or in the case of live performances, actually influence the performers. At the macro level, we might examine broader societal consequences of the media, such as the early childhood education delivered through programming like *Sesame Street*.

Even if an audience is spread out over a wide geographic area and members don't know one another, it is still distinctive in terms of age, gender, income, political party, formal schooling, race, and ethnicity. The audience for a ballet, for example, would likely differ substantially from the audience for alternative music.

The Segmented Audience

Increasingly, the media are marketing themselves to a *particular* audience. Once a media outlet, such as a radio station or a magazine, has identified its audience, it targets that group. To some degree, this specialization is driven by advertising. Media specialists have sharpened their ability, through survey research, to identify particular target audiences. Thus, during the midterm elections in 2010, the two major political parties placed TV advertisements in markets where surveys indicated they would find support. For example, the Republican Party placed ads on college football games and *America's Funniest Home Videos*. The Democratic Party bought time on *Brothers & Sisters* and *Dr. Phil* (A. Parker 2010).

 use your **sociological imagination**

Think about the last time you were part of an audience. Describe the performance. How similar to or different from yourself were the other audience members? What might account for whatever similarities or differences you noticed?

The specialized targeting of audiences has led some scholars to question the "mass" in mass media. For example, the British social psychologist Sonia Livingstone (2004) has written that the media have become so segmented, they have taken on the appearance almost of individualization. Are viewing audiences so segmented that large collective audiences are a thing of the past? That is not yet clear. Even though we seem to be living in an age of *personal* computers and *personal* digital assistants (PDAs), large formal organizations still do transmit public messages that reach a sizable, heterogeneous, and scattered audience.

trend|spotting

Who's on the Internet?

Everyone seems to be on the Internet, but not quite. Overall, about three-quarters of U.S. residents are connected to the Internet. Rural residents, as well as the poor, minorities, and the elderly, trail behind other groups in their use of the Internet.

The age gap in Internet usage is closing, however. In 2000, only 20 percent of people age 65 or older were on the web, compared to 78 percent of those in their 20s. Ten years later, 42 percent of those 65 and over were on the web, compared to about 88 percent of 20-somethings. This gap is expected to narrow further in coming years.

Likewise, the racial-ethnic and income gaps in Internet usage are closing. Internet use rose from 52 percent of Blacks and 66 percent of Whites in the year 2000 to 67 percent of Blacks and 79 percent of Whites in 2011. Low-income people and rural residents are making similar strides.

use your sociological imagination

How might you use the concept of audience segmentation in your future occupation?

Audience Behavior

Sociologists have long researched how audiences interact with one another and how they share information after a media event. The role of audience members as opinion leaders particularly intrigues social researchers. An **opinion leader** is someone who influences the opinions and decisions of others through day-to-day personal contact and communication. For example, a movie or theater critic functions as an opinion leader. Sociologist Paul Lazarsfeld and his colleagues (1948) pioneered the study of opinion leaders in their research on voting behavior in the 1940s. They found that opinion leaders encourage their relatives, friends, and co-workers to think positively about a particular candidate, perhaps pushing them to listen to the politician's speeches or read the campaign literature.

Despite the role of opinion leaders, members of an audience do not all interpret media in the same way. Often their response is influenced by their social characteristics, such as occupation, race, education, and income. Take the example of the televised news coverage of the riots in Los Angeles in 1992. The riots were an angry response to the acquittal of two White police officers accused of severely beating a Black motorist. Sociologist Darnell Hunt (1997) wondered how the social composition of audience members would affect the way they interpreted the news coverage. Hunt gathered 15 groups from the Los Angeles area, whose members were equally divided among Whites, Blacks, and Latinos. He showed each group a 17-minute clip from the

Sociology in the Global Community

BOX 21-1

Charity Begins Online

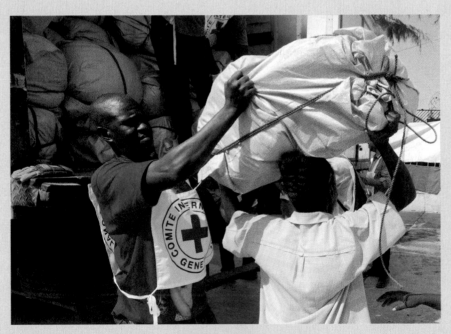

Increasingly, technology plays a part in the contributions people make to the causes and organizations they support. Research shows that in the United States, 20 percent of adults have contributed to charities online. Ten percent have done so from their cell phones, using text messaging. The new trend was especially noticeable in 2010, after the massive earthquake in Haiti, when cell phone owners used text messaging to contribute an estimated $43 million to relief efforts. The story of the disaster, which displaced millions of people, dominated the news and social media for weeks afterward.

For charities, mobile giving opened up a new way to reach donors, and a friend network that could spread news of natural disasters almost instantaneously. Most of those who made text donations to Haiti—almost 9 out of 10—responded quickly to television news reports, without stopping to investigate the charities. About half of them donated immediately; another quarter did so later in the day. Unlike traditional contributors, many of these donors shared their decisions through their electronic friend networks. In a survey, 43 percent of respondents who had made text donations to Haiti said they had encouraged friends or relatives to do the same. Of that group, 76 percent said that their friends or family had complied. Young and non-White donors were particularly active in spreading the word.

> For charities, mobile giving opened up a new way to reach donors, and a friend network that could spread news of natural disasters almost instantaneously.

Unfortunately, text donors' interest in the island nation's fate seemed to evaporate just as quickly as it had developed. Less than half of them have stayed informed on the charities' reconstruction efforts, and 15 percent have lost all interest. For the charities, the new donors' fickleness spells uncertainty about the success of future fundraising efforts. Traditional donors—those who research charities online before donating, and follow up on their effectiveness over the years—are more likely to stay involved and to support charities over the long term, regardless of what is or is not in the news.

LET'S DISCUSS

1. Have you ever texted a donation to a charity and then shared your concern with friends and family? If so, did you or anyone you know ever follow up on the charity's efforts? If not, why not?

2. If you worked for a charity, how would you deal with the here-today, gone-tomorrow nature of text donations?

Sources: Choney 2010; A. Smith 2012.

televised coverage of the riots and asked members to discuss how they would describe what they had just seen to a 12-year-old. In analyzing the discussions, Hunt found that although gender and class did not cause respondents to vary their answers much, race did.

Hunt went beyond noting simple racial differences in perceptions; he analyzed how the differences were manifested. For example, Black viewers were much more likely than Latinos or Whites to refer to the events in terms of "us" versus "them."

Another difference was that Black and Latino viewers were more animated and critical than White viewers as they watched the film clip. White viewers tended to sit quietly, still and unquestioning, suggesting that they were more comfortable with the news coverage than the Blacks or Latinos.

Social networking is continually allowing for new ways for audiences to get involved through use of mass media. As Box 21-1 shows, texting became a new source of philanthropy in the aftermath of the devastating 2010 earthquake in Haiti.

MODULE 21 | Recap and Review

Summary

The need for an audience distinguishes the mass media from other social institutions.

1. An audience may be small and well defined or large and amorphous. With increasing numbers of media outlets has come more and more targeting of segmented (or specialized) audiences.

2. Social researchers have studied the role of **opinion leaders** in influencing audiences.

Thinking Critically

1. What kind of audience is targeted by the producers of televised professional wrestling? By the creators of an animated film? By a rap group? What factors determine who makes up a particular audience?

2. Who do you consider to be opinion leaders to you? Why are those individuals influential to you? Would your parents, friends, or teachers select the same opinion leaders?

Key Term

Opinion leader 158

MODULE 22 | The Media's Global Reach

Has the rise of the electronic media created a *global village?* Canadian media theorist Marshall McLuhan predicted it would nearly 50 years ago. Today, physical distance is no longer a barrier, and instant messaging is possible across the world. The mass media have indeed created a global village. Not all countries are equally connected, as Figure 22-1 shows, but the progress has been staggering, considering that voice transmission was just beginning 100 years ago (McLuhan 1964, 1967).

Sociologist Todd Gitlin considers *global torrent* a more apt metaphor for the media's reach than *global village*. The media permeate all aspects of everyday life. Take advertising, for example. Consumer goods are marketed vigorously worldwide, from advertisements on airport baggage carriers to imprints on sandy beaches. Little wonder that people around the world develop loyalty to a brand and are as likely to sport a Nike, Coca-Cola, or Harley-Davidson logo as they are their favorite soccer or baseball insignia (Gitlin 2002; Klein 1999).

The Internet has facilitated all forms of communication. Reference materials and data banks can now be made accessible across national boundaries. Information related to international finance, marketing, trade, and manufacturing is literally just a keystroke away. We have seen the emergence of true world news outlets and the promotion of a world music that is not clearly

FIGURE 22-1 Media Penetration in Selected Countries

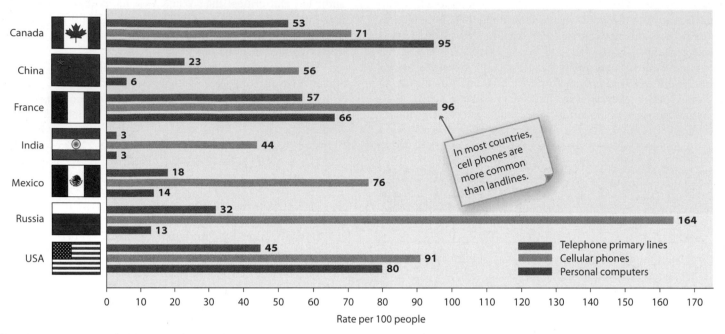

Canada — Telephone primary lines: 53, Cellular phones: 71, Personal computers: 95

China — Telephone primary lines: 23, Cellular phones: 56, Personal computers: 6

France — Telephone primary lines: 57, Cellular phones: 96, Personal computers: 66

India — Telephone primary lines: 3, Cellular phones: 44, Personal computers: 3

Mexico — Telephone primary lines: 18, Cellular phones: 76, Personal computers: 14

Russia — Telephone primary lines: 32, Cellular phones: 164, Personal computers: 13

USA — Telephone primary lines: 45, Cellular phones: 91, Personal computers: 80

In most countries, cell phones are more common than landlines.

Legend:
- Telephone primary lines
- Cellular phones
- Personal computers

Rate per 100 people (scale 0 to 170)

Note: Personal computer data for 2006, released in 2009; all other data for 2009, released in 2012.
Sources: Bureau of the Census 2009a:Table 1345; 2011a:Table 1392 on page 868.

Think about It

What is the economic and political significance of media penetration?

identifiable with any single culture. Even the most future-oriented thinker would find the growth in the reach of the mass media in postindustrial and postmodern societies remarkable (Castells 2001, 2010b; Croteau and Hoynes 2003, 2006; Croteau et al. 2012).

In 2011, "Black and Yellow" by rapper Wiz Khalifa (left) was one of the most frequently downloaded cell phone ringtones. Because today's media provide multiple services, music fans can use the Internet to access recorded music and listen to it on their cell phones.

Although in the United States we may take television for granted, even thinking of it as an old-fashioned medium, worldwide that is not necessarily the case. In India, half of all households do not have television; in Nigeria and Bangladesh, more than 70 percent of households go without. Two technological advances are likely to change this pattern, however. First, advances in battery power now allow viewers to watch television even in areas where there is no electricity. Second, digital signal transmission permits television reception via cable or satellite.

In some developing countries, people manage to watch television even though they don't own one. Consider the town of Gurupá, in the remote Amazon area of Brazil. In 1982, the wealthiest three households in this community bought televisions. To please the rest of the town, they agreed to place their TVs near the window so that their neighbors could watch them as well. As the TV owners proudly displayed their new status symbol, TV watching became a community social activity. The introduction of a new technology had created a new social norm (Kenny 2009; Pace 1993, 1998).

Around the world, people rely increasingly on digital media, from cell phones to the Internet. This trend toward online communication has raised new concerns about the right to privacy. The Social Policy section that follows examines the social implications of digital media, from censorship to criminal activity.

New technologies can create new social norms. In Gurupá, Brazil, television watching became a community social activity when three new TV owners agreed to share their sets with the community of 3,000.

social

policy and the Mass Media | The Right to Privacy

In 2010, humans added 1.2 zettabytes of digital information to the world's already huge data library. A zettabyte equals 1 trillion gigabytes—a quantity which, if placed on DVDs, would require a stack of disks stretching to the moon and back. By 2020, the size of this imaginary DVD tower will triple, quadruple, or even quintuple (Acohido 2010).

Within this mound of data lies personal information about people's finances, health, and individual tastes. In the postmodern digital age, do people have a right to keep that kind of information private? If so, can they expect others to respect that right?

Looking at the Issue

Although much of the sweeping change that accompanied the transition to digital media has benefited society, scholars have noted some negative effects. In particular, recent advances in computer technology have made it increasingly easy for business firms, government agencies, and even criminals to retrieve and store information about private individuals. In public places, at work, and on the Internet, surveillance devices track our every move, whether it is a keystroke or an ATM withdrawal. The information they accumulate includes everything from our buying habits to our web-surfing patterns.

As these technologies increase the power to monitor our behavior, they raise fears of their misuse for criminal or even undemocratic purposes. In short, they threaten not just our privacy, but our freedom from crime and censorship as well. Some obvious violations of privacy, such as identity theft—the misuse of credit card and Social Security numbers to masquerade as another person—have been well documented. Other violations involve online surveillance of dissident political groups by authoritarian regimes and the unauthorized release of classified government documents. In 2010, WikiLeaks released thousands of classified U.S. foreign policy documents on its website, causing some people to condemn the action as treasonous and others to praise it as a blow against government censorship (O'Harrow Jr. 2005).

Other privacy violations are subtler, and not strictly illegal. For example, many commercial websites use "cookies"

—*Continued*

Our society's growing dependence on electronic transactions has greatly increased concerns about our privacy.

empowering people with few resources—from hate groups to special-interest organizations—to communicate with the masses.

In contrast, conflict theorists stress the danger that the most powerful groups in a society will use technology to violate the privacy of the less powerful.

Initiating Policy

Legislation regarding the surveillance of electronic communications has not always upheld citizens' right to privacy. In 1986, the federal government passed the Electronic Communications Privacy Act, which outlawed the surveillance of telephone calls except with the permission of both the U.S. attorney general and a federal judge. Telegrams, faxes, and e-mails did not receive the same degree of protection, however. In 2001, one month after the terrorist attacks of September 11, Congress passed the Patriot Act, which relaxed existing legal checks on surveillance by law enforcement officers. Federal agencies are now freer to gather data electronically, including people's credit card receipts and banking records (Gertner 2005).

and tracking technology to monitor visitors' websurfing. Using that information, marketers can estimate a visitor's age, gender, and zip code, and from that data, the person's income. They can then select advertisements that will appeal specifically to that person. So depending on who we are, or at least appear to be, one of us might see ads about weight-loss products and another, ads about travel to exotic locations.

Is this approach to online marketing just effective advertising, or is it an invasion of privacy? Because the information that marketers gather in this way can be tied to other devices a person uses, such as a cell phone or computer, some critics see online tracking as a form of fingerprinting (Angwin 2010; Angwin and Valentino-DeVries 2010a).

Applying Sociology

From a sociological point of view, the complex issues of privacy and censorship can be considered illustrations of culture lag. As usual, the material culture (technology) is changing faster than the nonmaterial culture (norms for controlling the use of technology). Too often, the result is an anything-goes approach to the use of new technologies.

Sociologists' views on the use and abuse of new technologies differ depending on their theoretical perspective. Functionalists take a generally positive view of the Internet, pointing to its manifest function of facilitating communication. From their perspective, the Internet performs the latent function of

Today, most other types of online monitoring have yet to be tested in court, including the use of tracking technologies and the compilation and sale of personal profiles to merchandisers. Consistent with the concept of culture lag, privacy advocates complain that the law hasn't kept pace with advancing technology. In 2010, Congress began to draft federal legislation to inform cell phone and computer owners that their devices are being "fingerprinted," and to allow them to opt out of being monitored. The next year, seeking to head off the measure, some tracking organizations began voluntarily to allow people to edit the information collected in their online profiles. At the same time, the Federal Trade Commission issued a report that faulted the industry for not doing enough to protect consumers' privacy online (Angwin and Valentino-DeVries 2010b; Federal Trade Commission 2010; Steel 2010; *The Week* 2010b).

If anything, however, people seem to be less vigilant about maintaining their privacy today than they were before the information age. Young people who have grown up browsing the Internet seem to accept the existence of the "cookies" and "spyware" they may pick up while surfing. They have become accustomed to adult surveillance of their conversation in electronic chat rooms. And many see no risk in providing personal information about themselves to strangers they meet online. Little wonder that college professors find their students do not appreciate the political significance of their right to privacy (Turkle 2004, 2011).

a. television
b. the Internet
c. publishing
d. music

6. Which sociological perspective is especially concerned with the media's ability to decide what gets transmitted through gatekeeping?
    a. the functionalist perspective
    b. the conflict perspective
    c. the interactionist perspective
    d. the dramaturgical perspective

7. Which of the following is *not* a problem feminist theorists see with media coverage?
    a. Women are underrepresented, suggesting that men are the cultural standard and that women are insignificant.
    b. Men and women are portrayed in ways that reflect and perpetuate stereotypical views of gender.
    c. Female athletes are treated differently from male athletes in television commentary.
    d. The increasing frequency of single moms in the media is providing a negative role model for women.

8. Which of the following is *not* true concerning how men and women use the Internet?
    a. Men are more likely to use the Internet daily.
    b. Women are more likely to use e-mail to maintain friendships.
    c. Men account for 100 percent of players in online sports fantasy leagues.
    d. Men are slightly more likely to have ever used the Internet than women are.

9. Sociologist Paul Lazarsfeld and his colleagues pioneered the study of
    a. the audience.
    b. opinion leaders.
    c. the media's global reach.
    d. media violence.

10. In his study of how the social composition of audience members affected how they interpreted the news coverage of riots in Los Angeles in 1992, sociologist Darnell Hunt found what kind of differences in perception?
    a. racial
    b. gender
    c. class
    d. religious

11. The mass media increase social cohesion by presenting a more or less standardized, common view of culture through mass communication. This statement reflects the _____ perspective.

12. Paul Lazarsfeld and Robert Merton created the term _____ _____ to refer to the phenomenon in which the media provide such massive amounts of information that the audience becomes numb and generally fails to act on the information, regardless of how compelling the issue.

13. _____ _____ is the term used to describe the set of cultural beliefs and practices that helps to maintain powerful social, economic, and political interests.

14. Sociologists blame the mass media for the creation and perpetuation of _____, or generalizations about all members of a group that do not recognize individual differences within the group.

15. The _____ perspective contends that television distorts the political process.

16. We risk being _____ if we overstress U.S. dominance and assume that other nations do not play a role in media cultural exports.

17. Both _____ and _____ theorists are troubled that the victims depicted in violent imagery are often those who are given less respect in real life: women, children, the poor, racial minorities, citizens of foreign countries, and even the physically disabled.

18. The _____ perspective examines the media on the micro level to see how they shape day-to-day social behavior.

19. From a sociological point of view, the current controversy over privacy and media censorship illustrates the concept of _____ _____.

20. Nearly 50 years ago, Canadian media theorist _____ _____ predicted that the rise of the electronic media would create a "global village."

Answers

1 (c); 2 (a); 3 (d); 4 (d); 5 (b); 6 (b); 7 (d); 8 (c); 9 (b); 10 (a); 11 functionalist; 12 narcotizing dysfunction; 13 Dominant ideology; 14 stereotypes; 15 conflict; 16 ethnocentric; 17 conflict, feminist; 18 interactionist; 19 culture lag; 20 Marshall McLuhan.

thinking about movies

The Social Network

This dramatization of the rise of Facebook illustrates the way people connect to one another in the 21st century.

Pirate Radio

In the 1960s, an independent English radio station broadcasts from international waters, threatening the British Broadcasting Corporation's monopoly of the airwaves.

We Live in Public

This documentary traces the rise and fall of an Internet entrepreneur.

The need for online privacy seems only to be increasing, however. In a new practice called *weblining,* data-gathering companies are monitoring people's online activities not so much for merchandising purposes, but to collect negative personal information. Based on this information, collected from the websites people search or the products and people they friend, a person may be denied a job opportunity or assigned a low credit rating. Data-gathering companies also offer information on searches having to do with mental issues like bipolar disorder and anxiety, which can make it difficult for a person to secure affordable health insurance. Although weblining has not yet drawn policymakers' attention, it is sure to do so in the future (Andrews 2012).

Compared to online tracking, most people seem more worried about government surveillance and crimes like identity theft. Although online piracy is a real threat, in the long run, online tracking and other questionable forms of surveillance may pose a greater threat to society. As Nicholas Carr (2010:W2), former editor of the *Harvard Business Review,* has noted, "The continuing erosion of personal privacy . . . may lead us as a society to devalue the concept of privacy, to see it as outdated and unimportant . . . merely as a barrier to efficient shopping and socializing." From the point of view of many technology companies, however, abandoning the right to privacy is only realistic. As Sun Microsystems CEO Scott McNealy remarked in 1999, "You have no privacy. Get over it" (N. Carr 2010:W2).

TAKE THE ISSUE WITH YOU

1. How would you react if you discovered that the government was monitoring your use of the mass media?
2. If your safety were in jeopardy, would you be willing to sacrifice your privacy?
3. Which do you consider the greatest threat to society: government censorship, cybercrime, or Internet surveillance? Explain.

MODULE 22 | Recap and Review

Summary

The media have a global reach thanks to new communications technologies, especially the Internet.

1. Some people are concerned that the media's global reach will spread unhealthy influences to other cultures.

2. The media industry is becoming more and more concentrated, creating media conglomerates. This raises concerns about how innovative and independent the media can be. In some countries, governments own and control the media.

3. The Internet is the one significant exception to the trend toward media concentration, allowing millions of people to produce their own media content.

Thinking Critically

1. Use the functionalist, conflict, and interactionist perspectives to assess the effects of global TV programming on developing countries.

2. Give one example of how individualization of the media, through the Internet, and media concentration, through journalism, films, TV, and radio, have affected your life.

Mastering This Chapter

taking sociology with you

1 For one day, categorize every media message you receive in terms of its function: Does it socialize, enforce a social norm, confer status, or promote consumption? Keep a record and tally the results. Which function was the most common? What can you conclude from the results?

2 Pick a specific audience—residents of your dorm, for example—and track their media preferences over the

next day or two. Which mass media are they watching, reading, or listening to? Which media are the most popular and which the least popular? How segmented is this particular mass media audience?

3 Pick a foreign film, television program, or Internet site and study it from the point of view of a sociologist. What does it tell you about the culture that produced it?

key terms

Cultural convergence The flow of content across multiple media, and the accompanying migration of media audiences. (page 145)

Digital divide The relative lack of access to the latest technologies among low-income groups, racial and ethnic minorities, rural residents, and the citizens of developing countries. (153)

Dominant ideology A set of cultural beliefs and practices that helps to maintain powerful social, economic, and political interests. (151)

Gatekeeping The process by which a relatively small number of people in the media industry control what material eventually reaches the audience. (148)

Mass media Print and electronic means of communication that carry messages to widespread audiences. (145)

Narcotizing dysfunction The phenomenon in which the media provide such massive amounts of coverage that the audience becomes numb and fails to act on the information, regardless of how compelling the issue. (148)

Netizen A person who is actively involved in online communities and is committed to the free flow of information, with few outside controls. (149)

Opinion leader Someone who influences the opinions and decisions of others through day-to-day personal contact and communication. (158)

Stereotype An unreliable generalization about all members of a group that does not recognize individual differences within the group. (151)

self-quiz

Read each question carefully and then select the best answer.

1. From the functionalist perspective, the media can be dysfunctional in what way?
   a. They enforce social norms.
   b. They confer status.
   c. They desensitize us to events.
   d. They are agents of socialization.

2. Sociologist Robert Park studied how newspapers helped immigrants to the United States adjust to their environment by changing their customary habits and by teaching them the opinions held by people in their new home country. His study was conducted from which sociological perspective?
   a. the functionalist perspective
   b. the conflict perspective
   c. the interactionist perspective
   d. the dramaturgical perspective

3. There are problems inherent in the socialization function of the mass media. For example, many people worry about
   a. the effect of using the television as a babysitter.
   b. the impact of violent programming on viewer behavior.
   c. the unequal ability of all individuals to purchase televisions.
   d. both a and b.

4. Media advertising has several clear functions, but it also has dysfunctions. Sociologists are concerned that
   a. it creates unrealistic expectations of what is required to be happy.
   b. it creates new consumer needs.
   c. advertisers are able to influence media content.
   d. all of the above.

5. Gatekeeping, the process by which a relatively small number of people control what material reaches an audience, is largely dominant in all but which of the following media?

What do you think (or know) life is like in a high-crime area?

To learn about crime firsthand, sociologist Peter Moskos became a Baltimore police officer.

66 Living in Baltimore City, I was required to carry my gun both on and off duty. I never fired a shot outside of training. Only rarely was my service weapon—a charged semi-automatic nine-millimeter Glock-17 with no safety and a seventeen-round clip—pointed at somebody. But in my police duties, my gun was very routinely removed from its holster, probably every other shift. I did occasionally chase people down alleys and wrestled a few suspects. I maced one person, but did not hit anybody. As a police officer, I tried to speak softly and carry a big stick. The department issued a twenty-nine-inch straight wooden baton just for this purpose. I brought it along to all my calls.

In any account of police work, inevitably the noncriminal public, the routine, and the working folks all get short shrift. Police don't deal with a random cross-section of society, even within the areas they work. And this book reflects that. The ghetto transcends stereotypes. Families try to make it against the odds. Old women sweep the streets. People rise before dawn to go to work. On Sundays, ladies go to church wearing beautiful hats and preachers preach to the choir. But if you're looking for stereotypes, they're there. Between the vacant and abandoned buildings you'll find liquor stores, fast food, Korean corner stores, and a Jewish pawn shop. Living conditions are worse than third-world shanty towns: children in filthy apartments without plumbing or electricity, entire homes put out on eviction day, forty-five-year-old great-grand parents, junkies not raising their kids, drug dealers, and everywhere signs of violence and despair.

As a middle-class white man policing the ghetto, I should address the charge of "exoticism," that I use poor residents for my own advantage. I plead no-contest. If you're not from the ghetto, and though it may not be politically correct to say so, the ghetto *is* exotic. One field-training officer accused me of being "*fascinated* by the ghetto." I am. There are very few aspects of urban life that don't fascinate me. But it is not my intent to sensationalize the ghetto. This is a book about police.

If you want to read about the ghetto, good books are out there. Ghettos are diverse and encompass many cultures and classes. Some object to the very term ghetto. I use the word because it is the vernacular of police officers and many (though by no means all) of the residents. If you really want to learn about the ghetto, go there. There's probably one near you. Visit a church; walk down the street; buy something from the corner store; have a beer; eat. But most importantly, talk to people. That's how you learn. When the subject turns to drugs and crime, you'll hear a common refrain: "It just don't make sense."

Twenty months in Baltimore wasn't very long, but it was long enough to see five police officers killed in the line of duty. And there were other cops, friends of mine, who were hurt, shot, and lucky to live. A year after I quit the force, my friend and academy classmate became the first Baltimore police woman killed in the line of duty, dying in a car crash on the way to back up another police officer. 99

Twenty months in Baltimore wasn't very long, but it was long enough to see five police officers killed in the line of duty.

(Moskos 2008:15–17) Additional information about this excerpt can be found on the Online Learning Center at www.mhhe.com/schaefermod2e.

Peter Moskos's route to becoming a sworn police officer was unusual. None of his friends or relatives were on the force: his father was a sociologist. During his graduate studies, however, Moskos persuaded Baltimore's police commissioner to let him attend the police academy, as both a student and a sociologist. On the second day of class, the commissioner was ousted from office, to be replaced by a new commissioner who questioned Moskos's motives. "Why don't you want to be a cop for real?" he challenged. That was the beginning of Moskos's 20-month tour of duty with the Baltimore Police Department. In this excerpt from his book *Cop in the Hood: My Year Policing Baltimore's Eastern District*, Moskos describes his beat as seen through the eyes of a sociologist, taking sociology with him to the academy, the station house, and the street. Moskos notes that the residents he served could not fathom the crime that plagued their inner-city neighborhood. What does explain it? Although drug dealing, prostitution, and selling stolen goods are illegal, they provide some stability to those who live on the edge. Only a thin line separates their *deviant behavior*—behavior that violates social norms—from their illegal activities.

Crime is functional in their subculture, even if it is socially unacceptable to the rest of the neighborhood.

Another example of a behavior that can be seen as either socially acceptable or socially unacceptable is binge drinking. On the one hand, we can view binge drinking as *deviant,* violating a school's standards of conduct and endangering a person's health. On the other hand, we can see it as *conforming,* or complying with peer culture.

These modules examine the relationship between conformity, deviance, and social control. When does conformity verge on deviance? How does a society control its members? What are the consequences of deviance? We will begin by distinguishing between conformity and obedience and then look at

an experiment on obedience to authority. Next, we will analyze the informal and formal mechanisms societies use to encourage conformity and discourage deviance and focus on theoretical explanations for deviance. The final module focuses on crime, a specific type of deviant behavior subject to official, written norms. We will look at various types of crime found in the United States, the ways crime is measured, and international crime rates, and will consider the controversial topic of the death penalty.

MODULE 23 | Social Control

As we saw in Module 12, each culture, subculture, and group has distinctive norms governing appropriate behavior. Laws, dress codes, organizational bylaws, course requirements, and the rules of sports and games all express social norms.

How does a society bring about acceptance of basic norms? The term **social control** refers to the techniques and strategies for preventing deviant human behavior in any society. Social control occurs on all levels of society. In the family, we are socialized to obey our parents simply because they are our parents. Peer groups introduce us to informal norms, such as dress codes, that govern the behavior of their members. Colleges establish standards they expect of students. In bureaucratic organizations, workers encounter a formal system of rules and regulations. Finally, the government of every society legislates and enforces social norms.

Most of us respect and accept basic social norms and assume that others will do the same. Even without thinking, we obey

the instructions of police officers, follow the day-to-day rules at our jobs, and move to the rear of elevators when people enter. Such behavior reflects an effective process of socialization to the dominant standards of a culture. At the same time, we are well aware that individuals, groups, and institutions *expect* us to act "properly." This expectation carries with it **sanctions,** or penalties and rewards for conduct concerning a social norm. If we fail to live up to the norm, we may face punishment through informal sanctions such as fear and ridicule or formal sanctions such as jail sentences or fines.

The challenge to effective social control is that people often receive competing messages about how to behave. While the state or government may clearly define acceptable behavior, friends or fellow employees may encourage quite different behavior patterns. Historically, legal measures aimed at blocking discrimination based on race, religion, gender, age, and sexual orientation

In Finland (left), a young man relaxes in his prison cell, which resembles a college dorm room. In the United States (right), prisoners at a super-maximum-security prison watch television in cages that prevent them from making physical contact with guards or other prisoners. The rate of imprisonment in Finland is less than one-half that of England and one-fourth that of the United States.

have been difficult to implement, because many people tacitly encourage the violation of such measures.

Functionalists maintain that people must respect social norms if any group or society is to survive. In their view, societies literally could not function if massive numbers of people defied standards of appropriate conduct. In contrast, conflict theorists contend that the successful functioning of a society will consistently benefit the powerful and work to the disadvantage of other groups. They point out that in the United States, widespread resistance to social norms was necessary to win our independence from England, to overturn the institution of slavery, to allow women to vote, to secure civil rights, and to force an end to the war in Vietnam.

■ Conformity and Obedience

Techniques for social control operate on both the group level and the societal level. People we think of as peers or equals influence us to act in particular ways; the same is true of people who hold authority over us or occupy awe-inspiring positions. Social psychologist Stanley Milgram (1975) made a useful distinction between these two levels of social control.

The Milgram Experiment

Milgram used the term **conformity** to mean going along with peers—individuals of our own status who have no special right to direct our behavior. In contrast, **obedience** is compliance with higher authorities in a hierarchical structure. Thus, a recruit entering military service will typically *conform* to the habits and language of other recruits and *obey* the orders of superior officers. Students will *conform* to the drinking behavior of their peers and *obey* the requests of campus security officers.

If ordered to do so, would you comply with an experimenter's instruction to administer increasingly painful electric shocks to a subject? Most people would say no; yet Milgram's research (1963, 1975) suggests that most of us *would* obey such orders. In his words (1975:xi), "Behavior that is unthinkable in an individual . . . acting on his own may be executed without hesitation when carried out under orders."

Milgram placed advertisements in New Haven, Connecticut, newspapers to recruit subjects for a learning experiment at Yale University. Participants included postal clerks, engineers, high school teachers, and laborers. They were told that the purpose of the research was to investigate the effects of punishment on learning. The experimenter, dressed in a gray technician's coat, explained that in each test, one subject would be randomly selected as the "learner," while another would function as the "teacher." However, the experiment was rigged so that the real subject would always be the teacher, while an associate of Milgram's served as the learner.

At this point, the learner's hand was strapped to an electric apparatus. The teacher was taken to an electronic "shock generator" with 30 levered switches labeled from 15 to 450 volts. Before beginning the experiment, all subjects received sample shocks of 45 volts, to convince them of the authenticity of the experiment. The experimenter then instructed the teacher to apply shocks of increasing voltage each time the learner gave an incorrect answer on a memory test. Teachers were told that "although the shocks can be extremely painful, they cause no permanent tissue damage." In reality, the learner did not receive any shocks.

In a prearranged script, the learner deliberately gave incorrect answers and expressed pain when "shocked." For example, at 150 volts, the learner would cry out, "Get me out of here!" At 270 volts, the learner would scream in agony. When the shock reached 350 volts, the learner would fall silent. If the teacher wanted to stop the experiment, the experimenter would insist that the teacher continue, using such statements as "The experiment requires that you continue" and "You have no other choice; you *must* go on" (Milgram 1975:19–23).

Reflecting on the Milgram Experiment

The results of this unusual experiment stunned and dismayed Milgram and other social scientists. A sample of psychiatrists had predicted that virtually all subjects would refuse to shock innocent victims. In their view, only a "pathological fringe" of less than 2 percent would continue administering shocks up to the maximum level. Yet almost *two-thirds* of participants fell into the category of "obedient subjects."

Why did these subjects obey? Why were they willing to inflict seemingly painful shocks on innocent victims who had never done them any harm? There is no evidence that these subjects were unusually sadistic; few seemed to enjoy administering the shocks. Instead, in Milgram's view, the key to obedience was the experimenter's social role as a "scientist" and "seeker of knowledge."

Milgram pointed out that in the modern industrial world, we are accustomed to submitting to impersonal authority figures whose status is indicated by a title (professor, lieutenant, doctor) or by a uniform (the technician's coat). Because we view the authority as larger and more important than the individual, we shift responsibility for our behavior to the authority figure. Milgram's subjects frequently stated, "If it were up to me, I would not have administered shocks." They saw themselves as merely doing their duty (Milgram 1975).

From a conflict perspective, our obedience may be affected by the value we place on those whom our behavior affects. While Milgram's experiment shows that in general, people are willing to obey authority figures, other studies show that they are even more willing to obey if they feel the "victim" is deserving of punishment. Sociologist Gary Schulman (1974) re-created Milgram's experiment and found that White students were significantly more likely to shock Black learners than White learners. By a margin of 70 percent to 48 percent, they imposed more shocks on the Black learners than on the White learners.

From an interactionist perspective, one important aspect of Milgram's findings is the fact that subjects in follow-up studies were less likely to inflict the supposed shocks as they were moved physically closer to their victims. Moreover, interactionists emphasize the effect of *incrementally* administering additional dosages of 15 volts. In effect, the experimenter negotiated with the teacher and convinced the teacher to continue inflicting higher levels of punishment. It is doubtful that anywhere near the two-thirds rate of obedience would have been reached had the experimenter told the teachers to administer 450 volts immediately (B. Allen 1978; Katovich 1987).

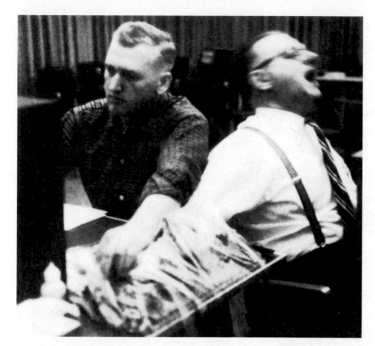

In one of Stanley Milgram's experiments, the learner supposedly received an electric shock from a shock plate when he answered a question incorrectly. At the 150-volt level, the learner would demand to be released and would refuse to place his hand on the shock plate. The experimenter would then order the actual subject, the teacher, to force the hand onto the plate, as shown in the photo. Though 40 percent of the true subjects stopped complying with Milgram at this point, 30 percent did force the learner's hand onto the shock plate, despite his pretended agony.

Milgram launched his experimental study of obedience to better understand the involvement of Germans in the annihilation of 6 million Jews and millions of other people during World War II. In an interview conducted long after the publication of his study, he suggested that "if a system of death camps were set up in the United States of the sort we had seen in Nazi Germany, one would be able to find sufficient personnel for those camps in any medium-sized American town." Though many people questioned his remark, the revealing photos taken at Iraq's Abu Ghraib prison in 2004, showing U.S. military guards humiliating if not torturing Iraqi prisoners, recalled the experiment Milgram had done two generations earlier. Under conducive circumstances, otherwise normal people can and often do treat one another inhumanely (CBS News 1979:7–8; Hayden 2004; Zimbardo 2007a).

How willing would participants in this experiment be to shock learners today? Although many people may be skeptical of the high levels of conformity Milgram found, recent replications of his experiment confirm his findings. In 2006, using additional safeguards to protect participants' welfare, psychologist Jerry Burger (2009) repeated part of Milgram's experiment with college undergraduates. To avoid biasing the participants, Burger was careful to screen out students who had heard of Milgram's study. The results of the replication were startlingly similar to Milgram's: participants showed a high level of willingness to shock the learner, just as the participants in Milgram's experiment had almost half a century earlier. At the most comparable point in the two studies, Burger measured a rate of 70 percent full obedience—lower, but not significantly so, than the rate of 82.5 percent measured two generations earlier.

💡 use your **sociological imagination**

If you were a participant in Milgram's research on conformity, how far do you think you would go in carrying out orders? Do you see any ethical problem with the experimenter's manipulation of the subjects?

⬤ Informal and Formal Social Control

The sanctions that are used to encourage conformity and obedience—and to discourage violation of social norms—are carried out through both informal and formal social control. As the term implies, people use **informal social control** casually to enforce norms. Examples include smiles, laughter, a raised eyebrow, and ridicule.

In the United States and many other cultures, adults often view spanking, slapping, or kicking children as a proper and necessary means of informal social control. Child development

Though formal social control usually involves fines, probation, or incarceration, some judges have used public humiliation as a sanction.

Sociology on Campus

BOX 23-1

Binge Drinking

About 1,700 college students die each year of unintentional alcohol-related injuries. According to a study published by the Harvard School of Public Health, 44 percent of college students indulge in binge drinking (defined as at least five drinks in a row for men and four in a row for women). These numbers represent an increase from 1990s data, despite efforts on many campuses across the nation to educate students about the risks of binge drinking.

The problem is not confined to the United States—Britain, Russia, and South Africa all report regular "drink till you drop" alcoholic consumption among young people. According to a study that compared data from 22 countries, however, college students in the United States have the highest rate of drinking and driving. Nor does binge drinking begin in college. A national study found that over a 30-day period, 29 percent of high school students engaged in binge drinking.

Binge drinking on campus presents a difficult social problem. On the one hand, it can be regarded as *deviant,* violating the standards of conduct expected of those in an academic setting. In fact, Harvard researchers consider binge drinking the most serious public health hazard facing colleges. On the other hand, binge drinking represents *conformity* to the peer culture, especially in fraternities and sororities, which serve as social centers on many campuses. Most students seem to take an "everybody does it—no big deal" attitude toward the behavior.

Some colleges and universities are taking steps to make binge drinking a bit less "normal" by means of *social control*—banning kegs, closing fraternities and sororities, encouraging

liquor retailers not to sell in high volume to students, and expelling students after three alcohol-related infractions. Despite privacy laws, many schools are notifying parents whenever their underage children are caught drinking. Even with these measures, however, curbing underage drinking is a challenge.

Forty-four percent of college students indulge in binge drinking.

LET'S DISCUSS

1. Why do you think most college students regard binge drinking as a normal rather than a deviant behavior?

2. Which do you think would be more effective in stopping binge drinking on your campus, informal or formal social control?

Sources: Bernstein 2007; Centers for Disease Control and Prevention 2010, 2012a; J. Miller et al. 2007; National Center on Addiction and Substance Abuse at Columbia University 2007; Outside the Classroom 2009; Parker-Pope 2012; Wechsler et al. 2002, 2004.

---

specialists counter that such corporal punishment is inappropriate because it teaches children to solve problems through violence. They warn that slapping and spanking can escalate into more serious forms of abuse. Yet, despite a policy statement by the American Academy of Pediatrics that corporal punishment is not effective and can indeed be harmful, 59 percent of pediatricians support the use of corporal punishment, at least in certain situations. Our culture widely accepts this form of informal social control (Chung et al. 2009).

Formal social control is carried out by authorized agents, such as police officers, judges, school administrators, employers, military officers, and managers of movie theaters. It can serve as a last resort when socialization and informal sanctions do not bring about desired behavior. Sometimes, informal social control can actually undermine formal social control, encouraging people to violate social norms. Box 23-1 examines binge drinking among college students, who receive conflicting messages about the acceptability of the behavior from sources of social control.

An increasingly significant means of formal social control in the United States is to imprison people. During the course of a year, over 7 million adults undergo some form of correctional supervision—jail, prison, probation, or parole. Put another way, almost 1 out of every 30 adult Americans is subject to this very formal type of social control every year (Sabol et al. 2009).

In 2007, in the wake of the mass shootings at Virginia Tech, many college officials reviewed security measures on their campuses. Administrators were reluctant to end or even limit the relative freedom of movement students on their campuses enjoyed. Instead, they concentrated on improving emergency communications between campus police and students, faculty, and staff. Reflecting a reliance on technology to maintain social control, college leaders called for replacement of the "old" technology of e-mail with instant alerts that could be sent to people's cell phones via instant messaging.

In the aftermath of September 11, 2001, new measures of social control became the norm in the United States. Some of them, such as stepped-up security and surveillance at airports and high-rise buildings, were highly visible to the public. The federal government has also publicly urged citizens to engage in informal social control by watching for and reporting people whose actions seem suspicious (Monahan 2011).

Many people think this kind of social control goes too far. Civil rights advocates worry that the government's request for information on suspicious activities may encourage negative stereotyping of Muslims and Arab Americans. Clearly, there is a trade-off between the benefits of surveillance and the right to privacy.

● Law and Society

Some norms are so important to a society that they are formalized into laws regarding people's behavior. **Law** may be defined as governmental social control (Black 1995). Some laws, such as the prohibition against murder, are directed at all members of society. Others, such as fishing and hunting regulations, affect particular categories of people. Still others govern the behavior of social institutions (for instance, corporate law and laws regarding the taxing of nonprofit enterprises).

Sociologists see the creation of laws as a social process. Because laws are passed in response to a perceived need for formal social control, sociologists have sought to explain how and why such a perception arises. In their view, law is not merely a static body of rules handed down from generation to generation. Rather, it reflects continually changing standards of what is right and wrong, of how violations are to be determined, and of what sanctions are to be applied (Schur 1968).

Sociologists representing varying theoretical perspectives agree that the legal order reflects the values of those in a position to exercise authority. Therefore, the creation of civil and criminal law can be a most controversial matter. Should it be against the law to employ illegal immigrants, to have an abortion (see Module 35), to allow prayer in public schools, or to smoke on an airplane? Such issues have been bitterly debated, because they require a choice among competing values. Not surprisingly, laws that are unpopular—such as the one-time prohibition of alcohol under the Eighteenth Amendment and the widespread establishment of a 55-mile-per-hour speed limit on highways—become difficult to enforce when there is no consensus supporting the norms.

One current and controversial debate over laws governing behavior is whether people should be allowed to use marijuana legally, for medical purposes. Although the majority of adults polled in national surveys support such a use, the federal government continues to regard all uses of marijuana as illegal. In 2005 the Supreme Court upheld the federal government's position. Nevertheless, 15 states and the District of Columbia have granted citizens the right to use marijuana for medical purposes—even if that privilege rests on dubious legal grounds (Figure 23-1).

Socialization is the primary source of conforming and obedient behavior, including obedience to law. Generally, it is not

In Singapore, a custodian removes a bit of litter from an otherwise spotless floor. Strict social controls prevail in the city-state, where the careless disposal of a cigarette butt or candy wrapper carries a $200 fine.

external pressure from a peer group or authority figure that makes us go along with social norms. Rather, we have internalized such norms as valid and desirable and are committed to observing them. In a profound sense, we want to see ourselves (and to be seen) as loyal, cooperative, responsible, and respectful of others. In the United States and other societies around the world, people are socialized both to want to belong and to fear being viewed as different or deviant.

Control theory suggests that our connection to members of society leads us to systematically conform to society's norms. According to sociologist Travis Hirschi and other control theorists, our bonds to family members, friends, and peers induce us

trend|spotting

Incarceration Nation

Since 1980, through prosperity and recession, war and peace, the United States has been sending more and more people to prison. Today, about 1.6 million people reside in federal or state institutions. That number is higher than the population of the fifth largest U.S. city, Phoenix.

Both the number of prisoners and the rate of incarceration have grown steadily. From 1980 through the end of 2010, the prison population increased from just over 1 in 1,000 to 1 in 231. If only adults are counted, the current proportion is 1 in every 33. The trend becomes even more disturbing when we consider the growing reliance on early-release programs. If cash-strapped states were not using electronic monitoring devices, like ankle bracelets, to lower their prison populations, the statistics would be even more dismal.

Internationally, the United States' incarceration rate stands out as one of the highest in the world—more than three times as high as that of Mexico or Canada. Even China with its huge population does not have as many people behind bars as the United States.

FIGURE 23-1 **The Status of Medical Marijuana**

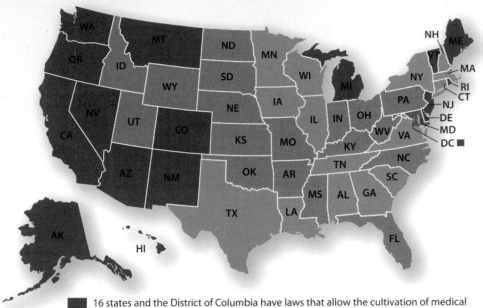

16 states and the District of Columbia have laws that allow the cultivation of medical marijuana and that protect patients who possess medical marijuana (with their doctors' recommendations or certifications) from criminal penalties.

Maryland protects medical marijuana patients from jail, but not from the threat of arrest.

15 states have laws that recognize marijuana's medical value, but these laws are ineffective because they rely on federal cooperation.

18 states have no provisions for medical marijuana.

to follow the mores and folkways of our society. We give little conscious thought to whether we will be sanctioned if we fail to conform. Socialization develops our self-control so well that we don't need further pressure to obey social norms. Although control theory does not effectively explain the rationale for every conforming act, it nevertheless reminds us that while the media may focus on crime and disorder, most members of most societies conform to and obey basic norms (Brewis et al. 2011; Gottfredson and Hirschi 1990; Hirschi 1969).

Source: NORML 2012.
The actions some states have taken to legalize marijuana are largely symbolic. Federal law still prohibits doctors from writing prescriptions for marijuana, and pharmacies from distributing the substance. Although patients can still be prosecuted by the federal government for possessing or using marijuana, the Obama administration has decided not to prosecute medical marijuana users who comply with state laws.

MODULE 23 | Recap and Review

Summary

This module examines the relationship between conformity and mechanisms of **social control.**

1. A society uses **social control** to encourage the acceptance of basic norms.

2. Stanley Milgram defined **conformity** as going along with one's peers; **obedience** is compliance with higher authorities in a hierarchical structure.

3. Some norms are so important to a society that they are formalized into **laws.** Socialization is a primary source of conforming and obedient behavior, including obedience to laws.

Thinking Critically

1. Think about a job you once held. How did your employer exercise social control over the employees?

How did you, as an employee, use social control in relating to those around you?

2. Should some illegal drugs be decriminalized? Why or why not?

Key Terms

Conformity 170

Control theory 173

Formal social control 172

Informal social control 171

Law 173

Obedience 170

Sanction 169

Social control 169

For sociologists, the term *deviance* does not mean perversion or depravity. **Deviance** is behavior that violates the standards of conduct or expectations of a group or society. In the United States, alcoholics, compulsive gamblers, and the mentally ill would all be classified as deviants. Being late for class is categorized as a deviant act; the same is true of wearing jeans to a formal wedding. On the basis of the sociological definition, we are all deviant from time to time. Each of us violates common social norms in certain situations (Best 2004).

Is being overweight an example of deviance? In the United States and many other cultures, unrealistic standards of appearance and body image place a huge strain on people—especially women and girls—based on how they look. Journalist Naomi Wolf (1992) has used the term *beauty myth* to refer to an exaggerated ideal of beauty, beyond the reach of all but a few females, which has unfortunate consequences. In order to shed their "deviant" image and conform to unrealistic societal norms, many women and girls become consumed with adjusting their appearances. Yet what is deviant in one culture may be celebrated in another.

Deviance involves the violation of group norms, which may or may not be formalized into law. It is a comprehensive concept that includes not only criminal behavior but also many actions that are not subject to prosecution. The public official who takes a bribe has defied social norms, but so has the high school student who refuses to sit in an assigned seat or cuts class. Of course, deviation from norms is not always negative, let alone criminal. A member of an exclusive social club who speaks out against a traditional policy of not admitting women, Blacks, and Jews is deviating from the club's norms. So is a police officer who blows the whistle on corruption or brutality within the department.

From a sociological perspective, deviance is hardly objective or set in stone. Rather, it is subject to social definition within a particular society and at a particular time. For that reason, what is considered deviant can shift from one social era to another. In most instances, those individuals and groups with the greatest status and power define what is acceptable and what is deviant. For example, despite serious medical warnings against the dangers of tobacco, made since 1964, cigarette smoking continued to be accepted for decades—in good part because of the power of tobacco farmers and cigarette manufacturers. Only after a long campaign led by public health and anticancer activists did cigarette smoking become more of a deviant activity. Today, many state and local laws limit where people can smoke.

Deviance and Social Stigma

A person can acquire a deviant identity in many ways. Because of physical or behavioral characteristics, some people are unwillingly cast in negative social roles. Once assigned a deviant role, they have trouble presenting a positive image to others and may even experience lowered self-esteem. Whole groups of people—for instance, "short people" or "redheads"—may be labeled in this way. The interactionist Erving Goffman coined the term **stigma** to describe the labels society uses to devalue members of certain social groups (Goffman 1963; Heckert and Best 1997).

Prevailing expectations about beauty and body shape may prevent people who are regarded as ugly or obese from advancing as rapidly as their abilities permit. Both overweight and anorexic people are assumed to be weak in character, slaves to their appetites or to media images. Because they do not conform to the beauty myth, they may be viewed as "disfigured" or "strange" in appearance, bearers of what Goffman calls a "spoiled identity." However, what constitutes disfigurement is a matter of interpretation. Of the 17 million cosmetic procedures done every year in the United States alone, many are performed on women who

In 2009, baseball fans were shocked by the revelation that, like several other baseball greats, superstar Alex Rodriguez had used banned substances and lied about it.

Think about It

If your friends or teammates violate a social norm, is their behavior deviant?

Deviant or normal? Television personality and recording artist Heidi Montag shocked fans in 2010 by revealing that she had undergone 10 plastic surgery procedures in a single day. Montag had already undergone breast augmentation, collagen lip injections, and rhinoplasty. Would you consider her behavior deviant?

Deviance and Technology

Technological innovations such as pagers and voice mail can redefine social interactions and the standards of behavior related to them. When the Internet was first made available to the general public, no norms or regulations governed its use. Because online communication offers a high degree of anonymity, uncivil behavior—speaking harshly of others or monopolizing chat room space—quickly became common. Online bulletin boards designed to carry items of community interest became littered with commercial advertisements. Such deviant acts are beginning to provoke calls for the establishment of formal rules for online behavior. For example, policymakers have debated whether to regulate the content of websites featuring hate speech and pornography.

Some deviant uses of technology are criminal, though not all participants see it that way. On the street, the for-profit pirating of software, motion pictures, and music has become a big business. On the Internet, the downloading of music by individual listeners, which is typically forbidden by copyright, is widely accepted. The music and motion picture industries have waged much publicized campaigns to stop these illegal uses of their products, yet among many people, no social stigma attaches to them. Deviance, then, is a complex concept. Sometimes it is trivial, sometimes profoundly harmful. Sometimes it is accepted by society and sometimes soundly rejected.

Sociological Perspectives on Deviance

Why do people violate social norms? We have seen that deviant acts are subject to both informal and formal social control. The nonconforming or disobedient person may face disapproval, loss of friends, fines, or even imprisonment. Why, then, does deviance occur?

Early explanations for behavior that deviated from societal expectations blamed supernatural causes or genetic factors (such as "bad blood" or evolutionary throwbacks to primitive ancestors). By the 1800s, substantial research efforts were being made to identify biological factors that lead to deviance, and especially to criminal activity. Though such research was discredited in the 20th century, contemporary studies, primarily by biochemists, have sought to isolate genetic factors that suggest a likelihood of certain personality traits. Although criminality (much less deviance) is hardly a personality characteristic, researchers have focused on traits that might lead to crime, such as aggression. Of course, aggression can also lead to success in the corporate world, in professional sports, or in other walks of life.

The contemporary study of the possible biological roots of criminality is but one aspect of the larger debate over sociobiology. In general, sociologists reject any emphasis on the genetic roots of crime and deviance. The limitations of current knowledge, the possibility of reinforcing racist and sexist assumptions, and the disturbing implications for the rehabilitation of criminals have led sociologists to draw largely on other approaches to explain deviance (Sagarin and Sanchez 1988).

would be defined objectively as having a normal appearance. And while feminist sociologists have accurately noted that the beauty myth makes many women feel uncomfortable with themselves, men too lack confidence in their appearance. The number of males who choose to undergo cosmetic procedures has risen sharply in recent years (American Academy of Cosmetic Surgery 2010).

Often people are stigmatized for deviant behaviors they may no longer engage in. The labels "compulsive gambler," "ex-convict," "recovering alcoholic," and "ex–mental patient" can stick to a person for life. Goffman draws a useful distinction between a prestige symbol that draws attention to a positive aspect of one's identity, such as a wedding band or a badge, and a stigma symbol that discredits or debases one's identity, such as a conviction for child molestation. While stigma symbols may not always be obvious, they can become a matter of public knowledge. Starting in 1994, many states required convicted sex offenders to register with local police departments. Some communities publish the names and addresses, and in some instances even the pictures, of convicted sex offenders on the web.

While some types of deviance will stigmatize a person, other types do not carry a significant penalty. Examples of socially tolerated forms of deviance can be found in the world of high technology.

Functionalist Perspective

According to functionalists, deviance is a common part of human existence, with positive as well as negative consequences for social stability. Deviance helps to define the limits of proper behavior. Children who see one parent scold the other for belching at the dinner table learn about approved conduct. The same is true of the driver who receives a speeding ticket, the department store cashier who is fired for yelling at a customer, and the college student who is penalized for handing in papers weeks overdue.

Durkheim's Legacy Émile Durkheim ([1895] 1964) focused his sociological investigations mainly on criminal acts, yet his conclusions have implications for all types of deviant behavior. In Durkheim's view, the punishments established within a culture (including both formal and informal mechanisms of social control) help to define acceptable behavior and thus contribute to stability. If improper acts were not sanctioned, people might stretch their standards of what constitutes appropriate conduct.

Sociologist Kai Erikson (1966) illustrated the boundary-maintenance function of deviance in his study of the Puritans of 17th-century New England. By today's standards, the Puritans placed tremendous emphasis on conventional morals. Their persecution and execution of women as witches represented a continuing attempt to define and redefine the boundaries of their community. In effect, their changing social norms created crime waves, as people whose behavior was previously acceptable suddenly faced punishment for being deviant (R. Schaefer and Zellner 2011).

Durkheim ([1897] 1951) introduced the term **anomie** into sociological literature to describe the loss of direction felt in a society when social control of individual behavior has become ineffective. Anomie is a state of normlessness that typically occurs during a period of profound social change and disorder, such as a time of economic collapse. People become more aggressive or depressed, which results in higher rates of violent crime and suicide. Since there is much less agreement on what constitutes proper behavior during times of revolution, sudden prosperity, or economic depression, conformity and obedience become less significant as social forces. It also becomes much more difficult to state exactly what constitutes deviance.

Merton's Theory of Deviance What do a mugger and a teacher have in common? Each is "working" to obtain money that can then be exchanged for desired goods. As this example illustrates, behavior that violates accepted norms (such as mugging) may be based on the same basic objectives as the behavior of people who pursue more conventional lifestyles.

On the basis of this kind of analysis, sociologist Robert Merton (1968) adapted Durkheim's notion of anomie to explain why people accept or reject the goals of a society, the socially approved means of fulfilling their aspirations, or both. Merton maintained that one important cultural goal in the United States is success, measured largely in terms of money. In addition to providing this goal for people, our society offers specific instructions on how to pursue success—go to school, work hard, do not quit, take advantage of opportunities, and so forth.

What happens to individuals in a society with a heavy emphasis on wealth as a basic symbol of success? Merton reasoned that people adapt in certain ways, either by conforming to or by deviating from such cultural expectations. His **anomie theory of deviance** posits five basic forms of adaptation (Table 24-1).

Conformity to social norms, the most common adaptation in Merton's typology, is the opposite of deviance. It involves acceptance of both the overall societal goal ("become affluent") and the approved means ("work hard"). In Merton's view, there must be some consensus regarding accepted cultural goals and the legitimate means for attaining them. Without such a consensus, societies could exist only as collectives of people rather than as unified cultures, and might experience continual chaos.

The other four types of behavior represented in Table 24-1 all involve some departure from conformity. The "innovator" accepts the goals of society but pursues them with means that are regarded as improper. For instance, a safecracker may steal money to buy consumer goods and expensive vacations.

In Merton's typology, the "ritualist" has abandoned the goal of material success and become compulsively committed to the institutional means. Work becomes simply a way of life rather than a means to the goal of success. An example would be the bureaucratic official who blindly applies rules and regulations without remembering the larger goals of the organization. Certainly that would be true of a welfare caseworker who refuses to assist a homeless family because their last apartment was in another district.

The "retreatist," as described by Merton, has basically retreated (or withdrawn) from both the goals and the means of society. In the United States, drug addicts and vagrants are typically portrayed as retreatists. Concern has been growing that adolescents who are addicted to alcohol will become retreatists at an early age.

The final adaptation identified by Merton reflects people's attempts to create a *new* social structure. The "rebel" feels alienated from the dominant means and goals and may seek a dramatically different social order. Members of a revolutionary political organization, such as a militia group, can be categorized as rebels according to Merton's model.

Table **24-1** Modes of Individual Adaptation

Mode	Institutionalized Means (hard work)	Societal Goal (acquisition of wealth)
Nondeviant	Accept	Accept
Conformity		
Deviant		
Innovation	Reject	Accept
Ritualism	Accept	Reject
Retreatism	Reject	Reject
Rebellion	Replace with new means	Replace with new goals

Source: Adapted from Merton 1968:194.

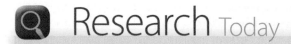
Does Crime Pay?

A driver violates the speed limit to get to a job interview on time. A financially strapped parent shoplifts goods that her family needs. These people may feel justified in violating the law because they do so to meet a reasonable objective. In Robert Merton's terms, they are *innovators*— people who violate social norms to achieve a commonly shared societal goal. Although their actions are criminal and potentially hurtful to others, from their own short-term perspective, their actions are functional.

Carried to its logical conclusion, innovation can and does become a career for some people. Yet from a purely economic point of view, even considering the fact that crime may pay is controversial, because doing so may seem to tolerate or encourage rule violation. Nothing is more controversial than the suggestion that gang-run drug deals are profitable and produce "good jobs." Although some people may see drug dealers as a cross between MBA-educated professionals and streetwise entrepreneurs, society in general does not admire these innovators.

Sociologist Sudhir Venkatesh collected detailed data on the illegal drug trade during his observation research on a Chicago street gang. Working with economist Steven Levitt,

coauthor of the best seller *Freakonomics,* to analyze the business of selling crack cocaine, he found that less than 5 percent of even the gang leaders earned $100,000 per year. The rest of the leaders and virtually all the rank and file earned less than the minimum wage. In fact, most were unpaid workers seeking to move up in the gang hierarchy. (Thus the title of a chapter in Levitt's book, "Why Do Drug Dealers Still Live with Their Moms?") As Levitt notes, the drug gang is like most corporations: the top 2 percent of workers take home most of the money.

Why, from a sociological *and* an economic perspective, do these nonprofitable practices persist, especially considering that one in every four members of drug-oriented

> Less than 5 percent of even the gang leaders earned $100,000 per year. The rest of the leaders and virtually all the rank and file earned less than the minimum wage.

street gangs is eventually killed? One reason, of course, is the public's almost insatiable demand for illegal drugs. And from the drug peddler's perspective, few legitimate jobs are available to young adults in poverty-stricken areas, urban or rural. Functionally, these youths are contributing to their household incomes by dealing drugs.

Scholars see a need for further research on Merton's concept of innovation. Why, for example, do some disadvantaged groups have lower rates of reported crime than others? Why do many people who are caught in adverse circumstances reject criminal activity as a viable alternative? Merton's theory of deviance does not easily answer such questions.

LET'S DISCUSS

1. Do you know anyone who has stolen out of need? If so, did the person feel justified in stealing, or did he or she feel guilty? How long did the theft continue?

2. Economically, profit is the difference between revenues and costs. What are the costs of the illegal drug trade, both economic and social? Is this economic activity profitable for society?

Sources: Clinard and Miller 1998; Kingsbury 2008; S. Levitt and Dubner 2006; S. Levitt and Venkatesh 2000; Rosen and Venkatesh 2008; Venkatesh 2008.

Merton made a key contribution to the sociological understanding of deviance by pointing out that deviants such as innovators and ritualists share a great deal with conforming people. The convicted felon may hold many of the same aspirations as people with no criminal background. The theory helps us to understand deviance as a socially created behavior rather than as the result of momentary pathological impulses. However, this theory of deviance has not been applied systematically to real-world crime. Box 24-1 examines scholars' efforts to confirm the theory's validity.

Interactionist Perspective

The functionalist approach to deviance explains why rule violations continue to happen despite pressure to conform and obey. However, functionalists do not indicate how a given person comes to commit a deviant act or why on some occasions crimes do or do not occur. The emphasis on everyday behavior that is the focus of the interactionist perspective offers two explanations of crime: cultural transmission and routine activities theory.

Cultural Transmission In the course of studying graffiti writing by gangs in Los Angeles, sociologist Susan A. Phillips (1999) discovered that the writers learned from one another. In

fact, Phillips was surprised by how stable their focus was over time. She also noted how other ethnic groups built on the models of the African American and Chicano gangs, superimposing Cambodian, Chinese, or Vietnamese symbols.

Humans *learn* how to behave in social situations, whether properly or improperly. There is no natural, innate manner in which people interact with one another. These simple ideas are not disputed today, but such was not the case when sociologist Edwin Sutherland (1883–1950) first advanced the idea that an individual undergoes the same basic socialization process in learning conforming and deviant acts.

Sutherland's ideas have been the dominating force in criminology. He drew on the **cultural transmission** school, which emphasizes that one learns criminal behavior by interacting with others. Such learning includes not only the techniques of lawbreaking (for example, how to break into a car quickly and quietly) but also the motives, drives, and rationalizations of the criminal. The cultural transmission approach can also be used to explain the behavior of those who habitually abuse alcohol or drugs.

Sutherland maintained that through interactions with a primary group and significant others, people acquire definitions of proper and improper behavior. He used the term differential association to describe the process through which exposure to attitudes *favorable* to criminal acts leads to the violation of rules. Research suggests that this view of differential association also applies to noncriminal deviant acts, such as smoking, truancy, and early sexual behavior.

Sutherland offers the example of a boy who is sociable, outgoing, and athletic and who lives in an area with a high rate of delinquency. The youth is very likely to come into contact with peers who commit acts of vandalism, fail to attend school, and so forth, and may come to adopt such behavior. However, an introverted boy who lives in the same neighborhood may stay away from his peers and avoid delinquency. In another community, an outgoing and athletic boy may join a Little League baseball team or a scout troop because of his interactions with peers. Thus, Sutherland views improper behavior as the result of the types of groups to which one belongs and the kinds of friendships one has.

According to critics, the cultural transmission approach may explain the deviant behavior of juvenile delinquents or graffiti artists, but it fails to explain the conduct of the first-time impulsive shoplifter or the impoverished person who steals out of necessity. While it is not a precise statement of the process through which one becomes a criminal, differential association theory does direct our attention to the paramount role of social interaction in increasing a person's motivation to engage in deviant behavior (Harding 2009; Sutherland et al. 1992).

Social Disorganization Theory

The social relationships that exist in a community or neighborhood affect people's behavior. Philip Zimbardo (2007a:24–25), author of the mock prison experiment described in Chapter 5, once did an experiment that demonstrated the power of communal relationships. He abandoned a car in each of two different neighborhoods, leaving its hood up and removing its hub caps. In one neighborhood, people started to strip the car for parts before Zimbardo had finished setting up a remote video camera to record their behavior. In the other neighborhood, weeks passed without the car being touched, except for a pedestrian who stopped to close the hood during a rainstorm.

Under cover of darkness, drag racers await the start signal on a deserted Los Angeles street. Sutherland's concepts of differential association and cultural transmission would both apply to the practice of drag racing on city streets.

What accounts for the strikingly different outcomes of Zimbardo's experiment in the two communities? According to **social disorganization theory,** increases in crime and deviance can be attributed to the absence or breakdown of communal relationships and social institutions, such as the family, school, church, and local government. This theory was developed at the University of Chicago in the early 1900s to describe the apparent disorganization that occurred as cities expanded with rapid immigration and migration from rural areas. Using the latest survey techniques, Clifford Shaw and Henry McKay literally mapped the distribution of social problems in Chicago. They found high rates of social problems in neighborhoods where buildings had deteriorated and the population had declined. Interestingly, the patterns persisted over time, despite changes in the neighborhoods' ethnic and racial composition.

This theory is not without its critics. To some, social disorganization theory seems to "blame the victim," leaving larger societal forces, such as the lack of jobs or high-quality schools, unaccountable. Critics also argue that even troubled neighborhoods have viable, healthy organizations, which persist despite the problems that surround them.

More recently, social disorganization theorists have taken to emphasizing the effect of social networks on communal bonds. These researchers acknowledge that communities are not isolated islands. Residents' bonds may be enhanced or weakened by their ties to groups outside the immediate community (Jensen 2005; Sampson and Graves 1989; Shaw and McKay 1942).

Labeling Perspective

The Saints and the Roughnecks were groups of high school males who were continually engaged in excessive drinking, reckless driving, truancy, petty theft, and vandalism. There the similarity ended. None of the Saints was ever arrested, but every Roughneck was frequently in trouble with police and townspeople. Why the disparity in their treatment? On the basis of observation research in their high school, sociologist William Chambliss (1973) concluded that social class played an important role in the varying fortunes of the two groups.

The Saints hid behind a facade of respectability. They came from "good families," were active in school organizations, planned on attending college, and received good grades. People generally viewed their delinquent acts as a few isolated cases of sowing wild oats. The Roughnecks had no such aura of respectability. They drove around town in beat-up cars, were generally unsuccessful in school, and aroused suspicion no matter what they did.

We can understand such discrepancies by using an approach to deviance known as **labeling theory.** Unlike Sutherland's work, labeling theory does not focus on why some individuals come to commit deviant acts. Instead, it attempts to explain why certain people (such as the Roughnecks) are *viewed* as deviants, delinquents, bad kids, losers, and criminals, whereas others whose behavior is similar (such as the Saints) are not seen in such harsh terms. Reflecting the contribution of interactionist theorists, labeling theory emphasizes how a person comes to be labeled as deviant or to accept that label. Sociologist Howard Becker (1963:9; 1964), who popularized this approach, summed it up with this statement: "Deviant behavior is behavior that people so label."

Labeling theory is also called the **societal-reaction approach,** reminding us that it is the *response* to an act, not the behavior itself, that determines deviance. For example, studies have shown that some school personnel and therapists expand educational programs designed for learning-disabled students to include those with behavioral problems. Consequently, a "troublemaker" can be improperly labeled as "learning-disabled," and vice versa (Grattet 2011).

Labeling and Agents of Social Control   Traditionally, research on deviance has focused on people who violate social norms. In contrast, labeling theory focuses on police, probation officers, psychiatrists, judges, teachers, employers, school officials, and other regulators of social control. These agents, it is argued, play a significant role in creating the deviant identity by designating certain people (and not others) as deviant. An important aspect of labeling theory is the recognition that some individuals or groups have the power to *define* labels and *apply* them to others. This view ties into the conflict perspective's emphasis on the social significance of power.

In recent years the practice of *racial profiling,* in which people are identified as criminal suspects purely on the basis of their race, has come under public scrutiny. Studies confirm the public's suspicions that in some jurisdictions, police officers are much more likely to stop Black males than White males for routine traffic violations, in the expectation of finding drugs or guns in their cars. Civil rights activists refer to these cases sarcastically as DWB (Driving While Black) violations. Beginning in 2001, profiling took a new turn as people who appeared to be Arab or Muslim came under special scrutiny. (Racial profiling will be examined in more detail in Chapter 10).

The popularity of labeling theory is reflected in the emergence of a related perspective, called social constructionism. According to the **social constructionist perspective,** deviance is the product of the culture we live in. Social constructionists focus specifically on the decision-making process that creates the deviant identity. They point out that "child abductors," "deadbeat dads," "spree killers," and "date rapists" have always been with us, but at times have become *the* major social concern of policymakers because of intensive media coverage (Liska and Messner 1999; E. R. Wright et al. 2000).

How do certain behaviors come to be viewed as a problem? Cigarette smoking, which was once regarded as a polite, gentlemanly activity, is now considered a serious health hazard, not only to the smoker but also to others nearby who don't smoke. Recently, people have become concerned about the danger, especially to children, posed by *thirdhand smoke*—smoke-related chemicals that cling to clothes and linger in rooms, cars, even elevators (Winickoff et al. 2009).

 use your **sociological imagination**

You are a teacher. What labels, freely used in education, might you attach to your students?

Conflict Perspective

Conflict theorists point out that people with power protect their interests and define deviance to suit their needs. Sociologist Richard Quinney (1974, 1979, 1980) was a leading exponent of the view that the criminal justice system serves the interests of the powerful. Crime, according to Quinney (1970), is a definition of conduct created by authorized agents of social control—such as legislators and law enforcement officers—in a politically organized society. He and other conflict theorists argue that lawmaking is often an attempt by the powerful to coerce others into their morality (see also Spitzer 1975).

This theory helps to explain why our society has laws against gambling, drug use, and prostitution, many of which are violated on a massive scale. (We will examine these "victimless crimes" later in the chapter.) According to conflict theorists, criminal law does not represent a consistent application of societal values, but instead reflects competing values and interests. Thus, the U.S. criminal code outlaws marijuana because of its alleged harm to users, yet cigarettes and alcohol—both of which can be harmful to users—are sold legally almost everywhere.

In the 1930s, the Federal Bureau of Narcotics launched a campaign to portray marijuana as a dangerous drug rather than a pleasure-inducing substance. From a conflict perspective, those in power often use such tactics to coerce others into adopting a different point of view.

Table **24-2**   **Sociological Perspectives on Deviance**

Tracking Sociological Perspectives

Approach	Theoretical Perspective	Proponents	Emphasis
Anomie	Functionalist	Émile Durkheim Robert Merton	Adaptation to societal norms
Cultural transmission/ Differential association	Interactionist	Edwin Sutherland	Patterns learned through others
Social disorganization	Interactionist	Clifford Shaw Henry McKay	Communal relationships
Labeling/Social constructionist	Interactionist	Howard Becker	Societal response to acts
Conflict	Conflict	Richard Quinney	Dominance by authorized agents Discretionary justice
Feminist	Conflict/Feminist	Freda Adler Meda Chesney-Lind	Role of gender Women as victims and perpetrators

In fact, conflict theorists contend that the entire criminal justice system in the United States treats suspects differently based on their racial, ethnic, or social-class background. In many cases, officials in the system use their own discretion to make biased decisions about whether to press charges or drop them, whether to set bail and how much, whether to offer parole or deny it. Researchers have found that this kind of **differential justice**—differences in the way social control is exercised over different groups—puts African Americans and Latinos at a disadvantage in the justice system, both as juveniles and as adults. On average, White offenders receive shorter sentences than comparable Latino and African American offenders, even when prior arrest records and the relative severity of the crime are taken into consideration (Brewer and Heitzeg 2008; Sandefur 2008; Schlesinger 2011).

The perspective advanced by conflict and labeling theorists forms quite a contrast to the functionalist approach to deviance. Functionalists see standards of deviant behavior as merely reflecting cultural norms; conflict and labeling theorists point out that the most powerful groups in a society can shape laws and standards and determine who is (or is not) prosecuted as a criminal. These groups would be unlikely to apply the label "deviant" to the corporate executive whose decisions lead to large-scale environmental pollution. In the opinion of conflict theorists, agents of social control and other powerful groups can impose their own self-serving definitions of deviance on the general public.

Feminist Perspective

Feminist criminologists such as Freda Adler and Meda Chesney-Lind have suggested that many of the existing approaches to deviance and crime were developed with only men in mind. For example, in the United States, for many years any husband who forced his wife to have sexual intercourse—without her consent and against her will—was not legally considered to have committed rape. The law defined rape as pertaining only to sexual relations between people who were not married to each other, reflecting the overwhelmingly male composition of state legislatures at the time.

It took repeated protests by feminist organizations to get changes in the criminal law defining rape. Beginning in 1993, husbands in all 50 states could be prosecuted under most circumstances for the rape of their wives. There remain alarming exceptions in no fewer than 30 states, however. For example, the husband is exempt when he does not need to use force because his wife is asleep, unconscious, or mentally or physically impaired. These interpretations still rest on the notion that the marriage contract entitles a husband to sex (Bergen 2006).

In the future, feminist scholarship can be expected to grow dramatically. Particularly on topics such as white-collar crime, drinking behavior, drug abuse, and differential sentencing rates between the genders, as well as on the fundamental question of how to define deviance, feminist scholars will have much to say.

We have seen that over the past century, sociologists have taken many different approaches in studying deviance, arousing some controversy in the process. Table 24-2 summarizes the various theoretical approaches to this topic.

MODULE 24 | Recap and Review

Summary

Deviant behavior is behavior that violates social norms. A very wide range of behavior may be classified as deviant, and everyone violates social norms in some situations.

1. Some forms of **deviance** carry a negative social **stigma,** while other forms are more or less accepted.

2. From a functionalist point of view, deviance and its consequences help to define the limits of proper behavior.

3. Some interactionists maintain that people learn criminal behavior by interacting with others (**cultural transmission**). To them, deviance results from exposure to attitudes that are favorable to criminal acts (**differential association**).

4. Other interactionists attribute increases in crime and deviance to the absence or breakdown of communal relationships and social institutions, such as the family, school, church, and local government (**social disorganization theory**).

5. An important aspect of **labeling theory** is the recognition that some people are viewed as deviant, while others who engage in the same behavior are not.

6. From the conflict perspective, laws and punishments are a reflection of the interests of the powerful.

7. The feminist perspective emphasizes cultural attitudes and differential economic relationships to help explain gender differences in deviance and crime.

Thinking Critically

1. Do some research on a culture you are unfamiliar with. Do any of the customs seem deviant to you? Which of your own customs might seem deviant to members of that culture?

2. Using examples drawn from work or college life, illustrate each of Merton's five modes of individual adaptation.

3. Explain the presence of both criminals and law-abiding citizens in an inner-city neighborhood in terms of the interactionist perspective.

Key Terms

Anomie   177

Anomie theory of deviance   177

Cultural transmission   178

Deviance   175

Differential association   179

Differential justice   181

Labeling theory   179

Social constructionist perspective   180

Social disorganization theory   179

Societal-reaction approach   180

Stigma   175

MODULE 25   Crime

Crime is on everyone's mind. Until recently, college campuses were viewed as havens from crime. But as Box 25-1 on page 183 shows, at today's colleges and universities, crime goes well beyond cheating and senior class pranks.

Crime is a violation of criminal law for which some governmental authority applies formal penalties. It represents a deviation from formal social norms administered by the state. Laws divide crimes into various categories, depending on the severity of the offense, the age of the offender, the potential punishment, and the court that holds jurisdiction over the case.

● Types of Crime

Rather than relying solely on legal categories, sociologists classify crimes in terms of how they are committed and how society views the offenses. In this section we will examine six types of crime differentiated by sociologists: victimless crimes, professional crime, organized crime, white-collar and technology-based crime, hate crimes, and transnational crime.

Victimless Crimes

When we think of crime, we tend to think of acts that endanger people's economic or personal well-being against their will (or without their direct knowledge). In contrast, sociologists use the term **victimless crime** to describe the willing exchange among adults of widely desired but illegal goods and services, such as prostitution (Schur 1965, 1985).

Some activists are working to decriminalize many of these illegal practices. Supporters of decriminalization are troubled by the attempt to legislate a moral code for adults. In their view, prostitution, drug abuse, gambling, and other victimless crimes are impossible to prevent. The already overburdened criminal justice system should instead devote its resources to street crimes and other offenses with obvious victims.

Despite widespread use of the term *victimless crime*, however, many people object to the notion that there is no victim other than the offender in such crimes. Excessive drinking, compulsive gambling, and illegal drug use contribute to an enormous amount of personal and property damage. A person with a drinking problem may become abusive to a spouse or children; a compulsive gambler or drug user may steal to pursue his or her obsession. And feminist sociologists contend that prostitution, as well as the more disturbing aspects of pornography, reinforce the misconception that women are "toys" who can be treated as objects rather than people. According to critics of decriminalization, society must not give tacit approval to conduct that has such harmful consequences (Melissa Farley and Malarek 2008).

The controversy over decriminalization reminds us of the important insights of labeling and conflict theorists presented

earlier. Underlying this debate are two questions: Who has the power to label gambling, prostitution, and public drunkenness as "crimes"? and Who has the power to label such behaviors as "victimless"? The answer is generally the state legislatures, and in some cases, the police and the courts.

Professional Crime

Although the adage "Crime doesn't pay" is familiar, many people do make a career of illegal activities. A **professional criminal,** or *career criminal,* is a person who pursues crime as a day-to-day occupation, developing skilled techniques and enjoying a certain degree of status among other criminals. Some professional criminals specialize in burglary, safecracking, hijacking of cargo, pickpocketing, and shoplifting. Such people have acquired skills that reduce the likelihood of arrest, conviction,

Sociology on Campus

BOX 25-1

Campus Crime

According to a national survey released in 2008, 72 percent of college students consider campus safety "very important" in selecting a college. A generation earlier, would campus crime have been uppermost in the minds of prospective students?

Research on crime in college has focused on interpersonal violence ("date rape," as it is sometimes trivialized) and the way in which colleges handle such incidents. In 2007, two very different events brought campus crime to national attention. First, there was the April 16, 2007, rampage at Virginia Tech. In its aftermath, observers questioned whether campus officials should have notified students and employees of the first shootings, at a dormitory, during the two hours that passed before the gunman's second attack in a classroom building. The federal law known as the Clery Act, passed in 1990, requires timely warnings of campus crime, but how they should be delivered and how specific they should be (for example, whether the names of alleged assailants should be revealed) is unclear.

The second incident, the death of a girl in her dormitory room at Eastern Michigan University, led to the resignation of the university's president. For two months, officials had

> The federal law known as the Clery Act, passed in 1990, requires timely warnings of campus crime, but how they should be delivered and how specific they should be is unclear.

assured her parents that she died a natural death. Later, her family learned that she had been raped and murdered, and that her body had been missing for three days.

These and other less publicized incidents have prompted colleges to become more forthcoming about campus crime and to provide better security. However, the growing trend toward living (and partying) off campus poses a challenge to their efforts. Student safety at internship sites and study-abroad programs is even more difficult to ensure.

Making judgments about campus crime based on the reports mandated by the Clery Act is difficult. Because these documents include only reported incidents, they may or may not be accurate. The latest data from the University of California, which has over 20,000 students, for example, show that the total number of forcible sex offenses per year ranges from 2 to more than 62.

campus, and how does it compare to crime rates at other schools? Relate what you have learned to sociological theory.

2. What have officials at your college done to discourage campus crime?

LET'S DISCUSS

1. Do some research on campus crime. What is the crime rate on your college

Sources: Department of Justice 2009; Interface Group Report (Virginia Tech) 2007; Lipka 2009; National Institute of Justice 2005; *New York Times* 2007, 2008; Security on Campus 2008.

and imprisonment. As a result, they may have long careers in their chosen professions.

Edwin Sutherland (1937) offered pioneering insights into the behavior of professional criminals by publishing an annotated account written by a professional thief. Unlike the person who engages in crime only once or twice, professional thieves make a business of stealing. They devote their entire working time to planning and executing crimes, and sometimes travel across the nation to pursue their "professional duties." Like people in regular occupations, professional thieves consult with their colleagues concerning the demands of work, becoming part of a subculture of similarly occupied individuals. They exchange information on places to burglarize, on outlets for unloading stolen goods, and on ways of securing bail bonds if arrested.

Organized Crime

A 1976 government report devotes three pages to defining the term *organized crime*. For our purposes, we will consider **organized crime** to be the work of a group that regulates relations among criminal enterprises involved in illegal activities, including prostitution, gambling, and the smuggling and sale of illegal drugs. Organized crime dominates the world of illegal business just as large corporations dominate the conventional business world. It allocates territory, sets prices for goods and services, and acts as an arbitrator in internal disputes. A secret, conspiratorial activity, it generally evades law enforcement. It takes over legitimate businesses, gains influence over labor unions, corrupts public officials, intimidates witnesses in criminal trials, and even "taxes" merchants in exchange for "protection" (National Advisory Commission on Criminal Justice 1976).

Organized crime serves as a means of upward mobility for groups of people struggling to escape poverty. Sociologist Daniel Bell (1953) used the term *ethnic succession* to describe the sequential passage of leadership from Irish Americans in the early part of the 20th century to Jewish Americans in the 1920s and then to Italian Americans in the early 1930s. Ethnic succession has become more complex, reflecting the diversity of the nation's latest immigrants. Colombian, Mexican, Russian, Chinese, Pakistani, and Nigerian immigrants are among those who have begun to play a significant role in organized crime activities (Chin 1996; Kleinknecht 1996).

White-Collar and Technology-Based Crime

Income tax evasion, stock manipulation, consumer fraud, bribery and extraction of kickbacks, embezzlement, and misrepresentation in advertising—these are all examples of **white-collar crime,** illegal acts committed in the course of business activities, often by affluent, "respectable" people. Edwin Sutherland (1949, 1983) likened these crimes to organized crime because they are often perpetrated through occupational roles.

A new type of white-collar crime has emerged in recent decades: computer crime. The use of high technology allows criminals to carry out embezzlement or electronic fraud, often leaving few traces, or to gain access to a company's inventory without leaving home. According to a study by the FBI and the National White Collar Crime Center, over 300,000 Internet crimes are reported every year, ranging from scams on online auction sites to identity theft (Internet Crime Complaint Center 2011).

When Charles Horton Cooley spoke of the self and Erving Goffman of impression management, surely neither scholar could have envisioned the insidious crime of identity theft. Each year about 14 percent of all adults find that their personal information has been misused for criminal purposes. Unfortunately, with our society's growing reliance on electronic financial transactions, assuming someone else's identity has become increasingly easy (Vamosi et al. 2010).

Identity theft does not necessarily require technology. A criminal can obtain someone's personal information by pickpocketing or by intercepting mail. However, the widespread exchange of information online has allowed criminals to access large amounts of personal information. Public awareness of the potential harm from identity theft took a giant leap in the aftermath of September 11, 2001, when investigations revealed that several hijackers had used fraudulent IDs to open bank accounts, rent apartments, and board planes. A law enacted in 2004 makes identity theft punishable by a mandatory prison sentence if it is linked to other crimes. Still, unauthorized disclosures of information, even if accidental, persist (Brubaker 2008).

Sutherland (1940) coined the term *white-collar crime* in 1939 to refer to acts by individuals, but the term has been broadened more recently to include offenses by businesses and corporations as well. *Corporate crime,* or any act by a corporation that is punishable by the government, takes many forms and includes individuals, organizations, and institutions among its victims. Corporations may engage in anticompetitive behavior, environmental pollution, medical fraud, tax fraud, stock fraud and manipulation,

"KICKBACKS, EMBEZZLEMENT, PRICE-FIXING, BRIBERY... THIS IS AN EXTREMELY HIGH-CRIME AREA."

accounting fraud, the production of unsafe goods, bribery and corruption, and health and safety violations (J. Coleman 2006).

For many years, corporate wrongdoers got off lightly in court by documenting their long history of charitable contributions and agreeing to help law enforcement officials find other white-collar criminals. Unfortunately, that is still the case. The highly visible jailing of multimedia personality Martha Stewart in 2004, as well as recent disclosures of "Wall Street greed," may lead the casual observer to think that government is cracking down on white-collar crime. However, an independent analysis found that from 2000 through 2009, the number of white-collar crimes that were prosecuted increased only modestly (Transactional Records Access Clearinghouse 2009).

The leniency shown to white-collar criminals is not limited to the United States. Japan did not level a fine for insider trading on a major financial corporation until 2012. The profit from the crime was about $119,000; the penalty was $600 (Fukase and Inagaki 2012).

Even when a person is convicted of corporate crime, the verdict generally does not harm his or her reputation and career aspirations nearly so much as conviction for street crime would. Apparently, the label "white-collar criminal" does not carry the stigma of the label "felon convicted of a violent crime." Conflict theorists don't find such differential treatment surprising. They argue that the criminal justice system largely disregards the crimes of the affluent, focusing on crimes committed by the poor. Generally, if an offender holds a position of status and influence, his or her crime is treated as less serious, and the sanction is much more lenient.

Hate Crime

In contrast to other crimes, hate crimes are defined not only by the perpetrators' actions, but by the purpose of their conduct. The government considers an ordinary crime to be a **hate crime** when the offender is motivated to choose a victim based on race, religion, ethnic group, national origin, or sexual orientation, and when evidence shows that hatred prompted the offender to commit the crime. Hate crimes are sometimes referred to as *bias crimes* (Department of Justice 2008).

In 1990, Congress passed the Hate Crimes Statistics Act, which created a national mandate to identify crimes based on race, religion, ethnic group, and national origin. (Before that time, only 12 states had monitored such crimes.) Since then the act has been broadened to include disabilities, both physical and mental, and sexual orientation. In addition, some jurisdictions impose harsher sanctions (jail time or fines) for hate crimes than for other crimes. For example, if the penalty for assault is a year in jail, the penalty for an assault identified as a hate crime might be two years.

In 2011, law enforcement agencies submitted data on hate crimes to the federal government. The statistics included official reports of more than 7,600 hate crimes and bias-motivated incidents. As Figure 25-1 shows, race was the apparent motivation in approximately 47 percent of the reports. Although vandalism and intimidation were the most common crimes, 40 percent of the incidents involved assault, rape, or murder.

FIGURE 25-1 **Categorization of Reported Hate Crimes**

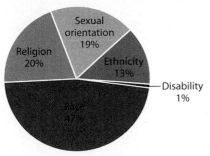

Source: Incidents reported for 2010 in 2011. Department of Justice 2011b.

The vast majority of hate crimes, although not all of them, are committed by members of the dominant group against those who are relatively powerless. One in every six racially based hate crimes is an anti-White incident. Except for the most horrific hate crimes, these offenses receive little media attention; anti-White incidents probably receive even less. Clearly, hostility based on race knows no boundaries (Department of Justice 2011b).

Transnational Crime

More and more, scholars and police officials are turning their attention to **transnational crime,** or crime that occurs across multiple national borders. In the past, international crime was often limited to the clandestine shipment of goods across the border between two countries. But increasingly, crime is no more restricted by such borders than is legal commerce. Rather than concentrating on specific countries, international crime now spans the globe.

Historically, probably the most dreadful example of transnational crime has been slavery. At first, governments did not regard slavery as a crime, but merely regulated it as they would the trade in goods. In the 20th century, transnational crime grew to embrace trafficking in endangered species, drugs, and stolen art and antiquities.

Transnational crime is not exclusive of some of the other types of crime we have discussed. For example, organized criminal networks are increasingly global. Technology definitely facilitates their illegal activities, such as trafficking in child pornography. Beginning in the 1990s, the United Nations began to categorize transnational crimes; Table 25-1 lists some of the more common types.

Bilateral cooperation in the pursuit of border criminals such as smugglers has been common for many years. The first global effort to control international crime was the International Criminal Police Organization (Interpol), a cooperative network of European police forces founded to stem the movement of political revolutionaries across borders. While such efforts to fight transnational crime may seem lofty—an activity with which any government should cooperate—they are complicated by sensitive legal and security issues. Most nations that have signed protocols issued by the United Nations, including the United States, have expressed concern over potential encroachments on their national judicial systems, as well as concern over their national

Table 25-1 Types of Transnational Crime

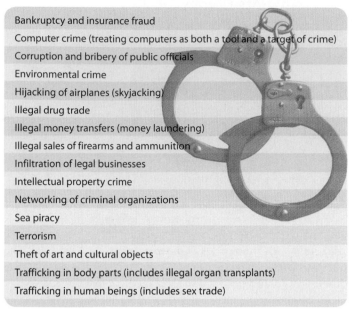

Bankruptcy and insurance fraud

Computer crime (treating computers as both a tool and a target of crime)

Corruption and bribery of public officials

Environmental crime

Hijacking of airplanes (skyjacking)

Illegal drug trade

Illegal money transfers (money laundering)

Illegal sales of firearms and ammunition

Infiltration of legal businesses

Intellectual property crime

Networking of criminal organizations

Sea piracy

Terrorism

Theft of art and cultural objects

Trafficking in body parts (includes illegal organ transplants)

Trafficking in human beings (includes sex trade)

Source: Compiled and updated by the author based on Mueller 2001 and United Nations Office on Drugs and Crime 2010.

security. Thus, they have been reluctant to share certain types of intelligence data. The terrorist attacks of September 11, 2001, increased both the interest in combating transnational crime and sensitivity to the risks of sharing intelligence data (Deflem 2005; Felson and Kalaitzidis 2005).

 use your **sociological imagination**

As the editor of an online news service, how might you treat stories on corporate or white-collar crime differently from those on violent crime?

Crime Statistics

Crime statistics are not as accurate as social scientists would like, especially since they deal with an issue of grave concern to the people of the United States. Unfortunately, they are frequently cited as if they were completely reliable. Such data do serve as an indicator of police activity, as well as an approximate indication of the level of certain crimes. Yet it would be a mistake to interpret these data as an exact representation of the incidence of crime.

Index Crimes and Victimization Surveys

Typically, the crime data reported in the United States are based on **index crimes,** or the eight types of crime tabulated each year by the Federal Bureau of Investigation (FBI). This category of criminal behavior generally consists of those serious offenses that people think of when they express concern about the nation's crime problem. Index crimes include murder, rape, robbery, and assault—all of which are violent crimes committed against people—as well as the property crimes of burglary,

larceny-theft, motor vehicle theft, and arson (Table 25-2). The crime index is published annually by the FBI as part of the *Uniform Crime Reports.*

Obviously, many serious offenses, such as white-collar crimes, are not included in this index (although they are recorded elsewhere). In addition, the crime index is disproportionately devoted to property crimes, whereas most citizens are more worried about violent crimes. Thus, a significant decrease in the number of rapes and robberies could be overshadowed by a slightly larger increase in the number of automobiles stolen, leading to the mistaken impression that *personal* safety is more at risk than before.

The most serious limitation of official crime statistics is that they include only those crimes actually *reported* to law enforcement agencies. Because members of racial and ethnic minority groups often distrust law enforcement agencies, they may not contact the police. Feminist sociologists and others have noted that many women do not report rape or spousal abuse out of fear they will be blamed for the crime.

Partly because of these deficiencies in official statistics, the National Crime Victimization Survey was initiated in 1972. The Bureau of Justice Statistics, in compiling this annual report, seeks information from law enforcement agencies, but also interviews households across the nation and asks if they were victims of a specific set of crimes during the preceding year. In general, those who administer **victimization surveys** question ordinary people, not police officers, to determine whether they have been victims of crime.

Unfortunately, like other crime data, victimization surveys have particular limitations. They require that victims understand what has happened to them and are willing to disclose such information to interviewers. Fraud, income tax evasion, and blackmail are examples of crimes that are unlikely to be reported in victimization studies.

Crime Trends

Crime fills the news reports on television, over the Internet, and in the newspaper. As a result, the public regards crime as a major social problem. Yet there has been a significant decline in violent crime in the United States in recent years, after many years of increases.

How much has crime declined? Consider this: the rate of crime being reported in 2012 was comparable to what it was back when gasoline cost 29 cents a gallon and the average person earned less than $6,000 a year. That was 1963.

Dramatic declines have occurred within the last decade. As Table 25-2 shows, both violent crime and property crime dropped 20 percent in the last 10 years. Although a tragic 14,748 people were murdered in 2010, in 1991 that number was a staggering 24,700. Declines have also been registered in victimization surveys (Figure 25-2).

What explains these declines in both index crimes and victimization rates? Possible explanations include the following:

- Community-oriented policing and crime prevention programs
- New gun control laws

Table 25-2 National Crime Rates and Percentage Change

Crime Index Offenses in 2010	Number Reported	Rate per 100,000 Inhabitants	Percentage Change in Rate since 2001
Violent crime			
Murder	14,748	5	−15
Forcible rape	84,767	28	−14
Robbery	367,832	119	−20
Aggravated assault	778,901	252	−21
Total	1,246,248	404	−20
Property crime			
Burglary	2,159,878	700	−6
Larceny-theft	6,185,867	2,004	−19
Motor vehicle theft	737,142	239	−40
Total	9,082,887	2,942	−20

Notes: Arson was designated an index offense beginning in 1979; data on arson were still incomplete as of 2012. Because of rounding, the offenses may not add to totals.
Source: Department of Justice 2011a: Tables 1, 1a.

- A massive increase in the prison population, which at least prevents inmates from committing crimes outside prison
- New surveillance technologies
- The decline of the crack cocaine epidemic, which soared in the late 1980s
- The aging of the population, as the number of people in their 50s increased and the number in their 20s decreased

No single explanation could account for such a marked change in crime rates. Taken together, however, these changes in public policy, public health, technology, and demographics may well explain it (Eckberg 2006:5- 223; Florida 2011; James Q. Wilson 2011; Wood 2012; Zimring 2007).

Feminist scholars draw our attention to one significant countertrend: the proportion of major crimes committed by women has increased. However, violent crimes committed by women, which have never been common, have declined. Despite the "mean girls" headlines in the tabloid magazines, every reliable measure shows that among women, fights, weapons possession, assaults, and violent injuries have plunged over the last decade (Males and Lind 2010).

International Crime Rates

If developing reliable crime data is difficult in the United States, making useful cross-national comparisons is even more difficult.

Taking Sociology to Work

Stephanie Vezzani, *Special Agent, U.S. Secret Service*

Stephanie Vezzani wasn't sure what she wanted to major in when she entered the University of Akron, but she did know what she wanted to do with her life: she wanted a career as a crime fighter. Vezzani began as an accounting major, but switched to sociology when she discovered the department offered a special concentration in law enforcement.

Vezzani is now an agent with the U.S. Secret Service, whose twofold mission is to protect high-ranking officials and their families and to investigate financial crimes, including counterfeiting, identity theft, and computer-based attacks on the financial, banking, and telecommunications

industries. She has tackled both aspects of the job. For her, a typical week would include working on a criminal investigation in a field office or traveling around the country with a government official in need of protection.

Vezzani finds that travel is one of the most exciting aspects of her job. Over the past six years she has visited Russia, Turkey, Jordan, Vietnam, and South Korea. She also attended the 2002 Winter Olympics in Salt Lake City, where she provided protection for the athletes living in the Olympic Village. Vezzani relishes meeting people from different cultures, and of course she loves the sights she gets to see. "The architecture in St. Petersburg, Russia, was amazing," she says.

Vezzani uses her training in sociology on a daily basis, as she interviews suspects, witnesses, and victims of crime. "It is critical in the

field of law enforcement to have an understanding of people's relationships and the beliefs and value systems that contribute to their decision making," she explains. "Sociology has provided me the knowledge to speak to and listen to people with different values and cultures in order to complete my job at the highest level possible."

LET'S DISCUSS

1. Besides an awareness of different beliefs, values, and cultures, what else might sociology offer to those who serve in law enforcement?

2. Law enforcement is a relatively new career option for women. What special strengths do you think a woman might bring to police work?

FIGURE 25-2 Victimization Rates, 1973–2010

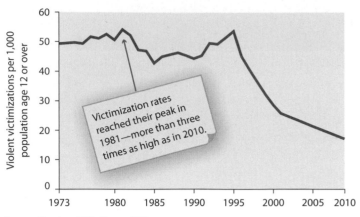

Sources: Rennison 2002; Truman 2011.

Nevertheless, with some care, we can offer preliminary conclusions about how crime rates differ around the world.

During the 1980s and 1990s, violent crimes were much more common in the United States than in western Europe. Murders, rapes, and robberies were reported to the police at much higher rates in the United States. Yet the incidence of certain other types of crime appears to be higher elsewhere. For example, England, Italy, Australia, and New Zealand all have higher rates of car theft than the United States. Developing nations have significant rates of reported homicide due to civil unrest and political conflict among civilians (International Crime Victim Survey 2004; World Bank 2003).

A particularly worrisome development has been the rapid escalation in homicide rates in developing countries that supply drugs to industrialized countries, especially the United States. The huge profits generated by cocaine exports to North America and Europe have allowed drug gangs to arm themselves to the point of becoming illegal armies. Homicide rates in Mexico are now about twice as high as those in the United States. Honduras, Guatemala, Venezuela, and El Salvador's homicide rates are three to five times those of Mexico (*The Economist* 2010c).

Why are rates of violent crime generally so much higher in the United States than in western Europe? Sociologist Elliot Currie (1985, 1998) has suggested that our society places greater emphasis on individual economic achievement than other societies. At the same time, many observers have noted that the culture of the United States has long tolerated, if not condoned, many forms of violence. Coupled with sharp disparities between poor and affluent citizens, significant unemployment, and substantial alcohol and drug abuse, these factors combine to produce a climate conducive to crime.

In the United States, high rates of violent crime, especially in the cities, have long fueled calls for greater use of the death penalty. We will take a close look at the controversy over the ultimate penalty in the Social Policy section that follows.

social
policy and Social control | The Death Penalty in the United States and Worldwide

On June 11, 2001, Timothy McVeigh—the man who killed hundreds of innocent people when he bombed the federal building in Oklahoma City in 1995—was executed by the U.S. government. McVeigh was the first federal prisoner to be put to death in nearly four decades. His execution, and that of others who received the death penalty for their crimes, has raised many questions, both from supporters and from critics of capital punishment. How can the government prevent the execution of innocent men and women? Is it right to resort to a punishment that imitates the crime it seeks to condemn? Is life in prison enough of a punishment for a truly heinous crime?

Looking at the Issue

Historically, execution has been a significant form of punishment, both for deviance from social norms and for criminal behavior. In North America, the death penalty has been used for centuries to punish murder, alleged witchcraft, and a few other crimes. Yet for most of that time, little thought was given to its justification; capital punishment was simply assumed to be morally and religiously right. Today, the death penalty is still on the books in most states, where it is used to a greater or lesser extent (Figure 25-3).

In other parts of the world, serious thought has been given to the ethical implications of the ultimate penalty. As of 2012, 97 nations had abolished capital punishment; many more use it only sparingly, if at all (Figure 25-4).

Applying Sociology

Traditionally, the debate over the death penalty has focused on its appropriateness as a form of punishment and its value in deterring crime. Viewed from Émile Durkheim's functionalist perspective, sanctions against deviant acts help to reinforce society's standards of proper behavior. Supporters of capital punishment insist that fear of execution will prevent at least some criminals from committing serious offenses. Moreover, even if it does not serve as a deterrent, they still see the death penalty as justified, because they believe the worst criminals deserve to die for their crimes.

The death penalty also creates some dysfunctions, however. Although many citizens are concerned that the alternative to execution, life in prison, is unnecessarily expensive,

—Continued

MAPPING LIFE NATIONWIDE

FIGURE 25-3 **Executions by State since 1976**

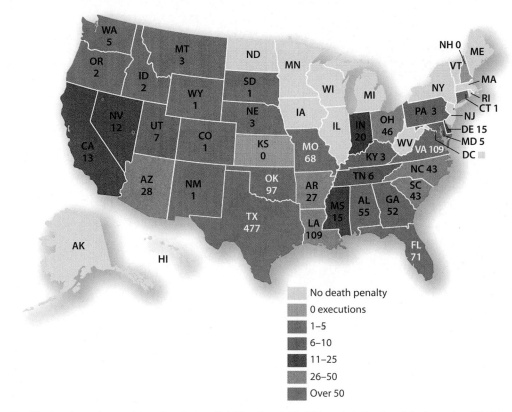

Legend:
- No death penalty
- 0 executions
- 1–5
- 6–10
- 11–25
- 26–50
- Over 50

Note: Number of executions carried out from January 17, 1977, to January 23, 2012, not including three federal executions. Illinois carried out 12 executions before abolishing the death penalty.
Source: Death Penalty Information Center 2012.

studies show that defendants are more likely to be sentenced to death if their victims were White rather than Black. About 76 percent of the victims in death penalty cases are White, even though only 50 percent of all murder victims are White. And there is some evidence that Black defendants, who constituted 42 percent of all death row inmates in 2012, are more likely to face execution than Whites in the same legal circumstance. About 60 percent of the 289 who have been exonerated for any reason, including poor legal defense, are members of minority groups. Evidence exists, too, that capital defendants receive poor legal services because of the racist attitudes of their own defense counsel. While racism is never acceptable, it is particularly devastating in the criminal justice system, where the legal process can result in an execution (Death Penalty Information Center 2012; Innocence Project 2012; Petrie and Coverdill 2010).

sentencing a person to death is not cheap. According to a recent analysis, in California, prosecuting death penalty cases costs $184 million more per year than prosecuting cases involving life without parole. Housing, health care, and legal representation also cost more for convicts on death row than for other inmates (Alarcón et al. 2011).

Conflict theorists counter that the persistence of social inequality in today's society puts poor people at a disadvantage in the criminal justice system. Simply put, the poor cannot afford to hire the best lawyers, but must rely instead on court-appointed attorneys, who typically are overworked and underpaid. This unequal access to legal resources may mean the difference between life and death for poor defendants. Indeed, the American Bar Association (1997) has repeatedly expressed concern about the limited defense most defendants who face the death penalty receive. As of late 2010, DNA analysis and other new technologies had exonerated 17 death row inmates.

Another issue of crucial concern to conflict theorists and researchers is the possibility of racial discrimination. Numerous

Initiating Policy

Many people hesitate to endorse the death penalty, yet when confronted with a horrendous crime, they feel the death penalty should be available, at least in some cases. In most people's minds, for example, Timothy McVeigh's sentence would be an appropriate use of the death penalty, although opinion on this point has fluctuated. In 2011, support for the death penalty was 62 percent—about the same level as when the question was first posed in 1936, in a national survey (Pew Research Center for the People and the Press 2012).

Recently, policy initiatives have moved in two different directions. In several death penalty states, legislators are considering broadening the range of offenses for which convicted criminals may be sentenced to execution. In these states, child molesters who did not murder their victims could become eligible for the death penalty, along with certain repeat offenders. The countertrend, a movement away from the death penalty, is based on doubts about whether an execution can be carried out humanely.

—Continued

MAPPING LIFE NATIONWIDE

FIGURE 25-4 **Death Penalty Status by Country**

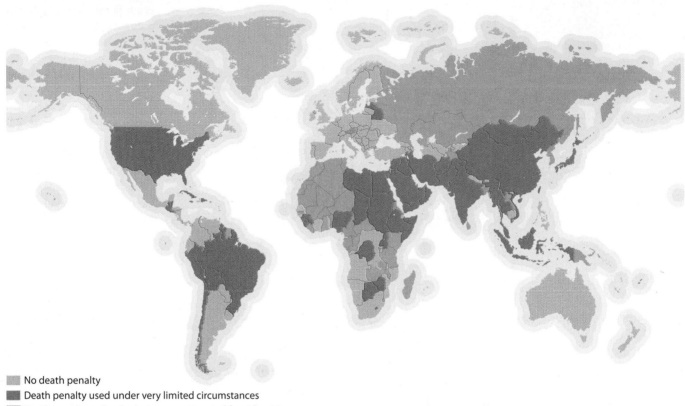

- No death penalty
- Death penalty used under very limited circumstances
- Death penalty on books, but no one executed for at least ten years
- Death penalty in use

Source: Amnesty International 2011.

Legal action has been taken on behalf of those convicted to die, especially by lethal injection, which is used in virtually all death penalty jurisdictions. Concerns about lethal injection range from medical ethics (the injection must be administered by a medical technician) to the effectiveness of the technique, which sometimes takes a long time to cause death. In 2008, the Supreme Court ruled that Kentucky's procedures were constitutional, but specified protocols for the use of chemicals, personnel training, medical supervision, and error risk that apply in all 35 states that use lethal injection (L. Greenhouse 2008).

Surprisingly, only about 40 to 50 death sentences are handed out for the more than 15,000 reported murders that occur every year. Courts continue to address the question of how this ultimate penalty can be administered in a judicially fair manner. Policymakers, however, do not seem concerned with such questions. In recent years, federal and state legislatures have declared additional crimes to be punishable by death, curtailed appeals by death row inmates, and reimbursed far fewer lawyers for their defense of condemned criminals.

Internationally, attention has focused on those nations where executions are relatively common, such as China and Iran. Foes of the death penalty see these nations as violators of human rights. In the United States, which usually regards itself as a champion of human rights, pressure to abolish capital punishment has grown both at home and abroad.

TAKE THE ISSUE WITH YOU

1. Does the death penalty deter crime? If so, why are crime rates in the United States high compared to those in other nations?

2. What is your position on the death penalty—should it be legal or should it be abolished? Explain your reasoning.

3. Should youths who have been convicted of violent crimes be subject to the death penalty? Why or why not?

Summary

Crime is deviation from formal social norms administered by the state.

1. Sociologists differentiate among **victimless crimes** (such as drug use and prostitution), crime committed by **professional criminals, organized crime, white-collar crime,** and **transnational crime.**

2. Crime statistics are among the least reliable social data, partly because so many crimes are not reported to law enforcement agencies. Rates of violent crime are higher in the United States than in other Western societies, although they have been dropping.

3. The death penalty is the ultimate sanction, one that functionalists believe deters serious crime. However, it is applied disproportionately to the economically disadvantaged and to racial minorities. Worldwide, many countries have renounced the death penalty

Thinking Critically

1. Why is it useful to sociologists to have victimization surveys in addition to reported crime data?

2. Apply at least two of the theories discussed in Module 24 to the problem of professional crime. Which theory seems to provide the best explanation?

Key Terms

Crime   182
Hate crime 185
Index crime   186
Organized crime   184
Professional criminal   183
Transnational crime   185
Victimization survey   186
Victimless crime   182
White-collar crime   184

Mastering This Chapter

taking sociology with you

1 Describe the mechanisms of social control, both formal and informal, on your campus. Which is more effective, formal or informal control?

2 Explain the presence of both criminals and law-abiding citizens in an inner-city neighborhood in terms of the interactionist perspective.

3 Pay a visit to your local courthouse and observe a trial by jury from the point of view of a sociologist. Then describe what you saw and heard using sociological concepts.

key terms

Anomie   Durkheim's term for the loss of direction felt in a society when social control of individual behavior has become ineffective. (page 177)

Anomie theory of deviance   Robert Merton's theory of deviance as an adaptation of socially prescribed goals or of the means governing their attainment, or both. (177)

Conformity   Going along with peers—individuals of our own status who have no special right to direct our behavior. (170)

Control theory   A view of conformity and deviance that suggests that our connection to members of society leads us to systematically conform to society's norms. (173)

Crime A violation of criminal law for which some governmental authority applies formal penalties. (182)

Cultural transmission A school of criminology that argues that criminal behavior is learned through social interactions. (178)

Deviance Behavior that violates the standards of conduct or expectations of a group or society. (175)

Differential association A theory of deviance that holds that violation of rules results from exposure to attitudes favorable to criminal acts. (179)

Differential justice Differences in the way social control is exercised over different groups. (181)

Formal social control Social control that is carried out by authorized agents, such as police officers, judges, school administrators, and employers. (172)

Hate crime A criminal offense committed because of the offender's bias against a race, religion, ethnic group, national origin, or sexual orientation. Also referred to as *bias crime*. (185)

Index crimes The eight types of crime tabulated each year by the FBI in the *Uniform Crime Reports:* murder, rape, robbery, assault, burglary, theft, motor vehicle theft, and arson. (186)

Informal social control Social control that is carried out casually by ordinary people through such means as laughter, smiles, and ridicule. (171)

Labeling theory An approach to deviance that attempts to explain why certain people are viewed as deviants while others engaged in the same behavior are not. (179)

Law Governmental social control. (173)

Obedience Compliance with higher authorities in a hierarchical structure. (170)

Organized crime The work of a group that regulates relations among criminal enterprises involved in illegal activities, including prostitution, gambling, and the smuggling and sale of illegal drugs. (184)

Professional criminal A person who pursues crime as a day-to-day occupation, developing skilled techniques and enjoying a certain degree of status among other criminals. (183)

Sanction A penalty or reward for conduct concerning a social norm. (169)

Social constructionist perspective An approach to deviance that emphasizes the role of culture in the creation of the deviant identity. (180)

Social control The techniques and strategies for preventing deviant human behavior in any society. (169)

Social disorganization theory The theory that crime and deviance are caused by the absence or breakdown of communal relationships and social institutions. (179)

Societal-reaction approach Another name for *labeling theory*. (180)

Stigma A label used to devalue members of certain social groups. (175)

Transnational crime Crime that occurs across multiple national borders. (185)

Victimization survey A questionnaire or interview given to a sample of the population to determine whether people have been victims of crime. (186)

Victimless crime A term used by sociologists to describe the willing exchange among adults of widely desired but illegal goods and services. (182)

White-collar crime Illegal acts committed by affluent, "respectable" individuals in the course of business activities. (184)

self quiz

Read each question carefully and then select the best answer.

1. Society brings about acceptance of basic norms through techniques and strategies for preventing deviant human behavior. This process is termed
   a. stigmatization.
   b. labeling.
   c. law.
   d. social control.

2. Which sociological perspective argues that people must respect social norms if any group or society is to survive?
   a. the conflict perspective
   b. the interactionist perspective
   c. the functionalist perspective
   d. the feminist perspective

3. Stanley Milgram used the word *conformity* to mean
   a. going along with peers.
   b. compliance with higher authorities in a hierarchical structure.
   c. techniques and strategies for preventing deviant human behavior in any society.
   d. penalties and rewards for conduct concerning a social norm.

4. Which sociological theory suggests that our connection to members of society leads us to conform systematically to society's norms?
   a. feminist theory
   b. control theory
   c. interactionist theory
   d. functionalist theory

5. Which of the following statements is true of deviance?
   a. Deviance is always criminal behavior.
   b. Deviance is behavior that violates the standards of conduct or expectations of a group or society.
   c. Deviance is perverse behavior.
   d. Deviance is inappropriate behavior that cuts across all cultures and social orders.

6. Which sociologist illustrated the boundary-maintenance function of deviance in his study of Puritans in 17th-century New England?
   a. Kai Erikson
   b. Émile Durkheim
   c. Robert Merton
   d. Edwin Sutherland

7. Which of the following is *not* one of the basic forms of adaptation specified in Robert Merton's anomie theory of deviance?
   a. conformity
   b. innovation
   c. ritualism
   d. hostility

8. Which sociologist first advanced the idea that an individual undergoes the same basic socialization process whether learning conforming or deviant acts?
   a. Robert Merton
   b. Edwin Sutherland
   c. Travis Hirschi
   d. William Chambliss

9. Which of the following theories contends that criminal victimization increases when communal relationships and social institutions break down?
   a. labeling theory
   b. conflict theory
   c. social disorganization theory
   d. differential association theory

10. Which of the following conducted observation research on two groups of high school males (the Saints and the Roughnecks) and concluded that social class played an important role in the varying fortunes of the two groups?
    a. Richard Quinney
    b. Edwin Sutherland
    c. Émile Durkheim
    d. William Chambliss

11. If we fail to respect and obey social norms, we may face punishment through informal or formal _____.

12. Police officers, judges, administrators, employers, military officers, and managers of movie theaters are all instruments of _____ social control.

13. Some norms are considered so important by a society that they are formalized into _____ controlling people's behavior.

14. It is important to underscore the fact that _____ is the primary source of conformity and obedience, including obedience to law.

15. _____ is a state of normlessness that typically occurs during a period of profound social change and disorder, such as a time of economic collapse.

16. Labeling theory is also called the _____ _____ approach.

17. _____ theorists view standards of deviant behavior as merely reflecting cultural norms, whereas _____ and _____ theorists point out that the most powerful groups in a society can shape laws and standards and determine who is (or is not) prosecuted as a criminal.

18. Feminists contend that prostitution and some forms of pornography are not _____ crimes.

19. Daniel Bell used the term _____ _____ to describe the process during which leadership of organized crime was transferred from Irish Americans to Jewish Americans and later to Italian Americans and others.

20. Consumer fraud, bribery, and income tax evasion are considered _____ _____ crimes.

 ## thinking about movies

Temple Grandin

An autistic woman fights for animal rights.

Shame

A man struggles to keep his life together while coping with a sex addiction.

American Gypsy

This documentary sheds light on the Romani, a minority group whose members are often stereotyped as criminals.

What does the Occupy Wall Street (OWS) movement say about American society?

Rana Foroohar, Assistant Managing Editor at *Time*, thinks that the movement voices our fear and anger over the loss of the American dream.

" America's story, our national mythology, is built on the idea of being an opportunity society. From the tales of Horatio Alger to the real lives of Henry Ford and Mark Zuckerberg, we have defined our country as a place where everyone, if he or she works hard enough, can get ahead. We may be poor today, but as long as there's a chance that we can be rich tomorrow, things are O.K.

But does America still work like that? The suspicion that the answer is no inspires not only the Occupy Wall Street (OWS) protests that have spread across the nation and beyond but also a movement as seemingly divergent as the Tea Party. While OWS may focus its anger on rapacious bankers, and the Tea Party on spendthrift politicians, both would probably agree that there's a cabal of entitled elites on Wall Street and in Washington who have somehow loaded the dice and made it impossible for average people to get ahead. The American Dream, like our economy, has become bifurcated.

Certainly the numbers support the idea that for most people, it's harder to get ahead than it's ever been in the postwar era. Inequality in the U.S., always high compared with that in other developed countries, is rising. The 1% decried by OWS takes home 21% of the country's income and accounts for 35% of its wealth. Wages, which have stagnated in real terms since the 1970s, have been falling for much of 2011, in part because of pervasively high unemployment. For the first time in 20 years, the percentage of the population employed in the U.S. is lower than in the U.K., Germany and the Netherlands.

We don't peg ourselves to our parents; we peg ourselves to the Joneses. . . . By that standard, we aren't doing very well at all.

The obvious question is, What happened? The answers, like social mobility itself, are nuanced and complex. You can argue about what kind of mobility really matters. Many conservatives, for example, would be inclined to emphasize absolute mobility, which means the extent to which people are better off than their parents were at the same age. That's a measure that focuses mostly on how much economic growth has occurred, and by that measure, the U.S. does fine. Two-thirds of 40-year-old Americans live in households with larger incomes, adjusted for inflation, than their parents had at the same age (though the gains are smaller than they were in the previous generation).

But just as we don't feel grateful to have indoor plumbing or multichannel digital cable television, we don't necessarily feel grateful that we earn more than our parents did. That's because we don't peg ourselves to our parents; we peg ourselves to the Joneses. Behavioral economics tells us that our sense of well-being is tied not to the past but to how we are doing compared with our peers. Relative mobility matters. By that standard, we aren't doing very well at all. Having the right parents increases your chances of ending up middle to upper middle class by a factor of three or four.

There are many reasons for the huge and growing wealth divide in our country. The rise of the money culture and bank deregulation in the 1980s and '90s certainly contributed to it. As the financial sector grew in relation to the rest of the economy (it's now at historic highs of about 8%), a winner-take-all economy emerged. Wall Street was less about creating new businesses—entrepreneurship has stalled as finance has become a bigger industry—but it did help set a new pay band for top talent. In the 1970s, corporate chiefs earned about 40 times as much as their lowest-paid worker (closer to the norm in many parts of Europe). Now they earn more than 400 times as much. "

(Foroohar 2011:77, 78, 79, 80) Additional information about this excerpt can be found on the Online Learning Center at www.mhhe.com/schaefermod2e.

The Occupy Wall Street movement began in Vancouver, Canada, after the editors of *Adbusters* magazine suggested a protest against "corporate rule" in lower Manhattan. Their call to action went out in a tweet ending with "#occupywallstreet."

On the first day of the movement, September 17, 2011, the 2,000 protesters who assembled in New York claimed to represent the vast majority of Americans. In their words, they were "the 99 percent" who had suffered as the wealthiest 1

percent—those earning roughly $500,000 a year—flourished. In the next few weeks, their movement spread across the United States to Honolulu and then throughout the world (Peralta 2011; M. Scherer 2011).

What did Americans make of this new movement? Opinions ran the gamut, from former New York City mayor Rudy Giuliani's sarcastic "How about you occupy a job?" to sociologist Craig Calhoun's comparison to student protests in China. The police response to Occupy Wall Street, Calhoun wrote, was "reminiscent of the Chinese government ousting protesters from Tiananmen." Native Americans observed that their land has been occupied for over five centuries without much notice from White protesters. And the homeless marveled over the sudden concern for people (protesters) sleeping in city parks (Calhoun 2011; K. Lawler 2011).

But is social inequality inescapable? How does government policy affect the life chances of the working poor? Is this country still a place where a hardworking person can move up the social ladder? These modules focus on the unequal distribution of socially valued rewards and its consequences. We will begin by examining four general systems of stratification, including the one most familiar to us, the social class system. We will examine three sociological perspectives on stratification, paying particular attention to the theories of Karl Marx and Max Weber. We'll also ask whether stratification is universal and see what sociologists have to say about that question. We will see how sociologists define social class and examine the consequences of class for people's wealth and income, safety, and educational opportunities. Then we will take a close look at poverty, particularly the question of who belongs to the underclass and why. And we will confront the question of social mobility, both upward and downward. Finally, in the Social Policy section, we will examine the issue of executive compensation—the huge salaries and bonuses that corporate executives earn even when their companies are losing money and employees are losing their jobs.

MODULE 26 | Systems of Stratification

Ever since people began to speculate about the nature of human society, they have wondered about the differences between individuals and groups. The term **social inequality** describes a situation where different people have different amounts of wealth, prestige, or power.

When a system of social inequality is based on a hierarchy of groups, sociologists refer to it as **stratification:** a structured ranking of entire groups of people that perpetuates unequal economic rewards and power in a society. These unequal rewards are evident, not only in the distribution of wealth and income, but even in the distressing mortality rates of impoverished communities. Stratification involves the ways in which one generation passes on social inequalities to the next, producing groups of people arranged in rank order, from low to high.

Stratification is a crucial subject of sociological investigation because of its pervasive influence on human interactions and institutions. It results inevitably in social inequality, because certain groups of people stand higher in social rankings, control scarce resources, wield power, and receive special treatment. As we will see in Module 27, the consequences of stratification are evident in the unequal distribution of both income and wealth in industrial societies.

Sociologists consider stratification on many levels, ranging from its impact on the individual to worldwide patterns of inequality. No matter where we look, however, disparities in wealth and income are substantial. Take income and poverty patterns in the United States, for example. As the top part of Figure 26-1 shows, in many states the median household income is 25 percent higher than that in other states. And as the bottom part of the figure shows, the poverty rate in many states is 200 percent that of other states. Later in this chapter we will address the meaning of such statistics. We'll begin our discussion here with an overview of the four basic systems of stratification. Then we'll see what sociologists have had to say on the subject of social inequality.

Look at the four general systems of stratification examined here—slavery, castes, estates, and social classes—as ideal types useful for purposes of analysis. Any stratification system may include elements of more than one type. For example, prior to the Civil War, you could find in the southern states of the United States both social classes dividing Whites from Whites and the institutionalized enslavement of Blacks.

To understand these systems better, it may be helpful to review the distinction between *achieved status* and *ascribed status,* explained in Module 16. **Ascribed status** is a social position assigned to a person by society without regard for the person's unique talents or characteristics. In contrast, **achieved status** is a social position that a person attains largely through his or her efforts. The two are closely linked. The nation's most affluent families generally inherit wealth and status, while many members of racial and ethnic minorities inherit disadvantaged status. Age and gender, as well, are ascribed statuses that influence a person's wealth and social position.

FIGURE 26-1 **The 50 States: Contrasts in Income and Poverty Levels**

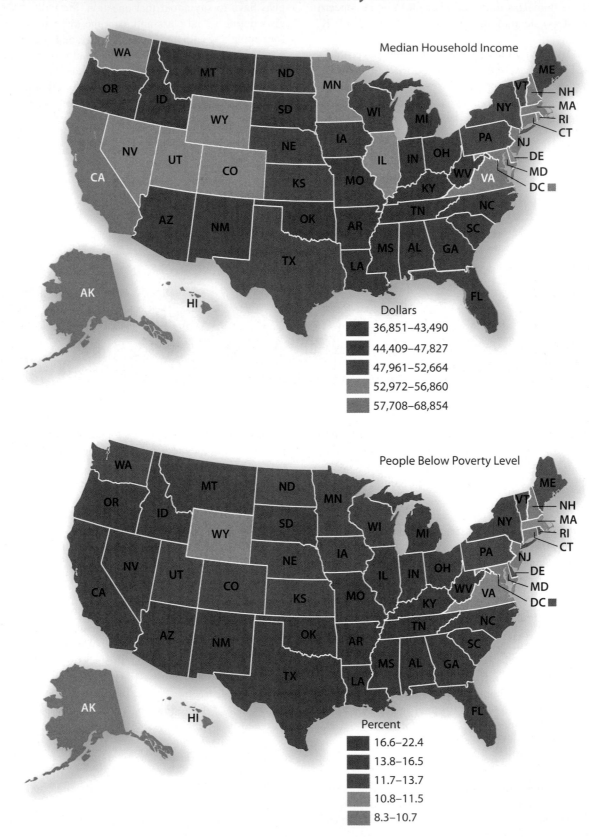

Median Household Income

Dollars

- 36,851–43,490
- 44,409–47,827
- 47,961–52,664
- 52,972–56,860
- 57,708–68,854

People Below Poverty Level

Percent

- 16.6–22.4
- 13.8–16.5
- 11.7–13.7
- 10.8–11.5
- 8.3–10.7

Note: National median household income was $51,914; national poverty rate, 13.9 percent.

Source: 2010 census data presented in American Community Survey 2011:Tables B19013, S1701.

Reactions to the Occupy movement varied with people's socioeconomic status. "How about you occupy a job?" former New York City mayor Rudy Giuliani (left) retorted. At the other extreme, Native American leaders observed that their lands have been occupied for five centuries.

Four Forms of Stratification

Slavery

The most extreme form of legalized social inequality for both individuals and groups is **slavery.** What distinguishes this oppressive system of stratification is that enslaved individuals are *owned* by other people, who treat these human beings as property, just as if they were household pets or appliances.

Slavery has varied in the way it has been practiced. In ancient Greece, the main source of slaves was piracy and captives of war. Although succeeding generations could inherit slave status, it was not necessarily permanent. A person's status might change, depending on which city-state happened to triumph in a military conflict. In effect, all citizens had the potential to become slaves or receive freedom, depending on the circumstances of history. In contrast, in the United States and Latin America, where slavery was an ascribed status, racial and legal barriers prevented the freeing of slaves.

Today, the Universal Declaration of Human Rights, which is binding on all members of the United Nations, prohibits slavery in all its forms. Yet more people are enslaved today than at any point in world history. In many developing countries, bonded laborers are imprisoned in virtual lifetime employment; in some countries, human beings are owned outright. But a form of slavery also exists in Europe and the United States, where guest workers and illegal immigrants have been forced to labor for years under terrible conditions, either to pay off debts or to avoid being turned over to immigration authorities.

Both these situations are likely to involve the transnational crime of trafficking in humans. Each year an estimated 600,000 to 800,000 men, women, and children are transported across international borders for slavery or sexual exploitation. In 2000, the U.S. Congress passed the Trafficking Victims Protection Act, which established minimum standards for the elimination of human trafficking. The act requires the State Department to monitor other countries' efforts to vigorously investigate, prosecute, and convict individuals who participate in trafficking—including government officials. Each year, the department reports its findings, some of which are shown in Table 26-1. Tier 1 and Tier 2 countries are thought to be largely in compliance with the act. Tier 2 Watch countries are making efforts to comply, though trafficking remains a significant concern. Tier 3 countries are not compliant and are not making significant efforts to comply (Bernat and Zhilina 2011).

Castes

Castes are hereditary ranks that are usually religiously dictated and that tend to be fixed and immobile. Caste membership is an ascribed status (at birth, children automatically assume the same position as their parents). Each caste is quite sharply defined, and members are expected to marry within that caste.

The caste system is generally associated with Hinduism in India and other countries. In India there are four major castes, called *varnas.* A fifth category of outcastes, referred to as the *untouchables,* represents 16 percent of the population; its members are considered so lowly and unclean as to have no place within this stratification system. In an effort to avoid perpetuating the historical stigma these people bear, the government now refers to the untouchables as *scheduled castes.* The untouchables themselves prefer *Dalit* ("the repressed"), a term that communicates their desire to overcome their disadvantaged status (P. Smith 2008).

In 1950, after gaining independence from Great Britain, India adopted a new constitution that formally outlawed the caste system. Over the past decade or two, however, urbanization and technological advances have brought more change to India's caste system than the government or politics has in more than half a century. The anonymity of city life tends to blur caste boundaries, allowing the *Dalit* to pass unrecognized in temples, schools, and places of employment. And the globalization of high technology has opened up India's social order, bringing new opportunities to those who possess the skills and ability to capitalize on them.

Table **26-1**   Human Trafficking Report

Tier 1 Full Compliance	Tier 2 Significant Effort	Tier 2 Watch List Some Effort, but Trafficking Remains a Concern	Tier 3 Noncompliant, No Effort
Australia	Bolivia	Afghanistan	Burma
Canada	Brazil	Bahamas	Congo (Dem. Rep.)
Colombia	Cambodia	China	Cuba
Denmark	Chile	Dominican Republic	Iran
France	Greece	Fiji	Mauritania
Germany	India	Malaysia	North Korea
Great Britain	Japan	Panama	Papua New Guinea
Norway	Mexico	Russia	Saudi Arabia
Poland	Philippines	Syria	Sudan
South Korea	South Africa	Ukraine	Venezuela
Spain	Turkey	Vietnam	Zimbabwe

Note: Table is incomplete; each tier lists only a sample of all nations classified. Since the *Human Trafficking Report* is created by the State Department, the level of compliance by the United States is considered to be "full compliance."

Source: Department of State 2011b.

The term *caste* can also be applied in recent historical contexts outside India. For example, the system of stratification that characterized the southern United States from the end of the Civil War through the 1960s resembled a caste system. So did the rigid system of segregation that prevailed in the Republic of South Africa under apartheid, from 1948 through the 1990s. In both cases, race was the defining factor that placed a person in the social hierarchy.

Taking Sociology to Work

Jessica Houston Su, *Research Assistant, Joblessness and Urban Poverty Research Program*

Jessica Houston Su chose sociology as her major "because it was the first class that appealed to my desire to understand the roots of inequality." It also helped her to make sense of what was going on around her at Dartmouth College. "I grew up in a rural, working-class community," she explains, "it was quite a culture shock to attend an affluent, Ivy League college." Learning about social structures and institutions helped Su to navigate through a new environment filled with people from many different backgrounds.

Su went through several potential majors before taking a sociology course and realizing that she was interested in almost every course the department offered. When she was hired for a work-study job in the department, she "soon realized that I was spending a lot of time reading all of the articles I was supposed to be photocopying," she jokes. "It became very obvious to me that I had found my major."

Su works with Harvard University's John F. Kennedy School of Government on a research program directed by the well-known sociologist William Julius Wilson. She is currently assigned to a large-scale longitudinal study of welfare reform in Boston, Chicago, and San Antonio. Her primary responsibility is to analyze the qualitative data from the study, gathered through ethnographic interviews with families who are affected by welfare reform, by searching for themes that might help to explain the study's quantitative data. She finds it exciting to be able to follow the same families over a long period. "I feel like I almost know some of the people," she explains.

Of all the things she learned as a sociology major, Su thinks one of the most important was the concept of social construction. "We consider many things to simply be facts of life," she explains, "but upon further investigation it is clear that most things have been socially constructed in some way." The concept of social construction has helped her to look more carefully at the world around her: "My worldview is much more nuanced and I've gained a much better understanding of how society works, both the good and the bad."

Su uses the research methods she learned in her sociology courses all the time. "I love going to work each day," she says. "I am challenged academically and I feel fulfilled knowing that I am working on something that will benefit society and perhaps influence future policy."

LET'S DISCUSS

1. Did you experience a sense of culture shock when you entered college and were exposed to students from different social classes? If so, has studying sociology helped you to adjust to the diversity in students' backgrounds?

2. Have you begun to see the world differently since you learned about the social construction of reality? If so, what in particular do you see in a different light?

Estates

A third type of stratification system, called *estates,* was associated with feudal societies during the Middle Ages. The **estate system**, or *feudalism,* required peasants to work land leased to them by nobles in exchange for military protection and other services. The basis for the system was the nobles' ownership of land, which was critical to their superior and privileged status. As in systems based on slavery and caste, inheritance of one's position largely defined the estate system. The nobles inherited their titles and property; the peasants were born into a subservient position within an agrarian society.

As the estate system developed, it became more differentiated. Nobles began to achieve varying degrees of authority. By the 12th century, a priesthood had emerged in most of Europe, along with classes of merchants and artisans. For the first time there were groups of people whose wealth did not depend on land ownership or agriculture. This economic change had profound social consequences as the estate system ended and a class system of stratification came into existence.

Social Classes

A **class system** is a social ranking based primarily on economic position in which achieved characteristics can influence social mobility. In contrast to slavery and caste systems, the boundaries between classes are imprecisely defined, and one can move from one stratum, or level, of society to another. Even so, class systems maintain stable stratification hierarchies and patterns of class division, and they, too, are marked by unequal distribution of wealth and power. Class standing, although it is achieved, is heavily dependent on family and ascribed factors, such as race and ethnicity.

Sociologist Daniel Rossides (1997) uses a five-class model to describe the class system of the United States: the upper class, the upper-middle class, the lower-middle class, the working class, and the lower class. Although the lines separating social classes in his model are not so sharp as the divisions between castes, members of the five classes differ significantly in ways other than just income level.

Upper and Lower Classes Rossides characterizes about 1 to 2 percent of the people of the United States as *upper class.* This group is limited to the very wealthy, who associate in exclusive clubs and social circles. In contrast, the *lower class,* consisting of approximately 20 to 25 percent of the population, disproportionately consists of Blacks, Hispanics, single mothers with dependent children, and people who cannot find regular work or must make do with low-paying work. This class lacks both wealth and income and is too weak politically to exercise significant power.

Both these classes, at opposite ends of the nation's social hierarchy, reflect the importance of ascribed status and achieved status. Ascribed statuses such as race and disability clearly influence a person's wealth and social position. People with disabilities are particularly vulnerable to unemployment, are often poorly paid, and tend to occupy the lower rungs of the occupational ladder. Regardless of their actual performance on

Worried about home foreclosures? Not the wealthy. The rich now spend $50,000 to $250,000 on their children's playhouses and tree houses.

the job, the disabled are stigmatized as not earning their keep. Such are the effects of ascribed status. We will look again at the plight of the lower class when we consider poverty and welfare policies.

The economist John Kenneth Galbraith (1977:44) observed that "of all classes the rich are the most noticed and the least studied." The poor receive a good deal of attention from reporters, social activists, and policymakers seeking to alleviate their poverty, but the very affluent, who live apart from the rest of the population, are largely a mystery. Since Galbraith's comment, moreover, the residential separation of the rich has grown. The newspaper's society page may give us a peek at members of this class, but we know very little about their everyday lives. Statistically, over 2 million households in the United States are worth more than $10 million each. Less than 10 percent of these people inherited their money, and very few of them are celebrities (Massey 2007).

Middle Class Sandwiched between the upper and lower classes in this model are the upper-middle class, the lower-middle class, and the working class. The *upper-middle class,* about 10 to 15 percent of the population, includes professionals such as doctors, lawyers, and architects. They participate extensively in politics and take leadership roles in voluntary associations. The *lower-middle class,* about 30 to 35 percent of the population, includes less affluent professionals (such as elementary school teachers and nurses), owners of small businesses, and a sizable number of clerical workers. While not all members of the middle class hold degrees from a college, they share the goal of sending their children there.

The middle class is currently under a great deal of economic pressure. Close analysis indicates that of those who lost their middle-class standing during the latter 20th century, about half rose to a higher ranking in the social class system, while half dropped to a lower position. These data mean that the United

Today, the once broadly based middle class is on the defensive and is slowly being squeezed by two growing groups, the rich and the poor.

States is moving toward a "bipolar income distribution." That is, a broadly based middle class is slowly being replaced by two growing groups of rich and poor.

Sociologists and other scholars have identified several factors that have contributed to the shrinking size of the middle class:

- *Disappearing opportunities for those with little education.* Today, most jobs require formal schooling, yet less than a third of adults between ages 35 and 44 have prepared themselves with a college degree.

- *Global competition and rapid advances in technology.* These two trends, which began several decades ago, mean that workers are more easily replaced now than they were in the past. Increasingly, globalization and technological advances are affecting the more complex jobs that were once the bread and butter of middle-class workers.

- *Growing dependence on the temporary workforce.* For those workers who have no other job, temporary positions are tenuous at best, because they rarely offer health care coverage or retirement benefits.

- *The rise of new growth industries and nonunion workplaces, like fast-food restaurants.* Industries may have added employment opportunities, but they are at the lower end of the wage scale.

Middle-class families want comfortable homes, college degrees for their children, occasional family vacations, affordable health care—the cost of which has been growing faster than inflation—and retirement security. The answer, for many people, is either to go without or to work longer hours at multiple jobs (Billitteri 2009; Blank 2010, 2011; Massey 2007; Thurow 1984).

Working Class Rossides describes the *working class*—about 40 to 45 percent of the population—as people who hold regular manual or blue-collar jobs. Certain members of this class, such as electricians, may have higher incomes than people in the lower-middle class. Yet even if they have achieved some degree of economic security, they tend to identify with manual workers and their long history of involvement in the labor movement of the United States. Of the five classes, the working class is declining noticeably in size. In the economy of the United States, service and technical jobs are replacing those involved in the actual manufacturing or transportation of goods.

Social class is one of the independent or explanatory variables most frequently used by social scientists to shed light on social issues. In later chapters, we will analyze the relationships between social class and child rearing (Module 40), religious affiliation (Module 42), and formal schooling (Module 48), as well as other relationships in which social class is a variable.

Class Warfare With Occupy Wall Street in the headlines, political leaders began to speak of class conflict. To some, the Occupy movement's call for a reduction in social inequality seemed a reply to the federal government's favorable tax treatment of the affluent. Before the recession began, the Bush administration had lowered the income tax rate paid by high-income filers. In 2009, the Tea Party pushed Congress to maintain that tax cut, despite a growing deficit. Others insisted that the affluent

actually paid less in taxes than the average citizen, given the many loopholes—offshore bank accounts, and so on—available to them. In Congress, the suggestion that the rich should pay the same effective tax rate as other citizens was met with an angry charge of class warfare.

As we will see shortly, by any statistical measure, the gulf between the rich and everyone else in the United States has grown over the last decade—indeed, over the last 50 years. Yet people do not tend to identify with or see themselves as members of a specific social class. Still, as the rhetoric heated up during the 2012 presidential campaign, and the Occupy Wall Street movement remained visible, a growing share of the population thought they saw evidence of class conflict. In December 2011, 66 percent of the public (compared to 47 percent in 2009) said they perceived "strong" conflict between the rich and the poor. Younger adults, women, and African Americans were most likely to hold this view. Interestingly, personal income had little to do with such perceptions: the rich were just as likely as the poor to agree with the existence of class conflict (Archer and Orr 2011; Pew Social and Demographic Trends 2012; Skocpol and Williamson 2012).

A miner peers into the dark at the Logan Orion coal mine in West Virginia's Logan County. Karl Marx would identify coal miners as members of the proletariat, or working class. Even today, miners are poorly compensated for the considerable dangers they face. Such exploitation of the working class is a core principle of Marxist theory.

● Sociological Perspectives on Stratification

Sociologists have hotly debated stratification and social inequality and have reached varying conclusions. No theorist stressed the significance of class for society—and for social change—more strongly than Karl Marx. Marx viewed class differentiation as the crucial determinant of social, economic, and political inequality. In contrast, Max Weber questioned Marx's emphasis on the overriding importance of the economic sector, arguing that stratification should be viewed as having many dimensions.

Karl Marx's View of Class Differentiation

Karl Marx was concerned with stratification in all types of human society, beginning with primitive agricultural tribes and continuing into feudalism. However, his main focus was on the effects of economic inequality on all aspects of 19th-century Europe. The plight of the working class made him feel that it was imperative to strive for changes in the class structure of society.

In Marx's view, social relations during any period of history depend on who controls the primary mode of economic production, such as land or factories. Differential access to scarce resources shapes the relationship between groups. Thus, under the feudal estate system, most production was agricultural, and the land was owned by the nobility. Peasants had little choice but to work according to terms dictated by those who owned the land.

Using this type of analysis, Marx examined social relations within **capitalism**—an economic system in which the means of production are held largely in private hands and the main incentive for economic activity is the accumulation of profits. Marx focused on the two classes that began to emerge as the feudal estate system declined, the bourgeoisie and the proletariat. The **bourgeoisie,** or capitalist class, owns the means of production, such as factories and machinery; the **proletariat** is the working class. In capitalist societies, the members of the bourgeoisie maximize profit in competition with other firms. In the process, they exploit workers, who must exchange their labor for subsistence wages. In Marx's view, members of each class share a distinctive culture. Marx was most interested in the culture of the proletariat, but he also examined the ideology of the bourgeoisie, through which that class justifies its dominance over workers.

According to Marx, exploitation of the proletariat will inevitably lead to the destruction of the capitalist system, because the workers will revolt. But first, the working class must develop **class consciousness**—a subjective awareness of common vested interests and the need for collective political action to bring about social change. Often, workers must overcome what Marx termed **false consciousness,** or an attitude held by members of a class that does not accurately reflect their objective position. A worker with false consciousness may adopt an individualistic viewpoint toward capitalist exploitation ("*I* am being exploited by *my* boss"). In contrast, the class-conscious worker realizes that all workers are being exploited by the bourgeoisie and have a common stake in revolution.

For Marx, class consciousness was part of a collective process in which the proletariat comes to identify the bourgeoisie as the source of its oppression. Revolutionary leaders will guide the working class in its struggle. Ultimately, the proletariat will overthrow the rule of both the bourgeoisie and the government (which Marx saw as representing the interests of capitalists) and will eliminate private ownership of the means of production.

In Marx's rather utopian view, classes and oppression will cease to exist in the postrevolutionary workers' state.

How accurate were Marx's predictions? He failed to anticipate the emergence of labor unions, whose power in collective bargaining weakens the stranglehold that capitalists maintain over workers. Moreover, as contemporary conflict theorists note, he did not foresee the extent to which political liberties and relative prosperity could contribute to false consciousness. Many workers came to view themselves as individuals striving for improvement within free societies that offer substantial mobility, rather than as downtrodden members of a social class who face a collective fate. Even today, "class warfare" seems to refer more to diminished individual expectations than to a collective identity. Finally, Marx did not predict that Communist Party rule would be established and later overthrown in the former Soviet Union and throughout Eastern Europe. Still, the Marxist approach to the study of class is useful in stressing the importance of stratification as a determinant of social behavior and the fundamental separation in many societies between two distinct groups, the rich and the poor

 use your **sociological imagination**

Have you ever been unaware of your true position in society—that is, have you experienced false consciousness? Explain.

Max Weber's View of Stratification

Unlike Karl Marx, Max Weber ([1913–1922] 1947) insisted that no single characteristic (such as class) totally defines a person's position within the stratification system. Instead, writing in 1916, he identified three distinct components of stratification: class, status, and power.

Weber used the term **class** to refer to a group of people who have a similar level of wealth and income. For example, certain workers in the United States try to support their families through minimum-wage jobs. According to Weber's definition, these wage earners constitute a class because they share the same economic position and fate. Although Weber agreed with Marx on the importance of this economic dimension of stratification, he argued that the actions of individuals and groups cannot be understood *solely* in economic terms.

Weber used the term **status group** to refer to people who have the same prestige or lifestyle. An individual gains status through membership in a desirable group, such as the medical profession. But status is not the same as economic class standing. In our culture, a successful pickpocket may belong to the same income class as a college professor. Yet the thief is widely regarded as holding low status, whereas the professor holds high status.

For Weber, the third major component of stratification has a political dimension. **Power** is the ability to exercise one's will over others. In the United States, power stems from membership in particularly influential groups, such as corporate boards of directors, government bodies, and interest groups. Conflict theorists generally agree that two major sources of power—big business and government—are closely interrelated. For instance, many of the heads of major corporations also hold powerful positions in the government or military. The Social Policy section at the end of this chapter examines the executive compensation that the powerful heads of corporations in the United States enjoy.

To summarize, in Weber's view, each of us has not one rank in society but three. Our position in a stratification system reflects some combination of class, status, and power. Each factor influences the other two, and in fact the rankings on these three dimensions often tend to coincide. John F. Kennedy came from an extremely wealthy family, attended exclusive preparatory schools, graduated from Harvard University, and went on to become president of the United States. Like Kennedy, many people from affluent backgrounds achieve impressive status and power.

Interactionist Perspective

Both Karl Marx and Max Weber looked at inequality primarily from a macrosociological perspective, considering the entire society or even the global economy. Marx did suggest the importance of a more microsociological analysis, however, when he stressed the ways in which individuals develop a true class consciousness.

Interactionists, as well as economists, have long been interested in the importance of social class in shaping a person's lifestyle. The theorist Thorstein Veblen (1857–1929) noted that those at the top of the social hierarchy typically convert part of their wealth into **conspicuous consumption**—that is, they purchase goods not to survive but to flaunt their superior wealth and social standing. For example, they may purchase more automobiles than they can reasonably use, or build homes with more rooms than they can possibly occupy. In an element of conspicuous consumption called *conspicuous leisure,* they may jet to a remote destination, staying just long enough to have dinner or view a sunset over some historic locale (Veblen [1899] 1964).

At the other end of the spectrum, behavior that is judged to be typical of the lower class is subject not only to ridicule but even to legal action. Communities have, from time to time, banned trailers from people's front yards and sofas from their front porches. In some communities, it is illegal to leave a pickup truck in front of the house overnight.

Is Stratification Universal?

Must some members of society receive greater rewards than others? Do people need to feel socially and economically superior to others? Can social life be organized without structured inequality? These questions have been debated for centuries, especially among political activists. Utopian socialists, religious minorities, and members of recent countercultures have all attempted to establish communities that to some extent or other would abolish inequality in social relationships.

Social scientists have found that inequality exists in all societies—even the simplest. For example, when anthropologist

With Mt. Everest in the background, a wealthy golfer plays a shot in a remote location, which he reached by helicopter. Traveling to exotic places to indulge in sports that most people play at home is an example of Thorstein Veblen's concept of conspicuous consumption, a spending pattern common to those at the very top of the social ladder.

Gunnar Landtman ([1938] 1968) studied the Kiwai Papuans of New Guinea, at first he noticed little differentiation among them. Every man in the village did the same work and lived in similar housing. However, on closer inspection, Landtman observed that certain Papuans—men who were warriors, harpooners, and sorcerers—were described as "a little more high" than others. In contrast, villagers who were female, unemployed, or unmarried were considered "down a little bit" and were barred from owning land.

Stratification is universal in that all societies maintain some form of social inequality among members. Depending on its values, a society may assign people to distinctive ranks based on their religious knowledge, skill in hunting, physical attractiveness, trading expertise, or ability to provide health care. But why has such inequality developed in human societies? And how much differentiation among people, if any, is actually essential?

Functionalist and conflict sociologists offer contrasting explanations for the existence and necessity of social stratification. Functionalists maintain that a differential system of rewards and punishments is necessary for the efficient operation of society. Conflict theorists argue that competition for scarce resources results in significant political, economic, and social inequality.

Functionalist Perspective

Would people go to school for many years to become physicians if they could make as much money and gain as much respect working as street cleaners? Functionalists say no, which is partly why they believe that a stratified society is universal.

In the view of Kingsley Davis and Wilbert Moore (1945), society must distribute its members among a variety of social positions. It must not only make sure that these positions are filled but also see that they are filled by people with the appropriate talents and abilities. Rewards, including money and prestige, are based on the importance of a position and the relative scarcity of qualified personnel. Yet this assessment often devalues work performed by certain segments of society, such as women's work in the home or in occupations traditionally filled by women, or low-status work in fast-food outlets.

Davis and Moore argue that stratification is universal and that social inequality is necessary so that people will be motivated to fill functionally important positions. But critics say that unequal rewards are not the only means of encouraging people to fill critical positions and occupations. Personal pleasure, intrinsic satisfaction, and value orientations also motivate people to enter particular careers. Functionalists agree, but they note that society must use some type of reward to motivate people to enter unpleasant or dangerous jobs and professions that require a long training period. This response does not address stratification systems in which status is largely inherited, such as slave or caste societies. Moreover, even if stratification is inevitable, the functionalist explanation for differential rewards does not explain the wide disparity between the rich and the poor (R. Collins 1975; Kerbo 2012).

Conflict Perspective

The writings of Karl Marx lie at the heart of conflict theory. Marx viewed history as a continuous struggle between the oppressors and the oppressed, which ultimately would culminate in an egalitarian, classless society. In terms of stratification, he argued that under capitalism, the dominant class—the bourgeoisie—manipulates the economic and political systems in order to maintain control over the exploited proletariat. Marx did not believe that stratification was inevitable, but he did see inequality and oppression as inherent in capitalism (E. O. Wright et al. 1982; E. O. Wright 2011).

Like Marx, contemporary conflict theorists believe that human beings are prone to conflict over scarce resources such as wealth, status, and power. However, Marx focused primarily on class conflict; more recent theorists have extended the analysis to include conflicts based on gender, race, age, and other dimensions. British sociologist Ralf Dahrendorf (1929–2009) is one of the most influential contributors to the conflict approach.

Dahrendorf (1959) has modified Marx's analysis of capitalist society to apply to modern capitalist societies. For Dahrendorf, social classes are groups of people who share common interests resulting from their authority relationships. In identifying the most powerful groups in society, he includes not only the bourgeoisie—the owners of the means of production—but also the managers of industry, legislators, the judiciary, heads of the government bureaucracy, and others. In that respect, Dahrendorf

As the reality television series *Ice Road Truckers* suggests, long-haul truck drivers take pride in their low-prestige job. According to the conflict perspective, the cultural beliefs that form a society's dominant ideology, such as the popular image of the truck driver as hero, help the wealthy to maintain their power and control at the expense of the lower classes.

has merged Marx's emphasis on class conflict with Weber's recognition that power is an important element of stratification (Cuff et al. 1990).

Conflict theorists, including Dahrendorf, contend that the powerful of today, like the bourgeoisie of Marx's time, want society to run smoothly so that they can enjoy their privileged positions. Because the status quo suits those with wealth, status,

and power, they have a clear interest in preventing, minimizing, or controlling societal conflict.

One way for the powerful to maintain the status quo is to define and disseminate the society's dominant ideology. The term **dominant ideology** describes a set of cultural beliefs and practices that helps to maintain powerful social, economic, and political interests. For Marx, the dominant ideology in a capitalist society served the interests of the ruling class. From a conflict perspective, the social significance of the dominant ideology is that not only do a society's most powerful groups and institutions control wealth and property; even more important, they control the means of producing beliefs about reality through religion, education, and the media (Abercrombie et al. 1980, 1990; Robertson 1988).

The powerful, such as leaders of government, also use limited social reforms to buy off the oppressed and reduce the danger of challenges to their dominance. For example, minimum-wage laws and unemployment compensation unquestionably give some valuable assistance to needy men and women. Yet these reforms also serve to pacify those who might otherwise rebel. Of course, in the view of conflict theorists, such maneuvers can never entirely eliminate conflict, since workers will continue to demand equality, and the powerful will not give up their control of society.

Conflict theorists see stratification as a major source of societal tension and conflict. They do not agree with Davis and Moore that stratification is functional for a society or that it serves as a source of stability. Rather, conflict sociologists argue that stratification will inevitably lead to instability and social change (R. Collins 1975; L. Coser 1977).

Table 26-2 summarizes and compares the three major perspectives on social stratification.

Lenski's Viewpoint

Let's return to the question posed earlier—Is stratification universal?—and consider the sociological response. Some form of differentiation is found in every culture, from the most primitive to the most advanced industrial societies of our time. Sociologist Gerhard Lenski, in his sociocultural evolution approach, described how economic systems change as their level of technology becomes more complex, beginning with hunting and gathering and culminating eventually with industrial society.

In subsistence-based hunting-and-gathering societies, people focus on survival. While some inequality and differentiation

Table **26-2** Sociological Perspectives on Social Stratification

Tracking Sociological Perspectives

	Functionalist	Conflict	Interactionist
Purpose of social stratification	Facilitates filling of social positions	Facilitates exploitation	Influences people's lifestyles
Attitude toward social inequality	Necessary to some extent	Excessive and growing	Influences intergroup relations
Analysis of the wealthy	Talented and skilled, creating opportunities for others	Use the dominant ideology to further their own interests	Exhibit conspicuous consumption and conspicuous leisure

are evident, a stratification system based on social class does not emerge because there is no real wealth to be claimed. As a society advances technologically, it becomes capable of producing a considerable surplus of goods. The emergence of surplus resources greatly expands the possibilities for inequality in status, influence, and power, allowing a well-defined, rigid social class system to develop. To minimize strikes, slowdowns, and industrial sabotage, the elites may share a portion of the economic surplus with the lower classes, but not enough to reduce their own power and privilege.

As Lenski argued, the allocation of surplus goods and services controlled by those with wealth, status, and power reinforces the social inequality that accompanies stratification systems. While this reward system may once have served the overall purposes of society, as functionalists contend, the same cannot be said for the large disparities separating the haves from the have-nots in current societies. In contemporary industrial society, the degree of social and economic inequality far exceeds what is needed to provide for goods and services (Lenski 1966; Nolan and Lenski 2009).

MODULE 26 | Recap and Review

Summary

Stratification is the structured ranking of entire groups of people that perpetuates unequal economic rewards and **power** in a society.

1. Some degree of **social inequality** characterizes all cultures.

2. Systems of social stratification include **slavery, castes,** the **estate system,** and social classes.

3. Karl Marx saw that differences in access to the means of production created social, economic, and political inequality, as well as two distinct classes, owners and laborers.

4. Max Weber identified three analytically distinct components of stratification: **class, status group,** and **power.**

5. Functionalists argue that stratification is necessary to motivate people to fill society's important positions. Conflict theorists see stratification as a major source of societal tension and conflict. Interactionists stress the importance of social class in determining a person's lifestyle.

Thinking Critically

1. What are the differences between slavery and caste systems? What are the similarities?

2. Give some examples of conspicuous consumption among your fellow college students. Which are obvious and which more subtle?

3. In your view, is the extent of social inequality in the United States helpful or harmful to society as a whole? Explain.

Key Terms

Achieved status   197

Ascribed status   197

Bourgeoisie   203

Capitalism   203

Caste   199

Class   204

Class consciousness   203

Class system   201

Conspicuous consumption   204

Dominant ideology   206

Estate system   201

False consciousness   203

Power   204

Proletariat   203

Slavery   199

Social inequality   197

Status group   204

Stratification   197

We continually assess how wealthy people are by looking at the cars they drive, the houses they live in, the clothes they wear, and so on. Yet it is not so easy to locate an individual within our social hierarchies as it would be in slavery or caste systems of stratification. To determine someone's class position, sociologists generally rely on the objective method.

Measuring Social Class

In the **objective method** of measuring social class, class is viewed largely as a statistical category. Researchers assign individuals to social classes on the basis of criteria such as occupation, education, income, and place of residence. The key to the objective method is that the *researcher,* rather than the person being classified, identifies an individual's class position.

The first step in using this method is to decide what indicators or causal factors will be measured objectively, whether wealth, income, education, or occupation. The prestige ranking of occupations has proved to be a useful indicator of a person's class position. For one thing, it is much easier to determine accurately than income or wealth. The term **prestige** refers to the respect and admiration that an occupation holds in a society. "My daughter, the physicist" connotes something very different from "my daughter, the waitress." Prestige is independent of the particular individual who occupies a job, a characteristic that distinguishes it from esteem. **Esteem** refers to the reputation that a specific person has earned within an occupation. Therefore, one can say that the position of president of the United States has high prestige, even though it has been occupied by people with varying degrees of esteem. A hairdresser may have the esteem of his clients, but he lacks the prestige of a corporate executive.

Table 27-1 ranks the prestige of a number of well-known occupations. In a series of national surveys, sociologists assigned prestige rankings to about 500 occupations, ranging from surgeon to panhandler. The highest possible prestige score was 100; the lowest was 0. Surgeon, physician, lawyer, dentist, and college professor were the most highly regarded occupations. Sociologists have used such data to assign prestige rankings to virtually all jobs and have found a stability in rankings from 1925 to the present. Similar studies in other countries have also developed useful prestige rankings of occupations (Nakao and Treas 1994).

Gender and Occupational Prestige

For many years, studies of social class tended to neglect the occupations and incomes of *women* as determinants of social rank. With more than half of all married women now working outside the home (see Module 35), this approach seems outmoded. How should we judge class or status in dual-career families—by the occupation regarded as having greater prestige, the average, or some other combination of the two? Sociologists—in particular, feminist sociologists in Great Britain—are drawing on new approaches to assess women's social class standing. One approach is to focus on the individual (rather than the family or household) as the basis for categorizing a woman's class position. Thus, a woman would be classified according to her own occupational status rather than that of her spouse (O'Donnell 1992).

Another feminist effort to measure the contribution of women to the economy reflects a more clearly political agenda. International Women Count Network, a global grassroots feminist organization, has sought to give a monetary value to women's unpaid work. Besides providing symbolic recognition of women's role in labor, this value would also be used to calculate pension and other benefits, which are usually based on wages received. The United Nations has placed an $11 trillion price tag on unpaid labor by women, largely in child care, housework, and agriculture. Whatever the figure, the continued undercounting of many workers' contributions to a family and to an entire economy means that virtually all measures of stratification are in need of reform (United Nations Development Programme 1995; United Nations Economic and Social Council 2010; Wages for Housework Campaign 1999).

Multiple Measures

Another complication in measuring social class is that advances in statistical methods and computer technology have multiplied the factors used to define class under the objective method. No longer are sociologists limited to annual income and education in evaluating a person's class position. Today, studies use as criteria the value of homes, sources of income, assets, years in present occupations, neighborhoods, and considerations regarding dual careers. Adding these variables will not necessarily paint a different picture of class differentiation in the United States, but it does allow sociologists to measure class in a more complex and multidimensional way. When researchers use multiple measures, they typically speak of **socioeconomic status (SES),** a measure of social class that is based on income, education, and occupation. To determine the socioeconomic status of a young person, such as a college student under age 25, they use *parental* income, education, and occupation.

Whatever the technique used to measure class, the sociologist is interested in real and often dramatic differences in power, privilege, and opportunity in a society. The study of

Table **27-1** Prestige Rankings of Occupations

Occupation	Score	Occupation	Score
Physician	86	Bank teller	50
College professor	78	Electrician	49
Lawyer	76	Farm manager	48
Dentist	74	Insurance agent	47
Banker	72	Secretary	46
Architect	71	Mail carrier	42
Airline pilot	70	Farmer	41
Clergy	69	Correctional officer	40
Registered nurse	66	Carpenter	40
High school teacher	63	Receptionist	39
Dental hygienist	61	Barber	38
Legislator	61	Child care worker	36
Pharmacist	61	Hotel clerk	32
Elementary school teacher	60	Bus driver	32
Veterinarian	60	Auto body repairer	31
Police officer or detective	60	Truck driver	30
Prekindergarten teacher	60	Salesworker (shoes)	28
Accountant	57	Waiter and waitress	28
Librarian	55	Cook (short-order)	28
Firefighter	53	Bartender	25
Funeral director	52	Garbage collector	17
Social worker	52	Janitor	16
Optician	51	Newspaper vendor	15

Note: 100 is the highest and 0 the lowest possible prestige score.
Source: General Social Survey 2012.

Think about It

Can you name what you think are two more high-prestige occupations? Two more low-prestige occupations?

stratification is a study of inequality. Nowhere is the truth of that statement more evident than in the distribution of income and wealth.

● Income and Wealth

By all measures, in the United States **income,** a term that refers to salaries and wages, is distributed unevenly. Nobel Prize–winning economist Paul Samuelson has described the situation in the following words: "If we made an income pyramid out of building blocks, with each layer portraying $500 of income, the peak would be far higher than Mount Everest, but most people would be within a few feet of the ground" (Samuelson and Nordhaus 2010:324).

Recent data support Samuelson's analogy. In 2010, the median household income in the United States was $49,445. In other words, half of all households had higher incomes that year and half had lower incomes. However, this fact does not fully convey the income disparities in our society. We can get some sense of income inequality by contrasting this median (middle) income with the mean arithmetic average, which in 2010 was $67,530. The mean is so much higher than the median because some people make a lot more money than others, which draws the mean up. Thus, the mean is a less useful statistic than the median for describing the average, or typical, income (DeNavas-Walt et al. 2011:33–34).

We can gain additional insight into income inequality in the United States by looking at the relative placement of households within the income distribution. One of the most common ways of doing so is to line up all income-earning households from low to high and then break them into quintiles, or fifths. Because there

time. In 1965, top executives earned only 24 times the average worker's pay. By 2010, the gap had widened to 325 times the average (S. Anderson et al. 2011).

Applying Sociology

From a functionalist perspective, such generous compensation seems reasonable given the potential for gain that a talented executive brings to a corporation. Today, even a small increase in a multibillion-dollar company's performance can add hundreds of millions of dollars to its bottom line. Not surprisingly, then, competition to attract top-performing executives to a company is fierce. Not all these executives are successful all the time, however; sometimes their leadership reduces profits. Critics point out that during the last decade, 7 of the top 25 highly paid executives presided over companies that lost money (Frank 2010; Thurm 2010).

Conflict theorists question not only the relatively high levels of executive compensation, but also the process through which executives' pay is determined. The board of directors, which holds the responsibility for determining executives' pay, has an incentive to go along with arrangements that are favorable to top executives. Board members themselves earned an average of about $228,000 in 2009, so they have a natural desire to avoid conflict over high salaries (Bebchuk and Fried 2010; Strauss 2011).

Taking an almost interactionist approach, sociologist Thomas DiPrete and his colleagues have observed that today, corporations must report executives' compensation relative to their peer group's compensation—that is, to the compensation received by leaders of similar businesses of similar size. Although members of such peer groups do not interact in the way that members of a primary group or even a secondary group would, they do form a social network. Thus, public comparisons of executive compensation within particular industries may influence board members' decisions, prompting them to tie executives' compensation more directly to their performance (DiPrete et al. 2010).

Initiating Policy

Although policymakers have long been concerned about executive compensation, until recently hard data have been difficult to obtain. Before 1992, corporations were required to disclose executives' pay, but not in a uniform manner. Many companies disguised the dollar amounts by literally spelling the words out in the midst of long, densely written documents. Today, the law mandates that companies publish "summary compensation tables." In 2006, reporting requirements were expanded to cover retirement packages, including the "golden parachute" clauses that protect executives who bail out of failing companies (Bebchuk and Fried 2010).

In 2011, as the U.S. economy began to pull out of a deep, long-lasting recession, corporate executives were still earning huge salaries and bonuses—despite the fact that many workers remained jobless.

During the economic downturn that began in 2008, the value of the stock that top executives received as part of their compensation packages did decline. Yet overall, CEOs' salaries in the 500 largest corporations still rose 3 percent in 2009. In response, the White House appointed a Treasury Department official, whom reporters quickly dubbed the "pay czar," to look into executive compensation. Given the deferred stock payments, expense accounts, and other perquisites executives typically receive, the assignment was a difficult one (D. Jones and Hansen 2009).

In the short time the pay czar has been in office, results have been mixed. Critics complain the office hasn't made significant progress in curbing executive pay, while companies claim that the government is hampering their ability to compete. Although the czar has managed to change some compensation practices, critics worry that companies may develop new ways to inflate executives' pay (Congressional Oversight Panel 2011; Edmans and Gabaix 2010; Grusky and Wimer 2010; Reuters 2010).

TAKE THE ISSUE WITH YOU

1. Should corporate executives earn high salaries even when their companies are losing money? Explain. How do you think functionalists would defend such a practice?

2. What do you think of the "golden parachute" clauses that allow executives to bail out of failing companies unharmed? What might be the effect of such clauses on executives' performance? On shareholders and on lower-level employees?

3. Relate the increases in executive compensation over the past half century to changes in U.S. social structure during that time. How have those changes affected you and your family?

Summary

Poverty is difficult to explain or define, although its effects are obvious and pervasive.

1. Many of those who live in poverty are full-time workers who struggle to support their families at minimum-wage jobs. The long-term poor—those who lack the training and skills to lift themselves out of poverty—form an **underclass.**

2. Functionalists find that the poor satisfy positive functions for many of the nonpoor in the United States.

3. One's **life chances** —opportunities for obtaining material goods, positive living conditions, and favorable life experiences—are related to one's social class. Occupying a high social position improves a person's life chances.

4. **Social mobility** is more likely to be found in an **open system** that emphasizes achieved status than in a **closed system** that emphasizes ascribed status. Race, gender, and family background are important factors in social mobility.

5. During the past half century, the gap between executive compensation and the average worker's pay has increased to 325 to 1. Although corporations claim that talented leaders enhance their performance, making executive pay packages well worth the money, they have gone to some trouble to disguise the expense from public scrutiny.

Thinking Critically

1. How do you identify areas of poverty in your own community or one nearby? Do you consider residents' achieved or ascribed characteristics?

2. How do people's life chances affect society as a whole?

3. Which factor—occupation, education, race and ethnicity, or gender—do you expect will have the greatest impact on your own social mobility? Explain.

Key Terms

Absolute poverty   212

Closed system   216

Feminization of poverty   213

Horizontal mobility   216

Intergenerational mobility   216

Intragenerational mobility   217

Life chances   215

Open system   216

Precarious work   213

Relative poverty   212

Social mobility   216

Underclass   214

Vertical mobility   216

Mastering This Chapter

taking sociology with you

1 Do some research on the educational and occupational levels in the city or town where you live. Based on what you have learned, describe the social-class stratification of your community.

2 Use census data to create a map showing the median income levels and/or property values in the geographic areas surrounding your home. What patterns does it show?

3 Talk with a parent or grandparent about your family's history. What can you learn about your forebears' life chances? About their social mobility? How do you hope to fit into the story?

Absolute poverty A minimum level of subsistence that no family should be expected to live below. (page 212)

Achieved status A social position that a person attains largely through his or her own efforts. (197)

Ascribed status A social position assigned to a person by society without regard for the person's unique talents or characteristics. (197)

Bourgeoisie Karl Marx's term for the capitalist class, comprising the owners of the means of production. (203)

Capitalism An economic system in which the means of production are held largely in private hands and the main incentive for economic activity is the accumulation of profits. (203)

Caste A hereditary rank, usually religiously dictated, that tends to be fixed and immobile. (199)

Class A group of people who have a similar level of wealth and income. (204)

Class consciousness In Karl Marx's view, a subjective awareness held by members of a class regarding their common vested interests and the need for collective political action to bring about social change. (203)

Class system A social ranking based primarily on economic position in which achieved characteristics can influence social mobility. (201)

Closed system A social system in which there is little or no possibility of individual social mobility. (216)

Conspicuous consumption Purchasing goods not to survive but to flaunt one's superior wealth and social standing. (204)

Dominant ideology A set of cultural beliefs and practices that helps to maintain powerful social, economic, and political interests. (206)

Estate system A system of stratification under which peasants were required to work land leased to them by nobles in exchange for military protection and other services. Also known as *feudalism.* (201)

Esteem The reputation that a specific person has earned within an occupation. (208)

False consciousness A term used by Karl Marx to describe an attitude held by members of a class that does not accurately reflect their objective position. (203)

Feminization of poverty A trend in which women constitute an increasing proportion of the poor people of both the United States and the world. (213)

Horizontal mobility The movement of an individual from one social position to another of the same rank. (216)

Income Salaries and wages. (209)

Intergenerational mobility Changes in the social position of children relative to their parents. (216)

Intragenerational mobility Changes in social position within a person's adult life. (217)

Life chances The opportunities people have to provide themselves with material goods, positive living conditions, and favorable life experiences. (215)

Objective method A technique for measuring social class that assigns individuals to classes on the basis of criteria such as occupation, education, income, and place of residence. (208)

Open system A social system in which the position of each individual is influenced by his or her achieved status. (216)

Power The ability to exercise one's will over others. (204)

Precarious work Employment that is poorly paid, and from the worker's perspective, insecure and unprotected. (213)

Prestige The respect and admiration that an occupation holds in a society. (208)

Proletariat Karl Marx's term for the working class in a capitalist society. (203)

Relative poverty A floating standard of deprivation by which people at the bottom of a society, whatever their lifestyles, are judged to be disadvantaged *in comparison with the nation as a whole.* (212)

Slavery A system of enforced servitude in which some people are owned by other people. (199)

Social inequality A condition in which members of society have differing amounts of wealth, prestige, or power. (197)

Social mobility Movement of individuals or groups from one position in a society's stratification system to another. (216)

Socioeconomic status (SES) A measure of social class that is based on income, education, and occupation. (208)

Status group People who have the same prestige or lifestyle, independent of their class positions. (204)

Stratification A structured ranking of entire groups of people that perpetuates unequal economic rewards and power in a society. (197)

Underclass The long-term poor who lack training and skills. (214)

Vertical mobility The movement of an individual from one social position to another of a different rank. (216)

Wealth An inclusive term encompassing all a person's material assets, including land, stocks, and other types of property. (211)

Read each question carefully and then select the best answer.

1. Which of the following describes a condition in which members of a society have different amounts of wealth, prestige, or power?
   a. stratification
   b. status inconsistency
   c. slavery
   d. social inequality

2. In Karl Marx's view, the destruction of the capitalist system will occur only if the working class first develops
   a. bourgeois consciousness.
   b. false consciousness.
   c. class consciousness.
   d. caste consciousness.

3. Which of the following were viewed by Max Weber as analytically distinct components of stratification?
   a. conformity, deviance, and social control
   b. class, status, and power
   c. class, caste, and age
   d. class, prestige, and esteem

4. Which sociological perspective argues that stratification is universal and that social inequality is necessary so that people will be motivated to fill socially important positions?
   a. the functionalist perspective
   b. the conflict perspective
   c. the interactionist perspective
   d. the labeling perspective

5. British sociologist Ralf Dahrendorf views social classes as groups of people who share common interests resulting from their authority relationships. Dahrendorf's ideology aligns best with which theoretical perspective?
    a. the functionalist perspective
    b. the conflict perspective
    c. the interactionist perspective
    d. sociocultural evolution

6. The respect or admiration that an occupation holds in a society is referred to as
    a. status.
    b. esteem.
    c. prestige.
    d. ranking.

7. Approximately how many out of every nine people in the United States live(s) below the poverty line established by the federal government?
    a. one
    b. two
    c. three
    d. four

8. Which sociologist has applied functionalist analysis to the existence of poverty and argues that various segments of society actually benefit from the existence of the poor?
    a. Émile Durkheim
    b. Max Weber
    c. Karl Marx
    d. Herbert Gans

9. A measure of social class that is based on income, education, and occupation is known as
    a. the objective method.
    b. stratification.
    c. socioeconomic status.
    d. the open system.

10. A plumber whose father was a physician is an example of
    a. downward intergenerational mobility.
    b. upward intergenerational mobility.
    c. downward intragenerational mobility.
    d. upward intragenerational mobility.

11. _____ is the most extreme form of legalized social inequality for individuals or groups.

12. In the _____ system of stratification, or feudalism, peasants were required to work land leased to them by nobles in exchange for military protection and other services.

13. Karl Marx viewed _____ differentiation as the crucial determinant of social, economic, and political inequality.

14. _____ _____ is the term Thorstein Veblen used to describe the extravagant spending patterns of those at the top of the class hierarchy.

15. _____ poverty is the minimum level of subsistence that no family should be expected to live below.

16. _____ poverty is a floating standard of deprivation by which people at the bottom of a society, whatever their lifestyles, are judged to be disadvantaged in comparison with the nation as a whole.

17. Sociologist William Julius Wilson and other social scientists have used the term _____ to describe the long-term poor who lack training and skills.

18. Max Weber used the term _____ _____ to refer to people's opportunities to provide themselves with material goods, positive living conditions, and favorable life experiences.

19. An open class system implies that the position of each individual is influenced by the person's _____ status.

20. _____ mobility involves changes in social position within a person's adult life.

Answers
1 (d); 2 (c); 3 (b); 4 (a); 5 (b); 6 (c); 7 (a); 8 (d); 9 (c); 10 (a); 11 Slavery; 12 estate; 13 class; 14 Conspicuous consumption; 15 Absolute; 16 Relative; 17 underclass; 18 life chances; 19 achieved; 20 Intragenerational

 thinking about movies

The Fighter

Two working-class brothers strive for upward mobility in the world of professional boxing.

Jumping the Broom

When two families come together to celebrate a wedding, social-class differences cause tension.

Dark Days

In this documentary, a community of homeless people in New York City copes with extreme poverty by living underground near a railroad station.

Could you live on less than $2 a day, including your rent or campus housing?

When a team of researchers asked poor people in developing countries how they spent their meager incomes, the results were surprising.

❝ To get a first sense of what the financial diaries [of the poor] reveal, consider Hamid and Khadeja. The couple married in a poor coastal village of Bangladesh where there was very little work for a poorly educated and unskilled young man like Hamid. Soon after their first child was born they gave up rural life and moved, as so many hundreds of thousands had done before them, to the capital city, Dhaka, where they settled in a slum. After spells as a cycle-rickshaw driver and construction laborer and many days of unemployment, Hamid, whose health was not good, finally got taken on as a reserve driver of a motorized rickshaw. That's what he was doing when we first met Hamid and Khadeja in late 1999, while Khadeja stayed home to run the household, raise their child, and earn a little from taking in sewing work. Home was one of a strip of small rooms with cement block walls and a tin roof, built by their landlord on illegally occupied land, with a toilet and kitchen space shared by the eight families that lived there.

In an average month they lived on the equivalent of $70, almost all of it earned by Hamid, whose income arrived in unpredictable daily amounts that varied according to whether he got work that day (he was only the reserve driver) and, if he did get work, how much business he attracted, how many hours he was allowed to keep his vehicle, and how often it broke down. A fifth of the $70 was spent on rent (not always paid on time), and much of the rest went toward the most basic necessities of life—food and the means to prepare it. By the couple's own reckoning, which our evidence agrees with, their income put them among the poor of Bangladesh, though not among the very poorest. By global standards they would fall into the bottom two-fifths of the world's income distribution tables.

An unremarkable poor household: a partly educated couple trying to stay alive, bring up a child, run a one-room home, and keep Ha-mid's health in shape—on an uncertain $0.78 per person per day. You wouldn't expect them to have much of a financial life. Yet the diversity of instruments in their year-end household balance sheet shows that Hamid and Khadeja, as part of their struggle to survive within their slim means, were active money managers.

Far from living hand-to-mouth, consuming every taka as soon as it arrived, Hamid and Khadeja had built up reserves in six different instruments, ranging from $2 kept at home for minor day-to-day shortfalls to $30 sent for safe-keeping to his parents, $40 lent out to a relative, and $76 in a life insurance savings policy. In addition, Hamid always made sure he had $2 in his pocket to deal with anything that might befall him on the road.

In addition to saving, borrowing, and repaying *money,* Hamid and Khadeja, like nearly all poor and some not-so-poor households, also saved, borrowed, and repaid in kind. Khadeja, sharing a crude kitchen with seven other wives, would often swap small amounts of rice or lentils or salt with her neighbors. She would keep a note of the quantities in her head, and so would her partners in these exchanges, to ensure that their transactions were fair over the long haul. Virtually all of the rural Bangladeshi households followed the well-established tradition of *musti chaul*—of keeping back one fistful of dry rice each time a meal was cooked, to hold against lean times, to have ready when a beggar called, or to donate to the mosque or temple when called on to do so. For rural respondents in India and Bangladesh, the intermediation of goods and services rather than cash was common, and included borrowing grain to be repaid after the harvest, repaying a loan with one's labor, or using labor to buy farm inputs. We recorded much of this activity. ❞

An unremarkable poor household: a partly educated couple trying to stay alive, bring up a child, run a one-room home, and keep Hamid's health in shape—on an uncertain $0.78 per person per day. You wouldn't expect them to have much of a financial life.

(D. Collins et al. 2009:7–8, 10–11) Additional information about this excerpt can be found on the Online Learning Center at www.mhhe.com/schaefermod2e.

Well over 2.5 billion people live on less than $2 a day—the widely recognized definition of poverty in the developing world. Incredibly, over 50 percent of them live on less than the extreme poverty level of $1.25 a day (World Bank 2012a:41). To find out how these poor households survive, four researchers conducted an intensive study of 250 families in Bangladesh, India, and South Africa. Daryl Collins, Jonathan Morduch, Stuart Rutherford, and Orlanda Ruthven wanted to know how best to use *microfinance*—small lending—to assist poor families in the developing world. As explained in the book *Portfolios of the Poor: How the World's Poor Live on $2 a Day,* rather than simply interviewing the families, Collins and his colleagues asked them to maintain financial diaries for a year.

Through the diaries, the research team discovered that the families were quite adept at managing their income. Because the stakes were high—there is no room for error on $1 or $2 a day—these mostly uneducated people had surprisingly sophisticated methods for managing their resources.

In developing countries like Bangladesh, most but not all the people are poor. Even in the poorest countries, the poor rub shoulders with the very wealthy. Inequality, then, exists within all countries, not just within the United States. On a global scale, inequality also exists *between* developing and developed nations, which is why a living allowance of $2 a day is so difficult for those of us in the developed world to comprehend. In these modules we will consider social inequality both within developing nations and between the developing and developed worlds.

What economic and political conditions explain the divide between rich nations and poor? Within developing nations, how are wealth and income distributed, and how much opportunity does the average worker have to move up the social ladder? How do race and gender affect social mobility in these countries? In Module 29 we will focus on global inequality, beginning with the global divide. We will consider the impact of colonialism and neocolonialism, globalization, the rise of multinational corporations, and the trend toward modernization. Then we will focus on stratification within nations, in terms of the distribution of wealth and income as well as social mobility. In a special case study, we will look closely at social stratification in Mexico, including the social impact of race and gender and the economic effects of industrialization. The chapter closes with a Social Policy section on welfare reform in Europe and North America.

The Global Divide

In some parts of the world, the people who have dedicated their lives to fighting starvation refer to what they call "coping mechanisms"—ways in which the desperately poor attempt to control their hunger. Eritrean women will strap flat stones to their stomachs to lessen their hunger pangs. In Mozambique, people eat the grasshoppers that have destroyed the crops, calling them "flying shrimp." Though dirt eating is considered a pathological condition (called *pica*) among the well-fed, the world's poor eat dirt to add minerals to their diet. And in many countries, mothers have been known to boil stones in water, to convince their hungry children that supper is almost ready. As they hover over the pot, these women hope that their malnourished children will fall asleep (McNeil 2004).

Around the world, inequality is a significant determinant of human behavior, opening doors of opportunity to some and closing them to others. Indeed, disparities in life chances are so extreme that in some places, the poorest of the poor may not be aware of them. Western media images may have circled the globe, but in extremely depressed rural areas, those at the bottom of society are not likely to see them.

A few centuries ago, such vast divides in global wealth did not exist. Except for a very few rulers and landowners, everyone in the world was poor. In much of Europe, life was as difficult as it was in Asia or South America. This was true until the Industrial Revolution and rising agricultural productivity produced explosive economic growth. The resulting rise in living standards was not evenly distributed across the world.

Figure 29-1 compares the industrialized nations of the world to the developing nations. Using total population as a yardstick, we see that the developing countries have more than their fair share of rural population, as well as of total births, disease, and childhood deaths. At the same time, the industrialized nations of the world, with a much smaller share of total population, have much more income and exports than the developing nations. Industrialized nations also spend more on health and the military than other nations, and they emit more carbon dioxide (CO_2; Sachs 2005; Sutcliffe 2002).

Although the divide between industrialized and developing nations is sharp, sociologists recognize a continuum of nations, from the richest of the rich to the poorest of the poor. For example, in 2008, the average value of goods and services produced per citizen (or per capita gross national income) in the industrialized countries of the United States, the Netherlands, Switzerland, France, and Norway was more than $47,000. In at least 39 poorer countries, the value was just $1,000 or less. However, most countries fell somewhere between those extremes, as Figure 29-2 shows.

Still, the contrasts are stark. Three forces discussed here are particularly responsible for the domination of the world marketplace by a few nations: the legacy of colonialism, the advent of multinational corporations, and modernization.

The Legacy of Colonialism

Colonialism occurs when a foreign power maintains political, social, economic, and cultural domination over a people for an

FIGURE 29-1 Fundamental Global Inequality

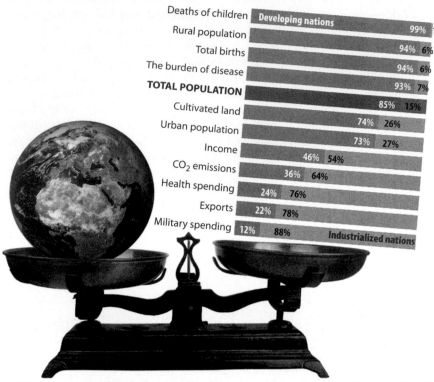

	Developing nations	Industrialized nations
Deaths of children	99%	1%
Rural population	94%	6%
Total births	94%	6%
The burden of disease	93%	7%
TOTAL POPULATION	85%	15%
Cultivated land	74%	26%
Urban population	73%	27%
Income	46%	54%
CO_2 emissions	36%	64%
Health spending	24%	76%
Exports	22%	78%
Military spending	12%	88%

Note: In this comparison, industrialized nations include the United States and Canada, Japan, western Europe, and Australasia. Developing nations include Africa, Asia (except for Japan), Latin America, eastern Europe, the Caribbean, and the Pacific.

Source: Adapted from Sutcliffe 2002:18.

Think about It

What is the relationship between health spending, disease, and deaths of children? Between CO_2 emissions, income, and exports?

extended period. In simple terms, it is rule by outsiders. The long reign of the British Empire over much of North America, parts of Africa, and India was an example of colonial domination. The same can be said of French rule over Algeria, Tunisia, and other parts of North Africa. Relations between the colonial nation and colonized people are similar to those between the dominant capitalist class and the proletariat, as described by Karl Marx.

By the 1980s, colonialism had largely disappeared. Most of the nations that were colonies before World War I had achieved political independence and established their own governments. However, for many of those countries, the transition to genuine self-rule was not yet complete. Colonial domination had established patterns of economic exploitation that continued even after nationhood was achieved—in part because former colonies were unable to develop their own industry and technology. Their dependence on more industrialized nations, including their former colonial masters, for managerial and technical expertise, investment capital, and manufactured goods kept former colonies in a subservient position. Such continuing dependence and foreign domination are referred to as **neocolonialism.**

The economic and political consequences of colonialism and neocolonialism are readily apparent. Drawing on the conflict perspective, sociologist Immanuel Wallerstein (1974, 1979a, 2000, 2012) views the global economic system as being divided between nations that control wealth and nations from which resources are taken. Through his **world systems analysis,** Wallerstein has described an interdependent global economy resting on unequal economic and political relationships. Critical to his analysis is the understanding that by themselves, nations do not, nor have they ever, constituted whole systems. Instead, they exist within a larger, global social context.

In Wallerstein's view, certain industrialized nations (among them the United States, Japan, and Germany) and their global corporations dominate the *core* of this system (Figure 29-3)

What do we stand in line for? People's needs and desires differ dramatically depending on where they live. On the left, eager customers line up outside a store in New York City to purchase the newly released iPhone 4S. On the right, residents of Ethiopia line up to receive water.

FIGURE 29-2 Gross National Income per Capita

GNI per capita in 2010

- Below $3,100
- $3,100–$7,995
- $8,000–$19,100
- Over $19,200
- No available data

Note: Country sizes and incomes based on 2010 estimates. Includes only those countries with 3 million or more people. The color for each country shows the gross national income (the total value of goods and services produced by the nation in a given year) per capita.

Sources: Haub 2010; Weeks 2012.

This stylized map reflects the relative population sizes of the world's nations. The color for each country shows the gross national income (the total value of goods and services produced by the nation in a given year) per capita.

Those who take a conflict perspective also urge policymakers and the general public to look closely at **corporate welfare**—the tax breaks, bailouts, direct payments, and grants that the government gives to corporations—rather than looking closely at the comparatively small allowances being given to mothers and their children. Yet any suggestion to curtail such corporate welfare brings a strong response from special-interest groups that are much more powerful than any coalition on behalf of the poor. One example of corporate welfare is the huge federal bailouts given to distressed financial institutions in fall 2008 and to bankrupt automobile companies in 2009. Although the outlay of hundreds of billions of dollars was vital to the nation's economic recovery, the measure received relatively little scrutiny

In northern and western Europe, following the deep worldwide recession that began in 2008, countries with strong social safety nets were forced to cut back benefits. These civil servants in Granada, Spain, are protesting salary cutbacks.

from Congress. Just a few months later, however, when legislation was proposed to extend the safety net for laid-off workers—unemployment compensation, food stamps, subsidized child care, assistance to the homeless, disability support, and infant nutrition—it met with loud demands for the monitoring of expenditures (DeParle 2009; Piven and Cloward 1996).

Initiating Policy

The government likes to highlight welfare-reform success stories. Though many people who once depended on tax dollars are now working and paying taxes themselves, it is much too soon to see if "workfare" will be successful. The new jobs that were generated by the booming economy of the late 1990s were an unrealistic test of the system. Prospects have faded for the hard-core jobless—people who are difficult to train or are encumbered by drug or alcohol abuse, physical disabilities, or child care needs—since that boom passed.

True, fewer people remain on the rolls since welfare reform was enacted in August 1996. By November 2011 just under 1.9 million families were still on the rolls, down 65 percent from a high of 5.1 million in 1994. But while those families that have left the rolls are modestly better off now, most of their breadwinners continue to hold low-paying, unskilled jobs. For them, the economic downturn that was well in place by 2009 made finding work tougher than ever. Of those adults who remain on welfare, nearly 60 percent are not in school or in welfare-to-work

programs, as the law requires them to be. This group tends to face the greatest challenges—substance abuse, mental illness, or a criminal record (Bitler and Hoynes 2010; Danziger 2010; Department of Health and Human Services 2012a).

European governments have encountered many of the same citizen demands as in North America: keep our taxes low, even if it means reducing services to the poor. However, nations in eastern and central Europe have faced a special challenge since the end of communism. Though governments in those nations traditionally provided an impressive array of social services, they differed from capitalist systems in several important respects. First, the communist system was premised on full employment, so there was no need to provide unemployment insurance; social services focused on the old and the disabled. Second, subsidies for housing and even utilities played an important role. With new competition from the West and tight budgets, some of these countries are beginning to realize that universal coverage is no longer affordable and must be replaced with targeted programs.

The reduction in state assistance to the unemployed is not limited to the former Soviet bloc. Even Sweden, despite its long history of social welfare programs, is feeling the pinch. Welfare payments have been reduced there over the past two years, and the number of sick days and other employment benefits trimmed. Yet by any standard, the European safety net is still significantly stronger than that of the United States (*The Economist* 2010d; Petrásóvá 2006; M. Walker and Thurow 2009).

—Continued

This decline in public assistance has not escaped public attention. Erik O. Wright, 2012 president of the American Sociological Society, has observed that the Occupy Wall Street movement (described at the beginning of Chapter 8) "is not a uniquely American event . . . it is part of a global wave of protests." Wright senses rising concern that "harsh inequalities" are becoming "increasingly illegitimate. It would appear the present trends in welfare policy are doing little to address these concerns" (E. O. Wright 2011).

MODULE 30 | Recap and Review

Summary

This module examines the effects of stratification within nations. The global economic system creates and perpetuates the gap between the rich and poor in developing nations.

1. Although Mexico is unquestionably a poor country, the gap between its richest and poorest citizens is one of the widest in the world.

2. The subordinate status of Mexico's Indians is but one reflection of the nation's color hierarchy, which links social class to the appearance of racial purity.

3. Growing recognition of the **borderlands** reflects the increasingly close and complex relationship between Mexico and the United States.

Thinking Critically

1. Contrast social mobility in developing and industrial nations. Do you think the differences will eventually disappear? Why or why not?

2. How do the borderlands increase social mobility within Mexico? How do they hinder it?

Key Terms

Borderlands   241

Corporate Welfare   244

Remittances   241

Mastering
This Chapter

taking sociology with you

1 Pick a multinational corporation whose products you are familiar with and look up its financial statements. In which countries does the corporation produce products and in which does it sell products? In which country does the corporation pay taxes? To which country do its profits flow? Why should the answers to these questions matter to you?

2 Choose a foreign country that you are interested in and do some research on social stratification in that

country. How equally or unequally are wealth and income distributed there, in comparison to the United States? How extensive is social mobility? Explain the reasons for any differences in stratification.

3 Choose a European country and a developing country and do some research on their welfare systems. How do the two systems differ? How does each reflect the culture and society it serves?

key terms

Borderlands The area of common culture along the border between Mexico and the United States. (page 241)

Colonialism The maintenance of political, social, economic, and cultural domination over a people by a foreign power for an extended period. (227)

Corporate welfare Tax breaks, bailouts, direct payments, and grants that the government gives to corporations. (244)

Dependency theory An approach that contends that industrialized nations continue to exploit developing countries for their own gain. (230)

Globalization The worldwide integration of government policies, cultures, social movements, and financial markets through trade and the exchange of ideas. (230)

Modernization The far-reaching process through which periphery nations move from traditional or less developed institutions to those characteristic of more developed societies. (235)

Modernization theory A functionalist approach that proposes that modernization and development will gradually improve the lives of people in developing nations. (235)

Multinational corporation A commercial organization that is headquartered in one country but does business throughout the world. (233)

Neocolonialism Continuing dependence of former colonies on foreign countries. (228)

Remittances The monies that immigrants return to their families of origin. Also called *migradollars*. (241)

World systems analysis The global economy as an interdependent system of economically and politically unequal nations. (228)

self-quiz

Read each question carefully and then select the best answer.

1. The maintenance of political, social, economic, and cultural domination over a people by a foreign power for an extended period is referred to as
   a. neocolonialism.
   b. government-imposed stratification.
   c. colonialism.
   d. dependency.

2. In viewing the global economic system as divided between nations that control wealth and those that are controlled and exploited, sociologist Immanuel Wallerstein draws on the
   a. functionalist perspective.
   b. conflict perspective.

   c. interactionist perspective.
   d. dramaturgical approach.

3. Which of the following nations would Immanuel Wallerstein classify as a *core* country within the world economic system?
   a. Germany
   b. South Korea
   c. Ireland
   d. Mexico

4. Which sociological perspective argues that multinational corporations can actually help the developing nations of the world?
   a. the interactionist perspective
   b. the feminist perspective

c. the functionalist perspective

d. the conflict perspective

5. Which of the following terms is used by contemporary social scientists to describe the far-reaching process by which peripheral nations move from traditional or less developed institutions to those characteristic of more developed societies?

    a. dependency

    b. globalization

    c. industrialization

    d. modernization

6. In at least 22 nations around the world, the most affluent 10 percent receives at least what percentage of all income?

    a. 20 percent

    b. 30 percent

    c. 40 percent

    d. 50 percent

7. Karuna Chanana Ahmed, an anthropologist from India who has studied developing nations, calls which group the most exploited of oppressed people?

    a. children

    b. women

c. the elderly

d. the poor

8. Which of the following terms is used to refer to Mexico's large, impoverished majority, most of whom have brown skin and a mixed racial lineage due to intermarriage?

    a. *criollo*

    b. *indio*

    c. *mestizo*

    d. *zapatista*

9. In Mexico, women now constitute what percentage of the labor force?

    a. 15 percent

    b. 23 percent

    c. 34 percent

    d. 48 percent

10. Which of the following terms refers to the foreign-owned factories established just across the border in Mexico, where the companies that own them don't have to pay taxes or provide insurance or benefits for their workers?

    a. *maquiladoras*

    b. *hombres*

    c. *mujeres*

    d. *toreadors*

11. Colonial domination established patterns of economic exploitation leading to former colonies remaining dependent on more industrialized nations. Such continuing dependence and foreign domination are referred to as _____.

12. According to Immanuel Wallerstein's analysis, the United States is at the _____ while neighboring Mexico is on the _____ of the world economic system.

13. Wallerstein's world systems analysis is the most widely used version of _____ theory.

14. _____ factories are factories found throughout the developing world that are run by multinational corporations.

15. As _____ industries become a more important part of the international marketplace, many companies have concluded that the low costs of overseas operations more than offset the expense of transmitting information around the world.

16. Viewed from a(n) _____ perspective, the combination of skilled technology and management provided by multinationals and the relatively cheap labor available in developing nations is ideal for a global enterprise.

17. In 2000 the United Nations launched the _____ _____; its objective is to eliminate extreme poverty worldwide by the year 2015.

18. Modernization theory reflects the _____ perspective.

19. At the top of the color hierarchy in Mexico are the _____, the 10 percent of the population who are typically White, well-educated members of the business and intellectual elites, and who have familial roots in Spain.

20. The term _____ refers to the area of a common culture along the border between Mexico and the United States.

thinking about movies

The End of Poverty?

This documentary asks whether we can close the gap between rich and poor nations by redistributing the world's wealth.

Hotel Rwanda

A hotel becomes a safe haven during the Rwandan genocide.

The Inheritors

Mexican agricultural laborers endure harsh working conditions in this documentary film.

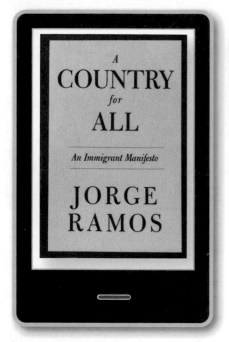

What kind of barriers to success have you faced in your life? Were they connected to your race, ethnicity, or citizenship status?

Many people have faced such barriers and overcome them, but few of them have risen as fast and as far as Alfredo Quiñones-Hinojosa.

" The life of Alfredo Quiñones-Hinojosa is an inspiring example of what an undocumented [illegal] immigrant can do in the United States when given the opportunity.

Alfredo came to the United States as an undocumented immigrant in 1987. He was just nineteen years old, and one of six children. "I was hopping back and forth," he told me, "between Calexico (in the United States) and Mexicali (in Mexico).... All I wanted to do back then was provide food and basic living essentials to a very poor Mexican family."

Alfredo crossed over the border without the aid of a coyote, or guide. His family didn't have the six-hundred-dollar going rate to hire one at the time.

His first job was as a farmhand, cultivating tomatoes, chili peppers, and cotton in central California's San Joaquin Valley. He earned $3.35 an hour. Later, he moved to a small city, where he tried his hand at other jobs: sweeping floors, shoeing horses, and soldering metal. That was where he learned English, and eventually he applied and was accepted to a local community college.

His next big step was when he accepted an offer to study at the University of California at Berkeley. Alfredo dreamed of becoming a doctor, and nothing was going to stop him.

After graduating from Berkeley, Alfredo was accepted to Harvard Medical School, where he graduated with honors. He then returned to California to complete his residency in neurosurgery at the University of California–San Francisco.

This young man, who started his working life harvesting cotton in the fields, now serves as the director of the brain tumor program at the Johns Hopkins Bayview campus.

After enduring a lengthy legal process, Alfredo became an American citizen in 1997. And in Boston, during his citizenship ceremony, he came to the realization that in a short time he had achieved something that takes most others an entire generation.

"The person who was speaking at the ceremony began to talk about how his great-grandfather had come here from Italy, and that his grandfather had worked hard so that his father could become a teacher, and how he eventually got to Harvard," he recalled. "And I realized that in less than ten years, I had jumped over all those generations."

As he told me, "A jump like that might seem incredible, but it's not impossible."

Today, Alfredo's expertise in treating spinal, brain stem, and brain tumors quite literally saves lives. Every single day. He is also heavily involved in researching the origins of tumors, and in developing new ways of treating brain cancer that might one day lead to a cure. "That would be my dream," he said. "Of course, many people consider that impossible. But that's also what people would have said about my life, back when I was only nineteen years old," and an undocumented farm worker.

There are many people like Dr. Quiñones-Hinojosa living among us, and with as much potential. But so many are not as lucky as he is.

These millions continue to live in the shadows. "

(Ramos 2010:xiii–xvi) Additional information about this excerpt can be found on the Online Learning Center at www.mhhe.com/schaefermod2e

His first job was as a farmhand, cultivating tomatoes, chili peppers, and cotton in central California's San Joaquin Valley. He earned $3.35 an hour.

In this excerpt from *A Country for All: An Immigrant Manifesto*, journalist Jorge Ramos writes about the remarkable life of Dr. Alfredo Quiñones-Hinojosa, or Dr. Q, as he has come to be known. Few people, even those who are privileged, attend Harvard University and then go on to become neurosurgeons and brain researchers. On the face of it, Dr. Q's rise from immigrant farm laborer to eminent neurosurgeon suggests that the United States is a land of opportunity for all, despite race or ethnicity. Yet immigrants like Quiñones-Hinojosa, who crossed the Mexican border illegally at age 19, are exactly the people that government policymakers now want to exclude from the United States (Quiñones-Hinojosa with Rivas 2011).

What sense are we to make of the issues of race, ethnicity, and immigration in the 21st century? Today, unlike Dr. Q, millions of African Americans, Asian Americans, Hispanic Americans, and many other racial and ethnic minorities experience an often bitter contrast between the "American dream" and the grim realities of poverty, prejudice, and discrimination. Like class, the social definitions of race and ethnicity still affect people's place and status in a stratification system, not only in this country, but throughout the world. High incomes, a good command of English, and hard-earned professional credentials do not always override racial and ethnic stereotypes or protect those who fit them from the sting of racism.

What is prejudice, and how is it institutionalized in the form of discrimination? In what ways have race and ethnicity affected the experience of immigrants from other countries? What are the fastest-growing minority groups in the United States today? In this chapter we will focus on the meaning of race and ethnicity. We will begin by identifying the basic characteristics of a minority group and distinguishing between racial and ethnic groups. Then we will examine the dynamics of prejudice and discrimination. After considering four sociological perspectives on race and ethnicity, we'll take a look at common patterns of intergroup relations. The following section will describe the major racial and ethnic groups in the United States. Finally, in the Social Policy section we will explore the issue of global immigration.

MODULE 31 | Minority, Racial, and Ethnic Groups

Sociologists frequently distinguish between racial and ethnic groups. The term **racial group** describes a group that is set apart from others because of physical differences that have taken on social significance. Whites, African Americans, and Asian Americans are all considered racial groups in the United States. While race does turn on physical differences, it is the culture of a particular society that constructs and attaches social significance to those differences, as we will see later. Unlike racial groups, an **ethnic group** is set apart from others primarily because of its national origin or distinctive cultural patterns. In the United States, Puerto Ricans, Jews, and Polish Americans are all categorized as ethnic groups (Table 31-1).

Minority Groups

A numerical minority is any group that makes up less than half of some larger population. The population of the United States includes thousands of numerical minorities, including television actors, green-eyed people, tax lawyers, and descendants of the Pilgrims who arrived on the *Mayflower*. However, these numerical minorities are not considered to be minorities in the sociological sense; in fact, the number of people in a group does not necessarily determine its status as a social minority (or a dominant group). When sociologists define a minority group, they are concerned primarily with the economic and political power, or powerlessness, of that group. A **minority group** is a subordinate group whose members have significantly less control or power over their own lives than the members of a dominant or majority group have over theirs.

Sociologists have identified five basic properties of a minority group: unequal treatment, physical or cultural traits, ascribed status, solidarity, and in-group marriage (Wagley and Harris 1958):

1. Members of a minority group experience unequal treatment compared to members of a dominant group. For example, the management of an apartment complex may refuse to rent to African Americans, Hispanics, or Jews. Social

inequality may be created or maintained by prejudice, discrimination, segregation, or even extermination.

2. Members of a minority group share physical or cultural characteristics that distinguish them from the dominant group. Each society arbitrarily decides which characteristics are most important in defining groups.

3. Membership in a minority (or dominant) group is not voluntary; people are born into the group. Thus, race and ethnicity are considered *ascribed* statuses.

4. Minority group members have a strong sense of group solidarity. William Graham Sumner, writing in 1906, noted that people make distinctions between members of their own group (the *in-group*) and everyone else (the *out-group*). When a group is the object of long-term prejudice and discrimination, the feeling of "us versus them" can and often does become extremely intense.

5. Members of a minority group generally marry others from the same group. A member of a dominant group is often unwilling to marry into a supposedly inferior minority group. In addition, the minority group's sense of solidarity encourages marriage within the group and discourages marriage to outsiders.

Race

Many people think of race as a series of biological classifications. However, research shows that is not a meaningful way of differentiating people. Genetically, there are no systematic differences between the races that affect people's social behavior and abilities. Instead, sociologists use the term *racial group* to refer to those minorities (and the corresponding dominant groups) who are set apart from others by obvious physical differences. But what is an "obvious" physical difference? Each society labels those differences that people consider important, while ignoring other characteristics that could serve as a basis for social differentiation.

In U.S. retail stores, Black customers have different experiences from White customers. They are more likely than Whites to have their checks or credit cards refused and more likely to be profiled by security personnel.

the **exploitation theory** (or *Marxist class theory*) to explain the basis of racial subordination in the United States. As we saw in Module 26, Karl Marx viewed the exploitation of the lower class as a basic part of the capitalist economic system. From a Marxist point of view, racism keeps minorities in low-paying jobs, thereby supplying the capitalist ruling class with a pool of cheap labor. Moreover, by forcing racial minorities to accept low wages, capitalists can restrict the wages of *all* members of the proletariat. Workers from the dominant group who demand higher wages can always be replaced by minorities who have no choice but to accept low-paying jobs.

The conflict view of race relations seems persuasive in a number of instances. Japanese Americans were the object of little prejudice until they began to enter jobs that brought them into competition with Whites. The movement to keep Chinese immigrants out of the United States became most fervent during

U.S. employers' demand for low-paid labor fuels illegal immigration.

the latter half of the 19th century, when Chinese and Whites fought over dwindling work opportunities. Both the enslavement of Blacks and the extermination and removal westward of Native Americans were economically motivated.

However, the exploitation theory is too limited to explain prejudice in its many forms. Not all minority groups have been exploited to the same extent. In addition, many groups (such as the Quakers and the Mormons) have been victimized by prejudice for other than economic reasons. Still, as Gordon Allport (1979:210) concludes, the exploitation theory correctly "points a sure finger at one of the factors involved in prejudice, . . . rationalized self-interest of the upper classes."

Labeling Perspective

One practice that fits both the conflict perspective and labeling theory is racial profiling. **Racial profiling** is any arbitrary action initiated by an authority based on race, ethnicity, or national origin rather than on a person's behavior. Generally, racial profiling occurs when law enforcement officers, including customs officials, airport security, and police, assume that people who fit a certain description are likely to be engaged in illegal activities. Beginning in the 1980s with the emergence of the crack cocaine market, skin color became a key characteristic in racial profiling. This practice is often based on very explicit stereotypes. For example, one federal antidrug initiative encouraged officers to look specifically for people with dreadlocks and for Latino men traveling together.

Today, authorities continue to rely on racial profiling, despite overwhelming evidence that it is misleading. A recent study showed that Blacks are still more likely than Whites to be frisked and handled with force when they are stopped. Yet Whites are more likely than Blacks to possess weapons, illegal drugs, or stolen property (A. Farrell and McDevitt 2010).

Research on the ineffectiveness of racial profiling, coupled with calls by minority communities to end the stigmatization, has led to growing demands to end the practice. But these efforts came to an abrupt halt after the September 11, 2001, terrorist attacks on the United States, when suspicions arose about Muslim and Arab immigrants. Foreign students from Arab countries were summoned for special questioning by authorities. Legal immigrants who were identified as Arab or Muslim were scrutinized for possible illegal activity and prosecuted for violations that authorities routinely ignored among immigrants of other ethnicities and faiths. National surveys have found little change since 2001 in public support for profiling of Arab Americans at airports. In 2010, 53 percent of Americans favored "ethnic and religious profiling" of air travelers—even those who are U.S. citizens—together with more intensive security checks of passengers who fit certain profiles (Zogby 2010).

Interactionist Perspective

A Hispanic woman is transferred from a job on an assembly line to a similar position working next to a White man. At first, the White man is patronizing, assuming that she must be incompetent. She is cold and resentful; even when she needs assistance, she refuses to admit it. After a week, the growing tension between the two leads to a bitter quarrel. Yet over time, each slowly comes to appreciate the other's strengths and talents. A year after they begin working together, these two workers become respectful friends. This story is an example of what interactionists call the *contact hypothesis* in action.

The **contact hypothesis** states that in cooperative circumstances, interracial contact between people of equal status will cause them to become less prejudiced and to abandon old stereotypes. People begin to see one another as individuals and discard the broad generalizations characteristic of stereotyping. Note the phrases *equal status* and *cooperative circumstances.* In the story just told, if the two workers had been competing for one vacancy as a supervisor, the racial hostility between them might have worsened (Allport 1979; Fine 2008).

As Latinos and other minorities slowly gain access to better-paying and more responsible jobs, the contact hypothesis may take on even greater significance. The trend in our society is toward increasing contact between individuals from dominant and subordinate groups. That may be one way of eliminating—or at least reducing—racial and ethnic stereotyping and prejudice. Another may be the establishment of interracial coalitions, an idea suggested by sociologist William Julius Wilson (1999). To work, such coalitions would obviously need to be built on an equal role for all members.

Table 32-1 summarizes the four major sociological perspectives on race. No matter what the explanation for racial and ethnic distinctions—functionalist, conflict, labeling, or interactionist—these socially constructed inequalities can have powerful consequences in the form of prejudice and discrimination. In the next section, we will see how inequality based on the ascribed characteristics of race and ethnicity can poison people's interpersonal relations, depriving whole groups of opportunities others take for granted.

Spectrum of Intergroup Relations

Racial and ethnic groups can relate to one another in a wide variety of ways, ranging from friendships and intermarriages to hostility, from behaviors that require mutual approval to behaviors imposed by the dominant group.

One devastating pattern of intergroup relations is **genocide**—the deliberate, systematic killing of an entire people or nation. This term describes the killing of 1 million Armenians by Turkey beginning in 1915. It is most commonly applied to Nazi Germany's extermination of 6 million European Jews, as well as gays, lesbians, and the Roma ("Gypsies"), during World War II. The term *genocide* is also appropriate in describing the United States' policies toward Native Americans in the 19th century. In 1800, the Native American (or American Indian) population of the United States was about 600,000; by 1850, it had been reduced to 250,000 through warfare with the U.S. cavalry, disease, and forced relocation to inhospitable environments.

The *expulsion* of a people is another extreme means of acting out racial or ethnic prejudice. In 1979, for example, the government of Vietnam expelled nearly 1 million ethnic Chinese from the country. The action resulted partly from centuries of hostility between Vietnam and neighboring China.

Tracking Sociological Perspectives

Table **32-1**   Sociological Perspectives on Race and Ethnicity

Perspective	Emphasis
Functionalist	The dominant majority benefits from the subordination of racial minorities.
Conflict	Vested interests perpetuate racial inequality through economic exploitation.
Labeling	People are profiled and stereotyped based on their racial and ethnic identity.
Interactionist	Cooperative interracial contacts can reduce hostility.

More recently (beginning in 2009), France expelled over 10,000 ethnic Roma (or Gypsies) who had immigrated from their home countries of Bulgaria and Romania. The action appeared to violate the European Union's ban against targeting ethnic groups, as well as its policy of "freedom of movement" throughout the EU. In 2011, the EU withdrew the threat of legal action when the French government modified its policy to apply only to those Roma who lived in "illegal camps." However, many observers saw the concession as a thinly veiled attempt to circumvent the EU's long-standing human rights policies.

In a variation of expulsion, called *secession,* failure to resolve an ethnic or racial conflict results in the drawing of formal boundaries between the groups. In 1947, India was partitioned into two separate countries in an attempt to end violent conflict between Hindus and Muslims. The predominantly Muslim areas in the north became the new country of Pakistan; the rest of India became predominantly Hindu.

Secession, expulsion, and genocide are extreme behaviors, clustered on the negative end of what is called the Spectrum of Intergroup Relations (Figure 32-1). More typical intergroup relations follow four identifiable patterns: (1) segregation, (2)

French police remove a member of the Roma minority who is resisting deportation to his home country. The expulsion of certain racial or ethnic groups is an extreme result of prejudice.

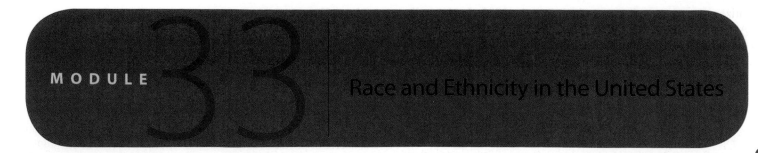

MODULE 33 | Race and Ethnicity in the United States

Few societies have a more diverse population than the United States; the nation is truly a multiracial, multiethnic society. Of course, that has not always been the case. The population of what is now the United States has changed dramatically since the arrival of European settlers in the 1600s, as Figure 31-1 (see page 253) shows. Immigration, colonialism, and in the case of Blacks, slavery determined the racial and ethnic makeup of our present-day society.

Today, the largest racial minorities in the United States are African Americans, Native Americans, and Asian Americans.

The largest ethnic groups are Latinos, Jews, and the various White ethnic groups. Figure 33-1 shows where the major racial and ethnic minorities are concentrated.

◼ African Americans

"I am an invisible man," wrote Black author Ralph Ellison in his novel *Invisible Man* (1952:3). "I am a man of substance, of flesh and

MAPPING LIFE NATIONWIDE

FIGURE 33-1 **The United States: The Image of Diversity**

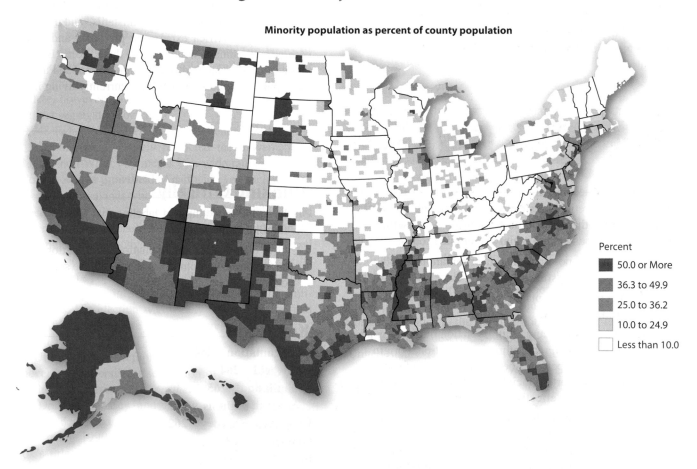

Minority population as percent of county population

Percent
◼ 50.0 or More
◼ 36.3 to 49.9
◼ 25.0 to 36.2
☐ 10.0 to 24.9
☐ Less than 10.0

Source: Humes et al. 2011:21.

Overall, 36.3 percent of the U.S. population belonged to a minority group in 2010. In four states (California, Hawai'i, New Mexico, and Texas) and the District of Columbia, minorities constitute the numerical majority. The 2010 Census also showed that 11 percent of the nation's counties already have become "majority minority"—less than 50 percent non-Hispanic white. Another 7 percent of the nation's counties have reached the "tipping point" toward becoming majority minority sometime in the next decade.

bone, fiber and liquids—and I might even be said to possess a mind. I am invisible, understand, simply because people refuse to see me."

Over five decades later, many African Americans still feel invisible. Despite their large numbers, they have long been treated as second-class citizens. Currently, by the standards of the federal government, more than 1 out of every 4 African Americans—as opposed to 1 out of every 11 White non-Hispanics—is poor (DeNavas-Walt et al. 2011:15).

Contemporary institutional discrimination and individual prejudice against African Americans are rooted in the history of slavery in the United States. Many other subordinate groups had little wealth and income, but as sociologist W. E. B. DuBois ([1909] 1970) and others have noted, enslaved African Americans were in an even more oppressive situation, because by law they could not own property and could not pass on the benefits of their labor to their children. Today, increasing numbers of African Americans and sympathetic Whites are calling for *slave reparations* to compensate for the injustices of forced servitude. Reparations could include official expressions of apology from governments such as the United States, ambitious programs to improve African Americans' economic status, or even direct payments to descendants of slaves (D. Williams and Collins 2004).

The end of the Civil War did not bring genuine freedom and equality for Blacks. The Southern states passed Jim Crow laws to enforce official segregation, and the Supreme Court upheld them as constitutional in 1896. In addition, Blacks faced the danger of lynching campaigns, often led by the Ku Klux Klan, during the late 1800s and early 1900s. From a conflict perspective, Whites maintained their dominance formally through legalized segregation and informally by means of vigilante terror and violence (Franklin and Higginbotham 2011).

During the 1960s, a vast civil rights movement emerged, with many competing factions and strategies for change. The Southern Christian Leadership Conference (SCLC), founded by Dr. Martin Luther King Jr., used nonviolent civil disobedience to oppose segregation. The National Association for the Advancement of Colored People (NAACP) favored use of the courts to press for equality for African Americans. But many younger Black leaders, most notably Malcolm X, turned toward an ideology of Black power. Proponents of **Black power** rejected

the goal of assimilation into White middle-class society. They defended the beauty and dignity of Black and African cultures and supported the creation of Black-controlled political and economic institutions (Ture and Hamilton 1992).

Despite numerous courageous actions to achieve Black civil rights, Black and White citizens are still separate, still unequal. From birth to death, Blacks suffer in terms of their life chances. Life remains difficult for millions of poor Blacks, who must attempt to survive in ghetto areas shattered by high unemployment and abandoned housing. Today the median household income of Blacks is still 60 percent that of Whites, and the unemployment rate among Blacks is more than twice that of Whites.

Some African Americans—especially middle-class men and women—have made economic gains over the past 50 years. For example, data show that the number of African Americans in management increased nationally from 2.4 percent of the total in 1958 to 6.4 percent in 2010. Yet Blacks still represent only 7 percent or less of all physicians, engineers, scientists, lawyers, judges, and marketing managers (Bureau of the Census 2011a:Table 616).

Native Americans

Today, about 2.5 million Native Americans represent a diverse array of cultures distinguishable by language, family organization, religion, and livelihood. The outsiders who came to the United States—European settlers—and their descendants came to know these native peoples' forefathers as "American Indians." By the time the Bureau of Indian Affairs (BIA) was organized as part of the War Department in 1824, Indian–White relations had already included more than two centuries of hostile actions that had led to the virtual elimination of native peoples (see Figure 33-1, page 266). During the 19th century, many bloody wars wiped out a significant part of the Indian population. By the end of the century, schools for Indians—operated by the BIA or by church missions—prohibited the practice of Native American cultures. Yet at the same time, such schools did little to make the children effective members of White society.

Today, life remains difficult for members of the 554 tribal groups in the United States, whether they live in cities or on reservations. For example, one Native American teenager in six has attempted suicide—a rate four times higher than the rate for other teenagers. Traditionally, some Native Americans have chosen to assimilate and abandon all vestiges of their tribal

Native American artists often break new ground to represent their life experiences. Dunne-Za member Brian Jungen used Nike shoes to make this three-dimensional piece, which suggests both his Pacific Northwest culture and his family's practice of stretching their modest means by reusing everything.

Asian Americans: A Model Minority?

Asian Americans are often held up as a **model**, or **ideal, minority group**, supposedly because they have succeeded economically, socially, and educationally, despite past prejudice and discrimination and without resorting to political and violent confrontations with Whites.. Proponents of this view add that because Asian Americans have achieved success, they are no longer disadvantaged. This portrayal of Asian Americans as a model minority ignores their economic diversity. Moreover, even those Asian Americans who are clustered at the high end of the social scale face some barriers to advancement.

The dramatic success of Asian Americans in the U.S. educational system has undoubtedly contributed to the model minority stereotype. Compared with their numbers in the population as a whole, Asian Americans are greatly overrepresented in the student bodies of the most prestigious universities, public and private. Their upward mobility in schooling can be attributed in part to a strong cultural belief in the value of education, to family pressure to succeed, and to the desire to escape discrimination through academic achievement.

The resulting perception of Asian Americans as academic stars does not always work to their advantage. Asian American students who do not excel in school may face criticism from parents or teachers for their failure to conform to the "whiz kid" image. In fact, the high school dropout rate among Asian Americans is increasing rapidly. In California's special program for low-income, academically disadvantaged

students, Asian Americans make up 30 percent of the students, and their proportion of all students in the program is rising.

Some observers see Asian Americans' supposed success as a reaffirmation of the cherished belief that with talent and hard work, anyone can get ahead in the United States. This view of Asian Americans as a successful minority carries an implicit critique of Blacks, Hispanics, and other groups who have not fared as well as the model minority. The tacit assumption is that minorities who have been less successful than Asian Americans are completely responsible for their failure to get ahead. Viewed from a conflict perspective, this flip side to the Asian American stereotype is yet another instance of "blaming the victim" (see Explaining Poverty in Module 28, p. 000).

> This view of Asian Americans as a successful minority carries an implicit critique of Blacks, Hispanics, and other groups who have not fared as well as the model minority.

LET'S DISCUSS

1. Are Asian Americans seen as "whiz kids" at your school? If so, how close to reality do you think that stereotype is?

2. Talk with some Asian American students about their grades and their study habits. Do they all have the same work ethic? How does your own work ethic compare to theirs?

Sources: Ryan 1976; Tachibana 1990; Takei and Sakamoto 2011; Teranishi 2010.

---

may contrast sharply in their degree of assimilation, desire to live in Chinatowns, and feelings about this country's relations with the People's Republic of China.

Currently, over 3 million Chinese Americans live in the United States. Some Chinese Americans have entered lucrative occupations, yet many immigrants struggle to survive under living and working conditions that belie the model-minority stereotype. New York City's Chinatown district is filled with illegal sweatshops in which recent immigrants—many of them Chinese women—work for minimal wages. Outside of Chinatown, 23 percent of Asian Americans fall into the low-income category. At the other end of the income distribution, barely 5 percent of Chinatown's residents earn more than $100,000 a year, compared to 25 percent of Asian Americans who live elsewhere in New York City (Logan et al. 2002; Wong 2006).

Asian Indians

After Chinese Americans, the second-largest Asian American group, immigrants from India and their descendants, numbers

over 2.9 million. It is difficult to generalize about Asian Indian Americans because Asian Indians are such a diverse population. India, a country of more than 1.2 billion people that is fast becoming the most populous nation in the world, is multiethnic. Perhaps because Asian Indian immigrants feel threatened by mainstream U.S. culture, religious orthodoxy is often stronger among first-generation immigrants to the United States than it is in India. New immigrants try to practice their religion just as they did in India rather than join congregations already established by other immigrant groups.

Maintaining family traditions is a major challenge for Asian Indian immigrants to the United States. Family ties remain strong despite their immigration—so much so that many Asian Indians feel more connected to their relatives in India than Americans do to relatives nearby. These *Desi* (pronounced day-see, colloquial for people who trace their ancestry to South Asia, especially India) are particularly concerned about the erosion of traditional family authority. Indian American children dress like their peers, go to fast-food restaurants, and even eat hamburgers, rejecting the vegetarian diet typical of both Hindus and many Asian Indian

Muslims. Sons do not feel the extent of responsibility to the family that tradition dictates. Daughters, whose occupations and marriage partners the family could control in India, assert their right to choose their careers, and even their husbands (Rangaswamy 2005).

Filipino Americans

Filipinos are the third-largest Asian American group in the United States, with over 2.6 million people. For geographic reasons, social scientists consider them to be of Asian extraction, but physically and culturally this group also reflects centuries of Spanish and U.S. colonial rule, as well as the more recent U.S. military occupation.

Filipinos began immigrating to the United States as American nationals when the U.S. government gained possession of the Philippine Islands at the end of the Spanish–American War (1899). When the Philippines gained their independence in 1948, Filipinos lost their unrestricted immigration rights, although farmworkers were welcome to work in Hawai'i's pineapple groves. Aside from this exception, immigration was restricted to 50 to 100 Filipinos a year until 1965, when the Immigration Act lifted the strict quotas.

Today, a significant percentage of Filipino immigrants are well-educated professionals who work in the field of health care. Although they are a valuable human resource in the United States, their immigration has long drained the medical establishment in the Philippines. When the U.S. Immigration and Naturalization Service stopped giving preference to physicians, Filipino doctors began entering the country as nurses—a dramatic illustration of the incredible income differences between the two countries. Like other immigrant groups, Filipino Americans save much of their income and send a significant amount of money, called *remittances,* back to their extended families (Zarembo 2004b).

For several reasons, Filipino Americans have not coalesced in a single formal social organization, despite their numbers. Their strong loyalty to the family (*sa pamilya*) and to the church—particularly Roman Catholicism—reduces their need for a separate organization. Moreover, their diversity complicates the task of uniting the Filipino American community, which reflects the same regional, religious, and linguistic distinctions that divide their homeland. Thus, the many groups that Filipino Americans have organized tend to be club-like or fraternal in nature. Because those groups do not represent the general population of Filipino Americans, they remain largely invisible to Anglos. Although Filipinos remain interested in events in their homeland, they also seek to become involved in broader, non-Filipino organizations and to avoid exclusive activities (Bonus 2000; Kang 1996; Lau 2006; Padilla 2008).

Vietnamese Americans

Vietnamese Americans came to the United States primarily during and after the Vietnam War—especially after U.S. withdrawal from the conflict in 1975. Refugees from the communist government in Vietnam, assisted by local agencies, settled throughout the United States, tens of thousands of them in small towns. Over time, however, Vietnamese Americans have gravitated toward the larger urban areas, establishing Vietnamese restaurants and grocery stores in their ethnic enclaves there.

In 1995, the United States resumed normal diplomatic relations with Vietnam. Gradually, the *Viet Kieu,* or Vietnamese living abroad, began to return to their old country to visit, but usually not to take up permanent residence. Today, more than 35 years after the end of the Vietnam War, sharp differences of opinion remain among Vietnamese Americans, especially the older ones, concerning the war and the present government of Vietnam (Pfeifer 2008).

Korean Americans

At over 1.4 million, the population of Korean Americans now exceeds that of Japanese Americans. Yet Korean Americans are often overshadowed by other groups from Asia.

Today's Korean American community is the result of three waves of immigration. The initial wave arrived between 1903 and 1910, when Korean laborers migrated to Hawai'i. The second wave followed the end of the Korean War in 1953; most of those immigrants were wives of U.S. servicemen and war orphans. The third wave, continuing to the present, has reflected the admissions priorities set up in the 1965 Immigration Act. These well-educated immigrants arrive in the United States with professional skills. Yet because of language difficulties and discrimination, many must settle at least initially for positions of lower responsibility than those they held in Korea and must suffer through a period of disenchantment. Stress, loneliness, and family strife may accompany the pain of adjustment.

In the early 1990s, the apparent friction between Korean Americans and another subordinate racial group, African Americans, attracted nationwide attention. Conflict between the two groups was dramatized in Spike Lee's 1989 movie *Do the Right Thing.* The situation stemmed from Korean Americans' position as the latest immigrant group to cater to the needs of inner-city populations abandoned by those who have moved up the economic ladder. This type of friction is not new; generations of Jewish, Italian, and Arab merchants have encountered similar hostility from what to outsiders seems an unlikely source—another oppressed minority (Kim 1999).

Japanese Americans

Approximately 842,000 Japanese Americans live in the United States. As a people, they are relatively recent arrivals. In 1880, only 148 Japanese lived in the United States, but by 1920 there were more than 110,000. Japanese immigrants—called the *Issei* (pronounced ee-say), or first generation—were usually males seeking employment opportunities. Many Whites saw them (along with Chinese immigrants) as a "yellow peril" and subjected them to prejudice and discrimination.

In 1941, the attack on Hawai'i's Pearl Harbor by Japan had severe repercussions for Japanese Americans. The federal government decreed that all Japanese Americans on the West Coast must leave their homes and report to "evacuation camps." In effect, Japanese Americans became scapegoats for the anger that other people in the United States felt concerning Japan's role in island—the paramount political issue is the destiny of Puerto Rico itself: should it continue in its present commonwealth status, petition for admission to the United States as the 51st state, or attempt to become an independent nation? This question has divided Puerto Rico for decades and remains a central issue in Puerto Rican elections. In a 1998 referendum, voters supported a "none of the above" option, effectively favoring continuation of the commonwealth status over statehood or independence.

Cuban Americans

Cuban immigration to the United States dates back as far as 1831, but it began in earnest following Fidel Castro's assumption of power in the Cuban revolution (1959). The first wave of 200,000 Cubans included many professionals with relatively high levels of schooling; these men and women were largely welcomed as refugees from communist tyranny. However, more recent waves of immigrants have aroused growing concern, partly because they were less likely to be skilled professionals. Throughout these waves of immigration, Cuban Americans have been encouraged to locate around the United States. Nevertheless, many continue to settle in (or return to) metropolitan Miami, Florida, with its warm climate and proximity to Cuba.

The Cuban experience in the United States has been mixed. Some detractors worry about the vehement anticommunism of Cuban Americans and the apparent growth of an organized crime syndicate that engages in the drug trade and ganglike violence. Recently, Cuban Americans in Miami have expressed concern over what they view as the indifference of the city's Roman Catholic hierarchy. Like other Hispanics, Cuban Americans are underrepresented in leadership positions within the church. Also—despite many individual success stories—as a group, Cuban Americans in Miami remain behind Whites in income, rate of employment, and proportion of professionals (Masud-Piloto 2008).

Central and South Americans

Immigrants from Central and South America are a diverse population that has not been closely studied. Indeed, most government statistics treat members of this group collectively as "other," rarely differentiating among them by nationality. Yet people from Chile and Costa Rica have little in common other than their hemisphere of origin and the Spanish language—if that. The fact is, not all Central and South Americans speak Spanish. Immigrants from Brazil, for example, speak Portuguese; immigrants from French Guyana speak French; and immigrants from Suriname speak Dutch.

Racially, many of the nations of Central and South America follow a complex classification system that recognizes a multitude of color gradients. Experience with this multiracial system does not prepare immigrants to the United States for the stark Black–White racial divide that characterizes U.S. society. Beyond their diversity in

color and language, immigrants from Central and South America are differentiated by social class distinctions, religious differences, urban or rural upbringings, and dialects. Some of them may come from indigenous populations, especially in Guatemala and Belize. If so, their social identity would be separate from any national allegiance.

In short, social relations among Central and South Americans, who collectively number nearly 7 million people, defy generalization. The same can be said about their relations with other Latinos and with non-Latinos. Central and South Americans do not form, nor should they be expected to form, a cohesive group. Nor do they easily form coalitions with Cuban Americans, Mexican Americans, or Puerto Ricans.

● Jewish Americans

Jews constitute about 2 percent of the population of the United States. They play a prominent role in the worldwide Jewish community, because the United States has the world's largest concentration of Jews. Like the Japanese, many Jewish immigrants came to this country and became white-collar professionals in spite of prejudice and discrimination.

Anti-Semitism—that is, anti-Jewish prejudice—has often been vicious in the United States, although rarely so widespread and never so formalized as in Europe. In many cases, Jews have been used as scapegoats for other people's failures. Not surprisingly, Jews have not achieved equality in the United States. Despite high levels of education and professional training, they are still conspicuously absent from the top management of large corporations (except for the few firms founded by Jews). Nonetheless, a national survey in 2009 showed that one out of four people in the United States blames "the Jews" for the financial crisis. In addition, private social clubs and fraternal groups frequently continue to limit membership to Gentiles (non-Jews), a

For practicing Jews, the Hebrew language is an important part of religious instruction. This young pupil learns the Hebrew alphabet with a Jewish teacher.

practice upheld by the Supreme Court in the 1964 case *Bell v. Maryland* (Malhotra and Margalit 2009).

The Anti-Defamation League (ADL) of B'nai B'rith coordinates an annual tally of reported anti-Semitic incidents. Although the number has fluctuated, in 2009 the tabulation of the total reported incidents of harassment, threats, vandalism, and assaults came to 1,211. Some incidents were inspired and carried out by neo-Nazi skinheads—groups of young people who champion racist and anti-Semitic ideologies. Such threatening behavior only intensifies the fears of many Jewish Americans, who remember the Holocaust—the extermination of 6 million Jews by the Nazi Third Reich during World War II (Anti-Defamation League 2010).

As is true for other minorities discussed in this chapter, Jewish Americans face the choice of maintaining ties to their long religious and cultural heritage or becoming as indistinguishable as possible from Gentiles. Many Jews have tended to assimilate, as is evident from the rise in marriages between Jews and Christians. In marriages that occurred in the 1970s, more than 70 percent of Jews married Jews or people who converted to Judaism. In marriages since 1996, that proportion has dropped to 53 percent. This trend means that today, American Jews are almost as likely to marry a Gentile as a Jew. For many, religion is a nonissue—neither parent practices religious rituals. Two-thirds of the children of these Jewish–Gentile marriages are not raised as Jews. Finally, in 2005, two-thirds of Jews felt that the biggest threat to Jewish life was anti-Semitism; only one-third named intermarriage as the biggest threat (American Jewish Committee 2005; Sanua 2007).

White Americans often express their ethnicity with special celebrations, such as this Scandinavian Festival parade in Junction City, Oregon. Participants proudly display the flag of Denmark.

● White Ethnics

A significant segment of the population of the United States is made up of White ethnics whose ancestors arrived from Europe within the past century. The nation's White ethnic population includes about 49 million people who claim at least partial German ancestry, 36 million Irish Americans, 17 million Italian Americans, and 10 million Polish Americans, as well as immigrants from other European nations. Some of these people continue to live in close-knit ethnic neighborhoods, whereas others have largely assimilated and left the "old ways" behind.

Many White ethnics today identify only sporadically with their heritage. **Symbolic ethnicity** refers to an emphasis on concerns such as ethnic food or political issues rather than on deeper ties to one's ethnic heritage. It is reflected in the occasional family trip to an ethnic bakery, the celebration of a ceremonial event such as St. Joseph's Day among Italian Americans, or concern about the future of Northern Ireland among Irish Americans.

Such practices are another example of the social construction of race and ethnicity. Except in cases in which new immigration reinforces old traditions, symbolic ethnicity tends to decline with each passing generation (Alba 1990; Winter 2008).

Although the White ethnic identity may be a point of pride to those who share it, they do not necessarily celebrate it at the expense of disadvantaged minorities. It is all too easy to assume that race relations are a zero-sum game in which one group gains at the expense of the other. Rather, the histories of several White ethnic groups, such as the Irish and the Italians, show that once marginalized people can rise to positions of prestige and influence (Alba 2009).

That is not to say that White ethnics and racial minorities have not been antagonistic toward one another because of economic competition—an interpretation that agrees with the conflict approach to sociology. As Blacks, Latinos, and Native Americans emerge from the lower class, they must compete with working-class Whites for jobs, housing, and educational opportunities. In times of high unemployment or inflation, any such competition can easily generate intense intergroup conflict.

In many respects, the plight of White ethnics raises the same basic issues as that of other subordinate people in the United States. How ethnic can people be—how much can they deviate from an essentially White, Anglo-Saxon, Protestant norm—before society punishes them for their willingness to be different? Our society does seem to reward people for assimilating, yet as we have seen, assimilation is no easy process. In the years to come, more and more people will face the challenge of fitting in, not only in the United States but around the world, as the flow of immigrants from one country to another continues to increase. In the Social Policy section that follows, we focus on global immigration and its implications for the future.

Worldwide, immigration is at an all-time high. Each year, about 191 million people move from one country to another—a number that is roughly the equivalent of the total populations of Russia and Italy. A million of these immigrants enter the United States legally, to join the 13 percent of the U.S. population who are foreign born. Perhaps more significantly, one-fourth of the U.S. labor force is foreign born—the largest proportion in at least 120 years (Passel and Cohn 2011).

Globally, these mass migrations have had a tremendous social impact. The constantly increasing numbers of immigrants and the pressure they put on job opportunities and welfare capabilities in the countries they enter raise troubling questions for many of the world's economic powers. Who should be allowed in? At what point should immigration be curtailed (United Nations 2009)?

Looking at the Issue

The migration of people is not uniform across time or space. At certain times, war or famine may precipitate large movements of people, either temporarily or permanently. Temporary dislocations occur when people wait until it is safe to return to their home areas. However, more and more migrants who cannot make an adequate living in their home nations are making permanent moves to developed nations. The major migration streams flow into North America, the oil-rich areas of the Middle East, and the industrial economies of western Europe and Asia. Currently, seven of the world's wealthiest nations (including Germany, France, the United Kingdom, and the United States) shelter about one-third of the world's migrant population, but less than one-fifth of the world's total population. As long as disparities in job opportunities exist among countries, there is little reason to expect this international trend to reverse.

One consequence of global immigration is the emergence of **transnationals**—immigrants who sustain multiple social relationships that link their societies of origin with the society of settlement. The industrial tycoons of the early 20th century, whose power outmatched that of many nation-states, were among the world's first transnationals. Today, millions of people, many of very modest means, move back and forth between countries much as commuters do between city and suburbs. More and more of these people have dual citizenship. Rather than being shaped by allegiance to one country, their identity is rooted in their struggle to survive—and in some instances prosper—by transcending international borders. We will take a closer look at these citizens of the world in the Social Policy section of Chapter 16 (Croucher 2004; Sassen 2005).

Countries that have long been a destination for immigrants, such as the United States, usually have policies regarding who has preference to enter. Often, clear racial and ethnic biases are built into these policies. In the 1920s, U.S. policy gave preference to people from western Europe, while making it difficult for residents of southern and eastern Europe, Asia, and Africa to enter the country. During the late 1930s and early 1940s, the federal government refused to lift or loosen restrictive immigration quotas in order to allow Jewish refugees to escape the terror of the Nazi regime. In line with this policy, the SS *St. Louis,* with more than 900 Jewish refugees on board, was denied permission to land in the United States in 1939. The ship was forced to sail back to Europe, where it is estimated that at least a few hundred of its passengers later died at the hands of the Nazis (Morse 1967; G. Thomas and Witts 1974).

Since the 1960s, U.S. policy has encouraged the immigration of relatives of U.S. residents as well as of people who have desirable skills. This change has significantly altered the pattern of sending nations. Previously, Europeans dominated, but for the past 40 years, immigrants have come primarily from Latin America and Asia. Thus, an ever-growing proportion of the U.S. population will be Asian or Hispanic (Figure 33-5). To a large degree, fear and resentment of growing racial and ethnic diversity is a key factor in opposition to immigration. In many nations, people are concerned that the new arrivals do not reflect their own cultural and racial heritage.

Applying Sociology

Research suggests that immigrants adapt well to life in the United States, becoming an asset to the nation's economy. In some areas, heavy immigration may drain a local community's resources, but in other areas it revitalizes the local economy.

Despite people's fears, immigration performs many valuable functions. For the receiving society, it alleviates labor shortages, as it does in health care and technology in the United States. For the sending nation, migration can relieve an economy unable to support large numbers of people. Often overlooked is the large amount of money *(remittances)* that immigrants send *back* to their home nations.

Immigration can be dysfunctional as well. Although studies generally show that it has a positive impact on the receiving nation's economy, areas that accept high concentrations of immigrants may find it difficult to meet short-term social service needs. And when migrants with skills or educational potential leave developing countries, their departure can be dysfunctional for those nations. No amount of payments sent back home can make up for the loss of valuable human resources from poor nations (Borjas et al. 2006; Kochhar 2006; Sum et al. 2006).

—Continued

FIGURE 33-5 Legal Migration to the United States, 1820–2010

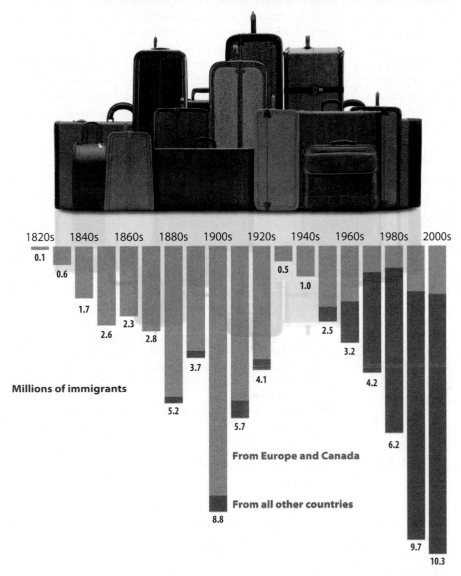

1820s 1840s 1860s 1880s 1900s 1920s 1940s 1960s 1980s 2000s

0.1
0.6
1.7
2.6 2.3
2.8
3.7
5.2
5.7
4.1
8.8
0.5
1.0
2.5
3.2
4.2
6.2
9.7
10.3

Millions of immigrants

From Europe and Canada

From all other countries

Source: Office of Immigration Statistics 2011.

For the past four decades, the majority of immigrants to the United States have come from outside Europe and Canada.

Fear and dislike of "new" ethnic groups divides countries throughout the world.

The feminist perspective pays special attention to the role that women play in global immigration. Immigrant women face all the challenges that immigrant men do, and some additional ones. Typically, they bear the responsibility for obtaining services for their families, particularly their children. Because the men are likely to be consumed with work, the women are left to navigate through the bureaucratic tangle of schools, city services, and medical facilities, as well as the unfamiliar stores and markets they must visit to feed their families. Women who need special medical services or are victims of domestic violence are often reluctant to seek outside help. Yet they are more likely than the men to serve as the liaison between their households and community and religious associations. Also, because many new immigrants view the United States as a dangerous place to raise a family, women must be especially watchful over their children's lives (Hondagneu-Sotelo 2003).

Initiating Policy

The long border with Mexico provides ample opportunity for illegal immigration into the United States. Throughout the 1980s, the public perception that the United States had lost control of its borders grew. Feeling pressure for immigration control, Congress ended a decade of debate by approving the Immigration Reform and Control Act of 1986. The act marked a historic change in the nation's immigration policy. For the first time, the hiring of illegal aliens was outlawed, and employers caught violating the law became subject to fines and even prison sentences. Just as significant a change was the extension of amnesty and legal status to many illegal immigrants already living in the United States. More than 20 years later, however, the act appears to have had mixed results. Substantial numbers of illegal immigrants continue to enter the country each year, with an estimated 11 million or more present at any given time—a marked increase since 2000, when their number was estimated at close to 8 million (Passel and Cohn 2011).

Conflict theorists note how much of the debate over immigration is phrased in economic terms. The debate intensifies when the arrivals are of a different racial or ethnic background from the host population. For example, Europeans often refer to "foreigners," but the term does not necessarily mean one of foreign birth. In Germany, "foreigners" refers to people of non-German ancestry, even if they were *born* in Germany; it does not refer to people of German ancestry born in another country, who may choose to return to their mother country.

—Continued

In 2010, frustrated by the continuing flow of illegal immigrants across the Mexican border, Arizona enacted a law empowering police to detain without authorization people whom they reasonably suspect of being illegal immigrants and to verify their immigration status. Immediately, opponents charged that the new law would lead to racial profiling. Legal experts questioned whether state enforcement of immigration law was constitutional. Although implementation of the law has been problematic, it has highlighted the resolve of those seeking to tighten control of the nation's borders. It has also galvanized those seeking to reform the nation's immigration law.

Recently, immigrants have staged massive marches to pressure Congress to speed the naturalization process and develop ways for illegal immigrants to gain legal residency. Counterdemonstrations by those who oppose illegal immigration have called for more resources with which to detect and deport illegal immigrants and to strengthen the U.S.–Mexican border. Despite this widespread public dissatisfaction with the nation's immigration policy, little progress has been made. Congress has had difficulty reaching a bipartisan compromise that pleases both sides: both supporters of strict social control and those who would allow illegal immigrants to remain in the country legally, under some circumstances.

The entire world feels the overwhelming impact of globalization on immigration patterns. The European Union agreement of 1997 gave the governing commission authority to propose a Europe-wide policy on immigration. An EU policy that allows residents of one EU country to live and work in another EU country is expected to complicate efforts by sending nations, such as Turkey, to become members of the EU. Immigrants from Turkey's predominantly Muslim population are not welcome in many EU countries (Denny 2004).

In the wake of the attacks of September 11, 2001, on the World Trade Center and the Pentagon, immigration procedures were complicated by the need to detect potential terrorists. Illegal immigrants especially, but even legal immigrants, have felt increased scrutiny by government officials around the world. For would-be immigrants to many nations, the wait to receive the right to enter a country—even to join relatives—has increased substantially, as immigration officials scrutinize more closely what were once routine applications.

The intense debate over immigration reflects deep value conflicts in the cultures of many nations. One strand of our culture, for example, has traditionally emphasized egalitarian principles and a desire to help people in time of need. At the same time, hostility to potential immigrants and refugees— whether the Chinese in the 1880s, European Jews in the 1930s and 1940s, or Mexicans, Haitians, and Arabs today—reflects not only racial, ethnic, and religious prejudice, but a desire to maintain the dominant culture of the in-group by keeping out those viewed as outsiders.

TAKE THE ISSUE WITH YOU

1. Did you or your parents or grandparents immigrate to the United States from another nation? If so, when and where did your family come from, and why?

2. On balance, do the functions of immigration to the United States outweigh the dysfunctions?

3. Do you live, work, or study with recent immigrants to the United States? If so, are they well accepted in your community, or do they face prejudice and discrimination?

MODULE 33 | Recap and Review

Summary

The U.S. population is highly diverse, both racially and ethnically.

1. Contemporary prejudice and discrimination against African Americans are rooted in the history of slavery in the United States.

2. Asian Americans are commonly viewed as a **model** or **ideal minority,** a false stereotype that is not necessarily beneficial to members of that group.

3. The various groups included under the general term *Latinos* represent the largest ethnic minority in the United States.

4. Worldwide, immigration is at an all-time high, fueling controversy not only in the United States but also in the European Union. A new kind of immigrant, the **transnational,** moves back and forth across international borders in search of a better job or education.

Thinking Critically

1. Mexican culture seems alive in many Mexican American communities. Native Americans routinely display their tribal identities. Why do White ethnic identities seem more elusive?

2. To what extent has U.S. society achieved pluralism? Give examples from your own experience to support your viewpoint.

Key Terms

Anti-Semitism 274

Mastering This Chapter

taking sociology with you

1 Consider one or more jobs you have had, or an occupation you aspire to. How diverse is the staff you worked or would work with? What about your clients or customers? Do you expect racial and ethnic diversity to play an important role in your future career?

2 Talk with an older relative about your family's past. Did your ancestors experience prejudice or discrimination because of their race or ethnicity, and if so, in what way? Did they ever use racial or ethnic slurs to refer to people of other races or ethnicities? Have your family's attitudes toward members of other groups changed over the years, and if so, why?

3 Look up the census statistics on the racial and ethnic composition of your community. What are the predominant racial and ethnic groups? How many other groups are represented? How many members of your community are immigrants, and where do they come from?

key terms

Affirmative action Positive efforts to recruit minority group members or women for jobs, promotions, and educational opportunities. (page 259)

Amalgamation The process through which a majority group and a minority group combine to form a new group. (264)

Anti-Semitism Anti-Jewish prejudice. (274)

Apartheid A former policy of the South African government, designed to maintain the separation of Blacks and other non-Whites from the dominant Whites. (264)

Assimilation The process through which a person forsakes his or her cultural tradition to become part of a different culture. (265)

Black power A political philosophy, promoted by many younger Blacks in the 1960s, that supported the creation of Black-controlled political and economic institutions. (267)

Color-blind racism The use of the principle of race neutrality to defend a racially unequal status quo. (255)

Contact hypothesis An interactionist perspective which states that in cooperative circumstances, interracial contact between people of equal status will reduce prejudice. (263)

Discrimination The denial of opportunities and equal rights to individuals and groups because of prejudice or other arbitrary reasons. (256)

Ethnic group A group that is set apart from others primarily because of its national origin or distinctive cultural patterns. (251)

Ethnocentrism The tendency to assume that one's own culture and way of life represent the norm or are superior to all others. (255)

Exploitation theory A Marxist theory that views racial subordination in the United States as a manifestation of the class system inherent in capitalism. (262)

Genocide The deliberate, systematic killing of an entire people or nation. (263)

Glass ceiling An invisible barrier that blocks the promotion of a qualified individual in a work environment because of the individual's gender, race, or ethnicity. (257)

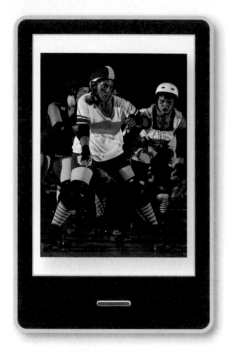

What do you think of women who engage in physically aggressive sports like roller derby? Are they different from other women?

To find out what life was like for roller-derby women, sociologist Nancy Finley began hanging out at the track. This is what she saw.

❝ Her hair is in child-like pigtails, her tattoos glare through strategically placed holes in fishnet stockings, and a short skirt reveals the pink panties that match the tight T-shirt altered to provide the most potent view of breast cleavage. The image portrays the outlandish, extravagant conventions of sexuality associated with the tawdriness of "pin-up girls." And yet the salience of knee pads, shin pads, elbow pads, and helmets resist simple assessments of sexualized femininity, as do facial scowls and the brutish postures through which she powers her way around the skating rink. This roller derby girl is ready to "kick ass," and she's going to do it in a sports environment that is described as "women's space" despite large numbers of burly roaring male fans.

The recent emergence of women's roller derby onto the popular scene provides an opportunity to explore the dynamics through which alternative femininities are constructed and reinforced within a social context. . . . At a derby bout, skaters . . . make conscious efforts to disassociate their sport from ones that are "feminized softer" sports where one does not play too rough. As one skater describes it, "We are tough girls fighting their way through it. Not like other sports." Another boasts, "This is not synchronized swimming. It feels good to hit a girl and you're still standing; that's the evil part." Taunting danger and injury is normative in derby. When designated emergency rescue teams, who are present at all the bouts due to the large number of injuries, carry off skaters, skaters complain that "I just want to get back in there and skate." Derby Web sites often contain pictures of bruises presented as works of art in an Internet gallery. Skaters wear injuries like badges of honor. A young skater who is usually serene

"This is not synchronized swimming. It feels good to hit a girl and you're still standing; that's the evil part."

off the rink explains, "We're mean. You have a flame inside you. I think the fans know it. I think they're scared of us." Ferocious intimidation is part of the performance; skulls and crossbones adorn clothing and are embedded in logos.

Yet their skulls and crossbones have pink bows. Skaters are not striving for the image of the "gender neutral" tough athlete; this image is intentionally feminized. The bruises have fishnet patterns made from sliding across a rink floor with hosiery on one's legs. "Rink rash is sexy," says the poster. Uniforms are complemented by gold panties, Catholic schoolgirl skirts, and heavy makeup; there are pink shoelaces in their black skates. The quintessential posturing of the derby girl juxtaposes caricatured expressions of physical strength with teasing exposure of cleavage and clothes that mock conventional feminine modesty but that also serve as markers of femininity. As one skater sees it, "It wouldn't be the same to me if I were wearing pants". . . .

One salient humorous pattern in derby is also one of the most bountiful areas for the juxtaposition of gender resistance and accommodation—the selection of a skater name. Everyone must select a skater name, such as "Harm School Teacher," "Maria Von Slap," "Calamity Jam," "Lola Fellonya," "Naturally Blood," and "Bomb Bastic," that mocks violence, sexuality, and convention while simultaneously claiming them. Names often blur the boundaries between masculine and feminine or reclaim pariah labels used to control women who are contaminating the gender order— "Wicked Wonder" or "Bitch Barbie." For some the name and character they use to skate becomes an alternate identity they can take off and put on with their skater garb. One skater said, "It definitely feels like being someone else; outfits and all." Several skaters said that they felt like a celebrity when they were in persona; several called it feeling like a "superhero" or "rock star." More than one mentioned that their persona made them feel "sexier than I ever have before." It is in sharp contrast to their daily lives, but as one confided, "I'm more like my derby self than people knew. ❞

(Finley 2010:359–360, 371–372, 377) Additional information about this excerpt can be found on the Online Learning Center at www .mhhe.com/schaefermod2e.

For two years Nancy Finley attended women's flat-track roller-derby games, practices, fund-raisers, and public appearances. A fan of the sport, Finley was fascinated by the roller skaters' seemingly contradictory gender images. Through her fieldwork, which included in-depth interviews with skaters, referees, and volunteers, she learned how the women manage to observe conventional definitions of femininity while mocking them. In this excerpt from her journal article "Skating Femininity," Finley explains how "derby girls" manipulate gender meanings, embracing heightened feminism even as they exhibit the masculine values traditionally associated with violent team sports (Finley 2010; Women's Flat Track Derby Association 2012).

Obviously, women with skater names like Wicked Wonder or Bomb Bastic don't fit the conventional gender roles played by female athletes, much less by women in general. What are the accepted gender roles in today's society? Have men's and women's positions in society changed? How do gender roles differ from one culture or subculture to another? In this chapter we will study these and other questions by looking first at how various cultures, including our own, assign women and men to particular social roles. Then we will consider sociological explanations for gender stratification. We will see that around the world, women constitute an oppressed majority of the population. We'll learn that only recently have women begun to develop a collective consciousness of their oppression and the way in which their gender combines with other factors to create social inequality. Finally, we will close Module 35 with a Social Policy section on the controversy over a woman's right to abortion.

How many airline passengers do you think are startled on hearing a female captain's voice from the cockpit? What do we make of a father who announces that he will be late for work because his son has a routine medical checkup? Consciously or unconsciously, we are likely to assume that flying a commercial plane is a *man's* job and that most parental duties are, in fact, a *woman's*. Gender is such a routine part of our everyday activities that we typically take notice only when someone deviates from conventional behavior and expectations.

Although a few people begin life with an unclear sexual identity, the overwhelming majority begin with a definite sex and quickly receive societal messages about how to behave. In fact, virtually all societies have established social distinctions between females and males that do not inevitably result from biological differences between the sexes (such as women's reproductive capabilities).

In studying gender, sociologists are interested in the gender-role socialization that leads females and males to behave differently. In Module 14, **gender roles** were defined as expectations regarding the proper behavior, attitudes, and activities of males and females. The application of dominant gender roles leads to many forms of differentiation between women and men. Both sexes are capable of learning to cook and sew, yet most Western societies determine that women should perform those tasks. Both men and women are capable of learning to weld and to fly airplanes, but those functions are generally assigned to men.

As we will see throughout this module, however, social behavior does not mirror the mutual exclusivity suggested by these gender roles. Nor are gender roles independent: in real life, the way men behave influences women's behavior, and the way women behave affects men's behavior. Thus, most people do not display strictly "masculine" or "feminine" qualities all the time. Indeed, such standards can be ambiguous. For instance, though men are supposed to be unemotional, they are allowed to become emotional when their favorite athletic team wins or loses a critical game. Yet our society still focuses on "masculine" and "feminine" qualities as if men and women must be evaluated in those terms. Despite recent inroads by women into male-dominated occupations, our construction of gender continues to define significantly different expectations for females and males.

Gender roles are evident not only in our work and behavior but also in how we react to others. We are constantly "doing gender" without realizing it. If the father mentioned earlier sits in the doctor's office with his son in the middle of a workday, he will probably receive approving glances from the receptionist and from other patients. "Isn't he a wonderful father?" runs through their minds. But if the boy's mother leaves *her* job and sits with the son in the doctor's office, she will not receive such silent applause.

We socially construct our behavior so as to create or exaggerate male/female differences. For example, men and women come in a variety of heights, sizes, and ages. Yet traditional norms regarding marriage and even casual dating tell us that in heterosexual couples, the man should be older, taller, and wiser than the woman. As we will see throughout this chapter, such social norms help to reinforce and legitimize patterns of male dominance.

Gender Roles in the United States

Gender-Role Socialization

Male babies get blue blankets; females get pink ones. Boys are expected to play with trucks, blocks, and toy soldiers; girls receive dolls and kitchen goods. Boys must be masculine—active, aggressive, tough, daring, and dominant—but girls must be feminine—soft, emotional, sweet, and submissive. These traditional gender-role patterns have been influential in the socialization of children in the United States.

An important element in traditional views of proper "masculine" and "feminine" behavior is **homophobia,** fear of and prejudice against homosexuality. Homophobia contributes significantly to rigid gender-role socialization, since many people stereotypically associate male homosexuality with femininity

Table 34-1 An Experiment in Gender Norm Violation by College Students

Norm If by Women	Norm If by Men
Send men flowers	Wear fingernail polish
Spit in public	Do needlepoint in public
Use men's bathroom	Throw Tupperware party
Buy jock strap	Cry in public
Buy/chew tobacco	Have pedicure
Talk knowledgeably about cars	Apply to babysit
Open doors for men	Shave body hair

Source: Nielsen et al. 2000:287.

In an experiment testing gender-role stereotypes, sociology students were asked to behave in ways that might be regarded as violations of gender norms, and to keep notes on how others reacted. This is a sample of their choices of behavior over a seven-year period. Do you agree that these actions test the boundaries of conventional gender behavior?

In our society, men and women receive different messages about the ideal body image. For women, the Miss America pageant promotes a very slim, statuesque physique. For men, "action figures" like the G.I. Joe doll promote an exaggerated muscularity typical of professional wrestlers (Angier 1998; Byrd-Bredbenner and Murray 2003).

and lesbianism with masculinity. Consequently, men and women who deviate from traditional expectations about gender roles are often presumed to be gay. Despite the advances made by the gay liberation movement, the continuing stigma attached to homosexuality in our culture places pressure on all males (whether gay or not) to exhibit only narrow masculine behavior and on all females (whether lesbian or not) to exhibit only narrow feminine behavior (Seidman 1994; see also Lehne 1995).

It is *adults,* of course, who play a critical role in guiding children into those gender roles deemed appropriate in a society. Parents are normally the first and most crucial agents of socialization. But other adults, older siblings, the mass media, and religious and educational institutions also exert an important influence on gender-role socialization, in the United States and elsewhere.

It is not hard to test how rigid gender-role socialization can be. Just try transgressing some gender norm—say, by smoking a cigar in public if you are female, or by carrying a purse if you are male. That was exactly the assignment given to sociology students at the University of Colorado and Luther College in Iowa. Professors asked students to behave in ways that they thought violated the norms of how a man or woman should act. The students had no trouble coming up with gender-norm transgressions (Table 34-1), and they kept careful notes on others' reactions to their behavior, ranging from amusement to disgust (Nielsen et al. 2000).

Women's Gender Roles

How does a girl come to develop a feminine self-image, while a boy develops one that is masculine? In part, they do so by identifying with females and males in their families and neighborhoods

and in the media. If a young girl regularly sees female television characters of all ages and body types, she is likely to grow up with a normal body image. And it will not hurt if the women she knows—her mother, sister, parents' friends, and neighbors—are comfortable with their body types, rather than constantly obsessed with their weight. In contrast, if this young girl sees only wafer-thin actresses and models on television, her self-image will be quite different. Even if she grows up to become a well-educated professional, she may secretly regret falling short of the media stereotype—a thin, sexy young woman in a bathing suit.

Television is far from alone in stereotyping women. Studies of children's books published in the United States in the 1940s, 1950s, and 1960s found that females were significantly underrepresented in central roles and illustrations. Virtually all female characters were portrayed as helpless, passive, incompetent, and in need of a strong male caretaker. Studies of picture books

Gender roles serve to discourage men from entering certain low-paying female-dominated occupations, such as child care. Only 5 percent of day care workers are male.

Males who do not conform to the socially constructed gender role face constant criticism and even humiliation, both from children when they are boys and from adults as men. It can be agonizing to be treated as a "chicken" or a "sissy" as a youth—particularly if such remarks come from one's father or brothers. And grown men who pursue nontraditional occupations, such as preschool teaching or nursing, must constantly deal with others' misgivings and strange looks. In one study, interviewers found that such men frequently had to alter their behavior in order to minimize others' negative reactions. One 35-year-old nurse reported that he had to claim he was "a carpenter or something like that" when he "went clubbing," because women weren't interested in getting to know a male nurse. The subjects made similar accommodations in casual exchanges with other men (Cross and Bagilhole 2002:215).

published from the 1970s through the present have found some improvement, but males still dominate the central roles. While males are portrayed as a variety of characters, females tend to be shown mostly in traditional roles, such as mother, grandmother, or volunteer, even if they also hold nontraditional roles, such as working professional (Etaugh 2003).

Traditional gender roles have restricted females more severely than males. This chapter shows how women have been confined to subordinate roles in the political and economic institutions of the United States. Yet it is also true that gender roles have restricted males.

Men's Gender Roles

Stay-at-home fathers? Until recent decades such an idea was unthinkable. Yet in a nationwide survey, 69 percent of respondents said that if one parent stays home with the children, it makes no difference whether that parent is the mother or the father. Only 30 percent thought that the mother should be the one to stay home. But while people's conceptions of gender roles are obviously changing, the fact is that men who stay home to care for their children are still an unusual phenomenon. For every stay-at-home dad there are 38 stay-at-home moms (Fields 2004: 11–12; Robison 2002).

While attitudes toward parenting may be changing, studies show little change in the traditional male gender role. Men's roles are socially constructed in much the same way as women's are. Family, peers, and the media all influence how a boy or man comes to view his appropriate role in society. The male gender role, besides being antifeminine (no "sissy stuff"), includes proving one's masculinity at work and sports—often by using force in dealing with others—as well as initiating and controlling all sexual relations.

At the same time, boys who successfully adapt to cultural standards of masculinity may grow up to be inexpressive men who cannot share their feelings with others. They remain forceful and tough, but as a result they are also closed and isolated. In fact, a small but growing body of scholarship suggests that for men as well as women, traditional gender roles may be disadvantageous. In many communities across the nation, girls seem to outdo boys in high school, grabbing a disproportionate share of the leadership positions, from valedictorian to class president to yearbook editor—everything, in short, except captain of the boys' athletic teams. Their advantage continues after high school. In the 1980s, girls in the United States became more likely than boys to go to college. By 2010, women accounted for over 57 percent of college students nationwide. And in 2002, for the first time, more women than men in the United States earned doctoral degrees (Bureau of the Census 2011a:Table 277 on page 177).

Aside from these disadvantages, many men find that traditional masculinity does not serve them well in the job market. The growth of a service economy over the past two generations has created a demand for skills, attitudes, and behaviors that are the antithesis of traditional masculinity. Increasingly, this sector is the place where low-skilled men must look for jobs. As a British study showed, many out-of-work men are reluctant to engage in the kind of sensitive, deferential behavior required by service sector jobs (Nixon 2009).

In the past 40 years, inspired in good part by the contemporary feminist movement (examined later in the chapter), increasing numbers of men in the United States have criticized the restrictive aspects of the traditional male gender role. Some men have taken strong public positions in support of women's struggle for full equality and have even organized voluntary associations for the purpose. However, their actions have been countered by other men who feel they are unfairly penalized by laws related to alimony, child support and custody, family violence, and affirmative action (Kimmel 2008; National Organization for Men Against Sexism 2012).

Recent research on gender roles has shown that in fact there is no single, simple characterization of the male gender role. Australian sociologist R. W. Connell (1987, 2002, 2005) has spoken of **multiple masculinities**, meaning that men play a variety of gender roles, including a nurturing-caring role and an effeminate-gay role, in addition to their traditional gender role of dominating women. Nevertheless, society reinforces their traditional, dominating role more than any other role (McCormack 2010).

Gender and Human Sexuality

How do gender roles affect a person's sexuality? Separating sex from gender is of course impossible. Yet it would be incorrect simply to equate males with stereotypically masculine expressions of sexuality, or females with stereotypically feminine expressions of sexuality.

Over time, social norms regarding sexual behavior have changed as gender roles have changed, becoming more ambiguous. Today, popularly coined words like *metrosexual* and *bromance* suggest that men should feel comfortable embracing traditionally feminine tastes or developing deep friendships with other men. Similarly, society is beginning to accept not only same-sex couples, but individuals whose gender and identity do not fit a simple either/or pattern, such as bisexuals and transgendered people.

As we saw in Module 24, society uses labels such as "good kids" and "delinquents" to condone or sanction certain behaviors by certain groups of people. The same is true of sexual behaviors. In Module 41, we will see how society uses labels to brand specific sexual behaviors as deviant. Traditionally, those labels have derived from gender-role distinctions.

 use your **sociological imagination**

What evidence can you see of women's changing roles over the past few generations?

Cross-Cultural Perspective

To what extent do actual biological differences between the sexes contribute to the cultural differences associated with gender? This question brings us back to the debate over "nature versus nurture." In assessing the alleged and real differences between men and women, it is useful to examine cross-cultural data.

Around the world, anthropologists have documented highly diverse constructions of gender that do not always conform to our ideals of masculinity and femininity. Beginning with the path-breaking work of Margaret Mead ([1935] 2001) and continuing

Conventional notions of femininity, masculinity, and gender roles do not begin to address the complexities of contemporary society. Consider transgendered persons, whose current gender identity no longer matches their physical identity at birth.

through contemporary fieldwork, these scholars have shown that gender roles can vary greatly from one physical environment, economy, and political system to the next.

In any society, gender stratification requires not only individual socialization into traditional gender roles within the family, but also the promotion and support of those traditional roles by other social institutions, such as religion and education. Moreover, even with all major institutions socializing the young into conventional gender roles, every society has women and men who resist and successfully oppose the stereotypes: strong women who become leaders or professionals, gentle men who care for children, and so forth. It seems clear that differences between the sexes are not dictated by biology. Indeed, the maintenance of traditional gender roles requires constant social controls—and those controls are not always effective.

We can see the social construction of gender roles in process in societies strained by war and social upheaval. U.S. troops were sent to Afghanistan primarily to quell terrorist operations, but also to improve women's rights in a country where social protections and the rule of law have broken down. In this patriarchal society wracked by poverty and war, Afghani women have never been secure; their appearance in public is especially dangerous. Not only is violence against women common in Afghanistan; it is seldom investigated or prosecuted, even in the most severe cases. Victims of violence risk being charged with adultery if they report the crime to authorities. Thanks to UN intervention on women's behalf, however, Afghanis are beginning to recognize that violence against women is a social problem (Organisation for Economic Co-operation and Development 2012b).

Being harassed or groped on public transit is a problem for women all over the world. In Tokyo, separate subway cars are reserved for women to protect them from sex offenses.

Sociological Perspectives on Gender

Cross-cultural studies indicate that societies dominated by men are much more common than those in which women play the decisive role. Sociologists have turned to all the major theoretical perspectives to understand how and why these social distinctions are established. Each approach focuses on culture rather than biology as the primary determinant of gender differences. Yet in other respects, advocates of these sociological perspectives disagree widely.

Functionalist Perspective

Functionalists maintain that gender differentiation has contributed to overall social stability. Sociologists Talcott Parsons and Robert Bales (1955) argued that to function most effectively, the family requires adults who specialize in particular roles. They viewed the traditional gender roles as arising out of the need to establish a division of labor between marital partners.

Parsons and Bales contended that women take the expressive, emotionally supportive role and men the instrumental, practical role, with the two complementing each other. **Expressiveness** denotes concern for the maintenance of harmony and the internal emotional affairs of the family. **Instrumentality** refers to an emphasis on tasks, a focus on more distant goals, and a concern for the external relationship between one's family and other social institutions. According to this theory, women's interest in expressive goals frees men for instrumental tasks, and vice versa. Women become anchored in the family as wives, mothers, and household managers; men become anchored in the occupational world outside the home. Of course, Parsons and Bales offered this framework in the 1950s, when many more women were full-time homemakers than is true today. These theorists did not explicitly endorse traditional gender roles, but they implied that dividing tasks between spouses was functional for the family as a unit.

Given the typical socialization of women and men in the United States, the functionalist view is initially persuasive. However, it would lead us to expect girls and women who have no interest in children to become babysitters and mothers. Similarly, males who love spending time with children might be programmed into careers in the business world. Such differentiation might harm the individual who does not fit into prescribed roles, as well as deprive society of the contributions of many talented people who feel confined by gender stereotyping. Moreover, the functionalist approach does not convincingly explain why men should be assigned categorically to the instrumental role and women to the expressive role.

Conflict Perspective

Viewed from a conflict perspective, the functionalist approach masks the underlying power relations between men and women. Parsons and Bales never explicitly presented the expressive and instrumental roles as being of unequal value to society, yet their

Conflict theorists emphasize that men's work is uniformly valued, whereas women's work (whether unpaid labor in the home or wage labor) is devalued. This woman is assembling computer parts in a factory in Austin, Texas.

inequality is quite evident. Although social institutions may pay lip service to women's expressive skills, men's instrumental skills are more highly rewarded, whether in terms of money or prestige. Consequently, according to feminists and conflict theorists, any division of labor by gender into instrumental and expressive tasks is far from neutral in its impact on women.

Conflict theorists contend that the relationship between females and males has traditionally been one of unequal power, with men in a dominant position over women. Men may originally have become powerful in preindustrial times because their size, physical strength, and freedom from childbearing duties allowed them to dominate women physically. In contemporary societies, such considerations are not so important, yet cultural beliefs about the sexes are long established, as anthropologist Margaret Mead and feminist sociologist Helen Mayer Hacker (1951, 1974) both stressed. Such beliefs support a social structure that places males in controlling positions.

Conflict theorists, then, see gender differences as a reflection of the subjugation of one group (women) by another group (men). If we use an analogy to Marx's analysis of class conflict, we can say that males are like the bourgeoisie, or capitalists; they control most of the society's wealth, prestige, and power. Females are like the proletariat, or workers; they can acquire valuable resources only by following the dictates of their bosses. Men's work is uniformly valued; women's work (whether unpaid labor in the home or wage labor) is devalued.

Feminist Perspective

A significant component of the conflict approach to gender stratification draws on feminist theory. Although use of the term *feminist theory* is comparatively recent, the critique of women's position in society and culture goes back to some of the earliest works that have influenced sociology. Among the most important are Mary Wollstonecraft's *A Vindication of the Rights of Women* (originally published in 1792), John Stuart Mill's *The Subjection of Women* (originally published in 1869), and Friedrich Engels's *The Origin of the Family, Private Property, and the State* (originally published in 1884).

Engels, a close associate of Karl Marx, argued that women's subjugation coincided with the rise of private property during industrialization. Only when people moved beyond an agrarian economy could males enjoy the luxury of leisure and withhold rewards and privileges from women. Drawing on the work of Marx and Engels, many contemporary feminist theorists view women's subordination as part of the overall exploitation and injustice that they see as inherent in capitalist societies. Some radical feminist theorists, however, view the oppression of women as inevitable in *all* male-dominated societies, whether they are labeled capitalist, socialist, or communist (Feuer 1989; Tuchman 1992; Tucker 1978:734–759).

Feminist sociologists would find little to disagree with in the conflict theorists' perspective, but are more likely to embrace a political agenda. Feminists would also argue that until the 1970s, the very discussion of women and society, however well meant, was distorted by the exclusion of women from academic thought, including sociology. We have noted the many accomplishments of Jane Addams and Ida Wells-Barnett, but they generally worked outside the discipline, focusing on what we would now call applied sociology and social work. At the time, their efforts, while valued as humanitarian, were seen as unrelated to the research and conclusions being reached in academic circles, which of course were male academic circles (Andersen 2007; J. Howard 1999).

Intersections with Race, Class, and Other Social Factors

Contemporary feminists recognize the differential treatment of some women not only because of their gender, but also because of the intersection of their race, ethnicity, and socioeconomic status. Simply put, Whites dominate these poor, non-White women because they are non-White; men dominate them because they are women; and the affluent dominate them because they are poor. The African American feminist theorist Patricia Hill Collins (2000) has termed the convergence of social forces that contributes to the subordinate status of these low-status women the **matrix of domination** (Figure 34-1).

Gender, race, and social class are not the only sources of oppression in the United States, though they profoundly affect women and people of color. Other forms of categorization and stigmatization that might be included in the matrix are sexual orientation, religion, disability, and age. If we apply the matrix to the world as a whole, we might add citizenship status or perceived colonial or neocolonial status to the list (Winant 2006).

Though feminists have addressed themselves to the needs of minority women, these women are oppressed much more by their race and ethnicity than by their gender. The question for Latinas (Hispanic women), African American women, Asian American women, and Native American women appears to be whether they should unite with their brothers against

FIGURE 34-1 **Matrix of Domination**

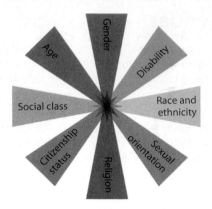

Source: Developed by author.

The matrix of domination illustrates how several social factors, including gender, social class, and race and ethnicity, can converge to create a cumulative impact on a person's social standing.

racism or challenge them for their sexism. The answer is that our society must eradicate both sexism and racism (Beisel and Kay 2004; Breines 2007; C. Epstein 1999).

The discussion of gender roles among African Americans has always provoked controversy. Advocates of Black nationalism contend that feminism only distracts women from participating fully in the African American struggle. The existence of feminist groups among Blacks, in their view, simply divides the Black community, thereby serving the dominant White majority. In contrast, Black feminists such as bell hooks (1994) argue that little is to be gained by accepting the gender-role divisions of the dominant society, which place women in a separate, subservient position. Though the media commonly portray Black women in a negative light—as illiterates, welfare queens, or prostitutes—Black feminists emphasize that it is not solely Whites and the White-dominated media who focus on such negative images. Black men (most recently, Black male rap artists) have also portrayed Black women in a negative way (Raybon 1989; Threadcraft 2008).

Historically, Native Americans stand out as an exception to the patriarchal tradition in North America. At the time of the European settlers' arrival, Native American gender roles varied greatly from tribe to tribe. Southern tribes, for reasons unclear to today's scholars, were usually matriarchal and traced their descent through the mother. European missionaries, who sought to make the native peoples more like Europeans, set out to transform this arrangement, which was not entirely universal. Like members of other groups, some Native American women have resisted gender stereotypes (Marubbio 2006).

Latinas are usually considered as part of either the Hispanic or feminist movements, and their distinctive experience ignored. In the past, they have been excluded from decision making in the two social institutions that most affect their daily lives: the family and the church. Particularly in the lower class, the Hispanic family suffers from the pervasive tradition of male domination.

And the Catholic Church relegates women to supportive roles, while reserving the leadership positions for men (Browne 2001; De Anda 2004).

Prior to this chapter, much of our discussion has focused on the social effects of race and ethnicity, coupled with poverty, low incomes, and meager wealth. The matrix of domination highlights the confluence of these factors with gender discrimination, which we must include to fully understand the plight of women of color.

 use your **sociological imagination**

Which elements of the matrix of domination privilege you? Which place you at a disadvantage?

Interactionist Perspective

While functionalists and conflict theorists who study gender stratification typically focus on macro-level social forces and institutions, interactionist researchers tend to examine gender stratification on the micro level of everyday behavior. The key to this approach is the way gender is socially constructed in everyday interactions. We "do gender" by reinforcing traditionally masculine and feminine actions. For example, a man "does masculinity" by opening a door for his girlfriend; she "does femininity" by consenting to his assistance. Obviously, the social construction of gender goes beyond these relatively trivial rituals. Interactionists recognize, too, that people can challenge traditional gender roles. A female golfer who uses the men's tees and a man who actively arranges a birthday luncheon at work are redoing gender (Deutsch 2007; West and Zimmerman 1987).

Tracking Sociological Perspectives

Table **34-2** **Sociological Perspectives on Gender**

Theoretical Perspective	Emphasis
Functionalist	Gender differentiation contributes to social stability
Conflict	Gender inequality is rooted in the female–male power relationship
Feminist	Women's subjugation is integral to society and social structure
Interactionist	Gender distinctions and "doing gender" are reflected in people's everyday behavior

One continuing subject of investigation is the role of gender in cross-sex conversations (sometimes referred to as "cross-talk"), specifically the idea that men interrupt women more than women interrupt men. Interestingly, empirical research does not clearly support this assertion. True, people in positions of authority or status—who are much more likely to be male than female—dominate interpersonal conversations. That does not necessarily mean that women per se cannot be heard, however. Future research results may deemphasize the clichéd advice that women must speak up and focus instead on the situational structures that cast men in dominant positions (Cameron 2007; Hyde 2005; Tannen 1990).

Table 34-2 summarizes the major sociological perspectives on gender.

MODULE 34 | Recap and Review

Summary

Gender is an ascribed status that provides a basis for social differentiation. This module examines the social construction of gender and theories of stratification by gender.

1. In the United States, the social construction of gender continues to define significantly different expectations for females and males.

2. **Gender roles** show up in our work and behavior and in how we react to others. Throughout history, these roles have constricted women much more than they have men.

3. Though men may exhibit a variety of different gender roles, or **multiple masculinities**, society reinforces their traditional role of dominating women.

4. Anthropological research points to the importance of cultural conditioning in defining the social roles of males and females.

5. Functionalists maintain that sex differentiation contributes to overall social stability, but conflict theorists charge that the relationship between females and males is one of unequal power, with men dominating women. This dominance shows up in people's everyday interactions.

6. Many women experience differential treatment, not only because of their gender but because of their race, ethnicity, and social class. This convergence of social forces is called the **matrix of domination**.

7. As an example of their micro-level approach to the study of gender stratification, interactionists have analyzed men's verbal dominance over women through conversational interruption.

Thinking Critically

1. Compare the social construction of gender with the social construction of race.

2. Which aspects of the functionalist and conflict perspectives on gender make the most sense to you? Explain.

MODULE 35 Women: The Oppressed Majority

Many people, both male and female, find it difficult to conceive of women as a subordinate and oppressed group. Yet take a look at the political structure of the United States: women remain noticeably underrepresented. As of mid-2012, for example, only 6 of the nation's 50 states had a female governor (Arizona, New Mexico, North Carolina, Oklahoma, South Carolina, and Washington).

Women have made slow but steady progress in certain political arenas. In 1981, out of 535 members of Congress, there were only 21 women: 19 in the House of Representatives and 2 in the Senate. In contrast, the Congress that held office in mid-2011 had 88 women: 71 in the House and 17 in the Senate. Yet the membership and leadership of Congress remain overwhelmingly male.

In October 1981, Sandra Day O'Connor was sworn in as the nation's first female Supreme Court justice. Still, no woman has ever served as president of the United States, vice president, or chief justice of the Supreme Court.

Sexism and Sex Discrimination

Just as African Americans are victimized by racism, women in our society are victimized by sexism. **Sexism** is the ideology that one sex is superior to the other. The term is generally used to refer to male prejudice and discrimination against women. In Module 31, we noted that Blacks can suffer from both individual acts of racism and institutional discrimination. **Institutional discrimination** was defined as the denial of opportunities and equal rights to individuals and groups that results from the normal operations of a society. In the same sense, women suffer from both individual acts of sexism (such as sexist remarks and acts of violence) and institutional sexism.

It is not simply that particular men in the United States are biased in their treatment of women. All the major institutions of our society—including the government, armed forces, large corporations, the media, universities, and the medical establishment—are controlled by men. These institutions, in their normal, day-to-day operations, often discriminate against women and perpetuate sexism. For example, if the central office of a nationwide bank sets a policy that single women are a bad risk for loans—regardless of their incomes and investments—that bank will discriminate against women in state after state. It will do so even at branches where loan officers hold no personal biases toward women, but are merely "following orders."

Our society is run by male-dominated institutions, yet with the power that flows to men come responsibility and stress. Men have higher reported rates of certain types of mental illness than women, and a greater likelihood of death due to heart attack or stroke. The pressure on men to succeed, and then to remain on top in the competitive world of work, can be especially intense. That is not to suggest that gender stratification is as damaging to men as it is to women. But it is clear that the power and privilege men enjoy are no guarantee of personal well-being.

 use your **sociological imagination**

Think of organizations or institutions you belong to whose leadership positions are customarily held by men. What would those organizations be like if they were led by women?

The Status of Women Worldwide

According to a detailed overview of the status of the world's women, issued by the World Bank in 2012, the lives of girls and women have changed dramatically over the past quarter century. Progress has been limited in some respects, however. In many parts of the world, women still lag far behind men in their earnings and in their ability to speak out politically (World Bank 2012b).

This critique applies to Western as well as non-Western countries. Although Westerners tend to view some societies—for example, Muslim countries—as being particularly harsh toward

BOX 35-1

The Head Scarf and the Veil: Complex Symbols

The wearing of a veil or head scarf by women is common to many but not all Middle Eastern societies. All Muslims, men and women alike, are expected to cover themselves and avoid revealing clothes designed to accentuate the body's contours or emphasize its physical beauty. The Koran does permit Muslims to wear revealing garments in private, with their families or with members of the same sex.

The Prophet Muhammad recommended that women cover all of their bodies except for the face, hands, and feet. The Koran adds that a woman's headcovering should fall over the neck and upper chest. A variety of women's outergarments comply with these guidelines for modest attire; collectively, they are referred to as the *hijab.* Face veils are dictated by cultural tradition, however—not by Islam.

In effect, the veil represents a rejection of the beauty myth (see Chapter 7), which is so prevalent in Western societies. By covering themselves almost completely, Muslim women assure themselves and their families that their physical appearance will not play a

> In effect, the veil represents a rejection of the beauty myth, which is so prevalent in Western societies.

role in their contacts outside the family. Rather, these women will be known only for their faith, their intellect, and their personalities.

The veil was politicized by modernization movements that pitted Western cultural values against traditional Islamic values. In Turkey, for instance, in the early 20th century, government officials attempted to subordinate traditional ethnic and religious influences to their nationalistic goals. Though women weren't forbidden to wear the veil, they were not allowed to veil themselves in public places like schools. Many Muslims resented these forced social changes.

In the United States today, Muslim women select from an array of traditional garments, including a long, loose tailored coat and a loose black overgarment that is worn with a scarf or perhaps a face veil. However, they are just as apt to wear an overblouse and a long skirt or loose pants, which they can buy at local clothing stores.

In some non-Muslim countries, notably France, officials have come under fire for banning the *hijab,* or the head scarf, in public schools, as well as a full-body, face-covering robe anywhere in public. The custom of covering generally has not been an issue in the United States, though one 11-year-old had to go to federal court to establish her right to wear a head scarf at school in Muskogee, Oklahoma. Interestingly, the U.S. Department of Justice supported her lawsuit.

The head scarf—an expression of modesty, a woman's right as an individual, or a sign of oppression?

LET'S DISCUSS

1. Consider life in a society in which women wear veils. Can you see any advantages, from the woman's point of view? From the man's?

2. Do you find the Western emphasis on physical beauty oppressive? If so, in what ways?

Sources: Charrad 2011; Gurbuz and Gurbuz-Kucuksari 2009; Killian 2003; Selod 2008b.

---

women, that perception is actually an overgeneralization. Muslim countries are exceedingly varied and complex and do not often fit the stereotypes created by the Western media. For a detailed discussion of the status of Muslim women today, see Box 35-1.

Regardless of culture, however, women everywhere suffer from second-class status. It is estimated that women grow half the world's food, but they rarely own land. They constitute one-third of the world's paid labor force, but are generally found in the lowest-paying jobs. Single-parent households headed by women, which appear to be on the rise in many nations, are typically found in the poorest sections of the population. The feminization of poverty has become a global phenomenon. As in the United States, women around the world are underrepresented politically.

Despite these challenges, women are not responding passively. They are mobilizing, individually and collectively. Given the significant underrepresentation of women in government offices and national legislatures, however, the task is difficult, as we shall see in Module 47.

Not surprisingly, there is a link between the wealth of industrialized nations and the poverty of women in developing countries. Viewed from a conflict perspective or through the lens of Immanuel Wallerstein's world systems analysis, the economies of developing nations are controlled and exploited by industrialized countries and multinational corporations based in those countries. Much of the exploited labor in developing nations, especially in the nonindustrial sector, is performed by women. Women workers typically toil long hours for low pay, but contribute significantly to their families' incomes (Chubb et al. 2008).

In industrialized countries, women's unequal status can be seen in the division of housework, as well as in the jobs they hold and the pay they earn. Sociologist Jan Paul Heisig analyzed gender inequality among the rich (the top decile in income) and the poor (the bottom decile) in 33 industrialized countries. Typically, poor men did more housework than rich men, but as Figure 35-1 shows, rich or poor, men did much less housework than women. The recent economic recession accentuated this unequal division of housework. Obviously, being unemployed leaves both men and women with more time for household chores. However, unemployed women do double the amount of extra housework as unemployed men (Gough and Killewald 2011).

FIGURE 35-1 **Gender Inequality in Housework**

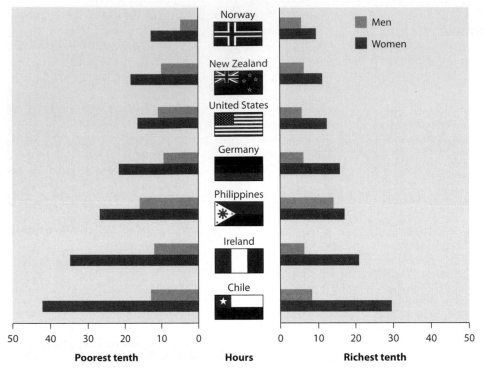

Poorest tenth   Hours   Richest tenth

Note: Housework includes laundry, grocery shopping, dinner preparation, and care for sick family members.
Source: Adapted from Heisig 2011:84.

Around the world, rich or poor, women do much more housework than men.

◼ Women in the Workforce of the United States

More than 30 years ago, the U.S. Commission on Civil Rights (1976:1) concluded that the passage in the Declaration of Independence proclaiming that "all men are created equal" has been taken too literally for too long—especially with respect to women's opportunities for employment. In this section we will see how gender bias has limited women's opportunities for employment outside the home, at the same time that it forces them to carry a disproportionate burden inside the home.

Labor Force Participation

Women's participation in the paid labor force of the United States increased steadily throughout the 20th century and into the 21st century (Figure 35-2). Today, millions of women—married or single, with or without children, pregnant or recently having given birth—are in the labor force.

Overall, 59 percent of adult women in the United States were in the labor force in 2010, compared to 41 percent in 1970. For men, the data were 71 percent in 2010, compared to 76 percent in 1970

(Bureau of the Census 2011a:Table 587 on page 377).

Still, women entering the job market find their options restricted in important ways. Women are *underrepresented* in occupations historically defined as "men's jobs," which often carry much greater financial rewards and prestige than women's jobs. For example, in 2010, women accounted for approximately 47 percent of the paid labor force of the United States, yet they constituted only 10 percent of civil engineers, 31 percent of computer systems analysts, and 32 percent of physicians (Table 35-1).

Such occupational segregation is not unique to the United States but typical of industrial countries. In Great Britain, for example, only 29 percent of computer analysts are women, while 81 percent of cashiers and 90 percent of nurses are women (Cross and Bagilhole 2002).

Women from all groups and men from minority groups sometimes encounter attitudinal or organizational bias that prevents them from reaching their full potential. As we saw in Module 31, the term **glass ceiling** refers to an invisible barrier that blocks the promotion of a qualified individual in a work environment because of the individual's gender, race, or ethnicity. A study of the *Fortune* 500 largest corporations in the United States showed that in 2011, barely 16 percent of the seats on their boards of directors were held by women. Women held the top-earning position in less than 8 percent of those corporations (Catalyst 2011).

When women do gain entry to corporate boards of directors, the response in the financial world is not entirely positive. Despite objective tests that show strong financial performance under gender-diverse leadership, some investors tend to balk. Research by Frank Dobbin and Jiwook Jung (2010) shows that

FIGURE 35-2 **Trends in U.S. Women's Participation in the Paid Labor Force, 1890–2010**

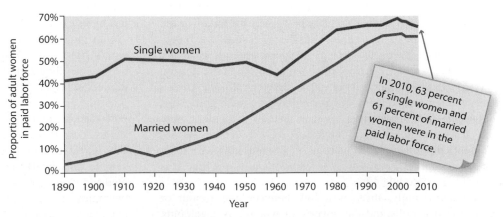

Source: Bureau of the Census 1975, 2011a:Table 597 on page 384.

Table 35-1 U.S. Women in Selected Occupations: Women as a Percentage of All Workers in the Occupation

Underrepresented		Overrepresented	
Firefighters	4%	High school teachers	57%
Aircraft pilots and engineers	5	Cashiers	74
Civil engineers	10	Social workers	81
Police officers	13	Elementary teachers	82
Clergy	18	File clerks	82
Chefs and head cooks	19	Librarians	83
Dentists	26	Tellers	88
Computer systems analysts	31	Registered nurses	91
Coaches and umpires	32	Receptionists	93
Lawyers	32	Word processors and typists	93
Physicians	32	Child care workers	95
Mail carriers	38	Dental assistants	98

Note: Women constitute 47 percent of the entire labor force.
Source: Data for 2010 reported in Bureau of the Census 2011a:Table 616 on pages 393–396.

small investors often sell their shares when women become corporate leaders, apparently falling for the stereotype that associates males with success. This sell pattern is not characteristic of larger investors, who have long argued that gender-diverse leadership is good for business.

This type of inequality is not unique to the United States. Worldwide, women hold less than 1 percent of corporate managerial positions. In recognition of the underrepresentation of women on boards of directors, the Norwegian legislature established minimum quotas for the number of female board members. As the architects of the plan put it, "instead of assuming what people *can't* do at work, provide opportunities for employees to prove what they can do." The goal was not complete equity for women, but 40 percent representation by 2008. By 2012 the percentage stood at 18 percent (European PWN 2012).

Compensation

He works. She works. Both are physicians—a high-status occupation with considerable financial rewards. He makes $140,000. She makes $88,000.

These median annual earnings for physicians in the United States were released by the Census Bureau. They are typical of the results of the bureau's detailed study of occupations and income. Take air traffic controllers. He makes $67,000; she makes $56,000. Or housekeepers: he makes $19,000; she makes $15,000. What about teachers' assistants? He makes $20,000; she makes $15,000. Statisticians at the bureau looked at the median annual earnings for no fewer than 821 occupations ranging from dishwasher to chief executive. After adjusting for workers' ages, education, and work experience, they came to an unmistakable conclusion: across the board, there is a substantial gender gap in the median earnings of full-time workers.

Men do not always earn more than women for doing the same work. Researchers at the Census Bureau found 2 occupations out of 821 in which women typically earn about 1 percent more income than men: hazardous materials recovery and telecommunications line installation. These two occupations employed less than 1 out of every 1,000 workers the bureau studied. Forecasting analyses show no convincing evidence that the wage gap is narrowing.

What accounts for these yawning wage gaps between men and women in the same occupation? Scholars at the Census Bureau studied the following characteristics of men and women in the same occupation:

- Age and degree of formal education
- Marital status and the presence of children at home
- Specialization within the occupation (for example, family practice versus surgical practice)
- Years of work experience
- Hours worked per year

Taking all these factors into consideration reduced the pay gap between men and women by only 3 cents. Women still earned 80 cents for every dollar earned by men. In sum, the disparity in pay between men and women cannot be explained by pointing to women's career choices (Government Accountability Office 2003; Weinberg 2004, 2007).

Legally, sex discrimination in wage payments is difficult to prove. Witness the case of former Goodyear worker Lilly Ledbetter, who learned 19 years after she was hired that she was being paid less than men doing the same job. Ledbetter sued and was awarded damages, only to have the Supreme Court overturn the decision on the grounds that she made her claim more than six months after the first discriminatory paycheck was issued. Congress relaxed this restriction in 2009 (Pear 2009).

Not all the obstacles women face in the workplace originate with management. Unfortunately, many workers, both male and female, would prefer not to work for a woman (Box 35-2).

While women are at a disadvantage in male-dominated occupations, the same is not true for men in female-dominated occupations. Sociologist Michelle Budig (2002) examined a national database containing career information on more than 12,000 men, collected over the course of 15 years. She found that men were uniformly advantaged in female occupations. Though male nurses, grade school teachers, and librarians may experience some scorn in the larger society, they are much more likely than women to be encouraged to become administrators. Observers of the labor force have termed this advantage for men in female-dominated occupations the *glass escalator*—quite a contrast to the glass ceiling (J. Jacobs 2003; C. L. Williams 1992, 1995).

Social Consequences of Women's Employment

Today, many women face the challenge of trying to juggle work and family. Their situation has many social consequences. For one thing, it puts pressure on child care facilities, public financing of day care, and even the fast-food industry, which provides by death threats and murders, have stopped performing abortions. For poor people in rural areas, this reduction in service makes it more difficult to locate and travel to a facility that will accommodate their wishes. Viewed from a conflict perspective, this is one more financial burden that falls especially heavily on low-income women.

Finally, some antiabortion activists have charged that family-planning agencies and health care professionals are targeting young African American women for abortions. These pro-life proponents use the emotion-laden phrase "womb lynchings" to call attention to the issue. Abortion rights advocates counter that the campaign falsely portrays young Black women as naive and not in control of their own decisions (Dewan 2010).

Initiating Policy

In 1973 the Supreme Court supported the general right to terminate a pregnancy by a narrow 5–4 majority. Although pro-life activists continue to hope for an overruling of *Roe v. Wade,*

they have focused in the interim on weakening the decision through tactics such as limiting the use of fetal tissue in medical experiments and prohibiting certain late-term abortions, which they term "partial-birth" abortions. The Supreme Court continues to hear cases involving such restrictions.

Pro-life activists have also focused on limiting abortion at the state level, where 61 new laws were enacted in 2011 alone. Typical provisions of these laws require women to view an ultrasound image of the fetus, and in some jurisdictions, to listen to the heartbeat. Although the Supreme Court upheld a 24-hour waiting period before an abortion in 1992, states are now calling for a 48-hour or 72-hour wait (D. Samuels 2011).

What is the policy in other countries? As in the United States, many European nations responded to public opinion and liberalized abortion laws beginning in the 1970s. However, many of those nations limit the procedure to the first 12 weeks of a pregnancy. (The United States, in contrast, allows abortions up to about the 24th week and beyond.) Inspired by the strong antiabortion movement in the United States,

MAPPING LIFE WORLDWIDE

FIGURE 35-5 **The Global Divide on Abortion**

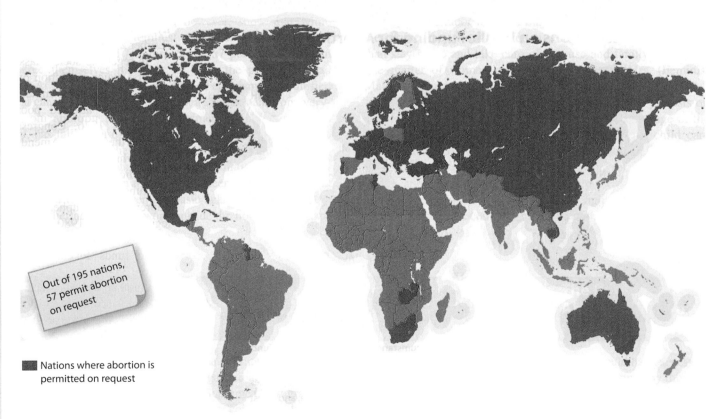

Out of 195 nations, 57 permit abortion on request

■ Nations where abortion is permitted on request

Note: Data current as of November 2011.
Source: Developed by the author based on United Nations Population Division 2011.

—Continued

antiabortion activists in Europe have become more outspoken, especially in Great Britain, France, Portugal, Spain, Italy, and Germany.

The policies of the United States are intertwined with those of developing nations. From the 1980s through January 2009, members of Congress who opposed abortion successfully blocked foreign aid to countries that might use the funds to encourage abortion. Yet developing nations generally have the most restrictive abortion laws. As Figure 35-5 shows, it is primarily in Africa, Latin America, and parts of Asia that women are not allowed to terminate a pregnancy on request. As might be expected, illegal abortions are most common in those nations. An estimated quarter of the world's women live in countries where abortion is illegal or is permitted only if a woman's life is in jeopardy. Indeed, the rate of abortions in countries with legal restrictions on the procedure matches the rate in countries that permit it. Hence, 40 percent of abortions worldwide—about 16 million procedures each year—are performed illegally (P. Baker 2009; Guttmacher Institute 2008).

TAKE THE ISSUE WITH YOU

1. How easy do you think it is for a young adult woman to obtain an abortion? What do you think should be the first step she takes in considering one?

2. Do you think teenage girls should be required to get their parents' consent before having an abortion? Why or why not?

3. Under what circumstances should abortions be allowed? Explain your reasoning.

MODULE 35 | Recap and Review

Summary

This module examines the status of women as an oppressed minority in the United States and around the world.

1. Women around the world suffer from **sexism** and **institutional discrimination**.

2. In the United States today, almost as many women as men participate in the paid labor force, but women are underrepresented in managerial positions and underpaid compared to men with the same jobs.

3. As women have taken on more and more hours of paid employment outside the home, they have been only partially successful in getting their husbands to take on more homemaking duties, including child care.

4. Many women agree with the positions of the feminist movement but reject the label *feminist.*

5. The issue of abortion has bitterly divided the United States (as well as other nations), pitting pro-choice activists against pro-life activists.

Thinking Critically

1. What are the challenges to comparing the status of women across different nations?

2. How would you argue that women have come either very far or not far enough in their labor force participation?

3. Today, is feminism more likely to produce social change or respond to social change? Explain.

Key Terms

Feminism   297

Glass ceiling   294

Institutional discrimination   292

Second shift   296

Sexism   292

Have you noticed how more and more older people are not "behaving elderly"?

Journalist Ted C. Fishman has devoted his skills to documenting how aging has changed across the world.

" Now in her eighties, my mother still dances at her grandsons' Led Zeppelin tribute concerts, swims Lake Michigan when the water is brisk, hikes among penguins in Patagonia, and dons cross-country skis as soon as the snow is deep enough. My late father, in contrast, was at the peak of his professional and creative success in his early sixties, but a barrage of ailments hit him hard at sixty-three. He began a cruel fifteen-year decline that left him blind, immobile, slow of speech, and utterly dependent. That he never lost his wit or kindness or his ability to hold on to the joys of life was, to me, heroic.

My parents' different experiences neatly represent what is happening to millions of Americans and to vast portions of the globe's population. The world is going gray. Getting not just older but *old*. Sometime after sixty, it seems to happen to everyone: life-altering events cascade one after another. In some combination, family nests are emptied; jobs end or change; spouses, friends, and kin grow gravely ill or die; bodies and minds decline; one's status and power in the family and in social circles inverts; money draws down; and, as remaining years grow fewer, relationships with time and eternity shift.

And yet new worlds can open up, too. Time can expand, social circles grow bigger, new passions take root. Freed from the relentless demands of family and work, older people may experience a sweet rejuvenation. People whom one might expect to be decrepit and infirm are, well, dancing at Led Zeppelin tribute concerts; Or even performing in them.

Meanwhile, although the world well understands how young people shape social life and business, it is just now beginning to see how the arrival of a historically enormous older population will affect all of us. Many old people, like my mother, will be healthy and vibrant, but many others, like my father, will need extraordinary resources to make it from one day to the next. The aging of the globe is having profound economic, political, cultural, and familial effects that are only going to intensify. Some of these changes will be welcome and others will not. Certain people will benefit and others will be harmed. Money and power are at stake, of course, as well as the well-being of millions of older people who have worked and loved and given themselves to all that life offers. But the well-being of the globe's young is also at stake, because it is they who need resources also required by the old, and because in the end, it is largely the young who, as family members, friends, and citizens traveling the continuum of an aging world, will eventually care for the old. And in time their older selves.

The signs of the shift, large and small, are everywhere, if we only will see them. Consider:

In a room full of telephones and flat-panel displays, where staff is on hand twenty-four hours a day, calls begin to pick up around 9:00 a.m. That's when the more than 6 million elderly customers of Philips Lifeline tend to begin their daily routines. The service allows its clients to alert the company if anything threatens them. The morning is rife with dangers. The average age of a customer is eighty-two, but thousands of centenarians use the service, too. The large majority are women, a predictable reality in an older group. The mornings see millions of Lifeline clients head to the showers, step out on slippery tiles, and then make their way to the kitchen, where fire, knives, tall cabinets, area rugs, and wood flooring are mortal threats. If customers slip and fall, or a sleeve catches fire, or if they are overcome with anxiety and fear as the day begins, devices around their necks or on their wrists let them send signals, sometimes automatically, to the Lifeline call center. By mid-morning on a beautiful fall day, Lifeline has handled nearly seven hundred thousand *calls*. "

The aging of the globe is having profound economic, political, cultural, and familial effects that are only going to intensify.

(Fishman 2010a:1–2) Additional information about this excerpt can be found on the Online Learning Center at www.mhhe.com/schaefermod2e.

J ournalist Ted C. Fishman, author of this excerpt, is known for his reporting on global trade and finance. He became aware of a powerful demographic trend, the aging of the world's population. In his book *Shock of Gray,* Fishman confronts the consequences of the rise in the proportion of elderly for entire societies and economies. He predicts a growing conflict between young and old, developed and developing nations, over limited resources.

Not all older people are frail and dependent, in need of support; many are healthy, energetic, and engaged. Unfortunately, younger people tend to stereotype the aged. Like race or gender, age is socially constructed, an ascribed status that dominates people's perceptions of others, obscuring individual differences. Rather than suggesting that a particular elderly person is no longer competent to drive, for instance, we may condemn the entire age group: "Those old codgers shouldn't be allowed on the road."

How do people's roles change as they age? What are the social implications of the growing number of elderly in the United States? In this chapter we will look at the process of aging throughout the life course and around the world. After exploring various theories of the impact of aging, we will discuss the role transitions typical of the major stages in the life course. We will consider the challenges facing the "sandwich generation," middle-aged people who care for both their children and their aging parents. We will pay particular attention to the effects of prejudice and discrimination on older people, and to the rise of a political consciousness among the elderly. Finally, in the Social Policy section we will discuss the controversial issue of the right to die.

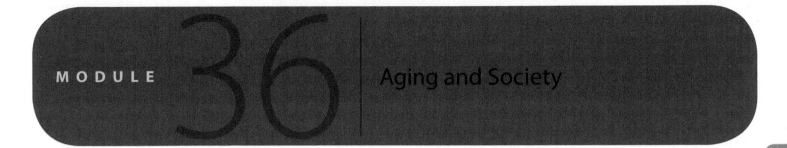

The Sherpas—a Tibetan-speaking Buddhist people in Nepal—live in a culture that idealizes old age. Almost all elderly members of the Sherpa culture own their homes, and most are in relatively good physical condition. Typically, older Sherpas value their independence and prefer not to live with their children. Among the Fulani of Africa, however, older men and women move to the edge of the family homestead. Since that is where people are buried, the elderly sleep over their own graves, for they are viewed socially as already dead. Like gender stratification, age stratification varies from culture to culture. One society may treat older people with great reverence, while another sees them as unproductive and "difficult" (M. Goldstein and Beall 1981; Stenning 1958; Tonkinson 1978).

contribute to their position as a minority group subject to discrimination, as we will see later in the chapter.

The model of five basic properties of a minority or subordinate group (introduced in Module 31) can be applied to older people in the United States to clarify their subordinate status:

1. Older people experience unequal treatment in employment and may face prejudice and discrimination.

2. Older people share physical characteristics that distinguish them from younger people. In addition, their cultural preferences and leisure-time activities often differ from those of the rest of society.

3. Membership in this disadvantaged group is involuntary.

Age Stratification

It is understandable that all societies have some system of age stratification that associates certain social roles with distinct periods in life. Some of this age differentiation seems inevitable; it would make little sense to send young children off to war, or to expect most older citizens to handle physically demanding tasks, such as loading freight at shipyards. However, as is the case with stratification by gender, in the United States age stratification goes far beyond the physical constraints on human beings at different ages.

"Being old" is a master status that commonly overshadows all others in the United States. Thus, the insights of labeling theory can help us in analyzing the consequences of aging. Once people have been labeled "old," the designation has a major impact on how others perceive them, and even on how they view themselves. Negative stereotypes of the elderly

Extended family arrangements are important to Americans, especially Latinos. Thirty-one percent of Hispanic women age 65 and older live with their relatives, compared to 13 percent of White non-Hispanic women. Among men of the same age, the rate is 15 percent for Hispanics, compared to 6 percent for White non-Hispanics (Jacobsen et al. 2011).

why social interaction must change or decrease in old age. In addition, they often ignore the impact of social class on the lives of elderly people.

The privileged upper class generally enjoys better health and vigor and less likelihood of dependency in old age. Affluence cannot forestall aging indefinitely, but it can soften the economic hardships people face in later years. Although pension plans, retirement packages, and insurance benefits may be developed to assist older people, those whose wealth allows them access to investment funds can generate the greatest income for their later years.

In contrast, the working class often faces greater health hazards and a greater risk of disability; aging is particularly difficult for those who suffer job-related injuries or illnesses. Working-class people also depend more heavily on Social Security benefits and private pension programs. During inflationary times, their relatively fixed incomes from these sources barely keep pace with the escalating costs of food, housing, utilities, and other necessities (Atchley and Barusch 2004).

According to the conflict approach, the treatment of older people in the United States reflects the many divisions in our society. The low status of older people is seen in prejudice and discrimination against them, in age segregation, and in unfair job practices—none of which are directly addressed by either disengagement or activity theory.

Conflict theorists have noted, too, that in the developing world, the transition from agricultural economies to industrialization and capitalism has not always been beneficial to the elderly. As a society's production methods change, the traditionally valued role of older people tends to erode. Their wisdom is no longer relevant in the new economy.

Tracking Sociological Perspectives

Table **36-1** **Sociological Perspectives on Aging**

Sociological Perspective	View of Aging	Social Roles	Portrayal of Elderly
Functionalist	Disengagement	Reduced	Socially isolated
Interactionist	Activity	Changed	Involved in new networks
Labeling	Socially constructed	Changing	Varies by audience
Conflict	Competition	Relatively unchanged	Victimized, organized to confront their victimization

In sum, the four perspectives considered here take different views of the elderly. Functionalists portray older people as socially isolated, with reduced social roles; interactionists see them as involved in new networks and changing social roles. Labeling theorists see old age as a life stage that is defined by society. Conflict theorists see it as a time when people are victimized and their social roles devalued. Table 36-1 summarizes these perspectives.

 use your **sociological imagination**

Have you noticed signs of second-class treatment of older people? If so, in what ways?

MODULE 36 | Recap and Review

Summary

Age, like gender and race, is an ascribed status that forms the basis for social differentiation.

1. Like other forms of stratification, age stratification varies from culture to culture.

2. In the United States, being old is a master status that seems to overshadow all others.

3. The particular problems of the aged have become the focus of a specialized area of research and inquiry known as **gerontology.**

4. **Disengagement theory** implies that society should help older people withdraw from their accustomed social roles. In contrast, **activity theory** suggests that the elderly person who remains active and socially involved will be better adjusted.

5. Labeling theorists note that people of the same age are labeled differently in different societies, based largely on difference in physical health, life opportunities, and life expectancy.

6. From a conflict perspective, the low status of older people is reflected in prejudice and discrimination against them and in unfair job practices.

Thinking Critically

1. Why is disengagement theory an example of functionalism?

2. Is labeling the same as stereotyping? Why or why not?

Key Terms

Activity theory   309
Disengagement theory   308
Gerontology   308

Today the world's population is evenly divided between those people who are under age 28 and those who are over age 28. By the middle of the 21st century, the median age will have risen to 40. Even though the United Nations held the first world assembly on aging in 1982, few people gave much thought to this prospect of whole populations—that is, nations—growing older until the 1990s. By 2010, the world had more than 551 million people age 65 and over. Together they constituted about 8 percent of the world's population. By 2045, nearly twice that proportion, or 15.2 percent of the world's people, will be over 65.

In an important sense, this trend toward the aging of the world's population represents a major success story, one that unfolded during the latter years of the 20th century. Through the efforts of national governments and international agencies, many societies have drastically reduced their incidence of disease, and with it their rate of death. As a result, these nations—particularly the industrialized countries of Europe and North America—have a high and steadily rising proportion of older members (Figure 37-1) (Fishman 2010b; Haub 2011).

Overall, Europe's population is older than that of any other continent. Though many European countries have long prided themselves on their generous pension programs, as the proportion of older people continues to rise, government officials have reluctantly begun to reduce pension benefits and raise the age at which workers can receive them. Japan, too, has a relatively old population; the Japanese enjoy a life expectancy of 83 years, compared to 78 in the United States. But though four more years of life may sound like a bonus, it presents a real and growing challenge to Japanese society (see Box 37-1 on page 315).

In most developing countries, people over 60 are likely to be in poorer health than their counterparts in industrialized nations. Yet few of those countries are in a position to offer extensive financial support to the elderly. Ironically, though the modernization of the developing world has brought many social and economic advances, it has undercut the traditionally high status of the elderly. In many cultures, the earning power of younger adults now exceeds that of their older relatives (Beck 2009).

Role Transitions throughout the Life Course

Socialization is a lifelong process. We simply do not experience things the same way at different points in the life course. For example, one study found that even falling in love differs according to where we are in the life course. Young unmarried adults tend to treat love as a noncommittal game or an obsession characterized by possessiveness and dependency. People over age 50 are much more likely to see love as involving commitment, and they tend to take a practical approach to finding a partner who meets a set of rational criteria. That does not mean that romance is dead among the older generation, however. Among those age 65 and over, 39 percent are "head over heels in love," compared to only 25 percent of those ages 18 to 34. While death of a partner or spouse marks a very significant life event, it does not mean the survivor becomes withdrawn. An analysis of widows and widowers age 65 and older found that within 18 months of the loss, 37% of men and 15% of women were interested in dating (Alterovitz and Mendelsohn 2009). The life course, then, affects the manner in which we relate to one another (G. Anderson 2009; Montgomery and Sorell 1997).

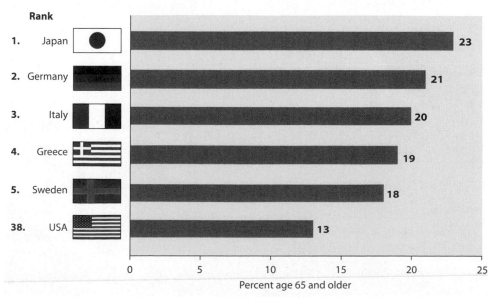

FIGURE 37-1 **World's "Oldest" Countries versus the United States**

Source: Data for 2009 or most recently available years from Haub 2011.

FIGURE 38-3 **Twenty-Eight Floridas by 2030**

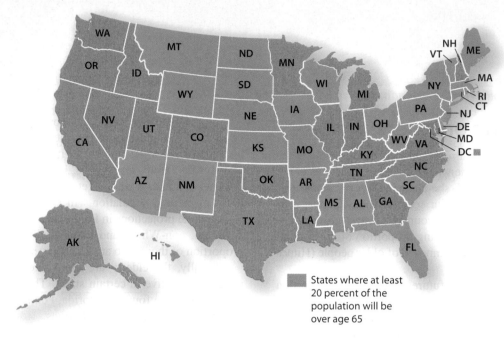

States where at least 20 percent of the population will be over age 65

Source: Bureau of the Census 2005a.

Wealth and Income

There is significant variation in wealth and poverty among the nation's older people. Some individuals and couples find themselves poor in part because of fixed pensions and skyrocketing health care costs (see Chapter 17). Nevertheless, as a group, older people in the United States are neither homogeneous nor poor. The typical elderly person enjoys a standard of living that is much higher now than at any point in the nation's past. Class differences among the elderly remain evident, but tend to narrow somewhat: those older people who enjoyed middle-class incomes while younger tend to remain better off after retirement, but less so than before (Denise Smith and Tillipman 2000).

To some extent, older people owe their overall improved standard of living to a greater accumulation of wealth—in the form of home ownership, private pensions, and other financial assets. Indeed, the median net worth of the elderly has increased by 42 percent over the past 25 years. But much of the improvement is due to more generous Social Security benefits. While modest when compared with other countries' pension programs, Social Security nevertheless provides 39 percent of all income received by older people in the United States. Still, about 9 percent of the nation's elderly population lives below the federal government's poverty line. At the extremes of poverty are those groups who were more likely to be poor at earlier points in the life cycle: female-headed households and racial and ethnic minorities (Richard Fry et al. 2011; He et al. 2005).

Viewed from a conflict perspective, it is not surprising that older women experience a double burden; the same is true of elderly members of racial and ethnic minorities. For example, in 2010 the proportion of older Latinos with incomes below the poverty level (18.0 percent) was almost three times as large as the proportion of older White non-Hispanics (6.8 percent). Moreover, 18.2 percent of older African Americans fell below the federal government's poverty line (DeNavas-Walt et al. 2011:Table B-2).

Ageism

Physician Robert Butler (1990) became concerned 49 years ago when he learned that a housing development near his home in metropolitan Washington, D.C., barred the elderly. Butler coined the term **ageism** to refer to prejudice and discrimination based on a person's age. Research shows that in the United States, a large majority of people over age 60—84 percent—have experienced ageism, from insulting jokes to outright disrespect (Roscigno 2010:7).

Ageism is especially difficult for the old, because at least youthful recipients of prejudice know that in time they will be "old enough." For many, old age symbolizes disease. While physical condition does weaken with age, today's older people are in much better shape than their counterparts even one generation ago. In any event, most jobs today require little brawn. Studies also indicate that older workers are better at jobs that require personnel skills, which comprise a growing proportion of the jobs available (*The Economist* 2011c).

Competition in the Labor Force

Although paid employment is not typical after age 65, since the 1980s it has become increasingly common. Concerned over their pension benefits, more and more people who are healthy enough to continue working have decided to postpone their retirement. Their decision has further eroded job opportunities for younger workers, already handicapped by the highest unemployment rates in a generation. Unfortunately, some people view older workers as "job stealers"—a biased judgment similar to that directed against illegal immigrants—instead of as experienced contributors to the labor force. Moreover, unemployed workers in their 50s find that potential employers rarely give them serious consideration. These difficulties not only intensify age conflict but lead to age discrimination as well (Jacobsen et al. 2011).

The federal Age Discrimination in Employment Act (ADEA), which went into effect in 1968, was passed to protect workers who are age 40 and older from being fired because of their age and replaced with younger workers, who would presumably receive lower salaries. The Supreme Court strengthened federal protection against age discrimination in 1996, ruling unanimously that such lawsuits can be successful even if an older worker is replaced by someone who is older than 40. Consequently, firing a 65-year-old employee to make way for a 45-year-old can be construed as age discrimination.

While firing people simply because they are old violates federal law, courts have upheld the right to lay off older workers for economic reasons. Critics contend that later, the same firms hire young, cheaper workers to replace experienced older workers. When economic growth began to slow in 2008 and companies cut back on their workforces, complaints of age bias grew sharply as older workers began to suspect they were bearing a disproportionate share of the layoffs (Roscigno 2010). Little wonder, then, in the wake of a bad economy, that workers are approaching their retirement warily. A national survey showed that only 14 percent of workers are confident of living comfortably in retirement, compared with 27 percent in 2007, before the recent recession (Ruth Helman et al. 2012:7).

Given recent legislative and legal advances, has the climate changed significantly for older workers? Box 38-1 presents several studies that have attempted to assess the extent of ageism, both in everyday life and in hiring.

The AARP is a major voice for the elderly. By featuring Bruce Springsteen (born in 1949) on the cover of its widely distributed magazine, the organization is signaling a desire to represent the younger members of the older generation, as well as to portray the active lives many older people lead.

 use your **sociological imagination**

It is September and you are channel-surfing through the new fall TV series. How likely are you to watch a television show that is based on older characters who spend a lot of time together?

The Elderly: Emergence of a Collective Consciousness

During the 1960s, students at colleges and universities across the country, advocating "student power," collectively demanded a role in the governance of educational institutions. In the following decade, many older people became aware that *they* were being treated as second-class citizens and turned to collective action.

The largest organization representing the nation's elderly is the AARP, founded in 1958 by a retired school principal who was having difficulty getting insurance because of age prejudice. Many of the AARP's services involve discounts and insurance for its 40 million members (43 percent of Americans age 50

and older), but the organization is also a powerful lobbying group. Recognizing that many elderly people are still gainfully employed, it has dropped its full name, American Association of *Retired* Persons (Donnelly 2007; Eggen 2009).

The potential power of the AARP is enormous. It is the third-largest voluntary association in the United States (behind only the Roman Catholic Church and the American Automobile Association), representing one out of every four registered voters in the United States. The AARP has endorsed voter registration campaigns, nursing home reforms, and pension reforms. In acknowledgment of its difficulties recruiting members of racial and ethnic minority groups, the AARP recently began a Minority Affairs Initiative. The spokeswoman for the initiative, Margaret Dixon, became the AARP's first African American president in 1996 (Birnbaum 2005).

People grow old in many different ways. Not all elderly people face the same challenges or enjoy the same resources. While the AARP lobbies to protect the elderly in general, other groups work in more specific ways. For example, the National Committee to Preserve Social Security and Medicare, founded in 1982, has successfully lobbied Congress to keep Medicare benefits for the ailing poor elderly. Other large special interest groups represent retired federal employees, retired teachers, and retired union workers (Quadagno 2011).

THE ACCORDION FAMILY

Boomerang Kids, Anxious Parents, and the Private Toll of Global Competition

KATHERINE S. NEWMAN

Do you know adult children in their 20s and 30s who continue to live at home or have returned to their parents' home? Are you one of them?

Some people call these families "accordion families" because they expand and contract as the adult children come and go.

❝ William Rollo and his wife arrived in Newton [Massachusetts] in 1989 after having lived in Seattle, Philadelphia, and Summit, New Jersey. A Brooklyn native, William married Janet at the age of twenty-two and set about completing a residency in podiatry. Their eldest son, John, grew up in Newton and did well enough in high school to attend the liberal arts college Williams, one of the nation's most selective. Even so, he beat it home after graduating and has lived with his parents for several years while preparing to apply to graduate school. "A lot of my friends are living at home to save money," he explains.

Tight finances are not all that is driving John's living arrangements. The young man had choices and decided he could opt for more of the ones he wanted if he sheltered under his parents' roof. John is saving money from his job in an arts foundation for a three-week trip to Africa, where he hopes to work on a mobile health-care project in a rural region. It's a strategic choice designed to increase his chances to be accepted into Harvard University's competitive graduate program in public health.

John needs to build up his credentials if he wants to enter a school like that. To get from here to there, he needs more experience working with patients in clinics or out in the field. It takes big bucks to travel to exotic locations, and a master's degree will cost him dearly, too. In order to make good on his

On his own, John could pay the rent on an apartment, especially if he had roommates. What he can't afford is to pay for both privacy and travel, to support himself and save for his hoped-for future.

aspirations, John needs his parents to cover him for the short run. On his own, John could pay the rent on an apartment, especially if he had roommates. What he can't afford is to pay for both privacy and travel, to support himself and save for his hoped-for future. Autonomy turns out to be the lesser priority, so he has returned to the bedroom he had before he left for college, and there he stays.

John sees few drawbacks to this arrangement. His parents don't nag him or curtail his freedom. Janet wonders if they should ask him to pay rent, to bring him down to earth a bit and teach him some life skills, like budgeting. William is not so sure. He enjoys his son's company and was happy when he moved back into his old bedroom. . . .

. . .

If John had no goals, no sense of direction, William would not be at ease with this "boomerang arrangement." Hiding in the basement playing video games would not do. Happily, that is not on John's agenda. William is glad to help his son realize his ambitions. He approves of John's career plans and doesn't really care if they don't involve making a handsome living. . . .

And it will cost this family, big time. William and Janet have invested nearly two hundred thousand dollars in John's education already. They will need to do more if John is going to become a public health specialist. They are easily looking at another fifty thousand dollars, even if John attends a local graduate program and continues to live with them. Fortunately, there are excellent options—some of the nation's finest—close by. Whatever it costs, they reason, the sacrifice is worth it. ❞

(Newman 2012:xv–xvii) Additional information about this excerpt can be found on the Online Learning Center at www.mhhe.com/schaefermod2e.

I n this excerpt from *The Accordion Family: Boomerang Kids, Anxious Parents, and the Private Toll of Global Competition,* sociologist Katherine S. Newman describes one of the major trends in family life today. In the United States as well as in many other countries, parenthood is being extended as single adult children remain at home, or return home after college or a brief foray into the job market. In the United States in 2011, 31 percent of single men and 15 percent of single women between the ages of 25 and 34 lived with their parents. Some of those adult children were still pursuing an education, but in many cases financial difficulties underlay their living arrangements. For younger job seekers, employment is often short term

or low paying—not secure enough to support a separate household. And with many marriages now ending in divorce—most commonly in the first seven years—divorced sons and daughters often return to their parents, sometimes with their own children in tow (Bureau of the Census 2011e:Table A2).

This trend is an example of the increasing complexity of family life. The family of today is not what it was a century ago, or even a generation ago. New roles, new gender distinctions, new child-rearing patterns have all combined to create new forms of family life. Today, for example, more and more women are taking the breadwinner's role, whether married or as a single parent. Blended families—the result of divorce and remarriage—are almost the norm. And many people are seeking intimate relationships without being married, whether in gay partnerships or in cohabiting arrangements (Cherlin 2009, 2011). The word *family* is inadequate to describe some of these arrangements, including cohabiting partners, same-sex marriages, and single-parent households. In 2011, the nation crossed a major threshold: the majority of births to women under age 30 occurred outside of marriage (Cherlin 2011; Wildsmith et al. 2011).

These modules address family and human sexuality in the United States as well as other parts of the world. As we will see, family patterns differ from one culture to another and even within the same culture. Despite the differences, however, the family is universal—found in every culture.

What are families in different parts of the world like? How do people select their mates? How does divorce affect the children? What are the alternatives to the nuclear family, and how prevalent are they? We will look at the family and intimate relationships from the functionalist, conflict, interactionist, and feminist points of view. We'll examine variations in marital patterns and family life, including child rearing, paying particular attention to the increasing numbers of people in dual-income and single-parent families. We'll examine divorce in the United States and consider diverse lifestyles such as cohabitation and marriage without children. We'll conclude by considering the complexity of human sexual behavior, and the growing acceptance of lesbian and gay relationships. Finally, in the Social Policy section we'll confront the controversial issue of gay marriage.

MODULE 39 Global View of the Family

Among Tibetans, a woman may be married simultaneously to more than one man, usually brothers. This system allows sons to share the limited amount of good land. Among the Betsileo of Madagascar, a man has multiple wives, each one living in a different village where he cultivates rice. Wherever he has the best rice field, that wife is considered his first or senior wife. Among the Yanomami of Brazil and Venezuela, it is considered proper to have sexual relations with your opposite-sex cousins if they are the children of your mother's brother or your father's sister. But if your opposite-sex cousins are the children of your mother's sister or your father's brother, the same practice is considered to be incest (Haviland et al. 2008; Kottak 2011).

Universal Principles

As these examples illustrate, there are many variations in the family from culture to culture. Yet the family as a social institution exists in all cultures. A **family** can be defined as a set of people related by blood, marriage, some other agreed-on relationship, or adoption, who share the primary responsibility for reproduction and caring for members of society. Moreover, certain general principles concerning its composition, kinship patterns, and authority patterns are universal.

Composition: What Is the Family?

If we were to take our information on what a family is from what we see on television, we might come up with some strange scenarios. The media do not always present a realistic view of the family. Moreover, many people still think of the family in very

narrow terms—as a married couple and their unmarried children living together, like the family in the old *Cosby Show*. However, this is but one type of family, what sociologists refer to as a **nuclear family.** The term *nuclear family* is well chosen, since this type of family serves as the nucleus, or core, on which larger family groups are built.

Most people in the United States see the nuclear family as the preferred family arrangement. Yet by 2000, only about a third of the nation's family households fit this model. The proportion of households in the United States that is composed of married couples with children at home has decreased steadily over the past 40 years and is expected to continue shrinking. At the same time, the number of single-parent households has increased (Figure 39-1).

A family in which relatives—such as grandparents, aunts, or uncles—live in the same home as parents and their children is known as an **extended family.** Although not common, such living arrangements do exist in the United States. The structure of the extended family offers certain advantages over that of the nuclear family. Crises such as death, divorce, and illness put less strain on family members, since more people can provide assistance and emotional support. In addition, the extended family constitutes a larger economic unit than the nuclear family. If the family is engaged in a common enterprise—a farm or a small business—the additional family members may represent the difference between prosperity and failure.

In considering these different family types, we have limited ourselves to the form of marriage that is characteristic of the United States—monogamy. The term **monogamy** describes

FIGURE 40-1 Median Age at First Marriage in Eight Countries

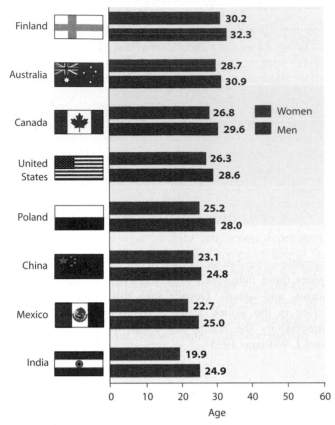

Finland — Women 30.2, Men 32.3
Australia — Women 28.7, Men 30.9
Canada — Women 26.8, Men 29.6
United States — Women 26.3, Men 28.6
Poland — Women 25.2, Men 28.0
China — Women 23.1, Men 24.8
Mexico — Women 22.7, Men 25.0
India — Women 19.9, Men 24.9

Age

Source: United Nations Statistics Division 2008.

Think about It

Why do people marry earlier in India than in Finland?

One unmistakable trend in mate selection is that the process appears to be taking longer today than in the past. A variety of factors, including concerns about financial security and personal independence, has contributed to this delay in marriage. Most people are now well into their 20s before they marry, both in the United States and in other countries (Figure 40-1).

Aspects of Mate Selection

Many societies have explicit or unstated rules that define potential mates as acceptable or unacceptable. These norms can be distinguished in terms of endogamy and exogamy. **Endogamy** (from the Greek *endon*, "within") specifies the groups within which a spouse must be found and prohibits marriage with others. For example, in the United States, many people are expected to marry within their racial, ethnic, or religious group, and are strongly discouraged or even prohibited from marrying outside the group. Endogamy is intended to reinforce the cohesiveness of the group by suggesting to the young that they should marry someone "of their own kind."

Even in the United States, interracial and interethnic marriages are still the exception. According to a report released in

2012, among newly married White couples, about 9 percent marry someone of a different race or ethnicity. Among African American couples the proportion is 17 percent; among Latinos, 26 percent; and among Asian Americans, 28 percent (W. Wang 2012).

In contrast, **exogamy** (from the Greek *exo*, "outside") requires mate selection outside certain groups, usually one's family or certain kinfolk. The **incest taboo,** a social norm common to virtually all societies, prohibits sexual relationships between certain culturally specified relatives. For those of us in the United States, this taboo means that we must marry outside the nuclear family. We cannot marry our siblings, and in most states we cannot marry our first cousins.

Another factor that influences the selection of a marriage partner is **homogamy,** the conscious or unconscious tendency to select a mate with personal characteristics similar to one's own. The "like marries like" rule can be seen in couples with similar personalities and cultural interests. However, mate selection is unpredictable. Though some people may follow the homogamous

Although most interracial marriages are not as visible as Robert De Niro and Grace Hightower's, such unions are becoming increasingly common and accepted. They are also blurring the definitions of race. Will the children of these couples be considered Black or White? Why do you think so?

pattern, others observe the "opposites attract" rule: one person is dependent and submissive—almost childishly so—while the other is dominant and controlling.

Recently, the concept of homogamy has been incorporated into the process of seeking a date or marital partner online. The Internet dating site eHarmony claims to be the first to use a "scientific approach" to matching people based on a variety of abilities and interests. As in real life, online searchers typically do not seek out people of a different race. According to one study of Yahoo daters, over 71 percent of women and 53 percent of men explicitly indicate their racial preferences (Robnett and Feliciano 2011).

The Love Relationship

Today's generation of college students seems more likely to hook up or cruise in large packs than to engage in the romantic dating relationships of their parents and grandparents. Still, at some point in their adult lives, the great majority of today's students will meet someone they love and enter into a long-term relationship that focuses on creating a family.

Parents in the United States tend to value love highly as a rationale for marriage, so they encourage their children to develop intimate relationships based on love and affection. Songs, films, books, magazines, television shows, and even cartoons and comic books reinforce the theme of love. At the same time, our society expects parents and peers to help a person confine his or her search for a mate to "socially acceptable" members of the opposite sex.

Though most people in the United States take the importance of falling in love for granted, the coupling of love and marriage is by no means a cultural universal. Many of the world's cultures give priority in mate selection to factors other than romantic feelings. In societies with *arranged marriages* engineered by parents or religious authorities, economic considerations play a significant role. The newly married couple is expected to develop a feeling of love *after* the legal union is formalized, if at all (Dayananda 2006).

Throughout the world, even where marital arrangements differ from our own, new media technologies are changing the mating game. In a rural Turkish village, where a small minority of the population still practices polygyny, the search for a second wife has moved from neighboring Syria to an Internet café where local men can contact prospective brides in faraway Morocco. Moroccan women watch Turkish soap operas on television and tend to see Turkish men as more romantic than others. They have become familiar with Turkey's culture and religion, politics and economy through the international news media. With a weak economy at home, many of these women must look elsewhere for marriage, so they turn to the Arabic website Habibti.com ("Mydear.com") to find a traditional marriage in an untraditional way (Schleifer 2009).

 use your **sociological imagination**

Your parents and/or a matchmaker are going to arrange a marriage for you. What kind of mate will they select? Will your chances of having a successful marriage be better or worse than if you selected your own mate?

Variations in Family Life and Intimate Relationships

Within the United States, social class, race, and ethnicity create variations in family life. Studying these variations will give us a more sophisticated understanding of contemporary family styles in our country.

Social Class Differences

Various studies have documented the differences in family organization among social classes in the United States. In the upper class, the emphasis is on lineage and maintenance of family position. If you are in the upper class, you are not simply a member of a nuclear family, but rather a member of a larger family tradition (think of the Rockefellers or the Kennedys). As a result, upper-class families are quite concerned about what they see as proper training for children.

Lower-class families do not often have the luxury of worrying about the "family name"; they must first struggle to pay their bills and survive the crises often associated with a life of poverty. Such families are more likely to have only one parent at home, which creates special challenges in child care and financial management. Children from lower-class families typically assume adult responsibilities—including marriage and parenthood—at an earlier age than children from affluent homes. In part, that is because they may lack the money needed to remain in school.

Social class differences in family life are less striking today than they once were. In the past, family specialists agreed that the contrasts in child-rearing practices were pronounced. Lower-class families were found to be more authoritarian in rearing children and more inclined to use physical punishment. Middle-class families were more permissive and more restrained in punishing their children. And compared to lower-class families, middle-class families tended to schedule more of their children's time, or even to overstructure it. However, these differences may have narrowed as more and more families from all social classes turned to the same books, magazines, and even television talk shows for advice on rearing children (Kronstadt and Favreault 2008; Luster et al. 1989; J. Sherman and Harris 2012).

Among the poor, women often play a significant role in the economic support of the family. Men may earn low wages, may be unemployed, or may be entirely absent from the family. In 2010, 32 percent of all families headed by women with no husband present fell below the federal government's poverty line. In comparison, the poverty rate for married couples was only 6.2 percent. The disproportionate representation of female-headed households among the poor is a persistent and growing trend, referred to by sociologists as the *feminization of poverty* (see Chapter 8; DeNavas-Walt et al. 2011:16).

Finally, in her book *The Accordion Family* (see the chapter-opening excerpt), Katherine S. Newman (2012) noted that the accordion or boomerang family differs by social class. An upper-middle-class family like the one described in the opening excerpt can afford to provide space to an adult child who is working

toward an advanced degree. Less privileged families tend to hang on to their adult children for the labor or income they can contribute to the family's welfare.

Many racial and ethnic groups appear to have distinctive family characteristics. However, racial and class factors are often closely related. In examining family life among racial and ethnic minorities, keep in mind that certain patterns may result from class as well as cultural factors.

Racial and Ethnic Differences

The subordinate status of racial and ethnic minorities in the United States profoundly affects their family lives. For example, the lower incomes of African Americans, Native Americans, most Hispanic groups, and selected Asian American groups make creating and maintaining successful marital unions a difficult task. The economic restructuring of the past 60 years, described by sociologist William Julius Wilson (1996, 2009) and others, has especially affected people living in inner cities and desolate rural areas, such as reservations. Furthermore, the immigration policy of the United States has complicated the successful relocation of intact families from Asia and Latin America.

The African American family suffers from many negative and inaccurate stereotypes. It is true that in a significantly higher proportion of Black than White families, no husband is present in the home (Figure 40-2). Yet Black single mothers often belong to stable, functioning kin networks, which mitigate the pressures of sexism and racism. Members of these networks—predominantly female kin such as mothers, grandmothers, and aunts—ease financial strains by sharing goods and services. In addition to these strong kinship bonds, Black family life has emphasized deep religious commitment and high aspirations for achievement (DuBois [1909] 1970; F. Furstenberg 2007).

Like African Americans, Native Americans draw on family ties to cushion many of the hardships they face. On the Navajo reservation, for example, teenage parenthood is not regarded as the crisis that it is elsewhere in the United States. The Navajo trace their descent matrilineally. Traditionally, couples reside with the wife's family after marriage, allowing the grandparents to help with the child rearing. While the Navajo do not approve of teenage parenthood, the deep emotional commitment of

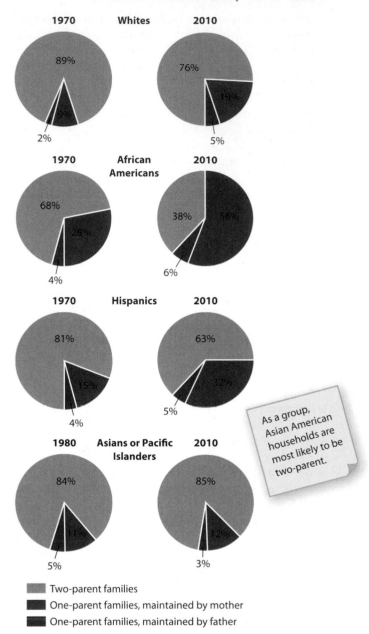

FIGURE 40-2 **Rise of Single-Parent Families in the United States, 1970–2010**

Legend:
- Two-parent families
- One-parent families, maintained by mother
- One-parent families, maintained by father

As a group, Asian American households are most likely to be two-parent.

Note: Families are groups with children under 18. Early data for Asian Americans are for 1980. Hispanics can be of any race. Not included are unrelated people living together with no children present. All data exclude the 11 percent of children in nonparental households.

Sources: Bureau of the Census 2008a:56, 2010c:Table FG10.

their extended families provides a warm home environment for children, even when no father is present or involved (Dalla and Gamble 2001; John 2012).

Sociologists also have taken note of differences in family patterns among other racial and ethnic groups. For example, Mexican American men have been described as exhibiting a sense of virility, personal worth, and pride in their maleness that is called **machismo.** Mexican Americans are also described as being more familistic than many other subcultures. **Familism** (or *familismo*) refers to pride in the extended family, expressed through the maintenance of close ties and strong obligations to kinfolk outside the immediate family. Traditionally, Mexican Americans have placed proximity to their extended families above other needs and desires.

Although familism is often seen as a positive cultural attribute, it may also have negative consequences. Sociologists who have studied the relatively low college application rates of Hispanic students have found they have a strong desire to stay at home. Even the children of college-educated parents express this preference, which diminishes the likelihood of their getting a four-year degree and dramatically reduces the possibility that they will apply to a selective college.

These family patterns are changing, however, in response to changes in Latinos' social class standing, educational achievements, and occupations. Like other Americans, career-oriented Latinos in search of a mate but short on spare time are turning to Internet sites. As Latinos and other groups assimilate into the dominant culture of the United States, their family lives take on both the positive and negative characteristics associated with White households (Negroni 2012; Suárez and Perez 2012).

● Child-Rearing Patterns

The Nayars of southern India acknowledge the biological role of fathers, but the mother's eldest brother is responsible for her children. In contrast, uncles play only a peripheral role in child care in the United States. Caring for children is a universal function of the family, yet the ways in which different societies assign this function to family members can vary significantly. Even within the United States, child-rearing patterns are varied. We'll take a look here at parenthood and grandparenthood, adoption, dual-income families, single-parent families, and stepfamilies.

Parenthood and Grandparenthood

The socialization of children is essential to the maintenance of any culture. Consequently, parenthood is one of the most important (and most demanding) social roles in the United States. Sociologist Alice Rossi (1968, 1984) has identified four factors that complicate the transition to parenthood and the role of socialization. First, there is little anticipatory socialization for the social role of caregiver. The normal school curriculum gives scant attention to the subjects most relevant to successful family life, such as child care and home maintenance. Second, only limited learning occurs during the period of pregnancy itself. Third, the transition to parenthood is quite abrupt. Unlike adolescence, it is not prolonged; unlike the transition to work, the duties of caregiving cannot be taken on gradually. Finally, in Rossi's view, our society lacks clear and helpful guidelines for successful parenthood. There is little consensus on how parents can produce happy and well-adjusted offspring—or even on what it means to be well adjusted. For these reasons, socialization for parenthood involves difficult challenges for most men and women in the United States.

In some homes, the full nest holds grandchildren. By 2009, 9 percent of White children, 17 percent of Black children, and 14 percent of Hispanic children lived with at least one grandparent. In about a third of these homes, no parent was present to assume responsibility for the youngsters. Special difficulties are inherent in such relationships, including legal custodial concerns, financial issues, and emotional problems for adults and youths alike. It is not surprising that support groups such as Grandparents as Parents have emerged to provide assistance (Kreider and Ellis 2011).

Adoption

In a legal sense, **adoption** is the transfer of the legal rights, responsibilities, and privileges of parenthood to a new legal parent or parents. In many cases, these rights are transferred from a biological parent or parents (often called birth parents) to an adoptive parent or parents. Every year, about 135,000 children are adopted (Child Welfare Information 2011).

Viewed from a functionalist perspective, government has a strong interest in encouraging adoption. Policymakers, in fact, have both a humanitarian and a financial stake in the process. In theory, adoption offers a stable family environment for children who otherwise might not receive satisfactory care. Moreover, government data show that unwed mothers who keep their babies tend to be of lower socioeconomic status and often require public assistance to support their children. The government can lower its social welfare expenses, then, if children are transferred to economically self-sufficient families. From an

When nine-year-old Blake Brunson shows up for a basketball game, so do his *eight* grandparents—the result of his parents' remarriages. Blended families can be very supportive to children, but what message do they send to them on the permanency of marriage?

often develop social networks, single fathers are typically more isolated. In addition, they must deal with schools and social service agencies that are more accustomed to women as custodial parents (Bureau of the Census 1994, 2011c).

 use your **sociological imagination**

What personal experience do you have with child rearing by grandparents, dual-income families, or single-parent families? Describe what you observed using sociological concepts.

Stepfamilies

Approximately 45 percent of all people in the United States will marry, divorce, and then remarry. The rising rates of divorce and remarriage have led to a noticeable increase in stepfamily relationships.

The exact nature of blended families has social significance for adults and children alike. Certainly resocialization is required when an adult becomes a stepparent or a child becomes a stepchild and stepsibling. Moreover, an important distinction must be made between first-time stepfamilies and households where there have been repeated divorces, breakups, or changes in custodial arrangements.

In evaluating the rise of stepfamilies, some observers have assumed that children would benefit from remarriage because they would be gaining a second custodial parent, and would potentially enjoy greater economic security. However, after reviewing many studies of stepfamilies, sociologist Andrew J. Cherlin (2010) concluded that children whose parents have remarried do not have higher levels of well-being than children in divorced single-parent families.

Stepparents can play valuable and unique roles in their stepchildren's lives, but their involvement does not guarantee

Most households in the United States do not consist of two parents living with their unmarried children.

an improvement in family life. In fact, standards may decline. Studies suggest that children raised in families with stepmothers are likely to have less health care, education, and money spent on their food than children raised by biological mothers. The measures are also negative for children raised by stepfathers, but only half as negative as in the case of stepmothers. These results don't mean that stepmothers are "evil"—it may be that the stepmother holds back out of concern for seeming too intrusive, or relies mistakenly on the biological father to carry out parental duties (Schmeeckle 2007; Schmeeckle et al. 2006).

 use your **sociological imagination**

What special challenges might stepfamilies face? What advantages might they enjoy? Explain using sociological concepts.

MODULE 40 | Recap and Review

Summary

People select mates in a variety of ways: in some societies, marriages are arranged, while in others, people select their own mates.

1. Some societies require mates to be chosen within a certain group (**endogamy**) or outside certain groups (**exogamy**). Consciously or unconsciously, many people look for a mate with similar personal characteristics (**homogamy**).

2. In the United States, family life varies with social class, race, and ethnicity.

3. Currently, in the majority of all married couples in the United States, both husband and wife work outside the home.

4. **Single-parent families** account for an increasing proportion of U.S. families.

Thinking Critically

1. How do both cultural and socioeconomic factors contribute to the following trends: later age of first marriage, the increasing number of extended-family households, and the boomerang generation?

2. Explain mate selection from the functionalist
   and interactionist perspectives.

Key Terms

Adoption   339

Endogamy   336

Exogamy   336

MODULE 41 Alternatives to Traditional Families

● Divorce

In the United States, the pattern of family life includes commitments both to marriage and to self-expression and personal growth. Needless to say, the tension between those competing commitments can undermine a marriage, working against the establishment of a lasting relationship. This approach to family life is distinctive to the United States. In some nations, such as Italy, the culture strongly supports marriage and discourages divorce. In others, such as Sweden, people treat marriage the same way as cohabitation, and both arrangements are just as lasting (Cherlin 2009).

Statistical Trends in Divorce

Just how common is divorce? Surprisingly, this is not a simple question; divorce statistics are difficult to interpret. The media frequently report that one out of every two marriages ends in divorce, but that figure is misleading. It is based on a comparison of all divorces that occur in a single year (regardless of when the couples were married) with the number of new marriages in the same year.

In many countries, divorce began to increase in the late 1960s but then leveled off; since the late 1980s, it has declined by 30 percent. (Figure 41-1 shows the pattern in the United States.) This trend is due partly to the aging of the baby boomer population and the corresponding decline in the proportion of people of marriageable age. But it also indicates an increase in marital stability in recent years (Coontz 2006).

Getting divorced obviously does not sour people on marriage. About 63 percent of all divorced people in the United States have remarried. Women are less likely than men to remarry because many retain custody of their children after a divorce, which complicates a new adult relationship (Bianchi and Spain 1996; Saad 2004).

Some people regard the nation's high rate of remarriage as an endorsement of the institution of marriage, but it does lead to the new challenges of a kin network composed of both current and prior marital relationships. Such networks can be particularly complex if children are involved or if an ex-spouse remarries.

Factors Associated with Divorce

Perhaps the most important factor in the increase in divorce over the past hundred years has been the greater social *acceptance* of divorce. It is no longer considered necessary to endure an

FIGURE 41-1 **Trends in Marriage and Divorce in the United States, 1920–2010**

Sources: Bureau of the Census 1975:64; Centers for Disease Control and Prevention 2012b.

Human sexuality spans a broad range of behaviors, including some that are not condoned by particular societies. From the sociologist's perspective, however, sexuality is not limited to physical behaviors, but includes the beliefs, values, and social norms that collectively govern its expression. For example, most societies seek to restrict sexual expression to marriage because of its effect on the family, particularly the welfare of women and children (C. Schneider 2008).

Although human sexuality is expressed in all societies, the way it is sanctioned differs widely, both geographically and historically. In South Africa, following the end of apartheid in 1990, legislators removed barriers to interracial cohabitation and marriage. Then in 1998 they passed the Recognition of Customary Marriages Act, which legalized polygamy among some African tribal groups, but not among Muslims and other religious groups. Finally, under the Civil Union Act of 2006, they granted gay and lesbian couples the same rights and responsibilities as opposite-sex couples (Stacey 2011).

Clearly, sexual attitudes and practices change over time. In Module 8 we saw how the publication of Alfred Kinsey's first study of human sexuality in 1948 profoundly shocked Americans. Today, online sites routinely solicit descriptions of almost any kind of human sexuality. Besides the new cultural openness about sex, medical advances have encouraged what many refer to as a

Lady Gaga's 2011 hit single "Born This Way," which includes the lyric "Don't be a drag, just be a queen," was written as an anthem to diversity and acceptance.

sexual revolution. For example, the development of oral contraceptives ("the pill") in 1965 and of remedies for erectile dysfunction (Viagra and other such drugs) in 1998 reduced the risk and increased the likelihood of frequent sexual activity. Today, young people engage in sexual practices that few people in earlier generations would have dared to participate in (see Box 42-1, which describes an interactionist study of the sexual networks in one American high school).

Labeling and Human Sexuality

In Chapter 7 we saw how society singles out certain groups of people by labeling them in positive or negative ways—as "good kids" or "delinquents," for example. Labeling theorists have also studied how labels are used to sanction certain sexual behaviors as "deviant."

The definition of deviant sexual behavior has varied significantly over time and from one culture to another. Until 1973, the American Psychiatric Association considered homosexuality a "sociopathic personality disorder," which in effect meant that homosexuals should seek therapy. Two years later, however, the association removed homosexuality from its list of mental illnesses. Today, the organization publicly proclaims that "being gay is just as healthy as being straight." To use Goffman's term, mental health professionals have removed the *stigma* from this form of sexual expression. As a result, in the United States and many other countries, consensual sex between same-sex adults is no longer a crime (American Psychological Association 2008; International Gay and Lesbian Human Rights Commission 2010).

Despite the change in health professionals' attitudes, however, the social stigma of homosexuality lingers. As a result, many people prefer the more positive terms *gay* and *lesbian*. Others, in defiance of the stigma, have proudly adopted the pejorative term *queer* in a deliberate reaction to the ridicule they have borne because of their sexual orientation. Still others maintain that constructing one's sexual orientation as either homosexual or heterosexual is too limiting. Indeed, such labels ignore those who are *bisexual*, or sexually attracted to both sexes.

Another group whose sexual orientation does not fit into the usual categories is *transgendered persons*, or those people whose current gender identity does not match their physical identity at birth. Some transgendered persons see themselves as both male and female. Others, called *transsexuals*, may take hormones or undergo surgery in an effort to draw physically closer to their chosen gender identity. Transgendered persons are

Adolescent Sexual Networks

If you drew a chart of the sexual network at a typical American high school, what would it look like? In the mid-1990s, sociologists Peter Bearman, James Moody, and Katherine Stovel asked themselves that question. While studying romantic relationships at a high school with 1,000 students, they found that about 61 percent of the boys and 55 percent of the girls had been sexually active over the past 18 months. Those percentages did not differ much from the results of similar studies done during the period. What surprised the research team was what they saw when they began to chart the students' relationships.

To obtain their data, Bearman and his colleagues conducted in-home interviews with the respondents. Instead of asking students for a face-to-face interview—a technique that might have embarrassed them or distorted their answers—the researchers gave them an audio recording of the questions, a pair of earphones, and a laptop computer on which to record their answers. The research team also asked respondents to look at a list of all the students at the high school and identify those with whom they had had romantic or sexual relationships.

The results showed that 573 of the 832 students surveyed had had at least one sexual relationship over the past 18 months. Among those respondents, the sociologists found only 63 steady couples, or pairs with no other partners. A much larger group of 288

Each dot represents a boy or girl at "Jefferson High." The lines that link them represent romantic and sexual relationships that occurred over an 18-month period. While most of the teenagers had had just one or two partners, 288 of the 832 kids interviewed were linked in a giant sexual network.

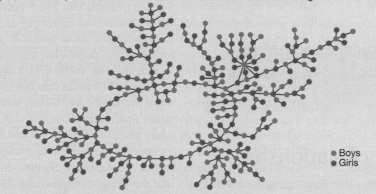

● Boys
● Girls

Other relationships (if a pattern was observed more than once, numeral indicates frequency)

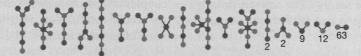

2   2   9   12   63

Sources: Bearman, Moody, and Stovel 2005:58

> A particularly significant implication of this study is the risk of sexually transmitted diseases (STDs) to those who participate in such a network.

students—almost a third of the sample—was involved in the free-flowing network of relationships shown on the accompanying chart. (Note the comparative absence of tightly closed loops of three to five individuals.) Not shown on the chart were another 90 students who were involved in relationships outside the school.

A particularly significant implication of this study is the risk of sexually transmitted diseases (STDs) to those who participate in such a network. Through the complicated chain of relationships, even students who have only one or two sexual partners are exposing themselves to a relatively high degree of risk. But while parents and even students may be alarmed by the data, public health officials are encouraged. Experts at the Centers for Disease Control who have reviewed the network charts from this and other studies see them as blueprints for change. If experts can alter participants' behavior anywhere along these chains—by counseling abstinence, condom use, or treatment of STDs—they can significantly reduce transmission of the diseases.

LET'S DISCUSS

1. Do the results of the study surprise you? How does the sexual network described in this study compare to the network where you went to high school?

2. Do you see any problems with the research method used in this study? Can you think of anything that might have compromised the validity of the data?

Sources: Bearman, Moody, and Stovel 2004; C. F. Turner et al. 1998; Wallis 2005.

---

sometimes confused with *transvestites,* or cross-dressers who wear the clothing of the opposite sex. Transvestites are typically men, either gay or heterosexual, who choose to wear women's clothing.

The use of these terms even in a positive or nonjudgmental way is problematic, since they imply that human sexuality can be confined in neat, mutually exclusive categories. Moreover, the destigmatization of these labels tends to reflect the influence of the socially privileged—that is, the affluent—who have the resources to overcome the stigma. In contrast, the traditional Native American concept of the *two spirit,* a personality that

blends the masculine and the feminine, has been largely ridiculed or ignored (Gilley 2006; Wentling et al. 2008).

What does constitute sexual deviance, then? The answer to this question seems to change with each generation. Today, U.S. laws allow married women to accuse their husbands of rape, when a generation ago such an offense was not recognized. Similarly, *pedophilia*—an adult having sex with a minor—is generally regarded with disgust today, even when it is consensual. Yet in many countries, fringe groups now speak positively of "intergenerational sex," arguing that "childhood" is not a biological given (Hendershott 2002).

MAPPING LIFE NATIONWIDE

FIGURE 42-2 **Gay Marriage by State**

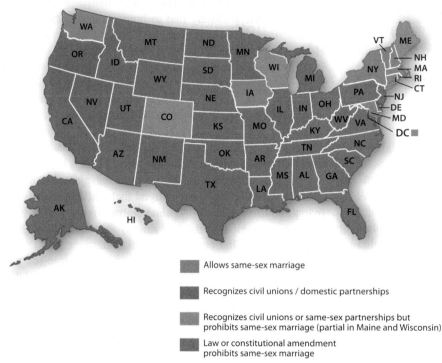

■ Allows same-sex marriage

■ Recognizes civil unions / domestic partnerships

■ Recognizes civil unions or same-sex partnerships but prohibits same-sex marriage (partial in Maine and Wisconsin)

■ Law or constitutional amendment prohibits same-sex marriage

Sources: As of June 2012, author based on news reports; Human Rights Campaign 2012; National Conference of State Legislatures 2012b.

defined as two unrelated adults who share a mutually caring relationship, reside together, and agree to be jointly responsible for their dependents, basic living expenses, and other common necessities. Domestic partnership benefits can apply to couples' inheritance, parenting, pensions, taxation, housing, immigration, workplace fringe benefits such as life insurance, and health care. Even though the most passionate support for domestic partnership legislation has come from lesbian and gay activists, the majority of those eligible for such benefits would be cohabiting heterosexual couples.

In the United States, marriage has traditionally been under the jurisdiction of state lawmakers. Recently, however, pressure has been mounting for national legislation. The Defense of Marriage Act, passed in 1996, provided that no state is obliged to recognize same-sex marriages performed in another state. However, some legal scholars doubt that the law could withstand a constitutional challenge, since it violates a provision in the Constitution that requires states to recognize one another's laws.

Within the United States, state courts in California, Iowa, and Massachusetts have ruled that there is no state law that precludes same-sex marriage. In California, 18,000 same-sex couples were married before voters amended the state constitution to prohibit such marriages in the future. In August 2010, a federal court weighed in for the first time on gay marriage, ruling that California's ban on same-sex marriage was unconstitutional. Ultimately, the Supreme Court will consider the issue. As of mid-2012, the District of Columbia and six states (Connecticut, Iowa, Massachusetts, New Hampshire, New York, and Vermont) were issuing marriage licenses to same-sex couples. (New laws in Maryland and Washington had not yet taken effect.) Gay rights activists claim their movement is gathering momentum, but opponents argue that their high-profile actions have galvanized conservatives who wish to define marriage as the union of one man and one woman.

TAKE THE ISSUE WITH YOU

1. If marriage is good for heterosexual couples and their families, why isn't it good for homosexual couples and their families?

2. How can interactionist studies of gay couples and their families inform policymakers who are dealing with the issue of gay marriage? Give a specific example.

3. Who are the stakeholders in the debate over gay marriage, and what do they stand to gain or lose? Whose interest do you think is most important?

Summary

Human sexuality spans a wide range of behaviors, and different societies condone different behaviors.

1. From the sociological perspective, sexuality is not limited to physical behaviors, but includes the beliefs, values, and social norms that collectively govern its expression.

2. Because homosexuality has traditionally been labeled as a deviant behavior, gay and lesbian couples face significant discrimination, including the denial of their right to marry.

3. The gay marriage movement, which would confer equal rights on gay and lesbian couples and their dependents, is strongly opposed by conservative religious and political groups.

Thinking Critically

1. What do you believe constitutes sexual deviance today? How might this change over the next decade or two?

2. How is cohabitation similar to marriage? How is it different? Could gay and lesbian couples achieve all the benefits of marriage without actually marrying?

Key Term

Domestic partnership   349

Mastering This Chapter

taking sociology with you

1 Go online and try tracing your family roots using one of the genealogical search sites. How far back can you go? Why might certain ancestral paths be more difficult to trace than others?

2 Do some research on the divorce law in your state. Has the law changed much over the past few decades, and if so, how? From a sociological perspective, why would the law change? Explain.

3 Talk to a marriage and family counselor or a professor of family law about the benefits of marriage versus cohabitation, or read what practical advice you can find on the Internet or in the library. What advantages does marriage offer that cohabitation does not? How important do those advantages seem to you?

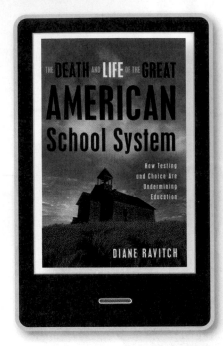

After a long career, Diane Ravitch lost faith in the educational reforms she had once championed as a way to rescue failing schools.

Searching for a better answer, she looked back on her own experience in high school, to her favorite English teacher.

" My favorite teacher was Mrs. Ruby Ratliff. She is the teacher I remember best, the one who influenced me most, who taught me to love literature and to write with careful attention to grammar and syntax. More than fifty years ago, she was my homeroom teacher at San Jacinto High School in Houston, and I was lucky enough to get into her English class as a senior.

Mrs. Ratliff was gruff and demanding. She did not tolerate foolishness or disruptions. She had a great reputation among students.... What I remember most about her was what she taught us. We studied the greatest writers of the English language.... We read Shakespeare, Keats, Shelley, Wordsworth, Milton, and other major English writers. Now, many years later, in times of stress or sadness, I still turn to poems that I first read in Mrs. Ratliff's class.

Mrs. Ratliff did nothing for our self-esteem. She challenged us to meet her exacting standards. I think she imagined herself bringing enlightenment to the barbarians (that was us). When you wrote something for her class, which happened with frequency, you paid close attention to proper English. Accuracy mattered. She had a red pen and she used it freely. Still, she was always sure to make a comment that encouraged us to do a better job. Clearly she had multiple goals for her students, beyond teaching literature and grammar. She was also teaching about character and personal responsibility. These are not the sorts of things that appear on any standardized test.

She loved her subject, and she enjoyed the respect the students showed her, especially since this was a large high school where students did not easily give respect to their teachers. Despite the passage of years, I still recall a class discussion of Shelley's "Ozymandias," and the close attention that thirty usually rowdy adolescents paid to a poem about a time and a place we could barely imagine. I wonder if Mrs. Ratliff has her counterparts today, teachers who love literature and love to teach it, or whether schools favor teachers who have been trained to elicit mechanical responses from their students about "text-to-self connections," "inferencing," "visualizing," and the other formalistic behaviors so beloved by au courant pedagogues. If Mrs. Ratliff were planning to teach these days, I expect that her education professors and supervisors would warn her to get rid of that red pen, to abandon her insistence on accuracy, and to stop being so judgmental. And they would surely demand that she replace those dated poems and essays with young adult literature that teaches adolescents about the lives of other adolescents just like themselves. . . .

I think of Mrs. Ratliff when I hear the latest proposals to improve the teaching force. Almost every day, I come across a statement by a journalist, superintendent, or economist who says we could solve all our problems in American education if we could just recruit a sufficient number of "great" teachers. I believe Mrs. Ratliff was a great teacher, but I don't think she would have been considered "great" if she had been judged by the kind of hard data that is used now. The policy experts who insist that teachers should be judged by their students' scores on standardized tests would have been frustrated by Mrs. Ratliff. Her classes never produced hard data. They didn't even produce test scores. How would the experts have measured what we learned? We never took a multiple-choice test. We wrote essays and took written tests, in which we had to explain our answers, not check a box or fill in a bubble. If she had been evaluated by the grades she gave, she would have been in deep trouble, because she did not award many A grades. An observer might have concluded that she was a very ineffective teacher who had no measurable gains to show for her work. "

Clearly she had multiple goals for her students, beyond teaching literature and grammar. She was also teaching about character and personal responsibility. These are not the sorts of things that appear on any standardized test.

(Ravitch 2010:169, 170, 171) Additional information about this excerpt can be found on the Online Learning Center at www.mhhe .com/schaefermod2e.

In her book *The Death and Life of the Great American School System*, education historian Diane Ravitch laments our failure in improving the quality of education in the United States. In recalling her favorite teacher, Ravitch questions what she sees as our current tendency to reduce the art of teaching to test cramming and relying solely on standardized tests as measures of students' performance. She is really asking the same questions that sociologists ask about education: what are its goals, and what is it supposed to accomplish, for individuals and for society as a whole? After considering how sociologists answer these questions, we will return to the issue of measuring school performance in the Social Policy section.

As we saw in Module 15, socialization can occur in the classroom or at home, through interactions with parents, teachers, friends, and even strangers. These modules focus in particular on the formal systems of education that characterize modern industrial societies. Do public schools offer everyone a way up the socioeconomic ladder, or do they reinforce existing divisions among social classes? What is the "hidden curriculum" in U.S. schools? And what have sociologists learned about the latest trends in education, such as competency testing? We will begin with discussion of four theoretical perspectives on education, and will then examine schools as formal organizations—as bureaucracies and subcultures of teachers and students. One contemporary educational trend, homeschooling, merits special mention. We close with a Social Policy section on the controversial charter-schools movement.

MODULE 43 | Sociological Perspectives on Education

Besides being a major industry in the United States, **education** is the social institution that formally socializes members of our society. In the past few decades, increasing proportions of people have obtained high school diplomas, college degrees, and advanced professional degrees. Figure 43-1 shows the proportion of the college-educated population in selected countries.

Throughout the world, education has become a vast and complex social institution that prepares citizens for the roles demanded by other social institutions, such as the family, government, and the economy. The functionalist, conflict, feminist, and interactionist perspectives offer distinctive views of education as a social institution.

■ Functionalist Perspective

Like other social institutions, education has both manifest (open, stated) and latent (hidden) functions. The most basic *manifest* function of education is the transmission of knowledge. Schools teach students how to read, speak foreign languages, and repair automobiles. Another important manifest function is

FIGURE 43-1 Current Higher Education Graduation Rates (BA/BS), Selected Countries

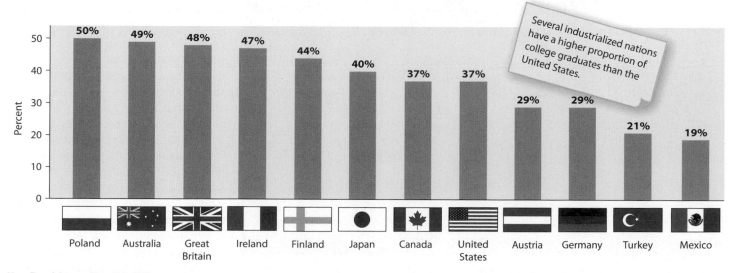

Note: For adults ages 25 to 64 in 2009.
Source: Organisation for Economic Co-Operation and Development 2012c:Table A3.

the bestowal of status. Because many believe this function is performed inequitably, we will consider it later, in the section on the conflict view of education.

In addition to these manifest functions, schools perform a number of *latent* functions: transmitting culture, promoting social and political integration, maintaining social control, and serving as an agent of change.

Transmitting Culture

As a social institution, education performs a rather conservative function—transmitting the dominant culture. Schooling exposes each generation of young people to the existing beliefs, norms, and values of their culture. In our society, we learn respect for social control and reverence for established institutions, such as religion, the family, and the presidency. Of course, this statement is true of many other cultures as well. While schoolchildren in the United States are hearing about the accomplishments of George Washington and Abraham Lincoln, British children are hearing about the distinctive contributions of Queen Elizabeth I and Winston Churchill.

Sometimes nations reassess the ways in which they transmit culture to students. In the last decade, the Chinese government revised the nation's history curriculum. Students are now taught that the Chinese Communist Party, not the United States, played a central role in defeating Japan in World War II. No mention is made of the estimated 30 million Chinese who died from famine because of party founder Mao Zedong's disastrous Great Leap Forward (1958–1962), a failed effort to transform China's agrarian economy into an industrial powerhouse. In the urban, Western-oriented areas of Shanghai, textbooks acknowledge the technological advances made in Western industrialized countries but avoid any criticism of past policies of the Chinese government (French 2004; J. Kahn 2006).

Culture has been transmitted to students in schools, through books and the spoken word, for centuries. Today, however, the Internet offers a new and potentially revolutionary way of transmitting culture. Box 43-1 discusses the educational impact of Google and other search engines.

Promoting Social and Political Integration

Many institutions require students in their first year or two of college to live on campus, to foster a sense of community among diverse groups. Education serves the latent function of promoting social and political integration by transforming a population composed of diverse racial, ethnic, and religious groups into a society whose members share—to some extent—a common identity. Historically, schools in the United States have played an important role in socializing the children of immigrants into the norms, values, and beliefs of the dominant culture. From a functionalist perspective, the common identity and social integration fostered by education contribute to societal stability and consensus (Touraine 1974).

In the past, the integrative function of education was most obvious in its emphasis on promoting a common language. Immigrant children were expected to learn English. In some instances, they were even forbidden to speak their native language on school grounds. More recently, bilingualism has been defended both for its educational value and as a means of encouraging cultural diversity. However, critics argue that bilingualism undermines the social and political integration that education has traditionally promoted.

Maintaining Social Control

In performing the manifest function of transmitting knowledge, schools go far beyond teaching skills like reading, writing, and mathematics. Like other social institutions, such as the family and religion, education prepares young people to lead productive and orderly lives as adults by introducing them to the norms, values, and sanctions of the larger society.

Through the exercise of social control, schools teach students various skills and values essential to their future positions in the labor force. They learn punctuality, discipline, scheduling, and responsible work habits, as well as how to negotiate the complexities of a bureaucratic organization. As a social institution, education reflects the interests of both the family and another social institution, the economy. Students are trained for what is ahead,

Although the school Harry Potter attends in the film *Harry Potter and the Deathly Hallows: Part 2* is fictitious, like real schools, it transmits a socially sanctioned culture to students.

Sociology on Campus

Box 43-1

Google University

From comic books, television, and fast-paced video games to educational films and online college courses, technological innovations in communication have been seen as both a threat to culture and a boon to education. Like these new media, the search engine called Google has been greeted with both praise and scorn. Founded by two students at Stanford University in 1998, Google handled some 65 percent of all Internet searches in the United States in early 2011. Its familiar multicolored logo stands for one of the most trusted brands in the world (see Figure 20-1, page 149).

Using Google or some other search engine, a researcher can now retrieve facts, viewpoints, images, and sounds within minutes. Just a few years ago, that task would have taken days. As Nicholas Carr (2008b:56), former editor of the *Harvard Business Review,* notes, "Once I was a scuba diver in the sea of words. Now I zip along the surface like a guy on a Jet Ski." Yet some critics of search engines charge that placing more and more of the world's knowledge just a mouse click away has made students lazy. Quick access to information, they point out, does not necessarily encourage concentration, let alone contemplation.

> Like the invention of the printing press, Google's advent is changing not just the university, but the universe of learning.

The availability of information online may also be changing the way people read. Educators worry that habitual skimming of the computer screen may carry over to students' print reading. Some have found that younger readers, faced with anything of length online, such as a short PDF file, simply ignore it. In response, researchers have begun to study whether those who read online in preference to books and other printed media still read sentence by sentence, as they were taught to do in school.

Other scholars are not disturbed by potential changes in what and how people read. They note that true literacy is not merely the ability to read to the end of an article or book, but to find the information you need amid a flood of sources—not all of them trustworthy—and use it correctly and responsibly. In other words, literacy includes critical thinking.

Ultimately, education is more than just collecting, organizing, and comprehending information. Accessing information and arguments

regarding political and social issues is a form of civic engagement. Thus, the search feature on a web page becomes a portal to a virtual town square. Perhaps that is why today's students are not only spending more time online than yesterday's students, but also doing more volunteer work.

Well before the advent of the Internet, much less Google, sociologist Daniel Bell (1973) wrote that *intellectual technologies* tend to institutionalize new approaches to the gathering and dissemination of information. Like the invention of the printing press, Google's advent is changing not just the university, but the universe of learning.

LET'S DISCUSS

1. Do you prefer to do your reading online or in a magazine, newspaper, or book? Has the availability of online information changed the way that you read the written word?

2. Have you participated in any social or political causes or volunteered your time while on campus? If so, did you use the Internet to organize or disseminate information about your activities?

Sources: Mark Bauerlein 2008; Brabazon 2007; Carr 2008a, 2008b; Maestretti 2009; Search Engine Watch 2011; Vaidhyanathan 2008; Workman 2008.

---

whether it be the assembly line or a physician's office. In effect, then, schools serve as a transitional agent of social control, bridging the gap between parents and employers in the life cycle of most individuals (Bowles and Gintis 1976; M. Cole 1988).

Schools direct and even restrict students' aspirations in a manner that reflects societal values and prejudices. School administrators may allocate ample funds for athletic programs but give much less support to music, art, and dance. Teachers and guidance counselors may encourage male students to pursue careers in the sciences but steer female students into careers as early childhood teachers. Such socialization into traditional gender roles can be viewed as a form of social control.

Serving as an Agent of Change

So far, we have focused on the conservative functions of education—on its role in transmitting the existing culture, promoting social and political integration, and maintaining

social control. Yet education can also stimulate or bring about desired social change. Sex education classes were introduced to public schools in response to the soaring pregnancy rate among teenagers. Affirmative action in admissions— giving priority to females or minorities—has been endorsed as a means of countering racial and sexual discrimination. And Project Head Start, an early childhood program that serves more than 904,000 children annually, has sought to compensate for the disadvantages in school readiness experienced by children from low-income families (Bureau of the Census 2011a:Table 574 on page 368).

These educational programs can and have transformed people's lives. For example, continued formal education has had a positive effect on the income people earn; median earnings rise significantly with each step up the educational ladder. Consider the significance of those increased earnings when they stretch over an entire lifetime. Obviously, racial, ethnic, and gender differences in income are also significant. Yet as

In response to a high pregnancy rate among adolescent girls, many schools now offer sex education courses that promote abstinence as well as safe sex. When schools attempt to remedy negative social trends, they are serving as an agent of social change.

significant as those inequalities are, the best indicator of a person's lifetime earnings is still the number of years of formal schooling that person has received (see Figure 43-2) (Julian and Kominski 2011; Wessel and Ranchero 2012).

Education also promotes social change by serving as a meeting ground where people can share distinctive beliefs and traditions. In 2009–2010, U.S. campuses hosted over 690,000 international students. That number, an all-time high, followed a temporary decline in foreign enrollments after September 11, 2001. Figure 43-3 on page 361 shows the major sending nations of foreign students in the United States (left) and the primary destinations of U.S. students seeking to enrich their college experience abroad (right).

Numerous sociological studies have revealed that additional years of formal schooling are also associated with openness to new ideas and liberal social and

FIGURE 43-2 **Lifetime Earnings by Race, Gender, and Degree Level**

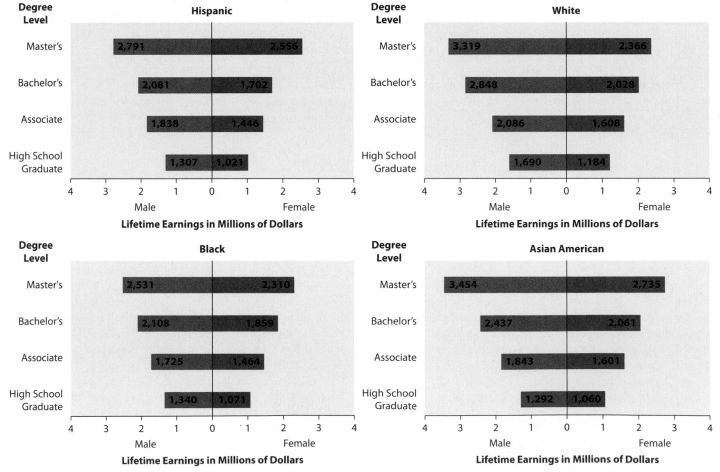

Note: Estimates for lifetime earnings for full-time, year-round workers ages 25 to 64 based on the American Community Survey for 2006–2008. Data are for non-Hispanic Whites, Blacks, and Asian Americans. Data points shown in thousands of dollars.
Source: Julian and Kominski 2011:6.

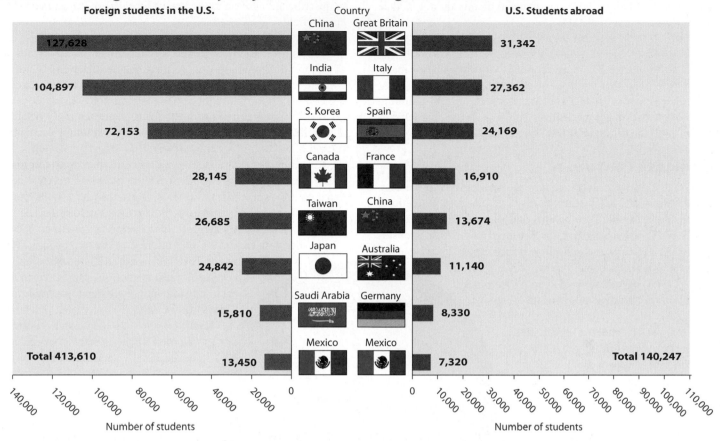

FIGURE 43-3 **Foreign Students by Major Countries of Origin and Destination**

Foreign students in the U.S. | Country | **U.S. Students abroad**

Foreign students in the U.S.	Country (origin)	Country (destination)	U.S. Students abroad
127,628	China	Great Britain	31,342
104,897	India	Italy	27,362
72,153	S. Korea	Spain	24,169
28,145	Canada	France	16,910
26,685	Taiwan	China	13,674
24,842	Japan	Australia	11,140
15,810	Saudi Arabia	Germany	8,330
13,450	Mexico	Mexico	7,320
Total 413,610			Total 140,247

Number of students (left): 140,000 120,000 100,000 80,000 60,000 40,000 20,000 0

Number of students (right): 0 10,000 20,000 30,000 40,000 50,000 60,000 70,000 80,000 90,000 100,000 110,000

political viewpoints. Sociologist Robin Williams points out that better-educated people tend to have greater access to factual information, to hold more diverse opinions, and to possess the ability to make subtle distinctions in analysis. Formal education stresses both the importance of qualifying statements (in place of broad generalizations) and the need at least to question (rather than simply accept) established truths and practices. The scientific method, which relies on *testing* hypotheses, reflects the questioning spirit that characterizes modern education (R. Williams et al. 1964).

● Conflict Perspective

The functionalist perspective portrays contemporary education as a basically benign institution. For example, it argues that schools rationally sort and select students for future high-status positions, thereby meeting society's need for talented and expert personnel. In contrast, the conflict perspective views education as an instrument of elite domination. Conflict theorists point out the sharp inequalities that exist in the educational opportunities available to different racial and ethnic groups. In 2004, the nation marked the 50th anniversary of the Supreme Court's landmark decision *Brown v. Board of Education,* which declared unconstitutional the segregation of public schools. Yet today, our schools are still characterized by racial

isolation. Nationwide, White students are the most isolated: only 23 percent of their classmates came from minority groups in the 2005–2006 school year. In comparison, Black and Latino

trend|spotting

Rising College Enrollment among Racial and Ethnic Minorities, Women

The past 30 years have brought a consistent increase in college enrollment among all racial and ethnic groups in the United States. The typical measure that researchers use to track college enrollments is the college participation rate, or the percentage of all 18- to 24-year-olds enrolled in 2-year and 4-year colleges or universities. For Whites, the participation rate increased from 28 percent to 44 percent between 1978 and 2008. For African Americans, the rate climbed from 20 percent to 32 percent; for Latinos, from 16 percent to 26 percent.

Across the board, growth has been greater among females than among males. In 1980, more men than women were in college, whether among Whites, Blacks and Hispanics, or Asian Americans. By 1995 that pattern had reversed, and women outnumbered men. Only among Native Americans have women historically outnumbered men on college campuses.

students have more classmates from different racial and ethnic backgrounds, although those classmates typically do not include Whites (Orfield and Lee 2007).

Conflict theorists also argue that the educational system socializes students into values dictated by the powerful, that schools stifle individualism and creativity in the name of maintaining order, and that the level of change they promote is relatively insignificant. From a conflict perspective, the inhibiting effects of education are particularly apparent in the "hidden curriculum" and the differential way in which status is bestowed.

The Hidden Curriculum

Schools are highly bureaucratic organizations, as we will see later. To maintain order, many teachers rely on rules and regulations. Unfortunately, the need for control and discipline can take precedence over the learning process. Teachers may focus on obedience to the rules as an end in itself, in which case students and teachers alike become victims of what Philip Jackson (1968) has called the *hidden curriculum.*

The term **hidden curriculum** refers to standards of behavior that are deemed proper by society and are taught subtly in schools. According to this curriculum, children must not speak until the teacher calls on them and must regulate their activities according to the clock or bells. In addition, they are expected to concentrate on their own work rather than to assist other students who learn more slowly. A hidden curriculum is evident in schools around the world. For example, Japanese schools offer guidance sessions that seek to improve the classroom experience and develop healthy living skills. In effect, these sessions instill values and encourage behavior that is useful in the Japanese business world, such as self-discipline and openness to group problem solving and decision making (Okano and Tsuchiya 1999).

In a classroom that is overly focused on obedience, value is placed on pleasing the teacher and remaining quiet rather than on creative thought and academic learning. Habitual obedience to authority may result in the type of distressing behavior documented by Stanley Milgram in his classic obedience studies.

 use your **sociological imagination**

In what ways did the high school you attended convey the hidden curriculum of education?

Credentialism

Sixty years ago, a high school diploma was the minimum requirement for entry into the paid labor force of the United States. Today, a college diploma is virtually the bare minimum.

This change reflects the process of **credentialism**—a term used to describe an increase in the lowest level of education needed to enter a field.

In recent decades, the number of occupations that are viewed as professions has risen. Credentialism is one symptom of this trend. Employers and occupational associations typically contend that such changes are a logical response to the increasing complexity of many jobs. However, in many cases, employers raise the degree requirements for a position simply because all applicants have achieved the existing minimum credential (David K. Brown 2001; Hurn 1985).

Conflict theorists observe that credentialism may reinforce social inequality. Applicants from poor and minority backgrounds are especially likely to suffer from the escalation of qualifications, since they lack the financial resources needed to obtain degree after degree. In addition, upgrading of credentials serves the self-interest of the two groups most responsible for this trend. Educational institutions profit from prolonging the investment of time and money that people make by staying in school. Moreover, as C. J. Hurn (1985) has suggested, current jobholders have a stake in raising occupational requirements, since credentialism can increase the status of an occupation and lead to demands for higher pay. Max Weber anticipated this possibility as early as 1916, concluding that the "universal clamor for the creation of educational certificates in all fields makes for the formation of a privileged stratum in businesses and in offices" (Gerth and Mills 1958:240–241).

use your **sociological imagination**

How would you react if the job you have or plan to pursue suddenly required a higher-level degree? If suddenly the requirements were lowered?

Bestowal of Status

Sociologists have long recognized that schooling is central to social stratification. Both functionalist and conflict theorists agree that education performs the important function of bestowing status. As noted earlier, an increasing proportion of people in the United States are obtaining high school diplomas, college degrees, and advanced professional degrees. From a functionalist perspective, this widening bestowal of status is beneficial not only to particular recipients but to society as a whole. According to Kingsley Davis and Wilbert E. Moore (1945), society must distribute its members among a variety of social positions. Education can contribute to this process by sorting people into appropriate levels and courses of study that will prepare them for positions in the labor force.

Conflict theorists are far more critical of the *differential* way in which education bestows status. They stress that schools sort pupils according to their social class backgrounds. Although the educational system helps certain poor children to move into middle-class professional positions, it denies most disadvantaged children the same educational opportunities afforded to children of the affluent. In this way, schools tend to preserve social class inequalities in each new generation. Higher education in particular acts more like a sieve that sorts people out of the educated classes than a social ladder that helps all with ambition to rise (Alon 2009; Giroux 1988; Sacks 2007).

The status that comes with advanced training is not cheap and has been getting progressively more expensive for several decades. Over the past 30 years, average tuition and fees at community colleges have risen at a relatively modest pace that matches the inflation rate (Figure 43-4). The increases have been greater at four-year institutions. At the same time as tuition has been increasing, financial aid has become more difficult to obtain (see Box 28-2 on page 217).

Even a single school can reinforce class differences by putting students in tracks. The term **tracking** refers to the practice of placing students in specific curriculum groups on the basis of their test scores and other criteria. Tracking begins very early, often in reading groups during first grade. The practice can reinforce the disadvantages that children from less affluent families may face if they haven't been exposed to reading materials, computers, and other forms of educational stimulation during their early childhood years. To ignore this connection between tracking and students' race and social class is to fundamentally misunderstand how schools perpetuate the existing social structure.

Not surprisingly, most recent research on tracking raises questions about its effectiveness, especially for low-ability students. In one study of low-income schools in California, researchers discovered a staggering difference between students who were tracked and those who were not. At one school, all interested students were allowed to enroll in advanced placement (AP) courses, not just those who were selected by the administration. Half the open enrollment students scored high enough to qualify for college credit—a much higher proportion than in selective programs, in which only 17 percent of students qualified for college credit. Tracking programs do not necessarily identify those students with the potential to succeed (B. Ellison 2008; Sacks 2007).

Conflict theorists hold that the educational inequalities produced by tracking are designed to meet the needs of modern capitalist societies. Samuel Bowles and Herbert Gintis (1976) have argued that capitalism requires a skilled, disciplined labor force, and that the educational system of the United States is structured with that objective in mind. Citing numerous studies, they offer support for what they call the **correspondence principle.** According to this approach, schools promote the values expected of individuals in each social class and perpetuate social class divisions from one generation to the next. Thus, working-class children, assumed to be destined for subordinate positions, are likely to be placed in high school vocational and general tracks, which emphasize close supervision and compliance with authority. In contrast, young people from more affluent families are likely to be directed to college preparatory tracks, which stress leadership and decision making—the skills they are expected to need as adults (McLanahan and Percheski 2008).

● Feminist Perspective

The educational system of the United States, like many other social institutions, has long been characterized by discriminatory treatment of women. In 1833, Oberlin College became the first institution of higher learning to admit female students—some 200 years after the first men's college was established. But Oberlin believed that women should aspire to become wives and mothers, not lawyers and intellectuals. In addition to attending classes, female students washed men's clothing, cared for their rooms, and served them at meals. In the 1840s, Lucy Stone, then an Oberlin undergraduate and later one of the nation's most outspoken feminist leaders, refused to write a commencement address because it would have been read to the audience by a male student.

In the 20th century, sexism in education showed up in many ways—in textbooks with negative stereotypes of women, counselors'

FIGURE 43-4 **Tuition Costs, 1976–2009**

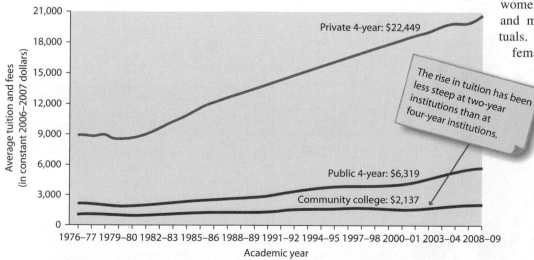

The rise in tuition has been less steep at two-year institutions than at four-year institutions.

Private 4-year: $22,449
Public 4-year: $6,319
Community college: $2,137

Average tuition and fees (in constant 2006–2007 dollars)

Academic year: 1976–77 1979–80 1982–83 1985–86 1988–89 1991–92 1994–95 1997–98 2000–01 2003–04 2008–09

Note: Data cover the entire academic year and represent the average total charges, including tuition and fees, for full-time attendance.
Sources: National Center for Education Statistics 2011; Provasnik and Planty 2008:7.

pressure on female students to prepare for "women's work," and unequal funding for women's and men's athletic programs. But perhaps nowhere was educational discrimination more evident than in the employment of teachers. The positions of university professor and college administrator, which hold relatively high status in the United States, were generally filled by men. Public school teachers, who earn much lower salaries, were largely female.

Women have made great strides in one area: the proportion of women who continue their schooling. As recently as 1969, twice as many men as women received college degrees; today, women outnumber men at college commencements. Moreover, women's access to graduate education and to medical, dental, and law schools has increased dramatically in the past few decades as a result of the Education Act of 1972. Box 43-2 examines the far-reaching effects of Title IX, the part of the act that concerns discrimination against women in education.

Much has been made of the superior academic achievement of girls and women. Today, researchers are beginning to examine the reasons for their comparatively strong performance in school—or to put it another way, for men's lackluster performance. Some studies suggest that men's aggressiveness, together with the fact that they do better in the workplace than women, even with less schooling, predisposes them to undervalue higher education. While the "absence of men" on many college campuses has captured headlines, it has also created a false crisis in public discourse. Few students realize their potential exclusively through formal education; other factors, such as ambition and personal talent, contribute to their success. And many students, including low-income and immigrant children, face much greater challenges than the so-called gender gap in education (Buchmann et al. 2008; Corbett et al. 2008; Kimmel 2006).

In cultures in which traditional gender roles remain the social norm, women's education suffers appreciably. Since September 11, 2001, the growing awareness of the Taliban's

Sociology on Campus

Box 43-2

The Debate over Title IX

Few federal policies have had such a visible effect on education as Title IX, which mandates gender equity in education in federally funded schools. Congressional amendments to the Education Act of 1972 have brought significant changes for both men and women at all levels of schooling. Title IX eliminated sex-segregated classes, prohibited sex discrimination in admissions and financial aid, and mandated that girls receive more opportunities to play sports, in proportion to their enrollment and interest.

Under this landmark legislation, to receive federal funds, a school or college must pass one of three tests. First, the numbers of male and female athletes must be proportional to the numbers of men and women enrolled at the school. Second, lacking that, the school must show a continuing history of expanding opportunities for female athletes. Or third, the school must demonstrate that the level of female participation in sports meets female students' level of interest or ability.

Today, Title IX is still one of the more controversial attempts ever made by the federal government to promote equality for all citizens. Its consequences for the funding of college athletics programs are hotly debated, while its

> Critics charge that men's teams have suffered from proportional funding of women's teams and athletic scholarships.

real and lasting effects on college admissions and employment are often forgotten. Critics charge that men's teams have suffered from proportional funding of women's teams and athletic scholarships, since schools with tight athletic budgets can expand women's sports only at the expense of men's sports.

From the women's point of view, however, the increased funding for women's sports has benefited men in some ways. In terms of coaching and administration, men have increasingly replaced women as directors of women's sports since Title IX was passed. Today only 19 percent of collegiate women's athletic administrators are women, compared to over 90 percent in the early 1970s. No national data exists for high school sports leadership, but an analysis of Minnesota youth soccer found that only 15 percent of head coaches were women.

Sociologists caution that the social effects of sports on college campuses are not all positive. Michael A. Messner, professor of sociology at the University of Southern California, points to some troubling results of a survey by the Women's Sports Foundation. The study shows that teenage girls who play sports simply for fun have more positive body images than girls who don't play sports. But those who are "highly involved" in sports are more likely than other girls to take steroids and to become risk takers. "Everyone has tacitly agreed, it seems, to view men's sports as the standard to which women should strive to have equal access," Messner writes. He is skeptical of a system that propels a lucky few college athletes to stardom each year while leaving the majority, many of them African American, without a career or an education. Certainly that was not the kind of equal opportunity legislators envisioned when they wrote Title IX.

LET'S DISCUSS

1. Has Title IX had an effect on you personally? If so, explain. On balance, do you think the increase in women's participation in sports has been good for society as a whole?

2. How might Title IX affect the way students and the public view gender roles?

Sources: Brady 2010; Cooky and LaVoi 2012; Messner 2002; Pennington 2008; Spencer 2008; Tigay 2011; Women's Sports Foundation 2011.

repression of Afghan women has dramatized the gender disparities in education in developing nations. Research has demonstrated that women are critical to economic development and good governance, and that education is instrumental in preparing them for those roles. Educating women, especially young girls, yields high social returns by lowering birthrates and improving agricultural productivity through better management (I. Coleman 2004).

● Interactionist Perspective

High school students know who they are—the kids who qualify for a free lunch. So stigmatized are they that in some schools, these students will buy a bit of food in the cash line or simply go without eating to avoid being labeled a "poor kid." School officials in San Francisco are so concerned about their plight that they are moving to cashless cafeterias, in which everyone, rich or poor, uses a debit card (Pogash 2008).

As we saw in Module 24, the labeling approach suggests that if we treat people in particular ways, they may fulfill our expectations. Children who are labeled as "troublemakers" may

In Tokyo, a mother escorts her daughter to an admissions interview at a highly competitive private school. Some Japanese families enroll children as young as 2 in cram schools. Like parents in the United States, Japanese parents know that higher education bestows status.

come to view themselves as delinquents. Similarly, a dominant group's stereotyping of racial minorities may limit their opportunities to break away from expected roles.

Can the labeling process operate in the classroom? Because interactionist researchers focus on micro-level classroom dynamics, they have been particularly interested in this question. Sociologist Howard S. Becker (1952) studied public schools in low-income and affluent areas of Chicago. He noticed that administrators expected less of students from poor neighborhoods, and wondered if teachers accepted their view. A decade later, in *Pygmalion in the Classroom,* psychologist Robert Rosenthal and school principal Lenore Jacobson (1968, 1992) documented what they referred to as a **teacher-expectancy effect**—the impact that a teacher's expectations about a student's performance may have on the student's actual achievements. This effect is especially evident in the lower grades (through Grade 3).

Studies in the United States have revealed that teachers wait longer for an answer from a student they believe to be a high achiever and are more likely to give such children a second chance. In one experiment, teachers' expectations were even shown to have an impact on students' athletic achievements. Teachers obtained better athletic performance—as measured in the number of sit-ups or push-ups performed—from those students of whom they *expected* higher numbers. Despite the controversial nature of these findings, researchers continue to document the existence of the teacher-expectancy effect. Interactionists emphasize that ability alone may be less predictive of academic success than one might think (Babad and Taylor 1992; Brint 1998; R. Rosenthal and Jacobson 1992:247–262).

Table 43-1 summarizes the four major theoretical perspectives on education.

Tracking Sociological Perspectives

Table **43-1** **Sociological Perspectives on Education**

Theoretical Perspective	Emphasis
Functionalist	Transmission of the dominant culture
	Integration of society
	Promotion of social norms, values, and sanctions
	Promotion of desirable social change
Conflict	Domination by the elite through unequal access to schooling
	Hidden curriculum
	Credentialism
	Bestowal of status
Interactionist	Teacher-expectancy effect
Feminist	Treatment of female students
	Role of women's education in economic development

Summary

Education is a cultural universal found in varied forms throughout the world.

1. The transmission of knowledge and bestowal of status are manifest functions of education. Among the latent functions are transmitting culture, promoting social and political integration, maintaining social control, and serving as an agent of social change.

2. In the view of conflict theorists, education serves as an instrument of elite domination by creating standards for entry into occupations, bestowing status unequally, and subordinating the role of women.

3. Although U.S. women attain higher levels of education than do men, their performance in the workplace continues to lag. In cultures that maintain traditional gender roles, education of women is critical to economic and social development.

4. Teacher expectations about a student's performance can sometimes affect the student's actual achievement.

Thinking Critically

1. How do the functions of integration and social control reinforce each other? How do they work against each other?

2. What are the functions and dysfunctions of tracking in schools? In what ways might tracking have a positive impact on the self-concepts of various students? In what ways might it have a negative impact?

Key Terms

Correspondence principle   363

Credentialism   362

Education   357

Hidden curriculum   362

Teacher-expectancy effect   365

Tracking   363

MODULE 44 | Schools as Formal Organizations

Nineteenth-century educators would be amazed at the scale of schools in the United States in the 21st century. The nation has about 15 million high school students today, compared to 10 million in 1961 and 5 million in 1931 (Bureau of the Census 2012c:Table H S-20; 2011a:Table 246 on page 161).

In many respects, today's schools, when viewed as an example of a formal organization, are similar to factories, hospitals, and business firms. Like those organizations, schools do not operate autonomously; they are influenced by the market of potential students. This statement is especially true of private schools, but could have broader impact if acceptance of voucher plans and other school choice programs increases. The parallels between schools and other types of formal organizations will become more apparent as we examine the bureaucratic nature of schools, teaching as an occupation, and the student subculture (K. Dougherty and Hammack 1992).

Bureaucratization of Schools

It simply is not possible for a single teacher to transmit culture and skills to children of varying ages who will enter many diverse occupations. The growing number of students being served by school systems and the greater degree of specialization required within a technologically complex society have combined to bureaucratize schools.

Max Weber noted five basic characteristics of bureaucracy, all of which are evident in the vast majority of schools, whether at the elementary, secondary, or even college level:

1. **Division of labor.** Specialized experts teach particular age levels and specific subjects. Public elementary and secondary schools now employ instructors whose sole responsibility is to work with children with learning disabilities or physical impairments.

2. **Hierarchy of authority.** Each employee of a school system is responsible to a higher authority. Teachers must report to principals and assistant principals and may also be supervised by department heads. Principals are answerable to a superintendent of schools, and the superintendent is hired and fired by a board of education.

3. **Written rules and regulations.** Teachers and administrators must conform to numerous rules and regulations in the performance of their duties. This bureaucratic trait can become dysfunctional; the time invested in completing required forms could instead be spent in preparing lessons or conferring with students.

4. **Impersonality.** As class sizes have swelled at schools and universities, it has become more difficult for teachers to give personal attention to each student. In fact, bureaucratic norms may actually encourage teachers to treat all students in the same way, despite the fact that students have distinctive personalities and learning needs.

5. **Employment based on technical qualifications.** At least in theory, the hiring of instructors is based on professional competence and expertise. Promotions are normally dictated by written personnel policies; people who excel may be granted lifelong job security through tenure.

Functionalists take a generally positive view of the bureaucratization of education. Teachers can master the skills needed to work with a specialized clientele, since they no longer are expected to cover a broad range of instruction. The chain of command within schools is clear. Students are presumably treated in an unbiased fashion because of uniformly applied rules. Finally, security of position protects teachers from unjustified dismissal. In general, then, functionalists stress that the bureaucratization of education increases the likelihood that students, teachers, and administrators will be dealt with fairly—that is, on the basis of rational and equitable criteria.

In contrast, conflict theorists argue that the trend toward more centralized education has harmful consequences for disadvantaged people. The standardization of educational curricula, including textbooks, will generally reflect the values, interests, and lifestyles of the most powerful groups in our society, and may ignore those of racial and ethnic minorities. In addition, the disadvantaged, more so than the affluent, will find it difficult to sort through complex educational bureaucracies and to organize effective lobbying groups. Therefore, in the view of conflict theorists, low-income and minority parents will have even less influence over citywide and statewide educational administrators than they have over local school officials (Bowles and Gintis 1976; Katz 1971).

Sometimes schools can seem overwhelmingly bureaucratic, with the effect of stifling rather than nourishing intellectual curiosity in students. This concern has led many parents and policymakers to push for school choice programs—allowing parents to choose the school that suits their children's needs, and forcing schools to compete for their "customers."

Taking Sociology to Work

Diane Belcher, *Assistant Director of Volunteer Services, New River Community College*

Not until Diane Belcher enrolled at New River Community College in Dublin, Virginia, did she realize that social work had always been part of her daily life. To this mother of two teenagers, helping people in need was something she just did, without even thinking about it.

Today, as assistant director of Volunteer Services at New River, Belcher assists Partners for Success, a mentoring program that matches struggling students with people in the community who have the time and energy to help them. With the director, she recruits and trains a "talent bank" of mentors, matches the mentors with student partners, and develops support programs for students experiencing problems with child care, transportation, and other necessities. The program's goal is to develop confident and successful learners who can take charge of their own studies.

Before she moved to Volunteer Services, Belcher was an administrative assistant in Workforce Development at New River, where she helped youths who lack direction and workers laid off from local factories to develop more marketable skills. In that job, she facilitated new students' transition to college, helping them to register and apply for financial aid and connecting them with professors in their fields of interest. Belcher also worked directly with the administration to develop a special fast-track program for laid-off workers.

As in all human services jobs, people skills, particularly sensitivity and compassion, are of paramount importance in Belcher's work. An understanding of the social and economic forces that affect the larger society is also essential. Belcher credits her sociology courses with helping her to "engage where needed." "Sociology exposed me to other people's situations and the role of society in creating them," she explains. "It helped me look beyond the individual level to understand societal impacts and solutions."

Asked what advice she might give to current sociology majors, Belcher says, "Drink it up, try and take it all in, relate it to the real world. Take notice of current cultural and economic conditions, understanding that when you attempt to 'fix' one part of society you must also be aware of how that will affect other parts of society."

LET'S DISCUSS

1. Have you, like Diane Belcher, realized through education that something you were doing without thinking about it has helped to prepare you for employment? Explain.

2. Do some research on Dublin, Virginia, and the surrounding area. What kind of economy does this community have? Relate the layoffs the community has been experiencing to larger societal forces.

Despite efforts to establish positive relationships among students and between teachers and students, many young people view their schools as impersonal institutions.

A teacher undergoes many perplexing stresses every day. While teachers' academic assignments have become more specialized, the demands on their time remain diverse and contradictory. Conflicts arise from serving as an instructor, a disciplinarian, and an employee of a school district at the same time. In too many schools, discipline means dealing with violence. Burnout is one result of these stresses: between a quarter and a third of new teachers quit within their first three years, and as many as half leave poor urban schools in their first five years (Wallis 2008).

Given these difficulties, does teaching remain an attractive profession in the United States? In 2011, 3.1 percent of first-year college students indicated that they were interested in becoming either elementary or high school teachers. These figures are dramatically lower than the 11 percent of first-year male students and 37 percent of first-year female students who held those occupational aspirations in 1966 (Pryor et al. 2007:122, 76; 2011a:29).

Undoubtedly, economic considerations enter into students' feelings about the attractiveness of teaching. In 2010, the average salary for all public elementary and secondary school teachers in the United States was reported at $55,350, placing teachers somewhere near the average of all the nation's wage earners. In most other industrial countries, teachers' salaries are higher in relation to the general standard of living. Of course, teachers' salaries vary considerably from state to state (Figure 44-1), and even more from one school district to another. Nevertheless, the economic reward for teaching is miniscule compared to some career options: the CEO of a major corporation makes more money in a day than the average teacher makes in a year.

In the United States, another significant countertrend to the bureaucratization of schools is the availability of education over the Internet. Increasingly, colleges and universities are reaching out via the web, offering entire courses and even majors to students in the comfort of their homes. Online curricula provide flexibility for working students and others who may have difficulty attending conventional classes because of distance or disability. Research on this type of learning is just beginning, so the question of whether teacher–student contact can thrive online remains to be settled. Computer-mediated instruction may also have an impact on instructors' status as employees, which we will discuss next, as well as on alternative forms of education like homeschooling.

 use your **sociological imagination**

How would you make your school less bureaucratic? What would it be like?

● Teachers: Employees and Instructors

Whether they serve as instructors of preschoolers or of graduate students, teachers are employees of formal organizations with bureaucratic structures. There is an inherent conflict in serving as a professional in a bureaucracy. The organization follows the principles of hierarchy and expects adherence to its rules, but professionalism demands the individual responsibility of the practitioner. This conflict is very real for teachers, who experience all the positive and negative consequences of working in bureaucracies (see Table 19-1, page 133).

U.S. EDUCATION: RACE TO the TOP!

From preschool through high school, teachers face a variety of challenges, including preparing students for standardized tests.

FIGURE 44-1 **Average Salary for Teachers**

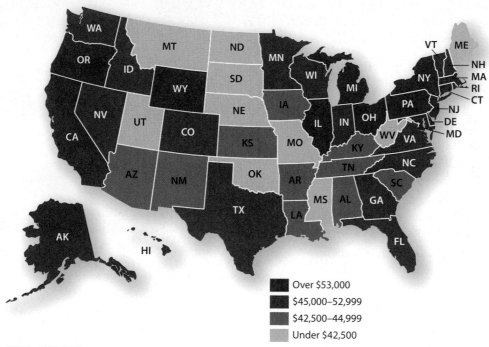

Over $53,000

$45,000–52,999

$42,500–44,999

Under $42,500

Note: Data released in 2009 for 2009–2010.
Source: National Education Association 2009.

State averages for teacher salaries range from a low of $35,136 in South Dakota to a high of $68,000 in Massachusetts.

The status of any job reflects several factors, including the level of education required, financial compensation, and the respect given the occupation by society. The teaching profession (see Table 27-1, page 209) is feeling pressure in all three of these areas. First, the level of formal schooling required for teaching remains high, and the public has begun to call for new competency examinations. Second, the statistics just cited demonstrate that teachers' salaries are significantly lower than those of many professionals and skilled workers. Third, the overall prestige of the teaching profession has declined in the past decade. Many teachers have become disappointed and frustrated and have left the educational world for careers in other professions.

● Student Subcultures

An important latent function of education relates directly to student life: schools provide for students' social and recreational needs. Education helps toddlers and young children to develop interpersonal skills that are essential during adolescence and adulthood. In their high school and college years, students may meet future husbands and wives and establish lifelong friendships.

When people observe high schools, community colleges, or universities from the outside, students appear to constitute a cohesive, uniform group. However, the student subculture is actually quite complex and diverse. High school cliques and social groups may crop up according to race, social class, physical attractiveness, placement in courses, athletic ability, and leadership roles in the school and community. In his classic community study of "Elmtown," August B. Hollingshead (1975) found some 259 distinct cliques in a single high school. The cliques, whose average size was five, were centered on the school itself, on recreational activities, and on religious and community groups.

Amid these close-knit and often rigidly segregated cliques, gay and lesbian students are particularly vulnerable. Peer group pressure to conform is intense at this age. Although coming to terms with one's sexuality is difficult for all adolescents, it can be downright dangerous for those whose sexual orientation does not conform to societal expectations.

Teachers and administrators are becoming more sensitized to these issues. Perhaps more important, some schools are creating gay–straight alliances (GSAs), school-sponsored support groups that bring gay teens together with sympathetic straight peers. Begun in Los Angeles in 1984, these programs numbered nearly 3,000 nationwide in 2005; most were founded after the murder of Matthew Shepard, a gay college student, in 1998. In some districts parents have objected to these organizations, but the same court rulings that protect the right of conservative Bible groups to meet on school grounds also protect GSAs. In 2003, the gay–straight movement reached a milestone when the New York City public schools moved an in-school program for gays, bisexuals, and transgendered students to a separate school. The Harvey Milk High School was named in memory of San Francisco's first openly gay city supervisor, who was assassinated in 1978 (Gay, Lesbian and Straight Education Network 2012).

We can find a similar diversity of student groups at the college level. Burton Clark and Martin Trow (1966) and more recently, Helen Lefkowitz Horowitz (1987) have identified four distinctive subcultures among college students:

1. The *collegiate* subculture focuses on having fun and socializing. These students define what constitutes a "reasonable" amount of academic work (and what amount of work is "excessive" and leads to being labeled as a "grind"). Members of the collegiate subculture have little commitment to academic pursuits. Athletes often fit into this subculture.

2. The *academic* subculture identifies with the intellectual concerns of the faculty and values knowledge for its own sake.

3. The *vocational* subculture is interested primarily in career prospects and views college as a means of obtaining degrees that are essential for advancement.

4. Finally, the *nonconformist* subculture is hostile to the college environment and seeks ideas that may or may not relate to academic studies. This group may find outlets through campus publications or issue-oriented groups.

Each college student is eventually exposed to these competing subcultures and must determine which (if any) seems most in line with his or her feelings and interests.

The typology used by the researchers reminds us that school is a complex social organization—almost like a community with different neighborhoods. Of course, these four subcultures are not the only ones evident on college campuses in the United States. For example, one might find subcultures of Vietnam veterans or former full-time homemakers at community colleges and four-year commuter institutions. And as more and more students from minority groups decide to continue their formal education beyond high school, subcultures based on race and ethnicity will become more evident. As Figure 44-2 shows, college campuses are becoming increasingly diverse.

Student subcultures are more diverse today than in the past. Many adults are returning to college to obtain further education, advance their careers, or change their line of work.

Sociologist Joe R. Feagin has studied a distinctive collegiate subculture: Black students at predominantly White universities. These students must function academically and socially within universities where there are few Black faculty members or administrators, where harassment of Blacks by campus police is common, and where curricula place little emphasis on Black contributions. Feagin (1989:11) suggests that "for minority students life at a predominantly White college or university means long-term encounters with pervasive whiteness." In Feagin's view, Black students at such institutions experience both blatant and subtle racial discrimination, which has a cumulative impact that can seriously damage the students' confidence (see also Feagin et al. 1996).

FIGURE 44-2 **College Campuses by Race and Ethnicity: Then, Now, and in the Future**

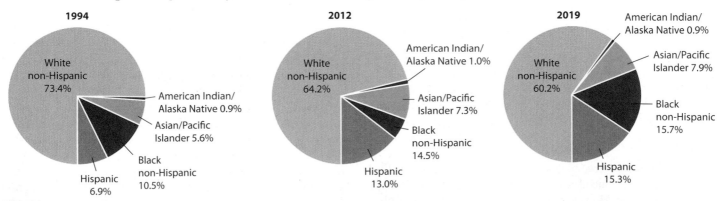

1994
- White non-Hispanic 73.4%
- American Indian/ Alaska Native 0.9%
- Asian/Pacific Islander 5.6%
- Black non-Hispanic 10.5%
- Hispanic 6.9%

2012
- White non-Hispanic 64.2%
- American Indian/ Alaska Native 1.0%
- Asian/Pacific Islander 7.3%
- Black non-Hispanic 14.5%
- Hispanic 13.0%

2019
- White non-Hispanic 60.2%
- American Indian/ Alaska Native 0.9%
- Asian/Pacific Islander 7.9%
- Black non-Hispanic 15.7%
- Hispanic 15.3%

Note: Percentages do not add to 100 due to rounding error. Nonresident aliens whose race/ethnicity is unknown excluded.
Source: Hussar and Bailey 2011:Table 29.

Homeschooling

When most people think of school, they think of bricks and mortar and the teachers, administrators, and other employees who staff school buildings. But for an increasing number of students in the United States, home is the classroom and the teacher is a parent. About 1.5 million students are now being educated at home. That is about 3 percent of the K–12 school population. For these students, the issues of bureaucratization and social structure are less significant than they are for public school students (Grady et al. 2010).

In the 1800s, after the establishment of public schools, families that taught their children at home lived in isolated environments or held strict religious views that were at odds with the secular environment of public schools. But today, homeschooling is attracting a broader range of families not necessarily tied to organized religion. Poor academic quality, peer pressure, and school violence are motivating many parents to teach their children at home. In addition, some immigrants choose homeschooling as a way to ease their children's transition to a new society. For example, the growing Arab American population recently joined the movement toward homeschooling (MacFarquhar 2008; National Center for Education Statistics 2009).

While supporters of homeschooling believe children can do just as well or better in homeschools as in public schools, critics counter that because homeschooled children are isolated from the larger community, they lose an important chance to improve their socialization skills. But proponents of homeschooling claim their children benefit from contact with others besides their own age group. They also see homeschools as a good alternative for children who suffer from attention-deficit/hyperactivity disorder (ADHD) and learning disorders (LDs). Such children often do better in smaller classes, which present fewer distractions to disturb their concentration.

Quality control is an issue in homeschooling. While homeschooling is legal in all 50 states, 10 states require no notification that a child will be homeschooled, and another 14 require notification only. Other states may require parents to submit their children's curricula or test scores for professional evaluation. Despite the lack of uniform standards, a research review by the Home School Legal Defense Association (2005) reports that homeschooled students score higher than others on standardized tests, in every subject and every grade.

Who are the people who are running homeschools? In general, they tend to have higher-than-average incomes and educational levels. Most are two-parent families, and their children watch less television than average—both factors that are likely to support superior educational performance. The same students, with the same support from their parents, would probably do just as well in the public schools. As research has repeatedly shown, small classes are better than big classes, and strong parental and community involvement is key (R. Cox 2003:28).

Whatever the controversy over homeschooling in the United States, it is much less serious than in some other nations. In 2010, the U.S. Immigration and Naturalization Service began granting political asylum to German families who homeschool their children, in violation of their country's constitution. German parents can be fined and imprisoned for homeschooling their children (Francis 2010).

social policy and Education | Charter Schools

Discontent with public schools stretches back for decades. In the 1970s, "classrooms without walls" were supposed to open up the curriculum to students' creativity. In 2002, the No Child Left Behind initiative was supposed to guarantee that all students would learn the basics. Although test scores inched up a bit in response, critics complained that schools were becoming too test-oriented, and scores on interactive science and math tests sank compared to those in other nations (K. Clark 2010).

Meanwhile, the charter school movement had been gathering strength. **Charter schools** are experimental schools that are developed and managed by individuals, groups of parents, or an educational management organization. Although these schools are typically considered to be public schools, they are administered outside the official public school system. Their charters (legal contracts) permit them to establish their own rules, curricula, and admissions and professional standards. Within their communities, however, charter schools must still abide by prevailing standards for health, public safety, and equal opportunity (Renzulli and Roscigno 2007).

Looking at the Issue

Charter schools first opened in Minnesota in 1992; by 2011, nearly 5,000 of them had been established in 40 different states (Figure 44-3). Advocates of charter schools claim that they offer parents accountability for their children's education. In effect, charter schools compete with public schools, offering an alternative that was once available only to the wealthy (National Alliance for Public Charter Schools 2011).

—*Continued*

MAPPING LIFE NATIONWIDE

FIGURE 44-3 **Charter Schools**

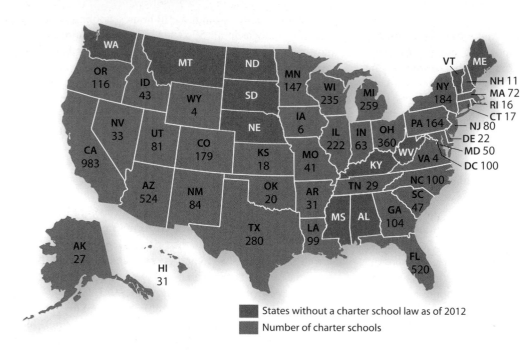

Legend:
- States without a charter school law as of 2012
- Number of charter schools

Map data:
WA, OR 116, ID 43, MT, WY 4, NV 33, UT 81, CA 983, AZ 524, NM 84, CO 179, ND, SD, NE, KS 18, OK 20, TX 280, MN 147, IA 6, MO 41, AR 31, LA 99, WI 235, IL 222, IN 63, MI 259, OH 360, KY, TN 29, MS, AL, GA 104, VT, ME, NH 11, MA 72, RI 16, CT 17, NY 184, PA 164, NJ 80, DE 22, MD 50, DC 100, WV 4, VA 4, NC 100, SC 47, FL 520, AK 27, HI 31

Source: National Alliance for Public Charter Schools. (2012). The Public Charter Schools Dashboard. Washington, DC: NAPCS.

Think about It

How does your state compare to others in terms of charter schools?

Charter Schools such as this one in Nampa, Idaho, are the latest answer to efforts to improve the quality of education.

Applying Sociology

Functionalists argue that charter schools meet society's need for education while serving a diverse student body. Despite criticism that charter schools are elitist institutions that serve the children of privileged White families, data show that 55 percent of the students enrolled in these schools are African American or Latino. More than a third of them qualify for free or reduced-price lunches (Gabriel 2010).

Although charter schools are publicly financed, most are not unionized. From a conflict perspective, charter schools do not represent teachers' interests well and are contributing to the decline of labor unions (see Module 19). Partly in response to this concern, public school districts in Denver, Detroit, Milwaukee, Boston, and Minnesota have empowered teachers to create their own charter schools (Dillon 2009; Hu 2010).

Because the charter school movement is a comparatively recent one, we do not have much research on the long-term impact of charter versus non-charter schools. Of course, there is great variation among both within the same city much less the same state. News stories about individual charter schools and high-profile advocates like the Bill and Melinda Gates Foundation suggest that these schools' outcomes are quite positive. However, the diversity in purpose, funding, organization, and curriculum that characterizes charter schools makes generalizing from one school or community to another very difficult.

As an example of the different conclusions that can be reached, many top school lists disproportionately identify charter schools as outperforming non-charter schools. Yet research released in 2012 shows that at least a third of charter schools do *worse* than the public schools they replaced. Similarly, research done at Stanford University on charter schools in 16 states shows that 37 percent of them produce test results that are worse than public schools. Only a small fraction of these schools have had their charters revoked, however (Center for Research on Education Outcomes 2009; Lubienski and Weitzel 2012; E. Thomas and Wingert 2010).

Initiating Policy

In the United States, unlike virtually all other industrial nations, school policy is driven at the local level. Although the federal government may encourage certain policies through public funding, and may dictate certain standards like nondiscrimination, school policy is created largely at the community level following statewide standards. Thus, in 2010, when the Department of Education began to expend $4.3 billion as part of a general educational stimulus program, it left the structure and organization of schools to local communities. Programs such as Race to the Top stressed only improvements in academic achievement (K. Clark 2010).

Today, the charter school movement is not the only approach to educational reform; other school choice programs are available to families. Homeschooling, described earlier in this chapter, could be viewed as the most complete alternative to public schools. In addition, some cities offer parents vouchers that allow them, in effect, to send their children to any local school, public, private, or religious, at taxpayers' expense. Yet as Karl Alexander (1997:17)

eloquently noted in his presidential address to the Southern Sociological Society, "The charter school movement, with its 'let 1,000 flowers bloom' philosophy, is certain to yield an occasional prize-winning rose. But is . . . [this approach to school choice] likely to prove a reliable guide for broad-based, systematic reform—the kind of reform that will carry the great mass of our children closer to where we want them to be? I hardly think so." Indeed, with such diversity in learning environments found among thousands of charter schools, the jury is still out on their effectiveness. As with most educational institutions, one cannot assume quality just based on a certain structure, size, affiliation, or funding source.

TAKE THE ISSUE WITH YOU

1. Do you have any experience with educational reform, either as a student yourself or as a parent? If so, describe the changes that you witnessed. Were they successful in improving educational outcomes?

2. Which type of school choice program, if any, would you favor— homeschooling, charter schools, or school vouchers? Explain your choice.

3. Are you concerned about educational standards in the United States? If so, do you think schools should be reformed at the local level? Should the federal government become more involved in school reform?

MODULE 44 | Recap and Review

Summary

Most schools in the United States are organized like formal organizations such as factories and hospitals.

1. Weber's five basic characteristics of bureaucracies are all evident in schools.

2. Teachers are professionals who serve as part of a bureaucracy. There is an inherent conflict in combining those two different roles.

3. Schools provide for students' social and emotional needs as well as their educational needs. Student subcultures within high schools and colleges are complex and varied.

4. Homeschooling has become a viable alternative to traditional public and private schools. In some countries homeschooling is illegal.

5. **Charter schools**—experimental schools that are developed and managed by individuals, groups of parents, or an educational management organization— are one of several recent attempts to reform the public

school system in the United States. Although charter schools are popular with parents, research shows that about a third of them do worse than the public schools they replaced.

Thinking Critically

1. Select two functions of education and suggest how they could be fulfilled through homeschooling.

2. What student subcultures can you identify on your campus? Which have the highest and lowest social status? How would functionalists, conflict theorists, and interactionists view the existence of student subcultures on a college campus?

Key Term

Charter school   317

Mastering This Chapter

taking sociology with you

1 Attend a meeting of a local Parent Teacher Association (PTA). What issues are parents talking about? Describe their concerns using one or more sociological perspectives.

2 Make a list of the student subcultures on your campus, then describe them using the concepts you learned in

Module 11. Do any of these subcultures serve as out-groups for other subcultures?

3 Does your school have a gay–straight alliance? If so, speak with one of the officers. What are members doing to reduce prejudice and foster better relations among gay and straight students? Explain their approach using sociological theory.

key terms

Charter school An experimental school that is developed and managed by individuals, groups of parents, or an educational management organization. (page 371)

Correspondence principle The tendency of schools to promote the values expected of individuals in each social class and to perpetuate social class divisions from one generation to the next. (363)

Credentialism An increase in the lowest level of education needed to enter a field. (362)

Education A formal process of learning in which some people consciously teach, while others adopt the social role of learner. (357)

Hidden curriculum Standards of behavior that are deemed proper by society and are taught subtly in schools. (362)

Teacher-expectancy effect The impact that a teacher's expectations about a student's performance may have on the student's actual achievements. (365)

Tracking The practice of placing students in specific curriculum groups on the basis of their test scores and other criteria. (363)

self-quiz

Read each question carefully and then select the best answer.

1. Which sociological perspective emphasizes that the common identity and social integration fostered by education contribute to overall societal stability and consensus?
   a. the functionalist perspective
   b. the conflict perspective
   c. the interactionist perspective
   d. labeling theory

2. Which one of the following was introduced into school systems to promote social change?
   a. sex education classes
   b. affirmative action programs
   c. Project Head Start
   d. all of the above

3. The correspondence principle was developed by
   a. Max Weber.
   b. Karl Marx and Friedrich Engels.
   c. Samuel Bowles and Herbert Gintis.
   d. James Thurber.

4. The student subculture that is hostile to the college environment and seeks out ideas that may or may not relate to studies is called the
   a. collegiate subculture.

   b. academic subculture.
   c. vocational subculture.
   d. nonconformist subculture.

5. Most recent research on ability grouping raises questions about its
   a. effectiveness, especially for lower-achieving students.
   b. failure to improve the prospects of higher-achieving students.
   c. ability to improve the prospects of lower- and higher-achieving students.
   d. both a and b

6. The most basic *manifest* function of education is
   a. transmitting knowledge.
   b. transmitting culture.
   c. maintaining social control.
   d. serving as an agent of change.

7. Sixty years ago, a high school diploma was the minimum requirement for entry into the paid labor force of the United States. Today, a college diploma is virtually the bare minimum. This change reflects the process of
   a. tracking.
   b. credentialism.
   c. the hidden curriculum.
   d. the correspondence principle.

8. Samuel Bowles and Herbert Gintis have argued that capitalism requires a skilled, disciplined labor force and that the educational system of the United States is structured with that objective in mind. Citing numerous studies, they offer support for what they call
    a. tracking.
    b. credentialism.
    c. the correspondence principle.
    d. the teacher-expectancy effect.

9. The teacher-expectancy effect is most closely associated with
    a. the functionalist perspective.
    b. the conflict perspective.
    c. the interactionist perspective.
    d. anomie theory.

10. Sociologist Max Weber noted five basic characteristics of bureaucracy, all of which are evident in the vast majority of schools, whether at the elementary, secondary, or even college level. Which of the following is *not* one of them?
    a. division of labor
    b. written rules and regulations
    c. impersonality
    d. shared decision making

11. The _____ perspective stresses the importance of education in transmitting culture, maintaining social control, and promoting social change.

12. In the past, the integrative function of education was most obvious through its emphasis on promoting a common _____.

13. The _____ subculture identifies with the intellectual concerns of the faculty and values knowledge for its own sake.

14. A _____ _____ is an experimental school that is developed and managed outside the public school system.

15. Women's education tends to suffer in those cultures with traditional _____ _____ .

16. Schools perform a variety of _____ functions, such as transmitting culture, promoting social and political integration, and maintaining social control.

17. Sociologist _____ _____ points out that better-educated people tend to have greater access to information, to hold more diverse opinions, and to possess the ability to make subtle distinctions in analysis.

18. The term _____ _____ refers to standards of behavior that are deemed proper by society and are taught subtly in schools. For example, children must not speak until the teacher calls on them and must regulate their activities according to the clock or the bell.

19. _____ is the practice of placing students in specific curriculum groups on the basis of their test scores and other criteria.

20. Of the four distinctive subcultures among college students discussed in the text, the _____ subculture is interested primarily in career prospects, and views college as a means of obtaining degrees that are essential for advancement.

thinking about movies

Waiting for Superman
This film documents failures in the American educational system and their personal consequences.

Teached Vol. I
This documentary explores why the American education system fails to provide basic literacy skills to a significant percentage of minority students.

To Be Heard
Four teens use writing and literacy as tools to improve their social circumstances.

Sociologists Nikki Bado-Fralick and Rebecca Sachs Norris used religiously themed toys and games to study contemporary religion.

They found that these seemingly frivolous items reveal a great deal about the way Americans practice their varied religious heritages today.

" There are many types of religious toys: stuffed torahs; Moses, David, and Jesus and the Tomb action figures; Noah's ark collections; and Resurrection Eggs, which supplement a young child's Easter book. 'Lead your kids on a fun, faith-filled Easter egg hunt this year—one that teaches them about Jesus' death and resurrection! Each egg carton is filled with a dozen colorful plastic eggs. Pop them open and find miniature symbols of the Easter story inside.' One of the dozen plastic eggs contains a crown of thorns, another is empty, representing the disappearance of the body of Jesus from the tomb, and pointing to his resurrection. Muslim toys include a mosque building set, mosque jewelry cases, and a prayer practice chart. Jewish toys include dreidels, wooden Shabbat sets, toy *sukkahs,* and a Plush Plagues Bag that includes 'all 10 Plagues!'

Religious dolls are part of this wonderland of sacred fun. There are plush and plastic talking Bible dolls, pumped-up Christian action figures, dolls designed to support a Jewish girl's religious identity and conform to religious requirements, Goddess dolls designed for affluent young feminists, talking Muslim dolls that teach Arabic phrases, and 'anti-Barbies'—Muslim dolls deliberately designed to compete with Barbie for the hearts and minds of young girls. There are plush Buddha and Siva dolls, and cuddly Jesus and Esther dolls as well.

Numerous card games and puzzles teach a variety of languages, including Hebrew, Arabic, and Punjabi. The Christian

Book Distributors Web site not only offers religiously themed educational materials, they also offer nonreligious toys that appeal to parents with religious consciences who may be looking for nonviolent toys, such as a food groups toy with hand-painted pieces in four wooden crates, a pizza party game with different toppings, and a car towing game.

Not all religious toys are meant for the edification of the young. Many religious games and toys are satirical or simply products meant to be amusing enough to sell in an era where we are oversatiated with things, and any cultural phenomenon is fair game for marketing purposes. These items amuse or appall us, depending on how clever or offensive the item is, and for whom it is intended. . . .

. . . .

. . . Games and toys not only transmit cultural values but reflect them as well. . . .

Contemporary religious games have their roots in ancient practices, but their flavor—their style and substance—as well as their commercial focus reveal a specifically twenty-first century American form of religiosity.

Games and religion have a long and complex history—they were used for divination and gambling, for this-worldly satire, and in the afterlife. Games were objects and methods used to interpret divine powers and influence supernatural forces. These religious and magical functions reflect the presence and movement of the sacred in the material world, indicators of a complex whole rather than a dualism where sacred and ordinary occupy separate realms.

Contemporary religious games have their roots in ancient practices, but their flavor—their style and substance—as well as their commercial focus reveal a specifically twenty-first century American form of religiosity. "

(Bado-Fralick and Norris 2010:7–8, 29–30) Additional information about this excerpt can be found on the Online Learning Center at www.mhhe.com/schaefermod2e.

I n this excerpt from *Toying with God: The World of Religious Games and Dolls,* religious studies scholars Nikki Bado-Fralick and Rebecca Sachs Norris consider how religiously themed toys and games reflect both popular and religious culture. Depending on their purpose and design, the authors note, as well as on the social context in which they are used, these dolls and board games can either reinforce or undermine organized religion. Their impact on the children who play with them parallels the broader influence of religion on society. Despite the much-publicized decline of organized religion over the past century, even a casual observer can see that religion still

permeates our social environment. As a result, nonbelievers are influenced by believers, whether they want to be or not. Similarly, believers are influenced by nonbelievers and by those of different faiths, despite any attempts they may make to screen out other points of view.

Religion plays a major role in people's lives, and religious practices of some sort are evident in every society. That makes religion a cultural universal, along with other common practices or beliefs found in every culture, such as dancing, food preparation, the family, and personal names. At present, an estimated 4 billion people belong to the world's many religious faiths.

What social purposes does religion serve? Does it help to hold society together or foster social change? What happens when religion mixes with politics? These modules concentrate on the formal systems of religion that characterize modern industrial societies. We begin with a brief description of the sociological perspectives on religion, followed by an overview of the world's major religions. We will also explore religion's role in societal integration, social support, social change, and social control. Next we'll examine three important components of religious behavior— belief, ritual, and experience. Finally, we will cover the basic forms of religious organization, including new religious movements. In a case study, we'll take a fascinating look at religion in India. We will close with a Social Policy section on the controversy over religion in the schools.

MODULE 45 The Sociological Approach to Religion

Durkheim and the Importance of Religion

If a group believes that it is being directed by a "vision from God," sociologists do not attempt to prove or disprove the revelation. Instead, they assess the effects of the religious experience on the group. What sociologists are interested in is the social impact of religion on individuals and institutions.

Émile Durkheim was perhaps the first sociologist to recognize the critical importance of religion in human societies. He saw its appeal for the individual, but more important, he stressed the *social* impact of religion. In Durkheim's view, religion is a collective act that includes many forms of behavior in which people interact with others. As in his work on suicide, Durkheim was not so interested in the personalities of religious believers as he was in understanding religious behavior within a social context.

Durkheim defined **religion** as a "unified system of beliefs and practices relative to sacred things." In his view, religion involves a set of beliefs and practices that are uniquely the property of religion, as opposed to other social institutions and ways of thinking. Durkheim ([1893] 1933; [1912] 2001) argued that religious faiths distinguish between certain transcending events and the everyday world. He referred to those realms as the *sacred* and the *profane.*

The **sacred** encompasses elements beyond everyday life that inspire awe, respect, and even fear. People become part of the sacred realm only by completing some ritual, such as prayer or sacrifice. Because believers have faith in the sacred, they accept what they cannot understand. In contrast, the **profane** includes the ordinary and commonplace. This concept can be confusing, however, because the same object can be either sacred or profane, depending on how it is viewed. A normal dining room table is profane, but it becomes sacred to some Christians if it bears the elements of a communion. A candelabra becomes sacred to Jews if it is a menorah. For Confucians and Taoists, incense sticks are not mere decorative items, but highly valued offerings to the gods in religious ceremonies that mark the new and full moons.

When religion's influence on other social institutions in a society diminishes, the process of **secularization** is said to be under way. During this process, religion will survive in the private sphere of individual and family life (as in the case of many Native American families); it may even thrive on a personal level. But at the same time, other social institutions—such as the economy, politics, and education—maintain their own sets of norms, independent of religious guidance. Even so, religion is enormously resilient. Although specific faiths or organizations may change, their transformation does not signal the demise of religious faith. Rather, it contributes to the diversity of religious expression and organization.

Following the direction established by Durkheim a century ago, contemporary sociologists view religion in two different ways. First, they study the norms and values of religious faiths by examining their substantive beliefs. For example, it is possible to compare the degree to which Christian faiths interpret the Bible literally, or Muslim groups follow the Qur'an (or Koran), the sacred book of Islam. At the same time, sociologists examine religion in terms of the social functions it fulfills, such as providing social support or reinforcing social norms. By exploring both the beliefs and the functions of religion, we can better understand its impact on the individual, on groups, and on society as a whole.

■ Sociological Perspectives on Religion

Since religion is a cultural universal, it is not surprising that it plays a basic role in human societies. In sociological terms, it performs both manifest and latent functions. Among its *manifest* (open and stated) functions, religion defines the spiritual world and gives meaning to the divine. It provides an explanation for events that seem difficult to understand, such as what lies beyond the grave. The *latent* functions of religion are unintended, covert, or hidden. Even though the manifest function of a church service is to offer a forum for religious worship, it might at the same time fulfill a latent social function as a meeting ground for unmarried members.

Functionalists and conflict theorists both evaluate religion's impact on human societies. We'll consider a functionalist view of religion's role in integrating society, providing social support, and promoting social change, and then look at religion from the conflict and feminist perspectives, as a means of social control. Note that for the most part, religion's impact is best understood from a macro-level viewpoint that is oriented toward the larger society. Its social support function is an exception: it is best understood on the micro, or individual, level.

The Integrative Function of Religion

Émile Durkheim viewed religion as an integrative force in human society—a perspective that is reflected in functionalist thought today. Durkheim sought to answer a perplexing question: "How can human societies be held together when they are generally composed of individuals and social groups with diverse interests and aspirations?" In his view, religious bonds often transcend these personal and divisive forces. Durkheim acknowledged that religion is not the only integrative force; nationalism or patriotism may serve the same end.

How does religion provide this "societal glue"? Religion, whether it be Buddhism, Islam, Christianity, or Judaism, gives meaning and purpose to people's lives. It offers certain ultimate values and ends to hold in common. Although they are subjective and not always fully accepted, these values and ends help society to function as an integrated social system. For example, funerals, weddings, bar and bat mitzvahs, and confirmations serve to integrate people into larger communities by providing shared beliefs and values about the ultimate questions of life.

The integrative power of religion can be seen, too, in the role that churches, synagogues, and mosques have traditionally played and continue to play for immigrant groups in the United

In 2010 Jose H. Gomez (at the podium) became archbishop of Los Angeles, the largest Roman Catholic archdiocese in the United States. Born in Mexico, Gomez became a U.S. citizen while serving as a priest in Texas. His elevation reflects the growth of the Hispanic faithful among Roman Catholics in the United States.

States. For example, Roman Catholic immigrants may settle near a parish church that offers services in their native language, such as Polish or Spanish. Similarly, Korean immigrants may join a Presbyterian church that has many Korean American members and follows religious practices like those of churches in Korea. Like other religious organizations, these Roman Catholic and Presbyterian churches help to integrate immigrants into their new homeland.

In recent years, the most talked about immigrant religious group has been Muslims. Throughout the world, including the United States, Muslims are divided into a variety of sects, including Sunni and Shia (or Shiite). However, inside and outside these sects, people express their Islamic faith in many different ways. To speak of Muslims as being either Sunni or Shia would be like speaking of Christians as either Roman Catholic or Baptist.

Depending on the circumstances, Islam in the United States can be integrative by faith, ethnicity, or both. The great majority of Muslims in the United States are Sunni Muslims—literally, those who follow the *Sunnah,* or way of the Prophet. Compared to other Muslims, Sunnis tend to be more moderate in their religious orthodoxy. The Shia, who come primarily from Iraq and Iran, are the second-largest group. Shia Muslims are more attentive to guidance from accepted Islamic scholars than are Sunnis. In sufficient numbers, these two Muslim groups will choose to worship separately, even if they must cross ethnic or linguistic lines to do so. Whatever group Muslims belong to, however, there has been a remarkable increase in the number of Islamic places of worship in the United States. Between 2000 and 2010, the number of mosques rose 74 percent (Bagby 2012; Selod 2008a).

In some instances, religious loyalties are *dysfunctional;* that is, they contribute to tension and even conflict between groups or nations. During the Second World War, the German Nazis attempted to exterminate the Jewish people; approximately 6 million European Jews were killed. In modern times, nations such as Lebanon (Muslims versus Christians), Israel (Jews versus Muslims, as well as Orthodox versus secular Jews), Northern Ireland (Roman Catholics versus Protestants), and India (Hindus versus Muslims, and more recently, Sikhs) have been torn by clashes that are in large part based on religion. (See the case study on page 392 for a more detailed discussion of religious conflict in India.)

Religion and Social Support

Most of us find it difficult to accept the stressful events of life—the death of a loved one, serious injury, bankruptcy, divorce, and so forth—especially when something "senseless" happens. How can family and friends come to terms with the death of a talented college student, not even 20 years old?

Through its emphasis on the divine and the supernatural, religion allows us to "do something" about the calamities we face. In some faiths, adherents can offer sacrifices or pray to a deity in the belief that such acts will change their earthly condition. On a more basic level, religion encourages us to view our personal misfortunes as relatively unimportant in the broader perspective of human history—or even as part of an undisclosed divine purpose. Friends and relatives of the deceased college student may see his death as being "God's will," or as having some ultimate benefit that we cannot understand now. This perspective may be much more comforting than the terrifying feeling that any of us can die senselessly at any moment—and that there is no divine answer to why one person lives a long and full life, while another dies tragically at a relatively early age.

The religious function of social support is also apparent in people's use of social media. Overall, 31 percent of Facebook users in the United States and 24 percent of them outside the United States identify their religion in their profiles. Tens of millions indicate that they are fans or "friends" of a religious figure or category. Consequently, religious organizations are turning to Twitter and Facebook to strengthen their connections with these followers and provide them with 24/7 social support (Preston 2011).

Religion and Social Change

The Weberian Thesis When someone seems driven to work and succeed, we often attribute the Protestant work ethic to that person. The term comes from the writings of Max Weber, who carefully examined the connection between religious allegiance and capitalist development. Weber's findings appeared in his pioneering work *The Protestant Ethic and the Spirit of Capitalism* ([1904] 2011).

Weber noted that in European nations with both Protestant and Catholic citizens, an overwhelming number of business leaders, owners of capital, and skilled workers were Protestant.

In his view, this fact was no mere coincidence. Weber pointed out that the followers of John Calvin (1509–1564), a leader of the Protestant Reformation, emphasized a disciplined work ethic, this-worldly concerns, and a rational orientation to life that have become known as the **Protestant ethic.** One by-product of the Protestant ethic was a drive to accumulate savings that could be used for future investment. This "spirit of capitalism," to use Weber's phrase, contrasted with the moderate work hours, leisurely work habits, and lack of ambition that Weber saw as typical of the times.

Few books on the sociology of religion have aroused as much commentary and criticism as Weber's work. It has been hailed as one of the most important theoretical works in the field and an excellent example of macro-level analysis. Like Durkheim, Weber demonstrated that religion is not solely a matter of intimate personal beliefs. He stressed that the collective nature of religion has consequences for society as a whole. Indeed, a recent analysis of historical economic data shows that the Protestant ethic was an important factor in the growth of capitalism from 1500 through 1870 (S. Sanderson et al. 2011).

Weber provided a convincing description of the origins of European capitalism. However, this economic system has now been adopted by non-Calvinists in many parts of the world. Studies done in the United States today show little or no difference in achievement orientation between Roman Catholics and Protestants. Apparently, the "spirit of capitalism" has emerged as a generalized cultural trait rather than a specific religious tenet (Greeley 1989).

Conflict theorists caution that Weber's theory—even if it is accepted—should not be regarded as an analysis of mature capitalism, as reflected in the rise of multinational corporations. Marxists would disagree with Weber not on the origins of capitalism, but on its future. Unlike Marx, Weber believed that

Television scripts often poke fun at organized religion, while presenting characters who are atheists as enlightened people. A notable exception is the character Booth (left) in *Bones,* who does not hide his Roman Catholicism. Like many others who are both thoughtful and religious, Booth receives social support from his faith.

capitalism could endure indefinitely as an economic system. He added, however, that the decline of religion as an overriding force in society opened the way for workers to express their discontent more vocally (R. Collins 1980).

Liberation Theology Sometimes the clergy can be found in the forefront of social change. Many religious activists, especially in the Roman Catholic Church in Latin America, support **liberation theology**—the use of a church in a political effort to eliminate poverty, discrimination, and other forms of injustice from a secular society. Advocates of this religious movement sometimes sympathize with Marxism. Many believe that radical change, rather than economic development in itself, is the only acceptable solution to the desperation of the masses in impoverished developing countries. Activists associated with liberation theology believe that organized religion has a moral responsibility to take a strong public stand against the oppression of the poor, racial and ethnic minorities, and women (Christian Smith 1991).

The term *liberation theology* dates back to the publication in 1973 of the English translation of *A Theology of Liberation*. The book was written by a Peruvian priest, Gustavo Gutiérrez, who lived in a slum area of Lima during the early 1960s. After years of exposure to the vast poverty around him, Gutiérrez concluded that "in order to serve the poor, one had to move into political action." Eventually, politically committed Latin American theologians came under the influence of social scientists who viewed the domination of capitalism and multinational corporations as central to the hemisphere's problems. One result was a new approach to theology that built on the cultural and religious traditions of Latin America rather than on models developed in Europe and the United States (R. M. Brown 1980:23; G. Gutiérrez 1990).

Liberation theology may be dysfunctional, however. Some Roman Catholic worshippers have come to believe that by focusing on political and governmental injustice, the clergy are no longer addressing their personal and spiritual needs. Partly as a result of such disenchantment, some Catholics in Latin America are converting to mainstream Protestant faiths or to Mormonism.

 use your **sociological imagination**

The social support that religious groups provide is suddenly withdrawn from your community. How will your life or the lives of others change? What will happen if religious groups stop pushing for social change?

Religion and Social Control: A Conflict Perspective

Liberation theology is a relatively recent phenomenon that marks a break with the traditional role of churches. It was this traditional role that Karl Marx ([1844] 1964) opposed. In his view, religion *impeded* social change by encouraging oppressed people to focus on otherworldly concerns rather than on their immediate poverty or exploitation. Marx described religion as an opiate

that was particularly harmful to oppressed peoples. He felt that religion often drugged the masses into submission by offering a consolation for their harsh lives on earth: the hope of salvation in an ideal afterlife. For example, during the period of slavery in the United States, White masters forbade Blacks to practice native African religions, while encouraging them to adopt Christianity, which taught them that obedience would lead to salvation and eternal happiness in the hereafter. Viewed from a conflict perspective, Christianity may have pacified certain slaves and blunted the rage that often fuels rebellion.

Today, however, people around the world see religion more as a source of support through adversity than a source of oppression. In a combination of public opinion polls taken across 114 nations, 95 percent of those living in the poorest nations felt that religion was important in daily life, compared to only 47 percent of those in the wealthiest countries (Crabtree 2010).

Religion does play an important role in propping up the existing social structure. The values of religion, as already noted, tend to reinforce other social institutions and the social order as a whole. From Marx's perspective, however, religion's promotion of social stability only helps to perpetuate patterns of social inequality. According to Marx, the dominant religion reinforces the interests of those in power.

For example, contemporary Christianity reinforces traditional patterns of behavior that call for the subordination of the less powerful. The role of women in the church is an example of this uneven distribution of power. Assumptions about gender roles leave women in a subservient position both within Christian churches and at home. In fact, women find it as difficult to achieve leadership positions in many churches as they do in large corporations. A "stained glass ceiling" tends to stunt clergywomen's career development, even in the most liberal denominations.

Like Marx, conflict theorists argue that to whatever extent religion actually does influence social behavior, it reinforces existing patterns of dominance and inequality. From a Marxist perspective, religion keeps people from seeing their lives and societal conditions in political terms—for example, by obscuring the overriding significance of conflicting economic interests.

Although the number of women clergy has increased, only about 1 in 6 spiritual leaders is a woman, and in many faiths women are still banned from serving.

Marxists suggest that by inducing a "false consciousness" among the disadvantaged, religion lessens the possibility of collective political action that could end capitalist oppression and transform society.

Feminist Perspective

Drawing on the feminist approach, researchers and theorists have stressed the fundamental role women play in religious socialization. Most people develop their allegiance to a particular faith in their childhood, with their mothers playing a critical role in the process. Significantly, nonworshipping mothers tend to influence their children to be highly skeptical of organized religion.

However, women generally take a subordinate role in religious governance. Indeed, most faiths have a long tradition of exclusively male spiritual leadership. Furthermore, because most religions are patriarchal, they tend to reinforce men's dominance in secular as well as spiritual matters. Women do play a vital role as volunteers, staff, and religious educators, but even today, religious decision making and leadership typically fall to the men. Exceptions to this rule, such as the Shakers and Christian Scientists, as well as Hinduism with its long goddess heritage, are rare (R. Schaefer and Zellner 2011).

In the United States, women are much more likely than men to be affiliated with religion, to pray, to believe in God, to claim that religion is important in their lives, and to attend weekly worship services. Yet organized religion typically does not give them leadership roles. Nationally, women compose 18 percent of U.S. clergy, though they account for 34 percent of students enrolled in theological institutions. Women clerics typically have shorter careers than men, often in related fields that do not involve congregational

A Protestant congregation worships at Sunday service. Although Weber traced the "spirit of capitalism" to Protestant teachings, in the United States today Protestants and Catholics share the same work ethic.

leadership, such as counseling. In faiths that restrict leadership positions to men, women serve unofficially. For example, about 4 percent of Roman Catholic congregations are led by women who hold nonordained pastoral positions—a necessity in a church facing a shortage of male priests (Association of Theological Schools 2011; Bureau of the Census 2011a:Table 616 on page 393).

Table 45-1 summarizes the four major sociological perspectives on religion.

Table 45-1 Sociological Perspectives on Religion

Tracking Sociological Perspectives

Theoretical Perspective	Emphasis
Functionalist	Religion as a source of social integration and unification
	Religion as a source of social support for individuals
Conflict	Religion as a potential obstacle to structural social change
	Religion as a potential source of structural social change (through liberation theology)
Feminist	Religion as an instrument of women's subordination, except for their role in religious socialization
Interactionist	Individual religious expression through belief, ritual, and experience

MODULE 45 | Recap and Review

Summary

Religion is a cultural universal found throughout the world in various forms.

1. Émile Durkheim stressed the social impact of religion in attempting to understand individual religious behavior within the context of the larger society.

FIGURE 46-1 **Test Your Religious Knowledge**

Compare your knowledge of religion with that of the U.S. population as a whole. In a 2010 national survey, the average respondent answered seven or eight questions correctly.

Religious Knowledge Quiz

1 Which Bible figure is most closely associated with leading the exodus from Egypt?

- ○ Job
- ○ Elijah
- ○ Moses
- ○ Abraham

2 What was Mother Teresa's religion?

- ○ Catholic
- ○ Jewish
- ○ Buddhist
- ○ Mormon
- ○ Hindu

3 Which of the following is NOT one of the Ten Commandments?

- ○ Do not commit adultery
- ○ Do unto others as you would have them do unto you
- ○ Do not steal
- ○ Keep the Sabbath holy

4 When does the Jewish Sabbath begin?

- ○ Friday
- ○ Saturday
- ○ Sunday

5 Is Ramadan . . . ?

- ○ The Hindu festival of lights
- ○ A Jewish day of atonement
- ○ The Islamic holy month

6 Which of the following best describes the Catholic teaching about the bread and wine used for Communion?

- ○ The bread and wine actually <u>become</u> the body and blood of Jesus Christ.
- ○ The bread and wine are <u>symbols</u> of the body and blood of Jesus Christ.

7 In which religion are Vishnu and Shiva central figures?

- ○ Islam
- ○ Hinduism
- ○ Taoism

8 Which Bible figure is most closely associated with remaining obedient to God despite suffering?

- ○ Job
- ○ Elijah
- ○ Moses
- ○ Abraham

9 What was Joseph Smith's religion?

- ○ Catholic
- ○ Jewish
- ○ Buddhist
- ○ Mormon
- ○ Hindu

10 According to rulings by the U.S. Supreme Court, is a public school teacher permitted to lead a class in prayer, or not?

- ○ Yes, permitted
- ○ No, not permitted

11 According to rulings by the U.S. Supreme Court, is a public school teacher permitted to read from the Bible as an example of literature, or not?

- ○ Yes, permitted
- ○ No, not permitted

12 What religion do <u>most</u> people in Pakistan consider themselves?

- ○ Buddhist
- ○ Hindu
- ○ Muslim
- ○ Christian

13 What was the name of the person whose writings and actions inspired the Protestant Reformation?

- ○ Martin Luther
- ○ Thomas Aquinas
- ○ John Wesley

14 Which of these religions aims at nirvana, the state of being free from suffering?

- ○ Islam
- ○ Buddhism
- ○ Hinduism

15 Which of these preachers participated in the period of religious activity known as the First Great Awakening?

- ○ Jonathan Edwards
- ○ Charles Finney
- ○ Billy Graham

ANSWERS: 1. Moses 2. Catholic 3. Do unto others as you would have them do unto you 4. Friday 5. The Islamic holy month 6. The bread and wine actually become the body and blood of Jesus Christ 7. Hinduism 8. Job 9. Mormon 10. No, not permitted 11. Yes, permitted 12. Muslim 13. Martin Luther 14. Buddhism 15. Jonathan Edwards

Sources: Pew Forum on Religion and Public Life 2010a, 2010b.

Fundamentalists vary immensely in their behavior. Some stress the need to be strict in their own personal faith but take little interest in broad social issues. Others are watchful of societal actions, such as government policies, that they see as conflicting with fundamentalist doctrine.

The Adam and Eve account of creation found in Genesis, the first book of the Old Testament, is an example of a religious belief. Many people in the United States strongly adhere to this biblical explanation of creation and even insist that it be taught in public schools. These people, known as *creationists,* are worried by the secularization of society, and oppose teaching that directly or indirectly questions biblical scripture.

In general, spirituality is not as strong in industrialized nations as in developing nations. The United States is an exception to the trend toward secularization, in part because the government encourages religious expression (without explicitly supporting it) by allowing religious groups to claim charitable status, and even to receive federal aid for activities such as educational services. And although belief in God is relatively weak in formerly communist states such as Russia, surveys show a growth in spirituality in those countries over the past 10 years (Norris and Inglehart 2004).

Ritual

Religious rituals are practices required or expected of members of a faith. Rituals usually honor the divine power (or powers) worshipped by believers; they also remind adherents of their religious duties and responsibilities. Rituals and beliefs can be interdependent; rituals generally affirm beliefs, as in a public or private statement confessing a sin. Like any social institution, religion develops distinctive norms to structure people's behavior. Moreover, sanctions are attached to religious rituals, whether rewards (bar mitzvah gifts) or penalties (expulsion from a religious institution for violation of norms).

In the United States, rituals may be quite simple, such as saying grace at a meal or observing a moment of silence to commemorate someone's death. Yet certain rituals, such as the process of canonizing a saint, are quite elaborate. Most religious rituals in our culture focus on services conducted at houses of worship. Attendance at a service, silent and spoken prayers, communion, and singing of spiritual hymns and chants are common forms of ritual behavior that generally take place in group settings. From an interactionist perspective, these rituals serve as important face-to-face encounters in which people reinforce their religious beliefs and their commitment to their faith.

For Muslims, a very important ritual is the *hajj,* a pilgrimage to the Grand Mosque in Mecca, Saudi Arabia. Every Muslim who is physically and financially able is expected to make this trip at least once. Each year 3 million pilgrims go to Mecca during the one-week period indicated by the Islamic lunar calendar. Muslims from all over the world make the *hajj,* including those in the United States, where many tours are arranged to facilitate the trip.

In recent decades, participation in religious rituals has tended to hold steady or decline in most countries. Figure 46-2 shows religious participation in selected countries.

Experience

In the sociological study of religion, the term **religious experience** refers to the feeling or perception of being in direct contact with the ultimate reality, such as a divine being, or of being overcome with religious emotion. A religious experience may be rather slight, such as the feeling of exaltation a person receives from hearing a choir sing Handel's "Hallelujah Chorus." But many religious experiences are more profound, such as a Muslim's experience on a *hajj.* In his autobiography, the late African American activist Malcolm X ([1964] 1999:338) wrote of his *hajj* and how deeply moved he was by the way that Muslims in Mecca came together across race and color lines. For Malcolm X, the color blindness of the Muslim world "proved to me the power of the One God."

Another profound religious experience, for many Christians, is being *born again*—that is, at a turning point in one's life, making a personal commitment to Jesus. According to a 2010 national

FIGURE 46-2 **Religious Participation in Selected Countries**

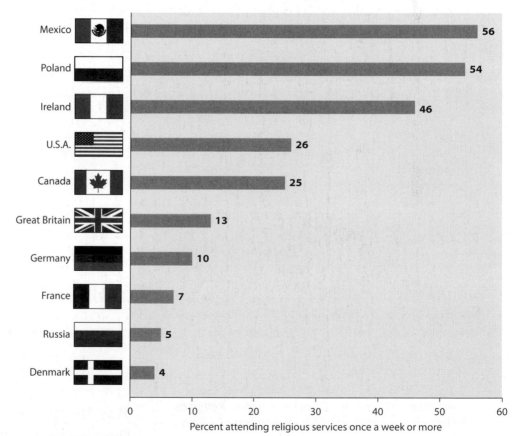

Percent attending religious services once a week or more

Note: Data are for 2006, except for Canada and Mexico, which are for 2004.
Source: Tom W. Smith 2009:28, 60, 72.

Think about It

Are you surprised by the variation in religious participation from one nation to another? Why or why not?

Pilgrims on *hajj* to the Grand Mosque in Mecca, Saudi Arabia. Islam requires all Muslims who are able to undertake this religious ritual at least once in a lifetime.

survey, 42 percent of people in the United States claim they have had a born-again Christian experience at some time in their lives. An earlier survey found that Southern Baptists (75 percent) were the most likely to report such experiences; in contrast, only 21 percent of Catholics and 24 percent of Episcopalians stated that they had been born again. The collective nature of religion, as emphasized by Durkheim, is evident in these statistics. The beliefs and rituals of a particular faith can create an atmosphere either friendly or indifferent to this type of religious experience. Thus, a Baptist would be encouraged to come forward and share such experiences with others, whereas an Episcopalian who claims to have been born again would receive much less interest (Gallup 2011a; Gallup Opinion Index 1978).

Table 46-2 summarizes the three components of religion.

Table **46-2**   Components of Religion

summing**up**

Element	Definition	Examples
Belief	Statement to which members of a particular religion adhere	Creation account Sacred characters or people
Ritual	Practice required or expected of members of a faith	Worship Prayer Singing or chanting
Experience	Feeling or perception of being in direct contact with the ultimate reality (such as a divine being) or of being overcome with religious emotion	Born-again experience Communion with holy spirit

MODULE 46 | Recap and Review

Summary

Tremendous diversity exists in religious beliefs and practices, although all religions share basic components.

1. Eighty-five percent of the world's population adheres to some form of religion.

2. Religious behavior is expressed through three major components: beliefs, rituals, and experience. **Religious beliefs** are statements to which all members of a faith adhere.

3. **Religious rituals** vary from the very simple to the highly complex.

4. **Religious experience,** or the feeling that one is having a direct encounter with the divine, is part of all major religions.

Thinking Critically

1. Which component of religion is easiest to measure? Which is hardest to measure? Explain.

2. What rituals—either religious or nonreligious—do you perform? Why do you perform them?

Key Terms

Fundamentalism   385

Religious belief   385

Religious experience   387

Religious ritual   387

The collective nature of religion has led to many forms of religious association. In modern societies, religion has become increasingly formalized. Specific structures such as churches and synagogues have been constructed for religious worship; individuals have been trained for occupational roles within various fields. These developments make it possible to distinguish clearly between the sacred and secular parts of one's life—a distinction that could not be made easily in earlier times, when religion was largely a family activity carried out in the home.

Four Basic Forms of Organization

Sociologists find it useful to distinguish between four basic forms of organization: the ecclesia, the denomination, the sect, and the new religious movement, or cult. We can see differences among these four forms of organization in their size, power, degree of commitment that is expected from members, and historical ties to other faiths.

Ecclesiae

An **ecclesia** (plural, *ecclesiae*) is a religious organization that claims to include most or all members of a society and is recognized as the national or official religion. Since virtually everyone belongs to the faith, membership is by birth rather than conscious decision. Examples of ecclesiae include Islam in Saudi Arabia and Buddhism in Thailand. However, significant differences exist within this category. In Saudi Arabia's Islamic regime, leaders of the ecclesia hold vast power over actions of the state. In contrast, the Lutheran Church in contemporary Sweden holds no such power over the Riksdag (parliament) or the prime minister.

Generally, ecclesiae are conservative, in that they do not challenge the leaders of a secular government. In a society with an ecclesia, the political and religious institutions often act in harmony and reinforce each other's power in their relative spheres of influence. In the modern world, ecclesiae are declining in power.

Denominations

A **denomination** is a large, organized religion that is not officially linked to the state or government. Like an ecclesia, it tends to have an explicit set of beliefs, a defined system of authority, and a generally respected position in society. Denominations claim as members large segments of a population. Generally, children accept the denomination of their parents and give little thought to membership in other faiths. Denominations also resemble ecclesiae in that they make few demands on members. However, there is a critical difference between these two forms of religious organization. Although the denomination is considered respectable and is not viewed as a challenge to the secular government, it lacks the official recognition and power held by an ecclesia (Doress and Porter 1977).

The United States is home to a large number of denominations. In good measure, this diversity is a result of our nation's immigrant heritage. Many settlers brought with them the religious commitments native to their homelands. Some Christian denominations in the United States, such as the Roman Catholics, Episcopalians, and Lutherans, are the outgrowth of ecclesiae established in Europe. New Christian denominations also emerged, including the Mormons and Christian Scientists. Within the past generation, immigrants have increased the number of Muslims, Hindus, and Buddhists living in the United States.

Although by far the largest denomination in the United States is Roman Catholicism, at least 24 other Christian faiths have 1 million or more members. Protestants collectively accounted for about 45 percent of the nation's adult population in 2010,

trend spotting

None of the Above: The Nonreligious

Many people noted and were dismayed by a statement in President Obama's 2009 inaugural address, "We are a nation of Christians and Muslims, Jews and Hindus, and nonbelievers." Yet the President was merely acknowledging a long-noted pattern, the gradual growth in the proportion of U.S. residents who indicate they have no religion.

National surveys reveal that between 1990 and 2008, the number of Americans who identify themselves as having no religion doubled. Moreover, the proportion of people who give no answer to questions about religion suggests that currently, about 20 percent of the adult population—well over 60 million people—has no overt religious identity.

The growth of the "none of the above" category does not mean that those respondents do not believe in God, however. A third of them say that they pray weekly or daily, and fewer than 1 percent call themselves atheists. Nevertheless, while the phrase "In God We Trust" still seems to apply, more and more people are choosing not to affiliate themselves with organized religion.

compared to 21 percent for Roman Catholics and 2 percent for Jews. There are also 5 million Muslims in the United States, and large numbers of people adhere to Eastern faiths such as Buddhism (3 million) and Hinduism (1 million) (Britannica Online 2011; Gallup 2011a; Lindner 2012).

Sects

A **sect** can be defined as a relatively small religious group that has broken away from some other religious organization to renew what it considers the original vision of the faith. Many sects, such as that led by Martin Luther during the Reformation, claim to be the "true church," because they seek to cleanse the established faith of what they regard as extraneous beliefs and rituals (Stark and Bainbridge 1985). Max Weber ([1916] 1958:114) termed the sect a "believer's church," because affiliation is based on conscious acceptance of a specific religious dogma.

Sects are fundamentally at odds with society and do not seek to become established national religions. Unlike ecclesiae and denominations, they require intensive commitments and demonstrations of belief by members. Partly owing to their outsider status, sects frequently exhibit a higher degree of religious fervor and loyalty than more established religious groups. Recruitment focuses mainly on adults, and acceptance comes through conversion.

Sects are often short-lived. Those that survive may become less antagonistic to society over time and begin to resemble denominations. In a few instances, sects have endured over several generations while remaining fairly separate from society. Sociologist J. Milton Yinger (1970:226–273) uses the term **established sect** to describe a religious group that is the outgrowth of a sect, yet remains isolated from society. Hutterites, Jehovah's Witnesses, Seventh-Day Adventists, and Amish are contemporary examples of established sects in the United States.

 use your **sociological imagination**

Choose a religious tradition other than your own. How would your religious beliefs, rituals, and experience differ if you had been raised in that tradition?

New Religious Movements or Cults

In 1997, 38 members of the Heaven's Gate cult were found dead in Southern California after a mass suicide timed to occur with the appearance of the Hale-Bopp comet. They believed the comet hid a spaceship on which they could catch a ride once they had broken free of their "bodily containers."

Partly as a result of the notoriety generated by such groups, the popular media have stigmatized the word *cult*, associating it with the occult and the use of intense and forceful conversion techniques. The stereotyping of cults as uniformly bizarre and unethical has led sociologists to abandon the term and refer instead to a *new religious movement (NRM)*. While some NRMs exhibit strange behavior, many do not. They attract new members just like any other religion, and often follow teachings similar to those of established Christian denominations, though with less ritual.

Sects are difficult to distinguish from cults. A **new religious movement (NRM)** or **cult** is generally a small, secretive religious group that represents either a new religion or a major innovation of an existing faith. NRMs are similar to sects in that they tend to be small and are often viewed as less respectable than more established faiths. Unlike sects, however, NRMs normally do not result from schisms or breaks with established ecclesiae or denominations. Some cults, such as those focused on UFO sightings, may be totally unrelated to existing faiths. Even when a cult does accept certain fundamental tenets of a dominant faith—such as a belief in Jesus as divine or in Mohammad as a messenger of God—it will offer new revelations or insights to justify its claim to being a more advanced religion (Stark and Bainbridge 1979, 1985).

Like sects, NRMs may be transformed over time into other types of religious organization. An example is the Christian Science Church, which began as a new religious movement under the leadership of Mary Baker Eddy. Today, this church exhibits the characteristics of a denomination. In fact, most major religions, including Christianity, began as cults. NRMs may be in the early stages of developing into a denomination or new religion, or they may just as easily fade away through the loss of members or weak leadership (R. Schaefer and Zellner 2011).

Comparing Forms of Religious Organization

How can we determine whether a particular religious group falls into the sociological category of ecclesia, denomination, sect, or NRM? As we have seen, these types of religious organization have somewhat different relationships to society. Ecclesiae are recognized as national churches; denominations, although not officially approved by the state, are generally widely respected. In contrast, sects and NRMs are much more likely to be at odds with the larger culture.

Still, ecclesiae, denominations, and sects are best viewed as types along a continuum rather than as mutually exclusive categories. Table 47-1 summarizes some of the primary characteristics of the ideal types. Since the United States has no ecclesiae, sociologists studying this country's religions have focused on the denomination and the sect. These religious forms have been pictured on either end of a continuum, with denominations accommodating to the secular world and sects protesting against established religions. Although NRMs also are included in the table, they lie outside the continuum, because they generally define themselves in terms of a new view of life rather than in terms of existing religious faiths. In fact, one of the most controversial NRMs, Wicca, may not fully qualify as a religion (Box 47-1).

Sociologists look at religion from an organizational perspective, which tends to stress the stability of religious adherence, but there are other ways to view religion. From an individual perspective, religion and spirituality are remarkably fluid. People often change their places of worship or move from one denomination to another. In many countries, including the United States, churches, temples, and mosques operate in a highly competitive market (Pew Forum on Religion and Public Life 2008; Wolfe 2008).

Characteristic	Ecclesia	Denomination	Sect	New Religious Movement (or Cult)
Size	Very large	Large	Small	Small
Wealth	Extensive	Extensive	Limited	Variable
Religious services	Formal, little participation	Formal, little participation	Informal, emotional	Variable
Doctrines	Specific, but interpretation may be tolerated	Specific, but interpretation may be tolerated	Specific, purity of doctrine emphasized	Innovative, pathbreaking
Clergy	Well-trained, full-time	Well-trained, full-time	Trained to some degree	Unspecialized
Membership	By virtue of being a member of society	By acceptance of doctrine	By acceptance of doctrine	By an emotional commitment
Relationship to the state	Recognized, closely aligned	Tolerated	Not encouraged	Ignored or challenged

Source: Adapted from Vernon 1962; see also Chalfant et al. 1994.

Research Today

BOX 47-1

Wicca: Religion or Quasi-Religion?

"I'm not a Witch," Christine O'Donnell famously declared in her 2010 campaign for the U.S. Senate. Eleven years earlier, she admitted, she had dabbled in Witchcraft. To most voters, the idea was beyond the pale. Yet today, thousands of people, both men and women, do view themselves as Witches; they practice a little-known religion called Wicca (which should not be confused with Satanism—there is no place in the Craft for devil worship).

Wicca (Anglo-Saxon for *witch* and *wizard*) is a modern form of Witchcraft, practiced for the last hundred years. The Englishman Gerald Gardner, born in 1884, drew on past rituals to found the Craft. Gardner stressed the importance of worshipping *skyclad,* or "clothed by the sky"—that is, naked. Being skyclad, he believed, helped a person to gain insight.

Not all Wiccans follow in Gardner's tradition. Today, Wiccan ritual takes on a dizzying variety of forms, ranging from the elementary to the highly detailed and sophisticated. A Wiccan circle or meeting can include a single heartfelt prayer or a highly complex and time-consuming ritual. Like members of more accepted religions, Wiccans observe several rituals associated with the life cycle. Parents name their children at a *Wiccaning,* which includes a dedication to the Goddess and the God. Contemporary Wiccans also celebrate a wedding-like ceremony called a *handfasting,* which is typically performed by a High Priest and/or Priestess.

Just as Wiccans' worship varies, so does their organization. Some Witches practice alone, as a *solitaire;* others practice in a group

of similarly minded Witches, called a *coven.* A coven may include just three or four Witches, male and/or female, or as many as thirty; members tend to come and go just as they do in a church or temple. In a mixed coven, the assembly is often governed by a High Priest or Priestess, or by both.

Revealing one's membership in any extraordinary group is always difficult, but perhaps especially so for Wiccans, who refer to the experience as "coming out of the broom closet." Many Wiccans are young, and so must

> *Some Witches practice alone, as a* solitaire; *others practice in a group of similarly minded Witches, called a* coven.

come out to their parents. Parental reactions range from cutting off contact with the Witch to wanting to learn more about the Craft. Many parents treat the religion as a "phase" in their child's spiritual journey.

Most scholars treat Wicca as a **quasi-religion,** a category that includes organizations that may see themselves as religious, but are seen by others as "sort of religious." National surveys that allow respondents to self-identify showed 8,000 Wiccans in 1990; 134,000 in 2001; and 342,000 in 2008, the latest year for which reliable national data are available. These estimates suggest either an

increase in willingness to identify as Wiccan or an absolute growth in the faithful—probably both.

LET'S DISCUSS

1. Do you know anyone who practices Wicca? If so, describe the person's practices.
2. Do you think that Wicca should be considered a religion? Why or why not?

Sources: Chase 2010; M. Howard 2009; Kosmin and Keysar 2009; Rabikovitch and Lewis 2004; R. Schaefer and Zellner 2011:347–377.

From a sociological point of view, the nation of India is large and complex enough that it might be considered a world of its own. Four hundred languages are spoken in India, 16 of which are officially recognized by the government. Besides the two major religions that originated there—Hinduism and Buddhism—several other faiths animate this society. Demographically the nation is huge, with over a billion residents. This teeming country is expected to overtake China as the most populous nation in the world in about three decades (Third World Institute 2007).

The Religious Tapestry in India

Hinduism and Islam, the two most important religions in India, were described in Module 46. Islam arrived in India in A.D. 1000, with the first of many Muslim invasions. It flowered there during the Mogul empire (1526–1857), the period when the Taj Mahal was built. Today, Muslims account for 12 percent of India's population; Hindus make up 83 percent.

The presence of one dominant faith influences how a society views a variety of issues, even secular ones. For example, India has emerged as a leader in biotechnology, due at least partly to the Hindu faith's tolerance of stem cell research and cloning—techniques that have been questioned in nations where Christianity dominates. Hinduism is open to the latest biomedical techniques, as long as no evil is intended. The only legal prohibition is that fetuses cannot be terminated for the purpose of providing stem cells. Because of its respect for life in all forms, Hinduism has no major conflict with engineered life-forms of any kind, such as clones (Religion Watch 2006; Sengupta 2006).

Another religion, the Sikh faith, originated in the 15th century with a Hindu named Nanak, the first of a series of gurus (prophets). Sikhism shows the influence of Islam in India, in that it is monotheistic (based on a belief in one god rather than many). It resembles Buddhism in its emphasis on meditation and spiritual transcendence of the everyday world. *Sikhs* (learners) pursue their goal of spiritual enlightenment through meditation with the help of a guru.

Sikh men have a characteristic mode of dress, which in the United States often causes them to be mistaken—and discriminated against—as Muslims. They are highly patriotic. Although the 20 million Sikhs in India make up just 2 percent of the country's population, they account for 25 percent of India's army. In 2004 Manmohan Singh, a Sikh, became Prime Minister of India—an event that is almost comparable to a Black man becoming President of the United States. He is now serving his second term (Fausset 2003; Watson 2005).

Another group that forms a small segment of the faithful, Christians, plays a disproportionate role in the country's social safety net. Christian schools, hospitals, and other social service organizations serve non-Christians as well as Christians. Interestingly, hundreds of priests who were trained at churches in India have since immigrated to the United States to ease the shortage of priests there. Together with Jains and Buddhists, Christians make up 3 percent of India's population (Embree 2003; Goodstein 2008).

Religion and the State in India

Religion was influential in India's drive to overturn British colonialism. The great Mohandas K. Gandhi (1869–1948) led the long struggle to regain India's sovereignty, which culminated in its independence in 1947. A proponent of nonviolent resistance, Gandhi persuaded Hindus and Muslims, ancient enemies, to join in defying British domination. But his influence as a peacemaker could not override the Muslims' demand for a separate state of their own. Immediately after independence was granted, India was partitioned into two states, Pakistan for the Muslims and India for the Hindus. The new arrangement caused large-scale migrations of Indians, especially Muslims, from one nation to the other, and

Adherents of the Hindu religion participate in fire worship at a celebration in Kerala, India. The Hindu faith is enormously influential in India, the country where most Hindus live.

sparked boundary disputes that continue to this day. In many areas, Muslims were forced to abandon places they considered sacred. In the chaotic months that followed, centuries of animosity between the two groups boiled over into riots, ending in Gandhi's assassination in January 1948.

Today, India is a secular state that is dominated by Hindus. Though the government is officially tolerant of the Muslim minority, tensions between Hindus and Muslims remain high in some states. Conflict also exists among various Hindu groups, from fundamentalists to more secular and ecumenical adherents (Embree 2003).

Many observers see religion as the moving force in Indian society. As in so many other parts of the world, religion is being redefined in India. To the dismay of Sikh spiritual leaders, increasing numbers of young Sikh men are trimming their long hair and abandoning the traditional turban. To show that the 300-year-old tradition is still cool in the 21st century, Sikh leaders now offer a CD-ROM called "Smart Turban 1.0" (Gentleman 2007).

One sign of this fluidity is the rapid rise of still another form of religious organization, the electronic church. Facilitated by cable television and satellite transmission, *televangelists* (as they are called) direct their messages to more people—especially in the United States—than are served by all but the largest denominations. While some televangelists are affiliated with religious denominations, most give viewers the impression that they are dissociated from established faiths.

At the close of the 1990s, the electronic church began to take on another dimension: the Internet. Today, rather than going to a service in person, many people shop online for a church or faith. Surfers can go to GodTube.com, a video-sharing and social-networking website, for spiritually oriented content. Even the Second Life virtual world (described in Chapter 5) has a rich spiritual landscape, with functioning congregations of Buddhist, Jewish, Muslim, and Christian avatars (Kiper 2008; MacDonald 2007; Simon 2007).

social policy and Religion | Religion in the Schools

Should public schools be allowed to sponsor organized prayer in the classroom? How about Bible reading, or just a collective moment of silence? Can athletes at public schools offer up a group prayer in a team huddle? Should students be able to initiate voluntary prayers at school events? Each of these situations has been an object of great dissension among those who see a role for prayer in the schools and those who want to maintain strict separation of church and state.

Another controversy concerns the teaching of theories about the origin of humans and the universe. Mainstream scientific thinking holds that humans evolved over billions of years from one-celled organisms, and that the universe came into being 15 billion years ago as a result of a huge cosmic explosion (the big bang theory). These theories are challenged by people who hold to the biblical account of the creation of humans and the universe some 10,000 years ago—a viewpoint known as **creationism.** Creationists, many of whom are Christian fundamentalists, want their belief taught in the schools as the only one—or at the very least, as an alternative to the theory of evolution.

—*Continued*

Looking at the Issue

The issues just described go to the heart of the First Amendment's provisions regarding religious freedom. On the one hand, the government must protect the right to practice one's religion; on the other, it cannot take any measures that would seem to establish one religion over another (separation of church and state).

In the key case of *Engle v. Vitale*, the Supreme Court ruled in 1962 that the use of nondenominational prayer in New York schools was "wholly inconsistent" with the First Amendment's prohibition against government establishment of religion. In finding that organized school prayer violated the Constitution—even when no student was required to participate—the Court argued, in effect, that promoting religious observance was not a legitimate function of government or education. Subsequent Court decisions have allowed *voluntary* school prayer by students, but forbid school officials to *sponsor* any prayer or religious observance at school events. Despite these rulings, many public schools still regularly lead their students in prayer recitations or Bible readings. Other states have enacted "moments of silence" during the public school day, which many see as prayer in disguise (Robelon 2007).

As with school prayer, the teaching of creationism has significant support among the general public. Unlike Europeans, many people in the United States seem highly skeptical of evolutionary theory, which is taught as a matter of course in science classes. In 2009, a national survey showed that 39 percent of adults believe that God created humans in their present form. Almost as many believe that humans developed their present form with divine guidance (Gallup 2009a; Newport 2009).

The controversy over whether the biblical account of creation should be presented in school curricula recalls the famous "monkey trial" of 1925. In that trial, high school biology teacher John T. Scopes was convicted of violating a Tennessee law making it a crime to teach the scientific theory of evolution in public schools. Today, creationists have gone beyond espousing fundamentalist religious doctrine; they are attempting to reinforce their position regarding the origins of humanity and the universe with quasi-scientific data.

In 1987, the Supreme Court ruled that states could not compel the teaching of creationism in public schools if the primary purpose was to promote a religious viewpoint. In response, those who believe in the divine origin of life have recently advanced a concept called **intelligent design (ID),** the idea that life is so complex that it could only have been created by intelligent design. Though this concept is not based explicitly on the biblical account of creation, fundamentalists feel comfortable with it. Supporters of intelligent design

People on both sides of the debate between science and creationism invoke the name of Albert Einstein. Evolutionists emphasize the need for verifiable scientific data, like that which confirmed Einstein's groundbreaking scientific theories. Advocates of intelligent design quote the Nobel Prize–winning physicist's assertion that religion and science should coexist.

consider it a more accurate account of the origin of life than Darwinism and hold that at the very least, ID should be taught as an alternative to the theory of evolution. But in 2005, in *Kitzmiller v. Dove Area School District,* a federal judge ended a Pennsylvania school district's plans to require teachers to present the concept in class. In essence, the judge found ID to be "a religious belief," a subtler but similar approach to creationism in that both find God's fingerprints in nature. The issue continues to be hotly debated and is expected to be the subject of future court cases (Clemmitt 2005; W. Tierney and Holley 2008).

Applying Sociology

Supporters of school prayer and of creationism feel that strict Court rulings have forced too great a separation between what Émile Durkheim called the *sacred* and the *profane*. They insist that the use of nondenominational prayer can in no way lead to the establishment of an ecclesia in the United States. Moreover, they believe that school prayer—and the teaching of creationism—can provide the spiritual guidance and socialization that many children today do not receive from parents or regular church attendance.

Many communities also believe that schools should transmit the dominant culture of the United States by encouraging prayer. Opponents of school prayer and creationism argue that a religious majority in a community might impose viewpoints specific to its faith at the expense of religious

—Continued

minorities. These critics question whether school prayer can remain truly voluntary. Drawing on the interactionist perspective and small-group research, they suggest that children will face enormous social pressure to conform to the beliefs and practices of the majority.

Initiating Policy

Public school education is fundamentally a local issue, so most initiatives and lobbying have taken place at the local or state level. Federal courts have taken a hard line on religion in the schools. In a decision that the Supreme Court reversed in 2004, a federal appeals court ruled that reciting the phrase "under God" during the Pledge of Allegiance that opens each school day violates the U.S. Constitution (Religion News Service 2003).

Religion–school debates show no sign of ending. The activism of religious fundamentalists in the public school system raises the question "Whose ideas and values deserve a hearing in classrooms?" Critics see this campaign as one step toward sectarian religious control of public education. They worry that at some point in the future, teachers may not be able to use books or make statements that conflict with fundamentalist interpretations of the Bible. For advocates of a liberal education and of intellectual (and religious) diversity, this is a genuinely frightening prospect (Wilgoren 2005).

TAKE THE ISSUE WITH YOU

1. Was there organized prayer in any school you attended? Was creationism part of the curriculum?

2. Do you think that promoting religious observance is a legitimate function of education?

3. How might a conflict theorist view the issue of organized school prayer?

MODULE 47 Recap and Review

Summary

Religious organizations grow and evolve over time and in reaction to social changes.

1. Four basic types of religious organizations are the **ecclesia,** the **denomination,** the **sect,** and the **new religious movement,** or **cult.**

2. Advances in communication have led to a new type of church organization, the electronic church. Televangelists now preach to more people than belong to many denominations, and every day millions of people use the Internet for religious purposes.

3. India is a secular state that is dominated by a religious majority, the Hindus. The creation of a separate nation, Pakistan, for the Muslim minority following India's independence in 1947 did not end the centuries-old strife between the two groups, which has worsened with political polarization.

4. Today, the question of how much religion, if any, should be permitted in the U.S. public schools is a matter of intense debate.

Thinking Critically

1. What do you think attracts people to new religious movements?

2. Aside from differences in religious affiliation, how does religious life in India differ from religious life in the United States?

Key Terms

Creationism   393

Denomination   389

Ecclesia   389

Established sect   390

Intelligent design   394

New religious movement (NRM) or **cult**   390

Quasi-religion   391

Sect   390

Mastering This Chapter

taking sociology with you

1 Make a list of the student subcultures on your campus, then describe them using the concepts you learned in Chapter 3. Do any of these subcultures serve as out-groups for other subcultures?

2 Find out how many different religious groups there are at your school or in your community. How many belong to mainstream denominations? How many are fundamentalist? Are there any sects or new religious movements?

3 If your school or community has an interfaith organization, attend a meeting. What issues are the members currently dealing with? What sociological concepts are relevant to those issues?

key terms

Creationism A literal interpretation of the Bible regarding the creation of humanity and the universe, used to argue that evolution should not be presented as established scientific fact. (page 393)

Denomination A large, organized religion that is not officially linked to the state or government. (389)

Ecclesia A religious organization that claims to include most or all members of a society and is recognized as the national or official religion. (389)

Established sect A religious group that is the outgrowth of a sect, yet remains isolated from society. (390)

Fundamentalism An emphasis on doctrinal conformity and the literal interpretation of sacred texts. (385)

Intelligent design (ID) The idea that life is so complex that it could only have been created by intelligent design. (394)

Liberation theology Use of a church, primarily Roman Catholic, in a political effort to eliminate poverty, discrimination, and other forms of injustice from a secular society. (382)

New religious movement (NRM) or **cult** A small, secretive religious group that represents either a new religion or a major innovation of an existing faith. (390)

Profane The ordinary and commonplace elements of life, as distinguished from the sacred. (379)

Protestant ethic Max Weber's term for the disciplined work ethic, this-worldly concerns, and rational orientation to life emphasized by John Calvin and his followers. (381)

Quasi-religion A scholarly category that includes organizations that may see themselves as religious but may be seen by others as "sort of religious." (391)

Religion A unified system of beliefs and practices relative to sacred things. (379)

Religious belief A statement to which members of a particular religion adhere. (385)

Religious experience The feeling or perception of being in direct contact with the ultimate reality, such as a divine being, or of being overcome with religious emotion. (387)

Religious ritual A practice required or expected of members of a faith. (387)

Sacred Elements beyond everyday life that inspire awe, respect, and even fear. (379)

Sect A relatively small religious group that has broken away from some other religious organization to renew what it considers the original vision of the faith. (390)

Secularization The process through which religion's influence on other social institutions diminishes. (379)

self-quiz

Read each question carefully and then select the best answer.

1. Which of the following sociologists stressed the social impact of religion and was perhaps the first to recognize the critical importance of religion in human societies?
   a. Max Weber
   b. Karl Marx
   c. Émile Durkheim
   d. Talcott Parsons

2. A Roman Catholic parish church offers services in the native language of an immigrant community. This is an example of
   a. the integrative function of religion.
   b. the social support function of religion.
   c. the social control function of religion.
   d. none of the above.

3. Sociologist Max Weber pointed out that the followers of John Calvin emphasized a disciplined work ethic, this-worldly concerns, and a rational orientation to life. Collectively, this point of view has been referred to as
   a. capitalism.
   b. the Protestant ethic.
   c. the sacred.
   d. the profane.

4. The use of a church, primarily Roman Catholic, in a political effort to eliminate poverty, discrimination, and other forms of injustice evident in a secular society is referred to as
   a. creationism.
   b. ritualism.
   c. religious experience.
   d. liberation theology.

5. Many people in the United States strongly adhere to the biblical explanation of the beginning of the universe. Adherents of this point of view are known as
   a. liberationists.
   b. creationists.
   c. ritualists.
   d. experimentalists.

6. The Adam and Eve account of creation found in Genesis, the first book of the Old Testament, is an example of a religious
   a. ritual.
   b. experience.

   c. custom.
   d. belief.

7. Which of the following is *not* an example of an ecclesia?
   a. the Lutheran church in Sweden
   b. Islam in Saudi Arabia
   c. Buddhism in Thailand
   d. the Episcopal church in the United States

8. Religion defines the spiritual world and gives meaning to the divine. These are _____ functions of religion.
   a. manifest
   b. latent
   c. positive
   d. negative

9. Which sociological perspective emphasizes the integrative power of religion in human society?
   a. functionalist perspective
   b. conflict perspective
   c. interactionist perspective
   d. all of the above

10. John Calvin, a leader of the Protestant Reformation, emphasized
    a. disciplined work ethic.
    b. this-worldly concerns.
    c. a rational orientation to life.
    d. all of the above.

11. The _____ encompasses elements beyond everyday life that inspire awe, respect, and even fear, as compared to the _____, which includes the ordinary and the commonplace.

12. Wicca is an example of a(n) _____.

13. _____ is the largest single faith in the world; the second largest is _____.

14. _____ _____ are statements to which members of a particular religion adhere.

15. A(n) _____ is a religious organization that claims to include most or all members of a society and is recognized as the national or official religion.

16. Because they are _____, most religions tend to reinforce men's dominance in secular as well as spiritual matters.

17. The single largest denomination in the United States is _____ _____.

18. The big bang theory is challenged by _____, who hold to the biblical account of creation of humans and the universe.

19. Unlike ecclesiae and denominations, _____ require intensive commitments and demonstrations of belief by members.

20. A possible dysfunction of _____ _____ would be the belief that when Roman Catholics focus on political and governmental injustice, the clergy are no longer addressing people's personal and spiritual needs.

thinking about movies

Monsieur Ibrahim

In this film, which draws comparisons between Islam and Judaism, a Muslim grocer befriends a Jewish boy.

Saved!

A young woman tries to find her own voice in a Christian high school.

Trembling Before G-D

This documentary explores the tension between religious belief and sexual orientation.

Have you ever wondered what the label "fair trade" means?

To John Bowes, fair trade means a fair shake for the farm workers who supply our groceries.

" It is rare in life to have a moment of personal epiphany. Mine came in the millennium year when, at the Co-op, we had just introduced the UK's first own brand Fairtrade product: a chocolate bar with its key ingredient sourced from Ghana. We had supported the concept of fair trade right from the beginning but, although always empathetic to the ethical agenda, my interest was primarily commercial; the intention was to develop responsible retailing, a holistic approach to this agenda, as a modern day reflection of cooperative values and a vehicle for differentiating the business from its competitors. But in concert with the chocolate initiative a BBC crew visited Kuapa Kokoo in Ghana and their 14-minute film changed my view of the world. At the end of their report they unwrapped a chocolate bar, which was starting to melt in the heat, and gave some to a young woman and her daughter. As they tasted the product their eyes lit up and their faces were transformed into bright smiles and the young woman said 'oh, it's so sweet, so sweet'. This lady had spent her whole life toiling in the fields for a pittance and had never tasted the product of her own labours; she had no concept of what it was about chocolate that made it so important and appealing to the people living thousands of miles away in the northern hemisphere. In one sense the film captured a joyous experience but in another it was extraordinarily sad. I felt a catch in my throat and knew I was hooked for the rest of my life.

. . .

It has been estimated that fair trade may, currently, be benefiting more than 7 million people in the developing world.

This is an impressive achievement but set in the context of the sheer scale of world poverty it still represents only a relatively small contribution towards addressing an enormous problem.

It is estimated that 1.4 billion people, one fifth of the world's population, are trying to survive at or below the World Bank's official poverty line of just $1.25 a day. And 2.6 billion people, about 40 per cent of humanity, are living on less than $2 a day.

These astonishing numbers are so large that it is difficult to fully comprehend them. They reflect the appalling collective failure of human society. And the scale of the failure becomes even more dramatic when we consider *disparities* in world income. The poorest 40 per cent account for just 5 per cent of global income whilst the richest 20 per cent take three quarters of the pot. The truth is that fair trade is still very much in its infancy. Those who are committed to making a real difference in the developing world will recognise that we are not at the end of a process, or anywhere near the end, but really only at the very beginning. If we strip away all of the commercial spin, and occasional wishful thinking, we might be left with the uncomfortable conclusion that, far from capitalising on a consumer movement, we have perhaps not yet recognised its full potential and have so far failed to put mechanisms into place to ensure that its momentum can be fully realised.

. . .

The United States of America is the largest consumer market on Earth. No other country on the planet could do more to address the climate problem and establish a fairer trading system. While fair trade has experienced strong growth in the States, which in absolute terms is the largest single market for fair trade products, overall market penetration is low. Yet, if we are to have a true revolution in trading practices it is difficult to see how it can be achieved without the US fully on board. This represents the greatest single challenge for fair trade campaigners. . . . "

(Bowes 2011:ix, 2–3, 231–232) Additional information about this excerpt can be found on the Online Learning Center at www.mhhe.com/schaefermod2e.

> *The United States of America is the largest consumer market on Earth. No other country on the planet could do more to address the climate problem and establish a fairer trading system.*

Bowes, editor of this excerpt from *The Fair Trade Revolution,* once served as a top executive in a British grocery chain. In the process, he became acutely aware of the low wages paid to those who harvest the food sold in grocery stores. To address their plight, he helped to originate a movement called *fair trade,* in which consumers in industrialized countries voluntarily pay above-market prices for certain foods so that the workers who plant, pick, and pack the crops can receive higher wages. Supporters of fair trade often seek to subsidize export crops grown in developing countries, such as coffee, bananas, and chocolate (A. Stark 2011).

While acknowledging Bowes's point of view, sociologists also try to see foreign agricultural laborers and farm owners from the perspective of their own cultures—an approach called cultural relativism (see Module 9). That is, besides comparing farm work in developing countries to similar work in industrial nations, sociologists would compare it to the other jobs available to foreign workers. For example, sweatshops certainly aren't the sort of places where people in industrial countries would want to work, but from the foreign worker's perspective, they may be preferable to a farm in an isolated rural area or a lower-paying job with a local employer. In sum, foreign workers and producers face a different *economic system* from the one in industrial nations, so their attitudes and the choices they make may differ from our own.

As with social institutions such as the family, religion, and government, the economic system shapes other aspects of the social order and is in turn influenced by them. Throughout this textbook, you have been reminded of the economy's impact on social behavior—for example, on individual and group behavior in factories and offices.

These modules will present a combined analysis of government and the economy. We begin with a general discussion of power and authority and specific descriptions of four major types of government in which that power and authority operates. We'll also touch briefly on war, peace, and terrorism. Next we'll see how politics works, and we'll look at two models of power in the United States. We'll then turn to a macro-level analysis of capitalism and socialism, followed by a case study of China's attempt to mix the two. We'll look at ways in which the U.S. economy is changing in response to globalization. Finally, in the Social Policy section, we'll explore the effects of a financial innovation called *microfinancing* on the lives of poor people in developing countries.

MODULE 48 — Government, Power, and Authority

Power and Authority

In any society, someone or some group—whether it be a tribal chief, a dictator, or a parliament—makes important decisions about how to use resources and how to allocate goods. One cultural universal, then, is the exercise of power and authority. Inevitably, the struggle for power and authority involves **politics,** which political scientist Harold Lasswell (1936) tersely defined as "who gets what, when, and how." In their study of politics and government, sociologists are concerned with social interactions among individuals and groups and their impact on the larger political and economic order.

The social institution that is responsible for implementing and achieving society's goals is the **political system.** Each country has a unique political system that is founded on a recognized set of procedures. The political system interacts closely with the **economic system,** the social institution through which goods and services are produced, distributed, and consumed. As we will see throughout the next four modules, the political and economic systems are inextricably intertwined, and together they regulate power and authority within society.

Power

Power lies at the heart of a political system. According to Max Weber, **power** is the ability to exercise one's will over others. To put it another way, whoever can overcome the resistance of others and control their behavior is exercising power. Power relations can involve large organizations, small groups, or even people in an intimate association.

Because Weber developed his conceptualization of power in the early 1900s, he focused primarily on the nation-state and its sphere of influence. Today scholars recognize that the trend toward globalization has brought new opportunities, and with them new concentrations of power. Power is now exercised on a global as well as a national stage, as countries and multinational corporations vie to control access to resources and manage the distribution of capital (R. Schaefer 2008b; Sernau 2001).

There are three basic sources of power within any political system: force, influence, and authority. **Force** is the actual or threatened use of coercion to impose one's will on others. When leaders imprison or even execute political dissidents, they are applying force; so, too, are terrorists when they seize or bomb an embassy or assassinate a political leader.

In the 21st century, force has taken on new meaning as nations clamp down on use of the Internet to oppose the central government or assert freedom of expression, human rights, and minority or religious views. When a military coup overthrew the democratically elected government of Thailand in September 2006, for example, citizens lost access to websites that criticized the takeover. Censorship of online content is just as much a use of force as closing down a newspaper or arresting dissidents (Deibert et al. 2008; Zittrain and Palfrey 2008).

Influence, on the other hand, refers to the exercise of power through a process of persuasion. A citizen may change his or her view of a Supreme Court nominee because of a newspaper editorial, the expert testimony of a law school dean before the Senate Judiciary Committee, or a stirring speech by a political activist at a rally. In each case, sociologists would view such efforts to persuade people as examples of influence. Now let's take a look at the third source of power, *authority*.

Types of Authority

The term **authority** refers to institutionalized power that is recognized by the people over whom it is exercised. Sociologists commonly use the term in connection with those who hold legitimate power through elected or publicly acknowledged positions. A person's authority is often limited. Thus, a referee has the authority to decide whether a penalty should be called during a football game, but has no authority over the price of tickets to the game.

Max Weber ([1913] 1947) developed a classification system for authority that has become one of the most useful and frequently cited contributions of early sociology. He identified three ideal types of authority: traditional, rational-legal, and charismatic. Weber did not insist that only one type applies to a given society or organization. All can be present, but their relative importance will vary. Sociologists have found Weber's typology valuable in understanding different manifestations of legitimate power within a society.

Traditional Authority
Until the middle of the past century, Japan was ruled by a revered emperor whose absolute power was passed down from generation to generation. In a political system based on **traditional authority,** legitimate power is conferred by custom and accepted practice. A king or queen is accepted as ruler of a nation simply by virtue of inheriting the crown; a tribal chief rules because that is the accepted practice. The ruler may be loved or hated, competent or destructive; in terms of legitimacy, that does not matter. For the traditional leader, authority rests in custom, not in personal characteristics, technical competence, or even written law. People accept the ruler's authority because that is how things have always been done. Traditional authority is absolute when the ruler has the ability to determine laws and policies.

Rational-Legal Authority
The U.S. Constitution gives Congress and our president the authority to make and enforce laws and policies. Power made legitimate by law is known as **rational-legal authority.** Leaders derive their rational-legal authority from the written rules and regulations of political systems, such as a constitution. Generally, in societies based on rational-legal authority, leaders are thought to have specific areas of competence and authority but are not thought to be endowed with divine inspiration, as in certain societies with traditional forms of authority.

Charismatic Authority
Joan of Arc was a simple peasant girl in medieval France, yet she was able to rally the French people and lead them into major battles against English invaders. How was this possible? As Weber observed, power can be legitimized by the *charisma* of an individual. The term **charismatic authority** refers to power made legitimate by a leader's exceptional personal or emotional appeal to his or her followers.

Charisma lets a person lead or inspire without relying on set rules or traditions. In fact, charismatic authority is derived more from the beliefs of followers than from the actual qualities of leaders. So long as people perceive a charismatic leader such as Jesus, Joan of Arc, Gandhi, Malcolm X, or Martin Luther King Jr. as having qualities that set him or her apart from ordinary citizens, that leader's authority will remain secure and often unquestioned.

Observing charismatic authority from an interactionist perspective, sociologist Carl Couch (1996) points out that the growth of the electronic media has facilitated the development of charismatic authority. During the 1930s and 1940s, the heads of state of the United States, Great Britain, and Germany all used radio to issue direct appeals to citizens. Now, television and the Internet allow leaders to "visit" people's homes and communicate with them. In both Taiwan and South Korea in 1996, troubled political leaders facing reelection campaigns spoke frequently to national audiences and exaggerated military threats from neighboring China and North Korea, respectively.

As we noted earlier, Weber used traditional, rational-legal, and charismatic authority as ideal types. In reality, particular leaders and political systems combine elements of two or more of these forms. Presidents Franklin D. Roosevelt, John F. Kennedy, and Ronald Reagan wielded power largely through the rational-legal basis of their authority. At the same time, they were unusually charismatic leaders who commanded the personal loyalty of large numbers of citizens.

Steve Jobs, visionary co–founder of Apple, was a charismatic figure not only to Apple employees but to Apple users. Max Weber would have agreed with Jobs's admirers; Weber considered any kind of leader with exceptional personal appeal to be charismatic.

Types of Government

Each society establishes a political system through which it is governed. In modern industrialized nations, these formal systems of government make a significant number of critical political decisions. We will survey five basic types of government here: monarchy, oligarchy, dictatorship, totalitarianism, and democracy.

Monarchy

A **monarchy** is a form of government headed by a single member of a royal family, usually a king, queen, or some other hereditary ruler. In earlier times, many monarchs claimed that God had granted them a divine right to rule. Typically, they governed on the basis of traditional forms of authority, sometimes accompanied by the use of force. By the beginning of the 21st century, however, monarchs held genuine governmental power in only a few nations, such as Monaco. Most monarchs now have little practical power; they serve primarily ceremonial purposes.

Oligarchy

An **oligarchy** is a form of government in which a few individuals rule. A rather old method of governing that flourished in ancient Greece and Egypt, oligarchy now often takes the form of military rule. In developing nations in Africa, Asia, and Latin America, small factions of military officers will forcibly seize power, either from legally elected regimes or from other military cliques.

Strictly speaking, the term *oligarchy* is reserved for governments that are run by a few selected individuals. However, the People's Republic of China can be classified as an oligarchy if we stretch the meaning of the term. In China, power rests in the hands of a large but exclusive ruling *group*, the Communist Party. In a similar vein, drawing on conflict theory, one might argue that many industrialized nations of the West should be considered oligarchies (rather than democracies), since only a powerful few—leaders of big business, government, and the military—actually rule. Later in this chapter, we will examine the *elite model* of the U.S. political system in greater detail.

Dictatorship and Totalitarianism

A **dictatorship** is a government in which one person has nearly total power to make and enforce laws. Dictators rule primarily through the use of coercion, which often includes torture and executions. Typically, they *seize* power rather than being freely elected (as in a democracy) or inheriting power (as in a monarchy). Some dictators are quite charismatic and manage to achieve a certain popularity, though their supporters' enthusiasm is almost certainly tinged with fear. Other dictators are bitterly hated by the people over whom they rule.

Frequently, dictators develop such overwhelming control over people's lives that their governments are called *totalitarian*. (Monarchies and oligarchies may also achieve this type of dominance.) **Totalitarianism** involves virtually complete government control and surveillance over all aspects of a society's social and political life. Germany during Hitler's reign, the Soviet Union in the 1930s, and North Korea today are classified as totalitarian states.

North Korea has a totalitarian government whose leadership attempts to control all aspects of people's lives. This old billboard, a blatant example of government propaganda, portrayed the country's ruthless leader as a benevolent father figure.

Democracy

In a literal sense, **democracy** means government by the people. The word *democracy* originated in two Greek roots—*demos,* meaning "the populace" or "the common people," and *kratia,* meaning "rule." Of course, in large, populous nations such as the United States, government by the people is impractical at the national level. Americans cannot vote on every important issue that comes before Congress. Consequently, popular rule is generally maintained through **representative democracy,** a form of government in which certain individuals are selected to speak for the people.

Democracy on the Rise?

The breakup of the Soviet Union in 1991 launched several new countries in Eastern Europe, whose citizens were eager to escape foreign domination. In parts of Europe and Asia, democracy seemed to bloom where it never had grown before. What has happened since then?

Applying our own standards of democracy to nations in other parts of the world can be difficult. If a country holds free elections that are open to all citizens, is that enough to qualify it as a democracy? What if the government bans certain political parties? What if the media cannot criticize the government or report on opposition parties?

Freedom House, founded in 1941, is an international organization that advocates for democracy. Although it receives significant funding from the U.S. government, its annual review of democratic trends is generally regarded as a reasonable barometer of the spread (or lack thereof) of democracy. According to Freedom House, in 1989, only 41 percent of the world's countries could be considered democracies. The percentage rose dramatically after the collapse of the Soviet Union, reaching 60 percent in 1995. Since then, however, little has changed; the number of new democracies has been offset by the number of democracies that were overthrown.

Although recently, citizen-led revolts in countries like Tunisia and Egypt have offered some optimism, the overall trend is not encouraging. The industrialized democracies of North America and Europe often shrink from pressuring developing countries to reform their governments. Furthermore, in some areas of the world, violence and organized crime make democratic reform difficult. On the other hand, although the recent worldwide recession might easily have unsettled some fragile democracies, that fortunately has not happened.

The United States is commonly classified as a representative democracy, since the elected members of Congress and state legislatures make our laws. However, critics have questioned whether our democracy really is representative. Even today, not everyone in the United States feels included. Conspicuous among those who view themselves as excluded are Native Hawaiians (Box 48-1).

Do Congress and the state legislatures genuinely represent the masses, including minorities? Are the people of the United States legitimately self-governing, or has our government become a forum for powerful elites? We will explore these issues in Module 49. First, however, we will turn to a central aspect of social relations: conflict.

● War and Peace

Conflict is a central aspect of social relations. Too often it becomes ongoing and violent, engulfing innocent bystanders as well as intentional participants. Sociologists Theodore Caplow and Louis Hicks (2002:3) have defined **war** as conflict between organizations that possess trained combat forces equipped with deadly weapons. This meaning is broader than the legal definition, which typically requires a formal declaration of hostilities.

War

Sociologists approach war in three different ways. Those who take a *global view* study how and why two or more nations become engaged in military conflict. Those who take a *nation-state view* stress the interaction of internal political, socioeconomic, and cultural forces. And those who take a *micro view* focus on the social impact of war on individuals and the groups they belong to (Kiser 1992).

From the nation-state perspective, there is little to be said for the supposed socioeconomic benefits of war. Although armed conflicts increase government expenditures on troops and weapons, which tends to stimulate the economy, they also divert workers from civilian health and medical services. Thus, they have a negative effect on civilians' life chances, causing higher levels of civilian mortality. It is exceedingly difficult for a society to engage in armed conflict while maintaining citizens' well-being at home (Carlton-Ford 2010).

Although the decision to go to war is made by government leaders, public opinion plays a significant role in its execution. By 1971, the number of U.S. soldiers killed in Vietnam had surpassed 50,000, and antiwar sentiment was strong. Surveys done at that time showed the public was split roughly equally on the question of whether war was an appropriate way to settle differences between nations (Figure 48-1). This division in public opinion continued until the United States became involved in the Gulf War following Iraq's invasion of Kuwait in 1990. Since then, U.S. sentiment has been more supportive of war as a means of resolving disputes.

A major change in the composition of the U.S. military is the growing presence of women. Over 206,000 women, or about 14 percent of active U.S. military forces, are now in uniform, serving not just as support personnel but as an integral part of combat units. The first casualty of the war in Iraq, in fact, was Private First Class Lori Piestewa, a member of the Hopi tribe and a descendant of Mexican settlers in the Southwest (Bureau of the Census 2011a:Table 510 on page 335).

From a micro view, war can bring out the worst as well as the best in people. In 2004, graphic images of the abuse of Iraqi prisoners by U.S. soldiers at Iraq's Abu Ghraib prison shocked the world. For social scientists, the deterioration of the guards' behavior brought to mind Philip Zimbardo's mock prison experiment, done in 1971. Although the results of the experiment, highlighted in Chapter 5, have been applied primarily to civilian correctional facilities, Zimbardo's study was actually funded by the Office of Naval Research. In July 2004, the U.S. military began using a documentary film about the experiment to train military interrogators to avoid mistreatment of prisoners (Zarembo 2004a; Zimbardo 2004).

Peace

Sociologists have considered **peace** both as the absence of war and as a proactive effort to develop cooperative relations among nations. While we will focus here on international relations, we should note that in the 1990s, 90 percent of the world's armed conflicts occurred *within* rather than between states.

BOX 48-1

Sovereignty in the Aloha State

The people of Hawai'i are definitely multiracial. Twenty-three percent of the population is White; 38 percent, Asian American; 9 percent, Hawaiian or other Pacific Islander; 9 percent, Hispanic; and 2 percent, African American. Another 19 percent of the population, including Hawai'i-born Barack Obama, declare themselves to be of two or more races. Yet Hawai'i is not a racial paradise: certain occupations and even social classes tend to be dominated by Whites, Chinese, or Japanese Americans. Nor is Hawai'i immune to intolerance, although compared to the mainland and much of the rest of the world, race relations there are more harmonious than discordant.

> *If the act passes, Native Hawaiians will become the last remaining indigenous group in the United States to be allowed to establish their own government.*

For one group in particular, Native Hawaiians, access to any kind of power has been severely limited for generations. Now, through the sovereignty movement, the indigenous people of Hawai'i are hoping to win self-government, as well as restoration of—or compensation for—1.2 million acres of ancestral lands they have lost over the last century. Their movement is comparable to efforts made by American Indian tribes in the continental United States, both in its roots and in its significance.

The sovereignty movement began in 1996, when Native Hawaiians held a referendum on the question "Shall the Hawaiian people elect delegates to propose a Native Hawaiian government?" The results indicated that 73 percent

of those who voted favored such an effort. Since then, the state Office of Hawaiian Affairs has sought to create a registry of the estimated 200,000 people of significant Hawaiian descent on the islands. Officials are about halfway to reaching their goal of convincing all Native Hawaiians to come forward and register.

In Washington, D.C., Hawai'i's congressional delegation is seeking passage of the Native Hawaiian Government Reorganization Act, also referred to as the Akaka Bill, after U.S. Senator Daniel Akaka. The act would give people of Hawaiian ancestry more say over the use of local resources, including land and fresh water; provide them with affordable housing; take steps to preserve their culture; and create ways for them to better express their grievances. If the act passes, Native Hawaiians will become the last remaining indigenous group in the United States to be allowed to establish their own government—a right already extended to Alaskan Natives and 564 Native American tribes. As of mid-2012, the measure had passed the U.S. House of Representatives, but had not yet been discussed on the floor of the Senate.

Meanwhile, Native Hawaiians do what they can to create political pressure for their cause. On occasion, they form alliances with environmental groups that want to halt commercial development on the islands. In 2008 and again in 2011, a Native Hawaiian independence group seized the royal palace in Honolulu to protest the U.S.-backed overthrow of the Hawaiian monarchy in 1893. Although these occupations lasted barely a day, the political discontent they revealed persists. Little

wonder that in 2009, the 50th anniversary of Hawai'i's statehood passed without a single government-sponsored celebration. Instead, Native Hawaiians concentrated their attention on Washington, D.C., and pushed for passage of the Akaka Bill.

LET'S DISCUSS

1. From a mainstream point of view, what might be the advantages and disadvantages of extending sovereignty to an indigenous group? Discuss using sociological concepts.

2. Do some research on the legal basis for tribal sovereignty. How did American Indian tribes gain the status of separate nations?

Sources: Halualani 2002; Kelleher 2011; Niesse 2008, 2011; Staton 2004; Toensing 2009; Welch 2011.

Often, outside powers became involved in these internal conflicts, either as supporters of particular factions or in an attempt to broker a peace accord. In at least 28 countries where such conflicts occurred—none of which would be considered core nations in world systems analysis—at least 10,000 people died (Kriesberg 1992; Dan Smith 1999).

Another way of picturing the relative peacefulness of nations around the world is the Global Peace Index (Figure 48-2). This index is based on 24 indicators, including organized internal conflict, violent crime, political instability, the potential for terrorist acts, and a nation's level of military expenditures compared to its neighbors'. Currently, Iceland and New Zealand are at the top

of the index (very peaceful); Sudan, Iraq, and Somalia are at the bottom (great civil unrest). The United States ranks 82 on this list of 153 nations, between Gabon and Bangladesh.

Sociologists and other social scientists who draw on sociological theory and research have tried to identify conditions that deter war. One of their findings is that international trade may act as a deterrent to armed conflict. As countries exchange goods, people, and then cultures, they become more integrated and less likely to threaten each other's security. Viewed from this perspective, not just trade but immigration and foreign exchange programs have a beneficial effect on international relations.

FIGURE 48-1 U.S. Public Opinion on the Necessity of War, 1971–2007

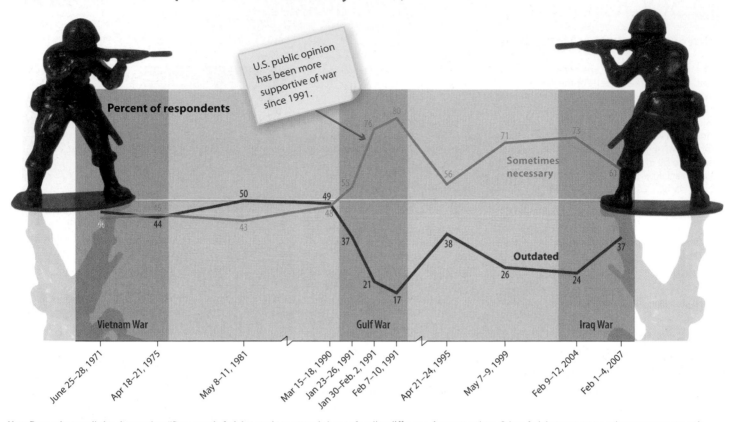

Percent of respondents

U.S. public opinion has been more supportive of war since 1991.

Sometimes necessary

Outdated

Vietnam War

Gulf War

Iraq War

June 25–28, 1971
Apr 18–21, 1975
May 8–11, 1981
Mar 15–18, 1990
Jan 23–26, 1991
Jan 30–Feb. 2, 1991
Feb 7–10, 1991
Apr 21–24, 1995
May 7–9, 1999
Feb 9–12, 2004
Feb 1–4, 2007

Note: Respondents replied to the question: "Some people feel that war is an outmoded way of settling differences between nations. Others feel that wars are sometimes necessary to settle differences. With which point of view do you agree?"
Source: Gallup 2009b.

Think about It

Do you think people today are less supportive or more supportive of war than they were in 2007? Why or why not? Would the survey responses have been different if people had been asked about the "war on terrorism" instead of "war"?

Another means of fostering peace is the activity of international charities and activist groups called nongovernmental organizations (NGOs). The Red Cross and Red Crescent, Doctors Without Borders, and Amnesty International donate their services wherever they are needed, without regard to nationality. In the past decade or more, these global organizations have been expanding in number, size, and scope. By sharing news of local conditions and clarifying local issues, they often prevent conflicts from escalating into violence and war. Some NGOs have initiated cease-fires, reached settlements, and even ended warfare between former adversaries.

Finally, many analysts stress that nations cannot maintain their security by threatening violence. Peace, they contend, can best be maintained by developing strong mutual security agreements between potential adversaries (Etzioni 1965; Shostak 2002).

In recent years, the United States has begun to recognize that its security can be threatened not just by nation-states, but by political groups that operate outside the bounds of legitimate authority. Indeed, terrorism is now considered the foremost threat to U.S. security—one the U.S. military is unaccustomed to fighting.

 use your **sociological imagination**

Do you hear much discussion of how to promote worldwide peace, or do the conversations you hear focus more on ending a particular conflict?

Terrorism

Acts of terror, whether perpetrated by a few or by many people, can be a powerful political force. Formally defined, **terrorism** is the use or threat of violence against random or symbolic targets in pursuit of political aims. For terrorists, the end justifies the means. They believe the status quo is oppressive and that desperate measures are essential to end the suffering of the deprived. Convinced that working through the formal political process will not effect the desired political change, terrorists insist that illegal actions—often directed against innocent people—are needed. Ultimately, they hope to intimidate society and thereby bring about a new political order.

FIGURE 48-2 **Global Peace Index**

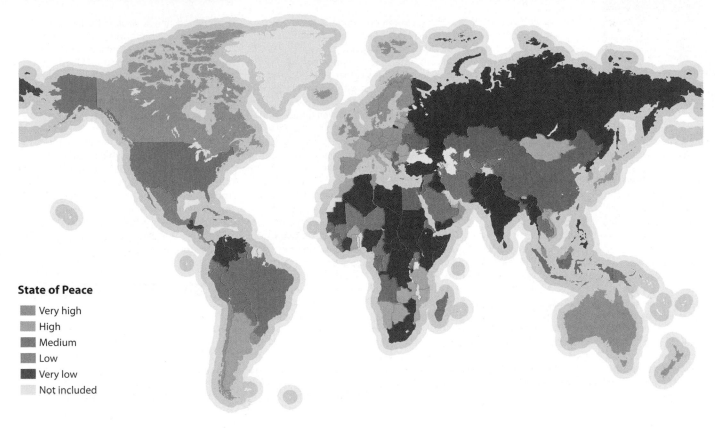

State of Peace

- Very high
- High
- Medium
- Low
- Very low
- Not included

Source: Institute for Economics and Peace 2011.

An essential aspect of contemporary terrorism involves use of the media. Terrorists may wish to keep secret their individual identities, but they want their political messages and goals to receive as much publicity as possible. Drawing on Erving Goffman's dramaturgical approach, sociologist Alfred McClung Lee has likened terrorism to the theater, where certain scenes are played out in predictable fashion. Whether through calls to the media, anonymous manifestos, or other means, terrorists typically admit responsibility for and defend their violent acts.

Sociologists and others have studied the role of different factors in the development of terrorism. They find that both democratic and repressive regimes can facilitate terrorism, although in different ways. The likelihood of violence is higher in youthful populations and among alienated groups, especially expatriate (overseas) communities (P. Davis and Cragin 2009).

Since September 11, 2001, governments worldwide have renewed their efforts to fight terrorism. Although the public generally regards

Global terrorism is just that—global in scope and impact. In March 2010, two female suicide bombers from the Caucasus region took 40 lives on the Moscow subway to call attention to their homeland's struggle for political independence from Russia.

Joseph W. Drummond, *Management Analyst, U.S. Army Space and Missile Defense Command*

When Joseph Drummond entered Morehouse College, he was planning to major in political science. But after taking an introductory sociology course, he felt that sociology gave him a clearer picture of the complexity and interconnectedness of society. "The career track that I had in mind was to enter the field of sociology as a researcher/policy maker," he explains. However, he soon ran into "a disconnect between academia and policy making," and an apparent lack of representation of sociologists at the policymaking level.

Drummond credits one of his sociology professors for steering him toward quantitative courses. "If you ever plan on having a job," the professor suggested, "make sure you have a lot of classes with quantitative analysis—for example, statistics and data analysis. These classes tell whatever company you want to work for that you have practical skills." Later, when Drummond asked his current employer why he had gotten the job he now holds, he was told that his data analysis and social statistics courses had made him competitive.

Today, Drummond works at the U.S. Army's Space and Missile Defense Command (SMDC), near Huntsville, Alabama. He began there as an intern, after responding to an email from Morehouse College's career office. Drummond is now a junior analyst with a team that formulates and develops doctrine, organization, and material requirements for Army units assigned to space and missile defense. In a typical workweek, he reviews military force structure—units, battalions, and so on—and helps to implement directives from Department of the Army headquarters. "A lot of what we do is attempting to translate very high-level guidance to something that's practical," he explains.

Drummond values the support and professional development he has received from the Army, including classes on program management, data analysis, national security, and force management. An Army-sponsored Technology and Government in Your Future event emphasized the need for interns to pursue graduate studies in math and science to land the best jobs. Drummond says the real-world experience he got as an intern at SMDC not only brought classroom theory to life; it also made him more attractive to future employers.

Asked how he uses sociology in his work, Drummond replies that his academic training has helped him to look critically at problems and to think about the second- and third-order effects of a decision. Seeing society from a macro-level view is also invaluable to him. "When U.S. leadership began to realize that a 'hearts and minds' campaign means that we need to understand the social-historical context of the people whose country we're occupying, that changed the way that we did business and also impacted the way U.S. military force structure was managed," he explains. "A lot of people had problems making the connection." Finally, sociology has taught Drummond not to take things at face value. "Most problems/issues that we come across very seldom have easy fixes," he notes. "Sociology taught me that thorough analysis means leaving no stone unturned."

LET'S DISCUSS

1. Have you ever considered a career in national defense? Do you know anyone with a college degree who works in the field?

2. Why do you think quantitative analysis is such an important skill to employers? How might you use it in your career?

---

increased surveillance and social control as a necessary evil, these measures have nonetheless raised governance issues. For example, some citizens in the United States and elsewhere have questioned whether measures such as the USA Patriot Act of 2001 threaten civil liberties. Citizens have also complained about the heightened anxiety created by the vague alerts issued by the federal government from time to time. Worldwide, immigration and the processing of refugees have slowed to a crawl, separating families and preventing employers from filling job openings. As these efforts to combat political violence illustrate, the term *terrorism* is an apt one (R. Howard and Sawyer 2003; A. Lee 1983; R. Miller 1988).

Increasingly, governments are becoming concerned about another form of political violence, the potential for malicious cyberattacks. In an age in which computer viruses can spread worldwide through the Internet, this kind of attack could render a nation's computer systems useless, or even shut down its power plants. A few years ago, such a scenario would have been considered pulp fiction, but it is now the subject of contingency planning throughout the world (Clayton 2011).

MODULE 48 | Recap and Review

Summary

Every society must have a **political system** to allocate valued resources.

1. There are three basic sources of **power** within any political system: **force, influence,** and **authority.**

2. Max Weber identified three ideal types of authority: **traditional, rational-legal,** and **charismatic.**

3. There are four basic types of government: **monarchy, oligarchy, dictatorship,** and **democracy.**

4. **War** may be defined as conflict between organizations that possess trained combat forces equipped with deadly weapons—a definition that includes conflict with terrorist organizations.

Thinking Critically

1. On your campus, what are some examples of the three types of authority?

2. Contrast the use of power in a dictatorship with its use in a democracy, as defined by Max Weber.

3. What is the greatest threat to world peace, and how would you counter it?

Key Terms

MODULE 49 | Political Behavior and Power in the United States

Citizens of the United States take for granted many aspects of their political system. They are accustomed to living in a nation with a Bill of Rights, two major political parties, voting by secret ballot, an elected president, state and local governments distinct from the national government, and so forth. Yet each society has its own ways of governing itself and making decisions. U.S. residents expect Democratic and Republican candidates to compete for public office; residents of Cuba and the People's Republic of China are accustomed to one-party rule by the Communist Party. In this section, we will examine several aspects of political behavior within the United States.

Participation and Apathy

In theory, a representative democracy will function most effectively and fairly if an informed and active electorate communicates its views to government leaders. Unfortunately, that is hardly the case in the United States. Virtually all citizens are familiar with the basics of the political process, and a small majority tend to identify to some extent with a political party. In 2012, about 29 percent of registered voters in the United States saw themselves as Democrats and 27 percent as Republicans; an impressive 43 percent were independent. However, only a small minority of citizens, often members of the higher social classes, actually participate in political organizations on a local or national level. Studies reveal that only 8 percent of Americans belong to a political club or organization. Not more than 20 percent have ever contacted an official of national, state, or local government about a political issue or problem (Gallup 2012; Orum and Dale 2009).

By the 1980s, it had become clear that many people in the United States were beginning to be turned off by political parties, politicians, and big government. The most dramatic indication of this growing alienation came from voting statistics. Today, voters of all ages and races appear to be less enthusiastic than ever about elections, even presidential contests. For example, in the presidential election of 1896, almost 80 percent of eligible voters in the United States went to the polls. Yet by the 2008 election, despite its drama and historic nature, turnout was only 62 percent of all eligible voters—well below the levels of the 1960s. Two years later, in the 2010 general election, turnout fell below 42 percent, lower than in most other nations (Figure 49-1).

Despite poor voter turnout, participation in politics may be increasing, especially on the Internet. In terms of both antigovernment activities and financial contributions to political parties, online participation rivals the political rallies and doorbell-ringing efforts of yesteryear. Fifty-five percent of the entire adult

FIGURE 49-1 **Voter Turnout Worldwide**

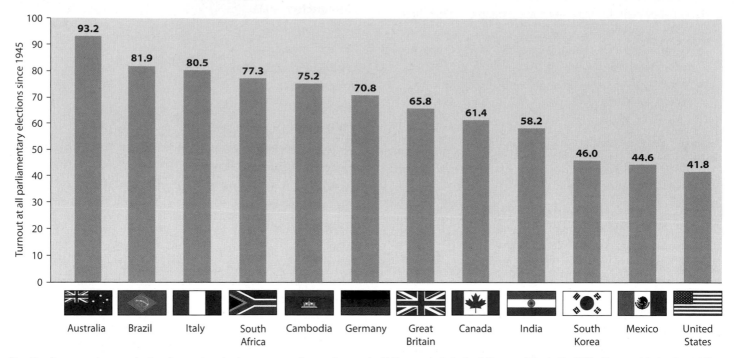

Note: Based on turnout in recent elections for seats in national congress or parliament. Data are for 2010 except for Italy, South Korea, and Cambodia (2008); Germany, Mexico, South Africa, and India (2009); and Canada (2011). USA 2010 data reflect correction in Bureau of the Census 2012c:Table A-1.
Source: International Institute for Democracy and Electoral Assistance 2012.

population of the United States went online in 2008 to get news and information about the presidential election. One in every five of those online participants went so far as to post comments for others to read (A. Smith 2009).

In the end, political participation makes government accountable to the voters. If participation declines, government operates with less of a sense of accountability to society. This issue is most serious for the least powerful individuals and groups in the United States. Voter turnout has been particularly low among members of racial and ethnic minorities. In postelection surveys, fewer African Americans and Hispanics than Whites report that they actually voted. Many more potential voters fail to register to vote. The poor—whose focus understandably is on survival—are traditionally underrepresented among voters as well. The low turnout found among these groups is explained at least in part by their common feeling of powerlessness. Yet these low statistics encourage political power brokers to continue to ignore the interests of the less affluent and the nation's minorities. The segment of the voting population that has shown the most voter apathy is the young, as discussed in Box 49-1 (Bureau of the Census 2012c; File and Crissey 2010).

 use your **sociological imagination**

Were you brought up to consider political involvement an important civic duty? If so, do you take that duty seriously by informing yourself about the issues and voting?

Race and Gender in Politics

Because politics is synonymous with power and authority, we should not be surprised that political strength is lacking in marginalized groups, such as women and racial and ethnic minorities. Nationally, women did not get the vote until 1920. Most Chinese Americans were turned away from the polls until 1926. And African Americans were disenfranchised until 1965, when national voting rights legislation was passed. Predictably, it has taken these groups some time to develop their political power and begin to exercise it effectively.

Progress toward the inclusion of minority groups in government has been slow. As of mid-2011, 17 out of 100 U.S. senators were women; 2 were Latino and 2 were Asian Americans, leaving 79 White non-Hispanic men. Among the 435 members of the U.S. House of Representatives, 310 were White non-Hispanic men; 71 were women, 42 were African Americans (including 13 women), 29 were Latinos (including 7 Latinas), and 7 were Asian Americans (including 4 women). These numbers, although low, represent a high-water mark for most of these groups.

Today, with record-high numbers of Blacks and Latinos holding elective office, many critics still decry what has been termed *fiesta politics*. White power brokers tend to visit racial and ethnic minority communities only when they need electoral support, making a quick appearance on a national or ethnic holiday to get their pictures taken and then vanishing. When the election is over, they too often forget to consult the residents who supported them about community needs and concerns.

Female politicians may be enjoying more electoral success now than in the past, but there is some evidence that the media

Why Don't More Young People Vote?

All through the 1960s, young people in the United States participated actively in a range of political issues, from pushing civil rights to protesting the Vietnam War. They were especially disturbed by the fact that young men were barred from voting but were being drafted to serve in the military and were dying for their country. In response to these concerns, the Twenty-Sixth Amendment to the Constitution was ratified in 1971, lowering the voting age from 21 to 18.

Now, more than 40 years later, we can consider the available research and see what happened. Frankly, what is remarkable is what did *not* happen. First, young voters (those between ages 18 and 21) have not united in any particular political sentiment. We can see in the way the young vote the same divisions of race, ethnicity, and gender that are apparent among older age groups.

Second, while the momentum for lowering the voting age came from college campuses, the majority of young voters are not students. Third, and particularly troubling, is their relatively low turnout. The 2008 presidential election, held against a background of war in Iraq, the historic candidacy of Barack Obama, and a global economic decline, did pique the

> *While the momentum for lowering the voting age came from college campuses, the majority of young voters are not students.*

interest of young voters. In that election, 51.4 percent of eligible voters under age 30 turned out, compared to 49 percent in 2004.

What lies behind voter apathy among the young? The popular explanation is that people—especially young people—are alienated from the political system, turned off by the shallowness and negativity of candidates and campaigns. However, young people do vote as they age.

Other explanations for the lower turnout among the young seem more plausible. First, the United States is virtually alone in requiring citizens to vote twice, in effect. They must first *register* to vote, often at a time when issues are not on the front burner and candidates haven't even declared. Second, though citizens in the United States tend to be more active in politics at the community level than those in other

countries, young people often feel unmoved by local issues such as public school financing.

One way in which youths *are* impacting elections is through their reliance on the Internet for information. Today, every political campaign maintains a presence on the Web, not only through an official website, but on social networking sites. During the 2008 presidential election, two-thirds of young adults with online profiles took part in some form of political activity on those sites. Time will tell whether the Internet will ultimately reduce political apathy among younger citizens.

LET'S DISCUSS

1. How often do you vote? If you do not vote, what accounts for your apathy? Are you too busy to register? Are community issues uninteresting to you?

2. Do you think voter apathy is a serious social problem? What might be done to increase voter participation in your age group and community?

Sources: Alwin 2002; Clymer 2000; Higher Education Research Institute 2004; McDonald 2009b; Niemi and Hanmer 2010; Patterson 2005; A. Smith 2009; Vargas 2007; Wattenberg 2008.

Reasons for Not Voting, 18- to 24-Year-Olds

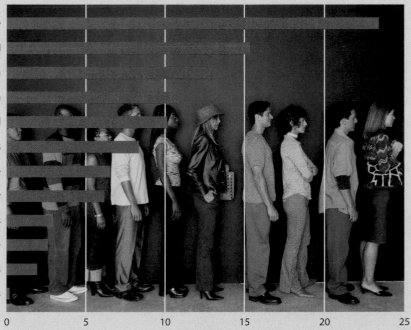

Source: Holder 2006:13.

Minnesota Democrat Keith Ellison created quite a stir in 2007 when he became the first person to take the congressional oath of office on a Qur'an. The newly elected member of the House of Representatives, who is Muslim, thought the Qur'an would make his oath more meaningful than a Bible. Speaker of the House Nancy Pelosi (left) borrowed Thomas Jefferson's two-volume Qur'an for the occasion—a reminder that acknowledging diversity is nothing new in U.S. politics.

government and the economic system? It is difficult to determine the location of power in a society as complex as the United States. In exploring this critical question, social scientists have developed two basic views of our nation's power structure: the power elite and the pluralist models.

Power Elite Models

Karl Marx believed that 19th-century representative democracy was essentially a sham. He argued that industrialized societies were dominated by relatively small numbers of people who owned factories and controlled natural resources. In Marx's view, government officials and military leaders were essentially servants of this capitalist class and followed their wishes. Therefore, any key decisions made by politicians inevitably reflected the interests of the dominant

cover them differently from male politicians. A content analysis of newspaper coverage of recent gubernatorial races showed that reporters wrote more often about a female candidate's personal life, appearance, or personality than a male candidate's, and less often about her political positions and voting record. Furthermore, when political issues were raised in newspaper articles, reporters were more likely to illustrate them with statements made by male candidates than by female candidates (Devitt 1999; Jost 2008).

Figure 49-2 shows the representation of women in selected national legislatures. While the proportion of women in national legislatures has increased in the United States and many other nations, in all but one country women still do not account for half the members of the national legislature. The African Republic of Rwanda, the exception, ranks the highest, with 56.3 percent of its legislative seats held by women. Overall, the United States ranked 94th among 190 nations in the proportion of women serving as national legislators at the end of 2011.

To remedy this situation, many countries have adopted quotas for female representatives. In some, the government sets aside a certain percentage of seats for women, usually from 14 to 30 percent. In others, political parties have decided that 20 to 40 percent of their candidates should be women. Thirty-two countries now have some kind of female quota system (Rubin and Dagher 2009; Vasagar 2005).

◼ Models of Power Structure in the United States

Who really holds power in the United States? Do "we the people" genuinely run the country through our elected representatives? Or is it true that behind the scenes, a small elite controls both the

FIGURE 49-2 **Women in National Legislatures, Selected Countries**

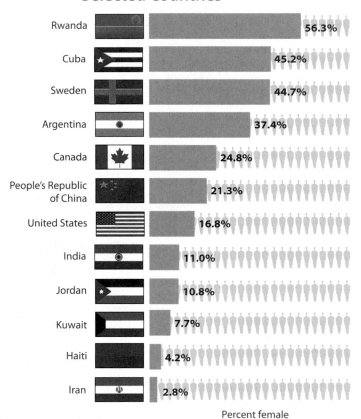

Country	Percent female
Rwanda	56.3%
Cuba	45.2%
Sweden	44.7%
Argentina	37.4%
Canada	24.8%
People's Republic of China	21.3%
United States	16.8%
India	11.0%
Jordan	10.8%
Kuwait	7.7%
Haiti	4.2%
Iran	2.8%

Percent female

Notes: Data are for lower legislative houses only, as of December 31, 2011; data on upper houses, such as the U.S. Senate, are not included. In 2005, the all-male Kuwaiti Parliament granted women the right to vote and serve in elected offices, which allowed women to run for office in 2007.
Source: Inter-Parliamentary Union 2012.

Think about It

Why do you think being elected to Congress is so difficult for women?

bourgeoisie. Like others who share an **elite model** of power relations, Marx believed that society is ruled by a small group of individuals who share a common set of political and economic interests.

Mills's Model   Sociologist C. Wright Mills took this model a step further in his pioneering work *The Power Elite* ([1956] 2000b). Mills described a small group of military, industrial, and government leaders who controlled the fate of the United States—the **power elite.** Power rested in the hands of a few, both inside and outside government.

A pyramid illustrates the power structure of the United States in Mills's model (Figure 49-3a). At the top are the corporate rich, leaders of the executive branch of government, and heads of the military (whom Mills called the "warlords"). Directly below are local opinion leaders, members of the legislative branch of government, and leaders of special-interest groups. Mills contended that these individuals and groups would basically follow the wishes of the dominant power elite. At the bottom of the pyramid are the unorganized, exploited masses.

The power elite model is in many respects similar to the work of Karl Marx. The most striking difference is that Mills believed that the economically powerful coordinate their maneuvers with the military and political establishments to serve their common interests. He rejected Marx's belief that by itself, the economic structure of capitalism could create a ruling class. Still, the powerless masses at the bottom of Mills's power elite model certainly bring to mind Marx's portrait of the oppressed workers of the world, who have "nothing to lose but their chains."

A fundamental element in Mills's thesis is that the power elite not only includes relatively few members but also operates as a self-conscious, cohesive unit. Although not necessarily diabolical or ruthless, the elite comprises similar types of people who interact regularly with one another and have essentially the same political and economic interests. Mills's power elite is not a conspiracy, but rather a community of interest and sentiment among a small number of influential people (A. Hacker 1964).

Admittedly, Mills failed to clarify when the elite opposes protests and when it tolerates them; he also failed to provide detailed case studies that would substantiate the interrelationships among members of the power elite. Nevertheless, his challenging theories forced scholars to look more critically at the democratic political system of the United States.

In commenting on the scandals that have rocked major corporations such as Enron and AIG over the past 15 years, observers have noted that members of the business elite *are* closely interrelated. In a study of the members of the boards of directors of *Fortune* 1000 corporations, researchers found that each director can reach *every* other board of directors in just 3.7 steps. That is, by consulting acquaintances of acquaintances, each director can quickly reach someone who sits on each of the other 999 boards. Furthermore, the face-to-face contact directors regularly have in their board meetings makes them a highly cohesive elite. Finally, the corporate elite is not only wealthy, powerful, and cohesive; it is also overwhelmingly White and male (G. Davis 2003, 2004; Kentor and Jang 2004; Mizruchi 1996; R. Schaefer 2008b; Strauss 2002).

One outgrowth of Mills's power elite model is current research on the presence of a *global* power elite—that is, those business, political, and former military leaders who exercise influence across national borders. Because this avenue of scholarship is relatively new, there is some disagreement on the definition of the term. Must the members of the global power elite demonstrate as much consensus as the members of Mills's power elite?

FIGURE 49-3   **Power Elite Models**

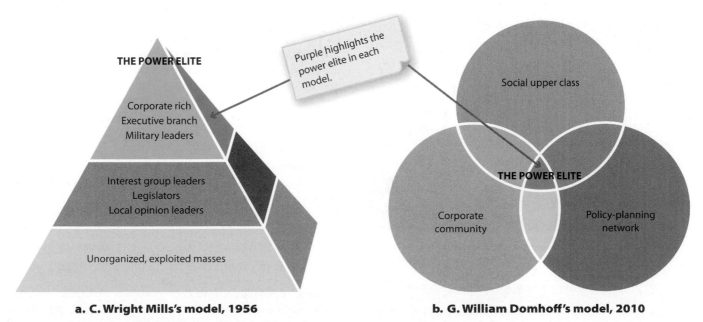

a. C. Wright Mills's model, 1956   **b. G. William Domhoff's model, 2010**

Source: Left, author based on Mills [1956] 2000b; right, Domhoff 2010:116.

Or can the global power elite include such diverse voices as publisher Rupert Murdoch, illegal arms dealer Viktor Bout, and former President Bill Clinton, in his role as head of the Clinton Global Initiative (L. Miller 2008; Rothkopf 2008)?

Domhoff's Model Over the past three decades, sociologist G. William Domhoff (2010) has agreed with Mills that a powerful elite runs the United States. He finds that it is still largely White, male, and upper class, as he wrote in his book with Richard L. Zweigenhaft (2006). However, Domhoff stresses the role played both by elites of the corporate community and by leaders of organizations in the policy-planning network, such as chambers of commerce and labor unions. Many of the people in both groups are also members of the social upper class. And he notes the presence of a small number of women and minority men in key positions—groups that were excluded from Mills's top echelon and are still underrepresented today.

Though the three groups in Domhoff's power elite model overlap, as Figure 49-3b shows, they do not necessarily agree on specific policies. Domhoff notes that in the electoral arena, two coalitions have exercised influence. A *corporate-conservative coalition* has played a large role in both political parties, generating support for particular candidates through direct-mail appeals. A *liberal-labor coalition* is based in unions, local environmental organizations, a segment of the minority group community, liberal churches, and the university and arts communities (Zweigenhaft and Domhoff 2006).

Pluralist Model

Several social scientists insist that power in the United States is shared more widely than the elite models indicate. In their view, a pluralist model more accurately describes the nation's political system. According to the **pluralist model,** many competing groups within the community have access to government, so that no single group is dominant.

Pluralism can be seen in action in the activity of lobbying groups attempting to influence public policy. The highly publicized battle over stem cell research is one example; it has pitted conservative religious groups against health advocacy groups, dividing political leaders in the process. Though legislation to support the controversial research technique had the backing of several prominent Republican lawmakers, including Senator Orrin Hatch (R-Utah), shown here with actor and activist Michael J. Fox, it fell victim to a presidential veto in 2006.

The pluralist model suggests that a variety of groups play a significant role in decision making. Typically, pluralists make use of intensive case studies or community studies based on observation research. One of the most famous—an investigation of decision making in New Haven, Connecticut—was reported by Robert Dahl (1961). Dahl found that although the number of people involved in any important decision was rather small, community power was nonetheless diffuse. Few political actors exercised decision-making power on all issues. One individual or group might be influential in a battle over urban renewal, but have little impact on educational policy.

The pluralist model, however, has not escaped serious questioning. Domhoff (1978, 2010) reexamined Dahl's study of decision making in New Haven and argued that Dahl and other pluralists had failed to trace how local elites who were prominent in decision making belonged to a larger national ruling class. In addition, studies of community power, such as Dahl's work in New Haven, can examine decision making only on issues that become part of the political agenda. They fail to address the potential power of elites to keep certain matters entirely out of the realm of government debate.

Dianne Pinderhughes (1987) has criticized the pluralist model for failing to account for the exclusion of African Americans from the political process. Drawing on her studies of Chicago politics, Pinderhughes points out that the residential and occupational segregation of Blacks and their long political disenfranchisement violates the logic of pluralism—which would hold that such a substantial minority should always have been influential in community decision making. This critique applies to many cities across the United States, where other large racial and ethnic minorities, among them Asian Americans, Puerto Ricans, and Mexican Americans, are relatively powerless.

Historically, pluralists have stressed ways in which large numbers of people can participate in or influence governmental decision making. New communications technologies like the Internet are increasing the opportunity to be heard, not just in countries such as the United States, but in developing countries the world over. One common point of the elite and pluralist perspectives stands out, however: in the political system of the United States, power is unequally distributed. All citizens may be equal in theory, yet those who are high in the nation's power structure are "more equal." New communications technology may or may not change that distribution of power (A. McFarland 2007).

Perhaps the ultimate test of power, no matter what a nation's power structure, is the decision to go to war. Because the rank and file of any army is generally drawn from the lower classes—the least powerful groups in society—such a decision has life-and-death consequences for people far removed from the center of power. In the long run, if the general population is not convinced that war is necessary, military action is unlikely to succeed. Thus, war is a risky way in which to address conflict between nations. In Module 48 we contrasted war and peace as ways of addressing societal conflict, and more recently, the threat of terrorism.

Summary

Political participation makes government accountable to citizens.

1. Both in the United States and in other countries, voters display a good deal of apathy toward the political system.

2. Women are still underrepresented in politics but are becoming more successful at winning election to public office.

3. Advocates of the **elite model** of the U.S. power structure see the nation as being ruled by a small group of individuals who share common political and economic interests (a **power elite**). Advocates of a **pluralist model** believe that power is shared more widely among conflicting groups.

Thinking Critically

1. In the United States, which plays a more significant role in political behavior, gender or race? Explain.

2. Which is a better model of the power structure in the United States, the power elite model or the pluralist model? Justify your answer.

Key Terms

Elite model   413

Pluralist model   414

Power elite   413

MODULE 50 | Economic Systems

The sociocultural evolution approach developed by Gerhard Lenski categorizes preindustrial society according to the way in which the economy is organized. The principal types of preindustrial society, as you recall, are hunting-and-gathering societies, horticultural societies, and agrarian societies.

As we noted in Module 17, the *Industrial Revolution*—which took place largely in England during the period 1760 to 1830—brought about changes in the social organization of the workplace. People left their homesteads and began working in central locations such as factories. As the Industrial Revolution proceeded, a new form of social structure emerged: the **industrial society,** a society that depends on mechanization to produce its goods and services.

Two basic types of economic system distinguish contemporary industrial societies: capitalism and socialism. As described in the following sections, capitalism and socialism serve as ideal types of economic system. No nation precisely fits either model. Instead, the economy of each individual state represents a mixture of capitalism and socialism, although one type or the other is generally more useful in describing a society's economic structure.

Capitalism

In preindustrial societies, land functioned as the source of virtually all wealth. The Industrial Revolution changed all that. It required that certain individuals and institutions be willing to take substantial risks in order to finance new inventions, machinery, and business enterprises. Eventually, bankers, industrialists, and other holders of large sums of money replaced landowners as the most powerful economic force. These people invested their funds in the hope of realizing even greater profits, and thereby became owners of property and business firms.

The transition to private ownership of business was accompanied by the emergence of the capitalist economic system. **Capitalism** is an economic system in which the means of production are held largely in private hands and the main incentive for economic activity is the accumulation of profits. In practice, capitalist systems vary in the degree to which the government regulates private ownership and economic activity (D. Rosenberg 1991).

Immediately following the Industrial Revolution, the prevailing form of capitalism was what is termed **laissez-faire** ("let them do"). Under the principle of laissez-faire, as expounded and endorsed by

For more than a century, the board game of Monopoly has entertained millions of people around the world. In the game, players strive to dominate the fictitious economy, gleefully bankrupting other players. Ironically, Monopoly was actually developed to demonstrate the weaknesses of capitalist economies, such as excessive rents and the tendency for money to accumulate in the hands of a few.

British economist Adam Smith (1723–1790), people could compete freely, with minimal government intervention in the economy. Business retained the right to regulate itself and operated essentially without fear of government interference (Smelser 1963).

Two centuries later, capitalism has taken on a somewhat different form. Private ownership and maximization of profits still remain the most significant characteristics of capitalist economic systems. However, in contrast to the era of laissez-faire, capitalism today features government regulation of economic relations. Without restrictions, business firms can mislead consumers, endanger workers' safety, and even defraud the companies' investors—all in the pursuit of greater profits. That is why the government of a capitalist nation often monitors prices, sets safety and environmental standards for industries, protects the rights of consumers, and regulates collective bargaining between labor unions and management. Yet under capitalism as an ideal type, government rarely takes over ownership of an entire industry.

Contemporary capitalism also differs from laissez-faire in another important respect: capitalism tolerates monopolistic practices. A **monopoly** exists when a single business firm controls the market. Domination of an industry allows the firm to effectively control a commodity by dictating pricing, quality standards, and availability. Buyers have little choice but to yield to the firm's decisions; there is no other place to purchase the product or service. Monopolistic practices violate the ideal of free competition cherished by Adam Smith and other supporters of laissez-faire capitalism.

Some capitalistic nations, such as the United States, outlaw monopolies through antitrust legislation. Such laws prevent any business from taking over so much of the competition in an industry that it controls the market. The U.S. federal government allows monopolies to exist only in certain exceptional cases, such as the utility and transportation industries. Even then, regulatory agencies scrutinize these officially approved monopolies to protect the public. The protracted legal battle between the Justice Department and Microsoft, owner of the dominant operating system for personal computers, illustrates the uneasy relationship between government and private monopolies in capitalistic countries.

Conflict theorists point out that although *pure* monopolies are not a basic element of the economy of the United States, competition is still much more restricted than one might expect in what is called a *free enterprise system.* In numerous industries, a few companies largely dominate the field and keep new enterprises from entering the marketplace.

During the severe economic downturn that began in 2008, the United States moved even further away from the laissez-faire ideal. To keep major financial institutions from going under, the federal government invested hundreds of billions of dollars in distressed banking, investment, and insurance companies. Then in 2009, the government bailed out the failing automobile industry, taking a 60 percent interest in General Motors. The Canadian government took another 12 percent.

As we have seen in earlier chapters, globalization and the rise of multinational corporations have spread the capitalistic pursuit of profits around the world. Especially in developing countries, governments are not always prepared to deal with the sudden influx of foreign capital and its effects on their economies. One particularly striking example of how unfettered capitalism can harm developing nations is found in the Democratic Republic of Congo (formerly Zaire). The Congo has significant deposits of the metal columbite-tantalite—coltan, for short—which is used in the production of electronic circuit boards. Until the market for cell phones, pagers, and laptop computers heated up recently, U.S. manufacturers got most of their coltan from Australia. But at the height of consumer demand, they turned to miners in the Congo to increase their supply.

Predictably, the escalating price of the metal—as much as $600 a kilogram at one point, or more than three times the average Congolese worker's yearly wages—attracted undesirable attention. Soon the neighboring countries of Rwanda, Uganda, and Burundi, at war with one another and desperate for resources to finance the conflict, were raiding the Congo's national parks, slashing and burning to expose the coltan beneath the forest floor. Indirectly, the sudden increase in the demand for coltan was financing war and the rape of the environment. U.S. manufacturers have since cut off their sources in the Congo in an effort to avoid abetting the destruction. But their action has only penalized legitimate miners in the impoverished country (*The Economist* 2011c; Friends of the Congo 2011).

 use your **sociological imagination**

Which aspects of capitalism do you personally appreciate? Which do you find worrisome?

Workers mine for coltan with sweat and shovels. The sudden increase in demand for the metal by U.S. computer manufacturers caused incursions into the Congo by neighboring countries hungry for capital to finance a war. Too often, globalization can have unintended consequences for a nation's economy and social welfare.

Socialism

Socialist theory was refined in the writings of Karl Marx and Friedrich Engels. These European radicals were disturbed by the exploitation of the working class that emerged during the Industrial Revolution. In their view, capitalism forced large numbers of people to exchange their labor for low wages. The owners of an industry profit from the labor of workers primarily because they pay workers less than the value of the goods produced.

As an ideal type, a socialist economic system attempts to eliminate such economic exploitation. Under **socialism,** the means of production and distribution in a society are collectively rather than privately owned. The basic objective of the economic system is to meet people's needs rather than to maximize profits. Socialists reject the laissez-faire philosophy that free competition benefits the general public. Instead, they believe that the central government, acting as the representative of the people, should make basic economic decisions. Therefore, government ownership of all major industries—including steel production, automobile manufacturing, and agriculture—is a primary feature of socialism as an ideal type.

In practice, socialist economic systems vary in the extent to which they tolerate private ownership. For example, in Great Britain, a nation with some aspects of both a socialist and a capitalist economy, passenger airline service was once concentrated in the government-owned corporation British Airways. Even before the airline was privatized in 1987, however, private airlines were allowed to compete with it.

Socialist nations differ from capitalist nations in their commitment to social service programs. For example, the U.S. government provides health care and health insurance to the elderly and poor through the Medicare and Medicaid programs. But socialist countries typically offer government-financed medical care to *all* citizens. In theory, the wealth of the people as a collectivity is used to provide health care, housing, education, and other key services to each individual and family.

Marx believed that socialist societies would eventually "wither away" and evolve into *communist* societies. As an ideal type, **communism** refers to an economic system under which all property is communally owned and no social distinctions are made on the basis of people's ability to produce. In recent decades, the Soviet Union, the People's Republic of China, Vietnam, Cuba, and nations in Eastern Europe were popularly thought of as examples of communist economic systems. However, this usage represents an incorrect application of a term with sensitive political connotations. All nations known as communist in the 20th century actually fell far short of the ideal type (Walder and Nguyen 2008).

By the early 1990s, Communist parties were no longer ruling the nations of Eastern Europe. Just two decades later, in 2012, Moscow had no fewer than 78 billionaires—more than New York (58) and London (39). That year, only China, Cuba, Laos, North Korea, and Vietnam remained socialist societies ruled by Communist parties. Yet even in those countries, capitalism had begun to make inroads. In Vietnam, for example, the Ho Chi Minh City Stock Exchange opened in 1990; the market now trades 600 stocks representing almost 40 percent of Vietnam's gross domestic product (GDP). Even in Cuba, a socialist stalwart, the government has begun to expand citizens' ability to own their own businesses and hire employees. By mid-2011, over 325,000 owners had received licenses for a range of businesses, including hairstyling, carpentry, shoemaking, and restaurant establishments (K. Chu 2010; Forbes 2012; Wilkinson 2011).

As we have seen, capitalism and socialism serve as ideal types of economic system. In reality, the economy of each industrial society—including the United States, the European Union, and Japan—includes certain elements of both capitalism and socialism (Table 50-1). Whatever the differences—whether a society more closely fits the ideal type of capitalism or socialism—all industrial societies rely chiefly on mechanization in the production of goods and services.

Table **50-1** Characteristics of the Three Major Economic Systems

Economic System	Characteristics	Contemporary Examples
Capitalism	Private ownership of the means of production Accumulation of profits the main incentive	Canada Mexico United States
Socialism	Collective ownership of the means of production Meeting people's needs the basic objective	Russia Sweden
Communism	Communal ownership of all property No social distinctions made on basis of people's ability to produce	Cuba North Korea Vietnam

Note: Countries listed in column 3 are typical of one of the three economic systems, but not perfectly so. In practice, the economies of most countries include a mix of elements from the three major systems.

Today's China is not the China of past generations; it is expected to become the world's largest economy by 2020. (Figure 50-1 shows the world's largest economies over the past 20 years.) In this country where the Communist Party once dominated people's lives, few now bother to follow party proceedings. Instead, after a decade of rapid economic growth, most Chinese are more interested in acquiring the latest consumer goods. Ironically, it was party officials' decision to transform China's economy by opening it up to capitalism that reduced the once-omnipotent institution's influence.

The Road to Capitalism

When the communists assumed leadership of China in 1949, they cast themselves as the champions of workers and peasants and the enemies of those who exploited workers, namely landlords and capitalists. Profit making was outlawed, and those who engaged in it were arrested. By the 1960s, China's economy was dominated by huge state-controlled enterprises, such as factories. Even private farms were transformed into community-owned organizations. Peasants essentially worked for the government, receiving payment in goods based on their contribution to the collective good. In addition, they could receive a small plot of land on which to produce food for their families or for exchange with others.

While the centralization of production for the benefit of all seemed to make sense ideologically, it did not work well economically. In the 1980s, the government eased restrictions on private enterprise somewhat, permitting small businesses with no more than seven employees. However, business owners could not hold policymaking positions in the party, at any level. Late in the decade, party leaders began to make market-oriented reforms, revising the nation's legal structure to promote private business. For the first time, private entrepreneurs were allowed to compete with some state-controlled businesses. By the mid-1990s, impressed with the results of the experiment, party officials had begun to hand some ailing state-controlled businesses over to private entrepreneurs, in hopes they could be turned around (D. Bell 2008).

The Chinese Economy Today

Today, the entrepreneurs who weathered government harassment during the Communist Party's early years are among the nation's wealthiest capitalists. Some even hold positions on government advisory boards. The growing free-market economy

FIGURE 50-1 **World's Largest Economies**

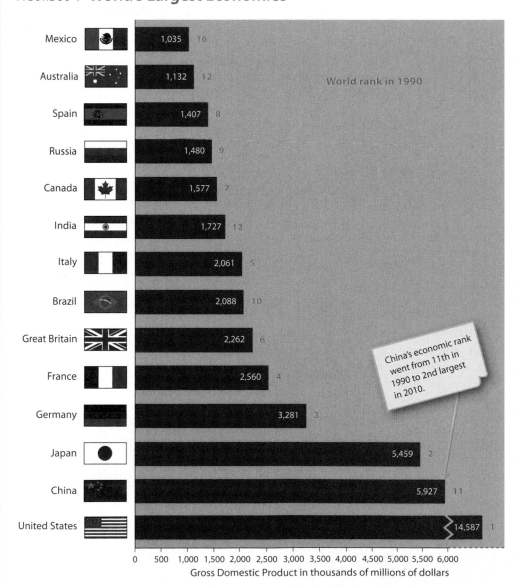

World rank in 1990

China's economic rank went from 11th in 1990 to 2nd largest in 2010.

Country	GDP	Rank
Mexico	1,035	16
Australia	1,132	12
Spain	1,407	8
Russia	1,480	9
Canada	1,577	7
India	1,727	13
Italy	2,061	5
Brazil	2,088	10
Great Britain	2,262	6
France	2,560	4
Germany	3,281	3
Japan	5,459	2
China	5,927	11
United States	14,587	1

Gross Domestic Product in thousands of millions of dollars

Note: 2010 data standardized in terms of estimated purchasing power parity to eliminate differences in buying power.
Sources: World Bank 2007:194–196; 2012a:218–220.

In Yuntan Province, China, agricultural workers divide up the meat from a steer they purchased jointly. Although some parts of China have seen massive manufacturing booms, in rural areas the economy is still based on traditional farming methods.

they spawned has brought significant inequality to Chinese workers, however, especially between urban and rural workers. Though the move toward market-driven development has been slowing, questions are still being raised about the accumulation of wealth by a few (Sicular et al. 2006).

Chinese capitalists have had to compete with multinational corporations, which can operate more easily in China now, thanks to government economic reforms. General Motors (GM) first became interested in China in 1992, hoping to use the nation's low-cost labor to manufacture cars for overseas markets. More and more, though, foreign-owned enterprises like GM are selling to the Chinese market. By 2009 the Chinese were buying more automobiles than people were in the United States (Terlep 2011).

Chinese Workers in the New Economy

For Chinese workers, the loosening of state control over the economy has meant a rise in occupational mobility, which was severely limited in the early days of Communist Party rule. The new markets created by private entrepreneurs are allowing ambitious workers to advance their careers by changing jobs or even cities. On the other hand, many middle-aged urban workers have lost their jobs to rural migrants seeking higher wages. Moreover, the privately owned factories that churn out lawn chairs and power tools for multinational corporations offer limited opportunities and very long hours. Wages average just below $400 a month for a six-day workweek. As low as wages

are in China, they are still double what workers earn in Indonesia, the Philippines, and Vietnam, where multinationals are now establishing factories (*The Economist* 2010b).

Serious social problems have accompanied China's massive economic growth. Because safety is not a priority in many businesses, workers suffer from high injury rates. Harsh working conditions contribute to rapid turnover in the labor force. There is no pension system in China, so retirees must struggle to find other ways to support themselves. Pollution is common in urban areas, and environmental problems are extraordinary (Barboza 2008; French 2008).

For the average worker, party membership is less important now than in the past. Instead, managerial skill and experience are much in demand. Hong Kong sociologist Xiaowei Zang (2002) surveyed 900 workers in a key industrial city and found that party members still had an advantage in government and state-owned companies, where they earned higher salaries than other workers. But in private businesses, seniority and either managerial or entrepreneurial experience were what counted. As might be expected, being male and well educated also helped.

Women have been slower to advance in the workplace than men. Traditionally, Chinese women have been relegated to subservient roles in the patriarchal family structure. Communist Party rule has allowed them to make significant gains in employment, income, and education, although not as quickly as promised. For rural women in China, the growth of a market economy has meant a choice between working in a factory or on a farm. Still, despite recent economic changes, emerging research shows that Chinese women receive lower wages than men who work in the same job sectors (M. Wang and Cai 2006).

With the growth of a middle class and increased education, many Chinese are seeking the same opportunities as their Western counterparts. The struggle has been particularly visible in the Chinese people's desire for open, unrestricted access to the World Wide Web. In most countries of the world, a web search for images of Tiananmen Square will call up photos of the 1989 crackdown on student protesters, in which soldiers in tanks attacked unarmed students. But on the other side of what has been dubbed the Great Firewall of China, the same search yields only photos of visiting diplomats—including those from the United States—posing in the square (Deibert et al. 2008).

The Informal Economy

In many countries, one aspect of the economy defies description as either capitalist or socialist. In the **informal economy,** transfers of money, goods, or services take place but are not reported to the government. Examples of the informal economy include trading services with someone—say, a haircut for a computer lesson; selling goods on the street; and engaging in illegal transactions, such as gambling or drug deals. The informal economy also includes off-the-books work in landscaping, child care, and housecleaning. Participants in this type of economy avoid taxes and government regulations.

In the United States, the informal economy accounts for about 8 percent of total economic activity. In other industrialized nations it varies, from 11 percent in Great Britain to 20 percent in Spain and Portugal and 25 percent in Greece. In developing nations, the informal economy represents a much larger (40 to 60 percent) and often unmeasured part of total economic activity. Yet because this sector of the economy depends to a large extent on the labor of women, work in the informal economy is undervalued or even unrecognized the world over (T. Barnes 2009; Schneider 2010).

Functionalists contend that bureaucratic regulations sometimes contribute to the rise of an informal, or underground, economy. In the developing world, governments often set up burdensome business regulations that overworked bureaucrats must administer. When requests for licenses and permits pile up, delaying business projects, legitimate entrepreneurs find they need to go underground to get anything done. Despite its apparent efficiency, this type of informal economy is dysfunctional for a country's overall political and economic well-being. Since informal firms typically operate in remote locations to avoid detection, they cannot easily expand when they become profitable. And given the limited protection for their property and contractual rights, participants in the informal economy are less likely than others to save and invest their income.

Whatever the functions an informal economy may serve, it is in some respects dysfunctional for workers. Working conditions in these illegal businesses are often unsafe or dangerous, and the jobs rarely provide any benefits to those who become ill or cannot continue to work. Perhaps more significant, the longer a worker remains in the informal economy, the less likely that person is to make the transition to the formal economy. No matter how efficient or productive a worker, employers expect to see experience in the formal economy on a job application. Experience as a successful street vendor or self-employed cleaning person does not carry much weight with interviewers (Venkatesh 2006).

MODULE 50 | Recap and Review

Summary

A society's economic system has an important influence on social behavior and on other social institutions.

1. With the Industrial Revolution, a new form of social structure emerged: the **industrial society.**

2. Systems of **capitalism** vary in the degree to which the government regulates private ownership and economic activity, but all emphasize the profit motive.

3. The basic objective of **socialism** is to eliminate economic exploitation and meet people's needs. Marx believed that **communism** would evolve naturally out of socialism.

4. In developing nations, the **informal economy** represents a significant part of total economic activity. Yet because this sector depends largely on women's work, it is undervalued.

5. In the 1980s, the Chinese Communist Party began allowing Chinese entrepreneurs to experiment with capitalist ventures. Today multinational corporations are capitalizing on China's huge workforce to produce goods and services for sale not just to those in industrial nations, but to the people of China.

Thinking Critically

1. In the United States, what factors might encourage the growth of the informal economy? Are those factors related to the country's economic system?

2. Why do you think China's economy has grown as fast as it has?

Key Terms

Capitalism   415

Communism   417

Industrial society   415

Informal economy   420

Laissez-faire   415

Monopoly   416

Socialism   417

MODULE 51 | Changing Economies

As advocates of the power elite model point out, the trend in capitalist societies has been toward concentration of ownership by giant corporations, especially multinational ones. In the following sections we will examine three outgrowths of this trend in the United States: the changing face of the workforce, deindustrialization, and offshoring. As these trends show, any change in the economy has social and political implications.

The Changing Face of the Workforce

The workforce in the United States is constantly changing. During World War II, when men were mobilized to fight abroad, women entered the workforce in large numbers. And with the rise of the civil rights movement in the 1960s, minorities found numerous job opportunities opening to them. Box 51-1 takes a closer look at the active recruitment of women and minorities into the workplace, known as *affirmative action.*

Although predictions are not always reliable, sociologists and labor specialists foresee a workforce increasingly composed of women and racial and ethnic minorities. In 1960 there were twice as many men in the labor force as women. From 1988 to 2018, however, 52 percent of new workers are expected to be women. The dynamics for minority group workers are even more dramatic, as the number of Black, Latino, and Asian American workers continues to increase at a faster rate than the number of White workers (Toossi 2009).

More and more, then, the workforce reflects the diversity of the population, as ethnic minorities enter the labor force and immigrants and their children move from marginal jobs or employment in the informal economy to positions of greater visibility and responsibility. The impact of this changing labor force is not merely statistical. A more diverse workforce means that relationships between workers are more likely to cross gender, racial, and ethnic lines. Interactionists note that people will soon find themselves supervising and being supervised by people very different from themselves.

Deindustrialization

What happens when a company decides it is more profitable to move its operations out of a long-established community to another part of the country, or out of the country altogether? People lose jobs; stores lose customers; the local government's tax base declines and it cuts services. This devastating process has occurred again and again in the past decade or so.

The term **deindustrialization** refers to the systematic, widespread withdrawal of investment in basic aspects of productivity, such as factories and plants. Giant corporations that deindustrialize are not necessarily refusing to invest in new economic opportunities. Rather, the targets and locations of investment change, and the need for labor decreases as advances in technology continue to automate production. First, companies may move their plants from the nation's central cities to the suburbs. The next step may be relocation from suburban areas of the Northeast and Midwest to the South, where labor laws place more restrictions on unions. Finally, a corporation may simply relocate *outside* the United States to a country with a lower rate of prevailing wages. General Motors, for example, decided to build a multibillion-dollar plant in China rather than in Kansas City or even in Mexico (Lynn 2003).

Although deindustrialization often involves relocation, in some instances it takes the form of corporate restructuring, as companies seek to reduce costs in the face of growing worldwide competition. When such restructuring occurs, the impact on the bureaucratic hierarchy of formal organizations can be significant. A large corporation may choose to sell off or entirely abandon less productive divisions and to eliminate layers of management viewed as unnecessary. Wages and salaries may be frozen and benefits cut—all in the name of restructuring. Increasing reliance on automation also spells the end of work as we have known it.

The term **downsizing** was introduced in 1987 to refer to reductions taken in a company's workforce as part of deindustrialization. Viewed from a conflict perspective, the unprecedented attention given to downsizing in the mid-1990s reflected the continuing importance of social class in the United States. Conflict theorists note that job loss has long been a feature of deindustrialization among blue-collar workers. But when large numbers of middle-class managers and other white-collar employees with substantial incomes began to be laid off, suddenly the media began expressing great concern over downsizing.

The extended economic downturn that began in 2008 accelerated the processes of deindustrialization and downsizing. As the recession deepened, many plants shut down either temporarily or permanently, leaving more and more workers without jobs. With those jobs and shuttered plants went any hope of restoring or expanding heavy industry, including automobile manufacturing. The bankruptcy of Chrysler and General Motors hit the midwestern states particularly hard.

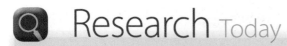
Affirmative Action

The term *affirmative action* first appeared in an executive order issued by President John F. Kennedy in 1961. That order called for contractors to "take affirmative action to ensure that applicants are employed, and that employees are treated during employment, without regard to their race, creed, color, or national origin." In 1967, the order was amended by President Lyndon Johnson to prohibit discrimination on the basis of sex as well, but affirmative action remained a vague concept. Currently, **affirmative action** refers to positive efforts to recruit minority group members or women for jobs, promotions, and educational opportunities.

> Critics warn against hiring and admissions quotas, complaining that they constitute a kind of "reverse discrimination" against White males.

Sociologists—especially conflict and feminist theorists—view affirmative action as a legislative attempt to reduce the inequality embedded in the social structure by increasing opportunities for groups who were deprived in the past, such as women and African Americans. Despite the clear disparity in earnings between White males and other groups, however, many people doubt that everything done in the name of affirmative action is desirable. Critics warn against hiring and admissions quotas, complaining that they constitute a kind of "reverse discrimination" against White males.

Affirmative action became a prominent issue in state and national political campaigns in 1996, when California's voters approved by a 54 to 46 percent margin the California Civil Rights Initiative. Better known as Proposition 209, this measure amends the state constitution to *prohibit* any program that gives preference to women and minorities in college admissions, hiring, promotion, or government contracts. In other words, it aims to abolish affirmative action programs. The courts have since upheld the measure. In 1998, voters in Washington State passed a similar anti–affirmative action measure.

In 2003, focusing specifically on college admissions in a pair of decisions involving policies at the University of Michigan, the Supreme Court ruled that colleges may consider race and ethnicity as one factor in their admissions decisions. However, they cannot assign a specific value to being a minority candidate in such a way that race becomes the overriding factor in a decision. The ruling allowed many colleges and universities to continue their existing affirmative action policies.

Increasingly, critics of affirmative action are calling for color-blind policies that would end affirmative action. Presumably, such policies would allow all applicants to be judged fairly. However, opponents warn against the danger of **color-blind racism**—the use of the principle of race neutrality to defend a racially unequal status quo (see Chapter 10). Will "color-blind" policies put an end to institutional practices that now favor Whites, they ask? According to the latest data, for example, Harvard University admits 40 percent of those applicants who are children of alumni—almost all of whom are White—compared to 11 percent of nonalumni children. Ironically, studies show that children of alumni are far more likely than either minority students or athletes to run into trouble academically.

The Supreme Court's many decisions on the constitutionality of affirmative action programs have made it difficult for organizations to encourage diversity without transgressing the law.

LET'S DISCUSS

1. Is affirmative action part of the admissions policy at the college or university you attend? If so, do you think the policy has helped to level the playing field? Might it have excluded some qualified White applicants?

2. Take a poll of your classmates. What percentage of the class supports affirmative action in hiring and college admissions? How does that group break down in terms of gender, race, and ethnicity?

Sources: Massey and Mooney 2007; Pincus 2003, 2008; University of Michigan 2003.

The social costs of deindustrialization and downsizing cannot be overemphasized. Plant closings lead to substantial unemployment in a community, which has a devastating impact on both the micro and macro levels. On the micro level, the unemployed person and his or her family must adjust to a loss of spending power. Painting or re-siding the house, buying health insurance or saving for retirement, even thinking about having another child must be put aside. Both marital happiness and family cohesion may suffer as a result. Although many dismissed workers eventually reenter the paid labor force, they must often accept less desirable positions with lower salaries and fewer benefits. Unemployment and underemployment are tied to many of the social problems discussed throughout this textbook, among them the need for child care and the controversy over welfare.

Offshoring

U.S. firms have been outsourcing certain types of work for generations. For example, moderate-sized businesses such as furniture stores and commercial laundries have long relied on outside

Gutted factories like this one in Boston, Massachusetts, contrast with the glamorous corporate campus of Google Corporation in Mountain View, California. Deindustrialization and the rise of high technology have shifted the U.S. labor market, displacing many workers in the process.

trucking firms to make deliveries to their customers. The new trend toward **offshoring** carries this practice one step further, by transferring other types of work to foreign contractors. Now, even large companies are turning to overseas firms, many of them located in developing countries. Offshoring has become the latest tactic in the time-worn business strategy of raising profits by reducing costs.

Significantly, the transfer of work from one country to another is no longer limited to manufacturing. Office and professional jobs are being exported, too, thanks to advanced telecommunications. Table 51-1 lists those occupations most likely to be offshored.

In 2012, complaints about working conditions in Apple's factories in China called attention to the fact that the company's financial success had been built on outsourced labor. At one time, Apple manufactured its computers in the United States.

Today the company still employs about 43,000 full-time workers in the United States, and another 20,000 full-time workers abroad. However, Apple contracts on a short-term basis with an additional 700,000 workers who both engineer and build its products overseas (Duhigg and Bradsher 2012).

Because offshoring, like outsourcing in general, tends to improve the efficiency of business operations, it can be viewed as functional to society. Offshoring also increases economic interdependence in the production of goods and services, both in enterprises located just across town and in those located around the globe. Still, conflict theorists charge that this aspect of globalization furthers social inequality. Although moving high-tech work to developing countries does help to lower a company's costs, the impact on technical and service workers at home is clearly devastating. Certainly middle-class workers are alarmed by the trend. Because offshoring increases efficiency, economists oppose efforts to block the practice and instead recommend assistance to displaced workers.

There is a downside to offshoring for foreigners, as well. Although outsourcing is a significant source of employment for the upper-middle class in developing countries, hundreds of millions of other foreign workers have seen little to no positive impact from the trend. Thus the long-term impact of offshoring on developing nations is difficult to predict. Another practice, *microfinancing,* is having a more positive impact on the lower classes in developing nations: see the Social Policy section that follows (Goering 2008b; Waldman 2004a, 2004b, 2004c).

Table **51-1** Occupations Most Vulnerable to Offshoring

Rank	Occupation
1	Computer programming
2	Data entry
3	Electrical and electronics drafting
4	Mechanical drafting
5	Computer and information science, research
6	Actuarial science
7	Mathematics
8	Statistics
9	Mathematical science (all other)
10	Film and video editing

Sources: Bureau of Labor Statistics data cited in Hira 2008; Moncarz et al. 2008.

 use your **sociological imagination**

Do you know anyone whose job has been transferred to a foreign country? If so, was the person able to find a comparable job in the same town, or did he or she have to relocate? How long was the person unemployed?

In India, a very small loan has made a big change in a young mother's life. Not many years ago Siyawati was dependent on what little income her husband could earn as a day laborer. Then a $212 microloan allowed her to buy a machine for making candles. Today, Siyawati's cottage venture has expanded into a factory with eight employees, and her monthly income has climbed from $42 to $425. Her increased earnings have allowed her to enroll her children in a good school—the dream of struggling parents in developing countries around the world (Glazer 2010:1).

Looking at the Issue

In some respects it offers a small solution to a big problem. **Microfinancing** is lending small sums of money to the poor so they can work their way out of poverty. Borrowers use the money to start small businesses in the informal economy—to buy yarn to weave into cloth, cows to produce milk, or tools, equipment, and bamboo to make stools. The products they produce are then sold in the local shops. Typically, microloans are less than $600, often as little as $20. The recipients are people who ordinarily would not be able to qualify for banking services.

Sometimes referred to as "banking the unbanked," microfinancing was the brainchild of Bangladeshi economist Muhammad Yunus (pronounced Iunus). In 1976, in the midst of a devastating famine in Bangladesh, Yunus founded the Grameen (meaning "Village") Bank, which he headed until 2011. The idea came to him when he reached into his pocket to lend money to a group of villagers who had asked him for help. Working through local halls or meeting places, the Grameen Bank has now extended credit to nearly 7 million people. The idea has spread, and has even been underwritten by over a thousand for-profit banks and multinational organizations. According to the most recent estimates, microfinancing is now reaching 91 million people in 100 countries (Microfinance Information Exchange 2011; Yunus 2010).

Although microfinancing has benefited many families, critics charge that some lenders are taking advantage of the poor. Especially in India, the extension of microloans to financially questionable projects with little chance for success has left some borrowers in debt. At the other extreme, some lenders have reaped extraordinary profits, both for themselves and for the investment banks they have created.

The microfinance movement is not a failure, however. It has evolved to offer borrowers scholarships, low-cost health care, and even solar power. Research supports the conclusion that the poorest of the poor can and do become entrepreneurs when they can obtain credit at acceptable interest rates (M. Fitzgerald 2011; D. Haase 2012).

In 2006 Muhammad Yunus, founder of the Grameen Bank, was awarded the Nobel Peace Prize for his work in championing the concept of microfinancing. The small loans his bank makes to the poor, many of them women, have improved the quality of life of countless families.

Applying Sociology

Researchers who draw on the interactionist approach have shown that there is more to microfinancing than money. A study done by microfinance expert Daryl Collins and his colleagues (2009), described in the opening excerpt to Chapter 9, shows how even with modest assistance, poor people can significantly improve their circumstances through mutual support. Collins asked villagers and slum dwellers in Bangladesh, India, and South Africa to keep diaries of how they spent every penny

—*Continued*

they earned. He and his team found that most of the poor households they studied did not live hand to mouth, spending everything they earned as soon as they got it. Instead, they used financial tools that were linked to their extended families and informal social networks. They saved money, squeezed it out of creditors whenever possible, ran sophisticated savings clubs, and took advantage of microfinancing whenever it was available. Their tactics suggested new methods of fighting poverty and encouraged the development of broader microfinance programs.

Because an estimated 90 percent of the recipients of microcredit are women, feminist theorists are especially interested in the growth of microfinancing. Women's economic status has been found to be critical to the well-being of their children, and the key to a healthy household environment. In developing countries, where women often are not treated as well as men, being entrusted with credit is particularly empowering to them. Research indicates that women recipients are more likely than men to participate in networks and collective action groups, perhaps because they must overcome resistance to women as economic decision makers (Karidesing 2010; Sanyal 2009).

Drawing on world systems analysis (see Module 29), sociologist Marina Karides (2010) contrasts microfinancing with the Western model of economic development, in which multinational corporations based in core countries take advantage of the low wages and natural resources in periphery and semi-periphery countries. The low-wage workers employed by the multinationals rarely escape subsistence living, while the vast majority of people in core nations enjoy a comparatively high standard of living. Microfinanciers hope that in contrast, the cottage industries they help to establish will contribute to the local economies in developing countries, and ultimately to the well-being of those societies, rather than merely serve the economic interests of core nations.

Some critics complain that the creation of small home-based industries reduces the demand for formal employment opportunities. Supporters of microenterprise counter that much time has passed without a significant change in job growth. Microfinancing, they claim, is the best way to create sustainable market opportunities for the poor in developing nations, even if those opportunities are much less attractive than those available in core nations.

Initiating Policy

Even supporters of microfinancing acknowledge the need to reduce overlending and monitor the success of small loans in helping borrowers to escape poverty. Some indicators suggest that many borrowers do not achieve self-sufficiency. If that is

At a workshop in Mumbai, India, Sharda Bhandare cuts the pieces for a pair of gloves from a towel. Microloans make such small businesses possible, and help them to become self-sustaining.

true, lenders should increase their oversight and attempt to identify best practices—that is, those types of assistance that are most effective in helping the poor. Less than a decade ago, microfinancing was hailed as the single best solution to world poverty. With modifications, it should continue to reduce hardship and suffering among the poor (Bajaj 2011a, 2011b; Glazer 2010).

Lenders also need to work with political leaders, and vice versa, to ensure that they do not regard one another as competitors for political support from the poor. Some government leaders have gone so far as to charge lenders with profiteering at the expense of the poor, and to take extraordinary measures for the protection of borrowers. In 2010, officials of one state in India required all loans to be approved by the government, and their eventual repayment to be made in person before a public official. To the degree that profiteering is truly a problem, some type of remedy, whether through legislation or self-monitoring, may need to be introduced. Given the cultural, political, and legal differences among nations where microfinanciers operate, the development of this type of government policy will be a major undertaking.

TAKING SOCIOLOGY WITH YOU

1. Do you think microfinancing might be useful in the United States? If so, how and under what conditions?

2. Using sociological concepts, explain why some politicians might resent microfinancing programs.

3. What obstacles might prevent poor people, either in the United States or elsewhere, from improving their lives through microfinancing? Might the government have a role to play in removing those obstacles?

Summary

Any change in the economy has both social and political implications.

1. In the United States, workers are coping with **deindustrialization** and **offshoring** and employers are training an increasingly diverse workforce.

2. **Affirmative action** is intended to remedy the effects of discrimination against minority groups and women. The concept is controversial, however, because some people see it as reverse discrimination against majority groups.

3. In developing countries, **microfinancing** is improving the lives of millions of poor people.

Thinking Critically

1. What are the implications of trends such as deindustrialization and offshoring on social institutions such as the family, education, and government in the United States?

2. What evidence of deindustrialization or downsizing do you see, specifically, in your own community? What broad economic shifts brought about those changes?

Key Terms

Affirmative action 422

Color-blind racism 422

Deindustrialization 421

Downsizing 421

Microfinancing 424

Offshoring 423

Mastering This Chapter

taking sociology with you

1 Pick a nongovernmental organization with worldwide recognition, such as the Red Cross, Doctors Without Borders, or Amnesty International. Go online and find out how the organization works on behalf of peace. What specifically has this NGO done to prevent or stop war?

2 If you aren't already familiar with it, visit your local community college and stop by the administration office. Ask what programs the college has to offer in workforce development. What skills is the college currently developing for tomorrow's workforce? What will those skills mean, not just for students, but for the community as a whole?

3 If your college has a club for young Republicans or Democrats, attend one of their meetings. What issues are members interested in, and why? How are they planning to put their beliefs into action? Are they concerned about voter apathy among young people?

Affirmative action Positive efforts to recruit minority group members or women for jobs, promotions, and educational opportunities. (page 422)

Authority Institutionalized power that is recognized by the people over whom it is exercised. (402)

Capitalism An economic system in which the means of production are held largely in private hands and the main incentive for economic activity is the accumulation of profits. (415)

Charismatic authority Power made legitimate by a leader's exceptional personal or emotional appeal to his or her followers. (402)

Color-blind racism The use of the principle of race neutrality to defend a racially unequal status quo. (422)

Communism As an ideal type, an economic system under which all property is communally owned and no social distinctions are made on the basis of people's ability to produce. (417)

Deindustrialization The systematic, widespread withdrawal of investment in basic aspects of productivity, such as factories and plants. (421)

Democracy In a literal sense, government by the people. (403)

Dictatorship A government in which one person has nearly total power to make and enforce laws. (403)

Downsizing Reductions taken in a company's workforce as part of deindustrialization. (421)

Economic system The social institution through which goods and services are produced, distributed, and consumed. (401)

Elite model A view of society as being ruled by a small group of individuals who share a common set of political and economic interests. (413)

Force The actual or threatened use of coercion to impose one's will on others. (401)

Industrial society A society that depends on mechanization to produce its goods and services. (415)

Influence The exercise of power through a process of persuasion. (401)

Informal economy Transfers of money, goods, or services that are not reported to the government. (420)

Laissez-faire A form of capitalism under which people compete freely, with minimal government intervention in the economy. (415)

Microfinancing Lending small sums of money to the poor so they can work their way out of poverty. (424)

Monarchy A form of government headed by a single member of a royal family, usually a king, queen, or some other hereditary ruler. (403)

Monopoly Control of a market by a single business firm. (416)

Offshoring The transfer of work to foreign contractors. (423)

Oligarchy A form of government in which a few individuals rule. (403)

Peace The absence of war, or more broadly, a proactive effort to develop cooperative relations among nations. (404)

Pluralist model A view of society in which many competing groups within the community have access to government, so that no single group is dominant. (414)

Political system The social institution that is founded on a recognized set of procedures for implementing and achieving society's goals. (401)

Politics In Harold Lasswell's words, "who gets what, when, and how." (401)

Power The ability to exercise one's will over others. (401)

Power elite A small group of military, industrial, and government leaders who control the fate of the United States. (413)

Rational-legal authority Power made legitimate by law. (402)

Representative democracy A form of government in which certain individuals are selected to speak for the people. (403)

Socialism An economic system under which the means of production and distribution are collectively owned. (417)

Sovereignty movement The effort by the indigenous people of Hawai'i to win self-government, as well as the restoration of—or compensation for—their ancestral lands. (405)

Terrorism The use or threat of violence against random or symbolic targets in pursuit of political aims. (406)

Totalitarianism Virtually complete government control and surveillance over all aspects of a society's social and political life. (403)

Traditional authority Legitimate power conferred by custom and accepted practice. (402)

War Conflict between organizations that possess trained combat forces equipped with deadly weapons. (404)

Read each question carefully and then select the best answer.

1. Which two basic types of economic system distinguish contemporary industrial societies?
   a. capitalism and communism
   b. capitalism and socialism
   c. socialism and communism
   d. capitalism and dictatorship

2. According to the discussion of capitalism in the text, which of the following statements is true?
   a. The means of production are held largely in private hands.
   b. The main incentive for economic activity is the accumulation of profits.
   c. The degree to which the government regulates private ownership and economic activity will vary.
   d. all of the above

3. G. William Domhoff's model is an example of a(n)
   a. elite theory of power.
   b. pluralist theory of power.
   c. functionalist theory of power.
   d. interactionist theory of power.

4. In terms of voter turnout, the United States typically ranks
   a. highest among all countries.
   b. highest among industrial nations.
   c. lowest among industrial nations.
   d. lowest among all countries.

5. What are the three basic sources of power within any political system?
   a. force, influence, and authority
   b. force, influence, and democracy
   c. force, legitimacy, and charisma
   d. influence, charisma, and bureaucracy

6. Which of the following is *not* part of the classification system of authority developed by Max Weber?
   a. traditional authority
   b. pluralist authority
   c. legal-rational authority
   d. charismatic authority

7. According to C. Wright Mills, power rests in the hands of the
   a. people.
   b. representative democracy.
   c. aristocracy.
   d. power elite.

8. The systematic, widespread withdrawal of investment in basic aspects of productivity such as factories and plants is called
   a. deindustrialization.
   b. downsizing.
   c. postindustrialization.
   d. gentrification.

9. Sociologists and labor specialists foresee a workforce increasingly composed of
   a. women.
   b. racial minorities.
   c. ethnic minorities.
   d. all of the above

10. Currently, _____ _____ refers to positive efforts to recruit minority group members or women for jobs, promotions, and educational opportunities.
   a. equal rights
   b. affirmative action
   c. work programs
   d. equal action

11. The principle of _____ _____, as expounded and endorsed by the British economist Adam Smith, was the prevailing form of capitalism immediately following the Industrial Revolution.

12. Under _____, the means of production and distribution in a society are collectively rather than privately owned, and the basic objective of the economic system is to meet people's needs rather than to maximize profits.

13. _____ is an economic system under which all property is communally owned and no social distinctions are made based on people's ability to produce.

14. _____ theorists point out that while pure monopolies are not a basic element of the economy of the United States, competition is much more restricted than one might expect in what is called a free enterprise system.

15. Some capitalist nations, such as the United States, outlaw _____ through antitrust legislation.

16. The elite model of political power implies that the United States has a(n) _____ as its form of government.

17. Sexism has been the most serious barrier to women interested in holding public office. To remedy this situation, many countries have adopted _____ for female representatives.

18. _____ is the exercise of power through a process of persuasion.

19. The United States is commonly classified as a(n) _____, because the elected members of Congress and state legislatures make our laws.

20. Advocates of the _____ model suggest that competing groups within the community have access to government, so that no single group is dominant.

Answers

1 (b); 2 (d); 3 (a); 4 (c); 5 (a); 6 (b); 7 (d); 8 (a); 9 (d); 10 (b); 11 laissez-faire; 12 socialism; 13 Communism; 14 Conflict; 15 monopolies; 16 oligarchy; 17 quotas; 18 Influence; 19 representative democracy; 20 pluralist

thinking about movies

Margin Call

Seen from the perspective of an investment banker, this drama explores the onset of the global financial crisis.

The Company Men

Corporate downsizing forces a white-collar worker to enter a blue-collar profession.

Countdown to Zero

This documentary explores the dangers of nuclear weapons in a global context.

Do you remember a time when you or your parents didn't worry about the food you ate and the water you drank?

Andrew Szasz does. It was a time before the environmental movement.

"" Not that long ago, hardly a generation back, people did not worry about the food they ate. They did not worry about the water they drank or the air they breathed. It never occurred to them that eating, drinking water, satisfying basic, mundane bodily needs, might be dangerous things to do. Parents thought it was good for their kids to go outside, get some sun.

That is all changed now. People see danger everywhere. Food, water, air, sun. We cannot do without them. Sadly, we now also fear them. We suspect that the water that flows from the tap is contaminated with chemicals that can make us ill. We have learned that conventionally grown fruits and vegetables have pesticide residues and that when we eat meat from conventionally raised animals, we are probably getting a dose of antibiotics and hormones, too. Contaminants can be colorless, tasteless, and odorless, invisible to the senses, and that fact increases the feeling of vulnerability.

People see danger everywhere. Food, water, air, sun. We cannot do without them. Sadly, we now also fear them.

According to the Environmental Protection Agency (EPA), indoor air is more toxic than outdoor air. That is because many household cleaning products and many contemporary home furnishings—carpets, drapes, the fabrics that cover sofas and easy chairs, furniture made of particle board—outgas toxic volatile organic chemicals. OK, we will go outside . . . only to inhale diesel exhaust, particulates suspended in the air, molecules of toxic chemicals wafting from factory smokestacks.

Even sunshine is now considered by many a hazard. Expose yourself to too much sun and your skin will age prematurely. You risk getting skin cancer. The ozone layer has thinned, making exposure to sunlight even more dangerous.

The incidence of melanoma, the deadliest form of skin cancer, is on the rise.

The response has been swift. Everywhere one looks, Americans are buying consumer products that promise to reduce their exposure to harmful substances.

In 1975, Americans were drinking, on average, one gallon of bottled water per person per year. By 2005, the latest year for which we have data, consumption had grown to twenty-six gallons per person per year, over seven and a half billion gallons of bottled water. Bottled water used to account for only a tiny fraction of beverage consumption, inconsequential when compared to soft drinks, coffee and tea, beer, milk, and juice. Today, after enjoying years of "enviable, unending growth," bottled water has become the "superstar [of] the beverage industry." In addition, nearly half of all households use some kind of water filter in the home.

A couple of decades back, organic foods had only a tiny share of the overall food market. Organically grown foods were sold, typically, in small "health food" stores. They were hard to find, even if you wanted them. Few people did. But now, after years of 20 percent annual growth, organic food is mainstream. There are not only organic fruits and vegetables but organic breads and cereals, organic meat, fish, and dairy, organic beer, organic snack food. One can find organic foods in large, attractive, upscale chain stores, such as Whole Foods, and also increasingly in mainstream supermarkets. Safeway and Wal-Mart both sell organic foods.

Those who can afford it buy "organic" or "natural" personal hygiene products, shampoo, soap, makeup; "nontoxic" home cleaning products; clothing made of natural fibers; furniture made of real wood; and rugs made of natural fiber. There is a new ritual in America (at least in middle-class America): applying 30 SPF sunscreen to our children's exposed skin every morning before they go to school, to summer camp, or to the beach. ""

(A. Szasz 2007:1–2) Additional information about this excerpt can be found on the Online Learning Center at www.mhhe.com/schaefermod2e.

I n this excerpt from *Shopping Our Way to Safety: How We Changed from Protecting the Environment to Protecting Ourselves*, sociologist Andrew Szasz links the ecological consciousness that arose from the environmental movement to a new kind of consumerism. Today, he notes, many people fear the everyday environmental hazards present in their immediate surroundings. Rather than work for the health of the environment, however, some try to quarantine themselves from these threats by shopping for supposedly pure, uncontaminated food, clothing, and cleaning products.

As Szasz notes, unless these individual responses go beyond self-protection, they won't improve society's health. What about the many people who cannot afford to drink bottled water or move to a healthier environment? Won't the environment eventually threaten everyone, no matter how much organic food they consume?

What defines a healthy environment? How does health care vary from one social class to another and from one nation to another? In these modules we begin by considering the relationship between culture and health. Then we present a sociological overview of health, illness, health care, and medicine as a social institution. We begin by examining how functionalists, conflict theorists, interactionists, and labeling theorists look at health-related issues. Next we study the distribution of diseases in a society by social class, race and ethnicity, gender, and age.

We'll also look at the evolution of the U.S. health care system. Sociologists are interested in the roles people play in the health care system and the organizations that deal with issues of health and sickness. Therefore, we will analyze the interactions among physicians, nurses, and patients; alternatives to traditional health care; and the role of government in providing health care services to the needy.

Finally, we examine the environmental problems facing the world in the 21st century, and we draw on the functionalist and conflict perspectives to better understand environmental issues. We'll see that it is important not to oversimplify the relationship between health and the environment. The Social Policy section explores the recently renewed interest in environmentalism.

MODULE 52 | Sociological Perspectives on Health and Illness

How can we define health? Imagine a continuum with health on one end and death on the other. In the preamble to its 1946 constitution, the World Health Organization defined **health** as a "state of complete physical, mental, and social well-being, and not merely the absence of disease and infirmity" (Leavell and Clark 1965:14). In this definition, the "healthy" end of the continuum represents an ideal rather than a precise condition.

Along the continuum, individuals define themselves as healthy or sick on the basis of criteria established by themselves and relatives, friends, co-workers, and medical practitioners. Health and illness, in other words, are socially constructed. They are rooted in culture and are defined by claims makers—people who describe themselves as healthy or ill—as well as by a broad range of interested parties, including health care providers, pharmaceutical firms, and even food providers (Conrad and Barker 2010).

Because health is socially constructed, we can consider how it varies in different situations or cultures. Why is it that you may consider yourself sick or well when others do not agree? Who controls definitions of health and illness in our society, and for what ends? What are the consequences of viewing yourself (or of being viewed) as ill or disabled? By drawing on four sociological perspectives—functionalism, conflict theory, interactionism, and labeling theory—we can gain greater insight into the social context that shapes definitions of health and the treatment of illness.

Functionalist Perspective

Illness entails breaks in our social interactions, both at work and at home. From a functionalist perspective, being sick must therefore be controlled, so that not too many people are released from their societal responsibilities at any one time. Functionalists contend that an overly broad definition of illness would disrupt the workings of a society.

Health practices vary from one country to another. Unlike people in most other societies, the Japanese often wear surgical masks in public, to protect themselves from disease or pollution. The practice began in 1919, when the worldwide Spanish flu epidemic became a public health menace. Today mask–wearing persists even when there is no public health threat.

Sickness requires that one take on a social role, if only temporarily. The **sick role** refers to societal expectations about the attitudes and behavior of a person viewed as being ill. Sociologist Talcott Parsons (1951, 1975), well known for his contributions to functionalist theory, outlined the behavior required of people who are considered sick. They are exempted from their normal, day-to-day responsibilities and generally do not suffer blame for their condition. Yet they are obligated to try to get well, which includes seeking competent professional care. This obligation arises from the common view that illness is dysfunctional, because it can undermine social stability. Attempting to get well is particularly important in the world's developing countries. Modern automated industrial societies can absorb a greater degree of illness or disability than horticultural or agrarian societies, in which the availability of workers is far more critical (Conrad 2009b).

According to Parsons's theory, physicians function as *gatekeepers* for the sick role. They verify a patient's condition either as "illness" or as "recovered." The ill person becomes dependent on the physician, because the latter can control valued rewards (not only treatment of illness, but also excused absences from work and school). Parsons suggests that the physician–patient relationship is somewhat like that between parent and child. Like a parent, the physician helps the patient to enter society as a full and functioning adult (Weitz 2009).

The concept of the sick role is not without criticism. First, patients' judgments regarding their own state of health may be related to their gender, age, social class, and ethnic group. For example, younger people may fail to detect warning signs of a dangerous illness, while elderly people may focus too much on the slightest physical malady. Second, the sick role may be more applicable to people who are experiencing short-term illnesses than to those with recurring, long-term illnesses. Finally, even simple factors, such as whether a person is employed, seem to affect one's willingness to assume the sick role—as does the impact of socialization into a particular occupation or activity. For example, beginning in childhood, athletes learn to define certain ailments as "sports injuries" and therefore do not regard themselves as "sick." Nonetheless, sociologists continue to rely on Parsons's model for functionalist analysis of the relationship between illness and societal expectations of the sick (Curry 1993).

 use your **sociological imagination**

Describe some situations you have witnessed that illustrate different definitions of the "sick role."

of a culture. Typically, we think of informal social control as occurring within families and peer groups, and formal social control as being carried out by authorized agents such as police officers, judges, school administrators, and employers. Viewed from a conflict perspective, however, medicine is not simply a "healing profession"; it is a regulating mechanism.

How does medicine manifest its social control? First, medicine has greatly expanded its domain of expertise in recent decades. Physicians now examine a wide range of issues, among them sexuality, old age, anxiety, obesity, child development, alcoholism, and drug addiction. We tolerate this expansion of the boundaries of medicine because we hope that these experts can bring new "miracle cures" to complex human problems, as they have to the control of certain infectious diseases.

The social significance of this expanding medicalization is that once a problem is viewed using a *medical model*—once medical experts become influential in proposing and assessing relevant public policies—it becomes more difficult for common people to join the discussion and exert influence on decision making. It also becomes more difficult to view these issues as being shaped by social, cultural, or psychological factors, rather than simply by physical or medical factors (Caplan 1989; Conrad 2009a).

Second, medicine serves as an agent of social control by retaining absolute jurisdiction over many health care procedures. It has even attempted to guard its jurisdiction by placing health care professionals such as chiropractors and nurse-midwives outside the realm of acceptable medicine. Despite the fact that midwives first brought professionalism to child delivery, they have been portrayed as having invaded the "legitimate" field of obstetrics, in both the United States and Mexico. Nurse-midwives have sought licensing as a way to achieve professional respectability, but physicians continue to exert power to ensure that midwifery remains a subordinate occupation (Scharnberg 2007).

■ Conflict Perspective

Conflict theorists observe that the medical profession has assumed a preeminence that extends well beyond whether to excuse a student from school or an employee from work. Sociologist Eliot Freidson (1970:5) has likened the position of medicine today to that of state religions yesterday—it has an officially approved monopoly of the right to define health and illness and to treat illness. Conflict theorists use the term *medicalization of society* to refer to the growing role of medicine as a major institution of social control (Conrad 2009a; McKinlay and McKinlay 1977; Zola 1972, 1983).

The Medicalization of Society

Social control involves techniques and strategies for regulating behavior in order to enforce the distinctive norms and values

The growing concern about obesity among the young has focused attention on their eating habits and their need for exercise. Concern about obesity is a sign of the medicalization of society.

Inequities in Health Care

The medicalization of society is but one concern of conflict theorists as they assess the workings of health care institutions. As we have seen throughout this textbook, in analyzing any issue, conflict theorists seek to determine who benefits, who suffers, and who dominates at the expense of others. Viewed from a conflict perspective, glaring inequities exist in health care delivery in the United States. For example, poor areas tend to be underserved because medical services concentrate where people are wealthy.

Similarly, from a global perspective, obvious inequities exist in health care delivery. Today, the United States has about 27 physicians per 10,000 people, while African nations have fewer than 1 per 10,000. This situation is only worsened by the **brain drain**—the immigration to the United States and other industrialized nations of skilled workers, professionals, and technicians who are desperately needed in their home countries. As part of this brain drain, physicians, nurses, and other health care professionals have come to the United States from developing countries such as India, Pakistan, and various African states. Conflict theorists view their emigration out of the Third World as yet another way in which the world's core industrialized nations enhance their quality of life at the expense of developing countries. One way the developing countries suffer is in lower life expectancy. In Africa and much of Latin America and Asia, life expectancy is far lower than in industrialized nations (Bureau of the Census 2010a; World Bank 2009).

Conflict theorists emphasize that inequities in health care have clear life-and-death consequences. From a conflict perspective, the dramatic differences in *infant mortality rates* around the world (Figure 52-1) reflect, at least in part, unequal distribution of health care resources based on the wealth or poverty of various nations. The **infant mortality rate** is the number of deaths of infants under 1 year old per 1,000 live births in a given year. This measure is an important indicator of a society's level of health care; it reflects prenatal nutrition, delivery procedures, and infant screening measures. Still, despite the wealth of the United States, at least 41 nations have *lower* infant mortality rates. Conflict theorists point out that unlike the United States, these countries offer some form of government-supported health care for all citizens, which typically leads to greater availability and use of prenatal care (Mathews and MacDorman 2011).

FIGURE 52-1 **Infant Mortality Rates in Selected Countries**

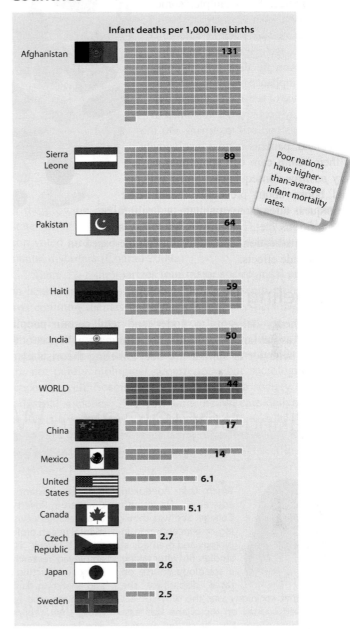

Source: Haub 2011.

 use your **sociological imagination**

From a sociological point of view, what might be the greatest challenge to reducing inequities in health care?

Interactionist Perspective

From an interactionist point of view, patients are not passive; often, they actively seek the services of a health care practitioner. In examining health, illness, and medicine as a social institution, then, interactionists engage in micro-level study of the roles played by health care professionals and patients. Interactionists are particularly interested in how physicians learn to play their occupational role. According to Brenda L. Beagan (2001), the technical language students learn in medical school becomes the basis for the script they follow as novice physicians. The familiar white coat is their costume—one that helps them to appear confident and professional at the same time that it identifies them as doctors to patients and other staff members. Beagan found that many medical students struggle to project the appearance of competence that they think their role demands.

Social epidemiology is the study of the distribution of disease, impairment, and general health status across a population. Initially, epidemiologists concentrated on the scientific study of epidemics, focusing on how they started and spread. Contemporary social epidemiology is much broader in scope, concerned not only with epidemics but also with nonepidemic diseases, injuries, drug addiction and alcoholism, suicide, and mental illness. Epidemiologists have taken on the new role of tracking bioterrorism. In 2001, they mobilized to trace the anthrax outbreak and prepare for any terrorist use of smallpox or other lethal microbes. Epidemiologists draw on the work of a wide variety of scientists and researchers, among them physicians, sociologists, public health officials, biologists, veterinarians, demographers, anthropologists, psychologists, and meteorologists.

Researchers in social epidemiology commonly use two concepts: *incidence* and *prevalence*. **Incidence** refers to the number of new cases of a specific disorder that occur within a given population during a stated period, usually a year. For example, the incidence of AIDS in the United States in 2010 was 48,079 cases. In contrast, **prevalence** refers to the total number of cases of a specific disorder that exist at a given time. The prevalence of HIV/AIDS in the United States is about 800,000 cases.

Worldwide, an estimated 33 million people were infected with HIV at the end of 2009. Women account for a growing proportion of new cases of HIV/AIDS, especially among racial and ethnic minorities. Although the spread of AIDS is stabilizing, with only gradual increases in reported cases, the disease is not evenly distributed. Those areas that are least equipped to deal with it—the developing nations of sub-Saharan Africa—face the greatest challenge (Centers for Disease Control and Prevention 2012c; Figure 53-1).

When disease incidence figures are presented as rates, or as the number of reports per 100,000 people, they are called **morbidity rates.** The term **mortality rate** refers to the incidence of *death* in a given population. Sociologists find morbidity rates useful because they reveal that a specific disease occurs more frequently in one segment of a population than another. As we shall see, social class, race, ethnicity, gender, and age can all affect a population's morbidity rates.

◼ Social Class

Social class is clearly associated with differences in morbidity and mortality rates. Studies in the United States and other countries have consistently shown that people in the lower classes have higher rates of mortality and disability than others.

Why is class linked to health? Crowded living conditions, substandard housing, poor diet, and stress all contribute to the ill health of many low-income people in the United States. In certain instances, poor education may lead to a lack of awareness of measures necessary to maintain good health. Financial strains are certainly a major factor in the health problems of less affluent people.

What is particularly troubling about social class differences is that they appear to be cumulative. Little or no health care in childhood or young adulthood is likely to mean more illness later in life. The longer that low income presents a barrier to adequate health care, the more chronic and difficult to treat illness becomes (Pampel et al. 2010; Phelan et al. 2010).

Another reason for the link between social class and health is that the poor—many of whom belong to racial and ethnic minorities—are less able than others to afford quality medical care. The affluent are more likely than others to have health insurance, either because they can afford it or because they have jobs that provide it. This situation has been deteriorating over time, as employer-provided coverage (the most common form of health insurance) declined steadily from 2000 through 2009. In 2008, 46.3 million people reported going without health care because they could not pay for it; in 2009, 50.7 million went without.

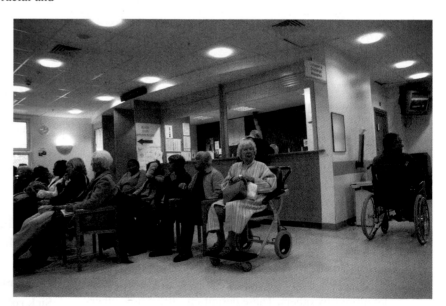

When people who do not have health insurance seek medical care, their condition is often more critical than it would be had they been receiving regular preventive care from a primary care provider. And the care they receive, especially in an emergency room, is much more expensive than the care in a doctor's office.

FIGURE 53-1 **People Living with HIV**

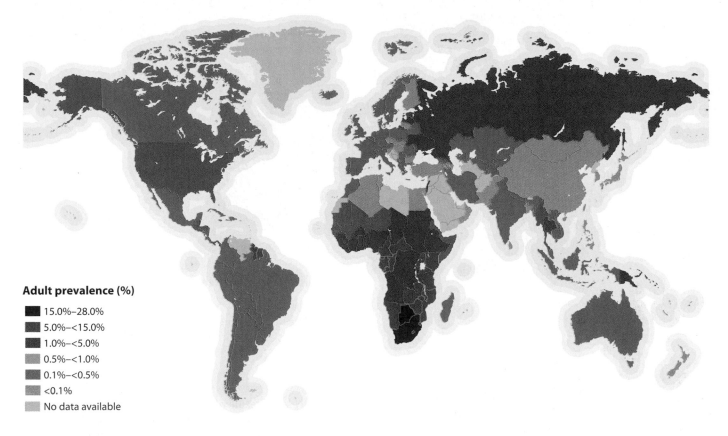

Adult prevalence (%)

- 15.0%–28.0%
- 5.0%–<15.0%
- 1.0%–<5.0%
- 0.5%–<1.0%
- 0.1%–<0.5%
- <0.1%
- No data available

Note: Data for the 33.3 million people (estimated range, 31.4–35.8 million) living with HIV at the end of 2009.
Source: UNAIDS 2010:23.

And increasingly, pharmacists reported that people were purchasing only those medications they "needed the most," or were buying in small quantities, such as four pills at a time. Even for children, many of whom are eligible for government-subsidized health insurance, coverage varies widely, ranging from 98.5 percent in Massachusetts to 81.6 percent in Nevada (Figure 53-2).

Finally, in the view of Karl Marx and contemporary conflict theorists, capitalist societies such as the United States care more about maximizing profits than they do about the health and safety of industrial workers. As a result, government agencies do not take forceful action to regulate conditions in the workplace, and workers suffer many preventable job-related injuries and illnesses. As we will see later in this chapter, research also shows that the lower classes are more vulnerable to environmental pollution than are the affluent, not only where they work but where they live.

 use your sociological imagination

Does the cost of health care affect the way you receive medical services?

trend|spotting

Longer Life Spans, More Social Change

Improved public health—a significant social change in itself—brings longer life expectancy. Ironically, this particular social change means that people living in the 21st century will experience more social change than past generations, and more stress because of it.

On average, a person born in the United States in 1900 could anticipate living to the age of 47. By 1927, life expectancy in the United States had been extended to age 60; by 1964, to age 70. By 1994, the birth year of many first-year college students today, average life expectancy had risen to 75 years. Those born in 2020 are expected to live—and experience social change—for over 79 years.

Significant differences in life expectancy exist among subgroups of the population. Women live longer than men, and Whites live longer than Blacks. Among those born in 1994, for example, a White female can anticipate living to 79.6 years of age, while a Black male can anticipate a life span of 64.9 years—the expected age of White females born in 1935.

FIGURE 53-2 **Percentage of Children without Health Insurance**

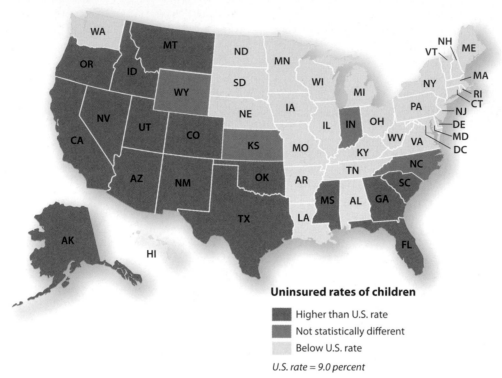

Uninsured rates of children

- ■ Higher than U.S. rate
- ■ Not statistically different
- □ Below U.S. rate

U.S. rate = 9.0 percent

Source: Mach and Blumenthal 2010:2.

Think about It

Do you know people whose children don't have health insurance? If so, how has the lack of insurance affected their decisions about their children's medical treatment?

■ Race and Ethnicity

The health profiles of many racial and ethnic minorities reflect the social inequality evident in the United States. The poor economic and environmental conditions of groups such as African Americans, Hispanics, and Native Americans are manifested in high morbidity and mortality rates for those groups. It is true that some diseases, such as sickle-cell anemia among Blacks, have a clear genetic basis. But in most instances, environmental factors contribute to the differential rates of disease and death.

As noted earlier, infant mortality is regarded as a primary indicator of health care. There is a significant gap in the United States between the infant mortality rates of African Americans and Whites. Generally, the rate of infant death is more than twice as high among Blacks (MacDorman and Mathews 2009).

The medical establishment is not exempt from racism. Unfortunately, the media often focus on obvious forms of racism, such as hate crimes, while overlooking more insidious forms in social institutions like the medical establishment. Minorities receive inferior medical care even when they are insured. Despite having access to care, Blacks, Latinos, and Native Americans are treated unequally as a result of racial prejudice and differences in the quality of various health care plans. Furthermore, national clinical studies have shown that even allowing for differences in income and insurance coverage, racial and ethnic minorities are less likely than other groups to receive both standard health care and life-saving treatment for conditions such as HIV infection (Centers for Disease Control and Prevention 2011b; Long and Masi 2009).

Drawing on the conflict perspective, sociologist Howard Waitzkin (1986) suggests that racial tensions also contribute to the medical problems of Blacks. In his view, the stress that results from racial prejudice and discrimination helps to explain the higher rates of hypertension found among African Americans (and Hispanics) compared to Whites. Hypertension—twice as common in Blacks as in Whites—is believed to be a critical factor in Blacks' high mortality rates from heart disease, kidney disease, and stroke (Centers for Disease Control and Prevention 2011b).

Some Mexican Americans and many other Latinos adhere to cultural beliefs that make them less likely than others to use the established medical system. They may interpret their illnesses according to ***curanderismo,*** or traditional Latino folk medicine—a form of holistic health care and healing. *Curanderismo* influences how one approaches health care and even how one defines illness. Most Hispanics probably use *curanderos,* or folk healers, infrequently, but perhaps 20 percent rely on home remedies. Some define such illnesses as *susto* (fright sickness) and *atague* (fighting attack) according to folk beliefs. Because these complaints often have biological bases, sensitive medical practitioners need to deal with them carefully in order to diagnose and treat illnesses accurately. Moreover, it would be a mistake to blame the poor health care that Latinos receive on cultural differences. Latinos are much more likely to seek treatment for pressing medical problems at clinics and emergency rooms than they are to receive regular preventive care through a family physician (Centers for Disease Control and Prevention 2011b; Durden and Hummer 2006; Trotter and Chavira 1997).

Gender

A large body of research indicates that compared with men, women experience a higher prevalence of many illnesses, although they tend to live longer. There are some variations—for example, men are more likely to have parasitic diseases, whereas women are more likely to become diabetic—but as a group, women appear to be in poorer health than men.

The apparent inconsistency between the ill health of women and their greater longevity deserves an explanation, and researchers have advanced a theory. Women's lower rate of cigarette smoking (reducing their risk of heart disease, lung cancer, and emphysema), lower consumption of alcohol (reducing the risk of auto accidents and cirrhosis of the liver), and lower rate of employment in dangerous occupations explain about one-third of their greater longevity than men. Moreover, some clinical studies suggest that the differences in morbidity may actually be less pronounced than the data show. Researchers argue that women are much more likely than men to seek treatment, to be diagnosed as having a disease, and thus to have their illnesses reflected in the data examined by epidemiologists.

From a conflict perspective, women have been particularly vulnerable to the medicalization of society, with everything from birth to beauty being treated in an increasingly medical context. Such medicalization may contribute to women's higher morbidity rates compared to those of men. Ironically, even though women have been especially affected by medicalization, medical researchers have often excluded them from clinical studies. Female physicians and researchers charge that sexism lies at the heart of such research practices, and insist there is a desperate need for studies of female subjects (Centers for Disease Control and Prevention 2011b; Rieker and Bird 2000).

Age

Health is the overriding concern of the elderly. Most older people in the United States report having at least one chronic illness, but only some of those conditions are potentially life threatening or require medical care. At the same time, health problems can affect the quality of life of older people in important ways. Almost half of older people in the United States are troubled by arthritis, and many have visual or hearing impairments that can interfere with the performance of everyday tasks.

Older people are also especially vulnerable to certain mental health problems. Alzheimer's disease, the leading cause of dementia in the United States, afflicts an estimated 5.4 million people age 65 or over—that is, 13 percent of that segment of the population. While some individuals with Alzheimer's exhibit only mild symptoms, the risk of severe problems resulting from the disease rises substantially with age (Alzheimer's Association 2012).

Not surprisingly, older people in the United States (age 75 and older) are five times more likely to use health services than younger people (ages 15–24). The disproportionate use of the U.S. health care system by older people is a critical factor in all discussions about the cost of health care and possible reforms of the health care system (Bureau of the Census 2011a).

In sum, to achieve greater access and reduce health disparities, federal health officials must overcome inequities that are rooted not just in age, but in social class, race and ethnicity, and gender. If that were not enough, they must also deal with a geographical disparity in health care resources.

MODULE 53 | **Recap and Review**

Summary

Social epidemiology is concerned both with epidemics and with nonepidemic diseases, injuries, drug addiction and alcoholism, suicide, and mental illness.

1. Studies consistently show that people from lower socioeconomic groups have higher rates of mortality and disability than others.

2. Racial and ethnic minorities have higher rates of **morbidity** and **mortality** than Whites.

3. Women tend to be in poorer health than men, but nevertheless they live longer.

4. Older people are especially vulnerable to mental health problems such as Alzheimer's disease, as well as to physical ailments.

Thinking Critically

1. Which is a more important factor in the adequate delivery of health care, race or gender?

2. What are some of the likely social consequences of passage of the Patient Protection and Affordable Care Act of 2010?

Key Terms

Curanderismo   **440**

Incidence   **438**

Morbidity rate   **438**

Mortality rate   **438**

Prevalence   **438**

Social epidemiology   **438**

As the entire nation is well aware, the costs of health care have skyrocketed. In 1997, total expenditures for health care in the United States crossed the trillion-dollar threshold—more than four times the 1980 total (Figure 54-1). In 2000, the amount spent on health care equaled that spent on education, defense, prisons, farm subsidies, food stamps, and foreign aid combined. By the year 2020, total expenditures for health care in the United States are expected to exceed $4.6 trillion. The rising costs of medical care are especially burdensome in the event of catastrophic illnesses or confinement to a nursing home. Bills of tens of thousands of dollars are not unusual in the treatment of cancer, Alzheimer's disease, and other chronic illnesses requiring custodial care.

The health care system of the United States has moved far beyond the days when general practitioners living in a neighborhood or community typically made house calls and charged modest fees for their services. How did health care become a big business involving nationwide hospital chains and marketing campaigns? How have these changes reshaped the interactions between doctors, nurses, and patients? We will address these questions in the next section of the chapter.

A Historical View

Today, state licensing and medical degrees confer an authority on medical professionals that is maintained from one generation to the next. However, health care in the United States has not always followed this model. The "popular health movement" of the 1830s and 1840s emphasized preventive care and what is termed "self-help." Strong criticism was voiced of "doctoring" as a paid occupation. New medical philosophies or sects established their own medical schools and challenged the authority and methods of more traditional doctors. By the 1840s, most states had repealed medical licensing laws.

FIGURE 54-1 **Total Health Care Expenditures in the United States, 1970–2019 (Projected)**

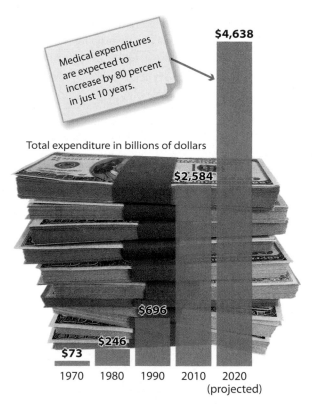

Medical expenditures are expected to increase by 80 percent in just 10 years.

$4,638

$2,584

Total expenditure in billions of dollars

$696

$246

$73

| 1970 | 1980 | 1990 | 2010 | 2020 (projected) |

Sources: Centers for Medicare and Medicaid Services 2011:Table 1 (2005–2020 data); Health Care Financing Administration 2001 (1970–1990 data).

Think about It

What social changes in the United States might account for the rise in health care costs from $73 billion in 1970 to almost $2.6 trillion in 2010?

"I'm going to hold up a number of outstanding medical bills. Tell me how many you see."

In response, through the leadership of the American Medical Association (AMA), founded in 1848, "regular" doctors attacked lay practitioners, sectarian doctors, and female physicians in general. Once they had institutionalized their authority through standardized programs of education and licensing, they conferred it on all who successfully completed their programs. The authority of the physician no longer depended on lay attitudes or on the person occupying the sick role; increasingly, it was built into the structure of the medical profession and the health care system. As the institutionalization of health care proceeded, the medical profession gained control over both the market for its services and the various organizational hierarchies that govern medical practice, financing, and policymaking. By the 1920s, physicians controlled hospital technology, the division of labor of health personnel, and indirectly, other professional practices such as nursing and pharmacy (R. Coser 1984).

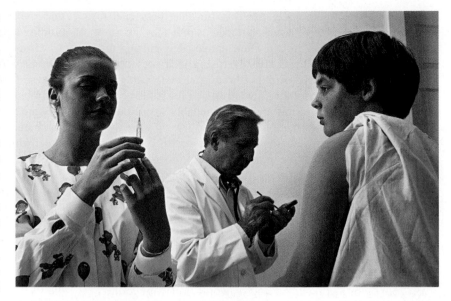

As if the status differences between nurses and physicians were not clear to all, the cheery uniform of nurses and the formal white doctor's coat reinforce the distinction.

 # RESEARCH TODAY

BOX 54-1

Health Care, Retail Style

Greeting cards are in aisle 7; vaccinations, in aisle 4. Today, over 1,200 health clinics are located in retail stores throughout the United States, including Walgreens, CVS, and Walmart. Staffed by nurse-practitioners and nurses with advanced degrees, these in-store clinics treat a limited menu of complaints, including sore throats, ear infections, pinkeye, and noncomplicated respiratory conditions. And the nurses do write prescriptions.

What are the implications of these new clinics for traditional health care? Having a regular physician is becoming less and less common in the United States, given the many people who lack health insurance, as well as the frequent changes in corporate health plans. Like it or not, the physician you see this year simply may not be available to you next year. Under these circumstances, retail medical care may not pose much of a challenge to traditional medical practices.

What about the quality of care offered at in-store clinics? Recently, researchers compared the care delivered in retail clinics to the care available in doctors' offices, urgent care departments, and emergency rooms. For three acute conditions—sore throat, middle ear infection, and urinary tract infection—they found that retail clinics delivered the same or better-quality care than traditional medical settings, including preventive care during or after the first visit. Costs were much lower, especially compared to those in emergency rooms.

In-store clinics are another example of **McDonaldization**, the process through which the principles of the fast-food restaurant are

> For three acute conditions— sore throat, middle ear infection, and urinary tract infection—retail clinics delivered the same or better-quality care than traditional medical settings.

coming to dominate more and more sectors of society. McDonaldization offers the benefit of clearly stated services and prices, but the drawback of impersonality. Family doctors note that 40 percent of clinic patients have a family physician. Yet given the shortcomings of health care delivery in the United States, it is difficult to argue against an innovative new method of providing health care.

LET'S DISCUSS

1. Have you ever been treated at an in-store clinic? If so, were you satisfied with the care you received? What about the price you paid—was it reasonable?

2. Evaluate the emergence of clinics from a functionalist and then a conflict perspective. On balance, do you think these clinics are a benefit to society?

Sources: Pickert 2009; RAND 2010; Ritzer 2011.

Patients have traditionally relied on medical personnel to inform them of health care issues, but increasingly they are turning to the media for health care information. Recognizing this change, pharmaceutical firms are advertising their prescription drugs directly to potential customers through television and magazines. The Internet is another growing source for patient information. Medical professionals are understandably suspicious of these new sources of information.

Today, consumers get more than their health care information in new ways. Over the past decade, they have discovered a new way to access traditional medicine: going to the store (Box 54-1).

 use your **sociological imagination**

If you were a patient, would you put yourself entirely in the physician's hands, or would you do some research on your own? If you were a doctor, would you want your patient checking medical information on the Internet? Explain your positions.

Physicians, Nurses, and Patients

Traditionally, physicians have held a position of dominance in their dealings with both patients and nurses. The functionalist and interactionist perspectives offer a framework for understanding the professional socialization of physicians as it relates to patient care. Functionalists suggest that established physicians and medical school professors serve as mentors or role models who transmit knowledge, skills, and values to the passive learner—the medical student. Interactionists emphasize that students are molded by the medical school environment as they interact with their classmates.

Both approaches argue that the typical training of physicians in the United States leads to rather dehumanizing physician–patient encounters. As Dr. Lori Arviso Alvord, a Navajo physician, writes in *The Scalpel and the Silver Bear,* "I had been trained by a group of physicians who placed much more emphasis on their technical abilities and clinical skills than on their abilities to be caring and sensitive" (Alvord and Van Pelt 1999:13). Despite many efforts to formally introduce a humanistic approach to patient care into the medical school curriculum, patient overload and cost-cutting by hospitals have tended to undercut positive relations. Moreover, widespread publicity about malpractice suits and high medical costs has further strained the physician–patient relationship. Interactionists have closely examined compliance and negotiation between physician and patient. They concur with Talcott Parsons's view that the relationship is generally asymmetrical, with doctors holding a position of dominance and controlling rewards.

Just as physicians have maintained dominance in their interactions with patients, they have controlled interactions with nurses. Despite their training and professional status, nurses commonly take orders from physicians. Traditionally, the relationship between doctors and nurses has paralleled the male dominance of the United States: most physicians have been male, while virtually all nurses have been female.

Like other women in subordinate roles, nurses have been expected to perform their duties without challenging the authority of men. Psychiatrist Leonard Stein (1967) refers to this process as the *doctor–nurse game.* According to the rules of this "game," the nurse must never openly disagree with the physician. When she has recommendations concerning a patient's care, she must communicate them indirectly, in a deferential tone. For example, if asked by a hospital's medical resident, "What sleeping medication has been helpful to Mrs. Brown in the past?" (an indirect request for a recommendation), the nurse will respond with a disguised recommendation, such as "Pentobarbital 100 mg was quite effective night before last." Her careful response allows the physician to authoritatively restate the same prescription as if it were *his* idea.

Like nurses, female physicians have traditionally found themselves in a subordinate position because of their gender, but that is slowly changing as their numbers increase. Box 54-2 on page 445 considers the social impact of the growing number of female physicians and surgeons on the medical field.

Alternatives to Traditional Health Care

In traditional forms of health care, people rely on physicians and hospitals for the treatment of illness. Yet at least one out of every three adults in the United States attempts to maintain good health or respond to illness through the use of alternative health care techniques. For example, in recent decades interest has been growing in *holistic* (also spelled *wholistic*) medical principles, first developed in China. **Holistic medicine** refers to therapies in which the health care practitioner considers the person's physical, mental, emotional, and spiritual characteristics. The individual is regarded as a totality rather than a collection of interrelated organ systems. Treatment methods include massage, chiropractic medicine, acupuncture (which involves the insertion of fine needles into surface points), respiratory exercises, and the use of herbs as remedies. Nutrition, exercise, and visualization may also be used to treat ailments that are generally treated through medication or hospitalization (Sharma and Bodeker 1998).

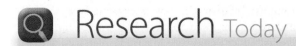
Women as Physicians and Surgeons

When Perri Klass told her four-year-old son she would be taking him to the pediatrician, he replied, "Is she a nice doctor?" Klass, a professor of pediatrics, was struck by his innocent assumption that like his mother, all pediatricians were female. "Boys can be doctors, too," she told him.

Not long ago, there would have been little potential for confusion on her son's part. Klass probably would not have been admitted to medical school, no less appointed a professor of medicine. Today, women represent nearly half of all medical students in the United States, where they account for one third of all physicians and two thirds of physician assistants. Yet female doctors make less income than men, even within the same specialty and even in the first years of their careers.

What has been the impact of this increase in the number of women in medicine? For one thing, female physicians may have improved physician–patient communication. Female primary care physicians spend an extra two minutes talking with patients—10 percent more time than male primary care physicians. They also engage in more patient-centered communication, listening more, asking questions about patients' personal well-being, and counseling patients about the concerns they bring to the doctor's office. Perhaps more important, female physicians tend to see their relationship with patients as an active partnership, one in which they discuss several treatment

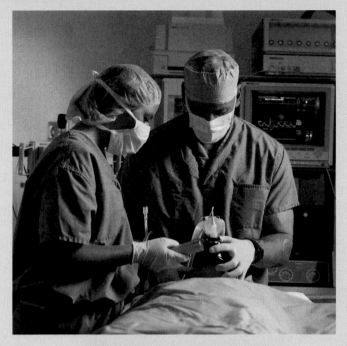

> Female physicians tend to see their relationship with patients as an active partnership, one in which they discuss several treatment options rather than recommending a single course of treatment.

options rather than recommending a single course of treatment. From an interactionist perspective, these differences between

female and male physicians correspond to typical gender differences in communication.

Women physicians may also have made medicine a more family-friendly profession. Nowadays, physicians who wish to, both male and female, can develop practices that allow them to spend more time at home. Despite this change in the medical field, female doctors still seem to experience more frustration than male doctors. A national study of nearly 8,000 surgeons found that 62 percent of women complained of a work–home conflict, compared to 49 percent of the men. Female surgeons were also three times as likely as male surgeons to believe that childrearing would slow their career advancement. That complaint may disappear over time, however. Ultimately, the growing participation of women in this traditionally male-dominated field has the potential to completely reshape the health profession.

LET'S DISCUSS

1. In your own experience, have you noted a gender difference in the way doctors communicate with patients? Explain.

2. Why is the quality of a doctor's communication with patients important? What might be the benefit of female physicians' superior communication style?

Sources: Tracey Adams 2010; Buddeberg-Fischer et al. 2012; Bureau of the Census 2011a:Table 616, page 394; Dyrbye et al. 2011; Klass 2003:319; Lo Sasso et al. 2011; Roter et al. 2002.

Practitioners of holistic medicine do not necessarily function totally outside the traditional health care system. Some have medical degrees and rely on X-rays and EKG machines for diagnostic assistance. Others who staff holistic clinics, often referred to as *wellness clinics,* reject the use of medical technology. The recent resurgence of holistic medicine comes amid widespread recognition of the value of nutrition and the dangers of over-reliance on prescription drugs (especially those used to reduce stress, such as Valium).

The medical establishment—professional organizations, research hospitals, and medical schools—has generally served as a

stern protector of traditionally accepted health care techniques. However, a major breakthrough occurred in 1992 when the federal government's National Institutes of Health—the nation's major funding source for biomedical research—opened the National Center for Complementary and Alternative Medicine, empowered to accept grant requests. NIH-sponsored national surveys conducted in 2002 and 2007 found that one in four adults in the United States had used some form of "complementary and alternative medicine" during the previous month or year. Examples included acupuncture, folk medicine, meditation, yoga, homeopathic treatments, megavitamin therapy, and chiropractic treatment. When prayer was included as an alternative or complementary form of medicine, the proportion of adults who used alternative medicine rose to over 62 percent (Figure 54-2).

On the international level, the World Health Organization (WHO) has begun to monitor the use of alternative medicine around the world. According to WHO, 80 percent of people who live in the poorest countries in the world use some form of alternative medicine, from herbal treatments to the services of a faith healer. In most countries, these treatments are largely unregulated, even though some of them can be fatal. For example, kava kava, an herbal tea used in the Pacific Islands to relieve anxiety, can be toxic to the liver in concentrated form. However, other alternative treatments have been found to be effective in the treatment of serious diseases, such as malaria and sickle-cell anemia. WHO's goal is to compile a list of such practices, as well as to encourage the development of universal training programs and ethical standards for practitioners of alternative medicine. To date, the organization has published findings on about 100 of the 5,000 plants believed to be used as herbal remedies (McNeil 2002).

assistance programs: Medicare, which is essentially a compulsory health insurance plan for the elderly, and Medicaid, which is a noncontributory federal and state insurance plan for the poor. These programs greatly expanded federal involvement in health care financing for needy men, women, and children.

Given the high rates of illness and disability among elderly people, Medicare has had a huge impact on the health care system. Initially, Medicare simply reimbursed health care providers such as physicians and hospitals for the billed costs of their services. However, in 1983, as the overall costs of Medicare increased dramatically, the federal government introduced a price-control system. Under this system, private hospitals often transfer patients whose treatment may be unprofitable to public facilities. In fact, many private hospitals have begun to conduct "wallet biopsies"— that is, to investigate the financial status of potential patients. Those judged undesirable are then refused admission or dumped. Although a federal law passed in 1987 made it illegal for any hospital receiving Medicare funds to dump patients, the practice continues (E. Gould 2007; Light 2004).

The Role of Government

Not until the 20th century did health care receive federal aid. The first significant involvement was the 1946 Hill-Burton Act, which provided subsidies for building and improving hospitals, especially in rural areas. A far more important change came with the enactment in 1965 of two wide-ranging government

FIGURE 54-2 **Use of Complementary and Alternative Medicine**

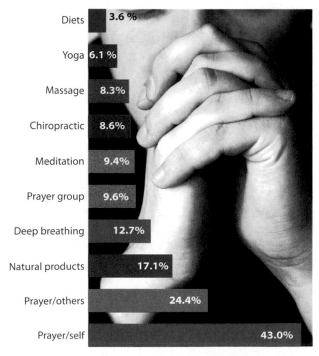

Diets	3.6%
Yoga	6.1%
Massage	8.3%
Chiropractic	8.6%
Meditation	9.4%
Prayer group	9.6%
Deep breathing	12.7%
Natural products	17.1%
Prayer/others	24.4%
Prayer/self	43.0%

Note: Data from 2007 survey, except for prayer data from 2002 survey.
Source: P. Barnes et al. 2004, 2008.

Tensions ran high as the Supreme Court heard arguments on the constitutionality of controversial new federal health care legislation. These citizens are indicating their opposition to the 2010 Affordable Care Act.

The 2010 Affordable Care Act improved health insurance coverage for people of all ages, especially young adults, who were allowed to remain longer on their parents' policies. President Obama's administration had pushed for the act in response to several problems, including high out-of-pocket costs for the uninsured and the inability of people with preexisting conditions to get insurance. However, critics complained that the act was too expensive for taxpayers, and unnecessarily—perhaps even unconstitutionally—dictated citizens' health care decisions (Budrys 2012; Skocpol and Williamson 2012).

MODULE 54 | Recap and Review

Summary

The health care system in the United States is a complex and expensive social institution that has evolved from relatively simple roots.

1. The preeminent role of physicians in the U.S. health care system gives them a position of dominance in their dealings with nurses and patients.

2. Many people use alternative health care techniques such as **holistic medicine** and self-help groups.

Thinking Critically

1. Explain the dominance of physicians in the health care system from a conflict perspective.

2. In the United States, a nation with a world-renowned medical system, why do so many people seek alternative forms of health care?

Key Terms

Holistic medicine   444

McDonaldization   443

MODULE 55 | Sociological Perspectives on the Environment

We have seen that the environment people live in has a noticeable effect on their health. Those who live in stressful, overcrowded places suffer more from disease than those who do not. Likewise, people have a noticeable effect on their environment. Around the world, increases in population, together with the economic development that accompanies them, have had serious environmental consequences. We can see signs of despoliation almost everywhere: our air, our water, and our land are being polluted, whether we live in St. Louis, Mexico City, or Lagos, Nigeria.

Though environmental problems may be easy to identify, devising socially and politically acceptable solutions to them is much more difficult. In this section we will see what sociologists have to say about the trade-off between economic growth and development and its effects on the environment. In the section that follows we will look more closely at specific environmental issues.

■ Human Ecology

Human ecology is an area of study that is concerned with the interrelationships between people and their environment. As the environmentalist Barry Commoner (1971:39) put it, "Everything is connected to everything else." Human ecologists focus on how the physical environment shapes people's lives and on how people influence the surrounding environment.

There is no shortage of illustrations of the interconnectedness of people and their environment. For example, scientific research has linked pollutants in the physical environment to people's health and behavior. The increasing prevalence of asthma, lead poisoning, and cancer have all been tied to human alterations to the environment. Similarly, the rise in melanoma (skin cancer) diagnoses has been linked to global warming. And ecological changes in our food and diet have been related to early obesity and diabetes.

With its view that "everything is connected to everything else," human ecology stresses the trade-offs inherent in every decision that alters the environment. In facing the environmental challenges of the 21st century, government policymakers and environmentalists must determine how they can fulfill humans' pressing needs for food, clothing, and shelter while preserving the environment.

▣ Conflict Perspective on the Environment

In Module 29, we drew on world systems analysis to show how a growing share of the human and natural resources of developing countries is being redistributed to the core industrialized nations. This process only intensifies the destruction of natural resources in poorer regions of the world. From a conflict perspective, less affluent nations are being forced to exploit their mineral deposits, forests, and fisheries in order to meet their debt obligations. The poor turn to the only means of survival available to them: they plow mountain slopes, burn plots in tropical forests, and overgraze grasslands (World Bank 2010b).

Brazil exemplifies this interplay between economic troubles and environmental destruction. Each year more than 5.7 million acres of forest are cleared for crops and livestock. The elimination of the rain forest affects worldwide weather patterns, heightening the gradual warming of the earth. These socioeconomic patterns, with their harmful environmental consequences, are evident not only in Latin America but in many regions of Africa and Asia.

Conflict theorists are well aware of the environmental implications of land use policies in the Third World, but they contend that focusing on the developing countries is ethnocentric. First, throughout most of history, developed countries have been the major source of greenhouse gas emissions. As Figure 55-1 shows, only recently have developing nations begun to emit greenhouse gases in the same quantities as developed nations.

FIGURE 55-1 Projected Greenhouse Gas Emissions

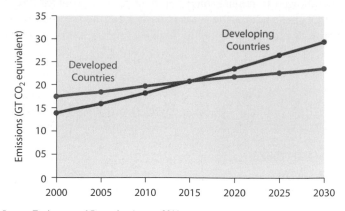

Source: Environmental Protection Agency 2011.
By 2015, total greenhouse gas emissions from developing countries are expected to exceed those from developed countries.

Think about It

Why do you think the contemporary debate about greenhouse gas emissions focuses on developing nations, when for decades industrial nations have been the main culprits?

(Greenhouse gas emissions will be discussed in more detail later.) Second, the industrialized nations of North America and Europe account for only 12 percent of the world's population but are responsible for 60 percent of worldwide consumption. Who, these theorists ask, is more to blame for environmental deterioration: the poverty-stricken and "food-hungry" populations of the world or the "energy-hungry" industrialized nations? The money that residents of developed countries spend on ocean cruises each year could provide clean drinking water for everyone on the planet. Ice cream expenditures in Europe alone could be used to immunize every child in the world. Thus, conflict theorists charge, the most serious threat to the environment comes from the global consumer class (Gardner et al. 2004; Shah 2009).

Allan Schnaiberg (1994) further refined this analysis by shifting the focus from affluent consumers to the capitalist system as the cause of environmental troubles. In his view, a capitalist system creates a "treadmill of production" because of its inherent need to build ever-expanding profits. This treadmill necessitates the creation of increasing demand for products, the purchase of natural resources at minimal cost, and the manufacturing of products as quickly and cheaply as possible—no matter what the long-term environmental consequences.

Can you identify these slowly sinking replicas of world-famous landmarks? Greenpeace staged the publicity stunt to draw attention to global warming during climate talks in Cancún, Mexico, in 2010.

Ecological Modernization

Critics of the human ecological and conflict models argue that they are too rooted in the past. People who take these approaches, they charge, have become bogged down in addressing existing practices. Instead, proponents of **ecological modernization,** an approach that emerged in the 1980s, focus on the alignment of environmentally favorable practices with economic self-interest through constant adaptation and restructuring (Mol 2010; Mol and Sonnenfeld 2000; Mol et al. 2009).

Ecological modernization can occur on both the macro and micro levels. On a macro level, adaptation and restructuring can mean reintegrating industrial waste back into the production process. On a micro level, it can mean reshaping individual lifestyles, including the consumption patterns described at the start of this chapter. In a sense, those who practice ecological modernization seek to refute the oft-expressed notion that being environmentally conscious means "going back to nature" or "living off the grid." Even modest changes in production and consumption patterns, they believe, can increase environmental sustainability (York et al. 2010).

Environmental Justice

In autumn 1982, nearly 500 African Americans participated in a six-week protest against a hazardous waste landfill in North Carolina. Their protests and legal actions against the dangerous cancer-causing chemicals continued until 2002, when decontamination of the site finally began. This 20-year battle could be seen as yet another "not in my backyard" (NIMBY) event. But today, the Warren County struggle is viewed as a transformative moment in contemporary environmentalism: the beginning of the *environmental justice* movement (Bullard 1993; McGurty 2000; North Carolina Department of Environmental and Natural Resources 2008).

Environmental justice is a legal strategy based on claims that racial minorities are subjected disproportionately to environmental hazards. Some observers have heralded environmental justice as the "new civil rights of the 21st century" (Kokmen 2008:42). Since the start of the environmental justice movement, activists and scholars have discovered other environmental disparities that break along racial and social class lines. In general, poor people and people of color are much more likely than others to be victimized by the everyday consequences of our built environment, including the air pollution from expressways and incinerators.

Sociologists Paul Mohai and Robin Saha (2007) examined over 600 identified hazardous waste treatment, storage, and disposal facilities in the United States. They found that non-Whites and Latinos make up 43 percent of the people who live within one mile of these dangerous sites. Skeptics often argue that minorities move near such sites because of low housing prices. However, two recent longitudinal (long-term) research studies, done over 30- and 50-year periods, found that toxic facilities tend to be located in minority communities (Mohai et al. 2009:413).

The environmental justice movement has become globalized, for several reasons. In many nations, activists have noticed similar patterns in the location of hazardous waste sites. These groups have begun to network across international borders, to share their tactics and remedies. Their unified approach is wise, because the offending corporations are often multinational entities (see Module 29); influencing their actions, much less prosecuting them, is difficult. As we have noted before, the global warming debate often focuses criticism on developing nations like China and India, rather than on established industrial giants with a long history of greenhouse gas emissions (Mohai et al. 2009; Shah 2009).

Sociologists, then, have emphasized both the interconnectedness of humans and the environment and the divisiveness of race and social class in their work on humans and their alteration of the environment. Scientists, too, have taken different

Environmental Justice draws attention to the fact that the poor, along with racial and ethnic minorities, are more likely than the rich to live near refineries, waste dumps, and other environmental hazards.

approaches, disagreeing sharply on the likely outcomes of environmental change. When these disagreements threaten to affect government policy and economic regulations, they become highly politicized.

● Environmental Issues

Around the world, people are recognizing the need to address challenges to the environment. Yet in the United States, survey respondents do not see environmental issues as the most pressing of concerns, and they often balk at proposed solutions. Unfortunately, framing environmental issues as "problems" may prevent people from seeing environmental deterioration as the by-product of both institutional practices and their own behavior. Thus, in a 2011 national survey, 41 percent of the respondents said they were unsure about the scientific evidence of global warming, and 43 percent thought the seriousness of the climate trend was generally exaggerated. Only 9 percent of those surveyed expected that they would see the effects of global warming in their lifetime (J. Jones and Saad 2011).

We will discuss the enormous challenge of global warming in this section, along with three broad areas of environmental concern. Two of them, air and water pollution, are thought to be contributors to global warming.

Air Pollution

Worldwide, more than 1 billion people are exposed to potentially health-damaging levels of air pollution. Unfortunately, in cities around the world, residents have come to accept smog and polluted air as normal. Urban air pollution is caused primarily by emissions from automobiles and secondarily by emissions from electric power plants and heavy industries. Smog not only limits visibility; it also can lead to health problems as uncomfortable as eye irritation and as deadly as lung cancer. Such problems are especially severe in developing countries.

Although people are capable of changing their behavior, they are unwilling to make such changes permanent. During the 1984 Olympics in Los Angeles, residents were asked to carpool and stagger their work hours to relieve traffic congestion and improve the quality of the air athletes would breathe. These changes resulted in a remarkable 12 percent drop in ozone levels. But when the Olympians left, people reverted to their normal behavior and the ozone levels climbed back up. Similarly, in the 2008 Olympics, China took drastic action to ensure that Beijing's high levels of air pollution did not mar the games. Construction work in the city ceased, polluting factories and power plants closed down, and roads were swept and sprayed with water several times a day. This temporary solution hardly solved China's ongoing problem, however (A. Jacobs 2010).

On an everyday basis—that is, when cities are not holding down their emissions because of global sports events—air pollution remains a serious issue. Today, half of all people live in countries where they are exposed to dangerously high levels of air pollution, either short-term or year-round. Solutions range from community efforts to clean up power plants and enforce

or strengthen air quality standards to individual actions, like driving less often or using less electricity (American Lung Association 2011).

Water Pollution

Throughout the United States, dumping of waste materials by industries and local governments has polluted streams, rivers, and lakes. Consequently, many bodies of water have become unsafe for drinking, fishing, and swimming. Around the world, pollution of the oceans is an issue of growing concern. Such pollution results regularly from waste dumping and is made worse by fuel leaks from shipping and occasional oil spills. When the oil tanker *Exxon Valdez* ran aground in Prince William Sound, Alaska, in 1989, its cargo of more than 11 million gallons of crude oil spilled into the sound and washed onto the shore, contaminating 1,285 miles of shoreline. All together, about 11,000 people joined in a massive cleanup effort that cost over $2 billion. Globally, oil tanker spills occur regularly. The oil spilled from BP's Deepwater Horizon oil platform in 2010 is estimated at *sixteen times* or more that of the *Exxon Valdez* (ITOPF 2006; Shapley 2010).

Less dramatic than large-scale accidents or disasters, but more common in many parts of the world, are problems with the basic water supply. The situation is worsened by heavy, widespread pollution of surface and groundwater by towns, industries, agriculture, and mining operations. In Egypt, a typical example, agricultural and industrial waste pours into the Nile. Every year about 17,000 Egyptian children die from diarrhea and dehydration after contact with the river's polluted water (Hengeveld 2012).

Global Warming

Based primarily on complex computer models, scientists have made hundreds of projections of global warming. The term *global warming* refers to the significant rise in the earth's surface temperatures that occurs when industrial gases like carbon

Images like this one have been combined with scientific data to draw attention to global warming.

dioxide turn the planet's atmosphere into a virtual greenhouse. These *greenhouse gas emissions,* which also include methane, nitrous oxide, and ozone, trap heat in the lower atmosphere. Even one additional degree of warmth in the globe's average surface temperature can increase the likelihood of wildfires, shrinkage of rivers and lakes, expansion of deserts, and torrential downpours, including typhoons and hurricanes (Giddens 2011; Lynas 2008).

Although scientific concern over global warming has heated up, climate change remains low on policymakers' list of concerns. The problem seems abstract, and in many countries, officials think that the real impact of any action they may take depends on decisive action by other nations. The Kyoto Protocol (1997) was intended to reduce global emissions of heat-trapped gases, which can contribute to global warming and climate change. To date, 190 countries are party to the accord, but the United States has failed to ratify it. Opponents of the protocol argue that doing so would place the nation at a disadvantage in the global marketplace.

In writing about the global environment, activists often assert, "We're all in this together." Though we are all in this together, the reality is that globally, the most vulnerable countries tend to be the poorest. Developing nations are more likely than others to have economies that are built on limited resources or on a small number of crops that are vulnerable to drought, flood, and

fluctuations in worldwide demand (Nordhaus and Shellenberger 2007; Revkin 2007).

We can view global warming from the point of view of world systems analysis. Historically, core nations have been the major emitters of greenhouse gases. Today, however, manufacturing has moved to semi-periphery and periphery nations, where greenhouse gas emissions are escalating. Ironically, many of the forces that are now calling for a reduction in the human activity that contributes to global warming are located in core nations, which have contributed disproportionately to the problem. We want our hamburgers, but we decry the destruction of the rain forests to create grazing land for cattle. We want inexpensive clothes and toys, but we condemn developing countries for depending on coal-fired power plants. Coal-fired power generation is expected to increase from 2 to 4 percent a year for decades to come, tripling between 2010 and 2050 and surpassing oil as the world's primary energy source (L. Smith 2011).

What are the causes of this global environmental crisis? Some observers, such as Paul Ehrlich and Anne Ehrlich, see the pressure of world population growth as the central factor in environmental deterioration. They argue that population control is essential in preventing widespread starvation and environmental decay.

Barry Commoner, a biologist, counters that the primary cause of environmental ills is the increasing use of technological innovations that are destructive to the environment—among them plastics, detergents, synthetic fibers, pesticides, herbicides, and chemical fertilizers. Conflict theorists see the despoliation of the environment through the lens of world systems analysis. And interactionists stress efforts by informed individuals and groups to reduce their carbon footprint—that is, their daily or even lifetime production of greenhouse gases—through careful selection of the goods they consume (Carbon Trust 2012; Commoner 1990, 2007; Ehrlich and Ellison 2002).

 use your **sociological imagination**

As you think about all the issues facing our society, how often do you consider global warming? How often do your friends give it much thought?

The Impact of Globalization

Globalization can be both good and bad for the environment. On the negative side, it can create a race to the bottom, as polluting companies relocate to countries with less stringent environmental standards. Similarly, globalization allows multinationals to reap the resources of developing countries for short-term profit. From Mexico to China, the industrialization that often accompanies globalization has increased pollution of all types.

Yet globalization can have a positive impact, as well. As barriers to the international movement of goods, services, and people fall, multinational corporations have an incentive to carefully consider the cost of natural resources. Overusing or wasting resources makes little sense, especially when they are in danger of depletion (Gallagher 2009; Kwong 2005).

One reflection of the interplay between globalization and the environment is the emergence of **environmental refugees,** people who have been displaced by rising seas, destructive storms, expanding deserts, water shortages, and high levels of toxic pollutants. Europe in particular is beginning to see an influx of such immigrants from developing nations. According to a European Union report, global warming can be viewed as a "threat multiplier" that exacerbates prolonged droughts and a shortage of arable land, and along with them, poverty, poor health, and poor living conditions. Viewed through the lens of world systems analysis, periphery countries may become overburdened by environmental problems, precipitating either migrations to industrial nations or conflicts that cause mass displacements of their populations. "Europe must expect substantially increased migratory pressure" from these environmental refugees, the report concludes (L. Brown 2011).

Against these potentially negative effects of globalization we must note the potential for new jobs in what are called green industries. Installing solar panels, weatherizing homes, brewing biofuels, building hybrid cars, growing organic foods, manufacturing organic garments, and erecting giant wind turbines are all classified as *green-collar jobs.* However, skeptics question how many

Vacation in an unspoiled paradise! Increasingly, people from developed countries are turning to ecotourism as an environmentally friendly way to see the world. The new trend bridges the interests of environmentalists and businesspeople, especially in developing countries. These birdwatchers are vacationing in Belize.

such jobs will be created, and to what degree they will offset job losses in pollution-prone industries like oil, gas, and coal mining (S. Greenhouse 2008b; R. Pinderhughes 2008).

social policy and the Environment | Environmentalism

On April 22, 1970, in a dramatic manifestation of growing grassroots concern over preservation of the environment, an estimated 25 million people turned out to observe the nation's first Earth Day. Two thousand communities held planned celebrations, and more than 2,000 colleges and 10,000 schools hosted environmental teach-ins. In many parts of the United States, citizens marched on behalf of specific environmental causes. That same year, the activism of these early environmentalists convinced Congress to establish the Environmental Protection Agency. The Clean Air, Clean Water, and Endangered Species acts soon followed (Brulle and Jenkins 2008).

Looking at the Issue

Sociologist Manual Castells (2010a:72) has declared environmentalism "the most comprehensive, influential movement of our time." Several social trends helped to mobilize the environmental movement. First, the activist subculture of the 1960s

and early 1970s encouraged people, especially young people, to engage in direct action regarding social issues. Second, the dissemination of scientific knowledge about serious environmental problems like oil spills and air pollution alarmed many Americans. And third, the growing popularity of outdoor recreation increased the number of people who were concerned about the environment. In this climate of broad-based interest in environmental issues, many organizations that had once focused narrowly on the conservation of natural resources evolved into full-fledged environmental groups (Dunlap and Mertig 1991).

Today, Earth Day has been enshrined on the calendars of city councils, zoos, and museums worldwide. Environmental issues have also moved up the agenda of mainstream political parties. Increasingly, efforts to publicize environmental concerns and create support for action have moved to the Internet. Although times have changed, two beliefs continue to galvanize environmentalists: the environment is in dire need of protection, and the government must take strong action

—Continued

FIGURE 55-2 The Environment versus Energy Production

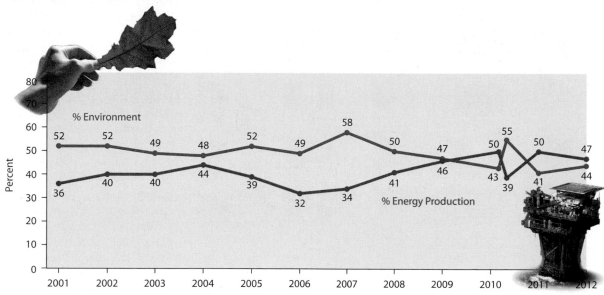

Source: Gallup Poll 2012; J. Jones and Saad 2012 in references.

in response. Although environmentalists recognize that they must "think locally" and monitor their own carbon footprints, they also see preservation of the environment as a global challenge. They note that while significant progress has been made toward environmental protection, government regulation of the environment has been curtailed in some ways (Brulle and Jenkins 2008; Rootes 2007; Sieber et al. 2006).

The general public has a mixed reaction to environmental issues. Many people question the scientific arguments behind the theory of global warming. And although the economic cost of environmental protection has always been an issue, the broad economic downturn that began in 2008 tipped the balance of public opinion in favor of energy production, at the expense of environmental protection (Figure 55-2). (A brief reversal occurred in spring 2010, when the BP oil spill created headlines on environmental damage in the Gulf of Mexico.) In times of economic stress, people tend to put off or ignore environmental concerns. Thus, there seems to be little public enthusiasm for the positive, forward-looking approach of ecological modernization. Not surprisingly, the political debate over the environmental movement grew more partisan between 2000 and 2012: Democrats became more sympathetic and Republicans more antagonistic (Dunlap 2010).

Today's college students also show less interest in the environment than students of past decades. In 2011, about 26 percent of first-year college students in the United States wanted to clean up the environment—down from 45.9 percent in 1972 (see Figure 10-1 on page 61). And as Figure 55-3 shows, U.S. high school students' interest in the issue does

not compare favorably with that of teens in other major countries. In a 30-nation comparative study, 15-year-olds in the United States tied those in another country for 22nd place in their knowledge of environmental issues.

Applying Sociology

Even those who support environmentalists' goals are troubled by the fact that nationwide, the most powerful environmental organizations are predominantly White, male-dominated, and affluent. One study notes that while women are overrepresented in the environmental movement (particularly in grassroots environmental groups), men continue to hold most of the high-profile upper-management positions in mainstream national organizations. The perceived middle-class orientation of the movement is especially relevant given the class, racial, and ethnic factors associated with environmental hazards. As we saw earlier in the context of environmental justice, low-income communities and areas with significant minority populations are more likely than affluent White communities to be located near waste sites. Sociologists Liam Downey and Brian Hawkins (2008) found that an average Black household with an income of $50,000 to $60,000 a year coped with higher levels of pollution than an average White household with an income of less than $10,000 a year.

Viewed from a conflict perspective, this disproportionate exposure of the poor and minorities to environmental

—Continued

FIGURE 55-3 Are U.S. Teens Green Enough?

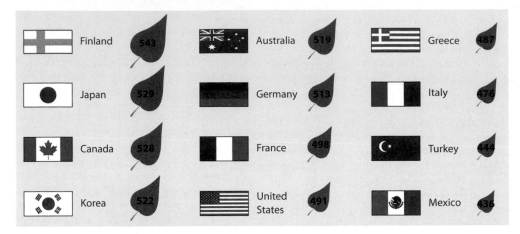

Note: Mean score for 15-year-old students' knowledge of environmental issues = 543.
Source: Organisation for Economic Co-operation and Development 2009b.

pollutants can act as a disincentive for others to take action. As Andrew Szasz (2007) noted in his book *Shopping Our Way to Safety* (see the chapter-opening excerpt), more affluent households can try to avoid exposing themselves and their children to health hazards by drinking bottled spring water, installing water and air filters in their homes, and buying organic food. Unfortunately, these individual actions have the unintended consequence of weakening collective environmental efforts.

Another concern, from the conflict perspective, is the fact that many environmental movements either do not include the poor and minorities or do not address their concerns. Although environmental justice issues have been well publicized, environmentalists do not always consider the implications of their demands for excluded groups (Rudel et al. 2011).

Initiating Policy

The global economic downturn that began in 2008 has been a mixed blessing for environmentalists. Currently, public opinion in the United States favors economic growth over environmental protection. Yet at the same time, the recent recession has sharply reduced the use of fossil fuels such as coal and oil. Moreover, the federal government's efforts to stimulate economic activity have emphasized the creation of green-collar jobs. By one estimate, every $1 billion invested in well-conceived green programs generates over 30,000 jobs and $450 million in cost savings per year. More specific environmental measures, such as raising federal gas mileage standards for automobiles, face a tough battle in Congress (Houser et al. 2009).

Environmentalism has moved onto a much bigger stage than the one it occupied on the first Earth Day. In 2008, for the first time, the leaders of the G8 economic powers (the United States, Japan, Germany, Great Britain, France, Italy, Canada, and Russia) set an explicit long-term target for eliminating greenhouse gases, which scientists have long warned were warming the planet. "Long-term" may be an understatement: their target date for cutting greenhouse gases in half is 2050. Environmentalists sharply criticized the G8's failure to set specific goals for the nearer term. The challenge is significant, given the fact that G8 emissions *increased* 35 percent over the preceding 15 years (Longhofer and Schofer 2010; Stolberg 2008).

Conventional wisdom holds that concern for environmental quality is limited to wealthy industrialized nations. However, the results of a 47-nation survey show that around the world, people are increasingly reluctant to ignore environmental issues. Concern has risen sharply in Latin America and Europe, as well as in Japan and India. The survey also noted a general increase in the percentage of people who cite pollution and environmental problems as a top global threat. Many people in other countries blame the United States, and to a lesser extent China, for environmental problems, and look to Washington, D.C., for a solution. Time will tell whether policymakers in the United States or elsewhere will address their concern for the environment (Pew Global Attitudes Project 2007).

TAKE THE ISSUE WITH YOU

1. In your community, how would you act locally to preserve the environment? Describe your community's environmental problems and explain how you would seek to solve them.

2. How do you see the trade-off between the economy and the environment? Which is more important? Is it possible to improve both at the same time? Explain.

3. Thinking globally about the environment, list what you consider the most pressing priorities. How important are world hunger and economic justice compared to global warming, clean air and water, and economic development? Are some of your priorities related? In what way?

Summary

The **human ecology** perspective suggests that the environment serves three basic functions: it provides essential resources, serves as a waste repository, and houses our species.

1. Conflict theorists charge that the most serious threat to the environment comes from Western industrialized nations.

2. **Environmental justice** addresses the disproportionate subjection of minorities to environmental hazards.

3. Four broad areas of environmental concern include air and water pollution, global warming, and globalization. Although globalization can contribute to environmental woes, it can also have beneficial effects.

4. Environmentalism is a social movement that is dominated by wealthy White people from industrialized countries. Increasingly, however, people of all races, ethnicities, social classes, and nationalities are becoming concerned about global warming and the threat it poses to our planet's health.

Thinking Critically

1. How are the physical and human environments connected in your neighborhood or community?

2. Which issue is more significant in your local community, air or water pollution? Why?

Key Terms

Ecological modernization   **449**

Environmental justice   **449**

Environmental refugee   **452**

Human ecology   **447**

Mastering This Chapter

taking sociology with you

1 Do some research on the incidence and prevalence of HIV/AIDS in your city or state. Now look up the corresponding morbidity and mortality rates. How do those rates compare to the rates in other cities or states? What might account for any differences in the rates from one place to another?

2 Visit the emergency room of your local hospital and observe what is going on in the waiting room. How crowded is the waiting room? How many people in the room appear to be severely ill or injured? How many do not seem to have an emergency? What else can you observe about the people who are gathered there, and how might that help to explain their presence?

3 Do an Internet search to locate the hazardous waste sites nearest your school or home. How many of them have been cleaned up, and at what cost? Who paid that cost? How many of these sites are still a problem?

key terms

Brain drain The immigration to the United States and other industrialized nations of skilled workers, professionals, and technicians who are desperately needed in their home countries. (page 435)

Curanderismo Latino folk medicine, a form of holistic health care and healing. (440)

Ecological modernization The alignment of environmentally favorable practices with economic self-interest through constant adaptation and restructuring. (449)

Environmental justice A legal strategy based on claims that racial minorities are subjected disproportionately to environmental hazards. (449)

Environmental refugee A person who has been displaced by rising seas, destructive storms, expanding deserts, water shortages, or high levels of toxic pollutants. (452)

Health As defined by the World Health Organization, a state of complete physical, mental, and social well-being, and not merely the absence of disease and infirmity. (433)

Holistic medicine Therapies in which the health care practitioner considers the person's physical, mental, emotional, and spiritual characteristics. (444)

Human ecology An area of study that is concerned with the interrelationships between people and their environment. (447)

Incidence The number of new cases of a specific disorder that occur within a given population during a stated period. (438)

Infant mortality rate The number of deaths of infants under 1 year old per 1,000 live births in a given year. (435)

McDonaldization The process through which the principles of the fast-food restaurant are coming to dominate more and more sectors of society. (443)

Morbidity rate The incidence of disease in a given population. (438)

Mortality rate The incidence of death in a given population. (438)

Prevalence The total number of cases of a specific disorder that exist at a given time. (438)

Sick role Societal expectations about the attitudes and behavior of a person viewed as being ill. (433)

Social epidemiology The study of the distribution of disease, impairment, and general health status across a population. (438)

self-quiz

Read each question carefully and then select the best answer.

1. Which sociologist developed the concept of the sick role?
   a. Émile Durkheim
   b. Talcott Parsons
   c. C. Wright Mills
   d. Erving Goffman

2. Regarding health care inequities, the conflict perspective would note that
   a. physicians serve as gatekeepers for the sick role, either verifying a patient's condition as "illness" or designating the patient as "recovered."
   b. patients play an active role in health care by failing to follow a physician's advice.
   c. emigration out of the Third World by physicians is yet another way that the world's core industrialized nations enhance their quality of life at the expense of developing countries.
   d. the designation "healthy" or "ill" generally involves social definition by others.

3. Which one of the following nations has the lowest infant mortality rate?
   a. the United States
   b. Mozambique
   c. Canada
   d. Sweden

4. Compared with Whites, Blacks have higher death rates from
   a. heart disease.
   b. diabetes.
   c. cancer.
   d. all of the above.

5. Which theorist notes that capitalist societies, such as the United States, care more about maximizing profits than they do about the health and safety of industrial workers?
   a. Thomas Szasz
   b. Talcott Parsons
   c. Erving Goffman
   d. Karl Marx

6. Which program is essentially a compulsory health insurance plan for the elderly?
   a. Medicare
   b. Medicaid
   c. Blue Cross
   d. Healthpac

7. Which of the following is a criticism of the sick role?
   a. Patients' judgments regarding their own state of health may be related to their gender, age, social class, and ethnic group.
   b. The sick role may be more applicable to people experiencing short-term illnesses than to those with recurring long-term illnesses.
   c. Even such simple factors as whether a person is employed or not seem to affect the person's willingness to assume the sick role.
   d. all of the above

8. Which of the following terms do conflict theorists use in referring to the growing role of medicine as a major institution of social control?
   a. the sick role
   b. the medicalization of society
   c. medical labeling
   d. epidemiology

9. Which of the following approaches stresses the alignment of environmentally favorable practices with economic self-interest?
   a. conflict theory
   b. human ecology
   c. ecological modernization
   d. environmental justice

10. Conflict theorists would contend that blaming developing countries for the world's environmental deterioration contains an element of
    a. ethnocentrism.
    b. xenocentrism.
    c. separatism.
    d. goal displacement.

11. A _____ _____ studies the effects of social class, race and ethnicity, gender, and age on the distribution of disease, impairment, and general health across a population.

12. From a(n) _____ perspective, "being sick" must be controlled so as to ensure that not too many people are released from their societal responsibilities at any one time.

13. The immigration to the United States and other industrialized nations of skilled workers, professionals, and technicians who are desperately needed by their home countries is known as the _____ _____.

14. Traditionally, the relationship between doctors and nurses has paralleled _____ dominance of the larger society.

15. Sociologists find it useful to consider _____ rates because they reveal that a specific disease occurs more frequently among one segment of a population compared with another.

16. The system of reimbursement used by Medicare has contributed to the controversial practice of "_____," under which patients whose treatment may be unprofitable are transferred by private hospitals to public facilities.

17. As defined by the World Health Organization,_____ is a "state of complete physical, mental, and social well-being, and not merely the absence of disease and infirmity."

18. The biologist _____ _____ blames environmental degradation primarily on technological innovations such as plastics and pesticides.

19. Regarding environmental problems, four broad areas of concern stand out:_____ pollution, _____ pollution, _____ _____, and _____.

20. _____ _____ is a legal strategy based on claims that racial minorities are subjected disproportionately to environmental hazards.

 ## thinking about movies

50/50

This dramatic comedy takes a humorous look at a young man's battle with cancer.

The City Dark

A documentary on light pollution, this film explores the consequences of an overreliance on unnatural light sources.

Food, Inc.

This documentary shows how the efficient, factory-like methods of multinational agricultural producers dehumanize laborers as they maximize corporate profits.

I live in
the future
&
here's how
it works

Why Your World, Work, and
Brain Are Being Creatively Disrupted

NICK BILTON

Lead Writer and Technology Reporter for the New York Times Bits Blog

Nick Bilton remembers a time when people didn't carry fully functioning GPS devices in their pockets.

It was a time when people talked about "getting on the map" as a sure sign of success.

" If you pull out your smart phone and click the button that says "locate me" on your Google or Yahoo! map application, you will see a small dot appear in the middle of your screen.

That's you!

If you start walking down the street in any direction, the whole screen will move right along with you, no matter where you go. This is a dramatic change from the print-on-paper world, where maps and locations are based around places and landmarks, not on you or your location. People don't go to the store and say, "Oh, excuse me, can I buy a map of me?" They go to the store and ask for a map of New York, or Amsterdam, or the subway system. You and I aren't anywhere to be seen on these maps. The maps are locations that we fit into.

But today's digital world has changed that. Kevin Slavin, a creator of location-based services and games and the cofounder of the gaming company Area/Code, put this succinctly at a technology conference last year: "We are always in the center of the map."

Though Slavin was talking about location-based games and Google maps, the center of the map, it turns out, is actually much bigger than a dot on the screen. It's a very powerful place to be.

> *Being in the center—instead of somewhere off to the side or off the page altogether—changes everything. It changes your conception of space, time, and location. It changes your sense of place and community.*

Being in the center—instead of somewhere off to the side or off the page altogether—changes everything. It changes your conception of space, time, and location. It changes your sense of place and community. It changes the way you view the information, news, and data coming in over your computer and your phone. And it changes your role in a transaction, empowering you to decide quite specifically what content to buy and how to buy and use it rather than simply accepting the traditional material that companies have packaged on your behalf.

Now you are the starting point. Now the digital world follows you, not the other way around.

. . .

I got my own hard lesson in this new Me! Now! world when some friends stopped by our house with their teenage cousin Lauren. As I started making coffee for our guests, Lauren asked if she could use my laptop to "check the news." I handed it over.

I was curious about which news sites she was going to, so I asked her, expecting to hear something like CNN or NYTimes, or maybe TMZ, the Hollywood gossip site. With a sincere face she looked up at me and said, "Facebook." Then she turned back to the computer and continued reading.

"I thought you were going to read the news," I said.

"This is my news," she replied.

To Lauren and many in her age group, news is not defined by newspapers, or broadcast television stations, or even bloggers or renegades. Instead, news is what is relevant to the individual. . . . "

(Bilton 2011:161–162, 164–165) Additional information about this excerpt can be found on the Online Learning Center at www.mhhe.com/schaefermod2e.

I n this excerpt from *I Live in the Future and Here's How It Works: Why Your World, Work, and Brain Are Being Creatively Disrupted,* technology writer Nick Bilton suggests that increasingly, new communications technologies are allowing us to center our communities, as well as our news and entertainment, on ourselves. So besides the global community—a virtual community knit together by new information technologies—we are creating a multitude of personal communities, each revolving around a single individual. How will this self-centered approach to information gathering change what we know (or do not know) about our society and other societies? More important, will our society change? The answers to these questions rest with each of us.

Social change often does follow the introduction of a new technology, in this case the computer. *Social change* has been defined as significant alteration over time in behavior patterns and culture (W. Moore 1967). But what constitutes a "significant" alteration? Certainly the dramatic rise in formal education documented in Module 43 represents a change that has had profound social consequences. Other social changes that have had long-term and important consequences include the emergence of slavery as a system of stratification (Module 16), the Industrial Revolution (Module 17), and the increased participation of women in the paid labor forces of the United States and Europe (Module 34).

How does social change happen? Is the process unpredictable, or can we make certain generalizations about it? Has globalization contributed to social change? In this chapter we examine the process of social change, with special emphasis on the impact of globalization. We begin with social movements—collective efforts to bring about deliberate social change. We will see that recent advances in communications technology have allowed some social movements to circle the world. Next, we examine three theories of social change and discuss vested interests, which often attempt to block changes they see as threatening. And we recognize the influence of globalization in spreading social change around the world. In a case study, we note the rapid social change that has occurred over a matter of decades in the Middle Eastern city-state of Dubai. Finally, we turn to the unanticipated social change that occurs when innovations such as new technologies sweep through society. The chapter closes with a Social Policy section on the creation of *transnationals*—immigrants with an allegiance to more than one nation.

MODULE 56 | Social Movements

Although such factors as the physical environment, population, technology, and social inequality serve as sources of change, it is the *collective* effort of individuals organized into social movements that ultimately leads to change. Sociologists use the term **social movement** to refer to an organized collective activity to bring about or resist fundamental change in an existing group or society (Benford 1992). Herbert Blumer (1955:19) recognized the special importance of social movements when he defined them as "collective enterprises to establish a new order of life."

In many nations, including the United States, social movements have had a dramatic impact on the course of history and the evolution of the social structure. Consider the actions of abolitionists, suffragists, civil rights workers, activists opposed to the war in Vietnam, and Occupy Wall Street protesters. Members of each social movement stepped outside traditional channels for bringing about social change, yet each had a noticeable influence on public policy. In Eastern Europe, equally dramatic collective efforts helped to topple communist regimes in a largely peaceful manner, in nations that many observers had thought were "immune" to such social change (Ramet 1991).

Though social movements imply the existence of conflict, we can also analyze their activities from a functionalist perspective. Even when they are unsuccessful, social movements contribute to the formation of public opinion. Initially, people thought the ideas of Margaret Sanger and other early advocates of birth control were radical, yet contraceptives are now widely available in the United States.

Because social movements know no borders, even nationalistic movements are deeply influenced by global events. Increasingly, social movements are taking on an international dimension from the start. Global enterprises, in particular, lend themselves to targeting through international mobilization, whether they are corporations like McDonald's or governmental bodies like the World Trade Organization. Global activism is not new, however; it began with the writing of Karl Marx, who sought to mobilize oppressed peoples in other industrialized countries. Today, activist networking is facilitated by the Internet. Participation in transnational activism is much more widespread now than in the past, and passions are quicker to ignite.

■ The Emergence of Social Movements

How and why do social movements emerge? Obviously, people are often discontented with the way things are. What causes them to organize at a particular moment in a collective effort to effect change? Sociologists rely on two explanations for why people mobilize: the relative deprivation and resource mobilization approaches.

 use your **sociological imagination**

What social movements are most visible on your campus? In the community where you live?

Relative Deprivation Approach

Those members of a society who feel most frustrated and disgruntled by social and economic conditions are not necessarily the worst off in an objective sense. Social scientists have long recognized that what is more significant is the way in which people *perceive* their situation. As Karl Marx pointed out, although the misery of the workers was important to their perception of their oppressed state, so was their position *in relation to* the capitalist ruling class (Marx and Engels [1847] 1955).

The term **relative deprivation** is defined as the conscious feeling of a negative discrepancy between legitimate expectations and present actualities (J. Wilson 1973). In other words,

Two members of People for the Ethical Treatment of Animals (PETA) protest against the killing of animals to make fur coats. Social movements like PETA seek public attention for the positions they espouse.

things aren't as good as you hoped they would be. Such a state may be characterized by scarcity rather than a complete lack of necessities (as we saw in the distinction between absolute and relative poverty in Module 28). A relatively deprived person is dissatisfied because he or she feels downtrodden relative to some appropriate reference group. Thus, blue-collar workers who live in two-family houses on small plots of land—though hardly at the bottom of the economic ladder—may nevertheless feel deprived in comparison to corporate managers and professionals who live in lavish homes in exclusive suburbs.

In addition to the feeling of relative deprivation, two other elements must be present before discontent will be channeled into a social movement. People must feel that they have a *right* to their goals, that they deserve better than what they have. At the same time, the disadvantaged group must perceive that its goals cannot be attained through conventional means. This belief may or may not be correct. Whichever is the case, the group will not mobilize into a social movement unless there is a shared perception that members can end their relative deprivation only through collective action (D. Morrison 1971).

Critics of this approach have noted that people don't need to feel deprived to be moved to act. In addition, this approach fails to explain why certain feelings of deprivation are transformed into social movements, whereas in similar situations, no collective effort is made to reshape society. Consequently, in recent years, sociologists have paid increasing attention to the forces needed to bring about the emergence of social movements (Alain 1985; Finkel and Rule 1987; Orum and Dale 2009).

 use your **sociological imagination**

Why might well-off people feel deprived?

Resource Mobilization Approach

It takes more than desire to start a social movement. It helps to have money, political influence, access to the media, and personnel. The term **resource mobilization** refers to the ways in which a social movement utilizes such resources. Indeed, the success of a movement for change will depend in good part on what resources it has and how effectively it mobilizes them. In other words, recruiting adherents and marshalling resources is critical to the growth and success of social movements (Gamson 1989; Tilly 1964, 2003; Walder 2009).

Sociologist Anthony Oberschall (1973:199) has argued that to sustain social protest or resistance, there must be an "organizational base and continuity of leadership." As people become part of a social movement, norms develop to guide their behavior. Members of the movement may be expected to attend regular meetings, pay dues, recruit new adherents, and boycott "enemy" products or speakers.

Leadership is a central factor in the mobilization of the discontented into social movements. Often, a movement will be led by a charismatic figure, such as Dr. Martin Luther King Jr. As Max Weber described it in 1904, *charisma* is that quality of an individual that sets him or her apart from ordinary people. Of course, charisma can fade abruptly, which helps to account for the fragility of certain social movements (Morris 2000).

Many social movements are mobilized by institutional insiders. During the nationwide debate of the Obama administration's plan for health care reform in 2009, for example, health insurance companies encouraged their employees to attend the forums arranged by the White House. Managers distributed "Town Hall Tips" that included a list of concerns employees could raise and suggestions on how to make their comments as personal as possible, by talking about their own health issues (E. Walker 2010).

Why do certain individuals join a social movement while others who are in similar situations do not? Some of them are recruited to join. Karl Marx recognized the importance of recruitment when he called on workers to become *aware* of their oppressed status and to develop a class consciousness. Like theorists of the resource mobilization approach, Marx held that a social movement (specifically, the revolt of the proletariat) would require leaders to sharpen the awareness of the oppressed. They would need to help workers to overcome feelings of **false consciousness,** or attitudes that did not reflect workers' objective position, in order to organize a revolutionary movement. Similarly, one of the challenges faced by women's liberation activists of the late 1960s and early 1970s was to convince women that they were being deprived of their rights and of socially valued resources.

Gender and Social Movements

Sociologists point out that gender is an important element in understanding social movements. In our male-dominated society, women find it more difficult than men to assume leadership positions in social movement organizations. Though women often serve disproportionately as volunteers in these movements, their work is not always recognized, nor are their voices as easily heard as men's. Gender bias causes the real extent of their influence to be overlooked. Indeed, traditional examination of the sociopolitical

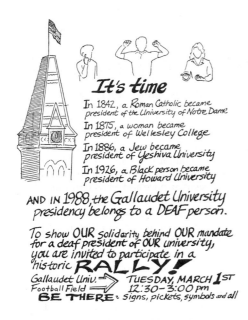

Gallaudet University in Washington, D.C., is the only four-year liberal arts college for deaf students in the United States. A leaflet (left) was distributed in 1988 as part of a successful effort by students, faculty, and alumni to force the appointment of the university's first deaf president. In 2007, after that president's retirement, students protested once again over the election process (right). The mobilization of resources, including leaflets, is one key to the success of a social movement.

system tends to focus on such male-dominated corridors of power as legislatures and corporate boardrooms, to the neglect of more female-dominated domains such as households, community-based groups, and faith-based networks. However, efforts to influence family values, child rearing, relationships between parents and schools, and spiritual values are clearly significant to a culture and society (Ferree and Merrill 2000; Noonan 1995).

Scholars of social movements now realize that gender can affect even the way we view organized efforts to bring about or resist change. For example, an emphasis on using rationality and cold logic to achieve goals helps to obscure the importance of passion and emotion in successful social movements. It would be difficult to find any movement—from labor battles to voting rights to animal rights—in which passion was not part of the consensus-building force. Yet calls for a more serious study of the role of emotion are frequently seen as applying only to the women's movement, because emotion is traditionally thought of as being feminine (Ferree and Merrill 2000; V. Taylor 1999, 2004).

 use your **sociological imagination**

Try to imagine a society without any social movements. Under what conditions could such a society exist? Would you want to live in it?

New Social Movements

Beginning in the late 1960s, European social scientists observed a change in both the composition and the targets of emerging social movements. Previously, traditional social movements had focused on economic issues, often led by labor unions or by people who shared the same occupation. However, many social

movements that have become active in recent decades—including the contemporary women's movement, the peace movement, and the environmental movement—do not have the social class roots typical of the labor protests in the United States and Europe over the past century (Tilly 1993, 2004).

The term **new social movement** refers to an organized collective activity that addresses values and social identities, as well as improvements in the quality of life. These movements may be involved in developing collective identities. Many have complex agendas that go beyond a single issue, and even cross national boundaries. Educated, middle-class people are significantly represented in some of these new social movements, such as the women's movement and the movement for lesbian and gay rights. Box 56-1 describes the women's movements in South Korea and India.

New social movements generally do not view government as their ally in the struggle for a better society. While they typically do not seek to overthrow the government, they may criticize, protest, or harass public officials. Researchers have found that members of new social movements show little inclination to accept established authority, even scientific or technical authority. This characteristic is especially evident in the environmental and anti–nuclear power movements, whose activists present their own experts to counter those of government or big business (Garner 1996; Polletta and Jasper 2001; A. Scott 1990).

The environmental movement is one of many new movements with a worldwide focus (see the Social Policy section in Module 55). In their efforts to reduce air and water pollution, curtail global warming, and protect endangered animal species, environmental activists have realized that strong regulatory measures within a single country are not sufficient. Similarly, labor union leaders and human rights advocates cannot adequately address exploitative sweatshop conditions in a developing country if multinational corporations can simply move their factories

Rural residents of Mongolia pose outside their home with their satellite dish. In the 21st century, technology links people in even the remotest areas. In 2008 protesters rocked Mongolia's capital in anger over election fraud. Two years later, they gathered to demand more equitable distribution of the nation's mining wealth. In both cases, people from rural areas organized for action on the Internet.

changing the way people relate to one another across vast distances, allowing small, focused audiences to become part of a global conversation. In doing so, they may find a common purpose. These social connections happen because of the Internet's technological structure. Websites are not autonomous and independent; they are connected by a global electronic network. One website generally lists a variety of other sites that serve as links. For example, seeking information on domestic partnerships may lead you to an electronic enclave that is supportive of cohabitation between men and women or to an enclave that is supportive of gay and lesbian couples. New developments in communications technology have clearly broadened the way we interact with one another (Calhoun 1998).

MODULE 56 | Recap and Review

Summary

Social movements are more structured than other forms of collective behavior and persist over longer periods.

1. A group will not mobilize into a social movement without a shared perception that its **relative deprivation** can be ended only through collective action.

2. The success of a social movement depends in good part on effective **resource mobilization.**

3. **New social movements** tend to focus on more than just economic issues and often cross national boundaries.

4. Advances in communications technology—especially the Internet—have had a major impact on social movements.

Thinking Critically

1. What might be some drawbacks of global communications technology?

2. What aspects of traditional gender roles explain the roles that women and men typically play in social movements?

Key Terms

Computer-mediated communication   465

False consciousness   462

New social movement   463

Relative deprivation   461

Resource mobilization   462

Social movement   461

MODULE 57 | Social Change

Theories of Social Change

A new millennium provides the occasion to offer explanations of **social change,** which we have defined as significant alteration over time in behavior patterns and culture. Social change can occur so slowly as to be almost undetectable to those it affects, but it can also happen with breathtaking rapidity. As Table 57-1 shows, some changes that have occurred in U.S. society over the past century and a half have been relatively slow or slight; others have been rapid or striking in magnitude.

Explanations of social change are clearly a challenge in the diverse and complex world we inhabit today. Nevertheless, theorists from several disciplines have sought to analyze social change. In some instances, they have examined historical events to arrive at a better understanding of contemporary changes. We will review three theoretical approaches to change—evolutionary, functionalist, and conflict—and then take a look at resistance to social change.

Evolutionary Theory

The pioneering work of Charles Darwin (1809–1882) in biological evolution contributed to 19th-century theories of social change. Darwin's approach stresses a continuing progression of successive life-forms. For example, human beings came at a later stage of evolution than reptiles and represent a more complex form of life. Social theorists seeking an analogy to this biological model originated **evolutionary theory,** in which society is viewed as moving in a definite direction. Early evolutionary theorists generally agreed that society was progressing inevitably toward a higher state. As might be expected,

they concluded in ethnocentric fashion that their behavior and culture were more advanced than those of earlier civilizations.

Table **57-1** **The United States: A Changing Nation**

Population	1850	1940	1960	2012
Total in millions	23.2	132.1	180.7	316.3
Percentage under age 15	41%	25%	31%	20%
Education	**1850**	**1940**	**1960**	**2010**
Percentage not completing high school	88%	18%	13%	13%
Percentage ages 19–24 enrolled in higher education	Under 1%	8%	40%	40%
Labor Force Participation	**1850**	**1940**	**1960**	**2010**
Men in their 20s	94%	88%	86%	82%
Women in their 20s	22%	39%	74%	73%
Health	**1850**	**1940**	**1960**	**2010**
Physicians per 100,000 population	176	133	150	273
Life expectancy at birth, in years	38	63	70	78.3
Technology	**1870**	**1940**	**1960**	**2010**
Copyrights issued	5,600	176,997	243,926	636,400
Patents issued	12,127	42,238	47,170	244,300
Family	**1890**	**1940**	**1960**	**2008**
Median age at first marriage				
Men	26	24	23	28
Women	22	22	20	26
Number of children born per family	3.25	2.7	3.65	2.09

Note: Data are comparable, although definitions vary. Definition of the United States changes between 1850 and 1940 and between 1940 and 1960. Earliest date for children born per family is 1905.

Sources: Author, based on federal data collected in Bureau of the Census 2011a:Tables 104, 165, 223, 229, 587, 774, 778, 780; Sutch and Carter 2006:1–28/29, 391, 401–402, 440, 541, 685, 697, 709, 2–441/442, and 3–424/425, 427/428.

Think about It

Which of the social changes shown in this table surprises you the most? Which category do you think will change the most in the next 20 years?

Auguste Comte (1798–1857), a founder of sociology, was an evolutionary theorist of change. He saw human societies as moving forward in their thinking, from mythology to the scientific method. Similarly, Émile Durkheim ([1893] 1933) maintained that society progressed from simple to more complex forms of social organization.

Today, evolutionary theory influences sociologists in a variety of ways. For example, it has encouraged sociobiologists to investigate the behavioral links between humans and other animals. It has also influenced human ecology, the study of the interaction between communities and their environment (Maryanski 2004).

Functionalist Perspective

Because functionalist sociologists focus on what *maintains* a system, not on what changes it, they might seem to offer little to the study of social change. Yet as the work of sociologist Talcott Parsons demonstrates, functionalists have made a distinctive contribution to this area of sociological investigation.

Parsons (1902–1979), a leading proponent of the functionalist perspective, viewed society as being in a natural state of equilibrium. By "equilibrium," he meant that society tends toward a state of stability or balance. Parsons would view even prolonged labor strikes or civilian riots as temporary disruptions in the status quo rather than as significant alterations in social structure. Therefore, according to his **equilibrium model,** as changes occur in one part of society, adjustments must be made in other parts. If not, society's equilibrium will be threatened and strains will occur.

Reflecting the evolutionary approach, Parsons (1966) maintained that four processes of social change are inevitable. *Differentiation* refers to the increasing complexity of social organization. The transition from medicine man to physician, nurse, and pharmacist is an illustration of differentiation in the field of health. This process is accompanied by *adaptive upgrading,* in which social institutions become more specialized in their purposes. The division of physicians into obstetricians, internists, surgeons, and so forth is an example of adaptive upgrading.

The next process Parsons identified is the *inclusion* of groups that were previously excluded because of their gender, race, ethnicity, or social class. Medical schools have practiced inclusion by admitting increasing numbers of women and African Americans. Finally, Parsons contends that societies experience *value generalization,* the development of new values that tolerate and legitimate a greater range of activities. The acceptance of preventive and alternative medicine is an example of value generalization: society has broadened its view of health care. All four processes identified by Parsons stress consensus—societal agreement on the nature of social organization and values (B. Johnson 1975; Wallace and Wolf 1980).

Although Parsons's approach explicitly incorporates the evolutionary notion of continuing progress, the dominant theme in his model is stability. Society may change, but it remains stable through new forms of integration. For example, in place of the kinship ties that provided social cohesion in the past, people develop laws, judicial processes, and new values and belief systems.

Conflict Perspective

The functionalist perspective minimizes the importance of change. It emphasizes the persistence of social life and sees change as a means of maintaining society's equilibrium (or balance). In contrast, conflict theorists contend that social institutions and practices persist because powerful groups have the ability to maintain the status quo. Change has crucial significance, since it is needed to correct social injustices and inequalities.

Karl Marx accepted the evolutionary argument that societies develop along a particular path. However, unlike Comte and Spencer, he did not view each successive stage as an inevitable improvement over the previous one. History, according to Marx, proceeds through a series of stages, each of which exploits a class of people. Ancient society exploited slaves; the estate system of feudalism exploited serfs; modern capitalist society exploits the working class. Ultimately, through a socialist revolution led by the proletariat, human society will move toward the final stage of development: a classless communist society, or "community of free individuals," as Marx described it in 1867 in *Das Kapital* (see Bottomore and Rubel 1956:250).

As we have seen, Marx had an important influence on the development of sociology. His thinking offered insights into such institutions as the economy, the family, religion, and government. The Marxist view of social change is appealing because it does not restrict people to a passive role in responding to inevitable cycles or changes in material culture. Rather, Marxist theory offers a tool for those who wish to seize control of the historical process and gain their freedom from injustice. In contrast

trend spotting

Social Change and Travel to the United States after 9/11

Catastrophic events can create significant social change. Americans are aware of changes that occurred after 9/11 in airport check-in procedures. However, most are unaware of changes in the way international tourists are treated when they want to visit the United States.

Imagine you are a foreign tourist. If you come from one of the 36 countries deemed U.S. allies, like Great Britain, Germany, or Japan, you will not need a visa to enter the United States. However, you will need to submit your travel plans in advance, and you will be fingerprinted when you arrive.

What if you are from China? You will wait up to four months for a tourist visa before being allowed to enter. If you are Brazilian, the wait may be five months.

What if you are an Afghan who risked your life working with U.S. troops or diplomats? You will wait two years or more for a background check before receiving a visa.

Although these changes do not have an effect on most Americans, they do affect U.S. citizens whose businesses depend on international travel and trade.

Source: New York Times 2011.

to functionalists' emphasis on stability, Marx argues that conflict is a normal and desirable aspect of social change. In fact, change must be encouraged as a means of eliminating social inequality (Lauer 1982).

One conflict theorist, Ralf Dahrendorf (1958), has noted that the contrast between the functionalist perspective's emphasis on stability and the conflict perspective's focus on change reflects the contradictory nature of society. Human societies are stable and long-lasting, yet they also experience serious conflict. Dahrendorf found that the functionalist and conflict perspectives were ultimately compatible, despite their many points of disagreement. Indeed, Parsons spoke of new functions that result from social change, and Marx recognized the need for change so that societies could function more equitably.

Table 57-2 summarizes the differences between the three major perspectives on social change.

On the outskirts of Buenos Aires, Argentina, a squatter settlement forms a stark contrast to the gleaming skyscrapers in the wealthy downtown area. Marxists and conflict theorists see social change as a way of overcoming the kind of social inequality evident in this photograph.

Resistance to Social Change

Efforts to promote social change are likely to meet with resistance. In the midst of rapid scientific and technological innovations, many people are frightened by the demands of an ever-changing society. Moreover, certain individuals and groups have a stake in maintaining the existing state of affairs.

Social economist Thorstein Veblen (1857–1929) coined the term **vested interests** to refer to those people or groups who will suffer in the event of social change. For example, in 2010 President Obama proposed scuttling NASA's Constellation project, whose primary goal was to return humans to the moon. Although many people expressed disappointment with the decision to abandon manned space flights, key opposition came from just 27 members of Congress. All represented districts in Alabama and Texas that were home to large suppliers to the project. Ironically, many of those representatives had gone on record as opponents of large federal spending projects. In general, those with a disproportionate share of society's wealth, status, and power, such as members of Congress and representatives of big business, have a vested interest in preserving the status quo (Friedman 2010; Veblen 1919).

Economic and Cultural Factors

Economic factors play an important role in resistance to social change. For example, it can be expensive for manufacturers to meet high standards for the safety of products and workers, and for the protection of the environment. Conflict theorists argue that in a capitalist economic system, many firms are not willing to pay the price of meeting strict safety and environmental standards. They may resist social change by cutting corners or by pressuring the government to ease regulations.

Communities, too, protect their vested interests, often in the name of "protecting property values." The abbreviation *NIMBY* stands for "not in my backyard," a cry often heard when people protest landfills, prisons, nuclear power facilities, and even bike trails and group homes for people with developmental disabilities. The targeted community may not challenge the need for the facility, but may simply insist that it be located elsewhere. The "not in my backyard" attitude has become so common that it is almost impossible for policymakers to find acceptable locations for facilities such as hazardous-waste dumps (Jasper 1997).

On the world stage, what amounts to a "not on planet Earth" campaign has emerged. Members of this movement stress many

Tracking Sociological Perspectives

Table **57-2** **Sociological Perspectives on Social Change**

Evolutionary	Social change moves society in a definite direction, frequently from simple to more complex.
Functionalist	Social change must contribute to society's stability.
	Modest adjustments must be made to accommodate social change.
Conflict	Social change can correct social injustices and inequalities.

A Google Street View car drives through Broughton, England, photographing it for use with Google's online map service. Residents of the rural village see the technology, which may encourage motorists and truckers to drive through their community, as an invasion of their privacy, but many others appreciate the innovation.

issues, from profiteering to nuclear proliferation, from labor rights to the eradication of poverty and disease. Essentially an antiglobalization movement, it manifests itself at international meetings of trade ministers and heads of state.

Like economic factors, cultural factors frequently shape resistance to change. William F. Ogburn (1922) distinguished between material and nonmaterial aspects of culture. *Material culture* includes inventions, artifacts, and technology; *nonmaterial culture* encompasses ideas, norms, communications, and social organization. Ogburn pointed out that one cannot devise methods for controlling and using new technology before the introduction of a technique. Thus, nonmaterial culture typically must respond to changes in material culture. Ogburn introduced the term **culture lag** to refer to the period of maladjustment when the nonmaterial culture is still struggling to adapt to new material conditions. One example is the Internet. Its rapid, uncontrolled growth raises questions about whether to regulate it, and if so, how much.

In certain cases, changes in material culture can strain the relationships between social institutions. For example, new means of birth control have been developed in recent decades.

Large families are no longer economically necessary, nor are they commonly endorsed by social norms. However, certain religious faiths, among them Roman Catholicism, continue to extol large families and to disapprove methods of limiting family size, such as contraception and abortion. This issue represents a lag between aspects of material culture (technology) and nonmaterial culture (religious beliefs). Conflicts may also emerge between religion and other social institutions, such as government and the educational system, over the dissemination of birth control and family-planning information (Riley et al. 1994a, 1994b).

use your **sociological imagination**

What kind of change do you find the hardest to accept? The easiest?

Resistance to Technology

Technology is cultural information about the ways in which the material resources of the environment may be used to satisfy human needs and desires. Technological innovations are examples of changes in material culture that often provoke resistance. The *Industrial Revolution,* which took place largely in England during the period 1760 to 1830, was a scientific revolution focused on the application of nonanimal sources of power to labor tasks. As this revolution proceeded, societies came to rely on new inventions that facilitated agricultural and industrial production and on new sources of energy, such as steam. In some industries, the introduction of power-driven machinery reduced the need for factory workers and made it easier for factory owners to cut wages.

Strong resistance to the Industrial Revolution emerged in some countries. In England, beginning in 1811, masked craft workers took extreme measures: they mounted nighttime raids on factories and destroyed some of the new machinery. The government hunted these rebels, known as **Luddites,** and ultimately banished or hung them. In a similar effort in France, angry workers threw their *sabots* (wooden shoes) into factory machinery to destroy it, giving rise to the term *sabotage.* While the resistance of the Luddites and the French workers was short-lived and unsuccessful, they have come to symbolize resistance to technology.

Are we now in the midst of a second industrial revolution, with a contemporary group of Luddites engaged in resisting? Many sociologists believe that we are living in a *postindustrial society.* It is difficult to pinpoint exactly when this era began. Generally, it is viewed as having begun in the 1950s, when for the first time the majority of workers in industrial societies became involved in services rather than in the actual manufacture of goods.

Just as the Luddites resisted the Industrial Revolution, people in many countries have resisted postindustrial technological changes. The term *neo-Luddites* refers to those who are wary of technological innovations and who question the incessant expansion of industrialization, the increasing destruction of the natural and agrarian world, and the "throw-it-away" mentality of contemporary capitalism, with its resulting pollution of the environment (Volti 2010).

A new slang term, *urban amish,* refers specifically to those who resist technological devices that have become part of our daily lives, such as cell phones. Such people insist that whatever the presumed benefits of industrial and postindustrial technology, such technology has distinctive social costs and may represent a danger to both the future of the human species and our planet (Bauerlein 1996; Rifkin 1995; Sale 1996; Slack and Wise 2007; Snyder 1996; Urban Dictionary 2012).

Other people will resist a new technology simply because they find it difficult to use or because they suspect that it will complicate their lives. Both these objections are especially true of new information and media technologies. Whether it is TiVo, the iPhone, or even the latest digital camera, many consumers are leery of these so-called must-have items.

MODULE 57 | Recap and Review

Summary

Social change is significant alteration over time in behavior patterns and culture, including mores and values.

1. Early advocates of the **evolutionary theory** of social change believed that society was progressing inevitably toward a higher state.

2. Talcott Parsons, a leading advocate of functionalist theory, viewed society as being in a natural state of equilibrium or balance.

3. Conflict theorists see change as having crucial significance, since it is needed to correct social injustices and inequalities.

4. In general, those with a disproportionate share of society's wealth, status, and power have a **vested interest** in preserving the status quo and will resist change.

5. The period of maladjustment when a nonmaterial culture is still struggling to adapt to new material conditions is known as **culture lag.**

Thinking Critically

1. Which perspective on social change do you find most convincing? Why?

2. Which do you think play more of a role in resistance to social change, economic or cultural factors? Why?

Key Terms

Culture lag   470

Equilibrium model   468

Evolutionary theory   467

Luddites   470

Social change   467

Technology   470

Vested interests   469

MODULE 58 | Global Social Change

The recent past has been a truly dramatic time in history to consider global social change. Maureen Hallinan (1997), in her presidential address to the American Sociological Association, asked those present to consider just a few of the recent events: the collapse of communism; terrorism in various parts of the world, including the United States; major regime changes and severe economic disruptions in Africa, the Middle East, and Eastern Europe; the spread of AIDS; and the computer revolution. Just a few months after her remarks came the first verification of the cloning of a complex animal, Dolly the sheep.

In this era of massive social, political, and economic change, global in scale, is it possible to predict change? Some technological changes seem obvious, but the collapse of communist governments in the former Soviet Union and Eastern Europe in

The story of Dubai, a Middle Eastern principality the size of Rhode Island, is a tale of two cities. When the Maktoum family took control of Dubai (pronounced Doo-Bye) in 1883, it was a pearl-fishing village on the Persian Gulf. But in 1966, the discovery of oil changed everything. When the state's oil reserves proved too limited to fund significant economic and social change, Dubai reinvented itself as a free-trade oasis. By 2000 it had become a tax-free information-technology hub. In less than a single generation—barely a decade—Dubai had transformed itself into what *Forbes* magazine calls the richest city in the world. This is a place that in the late 1950s had no electricity and no paved roads.

Wide-eyed journalists have described Dubai's air-conditioned indoor ski run, open year-round in a country where the daytime temperature averages 92 degrees. Then there is the 160-story Burj Khalifa, which opened in 2010; at a half-mile high, it is by far the world's tallest building. At one point, so much of the city was under construction that 10 percent of the world's construction cranes were located there.

A constitutional monarchy, Dubai is no democratic utopia—there are no contested elections, and there is little public opposition to the government. Socially, however, Dubai is relatively progressive for an Arab state. Women are encouraged to work, and there is little separation of the sexes, as is common in neighboring states. Alcohol is freely available, speech is relatively free, and the media are largely uncensored.

The citizens of Dubai share its affluence: they receive cheap electricity, free land and water, free health care and education (including graduate study abroad), as well as an average subsidy of $55,000 per year. They pay no income or property taxes. Ironically, the government handouts that citizens enjoy mean that most have little interest in competitive work, so high-skilled positions tend to go to foreigners. The social consequences of Dubai's wealth have been less than benign, however. Environmentally, the cost of its lavish lifestyle is exorbitant. Dubai ranks at the top of the list in terms of its greenhouse gas emissions, at twice the level of the United States and triple the global average.

Another significant social problem, hidden from the investment bankers and tourists who visit Dubai, is the treatment of immigrant laborers. About 95 percent of Dubaians are foreigners from India, Pakistan, the Philippines, Sri Lanka, North Korea, Bangladesh, China, and Yemen. A million of them—seven times the number of Dubai nationals—come from India alone. These migrant laborers sold everything they owned to come to Dubai and take jobs stacking bricks, watering lawns, and cleaning floors. The pay is good relative to their home countries—$275 a month for a skilled electrician—but very poor compared to what the lowest-paid citizen of Dubai earns. At best, an immigrant must work two years just to break even.

There is little government oversight of working or living conditions in Dubai, both of which are poor. For foreign

the early 1990s took people by surprise. Yet prior to the Soviet collapse, sociologist Randall Collins (1986, 1995), a conflict theorist, had observed a crucial sequence of events that most observers had missed.

In seminars as far back as 1980, and in a book published in 1986, Collins had argued that Soviet expansionism had resulted in an overextension of resources, including disproportionate spending on military forces. Such an overextension will strain a regime's stability. Moreover, geopolitical theory suggests that nations in the middle of a geographic region, such as the Soviet Union, tend to fragment into smaller units over time. Collins predicted that the coincidence of social crises on several frontiers would precipitate the collapse of the Soviet Union.

And that is just what happened. In 1979, the success of the Iranian revolution had led to an upsurge of Islamic fundamentalism in nearby Afghanistan, as well as in Soviet republics with substantial Muslim populations. At the same time, resistance to communist rule was growing both throughout Eastern Europe and within the Soviet Union itself. Collins had predicted that the rise of a dissident form of communism within the Soviet Union

might facilitate the breakdown of the regime. Beginning in the late 1980s, Soviet leader Mikhail Gorbachev chose not to use military power and other types of repression to crush dissidents in Eastern Europe. Instead, he offered plans for democratization and social reform of Soviet society, and seemed willing to reshape the Soviet Union into a loose federation of somewhat autonomous states. But in 1991, six republics on the western periphery declared their independence, and within months the entire Soviet Union had formally disintegrated into Russia and a number of other independent nations.

In her address, Hallinan (1997) cautioned that we need to move beyond the restrictive models of social change—the linear view of evolutionary theory and the assumptions about equilibrium in the functionalist perspective. She and other sociologists have looked to the "chaos theory" advanced by mathematicians to understand erratic events as a part of change. Hallinan noted that upheavals and major chaotic shifts do occur, and that sociologists must learn to predict their occurrence, as Collins did with the Soviet Union. Imagine, for example, the dramatic nonlinear social change that accompanies the transformation of a small,

From 1990 to 2008, the area surrounding the Emirates Golf Club in Dubai changed dramatically.

workers seeking to escape the slums in distant deserts, one-bedroom apartments rent for $1,400 per month. In 2008, fire investigators found 500 laborers living in a house built for a single family. Little wonder that late in 2009, when Dubai's economic expansion ground to a halt, foreign workers were heading home at an estimated rate of 5,000 a day.

The global economic downturn that began in 2008 has been particularly savage to Dubai. Having borrowed heavily and invested not always wisely, both the government and major companies are groaning under a debt load that is heavier than even the United States' or Europe's. By 2010, however,

Dubai's economy was back on the move, although a bit moderated. The state's story is hardly finished. At the beginning of the second decade of the 21st century, the well-to-do are still flying lobster in for extravagant parties. Overworked foreign laborers, although many fewer of them remain, are still earning wages well above those available in their home countries. Political analysts note that Dubai is the most stable country in the Arab world, with a measured tolerance for outside cultural influences and an intolerance for corruption (Alderman 2010; Ali 2010; Harman 2009; Krane 2009, 2010; McGirk 2009; Rogan 2009; Tatchell 2009).

undeveloped principality into a major financial and communications hub (see the Case Study on Dubai).

Technology and the Future

Technological advances—the airplane, the automobile, the television, the atomic bomb, and more recently, the computer, digital media, and the cell phone—have brought striking changes to our cultures, our patterns of socialization, our social institutions, and our day-to-day social interactions. Technological innovations are, in fact, emerging and being accepted with remarkable speed.

In the past generation alone, industrial countries have seen a major shift in consumer technologies. No longer do we buy electronic devices to last for even 10 years. Increasingly, we buy them with the expectation that within as little as 3 years, we will need to upgrade to an entirely new technology, whether it be a handheld device or a home computer. Of course, there are those people who either reject the latest gadgets or become frustrated trying to adapt to them. And then there are the

"tech-no's"—people who resist the worldwide movement toward electronic networking. Those who become tech-no's are finding that it is a life choice that sets them apart from their peers, much like deciding to be "child free" (Darlin 2006; Kornblum 2007).

In the following sections, we examine various aspects of our technological future and consider their impact on social change, including the social strain they will cause. We focus in particular on recent developments in computer technology, electronic censorship, and biotechnology.

Computer Technology

The past decade witnessed an explosion of computer technology in the United States and around the world. Its effects were particularly noteworthy with regard to the Internet, the world's largest computer network. In 2012 the Internet reached 2.3 billion users, compared to just 50 million in 1996. Box 58-1 sketches the worldwide access to and use of the Internet.

The Internet evolved from a computer system built in 1962 by the U.S. Defense Department to enable scholars and military researchers to continue their government work even if part of the

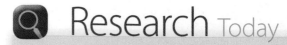
The Internet's Global Profile

The old notion of an Internet accessed primarily in the United States and dominated by English-only content is passé. In fact, usage patterns are changing so fast, generalizing about global use of the Internet requires careful research and phrasing.

For example, Figure A, Internet Users by World Region, shows an Internet that is dominated by users in Asia and Europe, two relatively populous continents. However, Figure B, Internet Penetration by World Region, shows

> *The old notion of an Internet accessed primarily in the United States and dominated by English-only content is passé.*

a dramatically different picture, one in which the *proportion* of people in each region who access the Internet is highest in North America and Australia. That is, numerically, most Internet users live in Asia and Europe, but the likelihood of a person being an Internet user is greatest in North America and Australia. Figure B shows dramatically low Internet use in Africa, where only 13.5 percent of residents access the global network.

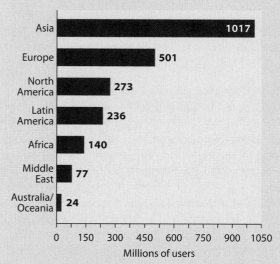

FIGURE A **Internet Users by World Region**

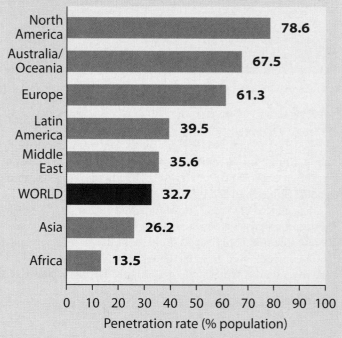

FIGURE B **Internet Penetration by World Region**

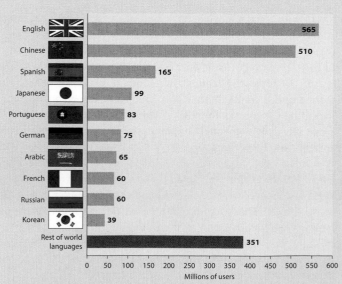

FIGURE C **Internet's Top 10 Languages**

Though English is still the primary language of Internet users, as Figure C shows, use of the Chinese language has become much more common. Interestingly, 78 percent of all Japanese speakers use the Internet, compared to 43 percent of all English speakers, though in absolute terms, speakers of Japanese are a significantly smaller group.

LET'S DISCUSS

1. Of the three figures shown here, which do you think presents the most sociologically significant statistics? Explain.

2. Why do you think the use of Chinese on the Internet has increased so dramatically in just a decade? What kind of information would you expect to find in Chinese? Who would use it?

Source: All data taken from Internet World Stats 2012 as of March 28, 2012.

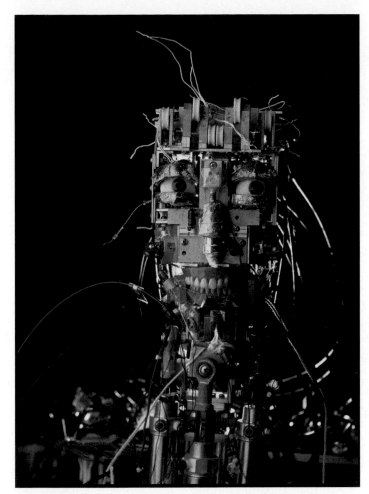

Happy, sad, or confused? This "face robot" was developed at the Science University of Tokyo during research on machines that can show and respond to human emotional expressions. Nonverbal communication is the latest innovation in robotics.

"We have to move - they're putting in a cell phone tower here."

Finding a place where you can't receive a text message is getting harder and harder.

 use your **sociological imagination**

Have you ever learned about a social movement outside the United States via the Internet?

nation's communications system were destroyed by a nuclear attack. Until a generation ago, it was difficult to gain access to the Internet without holding a position at a university or a government research laboratory. Today, however, virtually anyone can reach the Internet with a phone line, a computer, and a modem. People buy and sell cars, trade stocks, auction off items, research new medical remedies, vote, and track down long-lost friends online—to mention just a few of the thousands of possibilities. Earlier in this book we discussed the impact of the Internet on social interaction and the creation of new virtual worlds (see Module 16).

Unfortunately, not everyone can get onto the information highway, especially not the less affluent. Moreover, this pattern of inequality is global. The core nations that Immanuel Wallerstein described in his world systems analysis have a virtual monopoly on information technology; the peripheral nations of Asia, Africa, and Latin America depend on the core nations both for technology and for the information it provides. For example, North America, Europe, and a few industrialized nations in other regions possess almost all the world's *Internet hosts*—-computers that are connected directly to the worldwide network.

What is the solution to this global disconnect between the haves and the have-nots? Some people have suggested giving everyone a computer—or at least, everyone who can't afford one.

Privacy and Censorship in a Global Village

As we saw in the chapter-opening excerpt, new technologies like smartphones with map applications are bringing about sweeping social change. While much of that change is beneficial, there are some negative effects. Recent advances in computer technology have made it increasingly easy for business firms, government agencies, and even criminals to retrieve and store information about everything from our buying habits to our web-surfing patterns. In public places, at work, and on the Internet, surveillance devices now track our every move, be it a keystroke or an ATM withdrawal. At the same time that these innovations have increased others' power to monitor our behavior, they have raised fears that they might be misused for criminal or undemocratic purposes. In short, new technologies threaten not just our privacy, but our freedom from crime and censorship (O'Harrow Jr. 2005).

In recent years, concern about the criminal misuse of personal information has been underscored by the accidental loss of some huge databases. In 2006, for example, the theft of a laptop computer from the home of an employee of the Veterans' Administration compromised the names, Social Security numbers, and dates of birth of up to 26.5 million veterans. Unfortunately, technologies that facilitate the sharing of information have also created new types of crime.

From a sociological point of view, the complex issues of privacy and censorship can be considered illustrations of culture lag. As usual, the material culture (technology) is changing faster than the nonmaterial culture (norms for controlling the use of technology). Too often, the result is an anything-goes approach to the use of new technologies.

Legislation regarding the surveillance of electronic communications has not always upheld citizens' right to privacy. In 1986, the federal government passed the Electronic Communications Privacy Act, which outlawed the surveillance of telephone calls except with the permission of both the U.S. attorney general and a federal judge. Telegrams, faxes, and e-mail did not receive the same degree of protection, however. Then in 2001, one month after the terrorist attacks of September 11, Congress passed the Patriot Act, which relaxed existing legal checks on surveillance by law enforcement officers. As a result, federal agencies are now freer to gather electronic data, including credit-card receipts and banking records. In 2005, Americans learned that the National Security Agency was covertly monitoring phone calls with the cooperation of major U.S. telecommunications companies. Four years later, a federal court ruled that wiretapping without warrants is legal (Eckenwiler 1995; Lichtblau 2009; Vaidhyanathan 2008).

Sociologists' views on the use and abuse of new technologies differ depending on their theoretical perspective. Functionalists take a generally positive view of the Internet, pointing to its manifest function of facilitating communication. From their perspective, the Internet performs the latent function of empowering those with few resources—from hate groups to special-interest organizations—to communicate with the masses. Conflict theorists, in contrast, stress the danger that the most powerful groups in a society will use technology to violate the privacy of the less powerful. Indeed, officials in the People's Republic of China have attempted to censor online discussion groups and web postings that criticize the government. The same abuses can occur in the United States, civil liberties advocates remind us, if citizens are not vigilant in protecting their right to privacy (Magnier 2004).

Another source of controversy is the widespread use of GPS devices to track the location of cars or even people, not to mention the electronic tracking of handheld communications devices. Technology allows you to tweet your whereabouts to your friends, but should others, including the government, be able to home in on you? Put another way, is your location at any given moment covered by the Fourth Amendment to the U.S. Constitution, which protects your right to privacy? Both public opinion and court rulings on this question remain divided. The issue is yet another example of culture lag, or the time it takes for society to reconcile a new technology with traditional cultural values and behavior (Zipp 2009).

If anything, people seem to be less vigilant today about maintaining their privacy than they were before the information age. Young people who have grown up browsing the Internet seem to accept the existence of the cookies and spyware they may pick up while surfing. They have become accustomed to adult surveillance of their conversation in electronic chat rooms. Many see no risk in providing personal information about themselves to the strangers they meet online. Little wonder that college professors find their students do not appreciate the political significance of their right to privacy (Turkle 2004).

 use your **sociological imagination**

Do you hold strong views regarding the privacy of your electronic communications? When using a smartphone or similar device, do you ever suspect you are being watched or your actions monitored?

Biotechnology and the Gene Pool

Another field in which technological advances have spurred global social change is biotechnology. Sex selection of fetuses, genetically engineered organisms, cloning of sheep, cows, and some small animals—these have been among the significant yet controversial scientific advances in the field of biotechnology. George Ritzer's concept of McDonaldization applies to the entire area of biotechnology. Just as the fast-food concept has permeated society, no phase of life now seems exempt from therapeutic or medical intervention. In fact, sociologists view many aspects of biotechnology as an extension of the recent trend toward the medicalization of society, discussed in Module 52. Through genetic manipulation, the medical profession is expanding its turf still further (Clarke et al. 2003; Human Genome Project 2012).

One notable success of biotechnology—an unintended consequence of modern warfare—has been progress in the treatment of traumatic injuries. In response to the massive numbers of soldiers who survived serious injury in Iraq and Afghanistan, military doctors and therapists have come up with electronically controlled prosthetic devices. Their innovations include artificial limbs that respond to thought-generated nerve impulses, allowing amputees to move legs, arms, and even individual fingers.

These applications of computer science to the rehabilitation of the injured will no doubt be extended to civilians (J. Ellison 2008; Gailey 2007).

One startling biotechnological advance is the possibility of altering human behavior or physical traits through genetic engineering. Fish and plant genes have already been mixed to create frost-resistant potato and tomato crops. More recently, human genes have been implanted in pigs to provide humanlike kidneys for organ transplant. William F. Ogburn probably could not have anticipated such scientific developments when he wrote of culture lag over 80 years earlier. However, advances like these or even the successful cloning of sheep illustrate again how quickly material culture can change, and how nonmaterial culture moves more slowly in absorbing such changes.

Although today's biotechnology holds itself out as totally beneficial to human beings, it is in constant need of monitoring. Biotechnological advances have raised many difficult ethical and political questions, among them the desirability of tinkering with

A Ugandan farmer checks the price of coffee beans on his cell phone.

the gene pool, which could alter our environment in unexpected and unwanted ways. In particular, controversy has been growing concerning genetically modified (GM) food, an issue that arose in Europe but has since spread to other parts of the world, including the United States. The idea behind the technology is to increase food production and make agriculture more economical. But critics use the term *Frankenfood* (as in "Frankenstein") to refer to everything from breakfast cereals made from genetically engineered grains to fresh GM tomatoes. Members of the anti-biotech movement object to tampering with nature, and are concerned about the possible health effects of GM food. Supporters of genetically modified food include not just biotech companies, but those who see the technology as a way to help feed the burgeoning populations of Africa and Asia (Petersen 2009; World Health Organization 2009).

In contrast, less expensive and controversial technologies can further agriculture where it is needed more, in the developing world. Consider cell phones. Unlike most new technologies, the majority of the world's cell phones are used in *less* developed countries. Relatively cheap and not as dependent as computers on expensive communications infrastructure, cell phones are common in the world's poorest areas. In Uganda, farmers use them to check weather forecasts and commodity prices. In South Africa, laborers use them to look for work. Researchers at the London Business School have found that in developing countries, a 10 percent increase in cell phone use is correlated with a 0.6 percent rise in GDP (Bures 2011).

While farmers in the developing world use cell phones to improve their incomes, others set out for foreign countries. The Social Policy section that follows considers *transnationals*, immigrants who travel back and forth between the developing and developed worlds, forging human rather than technological links.

social
policy and Globalization | Transnationals

Around the world, new communications technologies—cell phones, the World Wide Web—have definitely hastened the process of globalization. Yet without human capital, these innovations would not have spurred the huge increase in global trade and development that occurred over the last several decades. Who are the people behind the trend toward globalization? Often, they are people who see a business opportunity abroad and strike out on their own to take advantage of it. In the process, many of them become migrants.

To facilitate trade and investment with other countries, migrants often exploit their social connections and their familiarity with their home language and culture. In Southeast Asia, for example, Chinese migrants dominate the trade with

—Continued

China; in Africa, Indian migrants dominate. Some migrants invest directly in their home countries to get the manufactured goods they sell abroad. Opportunities abound, and those with capital and good business skills can become quite wealthy (Guest 2011).

The millions of migrant laborers who leave home in search of a better life also play a role in the global economy, filling jobs where there are shortages in the labor market. Although they do not become wealthy working as landscapers or short-order cooks, they consider themselves better off than they were in the old country. Unfortunately, citizens of the host countries often react negatively to the migrants' arrival, worrying that they will take jobs away from the native-born.

Looking at the Issue

As of 2012, 214 million people, or about 3 percent of the world's population, were international migrants. That is more than double the number in 1970. The rest of the world's population were "stayers"—that is, people who continued to live in the countries where they were born (International Organization for Migration 2012).

Figure 58-1 shows the worldwide movement of workers with and without the legal right to immigrate. Several areas, such as the European Union, have instituted international agreements that provide for the free movement of laborers. But in most other parts of the world, immigration restrictions give foreign workers only temporary status. Despite such legal restrictions, the labor market has become an increasingly global one. Just as globalization has integrated government policies, cultures, social movements, and financial markets, it has unified what were once discrete national labor markets. So today, for example, immigrants from at least eight different countries work in one small Middle Eastern state, Dubai (see the case study on pages 472–473).

Globalization has changed the immigrant experience as well as the labor market. In generations past, immigrants read

MAPPING LIFE WORLDWIDE

FIGURE 58-1 **Labor Migration**

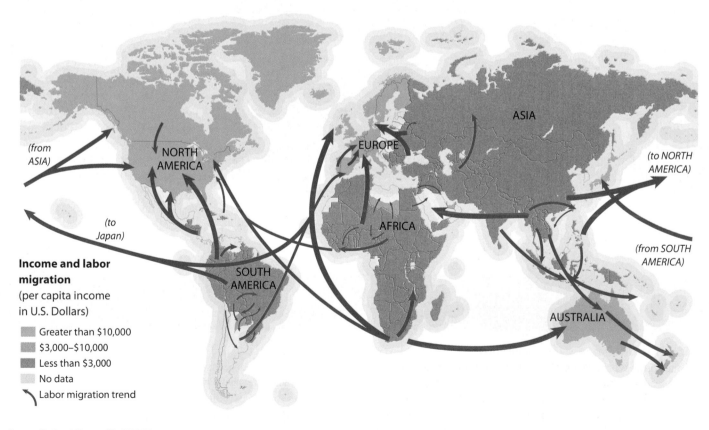

Income and labor migration (per capita income in U.S. Dollars)

Greater than $10,000
$3,000–$10,000
Less than $3,000
No data
Labor migration trend

Source: National Geographic 2005:16.

—*Continued*

foreign language newspapers to keep in touch with events in their home countries. Today, the Internet gives them immediate access to their countries and kinfolk. In this global framework, immigrants are less likely than they were in the past to think of themselves as residents of just one country. **Transnationals** are immigrants who sustain multiple social relationships that link their societies of origin with their societies of settlement (P. Levitt and Jaworsky 2007).

Applying Sociology

As with other issues, sociologists differ in their opinion of transnationals, depending on their theoretical perspective. Functionalists see the free flow of immigrants, even when it is legally restricted, as one way for economies to maximize their use of human labor. Given the law of supply and demand, they note, countries with too few workers will inevitably attract laborers, while those with too many will become unattractive to residents.

Conflict theorists charge that globalization and international migration have increased the economic gulf between developed and developing nations. Today, residents of North America, western Europe, Australia, and Japan consume 32 times more resources than the billions of people who live in developing countries. Through tourism and the global reach of the mass media, people in the poorer countries have become aware of the affluent lifestyle common in developed nations—and of course, many of them now aspire to it (L. Smith 2011).

Interactionists are interested in the day-to-day relationships transnationals have with the people around them, from those of their country of origin to those of the host country and fellow workers from other countries. These scholars are studying transnationals' involvement in local ethnic organizations, to see whether their membership facilitates or retards their integration into the host society. They have discovered that members of global social networks provide one another with mutual support and trust. Just as interesting is the question of how migrants see themselves—how they see their own identities as well as those of their children. In effect, transnationals negotiate their identities, depending on which social network they belong to at the moment. Some sociologists note that while being a transnational can be exhilarating, it can also isolate a person, even in a city of millions. Others worry that transnationals may become so cosmopolitan that they will lose touch with their national identities (Calhoun 2003; Evergeti and Zontini 2006; Plüss 2005; Portes et al. 2008; Rajan and Sharma 2006; Tilly 2007).

Initiating Policy

Although connecting to two societies can be an enriching experience, transnationals face continuing adjustment problems in their new home countries. As we saw in the case study of Dubai, immigrant laborers often face difficult living and working conditions. Some sending countries, such as Indonesia and the Philippines, have created national agencies to ensure the protection of their workers abroad. Their objective is ambitious, given that funding for the agencies is limited, and diplomatic and legal challenges complicate their task (United Nations Development Programme 2009:102–104).

Another unresolved transnational issue is voter eligibility. Not all nations allow dual citizenship; even those countries that do may not allow absent nationals to vote. The United States and Great Britain are rather liberal in this regard, permitting dual citizenship and allowing émigrés to continue to vote. Mexico, in contrast, has been reluctant to allow citizens who have emigrated to vote. Mexican politicians worry that the large number of Mexicans who live abroad (especially those in the United States) might vote differently from local voters, causing different outcomes (P. Levitt and Jaworsky 2007; Sellers 2004).

Finally, the controversial issue of illegal immigration has yet to be settled, perhaps because of culture lag. That is, both public attitudes and government policies (nonmaterial culture) have not kept pace with, much less adjusted to, the increasing ease of migration around the globe (material culture). Though globalization has created a global labor market—one that many countries depend on, legal or illegal—the general public's attitude toward illegal immigrants remains hostile, especially in the United States.

TAKE THE ISSUE WITH YOU

1. Suppose you live in an impoverished developing country and have the opportunity to earn a much higher income by immigrating to the United States. Will you do it, even if it means entering the country illegally and working long hours doing menial labor? If so, how will you justify your decision to those who condemn illegal immigration?

2. The U.S. economy depends on the cheap labor that immigrants provide. Should immigrants receive the same social services that U.S. citizens receive? What about their children who are born in the United States (and therefore are U.S. citizens)? Explain your reasoning.

3. Globalization has increased international trade and development at the same time that it has strained nations' social service systems, as migrant workers flow toward countries offering the most extensive social protection. On balance, do you think its overall effect has been beneficial or harmful? What might be done to alleviate the harmful effects of globalization?

Summary

We are living in a time of sweeping social, political, and economic change—change that occurs not just on a local or national basis but on a global scale.

1. Computer technology has made it increasingly easy for any individual, business, or government agency to retrieve more and more information about any of us, thereby infringing on our privacy.

2. Advances in biotechnology have raised difficult ethical questions about genetic engineering.

3. Dubai is a Middle Eastern principality that reinvented itself as an information technology hub, in the process undergoing massive social change.

4. Globalization has increased the international migration of laborers, producing a new kind of immigrant. **Transnationals** are immigrants who sustain multiple social relationships that link their societies of origin with their societies of settlement.

Thinking Critically

1. Using chaos theory, what kind of global social change might you predict for the 21st century?

2. Which aspect of biotechnology do you find most promising?

3. Do you sometimes see your future more in the electronic world than in the people and places around you?

Key Term

Transnational   479

Mastering This Chapter

taking sociology with you

1 Choose a social movement that you are interested in and do some research on it. If possible, visit with members of the movement in your local community. Which sociological theory fits this movement better, relative deprivation or resource mobilization? Would you describe the movement as a new social movement? What has been the role of communications in the movement?

2 Try turning off all your electronic devices—phone, laptop, and so on—for a specific period, say a day. Afterward, analyze the experiment from a sociological perspective. What functions did you lose while you were without the devices? Did you gain anything from the experience?

3 Choose a new technology that interests you and analyze it from a sociological point of view. What do you think this technology might contribute to society? What might be some negative effects of the technology? Have you noticed any resistance to it, and if so, on what grounds?

key terms

Computer-mediated communication Communicative interaction through two or more networked devices, such as a computer or cell phone. The term applies to a variety of text-based or video interactions, including e-mails, chat rooms, and text messages, some of which may be supported by social media. (page 465)

Culture lag A period of maladjustment when the nonmaterial culture is still struggling to adapt to new material conditions. (470)

Equilibrium model The functionalist view that society tends toward a state of stability or balance. (468)

Evolutionary theory A theory of social change that holds that society is moving in a definite direction. (467)

False consciousness A term used by Karl Marx to describe an attitude held by members of a class that does not accurately reflect their objective position. (462)

Luddites Rebellious craft workers in 19th-century England who destroyed new factory machinery as part of their resistance to the Industrial Revolution. (470)

New social movement An organized collective activity that addresses values and social identities, as well as improvements in the quality of life. (463)

Relative deprivation The conscious feeling of a negative discrepancy between legitimate expectations and present actualities. (461)

Resource mobilization The ways in which a social movement utilizes such resources as money, political influence, access to the media, and personnel. (462)

Social change Significant alteration over time in behavior patterns and culture, including norms and values. (467)

Social movement An organized collective activity to bring about or resist fundamental change in an existing group or society. (461)

Technology Cultural information about the ways in which the material resources of the environment may be used to satisfy human needs and desires. (470)

Transnational An immigrant who sustains multiple social relationships that link his or her society of origin with the society of settlement. (479)

Vested interests Those people or groups who will suffer in the event of social change, and who have a stake in maintaining the status quo. (469)

self-quiz

Read each question carefully and then select the best answer.

1. You are a student and do not own a car. All your close friends who are attending your college or university have vehicles of their own. You feel downtrodden and dissatisfied. You are experiencing
   a. relative deprivation.
   b. resource mobilization.
   c. false consciousness.
   d. depression.

2. It takes more than desire to start a social movement; it helps to have money, political influence, access to the media, and workers. The ways in which a social movement uses such things are referred to collectively as
   a. relative deprivation.
   b. false consciousness.
   c. resource mobilization.
   d. economic independence.

3. Karl Marx held that leaders of social movements must help workers overcome feelings of
   a. class consciousness.
   b. false consciousness.
   c. socialist consciousness.
   d. surplus value.

4. Organized collective activities that promote autonomy and self-determination, as well as improvements in the quality of life, are referred to as
   a. new social movements.
   b. social revolutions.
   c. resource mobilizations.
   d. crazes.

5. The text cites which of the following as a recognized definition of social change?
   a. tumultuous, revolutionary alternatives that lead to changes in leadership
   b. a significant alteration over time in behavior patterns and culture
   c. regular alteration in a consistent social frame of reference
   d. subtle alterations in any social system

6. Nineteenth-century theories of social change reflect the pioneering work in biological evolution done by
   a. Albert Einstein.
   b. Harriet Martineau.
   c. James Audubon.
   d. Charles Darwin.

7. According to Talcott Parsons's equilibrium model, during which process do social institutions become more specialized in their purposes?
   a. differentiation
   b. adaptive upgrading
   c. inclusion
   d. value generalization

8. Which of the following statements regarding Karl Marx is *not* true?
   a. Marx accepted the evolutionary argument that societies develop along a particular path.
   b. Marx believed that history proceeds through a series of stages, each of which exploits a class of people.
   c. Marx accepted Parsons's equilibrium model, which states that as changes occur in one part of society, there must be adjustments in other parts if stability is to be maintained.
   d. Marx argued that conflict is a normal and desirable aspect of social change.

9. Which of the following terms did William F. Ogburn use to refer to the period of maladjustment during which the nonmaterial culture is still struggling to adapt to new material conditions?
   a. economic shift
   b. political turmoil
   c. social change
   d. culture lag

10. Which sociological perspective sees transnationals as a way for economies to maximize their use of human labor?
    a. functionalist
    b. conflict
    c. interactionist
    d. feminist

11. _____ _____ are organized collective activities to bring about or resist fundamental change in an existing group or society.

12. A person suffering from relative deprivation is dissatisfied because he or she feels downtrodden relative to some appropriate _____ group.

13. Early evolutionary theorists concluded in a(n) _____ fashion that their own behavior and culture were more advanced than those of earlier civilizations.

14. Talcott Parsons used the term _____ to refer to the increasing complexity of social organization.

15. Social economist Thorstein Veblen coined the term _____ _____ to refer to those people or groups who will suffer in the event of social change.

16. The term _____ refers to those who are wary of technological innovations, and who question the incessant expansion of industrialization, the increasing destruction of the natural and agrarian world, and the "throw-it-away" mentality of contemporary capitalism.

17. In 2001, one month after the terrorist attacks of September 11, Congress passed the _____ Act, which relaxed existing legal checks on surveillance by law enforcement officers. Federal agencies are now free to gather data electronically, including credit card receipts and banking records.

18. The _____ is the world's largest computer network.

19. In developing countries, _____ _____ are a less expensive way of furthering agriculture than biotechnology.

20. The _____ _____ perspective would stress the danger that the most powerful groups in a society will use technology to violate the privacy of the less powerful.

thinking about movies

Life in a Day

This film was compiled from thousands of home movies from around the world, all shot on the same day.

Afghan Star

A documentary, this film gives viewers a glimpse into Afghanistan's version of *American Idol*.

Babies

This cross-cultural comparison shows the lives of several babies from around the world.

glossary

Numbers following the definitions indicate pages where the terms were identified. Consult the index for further page references.

a

Absolute poverty A minimum level of subsistence that no family should be expected to live below. (212)

Achieved status A social position that a person attains largely through his or her own efforts. (115, 197)

Activity theory An interactionist theory of aging that suggests that those elderly people who remain active and socially involved will be best adjusted. (309)

Adoption In a legal sense, the transfer of the legal rights, responsibilities, and privileges of parenthood to a new legal parent or parents. (339)

Affirmative action Positive efforts to recruit minority group members or women for jobs, promotions, and educational opportunities. (259, 422)

Ageism Prejudice and discrimination based on a person's age. (318)

Agrarian society The most technologically advanced form of preindustrial society. Members engage primarily in the production of food, but increase their crop yields through technological innovations such as the plow. (125)

Alienation A condition of estrangement or dissociation from the surrounding society. (132)

Amalgamation The process through which a majority group and a minority group combine to form a new group. (264)

Anomie Durkheim's term for the loss of direction felt in a society when social control of individual behavior has become ineffective. (11, 177)

Anomie theory of deviance Robert Merton's theory of deviance as an adaptation of socially prescribed goals or of the means governing their attainment, or both. (177)

Anticipatory socialization Processes of socialization in which a person rehearses for future positions, occupations, and social relationships. (97)

Anti-Semitism Anti-Jewish prejudice. (274)

Apartheid A former policy of the South African government, designed to maintain the separation of Blacks and other non-Whites from the dominant Whites. (264)

Applied sociology The use of the discipline of sociology with the specific intent of yielding practical applications for human behavior and organizations. (21)

Argot Specialized language used by members of a group or subculture. (77)

Ascribed status A social position assigned to a person by society without regard for the person's unique talents or characteristics. (114, 197)

Assimilation The process through which a person forsakes his or her cultural tradition to become part of a different culture. (265)

Authority Institutionalized power that is recognized by the people over whom it is exercised. (402)

b

Basic sociology Sociological inquiry conducted with the objective of gaining a more profound knowledge of the fundamental aspects of social phenomena. Also known as *pure sociology*. (22)

Bilateral descent A kinship system in which both sides of a person's family are regarded as equally important. (330)

Bilingualism The use of two languages in a particular setting, such as the workplace or schoolroom, treating each language as equally legitimate. (79)

Black power A political philosophy, promoted by many younger Blacks in the 1960s, that supported the creation of Black-controlled political and economic institutions. (267)

Borderlands The area of common culture along the border between Mexico and the United States. (241)

Bourgeoisie Karl Marx's term for the capitalist class, comprising the owners of the means of production. (203)

Brain drain The immigration to the United States and other industrialized nations of skilled workers, professionals, and technicians who are desperately needed in their home countries. (435)

Bureaucracy A component of formal organization that uses rules and hierarchical ranking to achieve efficiency. (131)

Bureaucratization The process by which a group, organization, or social movement becomes increasingly bureaucratic. (133)

c

Capitalism An economic system in which the means of production are held largely in private hands and the main incentive for economic activity is the accumulation of profits. (203, 415)

Caste A hereditary rank, usually religiously dictated, that tends to be fixed and immobile. (199)

Causal logic The relationship between a condition or variable and a particular consequence, with one leading to the other. (34)

Charismatic authority Max Weber's term for power made legitimate by a leader's exceptional personal or emotional appeal to his or her followers. (402)

Charter school An experimental school that is developed and managed by individuals, groups of parents, or an educational management organization. (371)

Class A group of people who have a similar level of wealth and income. (204)

Class consciousness In Karl Marx's view, a subjective awareness held by members of a class regarding their common vested interests and the need for collective political action to bring about social change. (203)

Class system A social ranking based primarily on economic position in which achieved characteristics can influence social mobility. (201)

Classical theory An approach to the study of formal organizations that views workers as being motivated almost entirely by economic rewards. (134)

Clinical sociology The use of the discipline of sociology with the specific intent of altering social relationships or restructuring social institutions. (22)

Closed system A social system in which there is little or no possibility of individual social mobility. (216)

Coalition A temporary or permanent alliance geared toward a common goal. (130)

Code of ethics The standards of acceptable behavior developed by and for members of a profession. (45)

Cognitive theory of development Jean Piaget's theory that children's thought progresses through four stages of development. (96)

Cohabitation The practice of living together as a male–female couple without marrying. (344)

Colonialism The maintenance of political, social, economic, and cultural domination over a people by a foreign power for an extended period. (227)

Color-blind racism The use of the principle of race neutrality to defend a racially unequal status quo. (255, 422)

Communism As an ideal type, an economic system under which all property is communally owned and no social distinctions are made on the basis of people's ability to produce. (417)

Computer-mediated communication Communicative interaction through two or more networked devices, such as a computer or cell phone. The term applies to a variety of text-based or video interactions, including e-mails, chat rooms, and text messages, some of which may be supported by social media. (465)

Conflict perspective A sociological approach that assumes that social behavior is best understood in terms of tension between groups over power or the allocation of resources, including housing, money, access to services, and political representation. (16)

Conformity Going along with peers—individuals of our own status who have no special right to direct our behavior. (170)

Conspicuous consumption Purchasing goods not to survive but to flaunt one's superior wealth and social standing. (204)

Contact hypothesis An interactionist perspective which states that in cooperative circumstances, interracial contact between people of equal status will reduce prejudice. (263)

Content analysis The systematic coding and objective recording of data, guided by some rationale. (43)

Control group The subjects in an experiment who are not introduced to the independent variable by the researcher. (43)

Control theory A view of conformity and deviance that suggests that our connection to members of society leads us to systematically conform to society's norms. (173)

Control variable A factor that is held constant to test the relative impact of an independent variable. (37)

Corporate welfare Tax breaks, bailouts, direct payments, and grants that the government gives to corporations. (244)

Correlation A relationship between two variables in which a change in one coincides with a change in the other. (34)

Correspondence principle A term used by Bowles and Gintis to refer to the tendency of schools to promote the values expected of individuals in each social class and to perpetuate social class divisions from one generation to the next. (363)

Counterculture A subculture that deliberately opposes certain aspects of the larger culture. (78)

Creationism A literal interpretation of the Bible regarding the creation of humanity and the universe, used to argue that evolution should not be presented as established scientific fact. (393)

Credentialism An increase in the lowest level of education needed to enter a field. (362)

Crime A violation of criminal law for which some governmental authority applies formal penalties. (182)

Cross-tabulation A table or matrix that shows the relationship between two or more variables. (52)

Cultural capital Noneconomic goods, such as family background and education, which are reflected in a knowledge of language and the arts. (14)

Cultural convergence The flow of content across multiple media, and the accompanying migration of media audiences. (145)

Cultural relativism The viewing of people's behavior from the perspective of their own culture. (62)

Cultural transmission A school of criminology that argues that criminal behavior is learned through social interactions. (178)

Cultural universal A common practice or belief found in every culture. (62)

Culture The totality of learned, socially transmitted customs, knowledge, material objects, and behavior. (61)

Culture industry The worldwide media industry that standardizes the goods and services demanded by consumers. (62)

Culture lag A period of maladjustment when the nonmaterial culture is still struggling to adapt to new material conditions. (76, 470)

Culture shock The feeling of surprise and disorientation that people experience when they encounter cultural practices that are different from their own. (79)

Culture war The polarization of society over controversial cultural elements. (71)

Curanderismo Latino folk medicine, a form of holistic health care and healing. (440)

d

Degradation ceremony An aspect of the socialization process within some total institutions, in which people are subjected to humiliating rituals. (98)

Deindustrialization The systematic, widespread withdrawal of investment in basic aspects of productivity, such as factories and plants. (421)

Democracy In a literal sense, government by the people. (403)

Denomination A large, organized religion that is not officially linked to the state or government. (389)

Dependency theory An approach that contends that industrialized nations continue to exploit developing countries for their own gain. (230)

Dependent variable The variable in a causal relationship that is subject to the influence of another variable. (34)

Deviance Behavior that violates the standards of conduct or expectations of a group or society. (175)

Dictatorship A government in which one person has nearly total power to make and enforce laws. (403)

Differential association A theory of deviance proposed by Edwin Sutherland that holds that violation of rules results from exposure to attitudes favorable to criminal acts. (179)

Differential justice Differences in the way social control is exercised over different groups. (181)

Diffusion The process by which a cultural item spreads from group to group or society to society. (74)

Digital divide The relative lack of access to the latest technologies among low-income groups, racial and ethnic minorities, rural residents, and the citizens of developing countries. (153)

Discovery The process of making known or sharing the existence of an aspect of reality. (73)

Discrimination The denial of opportunities and equal rights to individuals and groups because of prejudice or other arbitrary reasons. (256)

Disengagement theory A functionalist theory of aging that suggests that society and the aging individual mutually sever many of their relationships. (308)

Domestic partnership Two unrelated adults who share a mutually caring relationship, reside together, and agree to be jointly responsible for their dependents, basic living expenses, and other common necessities. (349)

Dominant ideology A set of cultural beliefs and practices that helps to maintain powerful social, economic, and political interests. (72, 151, 206)

Double consciousness The division of an individual's identity into two or more social realities. (13)

Downsizing Reductions taken in a company's workforce as part of deindustrialization. (421)

Dramaturgical approach A view of social interaction, popularized by Erving Goffman, in which people are seen as theatrical performers. (18, 94)

Dysfunction An element or process of a society that may disrupt the social system or reduce its stability. (16)

e

Ecclesia A religious organization that claims to include most or all members of a society and is recognized as the national or official religion. (389)

Ecological modernization The alignment of environmentally favorable practices with economic self-interest through constant adaptation and restructuring. (449)

Economic system The social institution through which goods and services are produced, distributed, and consumed. (401)

Education A formal process of learning in which some people consciously teach, while others adopt the social role of learner. (357)

Egalitarian family An authority pattern in which spouses are regarded as equals. (332)

Elite model A view of society as being ruled by a small group of individuals who share a common set of political and economic interests. (413)

Endogamy The restriction of mate selection to people within the same group. (336)

Environmental justice A legal strategy based on claims that racial minorities are subjected disproportionately to environmental hazards. (449)

Environmental refugee A person who has been displaced by rising seas, destructive storms, expanding deserts, water shortages, or high levels of toxic pollutants. (452)

Equilibrium model Talcott Parsons's functionalist view that society tends toward a state of stability or balance. (468)

Established sect J. Milton Yinger's term for a religious group that is the outgrowth of a sect, yet remains isolated from society. (390)

Estate system A system of stratification under which peasants were required to work land leased to them by nobles in exchange for military protection and other services. Also known as *feudalism*. (201)

Esteem The reputation that a specific person has earned within an occupation. (208)

Ethnic group A group that is set apart from others primarily because of its national origin or distinctive cultural patterns. (251)

Ethnocentrism The tendency to assume that one's own culture and way of life represent the norm or are superior to all others. (62, 255)

Ethnography The study of an entire social setting through extended systematic fieldwork. (40)

Euthanasia The act of bringing about the death of a hopelessly ill and suffering person in a relatively quick and painless way for reasons of mercy. (321)

Evolutionary theory A theory of social change that holds that society is moving in a definite direction. (467)

Exogamy The requirement that people select a mate outside certain groups. (336)

Experiment An artificially created situation that allows a researcher to manipulate variables. (42)

Experimental group The subjects in an experiment who are exposed to an independent variable introduced by a researcher. (43)

Exploitation theory A Marxist theory that views racial subordination in the United States as a manifestation of the class system inherent in capitalism. (262)

Expressiveness Concern for the maintenance of harmony and the internal emotional affairs of the family. (289)

Extended family A family in which relatives—such as grandparents, aunts, or uncles—live in the same home as parents and their children. (329)

f

Face-work A term used by Erving Goffman to refer to the efforts people make to maintain the proper image and avoid public embarrassment. (95)

False consciousness A term used by Karl Marx to describe an attitude held by members of a class that does not accurately reflect their objective position. (203, 462)

Familism (*Familismo*) Pride in the extended family, expressed through the maintenance of close ties and strong obligations to kinfolk outside the immediate family. (338)

Family A set of people related by blood, marriage or some other agreed-on relationship, or adoption, who share the primary responsibility for reproduction and caring for members of society. (329)

Feminism The belief in social, economic, and political equality for women. (297)

Feminist perspective A sociological approach that views inequity in gender as central to all behavior and organization. (17)

Feminization of poverty A trend in which women constitute an increasing proportion of the poor people of both the United States and the world. (213)

Folkway A norm governing everyday behavior whose violation raises comparatively little concern. (68)

Force The actual or threatened use of coercion to impose one's will on others. (401)

Formal norm A norm that has been written down and that specifies strict punishments for violators. (68)

Formal organization A group designed for a special purpose and structured for maximum efficiency. (131)

Formal social control Social control that is carried out by authorized agents, such as police officers, judges, school administrators, and employers. (172)

Functionalist perspective A sociological approach that emphasizes the way in which the parts of a society are structured to maintain its stability. (15)

Fundamentalism An emphasis on doctrinal conformity and the literal interpretation of sacred texts. (385)

g

Gatekeeping The process by which a relatively small number of people in the media industry control what material eventually reaches the audience. (148)

Gemeinschaft A term used by Ferdinand Tönnies to describe a close-knit community, often found in rural areas, in which strong personal bonds unite members. (123)

Gender role Expectations regarding the proper behavior, attitudes, and activities of males and females. (100, 285)

Generalized other A term used by George Herbert Mead to refer to the attitudes, viewpoints, and expectations of society as a whole that a child takes into account in his or her behavior. (94)

Genocide The deliberate, systematic killing of an entire people or nation. (263)

Gerontology The scientific study of the sociological and psychological aspects of aging and the problems of the aged. (308)

Gesellschaft A term used by Ferdinand Tönnies to describe a community, often urban, that is large and impersonal, with little commitment to the group or consensus on values. (123)

Glass ceiling An invisible barrier that blocks the promotion of a qualified individual in a work environment because of the individual's gender, race, or ethnicity. (257, 294)

Globalization The worldwide integration of government policies, cultures, social movements, and financial markets through trade and the exchange of ideas. (22, 230)

Goal displacement Overzealous conformity to official regulations of a bureaucracy. (132)

Group Any number of people with similar norms, values, and expectations who interact with one another on a regular basis. (117, 127)

h

Hate crime A criminal offense committed because of the offender's bias against a race, religion, ethnic group, national origin, or sexual orientation. Also referred to as *bias crime*. (185, 255)

Hawthorne effect The unintended influence that observers of experiments can have on their subjects. (43)

Health As defined by the World Health Organization, a state of complete physical, mental, and social well-being, and not merely the absence of disease and infirmity. (433)

Hidden curriculum Standards of behavior that are deemed proper by society and are taught subtly in schools. (362)

Holistic medicine Therapies in which the health care practitioner considers the person's physical, mental, emotional, and spiritual characteristics. (444)

Homogamy The conscious or unconscious tendency to select a mate with personal characteristics similar to one's own. (336)

Homophobia Fear of and prejudice against homosexuality. (285)

Horizontal mobility The movement of an individual from one social position to another of the same rank. (216)

Horticultural society A preindustrial society in which people plant seeds and crops rather than merely subsist on available foods. (125)

Hospice care Treatment of the terminally ill in their own homes, or in special hospital units or other facilities, with the goal of helping them to die easily, without pain. (315)

Human ecology An area of study that is concerned with the interrelationships between people and their environment. (447)

Human relations approach An approach to the study of formal organizations that emphasizes the role of people, communication, and participation in a bureaucracy and tends to focus on the informal structure of the organization. (135)

Hunting-and-gathering society A preindustrial society in which people rely on whatever foods and fibers are readily available in order to survive. (124)

Hypothesis A speculative statement about the relationship between two or more variables. (34)

i

Ideal type A construct or model for evaluating specific cases. (11, 131)

Impression management A term used by Erving Goffman to refer to the altering of the presentation of the self in order to create distinctive appearances and satisfy particular audiences. (94)

Incest taboo The prohibition of sexual relationships between certain culturally specified relatives. (336)

Incidence The number of new cases of a specific disorder that occur within a given population during a stated period. (438)

Income Salaries and wages. (209)

Independent variable The variable in a causal relationship that causes or influences a change in another variable. (34)

Index crimes The eight types of crime tabulated each year by the FBI in the *Uniform Crime Reports:* murder, rape, robbery, assault, burglary, theft, motor vehicle theft, and arson. (186)

Industrial society A society that depends on mechanization to produce its goods and services. (125, 415)

Infant mortality rate The number of deaths of infants under 1 year old per 1,000 live births in a given year. (435)

Influence The exercise of power through a process of persuasion. (401)

Informal economy Transfers of money, goods, or services that are not reported to the government. (420)

Informal norm A norm that is generally understood but not precisely recorded. (68)

Informal social control Social control that is carried out casually by ordinary people through such means as laughter, smiles, and ridicule. (171)

In-group Any group or category to which people feel they belong. (129)

Innovation The process of introducing a new idea or object to a culture through discovery or invention. (73)

Institutional discrimination The denial of opportunities and equal rights to individuals and groups that results from the normal operations of a society. (259, 292)

Instrumentality An emphasis on tasks, a focus on more distant goals, and a concern for the external relationship between one's family and other social institutions. (289)

Intelligent design (ID) The idea that life is so complex that it could only have been created by intelligent design. (394)

Interactionist perspective A sociological approach that generalizes about everyday forms of social interaction in order to explain society as a whole. (18)

Intergenerational mobility Changes in the social position of children relative to their parents. (216)

Interview A face-to-face, telephone, or online questioning of a respondent to obtain desired information. (39)

Intragenerational mobility Changes in social position within a person's adult life. (217)

Invention The combination of existing cultural items into a form that did not exist before. (73)

Iron law of oligarchy A principle of organizational life developed by Robert Michels, under which even a democratic organization will eventually develop into a bureaucracy ruled by a few individuals. (133)

k

Kinship The state of being related to others. (330)

l

Labeling theory An approach to deviance that attempts to explain why certain people are viewed as deviants while others engaged in the same behavior are not. (179)

Laissez-faire A form of capitalism under which people compete freely, with minimal government intervention in the economy. (415)

Language An abstract system of word meanings and symbols for all aspects of culture; includes gestures and other nonverbal communication. (65)

Latent function An unconscious or unintended function that may reflect hidden purposes. (16)

Law Governmental social control. (68, 173)

Liberation theology Use of a church, primarily Roman Catholic, in a political effort to eliminate poverty, discrimination, and other forms of injustice from a secular society. (382)

Life chances Max Weber's term for the opportunities people have to provide themselves with material goods, positive living conditions, and favorable life experiences. (215)

Life course approach A research orientation in which sociologists and other social scientists look closely at the social factors that influence people throughout their lives, from birth to death. (97)

Looking-glass self A concept used by Charles Horton Cooley that emphasizes the self as the product of our social interactions. (93)

Luddites Rebellious craft workers in 19th-century England who destroyed new factory machinery as part of their resistance to the Industrial Revolution. (470)

m

Machismo A sense of virility, personal worth, and pride in one's maleness. (338)

Macrosociology Sociological investigation that concentrates on large-scale phenomena or entire civilizations. (14)

Manifest function An open, stated, and conscious function. (16)

Mass media Print and electronic means of communication that carry messages to widespread audiences. (145)

Master status A status that dominates others and thereby determines a person's general position in society. (115)

Material culture The physical or technological aspects of our daily lives. (76)

Matriarchy A society in which women dominate in family decision making. (332)

Matrilineal descent A kinship system in which only the mother's relatives are significant. (331)

Matrix of domination The cumulative impact of oppression because of race and ethnicity, gender, and social class, as well as religion, sexual orientation, disability, age, and citizenship status. (290)

McDonaldization The process through which the principles of the fast-food restaurant are coming to dominate more and more sectors of society. (443)

Mean A number calculated by adding a series of values and then dividing by the number of values. (52)

Mechanical solidarity A collective consciousness that emphasizes group solidarity, characteristic of societies with minimal division of labor. (123)

Median The midpoint or number that divides a series of values into two groups of equal numbers of values. (52)

Microfinancing Lending small sums of money to the poor so they can work their way out of poverty. (424)

Microsociology Sociological investigation that stresses the study of small groups, often through experimental means. (14)

Midlife crisis A stressful period of self-evaluation that begins at about age 40. (312)

Minority group A subordinate group whose members have significantly less control or power over their own lives than the members of a dominant or majority group have over theirs. (251)

Mode The single most common value in a series of scores. (52)

Model, or ideal, minority A subordinate group whose members supposedly have succeeded economically, socially, and educationally despite past prejudice and discrimination, and without resorting to political and violent confrontations with Whites. (270)

Modernization The far-reaching process through which periphery nations move from traditional or less developed institutions to those characteristic of more developed societies. (235)

Modernization theory A functionalist approach that proposes that modernization and development will gradually improve the lives of people in developing nations. (235)

Monarchy A form of government headed by a single member of a royal family, usually a king, queen, or some other hereditary ruler. (403)

Monogamy A form of marriage in which one woman and one man are married only to each other. (329)

Monopoly Control of a market by a single business firm. (416)

Morbidity rate The incidence of disease in a given population. (438)

Mores Norms deemed highly necessary to the welfare of a society. (68)

Mortality rate The incidence of death in a given population. (438)

Multinational corporation A commercial organization that is headquartered in one country but does business throughout the world. (233)

Multiple masculinities A variety of male gender roles, including nurturing-caring and effeminate-gay roles, that men may play along with their more pervasive traditional role of dominating women. (288)

n

Narcotizing dysfunction The phenomenon in which the media provide such massive amounts of coverage that the audience becomes numb and fails to act on the information, regardless of how compelling the issue. (148)

Natural science The study of the physical features of nature and the ways in which they interact and change. (6)

Naturally occurring retirement community (NORC) An area that has gradually become an informal center for senior citizens. (314)

Neocolonialism Continuing dependence of former colonies on foreign countries. (228)

Netizen A person who is actively involved in online communities and is committed to the free flow of information, with few outside controls. (149)

New religious movement (NRM) or **cult** A small, secretive religious group that represents either a new religion or a major innovation of an existing faith. (390)

New social movement An organized collective activity that addresses values and social identities, as well as improvements in the quality of life. (463)

Nonmaterial culture Ways of using material objects, as well as customs, beliefs, philosophies, governments, and patterns of communication. (76)

Nonverbal communication The sending of messages through the use of gestures, facial expressions, and postures. (18)

Norm An established standard of behavior maintained by a society. (66)

Nuclear family A married couple and their unmarried children living together. (329)

o

Obedience Compliance with higher authorities in a hierarchical structure. (170)

Objective method A technique for measuring social class that assigns individuals to classes on the basis of criteria such as occupation, education, income, and place of residence. (208)

Observation A research technique in which an investigator collects information through direct participation, by closely watching a group or community. (40)

Offshoring The transfer of work to foreign contractors. (423)

Oligarchy A form of government in which a few individuals rule. (403)

Open system A social system in which the position of each individual is influenced by his or her achieved status. (216)

Operational definition An explanation of an abstract concept that is specific enough to allow a researcher to assess the concept. (33)

Opinion leader Someone who influences the opinions and decisions of others through day-to-day personal contact and communication. (158)

Organic solidarity A collective consciousness that rests on mutual interdependence, characteristic of societies with a complex division of labor. (123)

Organized crime The work of a group that regulates relations between criminal enterprises involved in illegal activities, including prostitution, gambling, and the smuggling and sale of illegal drugs. (184)

Out-group A group or category to which people feel they do not belong. (129)

p

Patriarchy A society in which men dominate in family decision making. (332)

Patrilineal descent A kinship system in which only the father's relatives are significant. (331)

Peace The absence of war, or more broadly, a proactive effort to develop cooperative relations among nations. (404)

Percentage A portion of 100. (52)

Personality A person's typical patterns of attitudes, needs, characteristics, and behavior. (89)

Peter principle A principle of organizational life, originated by Laurence J. Peter, according to which every employee within a hierarchy tends to rise to his or her level of incompetence. (132)

Pluralism Mutual respect for one another's cultures among the various groups in a society, which allows minorities to express their cultures without experiencing prejudice. (265)

Pluralist model A view of society in which many competing groups within the community have access to government, so that no single group is dominant. (414)

Political system The social institution that is founded on a recognized set of procedures for implementing and achieving society's goals. (401)

Politics In Harold Lasswell's words, "who gets what, when, and how." (401)

Polyandry A form of polygamy in which a woman may have more than one husband at the same time. (330)

Polygamy A form of marriage in which an individual may have several husbands or wives simultaneously. (330)

Polygyny A form of polygamy in which a man may have more than one wife at the same time. (330)

Postindustrial society A society whose economic system is engaged primarily in the processing and control of information. (126)

Postmodern society A technologically sophisticated society that is preoccupied with consumer goods and media images. (126)

Power The ability to exercise one's will over others. (204, 401)

Power elite A term used by C. Wright Mills to refer to a small group of military, industrial, and government leaders who control the fate of the United States. (413)

Precarious work Employment that is poorly paid, and from the worker's perspective, insecure and unprotected. (213)

Prejudice A negative attitude toward an entire category of people, often an ethnic or racial minority. (254)

Prestige The respect and admiration that an occupation holds in a society. (208)

Prevalence The total number of cases of a specific disorder that exist at a given time. (438)

Primary group A small group characterized by intimate, face-to-face association and cooperation. (128)

Profane The ordinary and commonplace elements of life, as distinguished from the sacred. (379)

Professional criminal A person who pursues crime as a day-to-day occupation, developing skilled techniques and enjoying a certain degree of status among other criminals. (183)

Proletariat Karl Marx's term for the working class in a capitalist society. (203)

Protestant ethic Max Weber's term for the disciplined work ethic, this-worldly concerns, and rational orientation to life emphasized by John Calvin and his followers. (381)

q

Qualitative research Research that relies on what is seen in field or naturalistic settings more than on statistical data. (40)

Quantitative research Research that collects and reports data primarily in numerical form. (39)

Quasi-religion A scholarly category that includes organizations that may see themselves as religious but are seen by others as "sort of religious." (391)

Questionnaire A printed or written form used to obtain information from a respondent. (39)

r

Racial formation A sociohistorical process in which racial categories are created, inhibited, transformed, and destroyed. (252)

Racial group A group that is set apart from others because of physical differences that have taken on social significance. (251)

Racial profiling Any arbitrary action initiated by an authority based on race, ethnicity, or national origin rather than on a person's behavior. (262)

Racism The belief that one race is supreme and all others are innately inferior. (255)

Random sample A sample for which every member of an entire population has the same chance of being selected. (35)

Rational-legal authority Power made legitimate by law. (402)

Reference group Any group that individuals use as a standard for evaluating themselves and their own behavior. (129)

Relative deprivation The conscious feeling of a negative discrepancy between legitimate expectations and present actualities. (461)

Relative poverty A floating standard of deprivation by which people at the bottom of a society, whatever their lifestyles, are judged to be disadvantaged *in comparison with the nation as a whole*. (212)

Reliability The extent to which a measure produces consistent results. (36)

Religion According to Émile Durkheim, a unified system of beliefs and practices relative to sacred things. (379)

Religious belief A statement to which members of a particular religion adhere. (385)

Religious experience The feeling or perception of being in direct contact with the ultimate reality, such as a divine being, or of being overcome with religious emotion. (387)

Religious ritual A practice required or expected of members of a faith. (387)

Remittances The monies that immigrants return to their families of origin. Also called *migradollars*. (241)

Representative democracy A form of government in which certain individuals are selected to speak for the people. (403)

Research design A detailed plan or method for obtaining data scientifically. (38)

Resocialization The process of discarding former behavior patterns and accepting new ones as part of a transition in one's life. (98)

Resource mobilization The ways in which a social movement utilizes such resources as money, political influence, access to the media, and personnel. (462)

Rite of passage A ritual marking the symbolic transition from one social position to another. (96)

Role conflict The situation that occurs when incompatible expectations arise from two or more social positions held by the same person. (115)

Role exit The process of disengagement from a role that is central to one's self-identity in order to establish a new role and identity. (116)

Role strain The difficulty that arises when the same social position imposes conflicting demands and expectations. (116)

Role taking The process of mentally assuming the perspective of another and responding from that imagined viewpoint. (94)

s

Sacred Elements beyond everyday life that inspire awe, respect, and even fear. (379)

Sample A selection from a larger population that is statistically representative of that population. (35)

Sanction A penalty or reward for conduct concerning a social norm. (69, 169)

Sandwich generation The generation of adults who simultaneously try to meet the competing needs of their parents and their children. (313)

Sapir-Whorf hypothesis A hypothesis concerning the role of language in shaping our interpretation of reality. It holds that language is culturally determined. (65)

Science The body of knowledge obtained by methods based on systematic observation. (6)

Scientific management approach Another name for the classical theory of formal organizations. (134)

Scientific method A systematic, organized series of steps that ensures maximum objectivity and consistency in researching a problem. (33)

Second shift The double burden—work outside the home followed by child care and housework—that many women face and few men share equitably. (296)

Secondary analysis A variety of research techniques that make use of previously collected and publicly accessible information and data. (43)

Secondary group A formal, impersonal group in which there is little social intimacy or mutual understanding. (128)

Sect A relatively small religious group that has broken away from some other religious organization to renew what it considers the original vision of the faith. (390)

Secularization The process through which religion's influence on other social institutions diminishes. (379)

Segregation The physical separation of two groups of people in terms of residence, workplace, and social events; often imposed on a minority group by a dominant group. (264)

Self According to George Herbert Mead, a distinct identity that sets us apart from others. (93)

Serial monogamy A form of marriage in which a person may have several spouses in his or her lifetime, but only one spouse at a time. (330)

Sexism The ideology that one sex is superior to the other. (292)

Sick role Societal expectations about the attitudes and behavior of a person viewed as being ill. (433)

Significant other A term used by George Herbert Mead to refer to an individual who is most important in the development of the self, such as a parent, friend, or teacher. (94)

Single-parent family A family in which only one parent is present to care for the children. (341)

Slavery A system of enforced servitude in which some people are owned by other people. (199)

Social capital The collective benefit of social networks, which are built on reciprocal trust. (14)

Social change Significant alteration over time in behavior patterns and culture, including norms and values. (467)

Social constructionist perspective An approach to deviance that emphasizes the role of culture in the creation of the deviant identity. (180)

Social control The techniques and strategies for preventing deviant human behavior in any society. (169)

Social disorganization theory The theory that crime and deviance are caused by the absence or breakdown of communal relationships and social institutions. (179)

Social epidemiology The study of the distribution of disease, impairment, and general health status across a population. (438)

Social inequality A condition in which members of society have differing amounts of wealth, prestige, or power. (22, 197)

Social institution An organized pattern of beliefs and behavior centered on basic social needs. (120)

Social interaction The ways in which people respond to one another. (113)

Social mobility Movement of individuals or groups from one position in a society's stratification system to another. (216)

Social movement An organized collective activity to bring about or resist fundamental change in an existing group or society. (461)

Social network A series of social relationships that links a person directly to others, and through them indirectly to still more people. (118)

Social role A set of expectations for people who occupy a given social position or status. (115)

Social science The study of the social features of humans and the ways in which they interact and change. (6)

Social structure The way in which a society is organized into predictable relationships. (113)

Socialism An economic system under which the means of production and distribution are collectively owned. (417)

Socialization The lifelong process in which people learn the attitudes, values, and behaviors appropriate for members of a particular culture. (89)

Societal-reaction approach Another name for *labeling theory*. (180)

Society A fairly large number of people who live in the same territory, are relatively independent of people outside their area, and participate in a common culture. (62)

Sociobiology The systematic study of how biology affects human social behavior. (63)

Sociocultural evolution Long-term social trends resulting from the interplay of continuity, innovation, and selection. (124)

Socioeconomic status (SES) A measure of social class that is based on income, education, and occupation. (208)

Sociological imagination An awareness of the relationship between an individual and the wider society, both today and in the past. (5)

Sociology The scientific study of social behavior and human groups. (5)

Sovereignty movement The effort by the indigenous people of Hawai'i to win self-government, as well as the restoration of—or compensation for—their ancestral lands. (405)

Status A term used by sociologists to refer to any of the full range of socially defined positions within a large group or society. (114)

Status group A term used by Max Weber to refer to people who have the same prestige or lifestyle, independent of their class positions. (204)

Stereotype An unreliable generalization about all members of a group that does not recognize individual differences within the group. (255)

Stigma A label used to devalue members of certain social groups. (175)

Stratification A structured ranking of entire groups of people that perpetuates unequal economic rewards and power in a society. (197)

Subculture A segment of society that shares a distinctive pattern of customs, rules, and traditions that differs from the pattern of the larger society. (77)

Survey A study, generally in the form of an interview or questionnaire, that provides researchers with information about how people think and act. (39)

Symbol A gesture, object, or word that forms the basis of human communication. (66)

Symbolic ethnicity An ethnic identity that emphasizes concerns such as ethnic food or political issues rather than deeper ties to one's ethnic heritage. (275)

t

Teacher-expectancy effect The impact that a teacher's expectations about a student's performance may have on the student's actual achievements. (365)

Technology Cultural information about the ways in which the material resources of the environment may be used to satisfy human needs and desires. (75, 124, 470)

Terrorism The use or threat of violence against random or symbolic targets in pursuit of political aims. (406)

Theory In sociology, a set of statements that seeks to explain problems, actions, or behavior. (8)

Total institution A term coined by Erving Goffman to refer to an institution that regulates all aspects of a person's life under a single authority, such as a prison, the military, a mental hospital, or a convent. (98)

Totalitarianism Virtually complete government control and surveillance over all aspects of a society's social and political life. (403)

Tracking The practice of placing students in specific curriculum groups on the basis of their test scores and other criteria. (363)

Traditional authority Legitimate power conferred by custom and accepted practice. (402)

Trained incapacity The tendency of workers in a bureaucracy to become so specialized that they develop blind spots and fail to notice obvious problems. (132)

Transnational An immigrant who sustains multiple social relationships that link his or her society of origin with the society of settlement. (276, 479)

Transnational crime Crime that occurs across multiple national borders. (185)

Transracial adoption The adoption of a non-White child by White parents or a Hispanic child by non-Hispanics. (340)

u

Underclass The long-term poor who lack training and skills. (214)

v

Validity The degree to which a measure or scale truly reflects the phenomenon under study. (36)

Value A collective conception of what is considered good, desirable, and proper—or bad, undesirable, and improper—in a culture. (69)

Value neutrality Max Weber's term for objectivity of sociologists in the interpretation of data. (46)

Variable A measurable trait or characteristic that is subject to change under different conditions. (34)

Verstehen The German word for "understanding" or "insight"; used by Max Weber to stress the need for sociologists to take into account the subjective meanings people attach to their actions. (11)

Vertical mobility The movement of an individual from one social position to another of a different rank. (216)

Vested interests Veblen's term for those people or groups who will suffer in the event of social change, and who have a stake in maintaining the status quo. (469)

Victimization survey A questionnaire or interview given to a sample of the population to determine whether people have been victims of crime. (186)

Victimless crime A term used by sociologists to describe the willing exchange among adults of widely desired but illegal goods and services. (182)

w

War Conflict between organizations that possess trained combat forces equipped with deadly weapons. (404)

Wealth An inclusive term encompassing all a person's material assets, including land, stocks, and other types of property. (211)

White-collar crime Illegal acts committed by affluent, "respectable" individuals in the course of business activities. (184)

White privilege Rights or immunities granted to people as a particular benefit or favor simply because they are White. (257)

World systems analysis The global economy as an interdependent system of economically and politically unequal nations. (228)

Brulle, Robert, and J. Craig Jenkins. 2008. "Fixing the Bungled U.S. Environmental Movement." *Contexts* 7 (Spring):14–18.

Buchmann, Claudia, Thomas A. DiPrete, and Anne McDaniel. 2008. "Gender Inequalities in Education." *Annual Review of Sociology* 34:319–337.

Buckingham, David. 2007. "Selling Childhood? Children and Consumer Culture." *Journal of Children and Media* 1 (1):15–24.

Buddeberg-Fischer, Barbara, Marina Stamm, Claus Buddeberg, Georg Bauer, Oliver Hämmig, Michaela Knecht, and Richard Klafhofer. 2012. "The Impact of Gender and Parenthood on Physicians' Careers—Professional and Personal Situation Seven Years After Graduation." *BMC Health Services Research* 10:40.

Budig, Michelle J. 2002. "Male Advantage and the Gender Composition of Jobs: Who Rides the Glass Escalator?" *Social Problems* 49 (2):258–277.

Budrys, Grace. 2012. *Our Unsystematic Health Care System.* 3rd ed. Lanham, MD: Rowman and Littlefield Publishers.

Bullard, Robert D. 1993. *Dumping in Dixie: Race, Class, and Environmental Quality.* 2nd ed. Boulder, CO: Westview Press.

———, and Beverly Wright. 2009. *Race, Place, and Environmental Justice after Hurricane Katrina.* Boulder, CO: Westview Press.

Burawoy, Michael. 2005. "For Public Sociology." *American Sociological Review* 70 (February):4–28.

Bureau of the Census. 1975. *Historical Statistics of the United States, Colonial Times to 1970.* Washington, DC: U.S. Government Printing Office.

———. 1994. *Statistical Abstract of the United States, 1994.* Washington, DC: U.S. Government Printing Office.

———. 2004a. *Statistical Abstract of the United States, 2004–2005.* Washington, DC: U.S. Government Printing Office.

———. 2004b. "Census 2000 Final Response Rates." Accessed January 16, 2010 (www.census.gov/dmd/www/response/2000response.html).

———. 2005b. "American Fact Finder: Places with United States." Accessed December 12 (http://factfinder.census.gov).

———. 2008a. *Statistical Abstract of the United States, 2008.* Washington, DC: U.S. Government Printing Office.

———. 2008c. "America's Families and Living Arrangements 2008." Accessed at www.census.gov/population/www/socdemo/hh-fam/ cps2008.html.

———. 2009a. *Statistical Abstract of the United States 2010.* Washington, DC: U.S. Government Printing Office.

———. 2010a. *Statistical Abstract of the United States 2011.* Washington, DC: U.S. Government Printing Office.

———. 2010b. "America's Families and Living Arrangements: 2010." Released January. Accessible at www.census.gov/population/www/socdemo/hh-fam/cps2010.html.

———. 2011a. *Statistical Abstract of the United States 2012.* Washington, DC: U.S. Government Printing Office.

———. 2011b. International Data Base (IDB). Accessible at http://www.census.gov/ipc/www/idb/informationGateway.php.

———. 2011c. "Census Bureau Releases Estimate of Same-Sex Married Couples." Accessible at www .census.gov/newsroom/releases/archives/2010 _census/cb11-cn181.html.

———. 2011d. "Current Population Survey, Annual Social and Economic Supplements." Washington, DC: U.S. Government Printing Office.

———. 2011e. "America's Families and Living Arrangements: 2011." November 3. Accessible at www.census.gov/newsroom/releases/archives/families_households/cb11-183.html.

———. 2011f. "2010 American Community Survey." Accessible at www.census.gov.

———. 2012a. "The Statistical Abstract of the United States 2013." Accessible at www.census .gov/.

———. 2012b. "The 2012 Statistical Abstract: Historical Statistics." Accessible at www.census.gov/compendia/statab/hist_stats.html.

———. 2012c. "Graphs on Historical Voting Trends." February 15. Accessible at www.census.gov/newsroom/releases/archives/voting/cb12-tps08 .html.

———. 2012d. "Census Bureau Releases Estimates of Undercount and Overcount in the 2010 Census." News Release CB12-95, May 22. Accessible at www.census.gov/newroom/releases/archives/2010_census/cb12-95.html.

———. 2012d. "Most Children Younger Than Age 1 are Minorities, Census Bureau Reports." May 17. Accessible at http://www.census.gov/newsroom/releases/archives/population/c12-90.html.

Bureau of Consular Affairs. 2011. FY2011 Annual Report on Intercountry Adoption, November 2011. Washington, DC: Bureau of Consular Affairs, U.S. Department of State.

Bureau of Justice Statistics. 2011. "U.S. Correctional Population Declined for Second Consecutive Year." Accessed April 24, 2012 (http://bjs.ojp .usdoj.gov/content/pub/press/p10cpus10pr.cfm).

Bureau of Labor Statistics. 2003. "Women at Work: A Visual Essay." *Monthly Labor Review* (October):45–50.

———. 2010. "Economic News Release: Number of Jobs Held." Accessible at www.bls.gov/news.release/nlsoy.nr0.htm.

———. 2011. "Labor Force Statistics: Table 3." Accessed March 21, 2011 (www.bls.gov/cps/tables.htm).

Bures, Frank. 2011. "Can You Hear Us Now?" *Utne Reader* (March–April):8–9, 11.

Burger, Jerry M. 2009. "Replicating Milgram: Would People Still Obey Today?" *American Psychologist* 64 (January):1–11.

Burger King. 2009. "Whopper Sacrifice." Accessed February 4 (www.whoppersacrifice.com/).

Burkitt, Laurie. 2011. "Wal-Mart China Woes Add Up." *Wall Street Journal,* October 18, p. B3.

Burns, Melinda. 2010. "Workfare and the Low-Wage Woman." *Miller-McClune* (November–December):76–81.

Butler, Daniel Allen. 1998. *"Unsinkable": The Full Story.* Mechanicsburg, PA: Stackpole Books.

Byrd-Bredbenner, Carol, and Jessica Murray. 2003. "Comparison of the Anthropometric Measurements of Idealized Female Body Images in Media Directed to Men, Women, and Mixed Gender Audiences." *Topics in Clinical Nutrition* 18 (2):117–129.

C

Calhoun, Craig. 1998. "Community without Propinquity Revisited." *Sociological Inquiry* 68 (Summer):373–397.

———. 2003. "Belonging in the Cosmopolitan Imaginary." *Ethnicities* 3 (December):531–553.

———. 2011. "Evicting the Public." Possible Futures: A Project of the Social Science Research Project. November 19. Accessed January 26, 2012 (www.possible-futures.org/2011/11/19/evicting-the-public-why-has-occupying-public-spaces-brought-such-heavy -handed-repression).

Cameron, Deborah. 2007. *The Myth of Mars and Venus.* Oxford: Oxford University Press.

Campbell, Mary, Robert Haveman, Gary Sandefur, and Barbara Wolte. 2005. "Economic Inequality and Educational Attainment across a Generation." *Focus* 23 (Spring):11–15.

Cañas, Jesus, Roberto Coronado, and Robert W. Gilman. 2007. "Southwest Economy." March/April. Accessed April 18 (http://dallasfed.org/research/swe/2007/swe0702b.cfm).

Caplan, Ronald L. 1989. "The Commodification of American Health Care." *Social Science and Medicine* 28 (11):1139–1148.

Caplow, Theodore, and Louis Hicks. 2002. *Systems of War and Peace.* 2nd ed. Lanham, MD: University Press of America.

Capriccioso, Rob. 2010. "Obama Mentions Tribes as Part of Oil Spill Restoration; Chief Testifies on Mess." *Indian Country Today,* June 23, pp. 1, 2.

Carbon Trust. 2012. "About the Carbon Trust." Accessed March 27 (www.carbontrust.co.uk/about-carbon-trust/pages/default.aspx).

Carey, Anne R., and Karl Gelles. 2010. "What Viewers Enjoy Most about Watching the Super Bowl on TV." *USA Today,* February 5, p. A1; *Gallup Poll* (May):3.

Carlton-Ford, Steve. 2010. "Major Armed Conflicts, Militarization, and Life Chances." *Armed Forces and Society* 36 (October):864–899.

Carr, Nicholas. 2010. "Tracking Is an Assault on Liberty, with Real Dangers." *Wall Street Journal,* August 7, pp. W1, W2.

———. 2008a. *The Big Switch: Revising the World: From Edison to Google.* New York: Norton.

———. 2008b. "Is Google Making Us Stoopid?" *Atlantic* (July/August):56–58, 60, 62–63.

Carroll, Joseph. 2006. "Public National Anthem Should Be Sung in English." *Gallup Poll* (May):3.

Caruso, Eugene M., Dobromir A. Rahnev, and Mahzarin R. Banaji. 2009. "Using Conjoint Analysis to Detect Discrimination: Revealing Covert Preferences from Overt Choices." *Social Cognition* 27 (1):128–137.

Castañeda, Jorge G. 1995. "Ferocious Differences." *Atlantic Monthly* 276 (July):68–69, 71–76.

Castells, Manuel. 2001. *The Internet Galaxy: Reflections on the Internet, Business, and Society.* New York: Oxford University Press.

———. 2009. *Communication Power.* New York: Oxford University Press.

———. 2010a. *The Rise of the Network Society.* 2nd ed. With a new preface. Malden, MA: Wiley-Blackwell.

———. 2010b. *The Power of Identity.* 2nd ed. With a new preface. Malden, MA: Wiley-Blackwell.

———. 2010c. *End of Millennium.* 2nd ed. With a new preface. Malden, MA: Wiley-Blackwell.

Catalyst. 2011. "No News Is Bad News: Women's Leadership Still Stalled in Corporate America." Accessed February 22, 2012 (www.catalyst .org/press-release/199/no-news-is-bad-news -womens-leadership-still-stalled-in-corporate -america).

Cauchon, Dennis. 2009. "Women Gain in Historic Job Shift." *USA Today,* September 3, p. A1.

CBS News. 1979. Transcript of *Sixty Minutes* segment, "I Was Only Following Orders." March 31, pp. 2–8.

Center for Academic Integrity. 2006. *CAI Research.* Accessed January 10 (www.academicintegrity .org).

Center for Community College Student Engagement. 2009. *Making Connections: Dimensions of Student Engagement* (2009 CCSS Findings). Austin: University of Texas at Austin, Community College Leadership Program. Accessible at www .ccsse.org/publications/national_report_2009/ccsse09_nationalreport.pdf.

Center for Community Initiatives. 2011. "Magnolia Project 2011 Reports." Accessed November 2 (www.unf.edu/coas/cci/magnilia/2011_Reports .aspx).

———. 2012a. "Northeast Florida Center for Community Initiatives (CCI)." Accessed January 3 (www.unf.edu/coas/cci/).

———. 2012b. "Magnolia Grant Objectives 2012." Accessed April 11 (htpp://aries.unfcsd.unf.edu/Magnolia/2012/objectives2012.php).

Center for Research on Education Outcomes. 2009. *Multiple Choice: Charter School Performances in 16 States.* Palo Alto, CA: CREDO, Stanford University. Accessible at http://credo.stanford.edu.

Centers for Disease Control and Prevention. 2010. "Binge Drinking among High School Students and Adults—United States, 2009." Washington, DC: CDC. Accessible at http://www.cdc.gov/mmwr/preview/mmwrhtml/mm5939a4.htm?s_cid=mm5939a4_w.

———. 2011b. *Health Disparities and Inequalities Report—United States, 2011.*

———. 2011c. *Multiple Births.* Accessible at www.cdc.gov/nchs/fstats/multiple.htm.

———. 2012a. *Vital Signs: Binge Drinking.* January 2012. Accessible at www.cdc.gov/vitalsigns/BingeDrinking.

———. 2012b. "National Marriage and Divorce Rate Trends." Accessed February 24 (www.cdc. gov/nchs/nvss/marriage_divorce_tables.htm).

———. 2012c. "HIV Surveillance-Epidemiology of HIV Infection (through 2010)." March 12. Accessible at www.cdc.gov/hiv/topics/surveillance/resources/slides/general/index/htm.

Centers for Medicare and Medicaid Services. 2011. "NHE Projections 2010–2020." Accessed March 22, 2012 (www.cms.hhs.gov).

Cerulo, Karen A., Janet M. Ruane, and Mary Chagko. 1992. "Technological Ties That Bind: Media Generated Primary Groups." *Communication Research* 19:109–129.

Chalfant, H. Paul, Robert E. Beckley, and C. Eddie Palmer. 1994. *Religion in Contemporary Society.* 3rd ed. Itasca, IL: F. E. Peacock.

Chambliss, William. 1973. "The Saints and the Roughnecks." *Society* 11 (November–December): 24–31.

Chamie, Joseph, and Barry Mirkin. 2011. "Same-Sex Marriage: A New Social Phenomenon." *Population and Development Review* 37 (September):529–551.

Chan, Sewell. 2009. "City Unveils Facebook Page to Encourage Condom Use." *New York Times,* February 12, p. A32.

Charrad, Mounira M. 2011. "Gender in the Middle East: Islam, State, Agency." *Annual Review of Sociology* 37:417–437

Chase, Randall. 2010. "O'Donnell: 'I'm Not a Witch.'" *Washington Times,* October 4. Accessed March 23 (http://www.washingtontimes.com/news/2010/oct/4/odonnell-im-not-witch/?page=2).

Chase-Dunn, Christopher, and Peter Grimes. 1995. "World-Systems Analysis." Pp. 387–417 in *Annual Review of Sociology,* 1995, edited by John Hagan. Palo Alto, CA: Annual Reviews.

———, Yukio Kawano, and Benjamin D. Brewer. 2000. "Trade Globalization Since 1795: Waves of Integration in the World System." *American Sociological Review* 65 (February):77–95.

Cheng, Shu-Ju Ada. 2003. "Rethinking the Globalization of Domestic Service." *Gender and Society* 17 (2):166–186.

Cherlin, Andrew J. 2003. "Should the Government Promote Marriage?" *Contexts* 2 (Fall):22–29.

———. 2006. "On Single Mothers 'Doing' Family." *Journal of Marriage and Family* 68 (November):800–803.

———. 2009. *The Marriage-Go-Round: The State of Marriage and the Family in America Today.* New York: Knopf.

———. 2010. *Public and Private Families: An Introduction.* 6th ed. New York: McGraw-Hill.

———. 2011. "The Increasing Complexity of Family Life in the United States." September 8. Accessible at www.prb.org/Articles/2011/us-complex-family-life.aspx?p=1.

Child Welfare Information. 2011. *How Many Children Were Adopted in 2007 and 2008?* Washington, DC: U.S. Government Printing Office.

Chin, Kolin. 1996. *Chinatown Gangs: Extortion, Enterprise, and Ethnicity.* New York: Oxford University Press.

Choney, Suzanne. 2010. "Mobile Giving for Chile Pales Compared to Haiti." MSNBC. March 12, 2010. Accessible at www.msnmb.msn.com/ ed/35822836/ns/technology_and_science -wireless/t/mobile-giving-chile-pales -compared-haiti.

Christakis, Nicholas A., and James H. Fowler. 2007. "The Spread of Obesity in a Large Social Network over 32 Years." *New England Journal of Medicine* 357 (July 26):370–379.

———, and ———. 2009. *Connected: The Amazing Power of Social Networks and How They Shape Our Lives.* New York: Harper.

Chronic Poverty Research Centre. 2009. *The Chronic Poverty Report 2008–09: Escaping Poverty Traps.* Geneva: Chronic Poverty Research Centre.

Chu, Henry. 2005. "Tractors Crush Heart of a Nation." *Los Angeles Times,* July 10, p. A9.

Chu, Kathy. 2010. "Vietnam's Market Grows Up." *USA Today,* August 23, p. B3.

Chubb, Catherine, Simone Melis, Louisa Potter, and Raymond Storry. 2008. *The Global Gender Pay Gap.* London: Incomes Data Services.

Chung, Esther K., Leny Mathew, Amy C. Rothkopf, Irma T. Elo, James C. Cayne, and Jennifer F. Culhane. 2009. "Parenting Attitudes and Infant Spanking: The Influence of Childhood Experiences." *Pediatrics* 124 (August):278–286.

Clark, Burton, and Martin Trow. 1966. "The Organizational Context." Pp. 17–70 in *The Study of College Peer Groups,* edited by Theodore M. Newcomb and Everett K. Wilson. Chicago: Aldine.

Clark, Candace. 1983. "Sickness and Social Control." Pp. 346–365 in *Social Interaction: Readings in Sociology,* 2nd ed., edited by Howard Robboy and Candace Clark. New York: St. Martin's Press.

Clark, Kim. 2010. "Can School Reform Even Really Work?" *US News and World Report* (January):23–26, 30–31.

Clarke, Adele E., Janet K. Shim, Laura Maro, Jennifer Ruth Fusket, and Jennifer R. Fishman. 2003. "Bio Medicalization: Technoscientific Transformations of Health, Illness, and U.S. Biomedicine." *American Sociological Review* 68 (April):161–194.

Clayton, Mark. 2011. "The New Cyber Arms Race." *Christian Science Monitor*, March 7, pp. 26–71.

Clemmitt, Marcia. 2005. "Intelligent Design." *CQ Researcher* 15 (July 29): 637–660.

Clifford, Stephanie. 2009a. "Teaching Teenagers about Harassment." *New York Times,* January 27, p. B1.

Clinard, Marshall B., and Robert F. Miller. 1998. *Sociology of Deviant Behavior.* 10th ed. Fort Worth, TX: Harcourt Brace.

Clymer, Adam. 2000. "College Students Not Drawn to Voting or Politics, Poll Shows." *New York Times,* January 2, p. A14.

Coates, Rodney. 2008. "Covert Racism in the USA and Globally." *Sociology Compass* 2:208–231.

Cockerham, William C. 2012. *Medical Sociology.* 12th ed. Upper Saddle River, NJ: Prentice Hall.

Cole, Mike. 1988. *Bowles and Gintis Revisited: Correspondence and Contradiction in Educational Theory.* Philadelphia: Falmer.

Coleman, Isobel. 2004. "The Payoff from Women's Rights." *Foreign Affairs* 83 (May–June):80–95.

Coleman, James William. 2006. *The Criminal Elite: Understanding White-Collar Crime.* 6th ed. New York: Worth.

College Board. 2009. *Trends in College Pricing.* New York: College Board.

Collins, Daryl, Jonathan Morduch, Stuart Rutherford, and Orlanda Ruthven. 2009. *Portfolios of* the Poor: How the World's Poor Live on $2 a Day. Princeton, NJ: Princeton University Press.

Collins, Patricia Hill. 2000. *Black Feminist Thought: Knowledge, Consciousness, and the Politics of Empowerment.* Revised 10th anniv. 2nd ed. New York: Routledge.

Collins, Randall. 1975. *Conflict Sociology: Toward an Explanatory Sociology.* New York: Academic Press.

———. 1980. "Weber's Last Theory of Capitalism: A Systematization." *American Sociological Review* 45 (December):925–942.

———. 1986. *Weberian Sociological Theory.* New York: Cambridge University Press.

———. 1995. "Prediction in Macrosociology: The Case of the Soviet Collapse." *American Journal of Sociology* 100 (May):1552–1593.

Colucci, Jim. 2008. "All the World's a Screen." *Watch!* (June):50–53.

Commission on Civil Rights. 1976. *A Guide to Federal Laws and Regulations Prohibiting Sex Discrimination.* Washington, DC: U.S. Government Printing Office.

———. 1981. *Affirmative Action in the 1980s: Dismantling the Process of Discrimination.* Washington, DC: U.S. Government Printing Office.

Commoner, Barry. 1971. *The Closing Circle.* New York: Knopf.

———. 1990. *Making Peace with the Planet.* New York: Pantheon.

———. 2007. "At 90, an Environmentalist from the 70's Still Has Hope." *New York Times,* June 19, p. D2.

Congressional Oversight Panel. 2011. "February Oversight Report: Executive Compensation Restrictions in the Troubled Asset Relief Program." Washington, DC: COP.

Conley, Dalton. 2010. *Being Black, Living in the Red.* 10th anniversary edition. Berkeley: University of California Press.

Connell, R. W. 1987. *Gendered Power: Society, the Person, and Sexual Politics.* Stanford, CA: Stanford University Press.

———. 2002. *Gender.* Cambridge, UK: Polity Press.

———. 2005. *Masculinities.* 2nd ed. Berkeley: University of California Press.

Conner, Thaddeus, and William A. Taggart. 2009. "The Impact of Gaming on the Indian Nations in New Mexico." *Social Science Quarterly* 90 (March):52–70.

Conrad, Peter, ed. 2009a. *The Medicalization of Society: On the Transformation of Human Conditions into Treatable Disorders.* 11th ed. Baltimore, MD: Johns Hopkins University.

———. 2009b. *The Sociology of Health and Illness: Cultural Perspectives.* 8th ed. New York: Worth.

———, and Kristin K. Barker. 2010. "The Social Construction of Illness: Key Insights and Policy Implications." *Journal of Health and Social Behavior* 51 (5):567–579.

Cooky, Cheryl, and Nicole M. LaVoi. 2012. "Playing but Losing." *Contexts* (Winter):42–46.

Cooley, Charles. H. 1902. *Human Nature and the Social Order.* New York: Scribner.

Coontz, Stephanie. 2006. "A Pop Quiz on Marriage." *New York Times,* February 19, p. 12.

Cooper, K., S. Day, A. Green, and H. Ward. 2007. "Maids, Migrants and Occupational Health in the London Sex Industry." *Anthropology and Medicine* 14 (April):41–53.

Copeland, Craig. 2012. "Labor-Force Participation Rates of the Population Age 55 and Older, 2011: After the Economic Downturn." *Employee Benefit Research Institute* Notes 33 (February).

Corbett, Christianne, Catherine Hill, and Andresse St. Rose. 2008. *Where the Girls Are: The Facts about Gender Equity in Education.* Washington, DC: American Association of University Women.

Coser, Lewis A. 1977. *Masters of Sociological Thought: Ideas in Historical and Social Context.* 2nd ed. New York: Harcourt, Brace and Jovanovich.

Coser, Rose Laub. 1984. "American Medicine's Ambiguous Progress." *Contemporary Sociology* 13 (January):9–13.

Côté, James E. 2000. *Arrested Adulthood: The Changing Nature of Identity and Maturity in the Late World.* New York: New York University.

Couch, Carl J. 1996. *Information Technologies and Social Orders.* Edited with an introduction by David R. Maines and Shing-Ling Chien. New York: Aldine de Gruyter.

Council on Ethical and Judicial Affairs, American Medical Association. 1992. "Decisions Near the End of Life." *Journal of the American Medical Association* 267 (April 22–29):2229–2333.

Council on Foreign Relations. 2009. "Public Opinion on Global Issues." Accessible at www.cfr.org/public-opinion.

Counts, Dorothy Ayers, and David Counts. 2012. "The Good, the Bad, and the Unresolved Death in Kaliai." *Social Science and Medicine* 58 (No. 5):887–897.

Cox, Oliver C. 1948. *Caste, Class, and Race: A Study in Social Dynamics.* Detroit: Wayne State University Press.

Cox, Rachel S. 2003. "Home Schooling Debate." *CQ Researcher* 13 (January 17):25–48.

Crabtree, Steve. 2010. *Religiosity Highest in World's Poorest Nations.* August 31. Accessible at www .gallup.com.

Cross, Simon, and Barbara Bagilhole. 2002. "Girls' Jobs for the Boys? Men, Masculinity and Non-Traditional Occupations." *Gender, Work, and Organization* 9 (April):204–226.

Croteau, David, and William Hoynes. 2003. *Media/Society: Industries, Images, and Audiences.* 3rd ed. Thousand Oaks, CA: Pine Forge Press.

———, and ———. 2006, *The Business of the Media: Corporate Media and the Public Interest.* 2nd ed. Thousand Oaks, CA: Pine Forge Press.

———, ———, and Stefania Milan. 2012. *Media/Society: Industries, Images, and Audiences.* 4th ed. Los Angeles: Sage.

Croucher, Sheila L. 2004. *Globalization and Belonging: The Politics of Identity in a Changing World.* Lanham, MD: Rowman and Littlefield.

Crouse, Kelly. 1999. "Sociology of the *Titanic.*" *Teaching Sociology Listserv.* May 24.

Crowe, Jerry, and Valli Herman. 2005. "NBA Lists Fashion Do's and Don'ts." *Los Angeles Times,* October 19, pp. A1, A23.

Crump, Andy. 2006. "Suicide in Japan." *Lancet* 367 (April 8):1143.

Cuff, E. C., W. W. Sharrock, and D. W. Francis, eds. 1990. *Perspectives in Sociology.* 3rd ed. Boston: Unwin Hyman.

Currie, Elliot. 1985. *Confronting Crime: An American Challenge.* New York: Pantheon.

———. 1998. *Crime and Punishment in America.* New York: Metropolis Books.

Curry, Timothy Jon. 1993. "A Little Pain Never Hurt Anyone: Athletic Career Socialization and the Normalization of Sports Injury." *Symbolic Interaction* 26 (Fall):273–290.

Cushing-Daniels, Brenda, and Sheila R. Zedlewski. 2008. "Tax and Spending Policy and Economic Mobility." Washington, DC: Economic Mobility Project. Also accessible at www.economic-mobility.org/reports_and_research/literature_reviews?id=0004.

Customs and Border Patrol. 2011. "U.S. Border Patrol Fiscal Year Apprehension Statistics—Southeast Border Sectors." Accessed January 29, 2012 (www.cbp.gov/xp/cgov/border_security/border_partol/usbp_statistics/).

d

Dade, Corey. 2012. "Battle Over Voter ID Laws Intensify." June 2. Accessible at www.wbur.org/npr/154152507/battles-over-voter-id-laws-intensify.

Dahl, Robert A. 1961. *Who Governs?* New Haven, CT: Yale University Press.

Dahrendorf, Ralf. 1958. "Toward a Theory of Social Conflict." *Journal of Conflict Resolution* 2 (June):170–183.

———. 1959. *Class and Class Conflict in Industrial Sociology.* Stanford, CA: Stanford University Press.

Dalla, Rochelle L., and Wendy C. Gamble. 2001. "Teenage Mothering and the Navajo Reservation: An Examination of Intergovernmental Perceptions and Beliefs." *American Indian Culture and Research Journal* 25 (1):1–19.

Daniel, G. Reginald. 2006. *Race and Multiraciality in Brazil and the United States: Converging Paths?* University Park: Pennsylvania State University Press.

Danziger, Sandra K. 2010. "The Decline of Cash Welfare and Implications for Social Policy and Poverty." *Annual Review of Sociology* 36:523–545.

Darlin, Damon. 2006. "It's O,K to Fall Behind the Technology Curve." *New York Times,* December 30, p. B6.

Darwin, Charles. 1859. *On the Origin of Species.* London: John Murray.

David, Gary. 2004. "Scholarship on Arab Americans Distorted Past 9/11." *Al Jadid* (Winter–Spring):26–27.

———. 2008. "Arab Americans." Pp. 84–87, vol. 1, in *Encyclopedia of Race, Ethnicity, and Society,* edited by Richard T. Schaefer. Thousand Oaks, CA: Sage.

Davidson, James D., and Ralph E. Pyle. 2011. *Ranking Faiths: Religious Stratification in America*. Lanham, MD: Rowman and Littlefield.

Davies, Christie. 1989. "Goffman's Concept of the Total Institution: Criticisms and Revisions." *Human Studies* 12 (June):77–95.

Davis, Darren W., and Brian D. Silver. 2003. "Stereotype Threat and Race of Interviewer Knowledge." *American Journal of Political Science* 47 (January):33–45.

Davis, Gerald. 2003. *America's Corporate Banks Are Separated by Just Four Handshakes*. Accessed March 7 (www.bus.umich.edu/research/davis .html).

———. 2004. "American Cronyism: How Executive Networks Inflated the Corporate Bubble." *Contexts* (Summer):34–40.

Davis, Kingsley. 1940. "Extreme Social Isolation of a Child." *American Journal of Sociology* 45 (January):554–565.

———. 1947. "A Final Note on a Case of Extreme Isolation." *American Journal of Sociology* 52 (March):432–437.

———, and Wilbert E. Moore. 1945. "Some Principles of Stratification." *American Sociological Review* 10 (April):242–249.

Davis, Martha F. 2010. "Abortion Access in the Global Marketplace." *North Carolina Law Review* 88:1657–1685.

Davis, Paul K., and Kim Cragin, eds. 2009. *Social Science for Counterterrorism: Putting the Pieces Together*. Santa Monica, CA: RAND.

Dayananda, Vanitha. 2006. *Sexuality and Love in Arranged Marriages in India: Why Arranged Marriages Last*. Leeds, England: Wisdom House Publications.

De Anda, Roberto M. 2004. *Chicanas and Chicanos in Contemporary Society*. 2nd ed. Lanham, MD: Rowman and Littlefield.

Death Penalty Information Center. 2012. "Facts About the Death Penalty (Updated January 23, 2012)." Accessible at www.deathpenaltyinfo.org.

Death with Dignity National Center. 2012. "Living with Dying." Accessed March 12 at http://www .deathwithdignity.org. Government Printing Office.

Deegan, Mary Jo, ed. 1991. *Women in Sociology: A Bio-Biographical Sourcebook*. Westport, CT: Greenwood.

———. 2003. "Textbooks, the History of Sociology, and the Sociological Stock of Knowledge." *Sociological Theory* 21 (November):298–305.

Deflem, Mathieu. 2005. "'Wild Beasts without Nationality': The Uncertain Origins of Interpol, 1898–1910." Pp. 275–285 in *Handbook of Transnational Crime and Justice*, edited by Philip Rerchel. Thousand Oaks, CA: Sage.

Deibert, Ronald J., John Palfrey, Rafal Rohozinski, and Jonathan Zittrain. 2008. *Access Denied: The Practice and Policy of Global Internet Filtering*. Cambridge, MA: MIT Press.

Delaney, Kevin J. 2005. "Big Mother Is Watching." *Wall Street Journal*, November 26, pp. A1, A6.

Della Porta, Donatella, and Sidney Tarrow, eds. 2005. *Transnational Protest and Global Activism*. Lanham, MD: Rowman and Littlefield.

DeNavas-Walt, Carmen, Bernadette D. Proctor, and Jessica C. Smith. 2010. "Income, Poverty, and Health Insurance Coverage in the United States: 2009." P60-238 in *Current Population Survey*. Washington, DC: U.S. Government Printing Office.

———. 2011. *Income, Poverty, and Health Insurance Coverage in the United States: 2010*. Washington, DC: U.S. Government Printing Office.

Denny, Charlotte. 2004. "Migration Myths Hold No Fears." *Guardian Weekly*, February 26, p. 12.

Denny, Kathleen E. 2011. "Gender in Context, Content, and Approach: Contemporary Gender Measures in Girl Scout and Boy Scout Handbooks." *Gender and Society* 25 (February): 27–47.

Denzin, Norman K. 2004. "Postmodernism." Pp. 581–583 in *Encyclopedia of Social Theory*, edited by George Ritzer. Thousand Oaks, CA: Sage.

DeParle, Jason. 2009. "The 'W' Word, Re-Engaged." *New York Times*, February 8, Week in Review, p. 1.

Department of Health and Human Services. 2011b. "AFCARS, Report." Accessed April 6 (www.acf .hhs.gov/programs/cb/stats_research/afcars/tar/report17.htm).

———. 2012a. "TANF: Total Number of Families." As of 1/30/2012. Accessible at www.acf.hhs.gov/programs/ofa/data-reports/caseload/2011/2012 _family_tan.htm.

Department of Homeland Security. 2010. *Haiti Social Media: Disaster Monitoring Initiative*. January 21. Washington, DC: U.S. Department of Homeland Security.

Department of Justice. 2000. *The Civil Liberties Act of 1988: Redress for Japanese Americans*. Accessed June 29 (www.usdoj.gov/crt/ora/main. html).

———. 2008. "Hate Crime Statistics, 2007." Accessible at www.Fbi.gov/ucr/ucr.htm.

———. 2009. *2008 Crime in the United States*. (Uniform Crime Report). Accessible at http://www.fbi.gov/ucr/cius2008/index.html.

———. 2011. "Labor Force Statistics: Table 3." Accessed March 21, 2011 (www.bls.gov/cps/tables.htm).

———. 2011a. "Crime in the United States, 2010." Accessed January 23, 2012 (www.fbi.gov/about-us/cjis/ucr/crime-in-the-u.s/2010/crime-in-the-u.s.-2010).

———. 2011b. "About Hate Crime Statistics, 2010." Accessed January 23, 2012 (www.fbi.gov .about-us/cjis/ucr/hate-crime/2010).

Department of State. 2011b. "Tier Placements." Accessed January 25, 2012 (www.state.gov/j/tip/rls/tiprpt/2011/164228.htm).

Desai, Rani A., Suchitra Krishnan-Sarin, Dana Cavallo, and Marc N. Potenza. 2010. "Video-Gaming among High School Students: Health Correlates, Gender Differences, and Problematic Gaming." *Pediatrics* 126 (November 15):1414–1424.

Deutsch, Francine M. 2007. "Undoing Gender." *Gender and Society* 21 (February):106–127.

Devitt, James. 1999. *Framing Gender on the Campaign Trail: Women's Executive Leadership and the Press*. New York: Women's Leadership Conference.

Dewan, Shaila. 2010. "To Court Blacks, Foes of Abortion Make Racial Case." *New York Times*, February 27, pp. A1, A13.

Diamond, Shari Seidman, and Mary R. Rose. 2005. "Real Juries." Pp. 255–284 in *Annual Review of Law and Social Science 2005*. Palo Alto, CA: Annual Reviews.

Dickler, Jessica. 2011. "Dig Deep to Buy Titanic Visit." *Chicago Tribune*, June 3, p. 25.

Dillon, Sam. 2009. "As More Charter Schools Unionize, Educators Debate the Effect." *New York Times*, July 27, pp. A1, A14.

DiPrete, Thomas A., Gregory M. Eirich, and Matthew Pittinsky. 2010. "Compensation Benchmarking, Leapfrogs, and the Surge in Executive Pay." *American Journal of Sociology* 115 (May):1671–1712.

Dobbin, Frank, and Jiwook Jung. 2010. "Corporate Board Gender Diversity and Stock Performance: The Competence Gap on Institutional Investor Bias?" *North Carolina Law Review* 89.

Dodds, Klaus. 2000. *Geopolitics in a Changing World*. Harlow, UK: Pearson Education.

Domhoff, G. William. 1978. *Who Really Rules? New Haven and Community Power Reexamined*. New Brunswick, NJ: Transaction.

———. 2010. *Who Rules America?* 6th ed. New York: McGraw-Hill.

Dominick, Joseph R. 2009. *The Dynamics of Mass Communication: Media in the Digital Age*. 10th ed. New York: McGraw-Hill.

Donadio, Rachel. 2009. "Facebook 'Fans' of the Mafia May Be More, Authorities Say." *New York Times*, January 20, pp. A1, A8.

Doress, Irwin, and Jack Nusan Porter. 1977. *Kids in Cults: Why They Join, Why They Stay, Why They Leave*. Brookline, MA: Reconciliation Associates.

Dougherty, Kevin, and Floyd M. Hammack. 1992. "Education Organization." Pp. 535–541 in *Encyclopedia of Sociology*, vol. 2, edited by Edgar F. Borgatta and Marie L. Borgatta. New York: Macmillan.

Downey, Liam, and Brian Hawkins. 2008. "Race, Income, and Environmental Inequality in the United States." *Sociological Perspectives* 50 (4):759–781.

DuBois, W. E. B. [1899] 1995. *The Philadelphia Negro: A Social Study*. Philadelphia: University of Pennsylvania Press.

———. [1900] 1969. "To the Nations of the World." Pp. 19–23 in *An ABC of Color*, edited by W. E. B. DuBois. New York: International Publishers.

———. [1903] 1961. *The Souls of Black Folks: Essays and Sketches*. New York: Fawcett.

———. [1903] 2003. *The Negro Church*. Walnut Creek, CA: AltaMira Press.

———. [1909] 1970. *The Negro American Family*. Atlanta University. Reprinted 1970. Cambridge, MA: MIT Press.

———. [1935] 1962. *Black Reconstruction in America 1860–1880*. New York: Athenaeum.

———. [1940] 1968. *Dusk of Dawn*. New York: Harcourt, Brace. Reprint. New York: Schocken Books.

Duhigg, Charles, and Keith Bradsher. 2012. "How U.S. Lost Out on iPhone Work." *New York Times*, January 22, p. A1.

Dukić, Vanja, Hedibert F. Lopes, and Nicholas G. Polson. 2011. "Tracking Flu Epidemics Using Google Flu Trends and Particle Learning." Accessible at http://faculty.chicagobooth.edu/ nicholas .polson/research/papers/Track.pdf.

Dundas, Susan, and Miriam Kaufman. 2000. "The Toronto Lesbian Family Study." *Journal of Homosexuality* 40 (20):65–79.

Duneier, Mitchell. 1994a. "On the Job, but Behind the Scenes." *Chicago Tribune,* December 26, pp. 1, 24.

———. 1994b. "Battling for Control." *Chicago Tribune,* December 28, pp. 1, 8.

Dunlap, Riley E. 2010. "At 40, Environmental Movement Endures with Less Consensus." April 22. Accessed April 27 (www.gallup.com/poll/ 127487/Environmental-Movement-Endures -Less-Consensus.aspx?version=print).

———, and Angela G. Mertig. 1991. "The Evolution of the U.S. Environmental Movement from 1970 to 1990: An Overview." *Society of National Resources* 4 (July–September):209–218.

Durden, T. Elizabeth, and Robert A. Hummer. 2006. "Access to Healthcare among Working-Aged Hispanic Adults in the United States." *Social Science Quarterly* 87 (December):1319–1343.

Durex. 2007. "The Face of Global Sex 2007—First Sex: An Opportunity of a Lifetime." Accessible at http://www.durexnetwork.org/SiteCollection- Documents/Research%20%20Face%20of%20 Global%20Sex%202007.pdf.

Durkheim, Émile. [1893] 1933. *Division of Labor in Society.* Translated by George Simpson. Reprint. New York: Free Press.

———. [1895] 1964. *The Rules of Sociological Method.* Translated by Sarah A. Solovay and John H. Mueller. Reprint. New York: Free Press.

———. [1897] 1951. *Suicide.* Translated by John A. Spaulding and George Simpson. Reprint. New York: Free Press.

———. [1912] 2001. *The Elementary Forms of Religious Life.* A new translation by Carol Cosman. New York: Oxford University Press.

Dutta, Soumitra, and Irene Mia. 2010. *The Global Information Technology Report 2009–2010.* Geneva: World Economic Forum and INSEAD. Accessible at http://networkedreadiness.com/gitr/ main/fullreport/index.html.

Dyrbye, Liselotte, N. Tait, D. Shanafelt, Charles M. Balch, Daniel Satele, and Julie Freischlag. 2011. "Relationship Between Work-Home Conflicts and Burnout Among American Surgeons." *Archives of Surgery* 146 (February):211–217.

Dzidzienyo, Anani. 1987. "Brazil." In *International Handbook on Race and Race Relations,* edited by Jay A. Sigler. New York: Greenwood Press.

e

Ebaugh, Helen Rose Fuchs. 1988. *Becoming an Ex: The Process of Role Exit.* Chicago: University of Chicago Press.

Eby, Lillian T., Charleen P. Maher, and Marcus M. Butts. 2010. "The Intersection of Work and Family Life: The Role of Affect." *Annual Review of Psychology* 61:599–622.

Eckberg, Douglas. 2006. "Crime, Law Enforcement, and Justice." Pp. 5-209–5-233 in *Historical Statistics of the United States*, Chapter Ec, edited by Richard Sutch and Susan Carter. New York: Cambridge University Press.

Eckenwiler, Mark. 1995. "In the Eyes of the Law." *Internet World* (August):74, 76–77.

Economic Mobility Project. 2009. *Findings from a National Survey and Focus Groups on Economic Mobility.* Washington, DC: Pew Charitable Trusts.

The Economist. 2003. "The One Where Pooh Goes to Sweden." (April 5):59.

———. 2004. "Battle on the Home Front." (February 21):8–10.

———. 2005b. "We Are Tous Québécois." (January 8):39.

———. 2005c. "Behind the Digital Divide." (March 2):22–25.

———. 2009a. "Burgeoning Bourgeoisie." (February 14):1–22.

———. 2010b. "Plus One Country." (September 4):46.

———. 2010c. "The Dark Side." (September 11):15.

———. 2010d. "The Strange Death of Social-Democratic Sweden." (September 18):16–17.

———. 2011c. "Digging for Victory." (September 24):60.

———. 2011c. "Age shall not wither them." (April 9):78.

Edmans, Alex, and Xavier Gabaix. 2010. "What's Right, What's Wrong, and What's Fixable." *Pathways* (Summer):13–16.

Ehrenreich, Barbara. 2001. *Nickel and Dimed: On (Not) Getting By in America.* New York: Metropolitan.

Ehrlich, Paul R. and Katherine Ellison. 2002. "A Looming Threat We Won't Face." *Los Angeles Times,* January 20, p. M6.

El Nasser, Haya, and Paul Overberg. 2009. "U.S. Making Sure Census Isn't Overcounted." *USA Today,* January 16.

———, and ———. 2011. "Recession Reshapes Life in the USA." USA Today, September 12, p. 3A.

———, and ———. 2012. "Census Shows Best Count Ever." *USA Today,* May 23, p. 3A.

Elgan, Mike. 2011. "How to Pop Your Internet 'Filter Bubble.'" *Computer World* (May 7). Accessed November 11 (www.computerworld. com/s/article/9216484/Elgan_How_to_pop_ your_Internet_filter_bubble).

Ellison, Brandy. 2008. "Tracking." Pp. 301–304, vol. 2, in *Encyclopedia of Race, Ethnicity, and Society,* edited by Richard T. Schaefer. Thousand Oaks, CA: Sage.

Ellison, Jesse. 2008. "A New Grip on Life." *Newsweek* 152 (December 15):64.

Ellison, Nicole, Charles Steinfield, and Cliff Lampe. 2007. "The Benefits of Facebook 'Friends': Exploring the Relationship between College Students' Use of Online Social Networks and Social Capital." *Journal of Computer-Mediated Communication* 12 (4):1143–1168.

Ellison, Nicole B., Jeffrey T. Hancock, and Catalina L. Toma. 2012. "Profile as Promise: A Framework for Conceptualizing the Veracity of Self Presentation in Online Dating Profiles." *New Media and Society*, 14 (February):45–62.

Ellison, Ralph. 1952. *Invisible Man.* New York: Random House.

Ely, Robin J. 1995. "The Power of Demography: Women's Social Construction of Gender Identity at Work." *Academy of Management Journal* 38 (3):589–634.

Embree, Ainslie. 2003. "Religion." Pp. 101–220 in *Understanding Contemporary India,* edited by Sumit Ganguly and Neil DeVotta. Boulder, CO: Lynne Rienner.

Engels, Friedrich [1884] 1959. "The Origin of the Family, Private Property, and the State." Pp. 392–394, excerpted in *Marx and Engels: Basic Writings on Politics and Philosophy,* edited by Lewis Feuer. Garden City, NY: Anchor Books.

Ennis, Sharon R., Merarys Rios-Vargas, and Nora G. Albert. 2011. *The Hispanic Population: 2010.* 2010 Census Brief BR-04. Washington, DC: U.S. Government Printing Office.

Entine, Jon, and Martha Nichols. 1996. "Blowing the Whistle on Meaningless 'Good Intentions.'" *Chicago Tribune,* June 20, sec. 1, p. 21.

Environmental Protection Agency. 2012. Global Greenhouse Gas Data. Accessible at http://epa .gov/climatechange/emissions/globalghg.html.

Epstein, Cynthia Fuchs. 1999. "The Major Myth of the Women's Movement." *Dissent* (Fall):83–111.

Epstein, Robert. 2009. "The Truth about Online Dating." *Scientific American* (Special Edition).

Erikson, Kai. 1966. *Wayward Puritans: A Study in the Sociology of Deviance.* New York: Wiley.

Esbenshade, Jill. 2008. "Giving Up Against the Global Economy: New Developments in the Anti-Sweatshops Movement." *Critical Sociology* 34 (3):453–470.

Escárcega, Sylvia. 2008. "Mexico." Pp. 898–902, vol. 2, in *Encyclopedia of Race, Ethnicity, and Society,* edited by Richard T. Schaefer. Thousand Oaks, CA: Sage.

Etaugh, Claire. 2003. "Witches, Mothers and Others: Females in Children's Books." *Hilltopics* (Winter):10–13.

Etzioni, Amitai. 1964. *Modern Organization.* Englewood Cliffs, NJ: Prentice Hall.

———. 1965. *Political Unification.* New York: Holt, Rinehart and Winston.

European Metalworkers' Federation. 2010. "What Is Precious Work?" Accessed March 1, 2011 (www .emf-fem.org).

European PWN. 2012. "Women on Boards: The Inside Story on Norway's 40% Target." Accessed February 22 (www.europeanpwn.net/index .php?article_id=150).

Evergeti, Venetia, and Elisabetta Zontini. 2006. "Introduction: Some Critical Reflections on Social Capital, Migration and Transnational Families." *Ethnic and Racial Studies* 29 (November):1025–1039.

f

Facebook. 2010. "Statistics." Accessed January 15 (www.facebook.com/press.info.php?statistics).

———. 2011. Statistics. Accessed January 21 (www.facebook.com/press/info.php?statistics).

Faiola, Anthony. 2005. "Their Husbands Made Them Sick." *Washington Post National Weekly Edition* 23 (October 24):18.

———. 2006. *Japan's Vulnerable Elderly. Washington Post National Weekly Edition* 23 (February 27):18.

Fairtrade Foundation. 2010. "Retail Products." Accessed Jan. 5 (www.fairtrade.org.uk/products/retail_products/default.aspx).

Faith, Nazila. 2005. "Iranian Cleric Turns Blogger in Campaign for Reform." *New York Times,* January 16, p. 4.

Fallows, Deborah. 2006. *Pew Internet Project Data.* Washington, DC: Pew Internet and American Life Project.

Farley, Maggie. 2004. "U.N. Gay Policy Is Assailed." *Los Angeles Times,* April 9, p. A3.

Farley, Melissa, and Victor Malarek. 2008. "The Myth of the Victimless Crime." *New York Times,* March 12, p. A27.

Farr, Grant M. 1999. *Modern Iran.* New York: McGraw-Hill.

Farrell, Amy, and Jack McDevitt. 2010. "Identifying and Measuring Racial Profiling by the Police." *Sociology Compass* 4:77–88.

Fausset, Richard. 2003. "Sikhs Mark New Year, Fight Post-September 11 Bias." *Los Angeles Times,* April 14, pp. B1, B7.

Favreault, Melissa. 2008. "Discrimination and Economic Mobility." Washington, DC: Economic Mobility Project. Also accessible at www.economicmobility.org/reports_and_research/literature_reviews?id=0004.

Feagin, Joe R. 1989. *Minority Group Issues in Higher Education: Learning from Qualitative Research.* Norman: Center for Research on Minority Education, University of Oklahoma.

———, Harnán Vera, and Nikitah Imani. 1996. *The Agony of Education: Black Students at White Colleges and Universities.* New York: Routledge.

Featherman, David L., and Robert M. Hauser. 1978. *Opportunity and Change.* New York: Aeodus.

Federal Trade Commission. 2010. "Protecting Consumer Privacy in an Era of Rapid Change: A Proposed Framework for Businesses and Policymakers." Accessible at http://www.ftc.gov/os/2010/12/101201privacyreport.pdf.

Felson, David, and Akis Kalaitzidis. 2005. "A Historical Overview of Transnational Crime." Pp. 3–19 in *Handbook of Transnational Crime and Justice,* edited by Philip Reichel. Thousand Oaks, CA: Sage.

Feminist Majority Foundation. 2007. "Feminists Are the Majority." Accessed February 25 (www.feminist.org).

Ferber, Abby L., and Michael S. Kimmel. 2008. "The Gendered Face of Terrorism." *Sociology Compass* 2:870–887.

Ferree, Myra Marx, and David A. Merrill. 2000. "Hot Movements, Cold Cognition: Thinking about Social Movements in Gendered Frames." *Contemporary Society* 29 (May):454–462.

Feuer, Lewis S. 1989. *Marx and Engels: Basic Writings on Politics and Philosophy.* New York: Anchor Books.

Field, John. 2008. *Social Capital.* 2nd ed. London: Routledge.

Fields, Jason. 2004. "America's Families and Living Arrangements: 2003." *Current Population Reports,* ser. P-20, no. 553. Washington, DC: U.S. Government Printing Office.

Fieser, Ezra. 2009. "What Price for Good Coffee?" *Time,* October 5, pp. 61–62.

Fiji TV. 2012. Home Page. Accessed January 10 (www.fijitv.com.fj).

File, Thom, and Sarah Crissey. 2010. "Voting and Registration in the Election of November 2008." *Current Population Reports,* ser. P-20, no. 562.

Finch, Emily, and Vanessa E. Munro. 2005. "Juror Stereotypes and Blame Attribution in Rape Cases Involving Intoxicants." *British Journal of Criminology* 45 (June):25–38.

——— and ———. 2007. "The Demon Drink and the Demonized Woman: Socio-Sexual Stereotypes and Responsibility Attribution in Rape Trials Involving Intoxicants." 16 (No. 4) 591–614.

——— and ———. 2008. "Lifting the Veil: The Use of Focus Groups and Trial Simulations in Legal Research." 30–51.

Fine, Gary C. 2008. "Robbers Cave." Pp. 1163–1164, vol. 3, in *Encyclopedia of Race, Ethnicity, and Society,* edited by Richard T. Schaefer. Thousand Oaks, CA: Sage.

Finkel, Steven E., and James B. Rule. 1987. "Relative Deprivation and Related Psychological Theories of Civil Violence: A Critical Review." *Research in Social Movements* 9:47–69.

Finley, Nancy J. 2010. "Skating Femininity: Gender Maneuvering in Women's Roller Derby." *Journal of Contemporary Ethnography* 39 (4):359–387.

Fiola, Jan. 2008. "Brazil." Pp. 200–204, vol. 2, in *Encyclopedia of Race, Ethnicity, and Society,* edited by Richard T. Schaefer. Thousand Oaks, CA: Sage.

Fiss, Peer C., and Paul M. Hirsch. 2005. "The Discourse of Globalization: Framing of an Emerging Concept." *American Sociological Review* (February):29–52.

Fitzgerald, Kathleen J. 2008. "White Privilege." Pp. 1403–1405, vol. 3, in *Encyclopedia of Race, Ethnicity, and Society,* edited by Richard T. Schaefer. Thousand Oaks, CA: Sage.

Fitzgerald, Michael. 2011. "Economics: Ends and Means." *The University of Chicago Magazine* (November–December):32–39.

Fitzpatrick, Maureen J., and Barbara J. McPherson. 2010. "Coloring within the Lines: Gender Stereotypes in Contemporary Coloring Books." *Sex Roles* 62:127–137.

Flacks, Richard. 1971. *Youth and Social Change.* Chicago: Markham.

Fletcher, Connie. 1995. "On the Line: Women Cops Speak Out." *Chicago Tribune Magazine,* February 19, pp. 14–19.

Florida, Richard. 2011. "Why Crime Is Down in America's Cities." *The Atlantic* (July). Accessible at www.theatlantic.com.

Fonseca, Felicia. 2008. "Dine College on Quest to Rename Navajo Cancer Terms." *News from Indian Country* 22 (January 7):11.

Forbes. 2011. "Carlos Slim Helu and Family." Accessed January 29, 2012 (www.forbes.com/profile/carlos-slim-helu/).

———. 2012. "Leaderboard: Billionaire Box Scores." 189 (March 26):34.

Foroohar, Rana. 2011. "What Ever Happened to Upward Mobility?" Pp. 77–85 in *Occupy. What Is Occupy?* New York: Times Books.

Francis, David. 2010. "Homeschoolers Seek Asylum in US." *Christian Science Monitor,* March 8, p. 12.

Frank, Robert H. 2010. "A Remedy Worse than the Disease." *Pathways* (Summer):17–21.

Franke, Richard Herbert, and James D. Kaul. 1978. "The Hawthorne Experiments: First Statistical Interpretation." *American Sociological Review* 43 (October):623–643.

Franklin, John Hope, and Evelyn Brooks Higginbotham. 2011. *From Slavery to Freedom.* 9th ed. New York: McGraw-Hill.

Freedom House. 2012. *Freedom in the World 2012.* Washington, DC: Freedom House.

Freese, Jeremy. 2008. "Genetics and the Social Science Explanation of Individual Outcomes." *American Journal of Sociology* 114 (Suppl.):51–535.

Freidson, Eliot. 1970. *Profession of Medicine.* New York: Dodd, Mead.

French, Howard W. 2004. "China's Textbooks Twist and Omit History." *New York Times,* December 6, p. A10.

———. 2008. "Lines of Grinding Poverty, Untouched by China's Boom." *New York Times,* January 13, p. 4.

Freudenburg, William, and Robert Gramling. 2010. *Blowout in the Gulf: The BP Oil Spill Disaster and the Future of Energy in America.* Cambridge: MIT Press.

Freudenburg, William R. 2005. "Seeing Science, Courting Conclusions: Reexamining the Intersection of Science, Corporate Cash, and the Law." *Sociological Forum* 20 (March):3–33.

Freundlich, Madelyn, and Joy Kim Lieberthal. 2000. "The Gathering of the First Generation of Adult Korean Adoptees: Adoptees' Perceptions of International Adoption." Accessible at www.adoptioninstitute.org/proed/korfindings.html.

Frey, William H. 2011. *A Demographic Tipping Point among America's Three-Year-Olds.* February 7. Accessible at http://www.brookings.edu/opinions/2011/0207_population_frey.aspx?p=1.

Fridlund, Alan J., Paul Erkman, and Harriet Oster. 1987. "Facial Expressions of Emotion; Review of Literature 1970–1983." Pp. 143–224 in *Nonverbal Behavior and Communication,* 2nd ed., edited by Aron W. Seigman and Stanley Feldstein. Hillsdale, NJ: Erlbaum.

Friedman, Louis. 2010. "NASA's Down-to-Earth Problems." *Star-Telegram* (Fort Worth), March 28. Accessible at http://www.star-telegram.com/2010/03/28/2072608/friedman-nasas-down-to-earth-problem.html.

Friends of the Congo. 2011. "Coltan: What You Should Know." Accessed May 21 (www.friendsofthecongo.org/new/coltan.php).

Fry, Richard, D'Vera Cohn, Gretchen Livingston, and Paul Taylor. 2011. "The Rising Age Gap in Economic Well-Being." Accessible at http://pewresearch.org/pubs/2124/age-gap-silent-generation-millennials-wealth-gap.

Fudge, Judy, and Rosemary Owens, eds. 2006. *Precarious Work, Women, and the New Economy: The Challenge to Legal Norms.* Oxford, UK: Hart.

Fukase, Atsuko, and Kana Inagaki. 2012. "Japan Insider Penalty: $600." *Wall Street Journal*, March 22, p. C2.

Furstenberg, Frank F, Jr., 2007. "The Making of the Black Family: Race and Class in Qualitative Studies in the Twentieth Century." *Annual Review of Sociology* 33:429–448.

———, and Andrew Cherlin. 1991. *Divided Families: What Happens to Children When Parents Part*. Cambridge, MA: Harvard University Press.

———, and Sheela Kennedy, Vonnie C. McCloyd, Rubén G. Rumbaut, and Richard A. Setterstein, Jr. 2004. "Growing Up Is Harder to Do." *Contexts* 3:33–41.

g

Gabriel, Trip. 2010. "Despite Push, Success at Charter Schools Is Mixed." *New York Times*, May 1, pp. A1, A24–A25.

Gailey, Robert. 2007. "As History Repeats Itself, Unexpected Developments Move Us Forward." *Journal of Rehabilitation Research and Development* 44 (4):vii–xiv.

Galbraith, John Kenneth. 1977. *The Age of Uncertainty*. Boston: Houghton Mifflin.

Galea, Sandro, Melissa Tracy, Katherine J. Hoggatt, Charles DiMaggio, and Adam Karpati. 2011. "Estimated Deaths Attributed to Social Factors in the United States." *American Journal of Public Health* 101 (August):1456–1465.

Gallagher, Kevin P. 2009. "Economic Globalization and the Environment." *Annual Review of Environmental Resources* 34:279–304.

Gallup. 2009a. "Religion:" Accessed April 9 at www .gallup.com.

———. 2009b. "Military and National Defense." Accessed April 17 (www.gallup.com/poll/1666/military-national-defense-aspx).

———. 2011a. "Religion." Accessed March 27 (www.gallup.com).

———. 2012. "Party Affiliation." Accessed March 8 (www.gallup.com/poll/15370/Party-Affiliation .aspx).

Gallup Opinion Index. 1978. "Religion in America, 1977–1978." 145 (January).

Gamson, Joshua. 1989. "Silence, Death, and the Invisible Enemy: AIDS Activism and Social Movement 'Newness.'" *Social Problems* 36 (October):351–367.

Gans, Herbert J. 1995. *The War against the Poor: The Underclass and Antipoverty Policy*. New York: Basic Books.

Garcia-Moreno, Claudia, Henrica A. F. M. Jansen, Mary Ellsberg, Lori Heise, and Charlotte Watts. 2005. *WHO Multi-Country Study on Women's Health and Domestic Violence against Women*. Geneva, Switzerland: WHO.

Gardner, Gary, Erik Assadourian, and Radhika Sarin. 2004. "The State of Consumption Today." Pp. 3–21 in *State of the World 2004*, edited by Brian Halweil and Lisa Mastny. New York: Norton.

Garfinkel, Harold. 1956. "Conditions of Successful Degradation Ceremonies." *American Journal of Sociology* 61 (March):420–424.

Garner, Roberta. 1996. *Contemporary Movements and Ideologies*. New York: McGraw-Hill.

———. 1999. "Virtual Social Movements." Presented at Zaldfest: A conference in honor of Mayer Zald. September 17, Ann Arbor, MI.

Garrett-Peters, Raymond. 2009. "'If I Don't Have to Work Anymore, Who Am I?': Job Loss and Collaborative Self-Concept Repair." *Journal of Contemporary Ethnography* 38 (5):547–583.

Gates, Gary J., and Abigail M. Cooke. 2011. "United States Census Snapshot: 2010." Accessible at http://williamsinstitute.law.ucla.edu/wp-content/uploads/Census2010Snapshot-US-v2.pdf.

Gaudin, Sharon. 2009. "Facebook Has Whopper of a Problem with Burger King Campaign." *Computerworld*, January 15.

Gay, Lesbian and Straight Education Network. 2012. "About GLSEN." Accessed March 1 (www.glsen.org).

Gecas, Viktor. 2004. "Socialization, Sociology of." Pp. 14525–14530 in *International Encyclopedia of the Social and Behavioral Sciences*, edited by Neil J. Smelser and Paul B. Baltes. Cambridge, MA: Elsevier.

Gelles, David. 2011. "It's All About the Algorithm." *Financial Times* (July 30).

General Social Survey. 2012. "GSS General Social Survey." Accessed January 25 (www3.norc.org/GSS+Website).

Gentile, Carmen. 2009. "Student Fights Record of 'Cyberbullying.'" *New York Times*, February 8, p. 20.

Gentleman, Amelia. 2006. "Bollywood Captivated by the Call Centre Culture." *Guardian Weekly*, June 2, p. 17.

———. 2007. "Young Sikh Men Get Haircuts, Annoying Their Elders." *New York Times*, March 29, p. A3.

Gerth, H. H., and C. Wright Mills. 1958. *From Max Weber: Essays in Sociology*. New York: Galaxy.

Gertner, Jon. 2005. "Our Ratings, Ourselves." *New York Times Magazine*, April 10, pp. 34–41, 56, 58, 64–65.

Gibbs, Nancy. 2009. "What Women Want Now." *Time* 174 (16):24–33.

Giddens, Anthony. 1991. *Modernity and Self-Identity: Self and Society in the Late Modern Age*. Cambridge, UK: Polity.

———. 2011. *The Politics of Climate Change*. 2nd ed. Cambridge, UK: Polity.

Giddings, Paul J. 2008. *Ida: A Sword among Lions*. New York: Amistad.

Gilley, Brian Joseph. 2006. *Becoming Two-Spirit: Gay Identity and Social Acceptance in Indian Country*. Lincoln: University of Nebraska Press.

Gillum, Jack. 2011. "How USA Today Analyzed Border Crime Trends." *USA Today*, July 16, p. 7A.

Gilsdorf, Ethan. 2010. "A Virtual World That Breaks Real Barriers." *Christian Science Monitor*, September 6, pp. 36–37.

Giordano, Peggy C. 2003. "Relationships in Adolescence." Pp. 257–281 in *Annual Review of Sociology, 2003*, edited by Karen S. Cook and John Hagan. Palo Alto, CA: Annual Reviews.

Girl Scouts of the USA. 2001. *Junior Girl Scout Badge Book*. New York: Girl Scouts of the United States of America.

Giroux, Henry A. 1988. *Schooling and the Struggle for Public Life: Critical Pedagogy in the Modern Age*. Minneapolis: University of Minnesota Press.

Gitlin, Todd. 2002. *Media Unlimited: How the Torrent of Images and Sounds Overwhelms Our Lives*. New York: Henry Holt.

Glanz, James, and John Markoff. 2011. "U.S. Underestimates Internet Detour Around Censors." *New York Times*, June 12, pp. 1, 8.

Glascock, Stuart. 2008. "A Town Confronts its Language Barrier." *Los Angeles Times* (May 25) p. A20.

Glazer, Susan. 2010. "Evaluating Microfinance." *EQ Global Research* 4 (April).

Glenn, David. 2007. "Anthropologists in a War Zone: Scholars Debate Their Role." *Chronicle of Higher Education* 54 (September 30):A1, A10–A12.

Goering, Laurie. 2008b. "Outsourced to India: Stress." *Chicago Tribune*, April 20, pp. 1, 18.

Goffman, Erving. 1959. *The Presentation of Self in Everyday Life*. New York: Doubleday.

———. 1961. *Asylums: Essays on the Social Situation of Mental Patients and Other Inmates*. Garden City, NY: Doubleday.

———. 1963. *Stigma: Notes on Management of Spoiled Identity*. Englewood Cliffs, NJ: Prentice Hall.

Goldman, David. 2012. "Are Landlines Doomed?" CNN Money. April 10. Accessed April 11 (http://money.cnn.com/2012/04/10/technology/att-verizon-landlines/index.htm).

Gomez, Alan, Jack Gillum, and Kevin Johnson. 2011. "On U.S. Side, Cities Are Havens from Drug Wars." *USA Today*, July 15, pp. 1A, 6A–7A.

Goode, Tawara D. 2011. *Cultural and Linguistic Competence: Implications for Statewide Independent Councils*. Washington, DC: National Center for Cultural Competence, Georgetown University.

Goodstein, Laurie. 2008. "India, Exporter of Priests, May Keep Them Home." *New York Times*, December 30, p. A1.

Gottfredson, Michael, and Travis Hirschi. 1990. *A General Theory of Crime*. Palo Alto, CA: Stanford University Press.

Gough, Margaret, and Alexandra Killewald. 2011. "Unemployment in Families: The Case of Housework." *Journal of Marriage and Family* 73 (October):1085–1100.

Gould, Elise. 2007. "The Health-Finance Debate Reaches a Fever Pitch." *Chronicle of Higher Education*, April 13, pp. B14, B15.

Gould, Larry A. 2002. "Indigenous People Policing Indigenous People: The Potential Psychological and Cultural Costs." *Social Science Journal* 39:171–188.

Government Accountability Office. 2003. "Women's Earnings: Work Patterns Partially Explain Difference between Men's and Women's Earnings." Washington, DC: U.S. Government. Printing Office.

Grady, Sarah, Stacy Bielick, and Susan Aud. 2010. *Trends in the Use of School Choice: 1993 to 2010*. Washington, DC: U.S. Government Printing Office.

Gramsci, Antonio. 1929. *Selections from the Prison Notebooks*. Edited and translated by Quintin Hoare and Geoffrey Nowell Smith. London: Lawrence and Wishort.

Grattet, Ryken. 2011. "Societal Reactions to Deviance." *Annual Review of Sociology* 37:185–204.

Grazian, David. 2010. *Mix It Up: Popular Culture, Mass Media, and Society.* New York: Norton.

Greeley, Andrew M. 1989. "Protestant and Catholic: Is the Analogical Imagination Extinct?" *American Sociological Review* 54 (August):485–502.

Greenemeier, Larry. 2010. "Gulf Spillover: Will BP's Deepwater Disaster Change the Oil Industry?" *Scientific American* (June 7). Accessible at http://www.scientificamerican.com/article.cfm?id=molotch-deepwater-environmental-sociology.

Greenhouse, Linda. 2008. "D.C. Ban Rejected. Landmark Decision on Covert Meaning of 2nd Amendment." *New York Times,* June 27, pp. A1, A12.

Greenhouse, Steven. 2008b. "Millions of Jobs of a Different Collar." *New York Times,* March 26.

Groza, Victor, Daniela F. Ileana, and Ivor Irwin. 1999. *A Peacock or a Crow: Stories, Interviews, and Commentaries on Romanian Adoptions.* Euclid, OH: Williams Custom Publishing.

Grusky, David, and Christopher Wimer. 2010. "Editor's Note." *Pathways* (Summer):2.

Guest, Robert. 2011. "Tribes Still Matter." *The Economist* (January 22):17–18.

Guo, Guang, Michael E. Roettger, and Tianji Cai. 2008. "The Integration of Genetic Propensities into Social-Control Models of Delinquency and Violence among Male Youths." *American Sociological Review* 73 (August):543–568.

Gurbuz, Mustafa, and Gulsum Gurbuz-Kucuksari. 2009. "Between Sacred Codes and Secular Consumer Society: The Practice of Headscarf Adoption among American College Girls." *Journal of Muslim Minority Affairs* 29 (September):387–399.

Gutiérrez, Gustavo. 1990. "Theology and the Social Sciences." Pp. 214–225 in *Liberation Theology at the Crossroads: Democracy or Revolution?* edited by Paul E. Sigmund. New York: Oxford University Press.

Guttmacher Institute. 2008. *Facts on Induced Abortion Worldwide.* New York: Guttmacher.

h

Haas, Steven A., David R. Schaefer, and Olga Kornienko. 2010. "Health and the Structure of Adolescent Social Networks." *Journal of Health and Social Behavior* 5 (4):424–439.

Haase, Dwight. 2012. "Banking on the Poor." *Contexts* (Winter):36–41.

Hacker, Andrew. 1964. "Power to Do What?" Pp. 134–146 in *The New Sociology,* edited by Irving Louis Horowitz. New York: Oxford University Press.

Hacker, Helen Mayer. 1951. "Women as a Minority Group." *Social Forces* 30 (October):60–69.

———. 1974. "Women as a Minority Group, Twenty Years Later." Pp. 124–134 in *Who Discriminates against Women?* edited by Florence Denmark. Beverly Hills, CA: Sage.

Hallinan, Maureen T. 1997. "The Sociological Study of Social Change." *American Sociological Review* 62 (February):1–11.

Halualani, Rona Tamiko. 2002. *In the Name of Hawaiians: Native Identities and Cultural Politics.* Minneapolis: University of Minnesota Press.

Hamm, Steve. 2007. "Children of the Web." *BusinessWeek,* July 2, pp. 50–56, 58.

Hani, Yoko. 1998. "Hot Pots Wired to Help the Elderly." *Japan Times Weekly International Edition* (April 13), p. 16.

Hank, Karsten. 2001. "Changes in Child Care Could Reduce Job Options for Eastern German Mothers." *Population Today* 29 (April):3, 6.

Hanson, Ralph E. 2005. *Mass Communication: Living in a Media World.* New York: McGraw-Hill.

Haq, Husna. 2011. "How Marriage Is Faring." *Christian Science Monitor,* February 14, p. 21.

Harden, Blaine. 2009. "Revising History: Japan helps immigrants find work, realizing that its aging population can't support itself." *Washington Post National Weekly Edition* (February) p. 20.

Harding, David J. 2009. "Violence, Older Peers, and the Socialization of Adolescent Boys in Disadvantaged Neighborhoods." *American Sociological Review* 74 (June):445–464.

Harlow, Harry F. 1971. *Learning to Love.* New York: Ballantine.

Harman, Donna. 2009. "Dubai's Glitz Lost in Grim Life." *Christian Science Monitor,* May 3, p. 8.

Harrington, Michael. 1980. "The New Class and the Left." Pp. 123–138 in *The New Class,* edited by B. Bruce Briggs. Brunswick, NJ: Transaction.

Harrisinteractive. 2008. "Cell Phone Usage Continues to Increase." Accessed January 13 (www.harrisinteractive.com).

Haub, Carl. 2010. "2010 World Population Data Sheet." Washington, DC: Population Reference Bureau.

———. 2011. *2011 World Population Data Sheet.* Washington, DC: Population Reference Bureau.

———, and Mary Mederius Kent. 2009. *2009 World Population Data Sheet.* Washington: Population Reference Bureau.

Haviland, William A., Harald E. L. Prins, Dana Walrath, and Bunny McBride. 2008. *Cultural Anthropology—The Human Challenge.* 12th ed. Belmont, CA: Wadsworth.

Hay, Andrew. 2009. "Spain's New Middle Classes Slip into Poverty." *Reuters.* April 8. Accessed May 11, 2011 (http://uk.reuters.com/article/email/ioUKTRE537029200904).

Hayden, H. Thomas. 2004. "What Happened at Abu Ghraib." Accessed August 7 (www.military .com).

Health Care Financing Administration. 2001. *National Health Care Expenditures Projections.* Accessed August 10 (www.hcfa.gov/stats/NHE-proj/).

Heckert, Druann, and Amy Best. 1997. "Ugly Duckling to Swan: Labeling Theory and the Stigmatization of Red Hair." *Symbolic Interaction* 20 (4):365–384.

Hedley, R. Alan. 1992. "Industrialization in Less Developed Countries." Pp. 914–920, vol. 2, in *Encyclopedia of Sociology,* edited by Edgar F. Borgatta and Marie L. Borgatta. New York: Macmillan.

Heilman, Madeline E. 2001. "Description and Prescription: How Gender Stereotypes Prevent Women's Ascent up the Organizational Ladder." *Journal of Social Issues* 57 (4):657–674.

Heisig, Jan Paul. 2011. "Who Does More Housework: Rich or Poor? A Comparison of 33 Countries." *American Sociological Review* 76 (1):74–99.

Hellmich, Nanci. 2001. "TV's Reality: No Vast American Waistlines." *USA Today,* October 8, p. D7.

Helman, Ruth, Mathew Greenwald, Craig Copeland, and Jack VanDerhel. 2012. "The 2012 Retirement Confidence Survey: Job Security, Debt Weigh on Retirement Confidence, Savings." *Employee Benefit Research Institute* Notes 33 (March).

Hendershott, Ann. 2002. *The Politics of Deviance.* San Francisco: Encounter Books.

Hengeveld, Rob. 2012. *Wasted World: How Our Consumption Challenges the Planet.* Chicago: University of Chicago Press.

Hertz, Rosanna. 2006. *Single by Chance. Mothers by Choice.* New York: Oxford University Press.

Hewlett, Sylvia Ann, and Carolyn Buck Luce. 2005. "Off-Ramps and On-Ramps: Keeping Talented Women on the Road to Success." *Harvard Business Review* (March):43–53.

Higgins, Chris A., Linda E. Duxbury, and Sean T. Lyons. 2010. "Coping with Overload in Stress: Men and Women in Dual-Earner Families." *Journal of Marriage and Family* 72 (August):847–859.

Higher Education Research Institute. 2004. *Trends in Political Attitudes and Voting Behavior among College Freshmen and Early Career College Graduates: What Issues Could Drive This Election?* Los Angeles: HERI, University of California, Los Angeles.

Hill, Michael R., and Susan Hoecker-Drysdale, eds. 2001. *Harriet Martineau: Theoretical and Methodological Perspectives.* New York: Routledge.

Hira, Ron. 2008. "An Overview of the Offshoring of U.S. Jobs." Pp. 14–15 in Marlene A. Lee and Mark Mather. "U.S. Labor Force Trends." *Population Bulletin* 63 (June).

Hirschi, Travis. 1969. *Causes of Delinquency.* Berkeley: University of California Press.

Hirst, Paul, and Grahame Thompson. 1996. *Globalization in Question: The International Economy and the Possibilities of Governance.* Cambridge, UK: Polity Press.

Hitlin, Steven, and Jane Allyn Piliavin. 2004. "Values: Reviving a Dormant Concept." Pp. 359–393 in *Annual Review of Sociology, 2004,* edited by Karen S. Cook and John Hagan. Palo Alto, CA: Annual Reviews.

Hochschild, Arlie Russell. 1990. "The Second Shift: Employed Women Are Putting in Another Day of Work at Home." *Utne Reader* 38 (March–April):66–73.

———. 2005. *The Commercialization of Intimate Life: Notes from Home and Work.* Berkeley: University of California Press.

———, with Anne Machung. 1989. *The Second Shift: Working Parents and the Revolution at Home.* New York: Viking Penguin.

Hoeffel, Elizabeth M., Sonya Rastogi, Myoung Ouk Kim, and Hasan Shahid. 2012. *The Asian Population: 2010.* C2101BR-11. Washington, DC: U.S. Government Printing Office.

Holden, Constance. 1980. "Identical Twins Reared Apart." *Science* 207 (March 21):1323–1328.
———. 1987. "The Genetics of Personality." *Science* 257 (August 7):598–601.

Holder, Kelly. 2006. "Voting and Registration in the Election of November 2004." *Current Population Reports,* ser. P-20, no. 556. Washington, DC: U.S. Government Printing Office.

Hollingshead, August B. 1975. *Elmtown's Youth and Elmtown Revisited.* New York: Wiley.

Holmes, Mary. 2009. "Commuter Couples and Distance Relationships: Living Apart Together." Sloan Work and Family Research Network. Accessible at http://wfnetwork.bc.edu/ encyclopedia_entry.php?id=15551&area=all.

Homans, George C. 1979. "Nature versus Nurture: A False Dichotomy." *Contemporary Sociology* 8 (May):345–348.

Home School Legal Defense Association. 2005. "State Laws" and "Academic Statistics on Homeschooling." Accessed May 12 (www .hslda.org).

Hondagneu-Sotelo, Pierrette, ed. 2003. *Gender and U.S. Immigration: Contemporary Trends.* Berkeley: University of California Press.

hooks, bell. 1994. *Feminist Theory: From Margin to Center.* 2nd ed. Boston: South End Press.

Horgan, John. 1993. "Eugenics Revisited." *Scientific American* 268 (June):122–128, 130–133.

Horkheimer, Max, and Theodore Adorno. [1944] 2002. *Dialectic of Enlightenment.* Palo Alto, CA: Stanford University Press.

Horowitz, Helen Lefkowitz. 1987. *Campus Life.* Chicago: University of Chicago Press.

Horrigan, John B. 2007. *A Typology of Information and Communication Technology Users.* Washington, DC: Pew Internet and American Life Project.

Hosokawa, William K. 1969. *Nisei: The Quiet Americans.* New York: Morrow.

Hospice Association of America. 2010. "Hospice Facts and Statistics." Accessed March 12, 2012 at www.nah.org/facts/HospiceStats/o.pdf.

Houser, Trevor, Shashank Mohamad, and Robert Heilmayer. 2009. *A Green Global Recovery? Assessing U.S. Economic Stimulus and the Prospects for International Coordination.* Washington, DC: World Resources Institute of Peterson Institute for International Economics.

Howard, Judith A. 1999. "Border Crossings between Women's Studies and Sociology." *Contemporary Sociology* 28 (September):525–528.

Howard, Michael. 2009. *Modern Wicca: A History from Gerald Gardner to the Present.* St. Paul, MN: Llewellyn Books.

Howard, Michael C. 1989. *Contemporary Cultural Anthropology.* 3rd ed. Glenview, IL: Scott, Foresman.

Howard, Russell D., and Reid L. Sawyer. 2003. *Terrorism and Counterterrorism: Understanding the New Security Environment.* Guilford, CT: McGraw-Hill/Dushkin.

Hu, Winnie. 2010. "In a New Role, Teachers Move to Run Schools." *New York Times,* September 7, pp. A1, A20.

Huang, Gary. 1988. "Daily Addressing Ritual: A Cross-Cultural Study." Presented at the annual meeting of the American Sociological Association, Atlanta.

Hughes, Everett. 1945. "Dilemmas and Contradictions of Status." *American Journal of Sociology* 50 (March):353–359.

Hughlett, Mike. 2008. "Sitting Pretty." *Chicago Tribune,* September 14, sec. 5, pp. 1, 7.

Human Genome Project. 2012. "Human Genome Project Information." Accessed April 4 (www .ornl.gov/sci/techresources/Human_Genome/ home.shtml).

Human Rights Campaign. 2012. "Marriage/Issues/ Human Rights." Accessible February 27 (www .hrc.org/issues/marriage).

Human Terrain System. 2011. "Welcome to the HTS Home Page." Accessed Novmber 18, 2011 (http://humanterrainsystem.army.mil).

Humes, Karen R., Nicholas A. Jones, and Roberto R. Ramirez. 2011. *Overview of Race and Hispanic Origin: 2010.* 2010 Census Brief BR-02. Accessible at http://www.census.gov/prod/ cen2010/briefs/c2010br-02.pdf.

Hundley, Tom, and Margaret Ramirez. 2008. "Young Muslims Put Faith in Facebook." *Chicago Tribune,* February 10, p. 12.

Hunt, Darnell. 1997. *Screening the Los Angeles "Riots": Race, Seeing, and Resistance.* New York: Cambridge University Press.

Hunter, Herbert M., ed. 2000. *The Sociology of Oliver C. Cox: New Perspectives: Research in Race and Ethnic Relations,* vol. 2. Stamford, CT: JAI Press.

Hunter, James Davison. 1991. *Culture Wars: The Struggle to Define America.* New York: Basic Books.

Huntington, Samuel P. 1993. "The Clash of Civilizations?" *Foreign Affairs* 72 (Summer):22–49.

Hur, Song-Woo. 2011. "Mapping South Korean Women's Movements During and After Democratization: Shifting Identities." *East Asian Social Movements,* edited by J. Broadbent and V. Brockman.

Hurn, Christopher J. 1985. *The Limits and Possibilities of Schooling,* 2nd ed. Boston: Allyn and Bacon.

Hussar, William J., and Tabitha M. Bailey. 2011. *Projections of Education Statistics to 2019.* Washington, DC: National Center for Education Statistics.

Hyde, Janet Shibley. 2005. "The Gender Similarities Hypothesis." *American Psychologist* 60 (6):581–592.

i

Igo, Sarah E. 2007. *The Average American: Surveys, Citizens, and the Making of a Mass Public.* Cambridge, MA: Harvard University Press.

Immervoll, Herwig, and David Barber. 2005. *Can Parents Afford to Work? Childcare Costs, Tax-Benefit Policies and Work Incentives.* Paris: Organisation for Economic Co-operation and Development.

Inglehart, Ronald, and Wayne E. Baker. 2000. "Modernization, Cultural Change, and the Persistence of Traditional Values." *American Sociological Review* 65 (February):19–51.

Innocence Project. 2012. "Facts on Post-Conviction DNA Exonerations." Accessed January 23 (www .innocenceproject.org/Content/Facts_on_ Post-Conviction_DNA_Exonerations.php).

Institute for American Values. 2011. *Why Marriage Matters. Thirty Conclusions from Social Sciences.* New York: Institute for American Values. Accessible at www.americanvalues.org.

Institute for Economics and Peace. 2011. "Global Peace Index 2011." March 2, 2012. Accessible March 7. (www.visionofhumanity.org/gpi/results/ world-map.php).

Institute of International Education. 2010. Open Doors "Fast Facts." Accessible at www.ies.org.

Interbrand. 2012. "Best Global Brands: 2011 Rankings." Accessed January 17. Accessible at www .interband.com/best_global_brands.aspx.

Interface Group Report (Virginia Tech) 2007. *Presidential Internal Review.* Blacksburg, Virginia Polytechnic Institute and State University.

International Crime Victim Survey. 2004. *Nationwide Surveys in the Industrialized Countries.* Accessed February 20 (www.ruljis.leidenuniv.nl/ group/jfcr/www/icvs).

International Gay and Lesbian Human Rights Commission. 2010. Home Page. Accessed February 11 (www.iglhrc.org).

International Institute for Democracy and Electoral Assistance. 2012. "Voter Turnout Database— Custom Query." Accessed March 7 (http://www .idea.int/vt/viewdata.cfm#).

International Monetary Fund. 2000. *World Economic Outlook: Asset Prices and the Business Cycle.* Washington, DC: International Monetary Fund.

International Organization for Migration. 2012. "Facts and Figures." Accessed March 29 (www .iom.int/jahia/jahia/about.migration/lang/en).

Internet Crime Complaint Center. 2011. *The 2010 Internet Crime Report.* Washington, DC: The National White Collar Crime Center. Accessible at www.ic3.gov/media/annualreport/2010_ IC3Report.pdf.

Internet World Stats. 2012. "Usage and Population Statistics" and "Internet World Users by Language." Updated on March 28. Accessed March 29 (www.internetworldstats.com).

Inter-Parliamentary Union. 2011. *Women in National Parliaments.* December 31. Accessed March 7 (www.ipu.org).

Isaacs, Julia B. 2007a. *Economic Mobility of Families across Generations.* Washington, DC: Economic Mobility Project, Pew Charitable Trusts.
———. 2007b. *Economic Mobility of Men and Women.* Washington, DC: Economic Mobility Project.
———, Isabel V. Sawhill, and Ron Haskins. 2008. *Getting Ahead or Losing Ground: Economic Mobility in America.* Washington, DC: Pew Charitable Trusts.

ITOPF. 2006. "Statistics: International Tanker Owners Pollution Federation Limited." Accessed May 2 (www.itopf.com/stats.html).

j

Jackson, Philip W. 1968. *Life in Classrooms.* New York: Holt.

Jacobs, Andres. 2010. "As China's Economy Grows, Pollution Worsens Despite New Efforts to Control It." *New York Times,* July 29, p. A4.

Jacobs, Jerry. 2003. "Detours on the Road to Equality: Women, Work and Higher Education." *Contexts* (Winter):32–41.

Jacobs, Tom. 2009. "Hot Men of the Links." *Miller-McCune* (May–June):79.

Jaffee, Daniel. 2007. *Brewing Justice: Fair Trade Coffee, Sustainability, and Survival*. Berkeley: University of California Press.

Jain, Saranga, and Kathleen Kurz. 2007. *New Insights on Preventing Child Marriage: A Global Analysis of Factors and Programs*. Washington, DC: International Center for Research on Women.

Jäntti, Markus. 2009. "Mobility in the United States in Comparative Perspectives." *Focus* 26 (Fall).

Japan Aisaika Organization. 2012. "Aisaika Organization Prospectus." Accessed January 15 (www.aisaika.org/en/prospectus.html).

Jasper, James M. 1997. *The Art of Moral Protest: Culture, Biography, and Creativity in Social Movements*. Chicago: University of Chicago Press.

Jayson, Sharon. 2009. "Holding Up the Value of Marriage." *USA Today*, February 18, pp. D1, D2.

Jenkins, Henry. 2006. *Convergence Culture: Where Old and New Media Collide*. New York: New York University Press.

Jensen, Gary F. 2005. "Social Organization Theory." In *Encyclopedia of Criminology*, edited by Richard A. Wright and J. Mitchell Miller. Chicago: Fitzrog Dearborn.

Jervis, Rick. 2008. "New Orleans Homicides up 30% over 2006 Level." *USA Today*, January 3, p. 3A.

Jesella, Kara. 2008. "Blogging's Glass Ceiling." *New York Times*, July 27, Style section, pp. 1, 2.

Jimenez, Maria. 2009. *Humanitarian Crisis: Migrant Deaths at the U.S.–Mexico Border*. San Diego: ACLU of San Diego and Imperial Countries.

Joas, Hans, and Wolfgang Knöbl. 2009. *Social Theory: Twenty Introductory Lectures*. Cambridge: Cambridge University Press.

John, Robert. 2012. "The Native American Family." Pp. 361–410 in *Ethnic Families in America: Patterns and Variations*. 5th ed., edited by Roosevelt Wright, Jr., Charles H. Mindel, Thanh Van Tran, and Robert W. Halsenstein. Upper Saddle River, NJ: Pearson.

Johnson, Benton. 1975. *Functionalism in Modern Sociology: Understanding Talcott Parsons*. Morristown, NJ: General Learning.

Johnson, Will. 2009. "Genie: The Wild Child." Accessed August 4, 2010 (http://knol.google.com/k/genie-the-wild-child-chapter-2#).

Jones, Del, and Barbara Hansen. 2009. "CEO Pay Packages Sink with Economy." *USA Today*, May 4, pp. B1–B2.

Jones, Jeff, and Lydia Saad. 2011. "Gallup News Service." *Gallup Poll Social Series: Environment* (March 3-6).

———, and ———. 2012. "Gallup News Service." *Gallup Poll Social Series: Environment* (March 8-11). Accessible at www.gallup.com/poll/153404/Americans-Split-Energy-Environment-Trade-OFF.aspx.

Jopling, John, and Reilly Morse. 2010. "The BP Oil Disaster and Its Disproportionate Impacts on Minorities and Communities of Color." *Focus* 36 (October–November):12–14.

Jordan, Miriam. 2009. "As U.S. Job Opportunities Fade, More Mexicans Look Homeward." *Wall Street Journal*, February 13, p. A14.

Joseph, Jay. 2004. *The Gene Illusion: Genetic Research in Psychiatry and Psychology under the Microscope*. New York: Algora Books.

Josephson Institute. 2011. "What Would Honest Abe Lincoln Say?" Accessed February 10 (www.CharacterCounts.org).

Jost, Kenneth. 2008. "Women in Politics." *CQ Researcher* 18 (March 21).

Julian, Tiffany, and Robert Kominski. 2011. *Education and Synthetic Work-Life Earnings Estimates*. ACS-14. Washington, DC: U.S. Government Printing Office.

K

Kahn, Joseph. 2006. "Where's Mao? Chinese Revise History Books." *New York Times*, September 1, pp. A1, A6.

Kalleberg, Arne L. 2009. "Precarious Work, Insecure Workers: Employment Relations in Transition." *American Sociological Review* 74 (February):1–22.

Kambayashi, Takehiko. 2008. "Japanese Men Shout the Oft-Unsaid 'I love you.'" *Christian Science Monitor*, February 13.

Kamenetz, Anya. 2006. *Generation Debt*. New York: Riverhead.

Kang, K. Connie. 1996. "Filipinos Happy with Life in U.S. but Lack United Voice." *Los Angeles Times*, January 26, pp. A1, A20.

Karides, Marina. 2010. "Theorizing the Rise of Microenterprise Development in Caribbean Context." *Journal of World-Systems Research* 16 (2):192–216.

Katovich, Michael A. 1987. Correspondence. June 1.

Katz, Michael. 1971. *Class, Bureaucracy, and the Schools: The Illusion of Educational Change in America*. New York: Praeger.

Kaufman, Sarah. 2006. "The Criminalization of New Orleanians in Katrina's Wake." Accessed April 4 (www.ssrc.org).

Kavada, Anastasia. 2005. "Exploring the Role of the Interest in the 'Movement for Alternative Globalization': The Case of the Paris 2003 European Social Forum." *Westminster Papers in Communication and Culture* 2 (1):72–95.

Keeter, Scott, and Courtney Kennedy. 2006. "The Cell Phone Challenge to Survey Research." Washington, DC: Pew Research Center.

Kelleher, Jennifer Sinco. 2011. "23 Arrested for Refusing to Leave Iolani Palace." *News from Indian Country*, November, p. 5.

Kennickell, Arthur B. 2009. *Ponds and Streams: Wealth and Income in the U.S., 1989 to 2007*. Washington, DC: Federal Reserve Board.

Kennicott, Philip. 2011. "Review: 9/11 Memorial in New York." Accessed August 26 (www.washingtonpost.com).

Kenny, Charles. 2009. "Revolution in a Box." *Foreign Policy* (November):68–74.

Kentor, Jeffrey, and Yong Suk Jang. 2004. "Yes, There Is a (Growing) Transnational Business Community." *International Sociology* 19 (September):355–368.

Kerbo, Harold R. 2006. *World Poverty: The Roots of Global Inequality and the World System*. New York: McGraw-Hill.

———. 2012. *Social Stratification and Inequality*. 8th ed. New York: McGraw-Hill.

Kesmodel, David, and Danny Yadron. 2010. "E-Cigarettes Spark New Smoking War." *Wall Street Journal*, August 25, pp. A1, A12.

Killian, Caitlin. 2003. "The Other Side of the Veil: North Africa Women in France Respond to the Headscarf Affair." *Gender and Society* (August 17):576–590.

Kim, Hyun Sik. 2011. "Consequences of Parental Divorce for Child Development." *American Sociological Review* 76 (3):487–511.

Kim, Kwang Chung. 1999. *Koreans in the Hood: Conflict with African Americans*. Baltimore: Johns Hopkins University Press.

Kimmel, Michael S. 2006. "A War against Boys?" *Dissent* (Fall):65–70.

———. 2008. *The Gendered Society*. 3rd ed. New York: State University of New York at Stony Brook.

King, Gary. 2011. "Ensuring the Data-Rich Future of the Social Sciences." *Science* (February 11):719–721.

King, Leslie. 1998. "France Needs Children: Pronatalism, Nationalism, and Women's Equity." *Sociological Quarterly* 39 (Winter):33–52.

King, Meredith L. 2007. *Immigrants in the U.S. Health Care System*. Washington, DC: Center for American Progress.

Kingsbury, Alex. 2008. "Q and A: Sudhir Venkatesh." *US News and World Report*, January 21, p. 14.

Kinsey, Alfred C., Wardell B. Pomeroy, and Paul H. Gebhard. 1953. *Sexual Behavior in the Human Female*. Philadelphia: Saunders.

———, ———, and Clyde E. Martin. 1948. *Sexual Behavior in the Human Male*. Philadelphia: Saunders.

Kiper, Dmitry. 2008. "GodTube.com Puts Christian Worship Online." *Christian Science Monitor*, February 6.

Kiser, Edgar. 1992. "War." Pp. 2243–2247 in *Encyclopedia of Sociology*, edited by Edgar F. Borgatta and Marie L. Borgatta. New York: Macmillan.

Kitchener, Richard F. 1991. "Jean Piaget: The Unknown Sociologist." *British Journal of Sociology* 42 (September):421–442.

Klass, Perri. 2003. "This Side of Medicine." P. 319 in *This Side of Doctoring Reflection for Women in Medicine*, edited by Eliza Lo Chin. New York: Oxford University Press.

Klein, Naomi. 1999. *No Logo: Money, Marketing, and the Growing Anti-Corporate Movement*. New York: Picador (St. Martin's Press).

Kleiner, Art. 2003. "Are You In with the In Crowd?" *Harvard Business Review* 81 (July):86–92.

Kleinknecht, William. 1996. *The New Ethnic Mobs: The Changing Face of Organized Crime in America*. New York: Free Press.

Klinenberg, Eric. 2012. *Going Solo: The Extraordinary Rise and Surprising Appeal of Living Alone.* New York: Penguin Press.

Kneebone, Elizabeth, Carey Nadeau, and Alan Berube. 2011. *The Re-Emergence of Concentrated Poverty Metropolitan Trends in the 2000s.* Washington, DC: Metropolitan Policy Program at Brookings.

Knudsen, Morten. 2010. "Surprised by Method— Functional Method and System Theory." *Forum: Qualitative Social Research* 11 (September): article 12.

Kochhar, Rakesh. 2006. "Growth in the Foreign-Born Workforce and Employment of the Native Born." Washington, DC: Pew Hispanic Center.

———. 2008. *Latino Workers in the Ongoing Recession: 2007–2008.* Washington, DC: Pew Hispanic Center.

Kohut, Andrew, et al. 2005. *American Character Gets Mixed Reviews: 16-Nation Pew Global Attitudes Survey.* Washington, DC: Pew Global Project Attitudes.

———, et al. 2007. *Global Unease with Major World Powers: Rising Environmental Concern in 47-Nation Survey.* Washington, DC: Pew Global Project Attitudes.

Kokmen, Leyla. 2008. "Environmental Justice for All." *Utne Reader* (March–April):42–46.

Korean Women's Association United. 2010. "Republic of Korea: Critical Issues on the Seventh Periodical Report on the Convention on the Elimination of All Forms of Discrimination against Women." November 10. Accessed March 27, 2010 (www2.ohchr.org/English/bodies/ cedaw/docs/ngos/Korean_Womens_Association_United(PSWG).pdf).

Kornblum, Janet. 2007. "Meet the 'Tech-No's': People Who Reject Plugging into the Highly Wired World." *USA Today,* January 11, pp. A1, A2.

Korzeniewicz, Roberto Patricio, and Timothy Patrick Moran. 2009. *Unveiling Inequality: A World Historical Perspective.* New York: Russell Sage Foundation.

Kosmin, Barry A., and Ariela Keysar. 2009. *American Religious Identification Survey.* Hartford, CT: Trinity College.

Kottak, Conrad. 2011. *Anthropology: Appreciating Human Diversity.* 14th ed. New York: McGraw-Hill.

Krane, Jim. 2009. *Dubai: The Story of the World's City.* London: Atlantic Books.

———. 2010. "To Spend or Not to Spend." Interviewed on Al Jazeera television, March 26. Accessed April 20 (http://english.aljazeera. net/ programmes/countingthecost/2010/03/ 201032510494187263.html).

Kraybill, Donald. 2001. *The Riddle of Amish Culture.* Rev. ed. Baltimore: Johns Hopkins University Press.

Kreider, Rose M. 2010. "Increase in Opposite-Sex Cohabiting Couples from 2009 to 2010 in the Annual Social and Economic Supplement (AEFC) to the Current Population Survey (CPS)." Working Paper. Washington, DC: U.S. Bureau of the Census.

———. 2011. "Contexts of Racial Socialization: Are Transracial Adoptive Families More Like Multiracial or White Monoracial Families?" March 1. Accessible at www.census.gov.

———, and Renee Ellis. 2011. "Living Arrangements of Children: 2009." *Current Population Reports,* ser. P70, no. 126. Washington, DC: U.S. Government Printing Office.

Kriesberg, Louis. 1992. "Peace." Pp. 1432–1436 in *Encyclopedia of Sociology,* edited by Edgar F. Borgatta and Marie L. Borgatta. New York: Macmillan.

Kristof, Nicholas D. 1998. "As Asian Economies Shrink, Women Are Squeezed Out." *New York Times,* June 11, pp. A1, A12.

Kroll, Luisa, and Kerry A. Dolan. 2012. "The Billionaires Issue." *Forbes* 189 (March 26):49–62.

Kronstadt, Jessica. 2008a. "Genetics and Economic Mobility." Washington, DC: Economic Mobility Project. Also accessible at www .economicmobility.org/reports_and_research/ literature_reviews?id=0004.

———, and Melissa Favreault. 2008. "Families and Economic Mobility." Washington, DC: Economic Mobility Project. Also accessible at www .economicmobility.org/reports_and_research/ literature_reviews?id=0004.

Kwong, Jo. 2005. "Globalization's Effects on the Environment." *Society* 42 (January– February): 21–28.

Ladner, Joyce. 1973. *The Death of White Sociology.* New York: Random Books.

Landler, Mark, and Michael Barbaro. 2006. "No, Not Always." *New York Times,* August 2, pp. C1, C4.

———, and David E. Sanger. 2009. "World Leaders Pledge $1.1 Trillion to Tackle Crisis." *New York Times,* April 3, pp. A1, A11.

Landtman, Gunnar. [1938] 1968. *The Origin of Inequality of the Social Class.* New York: Greenwood (original edition 1938, Chicago: University of Chicago Press).

Lansprey, Susan. 1995. "AAAs and 'Naturally Occurring Retirement Communities' (NORCs)." Accessed August 4, 2003 (www.aoa.gov/housing/norcs.html).

Lasswell, Harold D. 1936. *Politics: Who Gets What, When, How.* New York: McGraw-Hill.

Lau, Yvonne M. 2006. "Re-Visioning Filipino American Communities: Evolving Identities, Issues, and Organizations." Pp. 141–153 in *The New Chicago,* edited by John Koval et al. Philadelphia: Temple University Press.

Lauer, Robert H. 1982. *Perspectives on Social Change.* 3rd ed. Boston: Allyn and Bacon.

Laumann, Edward O., John H. Gagnon, and Robert T. Michael. 1994a. "A Political History of the National Sex Survey of Adults." *Family Planning Perspectives* 26 (February):34–38.

———, ———, ———, and Stuart Michaels. 1994b. *The Social Organization of Sexuality: Sexual Practices in the United States.* Chicago: University of Chicago Press.

Lavrakas, Paul J., Charles D. Shuttles, Charlotte Steel, and Howard Fienberg. 2007. "The State of Surveying Cell Phone Numbers in the United States: 2007 and Beyond." *Public Opinion Quarterly* 71 (5):840–854.

Lawler, Kristen. 2011. "Fear of a Slacker Revolution Futures: A Project of the Social Science Research Project." December 1. Accessed January 26, 2012 (www.possible-futures.org/2011/12/01/fear -slacker-revolution-occupy-wall-street-cultural -politics-class-struggle/).

Lawson, Sandra. 2008. *Girls Count.* New York: Goldman Sachs.

Lazarsfeld, Paul, Bernard Beretson, and H. Gaudet. 1948. *The People's Choice.* New York: Columbia University Press.

———, and Robert K. Merton. 1948. "Mass Communication, Popular Taste, and Organized Social Action." Pp. 95–118 in *The Communication of Ideas,* edited by Lymon Bryson. New York: Harper and Brothers.

Leavell, Hugh R., and E. Gurney Clark. 1965. *Preventive Medicine for the Doctor in His Community: An Epidemiologic Approach.* 3rd ed. New York: McGraw-Hill.

Lee, Alfred McClung. 1983. *Terrorism in Northern Ireland.* Bayside, NY: General Hall.

Lehman, Chris. 2012. "Retirement Communities Find Niche with Gay Seniors." February 16. Accessible at http://www.wbur.org/ npr/146713531/retirement-communities-find=niche-with-gay-seniors.

Lehne, Gregory K. 1995. "Homophobia among Men: Supporting and Defining the Male Role." Pp. 325–336 in *Men's Lives,* edited by Michael S. Kimmel and Michael S. Messner. Boston: Allyn and Bacon.

Lengermann, Patricia Madoo, and Jill Niebrugge-Brantley. 1998. *The Women Founders: Sociology and Social Theory, 1830–1930.* Boston: McGraw-Hill.

Lenhart, Amanda. 2009. "Pew Internet Project Data Memo: Adults and Social Network Websites." Accessible at www.pewinternet.org/PPF/r/272/ report_display.asp.

———, Mary Madden, Aaron Smith, Kristen Purcell, Kathryn Zickuhr, and Lee Rainie. 2011. *Teens, Kindness, and Cruelty on Social Network Sites.* Washington, DC: Pew Research Center's Internet and American Life Project.

Lenski, Gerhard. 1966. *Power and Privilege: A Theory of Social Stratification.* New York: McGraw-Hill.

Leonhardt, David. 2004. "As Wealthy Fill Top Colleges Concerns Grow over Fairness." *New York Times,* April 22, pp. A1, A12.

Levine, Nancy. 1988. *The Dynamics of Polyandry: Kinship, Domesticity, and Population on the Tibetan Border.* Chicago: University of Chicago Press.

Levinson, Daniel J. 1978. *The Seasons of a Man's Life.* With Charlotte N. Darrow et al. New York: Knopf.

———. 1996. *The Seasons of a Woman's Life.* With Judy D. Levinson. New York: Knopf.

Levitt, Peggy, and B. Nadya Jaworsky. 2007. "Transnational Migration Studies: Past Developments and Future Trends." *Annual Review of Sociology* 33:129–156.

Levitt, Steven D., and Stephen J. Dubner. 2006. *Freakonomics: A Rogue Economist Explores the Hidden Side of Everything.* Revised and expanded edition. New York: Morrow.

———, and Sudhir Venkatesh. 2000. "An Economic Analysis of a Drug-Selling Gang's Finances." *Quarterly Journal of Economics* (August):775–789.

Lewin, Tamar. 2011. "College Graduates' Debt Grew, Yet Again, in 2010." *New York Times,* November 3, p. A20.

Lichtblau, Eric. 2009. "Telecom Companies Win Dismissal of Wiretap Suits." *New York Times,* June 4, p. A14.

Light, Donald W. 2004. "Dreams of Success: A New History of the American Health Care System." *Journal of Health and Social Behavior* 45 (Extra issue):1–24.

Lim, Louisa. 2007. "Digital Culture: China's 'Gold Farmers' Play a Grim Game." May 14, 2007 broadcast on NPR. Accessible at www.npr.org.

Lindner, Eileen W. 2012. *Yearbook of American and Canadian Churches, 2012.* Nashville: Abingdon Press.

Link, Michael W., Ali H. Mokad, Herbert F. Stockhouse, and Nicole T. Flowers. 2006. "Race, Ethnicity, and Linguistic Isolation as Determinants of Participation in Public Heath Surveillance Surveys." *Presenting Chronic Disease* 3 (January).

Linn, Susan, and Alvin F. Poussaint. 1999. "Watching Television: What Are Children Learning about Race and Ethnicity?" *Child Care Information Exchange* 128 (July):50–52.

Lino, Mark. 2011. *Expenditures on Children by Families, 2011.* Washington, DC: U.S. Department of Agriculture, Center for Nutrition Policy and Promotion.

Lipka, Sara. 2009. "Do Crime Statistics Keep Students Safe?" *Chronicle of Higher Education* 55 (January 30):A15–A17.

Lipson, Karen. 1994. "'Nell' Not Alone in the Wilds." *Los Angeles Times,* December 19, pp. F1, F6.

Liptak, Adam. 2006. "The Ads Discriminate, but Does the Web?" *New York Times,* March 5, p. 16.

———. 2008. "From One Footnote, a Debate over the Tangles of Law, Science and Money." *New York Times,* November 25, p. A13.

———. 2010. "Study Finds Questioning of Nominees to Be Useful." *New York Times,* June 28, pp. A10, A11.

Liska, Allen E., and Steven F. Messner. 1999. *Perspectives on Crime and Deviance.* 3rd ed. Upper Saddle River, NJ: Prentice Hall.

Livingstone, Sonia. 2004. "The Challenge of Changing Audiences." *European Journal of Communication* 19 (March):75–86.

Llana, Sara Miller. 2009. "Mexico: Safety Comes in Park Taxes." December 24. Accessible at www.csmonitor.com.

Lo Sasso, Anthony T., Michael R. Richards, Chiu-Fang Chou, and Susan E. Gerber. 2011. "The $16,819 Pay Gap for Newly Trained Physicians: The Unexplained Trend of Men Earning More Than Women." *Health Affairs* 30 (February):193–201.

Loeb, Susanna, Bruce Fuller, Sharon Lynn Kagan, and Bidemi Carrol. 2004. "Child Care in Poor Communities: Early Learning Effects of Type, Quality, and Stability." *Child Development* 75 (January–February):47–65.

Lofland, Lyn H. 1975. "The 'Thereness' of Women: A Selective Review of Urban Sociology." Pp. 144–170 in *Another Voice,* edited by M. Millman and R. M. Kanter. New York: Anchor/Doubleday.

Lofquist, Daphne. 2011. *Same-Sex Couple Households.* ACSBR/10-03. Washington, DC: U.S. Government Printing Office.

———, Terry Lugaila, Martin O'Connell, and Sarah Feliz. 2012. "Households and Families: 2010. C2010BR-14." Accessible at www.census.gov/newsroom/releases/archives/1020_census/cb12-68.html.

Logan, John. R. 2011. *Separate and Unequal: The Neighborhood Gap for Blacks, Hispanics and Asians in Metropolitan America.* Providence RI: American Communities Project of Brown University and Russell Sage Foundation.

———, Richard D. Alba, and Werquan Zhang. 2002. "Immigrant Enclaves and Ethnic Communities in New York and Los Angeles." *American Sociological Review* 67 (April):299–322.

Long, Sharon K., and Paul B. Masi. 2009. *Access to and Affordability of Care in Massachusetts as of Fall 2008: Geographic and Racial/Ethnic Differences.* Washington, DC: Urban Institute.

Longhofer, Wesley, and Evan Schofer. 2010. "National and Global Origins of Environmental Association." *American Sociological Review* 75 (4):505–533.

Lopez, Mark Hugo. 2011. *The Latino Electorate in 2010: More Voters, More Non-Voters.* Washington, DC: Pew Hispanic Center.

Lorber, Judith. 2005. *Breaking the Bowls: Degendering and Feminist Change.* New York: Norton.

Lubienski, Christopher A., and Peter C. Weitzel. 2012. *The Charter School Experiment Expectations, Evidence, and Implications.* Cambridge MA: Harvard Education Press.

Ludwig, Jens, and Isabell Sawhill. 2007. *Success by Ten: Interviewing Early, Often, and Efficiently in the Education of Young Children.* Washington, DC: Brookings Institution.

Lukacs, Georg. 1923. *History and Class Consciousness.* London: Merlin.

Lundquist, Jennifer Hickes. 2006. "Choosing Single Motherhood." *Contexts* 5 (Fall):64–67.

Luster, Tom, Kelly Rhoades, and Bruce Haas. 1989. "The Relation between Parental Values and Parenting Behavior: A Test of the Kohn Hypothesis." *Journal of Marriage and the Family* 51 (February):139–147.

Luttinger, Nina, and Gregory Dicum. 2006. *The Coffee Book: Anatomy of an Industry from Crop to the Last Drop.* Revised and updated. New York: New Press.

Lyall, Sarah. 2002. "For Europeans, Love, Yes; Marriage, Maybe." *New York Times,* March 24, pp. 1–8.

Lynas, Mark. 2008. *Six Degrees: Our Future on a Hotter Planet.* Washington, DC: National Geographic.

Lynn, Barry C. 2003. "Trading with a Low-Wage Tiger." *American Prospect* 14 (February):10–12.

m

MacDonald, G. Jeffrey. 2007. "Go in Search of a Church by Way of the Web." *USA Today,* October 17, p. D8.

MacDorman, Marian F., and T. J. Mathews. 2009. *Behind International Rankings of Infant Mortality: How the United States Compares with Europe.* NCHS Date Brief (No. 23, November).

MacFarquhar, Neil. 2008. "Resolute or Fearful, Many Muslims Turn to Home Schooling." *New York Times,* March 26, p. A1.

Mach, Annie, and Laura Blumenthal. 2010. "Health Insurance Coverage of Children under 19: 2008 and 2009." 2009–2011 Census Brief BR-09–11. Accessible at http://www.census.gov/prod/2010pubs/acsbr09-11.pdf.

Machalek, Richard, and Michael W. Martin. 2010. "Evolution, Biology and Society: A Conversation for the 21st-Century Sociology Classroom." *Teaching Sociology* 38 (1):35–45.

Mack, Mick G. 2003. "Does Exercise Status Influence the Impressions Formed by College Students?" *College Student Journal* 37 (December).

Mack, Raymond W., and Calvin P. Bradford. 1979. *Transforming America: Patterns of Social Change.* 2nd ed. New York: Random House.

MacLeod, Calum. 2010. "Chinese Use Internet to Show Dissent." *USA Today,* December 29, p. 31.

Maestretti, Danielle. 2009. "Information Overload." *Utne Reader* (July-August) pp. 22–23.

Magga, Ole Henrik. 2006. "Diversity in Sami Terminology for Reindeer, Snow, and Ice." *International Social Science Journal* 58 (March):25–34.

Magnier, Mark. 2004. "China Clamps Down on Web News Discussion." *Los Angeles Times,* February 26, p. A4.

Malaby, Thomas M. 2009. *Making Virtual Worlds: Linden Lab and Second Life.* Ithaca, NY: Cornell University.

Malcolm X, with Alex Haley. [1964] 1999. *The Autobiography of Malcolm X.* Revised with Epilogue by Alex Haley and Afterword by Ossie Davis. New York: One World, Ballantine Books.

Males, Mike, and Meda-Chesney Lind. 2010. "The Myth of Mean Girls." *New York Times,* April 2, p. A21.

Malhotra, Neil, and Yotam Margalit. 2009. "State of the Nation: Anti-Semitism and the Economic Crisis." *Boston Review* (May–June). Accessible at http://bostonreview.net/BR34.3/malhotra_margalit.php.

Marable, Manning. 2011. *Malcolm X: A Life of Reinvention.* New York: Viking.

Margolis, Mac. 2009. "The Land of Less Contrast: How Brazil Reined in Inequality." *Newsweek,* November 28.

Markson, Elizabeth W. 1992. "Moral Dilemmas." *Society* 29 (July/August):4–6.

Marosi, Richard. 2007. "The Nation: A Once-Porous Border Is a Turning-Back Point." *Los Angeles Times,* March 21, pp. A1, A20.

Martin, Dominique, Jean-Luc Metzger, and Philippe Pierre. 2006. "The Sociology of Globalization:

Theoretical and Methodological Reflections." *International Sociology* 21 (July):499–521.

Martin, Joyce A., Brady E. Hamilton, Paul D. Sutton, Stephanie J. Ventura, Fay Menacker, Sharon Kirmeyer, and T. J. Mathews. 2009. "Births: Final Data for 2006." *National Vital Statistics Reports* 57 (January 7).

Martin, Karin A. 2009. "Normalizing Heterosexuality: Mothers' Assumptions, Talk, and Strategies with Young Children." *American Sociological Review* 74 (April):190–207.

Martin, Marvin. 1996. "Sociology Adapting to Changes." *Chicago Tribune,* July 21, sec. 18, p. 20.

Martin, Susan E. 1994. "Outsider within the Station House: The Impact of Race and Gender on Black Women Politics." *Social Problems* 41 (August):383–400.

Martineau, Harriet. [1837] 1962. *Society in America.* Edited, abridged, with an introductory essay by Seymour Martin Lipset. Reprint. Garden City, NY: Doubleday.

———. [1838] 1989. *How to Observe Morals and Manners.* Philadelphia: Leal and Blanchard. Sesquentennial edition, edited by M. R. Hill, Transaction Books.

Martinez, Elizabeth. 1993. "Going Gentle into That Good Night: Is a Rightful Death a Feminist Issue?" *Ms.* 4 (July/August):65–69.

Marubbio, M. Elise. 2006. *Killing the Indian Maiden: Images of Native American Women in Film.* Lexington: University Press of Kentucky.

Marx, Earl. 2009. "How Will Fair Fare?" *Christian Science Monitor,* April 19, pp. 30–31.

Marx, Karl. [1844] 1964. "Contribution to the Critique of Hegel's Philosophy of Right." In *On Religion, Karl Marx and Friedrich Engels.* New York: Schocker Books.

———, and Friedrich Engels. [1847] 1955. *Selected Work in Two Volumes.* Reprint. Moscow: Foreign Languages Publishing House.

Maryanski, Alexandra R. 2004. "Evaluation Theory." Pp. 257–263 in *Encyclopedia of Social Theory,* edited by George Ritzer. Thousand Oaks, CA: Sage.

Massey, Douglas S. 1998. "March of Folly: U.S. Immigration Policy after NAFTA." *American Prospect* (March–April):22–23.

———. 2007. *Categorically Unequal: The American Stratification System.* New York: Russell Sage Foundation.

———. 2008. "A Mexican Apartheid." Pp. 55–57, vol. 2, in *Encyclopedia of Race, Ethnicity, and Society,* edited by Richard T. Schaefer. Thousand Oaks CA: Sage.

———, and Nancy A. Denton. 1993. *American Apartheid: Segregation and the Making of the Underclass.* Cambridge, MA: Harvard University Press.

———, and Margarita Mooney. 2007. "The Effects of America's Three Affirmative Action Programs on Academic Performance." *Social Problems* 54 (1):99–117.

Masuda, Takahiko, Phoebe C. Ellsworth, Batja Mesquita, Janxin Leu, Shigehito Tanida, and Ellen Van de Veerdonk. 2008. "Attitudes and Social Cognition: Placing the Face in Context: Cultural Differences in the Perception of Facial Emotion."

Journal of Personality and Social Psychology 94 (3):365–381.

Masud-Piloto, Felix. 2008. "Cuban Americans." Pp. 357–359, vol. 1, in *Encyclopedia of Race, Ethnicity, and Society,* edited by Richard T. Schaefer. Thousand Oaks, CA: Sage.

Mathews, T. J., and Marian MacDorman. 2011. "Infant Mortality Statistics." *National Vital Statistics Reports* 59 (6).

Maylie, Devon. 2011. "Wal-Mart's Africa Foothold Shaky as Job Worries Mount." *Wall Street Journal,* May 10, p. 5.

Mazumder, Bhashkar. 2008. *Upward Intergenerational Economic Mobility in the United States.* Washington, DC: Economic Mobility Project.

McChesney, Robert W. 2008. *The Political Economy of Media: Enduring Issues, Emerging Dilemmas.* New York: Monthly Review Press.

McCormack, Mark. 2010. "Changing Masculinities in Youth Cultures." *Qualitative Sociology* 33:111–115.

McDonald, Michael P. 2009b. "2008 Current Population Survey Voting and Registration Supplement." Accessed April 16 (http://elections.gmu.edu/CPS_2008.html).

McDowell, Linda, Adina Batnitzky, and Sarah Dyer. 2009. "Precarious Work and Economic Migration: Emerging Immigrant Divisions of Labor in Greater London's Service Sector." *International Journal of Urban and Regional Research* 31 (March):3–25.

McFarland, Andrew S. 2007. "Neopluralism." *Annual Review of Political Science* 10:45–66.

McGirk, Tim. 2009. "Postcard: Dubai." *Time,* October 19, p. 6.

McGlynn, Clare, and Vanessa E. Munro (eds.) 2010. *Rethinking Rape Law: International and Comparative Perspective.* London: Routledge-Cavendish.

McGue, Matt, and Thomas J. Bouchard, Jr. 1998. "Genetic and Environmental Influence on Human Behavioral Differences." Pp. 1–24 in *Annual Review of Neurosciences.* Palo Alto, CA: Annual Reviews.

McGurty, Eileen Maura. 2000. "Warren County, NC, and the Emergence of the Environmental Justice Movement: Unlikely Coalitions and Shared Meanings in Local Collective Action." *Society and Natural Resources* 13:373–387.

McIntosh, Peggy. 1988. "White Privilege and Male Privilege: A Personal Account of Coming to See Correspondence through Work and Women's Studies." Working Paper No. 189, Wellesley College Center for Research on Women, Wellesley, MA.

McKinlay, John B., and Sonja M. McKinlay. 1977. "The Questionable Contribution of Medical Measures to the Decline of Mortality in the United States in the Twentieth Century." *Milbank Memorial Fund Quarterly* 55 (Summer):405–428.

McKinley, Jesse. 2012. "Ruling Extends Sex-Discrimination Protection to Transgender Women Denied Federal Jobs." *New York Times,* April 25, p. A14.

McLanahan, Sara, and Christine Percheski. 2008. "Family Structure and the Reproduction of Inequalities." *Annual Review of Sociology* 38:257–276.

McLuhan, Marshall. 1964. *Understanding Media: The Extensions of Man.* New York: New American Library.

———. 1967. *The Medium Is the Message: An Inventory of Effects.* New York: Bantam Books.

McNeil, Donald G., Jr. 2002. "W.H.O. Moves to Make AIDS Drugs More Accessible to Poor Worldwide." *New York Times,* August 23, p. D7.

———. 2004. "When Real Food Isn't an Option." *New York Times,* September 3, pp. A1, A5.

Mead, George H. 1934. In *Mind, Self and Society,* edited by Charles W. Morris. Chicago: University of Chicago Press.

———. 1964a. In *On Social Psychology,* edited by Anselm Strauss. Chicago: University of Chicago Press.

———. 1964b. "The Genesis of the Self and Social Control." Pp. 267–293 in *Selected Writings: George Herbert Mead,* edited by Andrew J. Reck. Indianapolis: Bobbs-Merrill.

Mead, Margaret. [1935] 2001. *Sex and Temperament in Three Primitive Societies.* New York: Perennial, HarperCollins.

Mehl, Matthias R., Simine Vazire, Nairán Ramírez-Esparza, Richard B. Slatcher, and James W. Pennebaker. 2007. "Are Women Really More Talkative than Men?" *Science* 317 (July 6):82.

Mendez, Jennifer Bickman. 1998. "Of Mops and Maids: Contradictions and Continuities in Bureaucratized Domestic Work." *Social Problems* 45 (February):114–135.

Merton, Robert. 1948. "The Bearing of Empirical Research upon the Development of Social Theory." *American Sociological Review* 13 (October):505–515.

———. 1968. *Social Theory and Social Structure.* New York Free Press.

———, and Alice S. Kitt. 1950. "Contributions to the Theory of Reference Group Behavior." Pp. 40–105 in *Continuities in Social Research: Studies in the Scope and Methods of the American Soldier,* edited by Robert K. Merton and Paul L. Lazarsfeld. New York: Free Press.

Messner, Michael A. 2002. "Gender Equity in College Sports: 6 Views." *Chronicle of Higher Education* 49 (December 6):B9–B10.

———, and Cheryl Cooky. 2010. *Gender in Televised Sports: News and Highlights Shows, 1989–2009.* Los Angeles: Center for Feminist Research, University of Southern California.

Meston, Cindy M., and David M. Buss. 2007. "Why Humanoids Have Sex." *Archives of Sexual Behavior* 36 (August).

Michals, Jennifer M. 2003. "The Price We Pay to Get Richer: A Look at Student Indebtedness." Unpublished M.A. paper, DePaul University, Chicago, IL.

Michels, Robert. 1915. *Political Parties.* Glencoe, IL: Free Press (reprinted 1949).

Microfinance Information Exchange. 2011. "MIX Market." Accessed May 24 (www.themix.org).

Migration News. 2012. "Remittance." *Migration News* (January).

Milgram, Stanley. 1963. "Behavioral Study of Obedience." *Journal of Abnormal and Social Psychology* 67 (October):371–378.

———. 1975. *Obedience to Authority: An Experimental View.* New York: Harper and Row.

Miller, David L., and JoAnne DeRoven Darlington. 2002. "Fearing for the Safety of Others: Disasters and the Small World Problem." Paper presented at Midwest Sociological Society, Milwaukee, WI.

Miller, Jacqueline W., Timothy S. Naimi, Robert D. Brewer, and Sherry Everett Jones. 2007. "Binge Drinking and Associated Health Risk Behaviors among High School Students." *Pediatrics* 119 (January):76–85.

Miller, Laura. 2008. "The Rise of the Superclass." Accessed in *Salon* May 2 (www.salon.com/books/review/2008/03/14/superclass/print .html).

Miller, Peter. 2012. "A Theory or Town About Twins." *National Geographic* (January).

Miller, Reuben. 1988. "The Literature of Terrorism." *Terrorism* 11 (1):63–87.

Mills, C. Wright. [1959] 2000a. *The Sociological Imagination.* 40th anniversary edition. New Afterword by Todd Gitlin. New York: Oxford University Press.

———. [1956] 2000b. *The Power Elite.* New edition. Afterword by Alan Wolfe. New York: Oxford University Press.

Miner, Horace. 1956. "Body Ritual among the Nacirema." *American Anthropologist* 58 (June): 503–507.

Minnesota Center for Twin and Family Research. 2012. "Research at the MCTFR." Accessed January 12 (http://mctfr.psych.umn.edu/research/).

Miyata, Kakuko, and Tetsuro Kobayashi. 2008. "Causal Relationship between Internet Use and Social Capital in Japan." *Asian Journal of Social Psychology* 11:42–52.

Mizruchi, Mark S. 1996. "What Do Interlocks Do? An Analysis, Critique, and Assessment of Research on Interlocking Directorates." Pp. 271–298 in *Annual Review of Sociology, 1996,* edited by John Hagan and Karen Cook. Palo Alto, CA: Annual Reviews.

Moeller, Philip. 2009. "Unique Havens for an Aging America." *US News and World Report* (October):62–68.

Moeller, Susan D. 1999. *Compassion Fatigue.* London: Routledge.

Mohai, Paul, David Pellow, and J. Timmons Roberts. 2009. "Environmental Justice." *Annual Review of Environmental Research* 34:405–430.

———, and Robin Saha. 2007. "Racial Inequality in the Distribution of Hazardous Waste: A National-Level Reassessment." *Social Problems* 54 (3):343–370.

Mol, A. J. 2010. "Ecological Modernization as a Social Theory of Environmental Reform." Pp. 63–71 in *The International Handbook of Environmental Sociology,* 2nd ed., edited by Michael R. Redcraft and Graham Woodgate. Cheltenham, UK: Edward Elgar.

———, and D. A. Sonnenfeld, eds. 2000. *Ecological Modernization around the World.* Portland, OR: Frank Cass.

———, ———, and G. Spaargaren, eds. 2009. *The Ecological Modernization Reader.* London: Routledge.

Molotch, Harvey. 1970. "Oil in Santa Barbara and Power in America." *Sociological Inquiry* 40 (Winter):131–144.

Monaghan, Peter. 1993. "Sociologist Jailed Because He 'Wouldn't Snitch' Ponders the Way Research Ought to Be Done." *Chronicle of Higher Education* 40 (September 1):A8, A9.

Monahan, Torin. 2011. "Surveillance as Cultural Practice." *The Sociological Quarterly* 52:495–508.

Moncarz, Roger J., Michael G. Wolf, and Benjamin Wright. 2008. "Service-Providing Occupations, Offshoring, and the Labor Market." *Monthly Labor Review* (December):71–86.

Montgomery, Marilyn J., and Gwendolyn T. Sorell. 1997. "Differences in Love Attitudes across Family Life Stages." *Family Relations* 46:55–61.

Moore, Molly. 2006. "Romance, but Not Marriage." *Washington Post National Weekly Edition,* November 27, p. 18.

Moore, Wilbert E. 1967. *Order and Change: Essays in Comparative Sociology.* New York: Wiley.

Morris, Aldon. 2000. "Reflections on Social Movement Theory: Criticisms and Proposals." *Contemporary Sociology* 29 (May):445–454.

Morrison, Denton E. 1971. "Some Notes toward Theory on Relative Deprivation, Social Movements, and Social Change." *American Behavioral Scientist* 14 (May–June):675–690.

Morrison, Peter A., and Thomas M. Bryan. 2010. "Targeting Spatial Centers of Elderly Consumers in the U.S.A." *Population Research Policy Review* 29:33–46.

Morse, Arthur D. 1967. *While Six Million Died: A Chronicle of American Apathy.* New York: Ace.

Moskos, Peter. 2008. *Cop in the Hood: My Year Policing Baltimore's Eastern District.* Princeton NJ: Princeton University Press.

Mosley, J., and E. Thomson. 1995. Pp. 148–165 in *Fatherhood: Contemporary Theory, Research and Social Policy,* edited by W. Marsiglo. Thousand Oaks, CA: Sage.

Mueller, G. O. 2001. "Transnational Crime: Definitions and Concepts." Pp. 13–21 in *Combating Transnational Crime: Concepts, Activities, and Responses,* edited by P. Williams and D. Vlassis. London: Franklin Cass.

Mufson, Steven. 2007. "Turning Down the Heat." *Washington Post National Weekly Edition* 24 (July):6–8.

Muñoz, José A. 2008. "Protest and Human Rights Networks: The Case of the Zapatista Movement." *Sociology Compass* (April):1045–1058.

Murdock, George P. 1945. "The Common Denominator of Cultures." Pp. 123–142 in *The Science of Man in the World Crisis,* edited by Ralph Linton. New York: Columbia University Press.

———. 1949. *Social Structure.* New York: Macmillan.

———. 1957. "World Ethnographic Sample." *American Anthropologist* 59 (August):664–687.

Murphy, Dean E. 1997. "A Victim of Sweden's Pursuit of Perfection." *Los Angeles Times,* September 2, pp. A1, A8.

Murray, Velma McBride, Amanda Willert, and Diane P. Stephens. 2001. "The Half-Full Glass: Resilient African American Single Mothers and Their Children." *Family Focus* (June):F4–F5.

Myers, Dowell, and John Pitkin. 2011. *Assimilation Tomorrow: How America's Immigrants Will Integrate by 2030.* Washington, DC: Centers for American Progress.

n

NAACP. 2008. *Out of Focus—Out of Sync Take 4.* Baltimore: NAACP.

NACCRRA (National Association of Child Care Resource and Referral Agencies). 2010. "Parents and the High Cost of Child Care: 2010 Update." Accessible at http://www.naccrra.org/docs/Cost_Report_073010-final.pdf.

Nakao, Keiko, and Judith Treas. 1994. "Updating Occupational Prestige and Socioeconomic Scores: How the New Measures Measure Up." *Sociological Methodology* 24:1–72.

NARAL Pro-Choice America. 2012. "Who Decides? Restrictions on Low-Income Women's Access to Abortion." Accessed February 22 (www .prochoiceamerica.org/what-is-choice/maps-and-charts/map.jsp?mapID=4).

Nash, Manning. 1962. "Race and the Ideology of Race." *Current Anthropology* 3 (June):285–288.

National Advisory Commission on Criminal Justice. 1976. *Organized Crime.* Washington, DC: U.S. Government Printing Office.

National Alliance for Caregiving. 2009. *Caregiving in the U.S.: Executive Summary.* Washington, DC: NAC and AARP.

National Alliance for Public Charter Schools. 2011. Number of Charter Schools 2009–2010 and 2010–2011. Communication to Schaefer from NAPCS. June 30.

———. 2012. "The Public Charter Schools Dashboard: Schools Overview 2011-2012 estimates." Accessed March 1 (http://dashboard.publiccharters.org/dashboard/schools/state/OR/year/2012).

National Center for Education Statistics. 2009. *Homeschooled Students.* Accessed May 31 (http://nces.ed.gov/programs/coe/2009/section1/indicator06.asp).

———. 2010. *Digest of Education Statistics 2009.* Accessible at http://nces.ed.gov/pubs2010/2010013.pdf.

———. 2011. *Average Undergraduate Tuition and Fees.* Accessed March 29 (http://nces.ed.gov/programs/digest/d09/tables/dt09_335.asp).

National Center on Addiction and Substance Abuse at Columbia University. 2007. *Wasting the Best and the Brightest: Substance Abuse at America's Colleges and Universities.* New York: NCASA at Columbia University.

National Conference of State Legislators. 2011. "Same-Sex Marriage, Civil Unions and Domestic Partnerships" and "Civil Unions & Domestic Partnership Statutes." Accessed March 21 (http://www.ncsl.org).

———. 2012a. "Voter Identification Requirements." Updated February 8. Accessed February 14 (www.ncsl.org/legislatures-elections/voter -id-state-requirements.aspx).

———. 2012b. "Defining Marriage: Defense of Marriage Acts and Same-Sex Marriage Laws." Accessed February 27 (www.ncsl.org/

issues-research/human-services/same-sex-marriage-overview .aspx).

National Education Association. 2009. *Rankings and Estimates: Rankings of the States 2009 and Estimates of School Statistics 2010.* Accessible at http://www.nea.org.assets/docs/010rankings.pdf.

National Gay and Lesbian Task Force. 2012. "Anti-Adoption Laws in the U.S." Accessed February 26 (http://thetaskforce.org/reports_and_research/adoption_laws).

National Geographic. 2005. *Atlas of the World.* 8th ed. Washington, DC: National Geographic.

National Institute of Justice. 2005. *Sexual Assault on Campus: What Colleges and Universities Are Doing about It.* Washington, DC: National Institute of Justice.

National Institute on Aging. 1999. *Early Retirement in the United States.* Washington, DC: U.S. Government Printing Office.

National Organization for Men Against Sexism. 2012. Home Page. Accessed February 22 (www .nomas.org).

Navarro, Mireya. 2005. "When You Contain Multitudes." *New York Times,* April 24, pp. 1, 2.

Needham, Paul. 2011. "9/11 Memorial Review: At Ground Zero, Staying Above Ground Matters." September 9. Accessible at www.huffingtonpost.com.

Negroni, Lirio K. 2012. "The Puerto Rican American Family." Pp. 129–147 in *Ethnic Families in America: Patterns and Variations.* 5th ed., edited by Roosevelt Wright, Jr., Charles H. Mindel, Thanh Van Tran, and Robert W. Halsenstein. Upper Saddle River, NJ: Pearson.

Nelson, Emily. 2004. "Goodbye, 'Friends'; Hello, New Reality." *Wall Street Journal,* February 9, pp. B6, B10.

Neuman, Lawrence W. 2009. *Understanding Research.* Boston: Allyn and Bacon.

New York Times. 2007. "University Officials Accused of Hiding Campus Homicide." June 24, p. 19.

———. 2011. "Welcome Rescinded." September 11, Section NY, p. 14.

Newman, Katherine S. 2012. *The Accordion Family: Boomerang Kids, Anxious Parents, and the Private Toll of Global Competition.* Boston: Beacon Press.

Newman, William M. 1973. *American Pluralism: A Study of Minority Groups and Social Theory.* New York: Harper and Row.

Newport, Frank. 2009. "Americans: Economy Takes Precedence Over Environment." Accessed April 27 at http://www.gallup.com/poll/116962/Americans-Economy-Takes-Precedence-Environment.aspx.

———. 2010b. *In U.S., Increasing Number Have No Religious Identity.* Accessed March 28, 2011 (www.gallup.com).

———. 2011a. "For First Time, Majority of Americans Favor Legal Gay Marriage." Accessed February 27, 2012 (www.gallup.com/poll/147662/First-Time-Majority-Americans-Favor-Legal-Gay-Marriage.aspx?version=print).

———. 2011b. "Record-High 50% of Americans Favor Legalizing Marijuana Use." October 17. Accessible at www.gallup.com.

Newsday. 1997. "Japan Sterilized 16,000 Women." September 18, p. A19.

———. 2008. "Law and Order." January 6, pp. 10–11.

NICHD. 2007. "Children Who Complete Intensive Early Childhood Program Show Gains in Adulthood: Greater College Attendance, Lower Crime and Depression." Accessed January 7, 2008 (www.nichd.nih.gov/news.releases/early_interventions_082107.cfm).

Nielsen Company. 2009. "The Nielsen Company's Guide to Super Bowl XLIII." Accessed February 7, 2010 (http://en-us.nielsen.com/main/news/news_releases/2009/january/the_nielsen_company0).

Nielsen, Joyce McCarl, Glenda Walden, and Charlotte A. Kunkel. 2000. "Gendered Heteronormativity: Empirical Illustrations in Everyday Life." *Sociological Quarterly* 41 (2):283–296.

Niemi, Richard G., and Michael J. Hanmer. 2010. "Voter Turnout among College Students: New Data and a Rethinking of Traditional Theories." *Social Science Quarterly* 91 (June):301–323.

Niesse, Mark. 2008. "Hawaiian Sovereignty Seekers Take Over Historic Iolani Palace in Honolulu." *News from Indian Country* (May 12):3.

———. 2011. "Native Hawaiian Self-Government May Be Set Up by State." *News from Indian Country* (March):3.

Niezen, Ronald. 2005. "Digital Identity: The Construction of Virtual Selfhood in the Indigenous Peoples' Movement." *Comparative Studies in Society and History* 47 (3):532–551.

Nixon, Darren. 2009. "'I Can't Put a Smiley Face On': Working-Class Masculinity, Emotional Labor and Service Work in the 'New Economy.'" *Gender, Work and Organization* 16 (3):300–322.

Noam, Eli. 2009. *Media Ownership and Concentration in America.* Cambridge, MA: Oxford University Press.

Nolan, Patrick, and Gerhard Lenski. 2009. *Human Societies: An Introduction to Macrosociology.* 11th ed. Boulder, CO: Paradigm.

Noonan, Rita K. 1995. "Women against the State: Political Opportunities and Collective Action Frames in Chile's Transition to Democracy." *Sociological Forum* 10:81–111.

Nordhaus, Ted, and Michael Shellenberger. 2007. *Break Through: From the Death of Environmentalism to the Politics of Possibility.* Boston: Houghton Mifflin.

Nordholt, Eric Schulte, Marijke Hartgers, and Rita Gircour, eds. 2004. "The Dutch Virtual Census of 2001." *Analysis and Methodology.* Voorburg: Statistics Netherlands.

NORML. 2012. "State Laws." Accessed June 1 (http://norml.org/laws).

Norris, Floyd. 2012. "The Number of Those Working Past 65 Is at a Record High." *New York Times,* May 19, p. B3.

Norris, Poppa, and Ronald Inglehart. 2004. *Sacred and Secular: Religion and Politics Worldwide.* Cambridge: Cambridge University Press.

North Carolina Department of Environmental and Natural Resources. 2008. "Warren County PCB Landfill Fact Sheet." Accessed April 9 (www .wastenotnc.org/WarrenCo_Fact_Sheet.htm).

O

Oberschall, Anthony. 1973. *Social Conflict and Social Movements.* Englewood Cliffs, NJ: Prentice Hall.

O'Connor, Anne-Marie. 2004. "Time of Blogs and Bombs." *Los Angeles Times,* December 27, pp. E1, E14–E15.

O'Donnell, Mike. 1992. *A New Introduction to Sociology.* Walton-on-Thames, UK: Thomas Nelson and Sons.

Office of Immigration Statistics. 2011. "Yearbook of Immigration Statistics: 2010." Accessible at www .dhs.gov/files/statistics/publications/LPR10.shtm.

Office of the United States Trade Representative. 2012. "Benefits of Trade." Accessed January 29 (www.ustr.gov/about-us/benefits-trade).

Ogas, Ogi, and Sai Gaddam. 2011. *A Billion Wicked Thoughts: What the World's Largest Experiment Reveals about Human Desire.* New York: Dutton.

Ogburn, William F. 1922. *Social Change with Respect to Culture and Original Nature.* New York: Huebsch (reprinted 1966, New York: Dell).

———, and Clark Tibbits. 1934. "The Family and Its Functions." Pp. 661–708 in *Recent Social Trends in the United States,* edited by Research Committee on Social Trends. New York: McGraw-Hill.

O'Harrow, Jr., Robert. 2005. "Mining Personal Data." *Washington Post National Weekly Edition,* February 6, pp. 8–10.

Okano, Kaori, and Motonori Tsuchiya. 1999. *Education in Contemporary Japan: Inequality and Diversity.* Cambridge: Cambridge University Press.

Okun, Barbara and Joseph Nowinski. 2011. *Saying Goodbye: How Families Can Find Renewal Through Loss.* Cambridge MA: Harvard Health Publications.

Oldenburg, Ray. 1999. *The Great Good Place Cafes, Coffee Shops, Bookstores, Bar, Hair Salons, and Other Hangouts at the Heart of a Community.* New York: Paragon House.

———. 2000. *Celebrating the Third Place: Inspiring Stories about the 'Great Good Places' at the Heart of Our Communities.* Marlowe and Company.

Oliver, Melvin L., and Thomas M. Shapiro. 2006. *Black Wealth/White Wealth: New Perspectives on Racial Inequality.* 2nd ed. New York: Routledge.

Omi, Michael, and Howard Winant. 1994. *Racial Formation in the United States.* 2nd ed. New York: Routledge.

Onishi, Norimitso. 2003. "Divorce in South Korea: Striking a New Attitude." *New York Times,* September 21, p. 19.

Orfield, Gary, and Chungmei Lee. 2007. *Historic Reversals, Accelerating Resegregation, and the Need for New Integration Strategies.* Los Angeles: Civil Rights Project, UCLA.

Organisation for Economic Co-operation and Development. 2008. *Growing Unequal? Income Distribution and Poverty in OECD Countries.* Geneva: OECD.

———. 2009b. "Green at Fifteen? How 15-Year-Olds Perform in Environmental Sciences and Geosciences in PISA 2006." PISA, OECD Publishing. Accessible at http://dx.doi.org/10.1787/9789264063600-en.

———. 2011. *Statistics on Resource Flows to Developing Countries.* Geneva: OECD. Accessible at http://www.oecd.org/dataoecd/53/43/47137659.pdf.

———. 2012a. "Poverty Rate After Taxes and Transfers from OECD." Stat extracts accessed January 20, 2012 (http://stats.oecd.org/Index.aspx?DataSetCode=Poverty).

———.2012b. "Gender Equality and Social Institutions in Afghanistan." Accessed February 22 (http://genderindex.org/country/Afghanistan).

———. 2012c. "Education at a Glance 2011: OECD Indicators." Accessible at www.oecd-ilibrary.org/education/education-at-a-glance-2011/how-many-students-finish-tertiary-education_eaf-2011-7-en.

Ormond, James. 2005. "The McDonaldization of Football." Accessed January 23, 2006 (http://courses.essex.ac.uk/sc/sc111).

Orum, Anthony M., and John G. Dale. 2009. *Political Sociology: Power and Participation in the Modern World.* 3rd ed. New York: Oxford University Press.

Outside the Classroom. 2009. "College Students Spend More Time Drinking than Studying." Accessed March 11 (www.outsidetheclassroom.com).

Oxford Poverty and Human Development Initiative. 2012. "Multidimensional Poverty Index." Accessed January 30 (www.ophi.org.uk).

p

Pace, Richard. 1993. "First-Time Televiewing in Amazonia: Television Acculturation in Gurupá, Brazil." *Ethnology* 32:187–205.

———. 1998. "The Struggle for Amazon Town." Boulder, CO: Lynne Rienner.

Padilla, Efren N. 2008. "Filipino Americans." Pp. 493–497 in vol. 1, *Encyclopedia of Race, Ethnicity, and Society,* edited by Richard T. Schaefer. Thousand Oaks, CA: Sage.

Page, Charles H. 1946. "Bureaucracy's Other Face." *Social Forces* 25 (October):89–94.

Pager, Devah. 2007. *Marked: Race, Crime, and Funding Work in an Era of Mass Incarceration.* Chicago: University of Chicago Press.

———, Bruce Weston, and Bart Bonikowski. 2009. "Discrimination in a Low-Wage Labor Market: A Field Experiment." *American Sociological Review* 74 (October):777–799.

Pampel, Fred C., Patrick M. Krueger, and Justin T. Denney. 2010. "Socioeconomic Disparities in Health Behaviors." *Annual Review of Sociology* 36:349–370.

Pariser, Ei. 2011a. *The Filter Bubble. What the Internet is Hiding from You.* New York: Penguin Press.

———. 2011b. "In Our Own Little Internet Bubbles." *Guardian Weekly,* June 24, p. 32.

Park, Robert E. 1922. *The Immigrant Press and Its Control.* New York: Harper.

Parker, Ashley. 2010. "Where Parties Look for an Audience." *New York Times,* October 30.

Parker-Pope, Tara. 2012. "America's Drinking Binge." January 11. Accessed January 18 (http://well.blogs.nytimes.com/2012/01/11/Americas-drinking-binge).

Parsons, Talcott. 1951. *The Social System.* New York: Free Press.

———. 1966. *Societies: Evolutionary and Comparative Perspectives.* Englewood Cliffs, NJ: Prentice Hall.

———. 1975. "The Sick Role and the Role of the Physician Reconsidered." *Milbank Medical Fund Quarterly Health and Society* 53 (Summer):257–278.

———, and Robert Bales. 1955. *Family: Socialization and Interaction Process.* Glencoe, IL: Free Press.

Passel, Jeffrey S., and D'Vera Cohn. 2011. "Unauthorized Immigrant Population National and State Trends, 2010." Washington, DC: Pew Research Center.

Passero, Kathy. 2002. "Global Travel Expert Roger Axtell Explains Why." *Biography* (July):70–73, 97–98.

Patel, Reena. 2010. *Working the Night Shift: Women in India's Call Center Industry.* Stanford CA: Stanford University Press.

Patterson, Thomas E. 2005. "Young Voters and the 2004 Election." Cambridge, MA: Vanishing Voter Project, Harvard University.

Pattillo-McCoy, Mary. 1999. *Black Picket Fences: Privilege and Peril among the Black Middle Class.* Chicago: University of Chicago Press.

Pear, Robert. 1997. "Now, the Archenemies Need Each Other." *New York Times,* June 22, sec. 4, pp. 1, 4.

———. 2009. "Congress Relaxes Rules on Suits over Pay Inequity." *New York Times,* January 28, p. A14.

Pendergrast, Mark. 1999. *Uncommon Grounds: The History of Coffee and How It Transformed Our World,* New York: Basic Books.

Pennington, Bill. 2008. "College Athletic Scholarships: Expectations Lose Out to Reality." *New York Times,* March 10, pp. A1, A15.

Peralta, Eyder. 2011. "Who Are the 1 Percent? Gallup Finds They're A Lot Like the 99 Percent." December 5. Accessed December 12 (www.wbur.org/npr/143143332/who-are-the-1-percent-gallup-finds-theyre-a-lot-like-the-99-percent).

Pesca, Mike. 2012. "Grading Charter Schools." Accessed February 24 (http://onpoint.wbur.org/2012/02/23/studying-charter-schools).

Peter, Laurence J., and Raymond Hull. 1969. *The Peter Principle.* New York: Morrow.

Petersen, John L. 2009. "How 'Wild Cards' May Reshape Our Future." *Futurist* (May–June): 19–20.

Petrášová, Alexandra. 2006. *Social Protection in the European Union.* Brussels: European Union.

Petrie, Michelle, and James E. Coverdill. 2010. "Who Lives and Dies on Death Row? Race, Ethnicity, and Post-Sentence Outcomes in Texas." *Social Problems* 57 (4):630–652.

Pew Forum on Religion and Public Life. 2008. *U.S. Religious Landscape Survey.* Washington, DC: Author.

———. 2010a. *U.S. Religious Knowledge Survey.* Washington, DC: Pew Forum. Accessible at http://pewforum.org.

———. 2010b. *Religious Knowledge Query.* Accessed March 23, 2011 (http://pewforum.org/ UploadedFiles/Topics/Belief-and-practices/religious-knowledge-quiz-handout.pdf).

Pew Global Attitudes Project. 2007. *Global Unease with Major World Powers.* Washington, DC: Pew Global.

Pew Hispanic Center. 2011. "The Mexican- American Boom: Births Overtake Immigration." Washington, DC: Pew Hispanic Center.

Pew Internet Project. 2000. "April 2000 Survey Data." Accessed January 17, 2010 (http://pewinternet.org/Shared-Content/Data-Sets/2000/April-2000-Survey-Data.aspx).

———. 2009. "Demographics of Internet Users." Accessed February 4 (www.pewinternet.org/trends/User_Demo_Jan_2009.htm).

———. 2012a. "Demographics of Internet Users." May 2011. Accessed January 17, 2012 (www.pewinternet.org/Trend-Data/Whos-Online .aspx).

———. 2012b. "Demographics of Teen Internet Users." September 2009. Accessed January 17, 2012 (www.pewinternet.org/Static-Pages/Trend-Data-for-Teens/Whos-Online.aspx).

———. 2012c. "Trend Data: Usage Over Time." Accessed January 17 (http://pewinternet.org/Trend-Data/Usage-Over-Time.aspx).

———. 2012d. "Demographics of Internet Users." Accessed May 28 (http://pewinternet.org/Static-Pages/Trend-Data-(Adults)/Whos-Online.aspx).

Pew Research Center for the People and the Press. 2012. "Continued Majority Support for Death Penalty, January 6." Accessed January 23 (www.people-press.org/2012/01/06/continued -majority-support-for-death-penalty/?src= prc-headline).

Pew Research Center. 2009. "Americans Now Divided Over Both Issues: Public Takes Conservative Turn on Gun Control, Abortion." News release. Washington, DC: Pew Research Center.

Pew Social and Demographic Trends. 2011. "Twenty-to-One: Wealth Caps Rise to Record Highs Between Whites, Black and Hispanics." Washington, DC: Pew Research Center.

———. 2012. "Rising Share of Americans See Conflict Between Rich and Poor." Washington, DC: Pew Research Center.

Pfeifer, Mark. 2008. "Vietnamese Americans" Pp. 1365–1368, vol. 3, in *Encyclopedia of Race, Ethnicity, and Society,* edited by Richard T. Schaefer. Thousand Oaks, CA: Sage.

Phelan, Jo C., Bruce G. Lint, and Parisha Tehranifar. 2010. "Social Conditions as Fundamental Causes of Health Inequalities: Theory, Evidence, and Policy Implications." *Journal of Health and Social Behavior* 51 (5):528–540.

Phillips, Susan A. 1999. *Wallbangin': Graffiti and Gangs in L.A.* Chicago: University of Chicago Press.

Piaget, Jean. 1954. *Construction of Reality in the Child.* Translated by Margaret Cook. New York: Basic Books.

Picca, Leslie Houts, and Joe R. Feagin. 2007. *Two-Faced Racism: Whites in Backstage and Frontstage.* New York: Routledge.

Pickert, Kate. 2009. "Getting Well While You Shop." *Time,* June 22, pp. 68–70.

Pincus, Fred L. 2003. *Reverse Discrimination: Dismantling the Myth.* Boulder, CO: Lynne Rienner.

———. 2008. "Reverse Discrimination." Pp. 1159–1161, vol. 3, in *Encyclopedia of Race, Ethnicity, and Society,* edited by Richard T. Schaefer. Thousand Oaks, CA: Sage.

Pinderhughes, Dianne. 1987. *Race and Ethnicity in Chicago Politics: A Reexamination of Pluralist Theory.* Urbana: University of Illinois Press.

Pinderhughes, Raquel. 2008. "Green Collar Jobs." Accessed June 29 (www.urbanhabitat.org/node/528).

Piven, Frances Fox, and Richard A. Cloward. 1996. "Welfare Reform and the New Class War." Pp. 72–86 in *Myths about the Powerless: Contesting Social Inequalities,* edited by M. Brinton Lykes, Ali Banuazizi, Ramsay Liem, and Michael Morris. Philadelphia: Temple University Press.

Plomin, Robert. 1989. "Determinants of Behavior." *American Psychologist* 44 (February):105–111.

Plüss, Caroline. 2005. "Constructing Globalized Ethnicity." *International Sociology* 20 (June):201–224.

Pogash, Carol. 2008. "Poor Students in High School Suffer Stigma from Lunch Aid." *New York Times,* March 1, pp. A1, A14.

Polletta, Francesca, and James M. Jasper. 2001. "Collective Identity and Social Movements." Pp. 283–305 in *Annual Review of Sociology, 2001,* edited by Karen S. Cook and Leslie Hogan. Palo Alto, CA: Annual Reviews.

Population Reference Bureau. 1996. "Speaking Graphically." *Population Today* 24 (June/July).

Portes, Alejandro, Cristina Escobar, and Renelinda Arana. 2008. "Bridging the Gap: Transnational and Ethnic Organizations in the Political Incorporation of Immigrants in the United States." *Ethnic and Racial Studies* 31 (September 6):1056–1090.

Powell, Brian, Catherine Bolzendahl, Claudia Geist, and Lola Carr Steelman. 2010. *Counted Out. Same-Sex Relationships and Americans' Definitions of Family.* New York: Russell Sage Foundation.

Powell, Gary N. 2010. *Women and Men in Management.* 4th ed. Thousand Oaks, CA: Sage.

Preston, Jennifer. 2011. "Facebook Page for Jesus with Highly Active Fans." *New York Times,* September 5, p. B3.

———, and Brian Stelter. 2011. "Cellphone Cameras Become World's Eyes and Ears on Protests across the Middle East." *New York Times,* February 19, p. A7.

Provasnik, Stephen, and Michael Planty. 2008. *Community Colleges: Special Supplement to the Condition of Education 2008.* Washington, DC: U.S. Government Printing Office.

Pryor, John H., Sylvia Hurtado, Victor B. Saenz, José Luis Santos, and William S. Korn. 2007. *The American Freshman: Forty Year Trends.* Los Angeles: Higher Education Research Institute, UCLA.

———, ———, Linda DeAngelo, Laura Palucki Blake, Sylvia Hurtado, and Serge Tran. 2011a. *The American Freshman: National Norms Fall 2011.* Los Angeles: Higher Education Research Institute, UCLA.

Putnam, Robert. 1995. *Bowling Alone: America's Declining Social Capital.* New York: Simon and Schuster.

q

Quadagno, Jill. 2011. *Aging and the Life Course: An Introduction to Social Gerontology.* 5th ed. New York: McGraw-Hill.

Quillian, Lincoln. 2006. "New Approaches to Understanding Racial Prejudice and Discrimination." *Annual Review of Sociology* 32:299–328.

Quinney, Richard. 1970. *The Social Reality of Crime.* Boston: Little, Brown.

———. 1974. *Criminal Justice in America.* Boston: Little, Brown.

———. 1979. *Criminology.* 2nd ed. Boston: Little, Brown.

———. 1980. *Class, State and Crime.* 2nd ed. New York: Longman.

Quiñones-Hinojosa, Alfredo with Mim Eichler Rivas. 2011. *Becoming Dr. Q: My Journey from Migrant Farm Worker to Brain Surgeon.* Berkeley: University of California Press.

r

Rabikovitch, Shelley, and James Lewis, eds. 2004. *The Encyclopedia of Modern Witchcraft and New Paganism.* New York: Citadel Press.

Rabinovitch, Simon. 2011. "China Labour Costs Soar as Wages Rise 22%." *Financial Times.* October 25. Accessed March 2, 2012 (www.ft.com/intl/cms/s/0/25f1c500-ff14-11e0-9b2f-00144feabdc0.html#axzz1nziV8URS).

Rainie, Lee. 2005. *Sports Fantasy Leagues Online.* Washington, DC: Pew Internet and American Life Project.

Rajan, Gita, and Shailja Sharma. 2006. *New Cosmopolitanisms: South Asians in the US.* Stanford, CA: Stanford University Press.

Ramet, Sabrina. 1991. *Social Currents in Eastern Europe: The Source and Meaning of the Great Transformation.* Durham, NC: Duke University Press.

Ramos, Jorge. 2010. *A Country for All.* New York: Vintage Books.

Ramstad, Evan. 2011. "Studying Too Much Is a New No-No In Upwardly Mobile South Korea." *Wall Street Journal,* October 6, p. A1.

RAND. 2010. "Retail Medical Clinics Perform Well Relative to Other Medical Settings." *RAND Review* (Winter 2009–2010). Accessed January 25 (www.rand.org/publications/randreview/issues/winter2009/news.html#medclinics).

Randolph, Tracey H., and Mellisa Holtzman. 2010. "The Role of Heritage Camps in Identity Development Among Korean Transnational Adoptees: A Relational Dialectics Approach." *Adoption Quarterly* 13:75–91.

Rangaswamy, Padma. 2005. "Asian Indians in Chicago." In *The New Chicago,* edited by John Koval et al. Philadelphia: Temple University Press.

Ratha, Dilip, Sanket Mohaptra, and Ani Silwat. 2010. "Outlook for Remittance Flows 2010–2011." *Migration and Development Brief,* World Bank.

Ratnesar, Romesh. 2011. "The Menace Within." *Stanford Magazine* (July/August). Accessible at www.stanfordalumni.org.

Ravitch, Diane. 2010. *The Death and Life of the Great American School System: How Testing and Choice Are Undermining Education.* New York: Basic Books.

Rawlinson, Linnie, and Nick Hunt. 2009. "Jackson Dies, Almost Takes Internet with Him." Accessed July 1 (www.cnn.com/2009/TECH/06/26/michael.jackson.internet/).

Raybon, Patricia. 1989. "A Case for 'Severe Bias.'" *Newsweek* 114 (October 2):11.

Reinharz, Shulamit. 1992. *Feminist Methods in Social Research.* New York: Oxford University Press.

Reitzes, Donald C., and Elizabeth J. Mutran. 2006. "Lingering Identities in Retirement." *Sociological Quarterly* 47:333–359.

Religion News Service. 2003. "New U.S. Guidelines on Prayer in Schools Get Mixed Reaction." *Los Angeles Times,* February 15, p. B24.

Religion Watch. 2006. "Hinduism Shaping India's Pragmatic Use of Biotechnology." April.

Rennison, Callie. 2002. *Criminal Victimization 2001. Changes 2000–01 with Trends 1993–2001.* Washington, DC: U.S. Government Printing Office.

Renzulli, Linda A., and Vincent J. Roscigno. 2007. "Charter Schools and Public Good." *Contexts* 6 (Winter):31–36.

Reuters. 2010. "Geoghegan Replaces Feinberg as Pay Czar." September 10. Accessed March 5, 2011 (http://www.reuters.com/assets/print?aid=USTRE6894ZH20100910).

Revkin, Andrew C. 2007. "Wealth and Poverty, Drought and Flood: Report from Four Fronts in the War on Warming." *New York Times,* April 3, pp. D4–D5.

Rice, Ronald E. 2008. *Media Ownership: Research and Regulation.* Cresskill, NJ: Hampton Press.

Rideout, Victoria K., Ulla G. Foehr, and Donald F. Roberts. 2010. Generation M: Media in the Lives of 8–18 Year-Olds. Kaiser Family Foundation. Accessible at www.kff.org/entmedia/mh012010pkg.cfm.

Riding, Alan. 1998. "Why 'Titanic' Conquered the World." *New York Times,* April 26, sec. 2, pp. 1, 28, 29.

———. 2005. "Unesco Adopts New Plan against Cultural Invasion." *New York Times,* October 21, p. B3.

Rieker, Patricia R., and Chloe E. Bird. 2000. "Sociological Explanations of Gender Differences in Mental and Physical Health." Pp. 98–113 in *Handbook of Medical Sociology,* edited by Chloe Bird, Peter Conrad, and Allan Fremont. New York: Prentice Hall.

Rifkin, Jeremy. 1995. *The End of Work; The Decline of the Global Labor Force and the Dawn of the Post-Market Era.* New York: Tarcher/Putnam.

Riley, Matilda White, Robert L. Kahn, and Anne Foner. 1994a. *Age and Structural Lag.* New York: Wiley InterScience.

———, Robert L. Kahn, and Anne Foner, in association with Karin A. Mock. 1994b. "Introduction: The Mismatch between People and Structures." Pp. 1–36 in *Age and Structural Lag,* edited by Matilda White Riley, Robert L. Kahn, and Anne Foner. New York: Wiley InterScience.

Ripley, Amanda. 2011. "Teacher, Leave Those Kids Alone." *Time,* December 5, pp. 46–49.

Ritzer, George. 1977. *Working: Conflict and Change.* 2nd ed. Englewood Cliffs, NJ: Prentice Hall.

———. 2002. *McDonaldization: The Reader.* Thousand Oaks, CA: Pine Forge Press.

———. 2004. *The Globalization of Nothing.* Thousand Oaks, CA: Pine Forge Press.

———. 2008. *The McDonaldization of Society 5.* Thousand Oaks, CA: Sage.

———. 2011. *McDonaldization of Society 6.* Thousand Oaks, CA: Sage.

Robelon, Erik W. 2008. 'Moment-of-Silence' Generates Loud Debate in Illinois." *Education Week* (October 24).

Robertson, Roland. 1988. "The Sociological Significance of Culture: Some General Considerations." *Theory, Culture, and Society* 5 (February):3–23.

Robinson, Kristopher, and Edward M. Crenshaw. 2010. "Reevaluating the Global Digital Divide: Socio-Demographic and Conflict Barriers to the Internet Revolution." *Sociological Inquiry* 80 (February):34–62

Robison, Jennifer. 2002. "Feminism—What's in a Name?" Accessed February 25, 2007 (www.galluppoll.com).

Robnett, Belinda, and Cynthia Feliciano. 2011. "Patterns of Racial-Ethnic Exclusion by Internet Daters." *Social Forces* 89 (March):807–828.

Rodman, George. 2011. *Mass Media in a Changing World.* 3rd ed. New York: McGraw-Hill.

Rogan, Eugene. 2009. "Sand, Sea and Shopping." *Guardian Weekly,* October 16, pp. 38–39.

Rootes, Christopher. 2007. "Environmental Movements." Pp. 608–640 in *The Blackwell Companion to Social Movements,* edited by David A. Snow, Sarah A. Sovle, and Hanspeter Kriesi. Malden, MA: Blackwell.

Rose, Arnold. 1951. *The Roots of Prejudice.* Paris: UNESCO.

Rose, Peter I., Myron Glazer, and Penina Migdal Glazer. 1979. "In Controlled Environments: Four Cases of Intense Resocialization." Pp. 320–338 in *Socialization and the Life Cycle,* edited by Peter I. Rose. New York: St. Martin's Press.

Rosen, Eva, and Sudhir Alladi Venkatesh. 2008. "A Perversion of Choice: Sex Work Offers Just Enough in Chicago's Urban Ghetto." *Journal of Contemporary Ethnography* (August):417–441.

Rosenberg, Douglas H. 1991. "Capitalism." Pp. 33–34 in *Encyclopedic Dictionary of Sociology,* 4th ed., edited by Dushkin Publishing Group. Guilford, CT: Dushkin.

Rosenbloom, Stephanie. 2011. "Love, Lies, and What They Learned." *New York Times,* November 13, pp. ST1, ST8.

Rosenfeld, Jake. 2010. "Little Labor." *Pathways* (Summer):4–6.

Rosenthal, Robert, and Lenore Jacobson. 1968. *Pygmalion in the Classroom.* New York: Holt.

———. 1992. *Pygmalion in the Classroom: Teacher Expectations and Pupils' Intellectual Development.* Newly expanded edition. Bancyfelin, UK: Crown House.

Rossi, Alice S. 1968. "Transition to Parenthood." *Journal of Marriage and the Family* 30 (February): 26–39.

———. 1984. "Gender and Parenthood." *American Sociological Review* 49 (February):1–19.

Rossi, Peter H. 1987. "No Good Applied Social Research Goes Unpunished." *Society* 25 (November–December):73–79.

Rossides, Daniel W. 1997. *Social Stratification: The Interplay of Class, Race, and Gender.* 2nd ed. Upper Saddle River, NJ: Prentice Hall.

Roszak, Theodore. 1969. *The Making of a Counterculture.* Garden City, NY: Doubleday.

Roter, Debra L., Judith A. Hall, and Yutaka Aoki. 2002. "Physician Gender Effects in Medical Communications: A Meta-analytic Review." *Journal of the American Medical Association* 288 (August 14):756–764.

Rothkopf, David. 2008. *Superclass: The Global Power Elite and the World They Are Making.* New York: Farrar, Straus and Giroux.

Rubin, Alissa J. 2003. "Pat-Down on the Way to Prayer." *Los Angeles Times,* November 25, pp. A1, A5.

———, and Sam Dagher. 2009. "Election Quotas for Iraqi Women Are Weakened, Provoking Anger as Vote Nears." *New York Times,* January 14, p. A13.

Rudel, Thomas K., J. Timmons Roberts, and Jo Ann Carmin. 2011. "Political Economy of the Environment." *Annual Review of Sociology* 37:221–238.

Ruiz, Rebecca. 2010. "Care for the Caregivers." *The American Prospect* (October):A17–A20.

Ryan, William. 1976. *Blaming the Victim.* Rev. ed. New York: Random House.

Rymer, Russ. 1993. *Genie: An Abused Child's Flight from Science.* New York: HarperCollins.

S

Saad, Lydia. 2004. "Divorce Doesn't Last." *Gallup Poll Tuesday Briefing.* March 30. Accessible at www.gallup.com.

———. 2011. "Americans Still Split Along 'Pro-Choice,' 'Pro-Life' Lines." May 23. Accessed February 22, 2012 (http://gallup.com/poll .147734/Americans-Split-Along-Pro-Choice -Pro-Life-Lines.aspx?version=print).

Sabol, William J., Heather C. West, and Matthew Cooper. 2009. "Prisoners in 2008." *Bureau of Justice Statistics Bulletin* (December).

Sachs, Jeffrey D. 2005. *The End of Poverty: Economic Possibilities for Our Time.* New York: Penguin.

Sacks, Peter. 2007. *Tearing Down the Gates: Confronting the Class Divide in American Education.* Berkeley: University of California Press.

Sagarin, Edward, and Jose Sanchez. 1988. "Ideology and Deviance: The Case of the Debate over the Biological Factor." *Deviant Behavior* 9 (1):87–99.

SAGE. 2012. "About Us: Services and Advocacy for Gay, Lesbian, Bisexual and Transgender Elders." Accessed March 12 at http://sageusa. org/about.

Saguy, Abigail, and Rene Almeling. 2008. "Fat in the Fire? Science, the News Media, and the 'Obesity Epidemic.'" *Sociological Forum* 23 (March):53–83.

Said, Edward W. 2001. "The Clash of Ignorance." *Nation,* October 22.

Sale, Kirkpatrick. 1996. *Rebels against the Future: The Luddites and Their War on the Industrial Revolution* (with a new preface by the author). Reading, MA: Addison-Wesley.

Salem, Richard, and Stanislaus Grabarek. 1986. "Sociology B.A.s in a Corporate Setting: How Can They Get There and of What Value Are They?" *Teaching Sociology* 14 (October):273–275.

Sampson, Robert J., and W. Byron Graves. 1989. "Community Structure and Crime: Testing Social-Disorganization Theory." *American Journal of Sociology* 94 (January):774–802.

Samuels, Dorothy. 2011. "Where Abortion Rights Are Disappearing." *New York Times,* September 25 (sect. SR), p. 14.

Samuels, Robert. 2010. "A Suicide Reminds Gulf Coast of Oil Spill." *Miami Herald,* June 28. Accessible at http://www.mcclatchydc. com/2010/06/ 28/96665/a-suicide-reminds-gulf-coast-of.html.

Samuelson, Paul A., and William D. Nordhaus. 2010. *Economics.* 19th ed. New York: McGraw-Hill.

Sandefur, Rebecca L. 2008. "Access to Civil Justice and Race, Class, and Gender Inequality." *Annual Review of Sociology* 34:339–358.

Sanders, Edmund. 2004. "Coming of Age in Iraq." *Los Angeles Times,* August 14, pp. A1, A5.

Sanderson, Stephen K., Seth A. Abrutyn, and Kristopher R. Proctor. 2011. "Testing the Protestant Ethic Thesis with Quantitative Historical Data: A Research Note." *Social Forces* 89 (March):905–912.

Santos, José Alcides Figueiredo. 2006. "Class Effects on Racial Inequality in Brazil." *Dados* 2:1–35.

Sanua, Marianne R. 2007. "AJC and Intermarriage: The Complexities of Jewish Continuity, 1960–2006." Pp. 3–32 in *American Jewish Yearbook 2007,* edited by David Singer and Lawrence Grossman. New York: American Jewish Committee.

Sanyal, Paromita. 2009. "From Credit to Collective Action: The Role of Microfinance in Promoting Women's Social Capital and Normative Influence." *American Sociological Review* 74 (August):529–550.

Sapir, Edward. 1929. "The State of Linguistics as a Science." *Language* 5 (4):207–214.

Saporito, Bill. 2007. "Restoring Wal-Mart." *Time* 170 (November 12):46–48, 50, 52.

Sassen, Saskia. 2005. "New Global Classes: Implications for Politics." Pp. 143–170 in *The New Egalitarianism,* edited by Anthony Giddens and Patrick Diamond. Cambridge: Polity.

Sawhill, Isabel, and Ron Haskins. 2009. "If You Can Make It Here . . ." *Washington Post National Weekly Edition,* November 9, p. 27.

———, and John E. Morton. 2007. *Economic Mobility: Is the American Dream Alive and Well?* Washington, DC: Economic Mobility Project, Pew Charitable Trusts.

Sayer, Liana C., Suzanne M. Bianchi, and John P. Robinson. 2004. "Are Parents Investing Less in Children? Trends in Mothers' and Fathers' Time with Children." *American Journal of Sociology* 110 (July):1–43.

Scarce, Rik. 2005. "A Law to Protect Scholars." *Chronicle of Higher Education,* August 12, p. 324.

Schadler, Ted. 2009. *US Telecommuting Forecast, 2009–2016.* Accessible at www.forester.com.

Schaefer, Peter. 2008. "Digital Divide." Pp. 388–389, vol. 1, in *Encyclopedia of Race, Ethnicity, and Society in the United States,* edited by Richard T. Schaefer. Thousand Oaks, CA: Sage.

Schaefer, Richard T. 1998. "Differential Racial Mortality and the 1995 Chicago Heat Wave." Presentation at the annual meeting of the American Sociological Association, August, San Francisco.

———. 2008b. "'Power' and 'Power Elite.'" In *Encyclopedia of Social Problems,* edited by Vincent Parrillo. Thousand Oaks, CA: Sage.

———. 2011. *Race and Ethnicity in the United States.* 12th ed. Census Update. Upper Saddle River, NJ: Prentice Hall.

———. 2012. *Racial and Ethnic Groups.* 13th ed. Upper Saddle River, NJ: Pearson.

———, and William Zellner. 2011. *Extraordinary Groups.* 9th ed. New York: Worth.

Scharnberg, Kirsten. 2007. "Black Market for Midwives Defies Bans." *Chicago Tribune,* November 25, pp. 1, 10.

Scherer, Michael. 2011. "Introduction: Taking It to the Streets." Pp. 5–12 in *Occupy: What Is Occupy?* New York: Time Books.

Scherer, Ron. 2010a. "A Long Struggle to Find Jobs." *Christian Science Monitor,* January 31, pp. 18–19.

———. 2010b. "For Jobless, Online Friends Can Be Lifelines." *Christian Science Monitor,* March 25, p. 21.

———. 2010c. "Jim Bunning Delays Vote; Unemployed Face First Week Without Check." *Christian Science Monitor* (March 2).

Schleifer, Yigal. 2009. "In Turkey, Surfing for Brides." *Christian Science Monitor,* July 5, p. 14.

Schlesinger, Traci. 2011. "The Failure of Race-Neutral Policies: How Mandatory Terms and Sentencing Enhancements Contribute to Mass Racialized Incarceration." *Crime & Delinquency* 57 (January):56–81.

Schmeeckle, Maria. 2007. "Gender Dynamics in Stepfamilies: Adult Stepchildren's Views." *Journal of Marriage and Family* 69 (February):174–189.

———, Roseann Giarrusso, Du Feng, and Vern L. Bengtson. 2006. "What Makes Someone Family? Adult Children's Perceptions of Current and Former Stepparents." *Journal of Marriage and Family* 68 (August):595–610.

Schnaiberg, Allan. 1994. *Environment and Society: The Enduring Conflict.* New York: St. Martin's Press.

Schneider, Christopher. 2008. "Sexuality." Pp. 847–848 in *Encyclopedia of Social Problems,* edited by Vincent Parrillo. Los Angeles: Sage.

Schneider, Friedrich. 2010. "Dues and Don'ts." *The Economist* (August 14):62.

Schram, Sanford F., Ruhard C. Fording, Joe Soss, and Linda Houser. 2009. "Deciding to Discipline: Race, Choice and Punishment at the Frontlines of Welfare Reform." *American Sociological Review* 74 (June):398–422.

Schulman, Gary I. 1974. "Race, Sex, and Violence: A Laboratory Test of the Sexual Threat of the Black Male Hypothesis." *American Journal of Sociology* 79 (March):1260–1272.

Schur, Edwin M. 1965. *Crimes without Victims: Deviant Behavior and Public Policy.* Englewood Cliffs, NJ: Prentice Hall.

———. 1968. *Law and Society: A Sociological View.* New York: Random House.

———. 1985. "'Crimes without Victims': A 20-Year Reassessment." Paper presented at the annual meeting of the Society for the Study of Social Problems.

Schwab, Klaus (ed). 2011. *The Global Competitiveness Report 2010-2011.* Geneva: World Economic Forum.

Schwartz, Howard D., ed. 1994. *Dominant Issues in Medical Sociology.* 3rd ed. New York: McGraw-Hill.

Schwartz, Shalom H., and Anat Bardi. 2001. "Value Hierarchies across Cultures: Taking a Similarities Perspective." *Journal of Cross-Cultural Perspective* 32 (May):268–290.

Scott, Alan. 1990. *Ideology and the New Social Movements.* London: Unwin Hyman.

Scott, Gregory. 2001. "Broken Windows behind Bars: Eradicating Prison Gangs through Ecological Hardening and Symbolic Cleansing." *Corrections Management Quarterly* 5 (Winter):23–36.

Scott, W. Richard, and Gerald F. Davis. 2007. *Organizations and Organizing: Rational, Natural and Open Systems Perspectives.* New York: Pearson.

Search Engine Watch. 2011. "comScore: Bing Grows for Sixth Straight Year." March 16. Accessible at http://searchenginewatch.com/3642049.

Seccombe, Karen. 2011. "So You Think I Drive a Cadillac?" Boston: Allyn and Bacon.

Second Life. 2010. "Current User Metrics for Second Life." Accessed February 2, 2010 (http://secondlife.com/xmlhttp/secondlife/php).

Security on Campus. 2008. "Complying with the Jeanne Clery Act." Accessed January 13 (www.securityoncampus.org/crimestats/index.html).

Seidman, Steven. 1994. "Heterosexism in America: Prejudice against Gay Men and Lesbians." Pp. 578–593 in *Introduction to Social Problems,* edited by Craig Calhoun and George Ritzer. New York: McGraw-Hill.

Sellers, Frances Stead. 2004. "Voter Globalization." *Washington Post National Weekly Edition,* November 29, p. 22.

Selod, Saher Farooq. 2008a. "Muslim Americans." Pp. 920–923, vol. 2, in *Encyclopedia of Race, Ethnicity, and Society,* edited by Richard T. Schaefer. Thousand Oaks, CA: Sage.

———. 2008b. "Veil." Pp. 1359–1360, vol. 3, in *Encyclopedia of Race, Ethnicity, and Society,* edited by Richard T. Schaefer. Thousand Oaks, CA: Sage.

Sengupta, Somini. 2006. "Report Shows Muslims Near Bottom of Social Ladder." *New York Times,* November 29, p. A4.

———. 2009. "An Empire for Poor Working Women, Guided by a Gandhian Approach." *New York Times,* March 7, p. A6.

Sernau, Scott. 2001. *Worlds Apart: Social Inequalities in a New Century.* Thousand Oaks, CA: Pine Forge Press.

Settersten, Richard, and Barbara Ray. 2011. *Not Quite Adults: Why 20-Somethings Are Choosing a Slower Path to Adulthood, and Why It's Good for Everyone.* New York: Bantam.

Shachtman, Tom. 2006. *Rumspringa: To Be or Not to Be Amish.* New York: North Point Press.

Shah, Anup. 2009. "Climate Justice and Equity." October 4. Accessed December 12 (www.globalissues.org/print/articles/231).

Shane, Scott. 2010. "Wars Fought and Wars Googled." *New York Times,* June 27, pp. PWK1–5.

Shapiro, Joseph P. 1993. *No Pity: People with Disabilities Forging a New Civil Rights Movement.* New York: Times Books.

Shapiro, Thomas M., Tatjana Meschede, and Laura Sullivan. 2010. "The Racial Wealth Gap Increases Fourfold." Research and Policy Brief, Institute on Assets and Social Policy, Brandeis University.

Shapley, Dan. 2010. "4 Dirty Secrets of the Exxon Valdez Oil Spill." Accessed May 3 (www.thedailygreen.com).

Sharkey, Patrick. 2009. *Neighbors and the Black-White Mobility Gap.* Washington, DC: Economic Mobility Project.

Sharma, Hari M., and Gerard C. Bodeker. 1998. "Alternative Medicine." Pp. 228–229 in *Britannica Book of the Year 1998.* Chicago: Encyclopaedia Britannica.

Shaw, Clifford R., and Henry D. McKay. 1942. *Juvenile Delinquency and Urban Areas.* Chicago: University of Chicago Press.

Sheehan, Charles. 2005. "Poor Seniors Take On Plans of Condo Giant." *Chicago Tribune,* March 22, pp. 1, 9.

Sherman, Arloc. 2007. *Income Inequality Hits Record Levels, New CBO Data Show.* Washington, DC: Center on Budget and Policy Priorities.

Sherman, Jennifer, and Elizabeth Harris. 2012. "Social Class and Parenting: Classic Debates and New Understandings." *Sociology Compass* 6:60–71.

Shin, Hyon B., and Robert A. Kominski. 2010. *Language Use in the United States: 2007.* Report ACS-12. Washington, DC: U.S. Government Printing Office.

Shostak, Arthur B. 2002. "Clinical Sociology and the Art of Peace Promotion: Earning a World without War." Pp. 325–345 in *Using Sociology: An Introduction from the Applied and Clinical Perspectives,* edited by Roger A. Straus. Lanham, MD: Rowman and Littlefield.

Sicular, Terry, Ximing Yue, Bjorn Gustafsson, and Shi Li. 2006. "The Urban-Rural Income Gap and Inequality in China." Research Paper No. 2006/135, United Nations University—World Institute for Development Economic Research.

Sieber, Renée E., Daniel Spitzberg, Hannah Muffatt, Kristen Brewer, Blanka Füleki, and Naomi Arbit. 2006. *Influencing Climate Change Policy: Environmental Non-Governmental Organizations (ENGOs) Using Virtual and Physical Activism.* Montreal: McGill University.

Siegel, Paul, Elizabeth Martin, and Rusalind Bruno. 2001. "Language Use and Linguistic Isolation: Historical Data and Methodological Issues." Paper presented at the Statistical Policy Seminar, Bethesda, MD.

Silverman, Rachel Emma. 2009. "As Jobs Grow Scarce, Commuter Marriages Rise." Accessed March 31, 2010 (http://blogs.wsj.com/juggle/2009/01/16/as-jobs-grow-scarce-commuter-marriages-rise/).

Silverstein, Ken. 2010. "Shopping for Sweat: The Human Cost of a Two-Dollar T-shirt." *Harpers* 320 (January):36–44.

Simon, Stephanie. 2007. "It's Easter; Shall We Gather at the Desktops?" *Los Angeles Times,* April 8, p. A13.

Sisson, Carmen K. 2007. "The Virtual War Family." *Christian Science Monitor,* May 29.

Skocpol, Theda, and Vanessa Williamson. 2012. *The Tea Party and the Remaking of Republican Conservatism.* New York: Oxford University Press.

Slack, Jennifer Daryl, and J. Macgregor Wise. 2007. *Culture + Technology.* New York: Peter Lang.

Slavin, Barbara. 2007. "Child Marriage Rife in Nations Getting U.S. Aid." *USA Today,* July 17, p. 6A.

Slavin, Robert E., and A. Cheung. 2003. *Effective Reading Programs for English Language Learners: A Best-Evidence Synthesis.* Baltimore: Johns Hopkins University, Center for Research on the Education of Students Placed at Risk.

Sloan, Allan. 2009. "What's Still Wrong with Wall Street." *Time,* November 9, pp. 24–29.

Slug-Lines.com. 2011a. "A Unique Commuter Solution." Accessed November 10, 2011. (www. slug-lines.com).

Smart, Barry. 1990. "Modernity, Postmodernism, and the Present." Pp. 14–30 in *Theories of Modernity and Postmodernity,* edited by Bryan S. Turner. Newbury Park, CA: Sage.

Smeeding, Timothy M. 2008. "Poorer by Comparison: Poverty, Work, and Public Policy in Comparative Perspective." *Pathways* (Winter):3–5.

Smelser, Neil. 1963. *The Sociology of Economic Life.* Englewood Cliffs, NJ: Prentice Hall.

Smith, Aaron. 2009. *The Internet's Role in Campaign 2000.* Washington, DC: Pew Internet and American Life Project.

———. 2012. *Real Time Charitable Giving.* Washington, DC: Pew Research Center's Internet and American Life Project. Accessible at www .pewinternet.org/Reports/2012/MobileGiving .aspx.

Smith, Christian. 1991. *The Emergence of Liberation Theology: Radical Religion and Social Movement Theory.* Chicago: University of Chicago Press.

———. 2007. "Getting a Life: The Challenge of Emerging Adulthood." *Books and Culture: A Christian Review* (November–December).

———. 2008. "Future Directions of the Sociology of Religion." *Social Forces* 86 (June):1564–1589.

Smith, Craig S. 2006. "Romania's Orphans Face Widespread Abuse, Group Says." *New York Times,* May 10, p. A3.

Smith, Dan. 1999. *The State of the World Atlas.* 6th ed. London: Penguin.

Smith, Lawrence C. 2011. *The World in 2050: Four Forces Shaping Civilizations Northern Future.* New York: A Plume Book.

Smith, Peter. 2008. "Going Global: The Transnational Politics of the Debt Movement." *Globalizations* 5 (March):13–33.

Smith, Tom W. 2003. *Coming of Age in 21st Century America: Public Attitudes toward the Importance and Timing of Transition to Adulthood.* Chicago: National Opinion Research Center.

———. 2009. *Religious Change around the World.* Chicago: NORC/University of Chicago.

Smith, Wesley J. 2011. "Euthanasia Spreads in Europe." October 26. Accessed March 12, 2012 at http://nationalreview.com/articles/281303/ euthanisa-spreads-europe-wesley-j-smith?pg=3.

Snyder, Thomas D. 1996. *Digest of Education Statistics 1996.* Washington, DC: U.S. Government Printing Office.

Somavia, Juan. 2008. "The ILO at 90 Working for Social Justice." *World of Work* 64 (December):4–5.

Sorokin, Pitirim A. [1927] 1959. *Social and Cultural Mobility.* New York: Free Press.

Southern Poverty Law Center. 2010. "Active 'Patriot' Groups in the United States in 2009." Accessed November 5 (www.splcenter.org/ patriot).

Spalter-Roth, Roberta, and Nicole Van Vooren. 2008a. "What Are They Doing with a Bachelor's Degree in Sociology?" Washington, DC: American Sociological Association. Accessible at http://asanet.org/galleries/research/ASA researchbrief_corrections.pdf.

———. 2008b. "Skills, Reasons and Jobs. What Happened to the Class of 2005." Washington, DC: American Sociological Association. Accessible at http://asanet.org.

———. 2010. *Mixed Success: Four Years of Experiences of 2005 Sociology Graduates.* Washington, DC: American Sociology Association.

Spencer, Nancy. 2008. "Title IX." Pp. 1308–1310, vol. 3, in *Encyclopedia of Race, Ethnicity, and Society,* edited by Richard T. Schaefer. Thousand Oaks, CA: Sage.

Spitzer, Steven. 1975. "Toward a Marxian Theory of Deviance." *Social Problems* 22 (June):641–651.

Sprague, Joey. 2005. *Feminist Methodologies for Critical Research: Bridging Differences.* Lanham, MD: AltaMira Press.

Stacey, Judith. 2011. *Unhitched.* New York: New York University Press.

Stahler-Sholk, Richard. 2008. "Zapatista Rebellion." Pp. 1423–1424, vol. 3, in *Encyclopedia of Race, Ethnicity, and Society,* edited by Richard T. Schaefer. Thousand Oaks, CA: Sage.

Stansell, Christine. 2011. *The Feminist Promise: 1792 to the Present.* New York: The Modern Library.

Stark, Andrew. 2011. "The Price of Moral Purity." *Wall Street Journal,* February 4.

Stark, Rodney. 2004. *Exploring the Religious Life.* Baltimore: Johns Hopkins University Press.

———, and William Sims Bainbridge. 1979. "Of Churches, Sects, and Cults: Preliminary Concepts for a Theory of Religious Movements." *Journal for the Scientific Study of Religion* 18 (June):117–131.

———, and ———. 1985. *The Future of Religion.* Berkeley: University of California Press.

Staton, Ron. 2004. "Still Fighting for National Hawaiian Recognition." *Asian Week,* January 22, p. 8.

Steel, Emily. 2010. "Some Data-Miners Ready to Reveal What They Know." *Wall Street Journal,* December 3, pp. B1, B2.

Steffen, Alex, ed. 2008. *World Changing: A User's Guide for the 21st Century.* New York: Harry N. Abrams.

Stein, Leonard I. 1967. "The Doctor-Nurse Game." *Archives of General Psychology* 16:699–703.

Stevick, Richard A. 2007. *Growing Up Amish: The Teenage Years.* Baltimore: Johns Hopkins University Press.

Stockard, Janice E. 2002. *Marriage in Culture.* Belmont, CA: Thomson Wadsworth.

Stolberg, Sheryl Gay. 1995. "Affirmative Action Gains Often Come at a High Cost." *Los Angeles Times,* March 29, pp. A1, A13–A16.

———. 2008. "Richest Nations Pledge to Halve Greenhouse Gas." *New York Times,* July 9, pp. A1, A13.

Strauss, Gary. 2002. "'Good Old Boys' Network Still Rules Corporate Boards." *USA Today,* November 1, pp. B1, B2.

———. 2011. "$228, 000 for a Part-Time Job? Apparently, That's Not Enough." *USA Today,* March 4, p. A1.

Suárez, Zulema E., and Rose M. Perez. 2012. "The Cuban American Family." Pp. 112–128 in *Ethnic Families in America: Patterns and Variations.* 5th ed., edited by Roosevelt Wright, Jr., Charles H. Mindel, Thanh Van Tran, and Robert W. Halsenstein. Upper Saddle River, NJ: Pearson.

Subramaniam, Mangala. 2006. *The Power of Women's Organization: Gender, Caste, and Class in India.* Lanham, MD: Lexington Books.

Suh, Doowon. 2011. "Institutionalizing Social Movements: The Dual Strategy of the Korean Women's Movement." *Sociological Quarterly* 52:442–471.

Suitor, J. Jill, Staci A. Minyard, and Rebecca S. Carter. 2001. "'Did You See What I Saw?' Gender Differences in Perceptions of Avenues to Prestige among Adolescents." *Sociological Inquiry* 71 (Fall):437–454.

Sullivan, Harry Stack. [1953] 1968. *The Interpersonal Theory of Psychiatry.* Edited by Helen Swick Perry and Mary Ladd Gawel. New York: Norton.

Sullivan, Kevin. 2006. "Bridging the Digital Divide." *Washington Post National Weekly Edition* 25 (July 17):11–12.

Sum, Andrew, Paul Harrington, and Ishwar Khatiwada. 2006. *The Impact of New Immigrants on Young Native-Born Workers, 2000–2005.* Washington, DC: Center for Immigration Studies.

Sumner, William G. 1906. *Folkways.* New York: Ginn.

Survival International. 2012. "Brazilian Indians." Accessed January 12 (www .survivialinternational.org/tribes/Brazilian).

SustainAbility. 2006. *Brazil—Country of Diversities and Inequalities.* London: SustainAbility.

Sutch, Richard, and Susan B. Carter. 2006. *Historical Statutes of US: Earliest Time to the Present.* Cambridge: Cambridge University Press.

Sutcliffe, Bob. 2002. *100 Ways of Seeing an Unequal World.* London: Zed Books.

Sutherland, Edwin H. 1937. *The Professional Thief.* Chicago: University of Chicago Press.

———. 1940. "White-Collar Criminality." *American Sociological Review* 5 (February):1–11.

———. 1949. *White Collar Crime.* New York: Dryden.

———. 1983. *White Collar Crime: The Uncut Version.* New Haven, CT: Yale University Press.

———, Donald R. Cressey, and David F. Luckenbill. 1992. *Principles of Criminology.* 11th ed. New York: Rowman and Littlefield.

Swartz, Jon. 2012. "Google's Personalized Search Charges Set Off Uproar." *USA Today,* January 12, p. B1.

Swatos, William H., Jr., ed. 1998. *Encyclopedia of Religion and Society.* Lanham, MD: AltaMira.

Sweet, Kimberly. 2001. "Sex Sells a Second Time." *Chicago Journal* 93 (April):12–13.

Swidler, Ann. 1986. "Culture in Action: Symbols and Strategies." *American Sociological Review* 51 (April):273–286.

Szasz, Andrew. 2007. *Shopping Our Way to Safety: How We Changed from Protecting the Environment to Protecting Ourselves.* Minneapolis: University of Minnesota Press.

Szasz, Thomas. 2010. *The Myth of Mental Illness: Foundations of a Theory of Personal Conduct.* 50th Anniversary Edition. New York: Harper Perennial.

t

Tachibana, Judy. 1990. "Model Minority Myth Presents Unrepresentative Portrait of Asian Americans, Many Educators Say." *Black Issues in Higher Education* 6 (March 1):1, 11.

Takei, Isao, and Arthur Sakamoto. 2011. "Poverty Among Asian Americans in the 21st Century." *Sociological Perspectives* 54 (Summer):251–276.

Tannen, Deborah. 1990. *You Just Don't Understand: Women and Men in Conversation.* New York: Ballantine.

Tatchell, Jo. 2009. *A Diamond in the Desert: Behind the Scenes in the World's Richest City.* London: Hodder and Stoughton.

Taylor, Chris. 2011. "Twitter Has 100 Million Active Users." December 8. Accessed January 15, 2012 (http://mashable.com/2011/09/08/twitter-has-100-million-active-users).

Taylor, Verta. 1999. "Gender and Social Movements: Gender Processes in Women's Self-Help Movements." *Gender and Society* 13:8–33.

———. 2004. "Social Movements and Gender." Pp. 14348–14352 in *International Encyclopedia of the Social and Behavioral Sciences,* edited by Neil J. Smelser and Paul B. Baltes. New York: Elsevier.

———, Leila J. Rupp, and Nancy Whittier. 2009. *Feminist Frontiers.* 8th ed. New York: McGraw-Hill.

Teaching Tolerance. 2012. "LGBT Content Access Denied." Accessed March 29 (www.tollerance.org/blog/lgbt-content-access-denied).

Tedeschi, Bob. 2006. "Those Born to Shop Can Now Use Cellphones." *New York Times,* January 2.

Telles, Edward E. 2004. *Race in America: The Significance of Skin Color in Brazil.* Princeton, NJ: Princeton University Press.

Teranishi, Robert T. 2010. *Asians in the Ivory Tower: Dilemmas of Racial Inequity in American Higher Education.* New York: Teachers College Press.

Terlep, Sharon. 2011. "Road Gets Bumpy for GM in China." *Wall Street Journal,* September 16, pp. A1, A10.

Therborn, Göran. 2010. Review of "Unveiling Inequality." *Contemporary Sociology* 39 (5):585–586.

Third World Institute. 2007. *The World Guide.* 11th ed. Oxford: New Internationalist Publications.

Thomas, Evan, and Pat Wingert. 2010. "Understanding Charter Schools." *Newsweek* 155 (June 21):46.

Thomas, Gordon, and Max Morgan Witts. 1974. *Voyage of the Damned.* Greenwich, CT: Fawcett Crest.

Thomas Jr., Landon. 2011. "Money Troubles Take Personal Toll in Greece." *New York Times,* May 16, pp. A1, A2. Accessible at www.nytimes.com/2011/05/16/business/global/16drachma.html?pagewanted=all.

Thomas, R. Murray. 2003. "New Frontiers in Cheating." In *Encyclopaedia Britannica 2003 Book of the Year.* Chicago: Encyclopaedia Britannica.

Thomas, William I. 1923. *The Unadjusted Girl.* Boston: Little, Brown.

Thomasrobb.com. 2007. "WhitePride TV." Accessed May 7 (http://thomasrobb.com).

Thompson, Ginger. 2001. "Why Peace Eludes Mexico's Indians." *New York Times,* March 11, sec. WK, p. 16.

Thompson, Tony. 2005. "Romanians Are Being Paid to Play Computer Games for Westerners." *Guardian Weekly,* March 25, p. 17.

Threadcraft, Shatema. 2008. "Welfare Queen." In *Encyclopedia of Race, Ethnicity and Society,* edited by Richard T. Schaefer. Thousand Oaks, CA: Sage.

Thurm, Scott. 2010. "Oracle's Ellison: Pay King." *Wall Street Journal,* July 27, pp. A1, A16.

Thurow, Lester. 1984. "The Disappearance of the Middle Class." *New York Times,* February 5, sec. 5, p. 2.

Tibbles, Kevin. 2007. "Web Sites Encourage Eating Disorders." *Today,* February 18. Accessed May 7 (www.msabc.msn.com).

Tierney, William G., and Karri A. Holley. 2008. "Intelligent Design and the Attack on Scientific Inquiry." *Cultural Studies Critical Methodologies* 8 (February):39–49.

Tigay, Chanan. 2011. "Women and Sports." *CQ Researcher* 21 (March 25).

Tilly, Charles. 1964. *The Vendée.* Cambridge, MA: Harvard University Press.

———. 1993. *Popular Contention in Great Britain 1758–1834.* Cambridge, MA: Harvard University Press.

———. 2003. *The Politics of Collective Violence.* New York: Cambridge University Press.

———. 2004. *Social Movements, 1768–2004.* Boulder, CO: Paradigm.

———. 2007. "Trust Networks in Transnational Migration." *Sociological Forum* 22 (March):3–24.

Timmerman, Kelsey. 2009. *Where Am I Wearing?* Hoboken NJ: Wiley.

Toensing, Gale Country. 2009. "Akaka Bill Gets Obama Approval." *Indian Country Today* (August 19):1, 2.

Toma, Catalina L., and Jeffrey T. Hancock. 2010. "Looks and Lies: The Role of Physical Attractiveness in Online Dating Self-Presentation

and Deception." *Community Research* 37 (3):335–351.

———, ———, and Nicole B. Ellison. 2008. "Separating Fact from Fiction: An Examination of Deceptive Self-Presentation in Online Dating Profiles." *Personality and Social Psychology Bulletin* 34:1023–1036.

Tönnies, Ferdinand. [1887] 1988. *Community and Society.* Rutgers, NJ: Transaction.

Toossi, Mitra. 2009. "Employment Outlook: 2008–2018." *Monthly Labor Review* (November):30–51.

Toppo, Greg. 2011. "The Search for a New Way to Test Schoolkids." *USA Today,* March 18, p. A4.

Torres, Lourdes. 2008. "Puerto Rican Americans" and "Puerto Rico." Pp. 1082–1089, vol. 3, in *Encyclopedia of Race, Ethnicity, and Society,* edited by Richard T. Schaefer. Thousand Oaks, CA: Sage.

Touraine, Alain. 1974. *The Academic System in American Society.* New York: McGraw-Hill.

Transactional Records Access Clearinghouse. 2009. "TRAC Monthly Bulletins by Topic, September 2009." Accessed February 11, 2010 (www.trac.syr.edu/tracreports/bulletins/white_collar_crime/monthly_sep09/fil).

Trimble, Lindsey B., and Julie A. Kmec. 2011. "The Role of Social Networks in Getting a Job." *Sociology Compass* 5 (2):165–178.

Trotter III, Robert T., and Juan Antonio Chavira. 1997. *Curanderismo: Mexican American Folk Healing.* Athens: University of Georgia Press.

Truman, Jennifer L. 2011. "Criminal Victimization Survey." *BJS Bulletin* (September).

Trumbull, Mark. 2006. "America's Younger Workers Losing Ground on Income." *Christian Science Monitor,* February 27.

Tschorn, Adam. 2010. "Parkour Ready to Launch." *Chicago Tribune,* July 25, sec. 6, pp. 20–21.

Tuan, Mia, and Jiannbin Lee Shiao. 2011. *Choosing Ethnicity, Negotiating Race: Korean Adoptees in America.* New York: Russell Sage Foundation.

Tuchman, Gaye. 1992. "Feminist Theory." Pp. 695–704 in *Encyclopedia of Sociology,* vol. 2, edited by Edgar F. Borgatta and Marie L. Borgatta. New York: Macmillan.

Tucker, Robert C. (ed.) 1978. *The Marx-Engels Reader.* 2nd ed. New York: Norton.

Ture, Kwame, and Charles Hamilton. 1992. *Black Power: The Politics of Liberation.* With new Afterword by authors. New York: Vintage Books.

Turkle, Sherry. 2004. "How Computers Change the Way We Think." *Chronicle of Higher Education* 50 (January 30):B26–B28.

———. 2011. *Alone Together: Why We Expect More from Technology and Less from Each Other.* New York: Basic Books.

Turner, Bryan S., ed. 1990. *Theories of Modernity and Postmodernity.* Newbury Park, CA: Sage.

Turner, C. F. L. Ku, S. M. Rogers, L. D. Lindberg, H. Pleck, and F. L. Sonenstein. 1998. "Adolescent Sexual Behavior, Drug Use, and Violence: Increased Reporting with Computer Survey Technology." *Science* 280 (May 8):867–873.

Turner, S. Derek, and Mark Cooper. 2006. *Out of the Picture: Minority and Female TV Station Ownership in the United States.* Washington, DC: Free Press.

U

UNAIDS. 2010. *Global Report: UNAIDS Report on the Global AIDS Epidemic 2010.* Geneva: UNAIDS.

UNICEF. 2010. "Child Marriage." Accessed January 15 (www.unicef.org/progressfprchildren/2007n6/index_41848.htm?q=printme).

United Nations. 2005. *The Millennium Development Goals Report.* Washington, DC: United Nations.

———. 2009. *International Migration Report 2006: A Global Assessment.* New York: United Nations, Economic and Social Affairs.

United Nations Development Programme. 1995. *Human Development Report 1995.* New York: Oxford University Press.

———. 2000. *Poverty Report 2000: Overcoming Human Poverty.* Washington, DC: UNDP.

———. 2009. *Overcoming Barriers: Human Mobility and Development.* New York: Palgrave Macmillan.

United Nations Economic and Social Council. 2010. "Review of the Implementation of the Beijing Declaration." New York: Economic and Social Council.

United Nations Office on Drugs and Crime. 2010. *The Globalization of Crime: A Transnational Organized Crime Threat Assessment.* New York: UNODO.

United Nations Population Division. 2011. "World Abortion Policies, 2011." Accessed February 22, 2012 (www.un.org/esa/population/publications/2011abortion/2011abortionwallchart.html).

United Nations Statistics Division. 2008. "Singulate Mean Age at Marriage." Accessed March 1, 2009 (http://data.un.org/search.aspx?q=marriage).

———. 2009. *Demographic Yearbook 2007.* Accessed April 1, 2010 (http://unstats.un.org/unsd/demographic/products/dyb/dyb2.htm).

United Way of King County. 2010. "Community Assessment." Accessed January 18 (www.uwkc/printver.asp?ref=kcca/data/languages/isolation.asp).

University of Michigan. 2003. *Information on Admissions Lawsuits.* Accessed August 8 (www.umich.edu/urel/admissions).

Urban Dictionary. 2012. "Urban Amish." Accessed March 29 (www.urbandictionary.com/define.php?term=urban+20amish).

U.S. English. 2012. "Making English the Official Language." Accessed January 12 (www.us-english.org/inc/).

V

Vaidhyanathan, Siva. 2008. "Generational Myth: Not All Young People Are Tech-Savvy." *Chronicle of Higher Education,* September 19, pp. B7–B9.

———. 2008. "Naked in the 'Nonopticon.'" *Chronicle of Higher Education* (February 15):B7–B10.

Vamosi, Robert, Mary Monahan, and Rachel Kim. 2010. *2010 Identity Fraud Survey Report.* Pleasanton, CA: Javelin Strategy.

Van Gennep, Arnold. [1909] 1960. *The Rites of Passage.* Translated by Monika B. Vizedom and Gabrielle L. Caffee. Chicago: University of Chicago Press.

van Vucht Tijssen, Lieteke. 1990. "Women between Modernity and Postmodernity." Pp. 147–163 in *Theories of Modernity and Postmodernity,* edited by Bryan S. Turner. London: Sage.

Vargas, Jose Antonio. 2007. "YouTube Gets Serious with Links to Candidates." *Washington Post,* March 2, p. C1.

Vasagar, Jeeran. 2005. "At Last Rwanda Is Known for Something Positive." *Guardian Weekly,* July 22, p. 18.

Vaughan, R. M. 2007. "Cairo's Man Show." *Utne Reader* (March–April):94–95.

Veblen, Thorstein. [1899] 1964. *Theory of the Leisure Class.* New York: Macmillan. New York: Penguin.

———. 1919. *The Vested Interests and the State of the Industrial Arts.* New York: Huebsch.

Venkatesh, Sudhir Alladi. 2006. *Off the Books: The Underground Economy of the Urban Poor.* Cambridge, MA: Harvard University Press.

———. 2008. *Gang Leader for a Day: A Rogue Sociologist Takes to the Streets.* New York: Penguin Press.

Vernon, Glenn. 1962. *Sociology and Religion.* New York: McGraw-Hill.

Vigdor, Jacob L. 2011. "Comparing Immigrant Assimilation in North American and Europe." May 2011. Accessible at www.manhattan-institute.org/cgl-bin/apMI/print.cgi.

Viramontes, Helena Maria. 2007. "Loyalty Spoken Here." *Los Angeles Times,* September 23, p. R7.

Volti, Rudi. 2010. *Society and Technological Change.* 6th ed. New York: Worth Publishers.

W

Wages for Housework Campaign. 1999. *Wages for Housework Campaign.* Circular. Los Angeles.

Wagley, Charles, and Marvin Harris. 1958. *Minorities in the New World: Six Case Studies.* New York: Columbia University Press.

Waite, Linda. 2000. "The Family as a Social Organization: Key Ideas for the Twentieth Century." *Contemporary Sociology* 29 (May):463–469.

Waitzkin, Howard. 1986. *The Second Sickness: Contradictions of Capitalist Health Care.* Chicago: University of Chicago Press.

Walder, Andrew. G. 2009. "Political Sociology and Social Movements." *Annual Review of Sociology* 35:393–412.

———, and Giang Hoang Nguyen. 2008. "Ownership, Organization, and Income Inequality: Market Transition in Rural Vietnam." *American Sociological Review* 73 (April):251–269.

Waldman, Amy. 2004a. "India Takes Economic Spotlight, and Critics Are Unkind." *New York Times,* March 7, p. 3.

———. 2004b. "Low-Tech or High, Jobs Are Scarce in India's Boom." *New York Times,* May 6, p. A3.

———. 2004c. "What India's Upset Vote Reveals: The High Tech Is Skin Deep." *New York Times,* May 15, p. A5.

Walker, Edward. 2010. "Activism Industry-Driven." *Contexts* (Spring):43–49.

Walker, Marcus, and Roger Thurow. 2009. "U.S., Europe Are Ocean Apart on Human Toll of Joblessness." *Wall Street Journal,* May 7, pp. A1, A14.

Wallace, Nicole. 2010. "Gifts for Oil Spill Total $4 Million, but More Is Needed." *The Chronicle of Philanthropy* 24 (14):1.

Wallerstein, Immanuel. 1974. *The Modern World System.* New York: Academic Press.

———. 1979a. *Capitalist World Economy.* Cambridge: Cambridge University Press.

———. 1979b. *The End of the World as We Know It: Social Science for the Twenty-First Century.* Minneapolis: University of Minnesota Press.

———. 2000. *The Essential Wallerstein.* New York: New Press.

———. 2012. "Reflections on an Intellectual Adventure." *Contemporary Sociology* 41 (1):6–12.

Wallis, Claudia. 2005. "A Snapshot of Teen Sex." *Time,* February 7, p. 58.

———. 2008. "How to Make Great Teachers." *Time* 171 (February 25):28–34.

Walmart. 2010. "The Ten-foot Attitude." Accessed January 17 (www.wal-martchina.com/english/walmart/rule/10.htm).

Wang, Meiyan, and Fand Cai. 2006. "Gender Wage Differentials in China's Urban Labor Market." Research Paper No. 2006/141. United Nations University World Institute for Development Economics Research.

Wang, Wendy. 2012. "The Rise of Intermarriage: Rates, Characteristics Vary by Race and Gender." Washington, DC: Pew Social and Demographic Trends.

Wasik, Bill. 2012. "Crown Control." *Wired* (January):76–83, 112–113.

Watson, Paul. 2005. "Defying Tradition." *Los Angeles Times,* April 24, p. 56.

Wattenberg, Martin P. 2008. *Is Voting for Young People?* New York: Pearson Longman.

Weber, Max. [1904] 1949. *Methodology of the Social Sciences.* Translated by Edward A. Shils and Henry A. Finch. Glencoe, IL: Free Press.

———. [1913–1922] 1947. *The Theory of Social and Economic Organization.* Translated by A. Henderson and T. Parsons. New York: Free Press.

———. [1916] 1958. *The Religion of India: The Sociology of Hinduism and Buddhism.* New York: Free Press.

———. [1904] 2011. *The Protestant Ethic and the Spirit Capitalism.* The Revised 1920 Edition. Translation by Stephen Kalberg. New York: Oxford University Press.

Wechsler, Henry, J. E. Lee, M. Kuo, M. Seibring, T. F. Nelson, and H. Lee. 2002. "Trends in College Binge Drinking during a Period of Increased Prevention Efforts: Findings from Four Harvard School of Public Health College Alcohol Surveys: 1993–2001." *Journal of American College Health* 50 (5):203–217.

———, Mark Seibring, I-Chao Liu, and Marilyn Ahl. 2004. "Colleges Respond to Student Binge Drinking: Reducing Student Demand or Limiting Access." *Journal of American College Health* 52 (4):159–168.

The Week. 2010b. "They're Watching You." (September 17):15.

———. 2011. "Fighting over Food." (March 4):15.

Weeks, John R. 2012. *Population: An Introduction to Concepts and Issues.* 11th ed. Belmont, CA: Cengage.

Wegner, Nina. 2010. "Nepal, Home of the Himalayas… and a Salsa Scene?" *Christian Science Monitor* (December 14).

Weinberg, Daniel H. 2004. *Evidence from Census 2000 About Earnings by Detailed Occupation for Men and Women.* CENSR-15. Washington, DC: U.S. Government Printing Office.

———. 2007. "Earnings by Gender: Evidence from Census 2000." *Monthly Labor Review* (July–August):26–34.

Weinraub, Bernard. 2004. "UPN Show Is Called Insensitive to Amish." *New York Times,* March 4, pp. B1, B8.

Weisberg, Jacob. 2011. "Bubble Trouble. Is Web Personalization Turning Us into Solipsistic Twits?" *Slate* (June). Accessible at www.slate.com.

Weitz, Rose. 2009. *The Sociology of Health, Illness, and Heath Care.* 5th ed. Belmont, CA: Cengage.

Welch, William M. 2011. "More Hawaii Residents Identify as Mixed Race." *USA Today,* February 28.

Wells-Barnett, Ida B. 1970. *Crusade for Justice: The Autobiography of Ida B. Wells.* Edited by Alfreda M. Duster. Chicago: University of Chicago Press.

Wentling, Tre, Elroi Windsor, Kristin Schilt, and Betsy Lucal. 2008. "Teaching Transgender." *Teaching Sociology* 36 (January):49–57.

Wentz, Laurel, and Claire Atkinson. 2005. "'Apprentice' Translators Hope for Hits All Over Globe." *Advertising Age,* February 14, pp. 3, 73.

Wessell, David. 2011. "Untangling the Long-Term-Unemployment Crisis." *Wall Street Journal,* October 20, p. A6.

———, and Stephanie Banchero. 2012. "Education Slowdown Threatens U.S." *Wall Street Journal,* April 26, p. A1.

West, Candace, and Don H. Zimmerman. 1987. "Doing Gender." *Gender and Society* 1 (June):125–151.

Westergaard-Nielsen, Niels. 2008. *Low-Wage Work in Denmark.* New York: Russell Sage Foundation.

White, David Manning. 1950. "'The Gatekeeper': A Case Study in the Selection of News." *Journalism Quarterly* 27 (Fall):383–390.

Whitlock, Craig. 2005. "The Internet as Bully Pulpit." *Washington Post National Weekly Edition* 22 (August 22):9.

Whittaker, Stephanie. 2006. "Who Would You Prefer to Work For?" *Gazette* (Montreal), November 4, p. 1.

Whyte, William Foote. 1981. *Street Corner Society: Social Structure of an Italian Slum.* 3rd ed. Chicago: University of Chicago Press.

Wilcox, W. Bradford. 2011. *Why Marriage Matters: Thirty Conclusions from the Social Sciences.* New York: Institute of American Values.

Wildsmith, Elizabeth, Nicole R. Steward-Streng, and Jennifer Manlove. 2011. "Childbearing Outside of Marriage: Estimates and Trends in the United States." *Child Trends Research Brief* #2011-29. Accessible at www.childtrends.org.

Wilford, John Noble. 1997. "New Clues Show Where People Made the Great Leap to Agriculture." *New York Times,* November 18, pp. B9, B12.

Wilkes, Rima, and John Iceland. 2004. "Hypersegregation in the Twenty-First Century." *Demography* 41 (February):23–36.

Wilkinson, Tracy. 2011. "Cuba: Now Open for Business." *Chicago Tribune,* August 15, p. 14.

Williams, Carol J. 1995. "Taking an Eager Step Back." *Los Angeles Times,* June 3, pp. A1, A14.

Williams, Christine L. 1992. "The Glass Escalator: Hidden Advantages for Men in the 'Female' Professions." *Social Problems* 39 (3):253–267.

———. 1995. *Still a Man's World: Men Who Do Women's Work.* Berkeley: University of California Press.

Williams, David R., and Chiquita Collins. 2004. "Reparations." *American Behavioral Scientist* 47 (March):977–1000.

Williams, Robin M., Jr. 1970. *American Society.* 3rd ed. New York: Knopf.

———, with John P. Dean and Edward A. Suchman. 1964. *Strangers Next Door: Ethnic Relations in American Communities.* Englewood Cliffs, NJ: Prentice Hall.

Wills, Jeremiah B., and Barbara J. Risman. 2006. "The Visibility of Feminist Thought in Family Studies." *Journal of Marriage and Family* 68 (August):690–700.

Wilson, Edward O. 1975. *Sociobiology: The New Synthesis.* Cambridge, MA: Harvard University Press.

———. 1978. *On Human Nature.* Cambridge, MA: Harvard University Press.

———. 2000. *Sociobiology: The New Synthesis.* Cambridge, MA: Belknap Press, Harvard University Press.

Wilson, James Q. 2011. "Hard Times, Fewer Crimes." *Wall Street Journal,* May 28, pp. C1–C2.

Wilson, John. 1973. *Introduction to Social Movements.* New York: Basic Books.

Wilson, William Julius. 1980. *The Declining Significance of Race: Blacks and Changing American Institutions.* 2nd ed. Chicago: University of Chicago Press.

———. 1987. *The Truly Disadvantaged: The Inner City, the Underclass and Public Policy.* Chicago: University of Chicago Press.

———. 1996. *When Work Disappears: The World of the New Urban Poor.* New York: Knopf.

———. 1999. *The Bridge over the Racial Divide: Rising Inequality and Coalition Politics.* Berkeley: University of California Press.

———. 2009. *More Than Just Race: Being Black and Poor in the Inner City.* New York: Norton.

———, J. M. Quane, and B. H. Rankin. 2004. "Underclass." In *International Encyclopedia of Social and Behavioral Sciences.* New York: Elsevier.

Wimer, Christopher, Barbara Bergmann, David Betson, John Coder, and David B. Grusky. 2011. "The Future of U.S. Poverty Measurement." *Pathways* (Fall) 20–25.

Winant, Howard B. 1994. *Racial Conditions: Politics, Theory, Comparisons.* Minneapolis: University of Minnesota Press.

———. 2006. "Race and Racism: Towards a Global Future." *Ethnic and Racial Studies* 29 (September):986–1003.

Winickoff, Jonathan P., Joan Friebely, Susanne E. Tanski, Cheryl Sherrod, George E. Matt, Melbourne F. Hovell, and Robert C. McMillen. 2009. "Beliefs about the Health Effects of 'Thirdhand' Smoke and Home Smoking Bans." *Pediatrics* 123 (January):74–79.

Winter, J. Allen. 2008. "Symbolic Ethnicity." Pp. 1288–1290, vol. 3, in *Encyclopedia of Race, Ethnicity, and Society,* edited by Richard T. Schaefer. Thousand Oaks, CA: Sage.

Wirth, Louis. 1931. "Clinical Sociology." *American Journal of Sociology* 37 (July):49–60.

Wolf, Naomi. 1992. *The Beauty Myth: How Images of Beauty Are Used against Women.* New York: Anchor Books.

Wolfe, Alan. 2008. "Pew in the Pews." *Chronicle of Higher Education,* March 21, pp. B5–B6.

Women's Flat Track Derby Association. 2012. "Women's Flat Track Derby Association." Accessible at http://www.wftda.com/about.html.

Women's Sports Foundation. 2011. *Title IX.* Accessed March 29 (http://www.womens sports-foundation.org/Issues-And-Research/Title-IX.aspx).

Wong, Morrison G. 2006. "Chinese Americans." Pp. 110–145 in *Asian Americans: Contemporary Trends and Issues,* 2nd ed., edited by Pyong Gap Min. Thousand Oaks, CA: Sage.

Wood, Daniel B. 2012. "How Serious Crime Fell in US." *Christian Science Monitor* (January 16):18.

Woon, Lee Kang. 2005. "Socialization of Transracially Adopted Korean Americans: A Self Analysis." *Human Architecture: Journal of the Sociology of Self-Knowledge* 3 (Spring):79–84.

Working Women's Forum. 2012. Home Page. Accessed March 27 (www.workingwomensforum.org).

Workman, Thomas A. 2008. "The Real Impact of Virtual Worlds." *Chronicle of Higher Education* (September 19), pp. B12–B13.

World Association of Girl Guides and Girl Scouts. 2011. "Our World." Accessed November 10 (www.wagggs.org/en/world).

World Bank. 2003. *World Development Report 2003: Sustainable Development in a Dynamic World.* Washington, DC: World Bank.

———. 2007. *World Development Indicators 2007.* Washington, DC: World Bank.

———. 2009. *World Development Indicators 2009.* Washington, DC: World Bank.

——— 2010b. *World Development Report 2010: Development and Climate Change.* Washington, DC: World Bank.

———. 2011. *Development Indicators 2011.* Washington, DC: World Bank.

———. 2012. *World Development Report 2012: Gender Equality and Development.* Washington, DC: World Bank.

———. 2012a. *World Development Indicators 2012.* Washington, DC: World Bank.

———. 2012b. *Gender Equality and Development.* Washington, DC: World Bank.

World Development Forum. 1990. "The Danger of Television." 8 (July 15):4.

World Health Organization. 2009. "Biotechnology (GM Foods)." Accessed May 11 (www.who.int/foodsafety/biotech/en/).

———. 2010. "Suicide Prevention." Accessed October 31 (http://www.who.int/mental_health/prevention/en/).

Worth, Robert F. 2008. "As Taboos Ease, Saudi Girl Group Dares to Rock." *New York Times,* November 24, pp. A1, A9.

Wortham, Robert A. 2008. "DuBois, William Edward Burghardt." Pp. 423–427, vol. 1, in *Encyclopedia of Race, Ethnicity, and Society,* edited by Richard T. Schaefer. Thousand Oaks, CA: Sage.

Wray, Matt, Matthew Miller, Jill Gurvey, Joanna Carroll, and Ichiro Kawachi. 2008. "Leaving Las Vegas: Exposure to Las Vegas and Risk of Suicide." *Social Science and Medicine* 67:1882–1888.

———, Cynthia Colen, and Bernice Pescosolido. 2011. "The Sociology of Suicide." *Annual Review of Sociology* 37:505–528.

Wright, Charles R. 1986. *Mass Communication: A Sociological Perspective.* 3rd ed. New York: Random House.

Wright, Erik O. 2011. "The Classical Marxist Theory of the History of Capitalism's Future." October 3. Accessed January 20, 2012 (www.ssc.wisc.edu/~wright/621-2011/lecture%208%202011%20--%20Classical%20Theory%20of%20Capitalisms%20future.pdf).

———, David Hachen, Cynthia Costello, and Joy Sprague. 1982. "The American Class Structure." *American Sociological Review* 47 (December):709–726.

Wright, Eric R., William P. Gronfein, and Timothy J. Owens. 2000. "Deinstitutionalization, Social Rejection, and the Self-Esteem of Former Mental Patients." *Journal of Health and Social Behavior* (March).

Wu, Tim. 2010. *The Master Switch.* New York: Knopf.

Wyatt, Edward. 2009. "No Smooth Ride on TV Networks' Road to Diversity." *New York Times,* March 18, pp. 1, 5.

Y

Yamagata, Hisashi, Kuang S. Yeh, Shelby Stewman, and Hiroko Dodge. 1997. "Sex Segregation and Glass Ceilings: A Comparative Statistics Model of Women's Career Opportunities in the Federal Government over a Quarter Century." *American Journal of Sociology* 103 (November):566–632.

Yinger, J. Milton. 1970. *The Scientific Study of Religion.* New York: Macmillan.

York, Richard, Eugene A. Rosa, and Thomas Dietz. 2010. "Ecological Modernization Theory: Theoretical and Empirical Challenges." Pp. 77–90 in *The International Handbook and Environmental Sociology,* 2nd ed., edited by Michael R. Redclift and Graham Woodgate. Cheltenham, UK: Edward Elgar.

Yunus, Muhammad. 2010. *Building Social Business.* New York: Perseus.

Z

Zakaria, Fareed. 2012. "Incarceration Nation." *Time,* April 2, p. 18.

Zang, Xiaowei. 2002. "Labor Market Segmentation and Income Inequality in Urban China." *Sociological Quarterly* 43 (1):27–44.

Zarembo, Alan. 2004a. "A Theater of Inquiry and Evil." *Los Angeles Times,* July 15, pp. A1, A24, A25.

———. 2004b. "Physician, Remake Thyself: Lured by Higher Pay and Heavy Recruiting, Philippine Doctors Are Getting Additional Degrees and Starting Over in the U.S. as Nurses." *Los Angeles Times,* January 10, pp. A1, A10.

Zeitzen, Miriam Koktvedgaard. 2008. *Polygamy: A Cross-Cultural Analysis.* Oxford, UK: Berg.

Zellner, William M. 1995. *Counter Cultures: A Sociological Analysis.* New York: St. Martin's Press.

Zernike, Kate. 2002. "With Student Cheating on the Rise, More Colleges Are Turning to Honor Codes." *New York Times,* November 2, p. A10.

Zi, Jui-Chung Allen. 2007. *The Kids Are OK: Divorce and Children's Behavior Problems.* Santa Monica, CA: RAND.

Zickuhr, Kathryn. 2011. *Generations and Their Gadgets.* Washington, DC: Pew Research Center's Internet and American Life Project.

Zimbardo, Philip G. 2004. "Power Turns Good Soldiers into 'Bad Apples.'" *Boston Globe,* May 9. Also accessible at www.prisonexp.org.

———. 2007. *The Lucifer Effect: Understanding How Good People Turn Evil.* New York: Random House.

———. 2007a. "Revisiting the Stanford Prison Experiment: A Lesson in the Power of the Situation." *Chronicle of Higher Education* 53 (March 20):B6, B7.

———, Robert L. Johnson, and Vivian McCann Hamilton. 2009. *Psychology: Core Concepts.* 6th ed. Upper Saddle River, NJ: Pearson.

Zimmerman, Ann, and Emily Nelson. 2006. "With Profits Elusive, Wal-Mart to Exit Germany." *Wall Street Journal,* July 29, pp. A1, A6.

Zimmerman, Seth. 2008a. "Globalization and Economic Mobility." Washington, DC: Economic Mobility Project. Also accessible at www.economicmobility.org/reports_and_research/literature_reviews?id=0004.

Zimring, Franklin E. 2007. *The Great American Crime Decline.* New York: Oxford University Press.

Zipp, Yvonne. 2009. "Courts Divided on Police Use of GPS Tracking." *Christian Science Monitor,* May 15.

Zittrain, Jonathan, and John Palfrey. 2008. "Reluctant Gatekeepers: Corporate Ethics on a Filtered Internet." Pp. 103–122 in *Access Denied,* edited by Ronald Deibert, John Palfrey, Rafal Rohozinski, and Jonathan Zittrain. Cambridge, MA: MIT Press.

Zogby. 2010. "Zogby Interactive: 54% Support Ethnic & Religious Profiling; 71% Favor Full-Body Scans." February 4. Accessed July 2, 2011 (http://www.zogby.com/news/2010/02/04/zogby-interactive-54-support-ethnic-religious-profiling-71-favor-full-body-scans/).

Zola, Irving K. 1972. "Medicine as an Institution of Social Control." *Sociological Review* 20 (November):487–504.

———. 1983. *Socio-Medical Inquiries.* Philadelphia: Temple University Press.

Zweigenhaft, Richard L., and G. William Domhoff. 2006. *Diversity in the Power Elite: How It Happened, Why It Matters.* 2nd ed. New York: Rowman and Littlefield.

Zywica, Jolene, and James Danowski. 2008. "The Faces of Facebookers: Investigating Social Enhancement and Social Compensation Hypotheses; Predicting Facebook and Offline Popularity from Sociability and Self-Esteem, and Mapping the Meanings of Popularity with Semantic Networks." *Journal of Computer-Mediated Communication* 14:1–34.

acknowledgments

Chapter 1

page 4: Quotation from Kelsey Timmerman. 2009. *Where Am I Wearing? A Global Tour to the Countries, Factories, and People that Make Our Clothes.* © 2009. Reproduced with permission of John Wiley & Sons, Inc.

page 23: Cartoon by Jim Morin / Morintoons Syndicate.

Chapter 2

page 32: Quotation from Patricia Adler and Peter Adler. 2011. *The Tender Cut: Inside the Hidden World of Self-Injury.* © 2011 New York University. All rights reserved. Used by permission of New York University Press.

page 39: Cartoon Doonesbury © 1989 G.B. Trudeau. Reprinted with permission of Universal Uclick. All rights reserved.

page 41: Cartoon F MINUS © 2007 Tony Carrillo. Reprinted by Universal Uclick for UFS. All rights reserved.

page 52: Figure A-3 From Gallup Poll, October 17, 2011, "Record High of 50% of Americans Favor Legalizing Marijuana Use," by Frank Newport. Copyright © 2011 Gallup, Princeton, NJ. Reprinted with permission.

Chapter 3

page 60: Quotation from Horace Miner. 1956. "Body Ritual among the Nacirema." *American Anthropologist*, vol. 58 (3), 1956:503–504. © 1956 American Anthropological Association.

page 63: Figure 9-1 Adapted in part from "The State of the World's Children 2009," UNICEF, and in part from "Progress for Children: A World Fit for Children Statistical Review," Number 6, December 2007, UNICEF global databases, UNICEF, NY.

Chapter 4

page 88: Quotation from Mary Pattillo-McCoy. 1999. *Black Picket Fences: Privilege and Peril among the Black Middle Class*:100–02. Copyright 1999. Reprinted by permission of University of Chicago Press.

page 90: Figure 13-1 From Susan Curtiss. 1977. *Genie: a Psycholinguistic Study of a Modern-Day "Wild Child,"* p. 275. Copyright Academic Press 1977. Reprinted with permission of Elsevier.

page 95: Cartoon by Scott Arthur Masear. Reprinted by permission of www.CartoonStock.com

page 95: Quotation from Daniel Albas and Cheryl Albas. 1988. "Aces and Bombers: The Post-Exam Impression Management Strategies of Students." *Symbolic Interaction.* University of California Press—Journals. Reproduced by permission of the authors.

page 97: Table 14-3 From Tom W. Smith. 2003. "Coming of Age in 21st Century America: Public Attitudes Toward the Importance and Timing of Transition to Adulthood." Based on the 2002 General Social Survey of 1,398 people. Used by permission of National Opinion Research Center.

page 102: Table 15-1 Adapted from Jill Suitor, Staci A. Minyard, and Rebecca S. Carter. 2001. "Did You See What I Saw? Gender Difference in Perceptions of Avenues to Prestige Among Adolescents," *Sociological Inquiry* 71 (Fall 2001):445, Table 2. University of Texas Press. Wiley-Blackwell Publishing Ltd.

page 102: Figure 15-1 From Henry J. Kaiser Family Foundation. 2010. Victoria J. Rideout et al., "Generation M^2: Media in the Lives of 8- to 18 Year-Olds," January 2010 (#8010). This information was reprinted with permission from the Henry J. Kaiser Family Foundation. The Kaiser Family Foundation, a leader in health policy analysis, health journalism and communication, is dedicated to filling the need for trusted, independent information on the major health issues facing our nation and its people. The Foundation is a non-profit private operating foundation, based in Menlo Park, CA.

page 104: STAHLER © 2010 Jeff Stahler. Reprinted by Universal Uclick for UFS. All rights reserved.

Chapter 5

page 112: Quotation from Philip G. Zimbardo. 2007. *The Lucifer Effect: Understanding How Good People Turn Evil.* Copyright © 2007 by Philip G. Zimbardo, Inc. Used by permission of Random House, Inc. and by Rider Books / Random House Group Ltd. For on-line information about other Random House, Inc. books and authors, see the Internet web site at http://www.randomhouse.com.

page 123: © Dean Vietor / The New Yorker Collection/www.cartoonbank.com

page 135: Cartoon © 2004 Daryl Cagle, MSNBC, and PoliticalCartoons.com

Chapter 6

page 144: Quotation from Sherry Turkle. *Alone Together: Why We Expect More from Technology and Less from Each Other.* NY: Basic Books. Copyright © 2011 Sherry Turkle. Reprinted by permission of Basic Books, a member of the Perseus Books Group.

page 146: Logo used by permission of New York City Department of Health and Mental Hygiene.

page 146: Table 20-1 Adapted from John B. Horrigan, *A Typology of Information and Communication Technology Users*, May 7, 2007, p. 5–11, www.pewinternet.org/Reports/2007/A-Typology-of-Information-and-Communication-Technology-Users.aspx. Pew Internet & American Life Project.

page 151: Cartoon by Dana Summers. © Tribune Media Services, Inc. All Rights Reserved. Reprinted with permission.

page 155: Figure 20-3 Adapted from "Demographics of teen internet users," accessed January 17, 2012, at http://www.pewinternet.org/Static-Pages/Trend-Data-for-Teens/Whos-Online.aspx and from "Demographics of Internet Users," accessed January 17, 2012, at http://www.pewinternet.org/Trend-Data/Whos-Online.aspx. Pew Internet & American Life Project.

page 162: Cartoon by Harley Schwadron. Reprinted with permission.

Chapter 7

page 168: Quotation from Peter Moskos. 2008. *Cop in the Hood: My Year Policing Baltimore's Eastern District.* © 2008 by Princeton University Press. Reprinted by permission of Princeton University Press.

page 174: Figure 23-1 Adapted from NORML 2012. Used by permission of the National Organization for the Reform of Marijuana Laws (NORML).

page 177: Table 24-1 From Robert K. Merton. 1968. *Social Theory and Social Structure*, Revised and Expanded Edition. Adapted by permission of The Free Press, a Division of Simon & Schuster, Inc. Copyright © 1967, 1968 by Robert K. Merton. Copyright renewed 1985 by Robert K. Merton. All rights reserved.

page 184: Cartoon by Sidney Harris. © ScienceCartoonsPlus.com

Chapter 8

page 196: Quotation from Rana Foroohar. 2011. "What Ever Happened to Upward Mobility?" in *What Is Occupy? Inside the Global Movement.* Published by TIME Books, an imprint of Time Home Entertainment Inc.

page 202: Cartoon © 2008 Pat Bagley, The Salt Lake Tribune, and PoliticalCartoons.com.

page 217: Cartoon by Matt Davies. © Tribune Media Services, Inc. All Rights Reserved. Reprinted with permission.

page 218: Figure 28-2 From Bhashkar Mazumder. 2008. *Upward Intergenerational Economic Mobility in the United States*. Washington DC: Economic Mobility Project, An initiative of the Pew Charitable Trusts. Used by permission of Dr. Bhashkar Mazumder.

page 220: Nick Anderson Editorial Cartoon used with the permission of Nick Anderson, the Washington Post Writers Group and the Cartoonist Group. All rights reserved.

Chapter 9

page 226: Quotation from Daryl Collins et al. 2009. *Portfolios of the Poor: How the World's Poor Live on $2 a Day*. © 2009 Princeton University Press. Reprinted by permission of Princeton University Press.

page 228: Figure 29-1 Adapted from Bob Sutcliffe. 2002. *100 Ways of Seeing an Unequal World*, Fig. 1, p. 18. London: Zed Books. Reprinted by permission.

page 229: Figure 29-2 Adapted in part from John R. Weeks. 2012. *Population* 11e. © 2012 Wadsworth, a part of Cengage Learning Inc. Reproduced by permission of www.cengage.com/permissions. And adapted in part from Carl Haub. 2010. *2010 World Population Data Sheet*. Used by permission of Population Reference Bureau.

page 232: Figure 29-4 From Chronic Poverty Research Centre. 2009. Administered by Institute for Development Policy and Management, School of Environment and Development, University of Manchester, UK. Used by permission.

page 234: Figure 29-5 Adapted from Table 1, p. 2 in OECD. February 2011. Statistics on Resource Flows to Developing Countries, www.oecd.org/dac/stats/dcrannex

page 237: Figure 30-1 Adapted from World Development Indicators 2012. © World Bank 2012a: 74–76, Table 2.9. Used under World Bank license CC BY 3.0 http://creativecommons.org/licenses/by/3.0/

page 238: Figure adapted from Edward Telles. 2004:108. *Race in Another America: The Significance of Skin Color*, Princeton University Press. Reprinted by permission of Princeton University Press.

Chapter 10

page 250: Quotation from Jorge Ramos. 2010. *A Country for All: An Immigrant Manifesto*. Translated from Spanish by Ezra Fitz, translation copyright © 2010 by Vintage Books, a division of Random House Inc. Used by permission of Vintage Books, a division of Random House Inc.

page 254: Nick Anderson Editorial Cartoon used with the permission of Nick Anderson, the Washington Post Writers Group and the Cartoonist Group. All rights reserved.

page 260: Figure 31-3 Adapted from "Voter ID Requirements." NCSL 2012a. © National Conference of State Legislatures.

page 262: Cartoon by STEIN © 2006. Reprinted with permission by Universal Uclick for UFS. All rights reserved.

page 272: Figure 33-3 © 2010 Arab American Institute.

Chapter 11

page 284: Quotation from Nancy J. Finley. 2010. "Skating Femininity: Gender Maneuvering in Women's Roller Derby," *Journal of Contemporary Ethnography*, 39(4):359–360, 371–372, 377. Copyright © 2010. Reprinted by permission of SAGE Publications.

page 286: Table 34-1 From Joyce McCarl Nielsen et al. 2000. "Gendered Heteronormativity: Empirical Illustrations in Everyday Life," *Sociological Quarterly* 41 (No. 2):287. © 2000. Blackwell Publishing. Reprinted by permission.

page 299: Figure 35-4 From NARAL Pro-Choice America Foundation. 2011. Used by permission of NARAL, Washington, DC.

Chapter 12

page 306: Quotation from Ted C. Fishman. 2010. Reprinted with the permission of Scribner, a Division of Simon & Schuster, Inc., from *Shock Of Gray: The Aging Of The World's Population And How It Pits Young Against Old, Child Against Parent, Worker Against Boss, Company Against Rival, And Nation Against Nation* by Ted C. Fishman. Copyright © 2010 by Ted C. Fishman. All rights reserved.

page 313: © Barbara Smaller / The New Yorker Collection / www.cartoonbank.com

page 314: Figure 37-2 Reprinted from *Baby Boomers Envision What's Next? Research and Strategic Analysis Integrated Value and Strategy, June, 2011*, Sources: AARP and GFK Custom Research North America 2011. All rights reserved.

page 317: Figure 38-1 From Linda Jacobsen, Mary Kent, Marlene Lee, and Mark Mather, "America's Aging Population," *Population Bulletin* 66 (Feb):3. Used by permission of Population Reference Bureau.

Chapter 13

page 328: Quotation from Katherine S. Newman. 2012. *The Accordion Family: Boomerang Kids, Anxious Parents, and the Private Toll of Global Competition*. Boston: Beacon Press, 2012. Used by permission of Beacon Press via Copyright Clearance Center.

page 342: Signe Wilkinson Editorial Cartoon used with the permission of Signe Wilkinson, the Washington Post Writers Group and the Cartoonist Group. All rights reserved.

page 347: Figure adapted from Peter S. Bearman, James Moody, and Katherine Stovel. 2004. "Chains of Affection: The Structure of Adolescent Romantic and Sexual Networks," Figure 2, p. 58. *American Journal of Sociology*. Copyright 2004. Used by permission of University of Chicago Press via Rightslink / Copyright Clearance Center.

page 348: Figure 42-1 From *United States Census Snapshot: 2010*. Used by permission of the Williams Institute, Los Angeles, CA.

page 349: Cartoon by Harley Schwadron. Reprinted with permission.

Chapter 14

page 356: Quotation from Diane Ravitch. 2010. *The Death and Life of the Great American School System: How Testing and Choice are Undermining Education*. Copyright © 2010 Diane Ravitch. Reprinted by permission of Basic Books, a member of the Perseus Books Group.

page 368: Signe Wilkinson Editorial Cartoon used with the permission of Signe Wilkinson, the Washington Post Writers Group and the Cartoonist Group. All rights reserved.

page 372: Figure 44-3 National Alliance for Public Charter Schools. (2011). *The public charter schools dashboard*. Washington, DC: NAPCS.

Chapter 15

page 378: Quotation from Nikki Bado-Fralick and Rebecca Sachs Norris. 2010. *Toying with God: The World of Religious Games and Dolls*, pp. 7–8, 29–30. © 2010. Reprinted by permission of Baylor University Press.

page 382: Cartoon © 2007 Riber Hansson, www.PoliticalCartoons.com

page 386: Figure 46-1 From The Pew Forum on Religion and Public Life, Pew Internet & American Life Project, Religious Knowledge Quiz, September 28, 2010, http://features.pewforum.org/quiz/us-religious-knowledge/

page 394: Cartoon © 2005 Sandy Huffaker, www.PoliticalCartoons.com.

Chapter 16

page 400: Quotation from John Bowes (ed.). 2011. *The Fair Trade Revolution*, pp. ix, 2–3, 231–232. Pluto Press. Reprinted by permission of Pluto Press.

page 406: Figure 48-1 From "Military and National Defense," The Gallup Poll. Copyright © 2009 The Gallup Organization, Princeton, NJ. Reprinted with permission.

page 407: Figure 48-2 From 2011 Global Peace Index, Institute for Economics and Peace.

page 412: Figure 49-2 Adapted from Inter-Parliamentary Union (IPU), 2012, Women in National Parliaments, www.ipu.org/wmn-e/classif.htm. Used by permission.

page 413 R: Figure 49-3 (right) From G. William Domhoff. 2010. *Who Rules America?* 6e. © 2010 by The McGraw-Hill Companies, Inc. Reproduced by permission.

page 422: Cartoon © 2003 Mike Keefe, The Denver Post, www. PoliticalCartoons.com

Chapter 17

page 432: Quotation from Andrew Szasz. 2007. *Shopping Our Way to Safety*. University of Minnesota Press. Copyright 2007 by the Regents of the University of Minnesota.

page 435: Figure 52-1 From Carl Haub. 2011. *World Population Data Sheet 2011*. Used by permission of Population Reference Bureau.

page 439: Figure 53-1 From UNAIDS. 2010. Adapted from Global Report: UNAIDS Report on the Global AIDS Epidemic 2010. Copyright © 2010 Joint UN Program on HIV/AIDS (UNAIDS). All rights reserved. Courtesy UNAIDS, Geneva, Switzerland.

page 442: © Michael Maslin / The New Yorker Collection / www.cartoonbank.com

page 449: Cartoon by Steve Greenberg, *Ventura County Reporter*, California, 2010. Used by permission.

page 453: Figure 55-2 From The Gallup Poll. 2012. Adapted from Energy Production vs. Environmental Protection, in "Americans Split on Energy vs. Environment Trade-Off." Methodology and results, Jeff Jones and Lydia Saad, 2012, Gallup News Service, Gallup Poll Social Series: Environment, March 8–11, 2012. Copyright © 2012 Gallup, Princeton, NJ. Reprinted with permission.

page 454: Figure 55-3 Adapted from OECD. 2009. *Green at Fifteen?: How 15-Year-Olds Perform in Environmental Science and Geoscience in PISA 2006*, PISA, OECD Publishing, http://dx.doi.org/10.1787/9789264063600-en

Chapter 18

page 460: Quotation from Nick Bilton. 2010. *I Live in the Future & Here's How It Works: Why Your World, Work, and Brain Are Being Creatively Disrupted*. Copyright © 2010 by Nick Bilton. Used by permission of Crown Business, a division of Random House, Inc.

page 463: Illustration reprinted by permission of the publisher from John B. Christiansen and Sharon N. Barnartt, *Deaf President Now! The 1988 Revolution at Gallaudet University*. Washington D.C.: Gallaudet University Press, 1995, p. 22. Copyright 1995 by Gallaudet University.

page 474: Figures A, B, C From www.InternetWorldStats.com. Copyright © 2001–2012, Miniwatts Marketing Group. All rights reserved worldwide.

page 475: Cartoon by Baloo, from *The Wall Street Journal*, permission Cartoon Features Syndicate.

page 478: Figure 58-1 Adapted from *National Geographic Atlas of the World* 8e. National Geographic Society, 2005. NG Maps / National Geographic Stock.

Trendspotting

Chapter 1: Oldenburg 1999, 2000; Putnam 1995. Chapter 2: Bureau of the Census 2004b, 2012d; El Nasser and Overburg 2009, 2012; Nordholt et al. 2004. Chapter 3: American Community Survey 2008; Table 1602; Goode 2011; Michael Link et al. 2006; P. Siegal et al. 2001; United Way of King County 2010. Chapter 4: Centers for Disease Control and Prevention 2011c; Knopmen et al. 2010; National Organization of Mothers of Twins Clubs 2010. Chapter 5: *The Economist* 2010a; Facebook 2012; Chris Taylor 2011. Chapter 6: Pew Internet and American Life Project 2012a, 2012b. Chapter 7: Bureau of Justice Statistics 2011; International Centre for Prison Studies 2010; William Sabol et al. 2009. Chapter 8: D. Cauchon 2009; H. Hartmann et al. 2010; Institute for Women's Policy Research 2009. Chapter 9: Bureau of the Census 2008b; *The Economist* 2011a; *The Week* 2011. Chapter 10: Alliance for Board Diversity 2008. Chapter 11: Bureau of Labor Statistics 2008b; 2010c; Toossi 2009. Chapter 12: Bureau of Labor Statistics 2008b; 2010c; Toossi 2009. Chapter 13: Kershaw 2009; Minyard and Ortyl 2010; Proulx et al. 2006. Chapter 14: Aud, Fox, and KewalRamani [sic] 2010. Chapter 15: Baker and Smith 2009; Kosmin et al. 2009; Lalli 2009. Chapter 16: Freedom House 2012. Chapter 17: Elizabeth Arias 2010: Table 12; Bureau of the Census 2010a: Table 102. Chapter 18: *New York Times* 2011.

photo credits

University Press. Reprinted by permission of Princeton University Press; 29.1(globe): © Rafael Laguillo/iStockphoto.com; 29.1(scale): © Jan Rysavy/iStockphoto.com; p. 228(bottom left): © AP Photo/Richard Drew; p. 228(bottom right): © Photofusion Picture Library/Alamy; p. 230: © Ingram Publishing/Alamy RF; p. 231: © AP Photo/Imaginechina; p. 233(top): © Frederic Soltan/Corbis; p. 233(bottom): © Photodisc/Getty Images RF; 29.5: © PhotoDisc Imaging/Getty Images RF; p. 236: The commercial titled JEANS was done by Springer & Jacoby Werbung advertising agency for AGAINST CHILD LABOUR (UNICEF company) in Germany. Copywriter: Sven Keitel; Art Director: Claudia Todt; Creative Director: Timm Weber/Bettina Olf; p. 239: © Stuart Franklin/Magnum Photos; p. 240: © Frances Stéphane/Hemis/Alamy; p. 244: © Pascal Saez/Alamy; p. 246: © D. Falconer/PhotoLink/Getty Images RF.

CHAPTER 10: Opener: © AP Photo/Steve Helber; p. 250: "Book Cover" © 2010 by Vintage Books, a division of Random House, Inc., from *A Country For All: An Immigrant Manifesto* by Jorge Ramos, translated by Ezra Fitz. Used by permission of Vintage Books, a division of Random House, Inc.; 31.1(top): © Library of Congress Prints and Photographs Division [LC-USZC2-1745]; 31.1(bottom): © Ken Usami/Getty Images RF; p. 254(left): © John Lund/Sam Diephuis/Getty Images RF; p. 254(right): © Motofish Images/Corbis; p. 255: © Jim McIsaac/Getty Images; p. 256(top): © Bob Daemmrich/The Image Works; p. 256(bottom): © Jay Freis / Getty Images; p. 258(top): © Enigma/Alamy; p. 258(bottom): Courtesy of Prudence Hannis; p. 259: Library of Congress Prints and Photographs Division [LC-USF33-020522-M2]; p. 262: © Tony Savino/The Image Works; p. 263: © Gaizka Iroz/AFP/Getty Images; p. 264: © Barbara Penoyar/Getty Images RF; p. 267: © Bram Belloni/Hollandse Hoogte/Redux Pictures; p. 268: © Michael Jensen/Auscape/The Image Works; p. 269: © Ariel Skelley/Blend Images/Corbis RF; p. 270: © New Line Cinema/PhotoFest; p. 272: © George Rose/Getty Images; p. 273: Courtesy of Sigma Pi Alpha Sorority, Inc.; p. 274: © Rachel Morton/Impact/HIP/The Image Works; p. 275: © David L. Moore – OR/Alamy; 33.5: © Steve Dibblee/iStockphoto.com; p. 279: © AP Photo/Steve Helber.

CHAPTER 11: Opener: © Michael Powell/Alamy; p. 284: © AP Photo/Charlie Riedel; p. 286(top): © AP Photo/Eric Jamison; p. 286(center): Picture provided by Harrison G. Pope, Jr. adapted from *The Adonis Complex* by Harrison G. Pope, Jr., Katherine Phillips, Roberto Olivardia. The Free Press © 2000; p. 287: © Gideon Mendel/Corbis; p. 288(top): © Katharine Andriotis Photography, LLC/Alamy; p. 288(bottom): © STR/EPA/Newscom; p. 289: © Bob Daemmrich/The Image Works; p. 290: © Inti St. Clair/Getty Images RF; p. 293: © John Birdsall/The Image Works; p. 295: © Thinkstock/Index Stock RF; p. 296: © Stefano Lunardi/Alamy RF; p. 297: © Steve Cole/Getty Images RF; p. 298: Courtesy of Abigail E. Drevs; p. 302: © Michael Powell/Alamy.

CHAPTER 12: Opener: © Gary Pearl/StockShot/Alamy; p. 306: Cover of *Shock of Gray: The Aging of the World's Population and How it Pits Young Against Old, Child Against Parent, Worker Against Boss, Company Against Rival, and Nation Against Nation* by Ted C. Fishman. Reprinted with the permission of Simon & Schuster, Inc. p. 307: © Hill Street Studios/Blend Images RF; p. 308: Courtesy of A. David Roberts; p. 309: © Catherine Karnow; p. 312: © Rex Moreton/Bubbles Photolibrary/Alamy; p. 314: © Gero Breloer/dpa/Corbis; p. 315: © Ron Sanford/Corbis; p. 319: Cover reprinted from the September–October 2009 issue of *AARP The Magazine*, a publication of AARP. © 2009. All rights reserved. Photo by Larry Busacca/WireImage/Getty Images; p. 320(top): © Masterfile RF; p. 320(bottom): © Stefan Kiefer/Imagebroker/Alamy; p. 321: © Detroit News; p. 323: © Gary Pearl/StockShot/Alamy.

CHAPTER 13: Opener: © Big Cheese Photo/PunchStock RF; p. 328: Image courtesy of Beacon Press © 2012 by Katherine Newman; p. 331: © Thomas L. Kelly; p. 332(top): © ImagesBazaar/Alamy RF; p. 332(bottom): © Burke/Triolo Productions/Brand X/Corbis RF; p. 333: © JupiterImages/Getty Images RF; p. 335: © Henry McGee/Globe Photos/Zumapress.com/Newscom; p. 336: © Dominique Charriau/WireImage/Getty Images; p. 338: © Hill Street Studios/Blend Images/Corbis RF; p. 339: © Lori Waselchuck/New York Times/Redux Pictures; p. 340: © Blend Images/Alamy RF; p. 341: © Cheryl Gerber for The New York Times/Redux

Pictures; p. 344: © Amos Morgan/Getty Images RF; p. 346: © Kevin Winter/Getty Images; p. 351: © Big Cheese Photo/PunchStock RF.

CHAPTER 14: Opener: © Bob Daemmrich/The Image Works; p. 356: *The Death and Life of the Great American School System* by Diane Ravitch. Publisher: Basic Books. Jacket design by Ariana Abud. Photo © Darrell Gulin/Getty Images; p. 358: Warner Bros. Pictures/Photofest © Warner Bros. Pictures; p. 360: © Mark Peterson/Redux Pictures; p. 361: © Ariel Skelley/Getty Images RF; p. 362: © Brand X Pictures/PunchStock RF; p. 363: © Comstock/PunchStock RF; p. 364: © Photodisc/Getty Images RF; p. 365: © Yuriko Nagano; p. 367: Courtesy Diane Belcher; p. 368: © Eirini Vourloumis/The New York Times/Redux Pictures; p. 370: © Ableimages/Getty Images; p. 372: © AP Photo/Troy Maben; p. 374: © Bob Daemmrich/The Image Works.

CHAPTER 15: Opener: © Jacob Silberberg/Panos Pictures; p. 378: "Book cover," *Toying With God, The World of Religious Games and Dolls* by Nikki Bado-Fralick and Rebecca Sachs Norris. © 2010. Reprinted with permission of Baylor University Press; p. 379: © Jonathan Nackstrand/AFP/Getty Images; p. 380: © Javier Rojas/Landov; p. 381: © Fox Broadcasting/Photo: Isabella Vosmikova/Photofest; p. 383: © Bob Daemmrich/Alamy; p. 388: © Kazuyoshi Nomachi/HAGA/The Image Works; p. 389: © Freedom From Religion Foundation, ffrg.org; p. 391: © Wes Pope KRT/Newscom; p. 392: © Dinodia Photo Library/The Image Works; p. 393: © AP Photo/Eric Gay; p. 396: © Jacob Silberberg/Panos Pictures.

CHAPTER 16: Opener: © George Frey/Bloomberg/Getty Images; p. 400: Book cover of *The Fair Trade Revolution* by John Bowes (ed). Reprinted with the permission of Pluto Press, London; p. 402(top): © C Squared Studios/Getty Images RF; p. 402(bottom): © Ryan Anson/AFP/Getty Images; p. 403(top): © Joren Gerhard; p. 403(bottom): © Frank Micelotta/Getty Images; p. 404: © Gamal Noman/AFP/Getty Images; p. 405: © AP Image/Marco Garcia; 48.1: © Valerie Loiseleux/iStockphoto.com; p. 407: © Tatyana Makeyeva/Reuters; p. 408: Courtesy of Joseph W. Drummond; p. 411: © Ryan McVay/Getty Images RF; p. 412: © Win McNamee/Getty Images; p. 414: © AP Photo/Haraz Ghanbari; p. 416: © The McGraw-Hill Companies, Inc./Mark Steinmetz, photographer; p. 417: © Eric Baccega/Minden Pictures; p. 419: © John Eastcott/Yva Momatiuk/Woodfin Camp & Associates; p. 423(left): © age fotostock/Superstock; p. 423(right): © Erin Lubin/Landov; p. 424: © Farjana K. Godhuly/AFP/Getty Images; p. 425: © Adeel Halim/Bloomberg via Getty Images; p. 426: © George Frey/Bloomberg/Getty Images.

CHAPTER 17: Opener: © Sonda Dawes/The Image Works; p. 432: *Shopping Our Way to Safety: How We Changed from Protecting the Environment to Protecting Ourselves* by Andrew Szasz. © 2007 University of Minnesota Press, publisher; p. 433: © Paul Souders/Corbis; p. 434: © Hill Street Studios/Blend Images/Getty Images RF; p. 436(top): Photodisc Collection/Getty Images RF; p. 436(bottom): Courtesy of Lola Adedokun; p. 438: © Janine Wiedel Photolibrary/Alamy; p. 439: © Polka Dot Images/Jupiterimages RF; 54.1: © Comstock Images/Alamy RF; p. 443(top): © Creatas/Superstock RF; p. 443(bottom): © Anthony Saint James/Getty Images RF; p. 444: © AP Photo/Nati Harnik; p. 445: © Photodisc/Getty Images RF; 54.2: © Duncan Walker/iStockphotos; p. 446: © AP Photo/John Bazemore; p. 448: © AP Photo/Eduardo Verdugo; p. 449: © Jeffrey Hamilton/Getty Images RF; p. 450: © Steve Allen/Brand X Pictures RF; p. 451: © Design Pics/Richard Wear RF; p. 452: © Macduff Everton/Corbis; 55.2(left): © Dynamicgraphics/Jupiterimages RF; 55.2(right): © Royalty-Free/Corbis; p. 455: © Sonda Dawes/The Image Works.

CHAPTER 18: Opener: © Oli Scarff/Getty Images; p. 460: Jacket Cover © 2010 by Crown Publishers, an imprint of the Crown Publishing Group, a division of Random House, Inc., from *I Live in the Future & Here's How It Works: Why Your World, Work, and Brain Are Being Creatively Disrupted* by Nick Bilton. Used by permission of Crown Business, a division of Random House, Inc.; p. 462: © AP Photo/Ed Andrieski; p. 463: © Joshua Roberts/Getty Images; p. 465: © Photodisc Collection/Getty Images RF; p. 466: © Pavel Filatov/Alamy; p. 468: © C Squared Studios/Getty Images RF; p. 469: © 2002 Joseph Rodriguez/Stockphoto.com; p. 470(top): © Caters News Agency; p. 470(bottom): © ScotStock/Alamy; p. 473(left): © Howard Boylan/Getty Images; p. 473(right): © David Cannon/Getty Images; p. 475: © Peter Menzel/Menzel Photography; p. 476: © Photodisc/Alamy RF; p. 477: © Trevor Snapp/Bloomberg via Getty Images; p. 480: © Oli Scarff/Getty Images.

name index

Wright, Eric R., 180
Wright, Erik O., 205, 245
Wu, Tim, 136
Wutich, Amber, 174
Wyatt, Edward, 152

y

Yadron, Danny, 76
Yamagata, Hisashi, 257
Yeh, Kuang S., 257

Yinger, J. Milton, 390
York, Richard, 449
Yue, Ximing, 419
Yufe, Jack, 91–92
Yunus, Muhammad, 424, *424*

Z

Zang, Ziaowei, 419
Zarembo, Alan, 404
Zedlewski, Sheila R., 105

Zeitzen, Miriam Koktvedgaard, 330, 331
Zellner, William M., 78, 100, 120, 177, 383, 390, 391
Zernike, Kate, 70
Zhang, Werquan, 270
Zhilina, Tatyana, 199
Zi, Jui-Chung Allen, 344
Zickuhr, Kathryn, 101
Zimbardo, Philip G., 112, 114, 115, 171, 179, 404
Zimmerman, Ann, 75

Zimmerman, Don H., 291
Zimmerman, Seth, 211
Zimring, Franklin E., 187
Zipp, Yvonne, 476
Zittrain, Jonathan, 401, 419
Zogby, 262
Zogby International Survey, 272
Zola, Irving K., 434, 437*t*
Zontini, Elisabetta, 479
Zuckerberg, Mark, 196, *398, 399*
Zweigenhaft, Richard L., 414
Zywica, Jolene, 103

subject index

Argentina, 229f, 235f, 349, 412f, 469
argot, 77
Arizona, 278
Arkansas, 317, 318f
Armenia, 229f
Armenians, genocide by Turks, 263
Army, U.S., 41, 42, 45, 408
arranged marriages, 335, 337
art, Native American, 267
arthritis, 441
artifacts of agrarian societies, 125
"artificial mothers," 91
Arunta tribe (Australia), 11
ASA. See American Sociological
　　Association
ascribed status, 114f, 114–115, 115,
　　122
　adoption and, 340
　in closed stratification systems, 216
　formal organizations and, 131
　in hunting-and-gathering societies,
　　125
　role conflict and, 116
　stratification and, 197, 199
　upper and lower classes, 201
Asia, 77, 474f, 478f. See also specific
　　countries
　abortion restriction in, 300f, 301
　AIDS education, 145
　immigration from, 276, 277f
　impact of globalization on, 231
　multinational corporations in, 419
　South Asia tsunami (2004), 23
Asian Americans, 252, 252t, 253f,
　　269f, 269–272
　Asian Indians, 252t, 269, 270–271
　Chinese Americans, 252t, 269–270
　Filipino Americans, 252t, 271
　interracial marriage among, 336
　Japanese Americans, 252t, 262,
　　269t, 271–272
　Korean Americans, 252t, 271
　median incomes of, 257, 257f
　as model minority, 270, 270, 278
　Vietnamese Americans, 252t, 271
Asian Indians, 252t, 269f, 269,
　　270–271
Asians, 370f
assimilation, 264f, 264–265
　of Jews, in U.S., 275
　by Native Americans, 267–268
atague (fighting attack), 440
atheists, 389
AT&T, 136
Attack the Block (film), 85
attention-deficit/hyperactivity
　　disorder (ADHD), 371
attitudinal bias, 294, 319
audience, 157–159
Australia, 200t, 229f, 336f, 357f, 454f
　Aboriginal people of, 268, 268
　aid to developing nations, 234f

Arunta tribe, 11
　assimilation in, 265
　human sexuality in, 50f
　income and labor migration, 478f
　Internet usage patterns in, 474f
　nonverbal communication in, 66
　poverty in, 214f
　property crimes in, 188
　size of economy, 418f
　subsidized child care in, 105
　U.S. students in, 361f
　voter turnout in, 410f
Austria, 229f, 357f
authority
　within families, 331–332
　hierarchy of. See hierarchy of
　　authority
　as source of power, 402, 402, 408
　submission to, 170–171, 171
Avatar (film), 119
avatars, 119, 119
averages, 52
AXA, 235f
Azerbaijan, 229f

b

Babies (documentary film), 482
baby boomers, 312, 314f, 320
"Baby Mama" (Barrino), 341
Bahamas, 200t
Bahrain, 149
Baja California, Mexico, 242f
Bangladesh, 63f, 229f, 237f, 405, 407f
　microfinancing in, 424, 424–425
　poverty in, 226–227, 232f
　television in, 161
Bank of America, 235f
barriers to success, 250
barter system, 226
basic sociology, 22, 24
BBC, 400
beauty myth, 175–176, 176, 293, 293
Beginners (film), 353
behavioral economics, 196
Beijing Olympics (2008), 450
Belarus, 229f
Belgium, 229f, 322, 349
Belize, 452
Bell v. Maryland (1964), 275
Beloved Wives Day, 114
Benin, 229f
bento box, 74
bereavement practices, 316
Berlitz method, 65
Betsileo people (Madagascar), 329
Bhutan, 229f
BIA (Bureau of Indian Affairs), 267
bias
　attitudinal, 294, 319
　gender bias, 294, 462–463

bias crimes, 185, 185f, 254
Big Boss (German TV series), 152
Big Brother (TV series), 152
Big Toe Crew, 75
bilateral descent, 330, 334
bilingual education, 79–80, 273
bilingualism, 79–81, 80f, 82, 358
Bill and Melinda Gates Foundation,
　　372
Bill of Rights, 409
binge drinking, 168–169, 172, 172
biotechnology, 471, 476–477, 480
bioterrorism, 438
"bipolar income distribution," 201–202
bisexuals, 288, 346
"Black and Yellow" (Wiz Khalifa), 160
BlackBerries, 144
Black Entertainment Television, 136
Black Picket Fences: Privilege and
　　Peril among the Black Middle
　　Class (Pattillo-McCoy), 88, 88
Blacks, 252, 252t, 253f, 266–267, 278
　achievements of, 254
　basic research on, 13, 20
　black middle class, 88, 88, 218, 267
　downward intergenerational
　　mobility, 218
　effects of Title IX on, 364
　friction with Korean Americans, 271
　incomes of, 211, 257f
　institutional discrimination against,
　　259, 267
　interracial marriage among, 336
　life expectancies of, 439
　lives of, as social problems, 46
　living near toxic waste sites, 449, 449
　lynchings of, 17, 267
　in Mexico, 240
　participation in diabetes testing, 22
　percentages of, in college, 370f
　poverty among older adults, 318
　at predominantly White schools, 370
　racial profiling of, 180
　single-parent families, 334, 338, 338f
　trends in college enrollment, 361
　unwed mothers, 341
　voter turnout among, 410
　women portrayed negatively, 290
"blaming the victims," 112, 128, 215,
　　255–256, 270
blended families, 328–329, 339, 339,
　　342
blogs (web logs), 120, 154
Bluefish, 215
Blue Valentine (film), 353
B'nai B'rith, 275
boards of directors, 259, 274,
　　294–295, 413
body image, 61
　beauty myth, 175–176, 176,
　　293, 293
　ideal, messages about, 286

"Body Ritual among the Nacirema"
　　(Miner), 60
Bolivia, 200t, 229f, 230f
Bones (TV series), 381
books, 286–287, 363–364
borderlands, 8, 241–242, 242f
born-again Christians, 387–388
Bosnia-Herzegovina, 229f
Boston, Mass., 372
Boston Pops orchestra, 131
Botswana, 116, 229f
bottled water, use of, 432
Bourdieu, Pierre, 14, 15
bourgeoisie, 203, 205
BP (British Petroleum), 150
　corporate revenue of, 235f
　Deepwater Horizon oil spill (2010),
　　18, 19, 19, 150, 450, 453
brain drain, 435
brand loyalty, 147–148, 159
Brazil, 200t, 229f, 237f, 410f, 418f
　environmental destruction in, 448
　human sexuality in, 50f
　income inequality in, 231
　middle class in, 239
　preindustrial societies in, 124
　stratification in, 238, 238f
　struggles of indigenous cultures, 76
　television as community activity,
　　161, 161
　Yanomami people, 329
breast cancer awareness, 298
British Airways, 417
British Empire, 228, 268, 392–393
bromance, 288
Brothers & Sisters (TV series), 157
Brown v. Board of Education (1954),
　　361
Buddhism, 384t, 385, 389, 390, 392
Bulgaria, 229f
bureaucracies, 137
　bureaucratization process, 133, 134,
　　134, 366–368
　characteristics of, 131–133, 133t,
　　134, 135, 137, 366–367
　oligarchy, 133–134
　organizational culture and, 134–135
　social control in, 169
bureaucratization process, 133, 134,
　　134, 366–368
Bureau of Indian Affairs (BIA), 267
Bureau of Justice Statistics, 186
Bureau of Labor Statistics, 39
Bureau of the Census, 26, 36, 295
Burger King, 155
Burj Khalifa, 472
Burkina Faso, 63f, 153t, 229f
Burma, 200t
burnout, in teaching, 368
Burundi, 153t, 229f, 416
business, private ownership of, 415
business practices, 68

C

California, 242f, 266f, 272, *423*, 450. *See also* Los Angeles, Calif.
- bilingualism in, 80, 80f, 81
- Civil Rights Initiative (Proposition 209), 422
- death penalty cases in, 189
- Heaven's Gate cult, 390
- research on discrimination in hiring, 256
- same-sex marriage in, 350
- "silver surfers," *309*
- Watts riots of 1992, 158–159

call centers, culture of, 78, *78*
Cambodia, 200t, 229f, 410f
Cameroon, 229f
Canada, 200t, 229f, 237f, 336f, 412f, 416
- aid to developing nations, 234f
- brand names from, 149f
- as capitalist country, 417t
- college graduation rates in, 357f
- at core of world systems, 230f
- First Nations, 258, *258*
- foreign students from, 361f
- human sexuality in, 50f
- income inequality in, 231
- infant mortality rates in, 435f
- Inuit tribes, 77
- knowledge of environmental issues, 454f
- media penetration in, 160f
- nuclear power generation in, *76*
- poverty in, 214f
- religious participation in, 387f
- same-sex marriage in, 349
- size of economy, 418f
- voter turnout in, 410f
- welfare in, 243

capital, 14
capitalism, 203, 415–416, *416*, 417t, 420
- case study of: China, 418f, 418–419
- in industrial societies, 415
- laissez-faire capitalism, 415–416
- Marxism on origins of, 381–382
- Marx on health in, 439
- Protestant ethic and, 381
- as "treadmill of production," 448

capital punishment, 188–190, 189f, 190f, 191
career criminals, 183–184
careers in sociology, 25f, 25–26, 26f
- academic careers, 26
- business careers, 117, *117*
- community services, 48, *48*
- criminal justice, 187
- health care research, 436, *436*
- human services positions, 367, *367*
- media consultant, 152, *152*
- military careers, 408, *408*

- in post-secondary institutions, 258, *258*
- program administration, 101, *101*
- program coordination, 298, *298*
- research assistantships, 200, *200*
- research coordinator, 48, *48*
- social media consulting, 151, *151*
- social work, 308, *308*

caregiving, 312, *312*
Carnegie Mellon University, *41*
case studies
- of capitalism in China, 418f, 418–419
- religion in India, *392*, 392–393
- Second Life®, 119, *119*, 393
- social change in Dubai, 472–473, *473*
- stratification in Mexico, *240*, 240–242, 242f
- Walmart culture, 75

castes, 199–200, 207
cattle, worship of, 15–16, *16*, 62
causal logic, 34, 36f
CBS Records, 135
CCI (Center for Community Initiatives), *21*, 21–22
CDC (Centers for Disease Control and Prevention), 347, 435
celebrities, 147, 147t
cell phones, 144, *160*, 162
- issues with phone surveys, 39, 40
- use in developing nations, 477

census, U.S., *30*, *31*, 253
- Bureau of the Census, 26, 36, 295
- estimate of gay households, 348, 348f
- overcounting and undercounting, 37
- urban segregation, 264

Center for Academic Integrity, 70
Center for Community Initiatives (CCI), *21*, 21–22
Centers for Disease Control and Prevention (CDC), 347, 435
Central African Republic, 63f, 229f
Central Americans, 273f, 274
Central Intelligence Agency (CIA), 132
Centre of Excellence on Women's Health, 258
Chad, 63f, 153t, 229f, 230f
"chaos theory" of social change, 472–473
charismatic authority, 402, *402*, 408
charismatic leadership, 462
"Charisse," 88
charitable giving, 158, *158*
charter schools
- social policy on, 371–373, 372f, *372*
- sociological perspectives of, 367, 372
cheating, culture of, 70, *70*
Chevron, 235f
Chicago, Illinois, 256, 414

- Arab American centers in, 272
- heat-related deaths in (1995), 309
- homelessness in, 47
- NORCs in, 314
- racial segregation in schools, 13

Chicago Coalition for the Homeless, 47
Chihuahua, Mexico, 242f
child care, 104–105, *105*, 106, 333
Child Care Law Center, 101
child-free marriage, 345
child marriage, 62–63, 63f
child-rearing patterns, 339–342
- adoption, 339–341, *340*
- dual-income families, 341, *341*
- in lower class, 337
- parenthood and grandparenthood, 339, *339*
- stepfamilies, 338f, 341–342

children, *93*, 344, 440f. *See also* adolescents; family(ies)
- child care, 104–105, *105*, 106, 333
- effect of media on, 146
- effects of early neglect on, 89–91
- exposed to negative messages, 99–100
- socialization of. *See* socialization
- stages of self in, 93–94

children's books, 286–287
Chile, 200t, 229f, 235f, 294f
China, People's Republic of, 200t, 229f, 230, 230f, *231*
- age at first marriage, 336f
- Apple's factories, conditions in, 423
- attempts to censor Internet, 476
- Beijing Olympics (2008), 450
- case study of capitalism in, 418f, 418–419
- as communist economic system, 417
- Communist Party in, 418, 420
- control of media in, 136
- death penalty common in, 190
- female infanticide in, 239
- foreign students from, 361f
- General Motors in, 419, 421
- immigrants from, 184, 262, 269f, 269–270
- income inequality in, 231, 239
- infant mortality rates in, 435f
- media penetration in, 160f
- as oligarchy, 403
- one-party rule in, 409
- political dissent in, 149–150
- poverty in, 232f
- revisionist history in, 358
- size of economy, 418f
- social policy on language, 81
- student protests in, 196–197
- U.S. students in, 361f
- value of ethnicity in, 71, 71f
- virtual societies in, 121
- Walmart's effect in, 75

- women in national legislature of, 412f

Chinese Americans, 252t, 269f, 269–270
Chinese Exclusion Act of 1882, 269
Chinese immigrants, 262, 269f, 269–270
chiropractors, 434
Christian Book Distributors, 378
Christianity, 71, 384t, 384–385
- born-again Christians, 387–388
- in India, 392
- music, *376*, *377*

Christian Science Church, 383, 389, 390
chronic fatigue syndrome, 437
Chrysler Corporation, 421
Church of Christ, Scientist, 383, 389, 390
Church of Jesus Christ of Latter-day Saints (Mormons), 262, 385, 389
CIA (Central Intelligence Agency), 132
cigarette smoking, 76, 175, 180
citizenship, *248*, *249*, 250, 273
City Dark, The (documentary film), 457
civic engagement, 359
civil liberties, 408
Civil Liberties Act of 1988, 282
Civil Rights Act of 1964, *256*, 259
civil rights model of disability, 116
civil rights movement, 267, 461
Civil Union Act of 2006, 346
class conflict, 16, *17*, 205–206
class consciousness, 203
class differentiation
- conflict perspective on, 204–206, 206t, 207
- functionalist perspective on, 205, 206t, 207
- interactionist perspective on, 204, *205*, 206t, 207
- Marxist perspective on, *203*, 203–204, 262
- sociocultural evolution approach to, 206–207

classical theory, 134–135
Classmates, 150
class system, 12, 201–202
class warfare, 202–203
Clean Air Act, 452
Clean Water Act, 452
Clemson University, 117
clergy, female, 383
Clery Act of 1990, 183
clinical sociology, 21–22, 24
Clinton Global Initiative, 414
closed stratification systems, 216, 221
CMC (computer-mediated communication), 464–466
CNN, 135, 152

Coahuila, Mexico, 242f
coal-fired power generation, 451
coalitions, 130, *130*
Coca-Cola, 159
code of ethics, 45
Code of Ethics (ASA), 45, 47
coercion, 403
coffee trade, 24
cognitive theory of development, 96, 96t, 98
cohabitation, 344, 345
Cold War era, 65
collective consciousness, 123, 297–298, 319–320
colleges and universities, 16, 26, 69f, 69–70, 357f. *See also specific schools*
    access to, 101
    admissions, 255, 259, 359, 422
    bias-related incidents, 254
    binge drinking on campus, 172, *172*
    costs of, 363, 363f
    crime on campus, 183, *183*
    culture of cheating, 70, *70*
    enrollment trends, 361
    financial aid, 217, *217*
    impression management by students, 95
    prospective students, *354, 355*
    racial discrimination in, 370
    social ranking in fraternities, 11
    sociology degrees conferred, 25f, 25–26
    subcultures within, 370, *370*
    Title IX issues, 364, *364*
    transition to, from high school, 117
college students. *See* students
collegiate subculture, 370
Colombia, 200t, 229f, 235f
colonialism
    of British Empire, 228, 268, 392–393
    global inequality and, 227–228, 230f, 230–231
    neocolonialism, 228, 235, 236
Colorado, 129, 150, 372
color-blind racism, 255–256, *256,* 260, 422
color hierarchy, 240–241, 274
coltan mining, 416, *417*
Columbia Pictures, 135
Columbia Records, 135–136
Columbine High School massacre, 129, 150
Comcast, 136
common sense, 8, 9
Communicare day care center, *105*
communication. *See also* language(s)
    computer-mediated (CMC), 464–466
    cultural variation and, 77
    facilitated by Internet, 159–160, *160*

nonverbal, 18, 66, *475*
    patient-centered, 444
communications technology
    distribution of power and, 414
    globalization and, 477
    privacy affected by, 475, *475*
    relationships and, 144
    use of ICTs, 145, 146t
communism, 417, 417t, 420, 472
Communist Manifesto, The (Marx & Engels), 12f, 22, 132
Communist Party, 204, 403, 409, 418, 420
communities, 32, 155f, 161, *161,* 314
community colleges, 217
Company Men, The (film), 429
comparison function, 129
compensation, 210
    employer wage violations, 212
    executive compensation, 219–220, *220,* 221
    minimum-wage laws, 206
    teacher salaries in U.S., 368, 369f
    of women, discrimination in, 295
computer crime, 184
computer-mediated communication (CMC), 464–466
computer-mediated instruction, 368
computer technology, 473, 475, *475,* 480
Comte, August, 10, 11, 15, 468
conclusions, 36–37, 37f
confidentiality, 45
conflict(s), 72, 275
    class conflict, 16, *17,* 205–206
    role conflict, 115–116
conflict of interest, 45–46, *46*
conflict perspective, 16–17, 20, 20t, 228
    on affirmative action, 422
    on aging, 309–310, 310t
    on bilingualism, 80
    on charter schools, 372
    on child care, 105
    on class differentiation, 204–206, 206t, 207
    on cultural variation, 78
    on culture and society, 72, 72t
    on death penalty, 189
    on deviance, 180–181, 181t, 182
    on downsizing, 421
    on education, 101, 361–363, 365t, 367
    on education-income relation, 37
    on environment, 448, 448f, 451, 455
    on environmental movement, 453–454
    on executive compensation, 220
    on family, 332, 333, 334, 334t
    on feminization of poverty, 214
    on gender, 289, 291t
    on global immigration, 277

on Gulf Coast oil spill (2010), 19, *19*
    on health and illness, 434–435, 435f, 437t
    on health care, 439, 440, 441
    on Internet, 162
    Marxist view, 16, *17,* 205–206, 461, 468
    on mass media, 148–153, 156, 156t
    on media concentration, 136
    on Milgram experiment, 170
    on modernization, 235
    on multinational corporations, 234, 236t
    on offshoring, 423
    on oligarchy, 133–134
    on physician-assisted suicide, 321–322
    on postindustrial society, 126
    on racial and ethnic inequality, 261–262, 263t
    on religion, 381–383, 383t
    on same-sex marriage, 349
    on schools as bureaucracies, 367
    on social change, 468–469, 469t, 471
    on social control, 170
    on social institutions, 17, 121, 122t
    on social movements, 461
    on transnationals, 479
    on welfare, 243–244
conformity
    binge drinking as, 168–169, 172, *172*
    individual adaptation, 177, 177t
    Milgram experiment, 170–171, *171,* 174
    nonconformist subculture, 370
Congo, Democratic Republic of, 200t, 229f, 232f, 416, *417*
Congo, Republic of, 229f
Congress, U.S., 292
Connecticut, 350
Conoco Phillips, 235f
consensus, 468
conspicuous consumption, 204
conspicuous leisure, 204, *205*
Constellation project (NASA), 469
Constitution, U.S.
    Bill of Rights, 409
    Eighteenth Amendment to, 173
    First Amendment to, 394
    Fourth Amendment to, 476
    Nineteenth Amendment to, 297
    rational-legal authority of, 402
    Twenty-Sixth Amendment to, 411
    "under God" a violation of, 395
consumers, 4, 400, 448
consumer technologies, 473
consumption, 448
    conspicuous, 204
    promoted by mass media, 147–148, 149f, 154–155
contact hypothesis, 262–263, 265
content analysis, 43, 43t, 44

control
    gatekeeping, 136, 148–150, 156, 434
    of mass media, *135,* 135–136
control group, 43–44
control theory, 173–174
control variables, 37
convenience samples, 36
convergence perspective, 235
"cookies," 161–162
Cooley, Charles Horton, 20t
    development of sociology and, 13, 15
    theory of self, 93, 95, 96, 96t, 98
Cop in the Hood: My Year Policing Baltimore's Eastern District (Moskos), 168
Copyright violation, 70
core nations, 228, 230, 230f, 475
Cornell University, 102t
"corner boys," 41
corporal punishment, 171–172
corporate-conservative coalition, 414
corporate crime, 184–185
corporate restructuring, 421
corporate welfare, 244
corporations, 413, 421
    big business and stratification, 204
    boards of directors, 259, 274
    multinational. *See* multinational corporations
correlations, 34
correspondence principle, 363
Cosby Show (TV series), 329
cosmetic surgery, 175–176, *176*
Costa Rica, 229f
Cote d'Ivoire, 229f
"cougars," 335
Countdown to Zero (documentary film), 429
countercultures, 78–79, *79,* 82
Country for All, A: An Immigrant Manifesto (Ramos), 250
courtship and mate selection, 335–337, 336f
coven, 391
covert racism, 255–256, *256*
Craigslist.org, 257
"cram schools," 71
Crash (film), 281
creationism, 386–387, 393, 394
creation of new identity, 117
credentialism, 362
Creek tribe, 315
crime, 182–191
    on campus, study of, 183, *183*
    corporate, 184–185
    decriminalization movement, 182–183
    following Hurricane Katrina, 8
    hate (bias) crimes, 185, 185f, 254
    human trafficking, 199, 200t, 348
    illegal immigration, 242f, 479
    illegal uses of technology, 176, 184

lack of profit in, 178
law enforcement, 116, 168, 187
marital rape, 181, 347
organized crime, 184, 185, 191, 404
pedophilia, 347–348
professional, 183–184
property crime, 187*t*, 188
related to 9/11 attacks, 184, 186
social policy: death penalty,
   188–190, 189*f*, 190*f*, 191
statistics on. *See* crime statistics
terrorism. *See* terrorism; terrorist
   attacks of 9/11
transnational, 185–186, 186*t*, 191,
   199, 200*t*, 348
trends in, 186–187, 188*f*
"victimless," 180, 182–183, 191
violent. *See* violence (violent crime)
white-collar, *184,* 184–185
crime statistics, 186–188, 191
index crimes, 186, 187*t*
international crime rates, 187–188
poverty and crime rates, 14
victimization surveys, 186
criollos, 240
critical thinking, 5, 25
Croatia, 229*f*
cross-cultural perspective, 288, *288*
cross-tabulation, 52
"cross-talk," 291
CSI (TV series), 128, 146
CSI: New York (TV series), 152
Cuba, 200*t*, 229*f*, 252*t*, 412*f*
as communist country, 417, 417*t*
control of media in, 136
immigrants from, 273*f*, 274
one-party rule in, 409
Cuban Americans, 96, 273*f*, 274
Cuban Revolution of 1959, 274
cults, 390, 391*t*, 395
cultural assumptions, 99–100
cultural capital, 14, 64
cultural convergence, 145
cultural differences, *61*
in aging, 309, 310
in death and dying, *314,* 315
cultural diffusion, *75,* 75–76
cultural goals, 177
cultural heritage, 151–152
cultural invasion, 152–153
cultural relativism, 62–63, 63*f,* 64, 72,
   400–401
cultural survival, 76
cultural traditions, 235
cultural transmission
of deviance, 178–179, 182
by groups, 127
by Internet, 358, 359
by socialization, 89
through education, 358, *358*
cultural universals, 62, 64,
   378–379, 380

cultural values, 69
cultural variation, 77, 78
culture, 58–81. *See also specific*
   cultures and peoples
countercultures, 78–79, *79,* 82
culture lag. *See* culture lag
culture shock, 79, 82
dominant ideology and, 69*f,* 71–72
elements of, 64–73
ethnocentrism and, 62
global culture war, 71–72
global development of, 73–77
indigenous cultures, 76, 268, *268*
material and nonmaterial, 76, *76,*
   162, 470, 476
merchandising and, 75
"Nacirema" culture, 60
nature of, 61–64
norms of. *See* norms
organizational, 75, 78, *78,* 134–135
resistance to social change and,
   469–470
role of diffusion and technology
   in, 74–76
role of language in. *See* language(s)
social policy: bilingualism,
   79–81, 80*f*
sociobiology and, 63–64
sociological perspectives of, 72, 72*t*
subcultures. *See* subcultures
variations in, 72*t*, 77–79
culture industry, 62
culture lag, 76, *76,* 470, 471
illegal immigration and, 479
privacy and censorship, 476
culture shock, 79, 82
culture war, 71–72
curanderismo, 440
Current Population Survey
   (Bureau of Census), 36
CVS, 443
cyberbullying, 146
Czech Republic, 229*f,* 237*f,* 435*f*

d

Dalit (untouchables), 16, 199
Dark Days (documentary film), 223
Dartmouth College, 200, 298, 435
Darwinism, 394
Das Kapital (Marx), 12*f,* 468
data collection and analysis, 33*f*
in report writing, 53
sample selection, 35–36
theft of databases, 475–476
validity and reliability in, 36
weblining, privacy and, 163
Data Truck (CMU), *41*
"date rape," 183
"daughter track," 312
day care centers, 104

death and dying, 314–316
capital punishment, 188–190, 189*f,*
   190*f,* 191
cultural differences in, *314,* 315, *315*
death due to poverty, 215
disengagement theory, 308, 309,
   310, 310*t*
hospice care, 316–317
stages of, 314–315
by suicide. *See* suicide
Death and Life of the Great American
   School System, The (Ravitch), 356
Death of White Sociology, The
   (Ladner), 46
death penalty, 188–190, 189*f,* 190*f,*
   191
"death with dignity," 316–317
Death with Dignity act of 1997, 322
decision making, 128, 414, 434
decriminalization movement,
   182–183
Deepwater Horizon oil spill (2010),
   18, 19, *19,* 150, 450, 453
Defense Department, 473, 475
Defense Intelligence Agency, 132
Defense of Marriage Act of 1996, 350
degradation ceremony, 98
dehumanization, 112, 113
deindustrialization, 421–422, *423,* 426
deinstitutionalization, 215
Delta Apparel Factory, 4
democracy, 403–404, 408
Democratic Party, 157
Democratic Republic of Congo, 200*t*,
   229*f,* 232*f,* 416, *417*
Denmark, 153, 153*t*, 200*t*, 229*f,* 275
aid to developing nations, 232–233
assistance to unemployed in, 213
income inequality in, 231
religious participation in, 387*f*
sexual norms, 332
subsidized child care in, 105
denominations, religious, 389–390,
   391*t,* 395
Denver, Colo., 372
Department of Education, 373
Department of Homeland Security, 151
departure stage, 117
DePaul University, 151
dependency theory, 230, 236, 236*t*
dependent variables, 34, 36*f*
depersonalization, 112
Desi, 270–271
developing nations, 236
abortion issue in, 301
aging in, 311
emigration from, 435
exploitation of women in, 293
foreign aid to, 232–233, 234*f*
industrialized nations compared,
   227, 228*f*
land use policies in, 448

social mobility in, 239, *239*
spirituality strong in, 387
technology use in, 102, 161, *161,* 477
television in, 161
deviance, 175–182
anomie theory of, 177*t,* 177–178,
   181*t*
conformity compared, 168–169,
   172, *172*
crime. *See* crime; crime statistics;
   violence
cultural transmission of, 178–179,
   182
Durkheim on, 177, 181*t,* 188–189
illness as, 436–437, 437*t*
poor identified as deviants, 215
social stigma and, 175–176, *176*
sociological perspectives on, 176–
   181, 181*t,* 182
sociological research on, 178
technology and, 176
deviant behavior, 14, 168–169, 172,
   172
Devoted Husband Organization,
   113–114
Dickinson College, 101
dictatorship, 403, 408
differential association, 178–179, 182
differential justice, 181
differentiation, 468
diffusion, 74–76, 233
digital divide, 153, 153*t*
Dilli (The Deal, Finnish TV series),
   152
disability, 201, 215*t*
hate crimes based on, 185, 185*f*
as master status, 115, 116, *116*
oppression of women due to, 290,
   290*f*
physician-assisted suicide and,
   321–322
disability rights activism, 116
discovery, 73
discrimination, 257, 260, 262
anti-discrimination measures,
   169–170
in compensation of women, 295
on corporate boards, 259, 274
cumulative disadvantage of, 218
discriminatory behavior, *256,*
   256–257, 257*f*
functions of bigotry in, 261
against gay and lesbian couples, 348
institutional. *See* institutional
   discrimination
against older adults, 310, 319
racial. *See* racial discrimination
sex discrimination, 239, 292, 295,
   364
against "underclass," 214
disenchantment phase of retirement,
   313

equilibrium model, 468
Eritrea, 63f, 229f
ESEA (Elementary and Secondary Education Act) of 1965, 81
established sects, 390
estate system, 201, 207
esteem, 208
Estonia, 229f
ethics
of biotechnology, 477
codes of, 45, 47
Protestant ethic, 381, 384
of sociological research, 40, 45–47, 46
Ethiopia, 63f, 229f, 232f
ethnic groups, 251, 252t, 260, 271
ethnic inequality. See racial and ethnic inequality
ethnicity, 252t, 254. See also race; racial and ethnic inequality
differential justice, 181
hate crimes based on, 185, 185f
health related to, 440–441
income inequality related to, 256, 257f
Internet use and, 157
poverty and, 215t
response to media, 158–159
social construction of, 275, 275
in social mobility, 218–219
use of Internet by, 155f
value of, 71, 71f
ethnic minorities, 266, 266f. See also racial and ethnic inequality
at disadvantage in networking, 119
family lives of, 338f, 338–339
higher death rates of, 317
living near toxic waste sites, 449, 449
in precarious work, 213
voter turnout among, 410
in workforce, 421
ethnic neighborhoods, 265, 270
ethnic slurs, 255
ethnic succession, 184
ethnocentrism, 62, 64, 72
in modernization, 235, 236
prejudice resulting from, 255
ethnography, 40–42, 44, 44t, 95, 101
Europe. See also specific countries
cohabitation common in, 344
concern for environment, 454
Eastern Europe, 417, 461
income and labor migration, 478f
Internet usage patterns in, 474f
welfare in, 244
European Union, 263, 452, 478
European Union agreement of 1997, 278
euthanasia, 321
evacuation camps (World War II), 271–272
evolution, theory of, 63

evolutionary theory of social change, 467–468, 469t, 471
executive compensation, 219–220, 220, 221
exogamy, 336, 342
expectations, 115
Expedia, 219
experiment(s), 42–43, 44, 44t
experimental group, 43–44
exploitation theory, 261–262, 265
exploitative conditions, 463–464
expressiveness, 289
expulsion, 263, 264f
extended families, 307, 329, 334, 339, 339
extremist groups, 155, 465
Exxon Mobil Corporation, 45–46, 46, 235f
Exxon Valdez oil spill (1989), 19, 45–46, 46, 450

f

Facebook, 103, 121, 145, 146, 146, 150, 151, 155, 381, 398, 399
"face robot," 475
face-work, 95, 96t
fair trade coffee, 24
fair trade movement, 400–401
Fair Trade Revolution, The (Bowes), 400, 400
false consciousness, 203, 297, 383, 462
familism (familismo), 338–339
family(ies), 326, 327, 329–344
"accordion families," 328
as agent of socialization, 86–87, 99, 99–100
authority patterns in, 331–332
blended families, 328–329, 339, 339, 342
changes in, 467t
child-rearing patterns, 338f, 339–342
complexity of family life, 328–329
composition of, 329–330, 330f
effects of divorce on, 5
egalitarian families, 332, 332, 333, 334
extended families, 307, 329, 334, 339, 339
functions of, 332, 333
kinship patterns in, 330–331
marriage and. See marriage
nuclear family, 329, 334
poverty and, 215t
racial and ethnic differences in, 338f, 338–339
role of stepparents, 333
single-parent households. See single-parent families

social class differences in, 330f, 337–338
sociological perspectives on, 332–334, 334t
stepfamilies, 338f, 341–342
traditional, alternatives to, 343–345
family traditions, 270–271
FBI (Federal Bureau of Investigation), 132, 184
FCC (Federal Communications Commission), 136
FDA (Food and Drug Administration), 76
federal bailouts, 244, 416
Federal Bureau of Investigation (FBI), 132, 184
Federal Bureau of Narcotics, 180
Federal Communications Commission (FCC), 136
federal government
anti-marijuana campaigns, 180, 180
corporate bailouts, 244, 416
environmental regulation by, 453, 453f
Medicare price control, 446
response to Hurricane Katrina, 7–8
role in health care, 446, 446–447
surveillance by, 71, 476
survey research by agencies of, 26
Federal Reserve Bank, 211, 211f
Federal Trade Commission (FTC), 162
feeding the world, 230
female-headed households, 330f, 337
female infanticide, 239
Feminine Mystique, The (Friedan), 297
feminism, 287, 297–298, 301, 333
feminist perspective, 17, 17, 19, 20
on abortion issue, 299–300
on affirmative action, 422
on child care, 105
on culture and society, 72, 72t
on decriminalization, 183
on deviance, 181, 181t, 182
on education, 363–365, 365t
on family, 333–334, 334t
on gender, 289–290, 291t
on gender-related language, 66
on global immigration, 277
on Gulf Coast oil spill (2010), 19, 19
on mass media, 154, 156, 156t
on religion, 383, 383t
on social institutions, 121
on violent crime, 186, 187
on White privilege, 257–258
on women's class position, 208
on women's status in Mexico, 241
feminist research methodology, 47–48
feminist theory, 289–290
feminization of poverty, 213–214, 215t, 337
feudalism, 201, 207

"fiesta politics," 410
50/50 (film), 457
Fighter, The (film), 223
Fiji, 60–61, 200t
Filipino Americans, 252t, 269f, 271
Filter Bubble, The (Pariser), 150
financial aid, 217, 217
Finland, 229f, 336f, 357f, 454f
brand names from, 149f
networked readiness of, 153t
prison facilities in, 169
First Nations (Canada), 258, 258
First Nations Post-Secondary Institution, 258
five-class model, 201–202
Flathead tribes, 315
Flickr, 155
Flight 93 memorial, 67
Florida, 19, 274, 341
Magnolia Project, 21, 21–22
older adults living in, 317, 318f
Florida State University, 308
folkways, 68, 73
Food, Inc. (documentary film), 457
Food and Drug Administration (FDA), 76
food supply, 230
Forbes magazine, 472
force, 401, 408
foreign investment, 234
foreign students, 360, 361f
foreign workers, 4, 24
formal norms, 68, 69t, 73, 321
formal organizations, 131, 137
classical theory of, 134–135
in religion. See religious organization
schools as. See school(s)
sociological research on, 135
formal social control, 171, 172
Fortune 500 companies, 294
Fortune 1000 corporations, 413
Fox Network Television, 135
France, 200t, 229, 229f, 230f, 454f
assimilation in, 264–265
brand names from, 149f
colonialism of, 228
expulsion of gypsies, 263, 263
French Revolution, 10
hijab banned in, 293
income inequality in, 231
media penetration in, 160f
nuclear power generation in, 76
poverty in, 214f
rate of single motherhood in, 344
religious participation in, 387f
resistance to technology, 470
size of economy, 418f
subsidized child care in, 105
TV series popular in, 152
U.S. students in, 361f
value of ethnicity in, 71, 71f

"Frankenfood," 477
fraternities, 11
Freakonomics (Levitt & Dubner), 178
Freedom House, 404
free enterprise system, 416
Freej (TV series), *151*
free school lunches, 365, 372
"friending," 103, 150
friendship networks, 14
Frozen River (film), 29
FTC (Federal Trade Commission), 162
Fulani tribe, 307
functionalist perspective, 15–16, 20, 20*t*
  on adoption, 339
  on aging, 308, 310*t*
  on bilingualism, 80
  on charter schools, 372
  on class differentiation, 205, 206*t*, 207
  on cultural variation, 78
  on culture and society, 72, 72*t*
  on death and dying, 315–316
  on death penalty, 188–189
  on deviance, 177–178, 181, 181*t*
  dysfunctions. *See* dysfunctions
  on education, 101, 357–361, 362, 365*t*
  on executive compensation, 220
  on family, 332–333, 334*t*
  on gender, 289, 291, 291*t*
  on global immigration, 276
  on Gulf Coast oil spill (2010), 19, *19*
  on health and illness, 433–434, 437*t*
  on informal economy, 420
  on Internet, 162, 476
  manifest and latent functions, 16, 357–358, 380, 476
  on mass media, 145–148, 156, 156*t*
  on media concentration, 136
  on multinational corporations, 233–234, 236*t*
  on online networking, 103
  on physicians, 444
  on postindustrial society, 126
  on poverty, 215, 221
  on racial and ethnic inequality, 261, 263*t*
  on religion, 380–381, 383*t*
  on same-sex marriage, 349
  on schools as bureaucracies, 367
  on social change, 468, 469*t*
  on social control, 170
  on social institutions, 120, 122*t*
  on social movements, 461
  on social roles, 115
  on transnationals, 479
fundamentalism
  Islamic, 62, 385, 472

religion in schools and, *393, 393*–395, *394*
  trend toward, 385–386
funding for sociological research, 45–46, *46*

g

Gabon, 229*f*, 405, 407*f*
Gallaudet University, *463*
Gambia, 229*f*
gambling, 9
game stage of self, 94, 94*t*
gangs, 16, 178, 274
garment workers, 4, *236*
Gasland (documentary film), 57
gatekeeping, 136, 148–150, 156, 434
gay liberation movement, 286
gay marriage. *See* same-sex marriage
gay relationships, 341, 348, 348*f*
gay rights activists, 350
gay-straight alliances, 369
Gaza Strip, 229*f*
G8 economic powers, 454
Gemeinschaft, 123–124, 124*t*, 125, 126, 127
gender, 23, 25*f*, 284
  as ascribed status, 115
  health related to, 441
  human sexuality and, 288, *288*
  inequalities in sports, 17
  inequality in housework, 293, 294*f*, 301
  in politics, 410, 412, 412*f*, *412*
  research on issues of. *See* sociological research
  rights of women, 10
  role in abortion issue, 299
  role in social mobility, 219, *219*, 239, 242
  social construction of, 285–291
  social factors in, 290*f*, 290–291
  social movements and, 462–463
  sociological perspectives on, 288, *288*, 289–291, 291*t*
  stratification by. *See* gender stratification
  transgendered persons, 288, *288*, 346–347
  trends in college enrollment, 361
  use of Internet by, 155*f*
  women's trade unions, 14
gender bias, 294, 462–463
gender differences
  in earnings from sports, 17
  in effects of South Asia tsunami, 23
  in social mobility, 239, 242
  in talkativeness, 8
gender messages, 42, 43
gender norm violations, 286, 286*t*
gender-related language, 66

gender roles, 285–288, 291
  among Latinos, 290–291
  among Native Americans, 290
  cross-cultural perspective on, 288, *288*
  human sexuality and, 288, *288*
  in Japan, changing, 312
  men's roles, *287*, 287–288
  socialization to, 100, 106, 285–286, 286*t*, 359
  sports and, 17
  survival skills and, 100
  traditional, education and, 364–365
  women's roles, 286–287
gender-role socialization, 285–286, 286*t*
gender-stereotyped behavior, 43
gender stereotyping, 154, 286–287
gender stratification, 282–301
  emergence of feminism, 297–298
  sexism and discrimination, 292
  single-parent families and, 293, 297
  social construction of gender, 285–291
  social policy: abortion, 298–301, 299*f*, 300*f*
  women as oppressed majority, 292–301
  in workforce, 294–297
  worldwide status of women, 292–293, 294*f*
General Electric, *219*, 235*f*
generalized other, 94, 96*t*, 98
General Motors (GM), 416, 419, 421
Generation Y, 217
genetically modified (GM) food, 477
genetic engineering, 477
genetic links in human behavior, 63
"Genie," 90, *90*
genocide, 263, 264*f*
gentile-only rules, 274–275
George Lopez (TV series), 151–152
Georgia (country), 229*f*
German Americans, 272
Germany, 200*t*, 229*f*, 294*f*, 387*f*, 454*f*
  brand names from, 149*f*
  college graduation rates in, 357*f*
  at core of world systems, 228, 230*f*
  homeschooling illegal in, 372
  immigration issue in, 277
  income inequality in, 231
  under Nazis. *See* Nazi Germany
  networked readiness of, 153*t*
  online networking in, 103
  poverty in, 214*f*
  proportion of older adults, 311*f*
  size of economy, 418*f*
  subsidized child care in, 105
  television in, 152
  U.S. students in, 361*f*
  voter turnout in, 410*f*
  Walmart's failure in, 75

gerontology, 308, 310
Gesellschaft, 123–124, 124*t*, 126, 127
Ghana, 229*f*, *314*, 400
G.I. Joe doll, *286*
Gifted LearningLinks program, 151
glass ceiling, *219*, 257, 269, 294
Glass Ceiling Commission, 257
glass escalator, 295
global activism, 461
global competition, 202
global culture war, 71–72
"global disconnect," 153, 153*t*
global economy, 4
"global factories," 233
global immigration, 276–278, 277*f*
global inequality, 209–210, 210*f*, 211*f*, 224–245
  dependency theory of, 230, 236, 236*t*
  global divide, 227, 228*f*, 229*f*
  global perspective on, 231
  global stratification, 227–236, 236*t*
  income inequality, 211, 231
  legacy of colonialism in, 227–228, 230*f*, 230–231
  modernization and, 234–235
  rise of multinational corporations, 233–234, 235*f*
  social mobility and, 237, 239, 242
  social policy: rethinking welfare, 243–245, *244*
  stratification within nations, 237–245
  wealth and income distribution, 237, 237*f*
  worldwide poverty, 229*f*, 232*f*, 232–233, 234*f*
globalization, 236
  coffee trade, 24
  communications technologies and, 477
  criticisms of, 74
  global social policy, 23
  global thinking, 22
  impact on environment, 451–452, *452*
  income inequality and, 211
  interests of core nations in, 230–231
  positive and negative effects of, *23*
  of social movements, 464–466
  social policy: transnationals, 477–479, 478*f*
Global Peace Index, 405, 407*f*
global power elite, 413–414
global reach of media, 159–163, 160*f*
global recession of 2008. *See also* economy(ies)
  assimilation and, 265
  bankruptcies, 421
  democratic reform and, 404
  effect on older adults, 314
  effects on Dubai, 473

effects on environmental issues, 454
effects on U.S. economic
    system, 416
executive compensation
    during, 220, *220*
growth of underclass and, 214
increase in precarious work
    due to, 213
study of impacts of, 6, *7*
unequal division of housework
    and, 293
global view of war, 404
"global village," 159
global warming, 450–451, *451*
GM (General Motors), 416, 419, 421
GM (genetically modified) food, 477
goal displacement, 132
GodTube.com, 393
"golden parachute" clauses, 220
"good death" concept, 315–316
goods and services, 120
Google Corporation, 48, 146, 150,
    358, 359, *423*
Google Earth, 145
Google Street View, *470*
Gossip Girl (TV series), 61
government(s), 401–408. *See also*
    federal government
inclusion of minority groups in, 410
move toward deregulation of media,
    136
ownership of industry, 417, 418
power and authority of, 401–402
regulation of economic relations, 416
socialization by, 104
stratification and, 204
subsidization of child care, 105, *105*
types of, *403*, 403–404
war and peace, 404–408
government documents, 53
GPS devices, 476
grade comparisons, 95
graffiti, 178
Grameen Bank, 424, *424*
Grand Mosque (Mecca), 387, *388*
grandparenthood, 339, *339*
Grandparents as Parents, 339
Gran Torino (film), 325
graphs, 48, 52, *52f*
Gray Panthers, 114
Great Britain, 153*t*, 200*t*, 229*f*, 357*f*,
    361*f*
aid to developing nations, 234*f*
binge drinking in, 172
brand names from, 149*f*
British colonialism, 228, 268,
    392–393
at core of world systems, 230*f*
distribution of income in, 237*f*
government ownership of industry,
    417
India's independence from, 199

informal economy in, 420
multiracial society, 265
online networking in, 103
poverty in, 214*f*
property crimes in, 188
rate of single motherhood in, 344
religious participation in, 387*f*
size of economy, 418*f*
TV series from, 152
voter eligibility issues, 479
voter turnout in, 410*f*
welfare in, 243
women in military, 282, 283
Great Depression, 210
"Great Firewall of China," 419
Great Leap Forward, 358
Greece, 200*t*, 229*f*, 311*f*, 454*f*
ancient, slavery in, 199
informal economy in, 420
unemployment in, 243
Greek Orthodox Church, 385
green-collar jobs, 452
greenhouse gas emissions, 448, 448*f*,
    450–451
green industries, 452
Greenpeace, 464
gross national income, 229, 229*f*,
    232–233
group(s), 117–118, 122, 127–130
bureaucratization in, 133
coalitions, 130, *130*
dominant. *See* dominant groups
ethnic groups, 251, 252*t*, 260, 271
extremist, use of Internet by,
    155, 465
genetic composition of, 64
influence on individuals, 12
in-groups and out-groups, 129,
    130, 251
intergroup conflict, 275
kinship groups, 330, 343
militia groups, 79, *79*
peer groups, 101, 102*t*, 106, 169
primary groups, 128, 128*t*, 130
pro-life groups, 298, 299
racial groups, 251, 252*t*, 260
reference groups, *129*, 129–130
religious groups, 74
secondary groups, *127*, 128,
    128*t*, 130
small groups, study of, 13, 14
social classes. *See* social class
special interest groups, 319
Spectrum of Intergroup Relations,
    263–265, 264*f*
group associations, 12
group behavior, 11, 128, 129
group life of society, 9
group solidarity, 11, 251
Grown Ups (film), 109
Guatemala, *99*, 188, 229*f*, 234,
    252*t*, 273*f*

Guinea, 63*f*, 229*f*
Guinea-Bissau, 229*f*
Gulf Coast
    Hurricane Katrina, 7–8, 23, 151, 215
    oil spill of 2010, 18, 19, *19,* 150,
        450, 453
Gulf War, 404
gypsies (Roma), 263, *263*

h

Habibti.com ("Mydear.com"), 337
Haiti, 229*f*, 230*f*, 412*f*, 435*f*
earthquake of 2010, 151, 158, *158,*
    340–341
networked readiness of, 153, 153*t*
hajj, 387, *388*
"Hallelujah Chorus" (Handel), 387
handfasting ceremony, 391
hand signals, 66
Hangover Part II, The (film), *148*
Hard Rock Cafe, *148*
Harley-Davidson, 159
Harold & Kumar movies, *269*
*Harry Potter and the Deathly
    Hallows, Part 2* (film), *358*
Hartland Financial Services, 259
Harvard Business Review, 163, 297,
    297*f*, 359
Harvard University, 200, 204, 250
    John F. Kennedy School of
        Government, 200
    Law School, 24
    Olin Center for Law, Economics,
        and Business, 46
    School of Public Health, 172
Harvey Milk High School, 369–370
hate crimes, 185, 185*f*, 254
Hate Crimes Statistics Act of
    1990, 185
hate speech, 176
Hawai'i, 252*t*, 266*f*, 271, 405, *405*
Hawthorne effect, 44
hazardous waste, 432, 449, 450
HBO, 135
Head Start programs, 104
health, 437
breast cancer awareness, 298
changes in, 467*t*
diseases infecting indigenous
    people, 268
effect of sports on, 17
effects of environment on, 447
of older adults, 309, *309,* 318, 441
"popular health movement,"
    442–443
social epidemiology and, 438–441,
    439*f*, 440*f*
sociological perspectives of,
    433–437, 437*t*
of working class, 310

health care, 442*f, 442,* 442–447
alternative medicine, 444–446, *446f*
conflict perspective on, 439, 440,
    441
costs of, 442, 442*f, 442*
historical view of, 442–444
inequities in, 435, 435*f*, 440–441
McDonaldization of, *134,* 443, *443*
mobile wellness van, *430, 431*
for older adults, 320, 441
patronizing attitude in, 320
physicians, nurses, and patients,
    443, 444
role of government in, *446,* 446–447
health insurance, 438–439, 440*f*
Healthy Marriage Initiative of
    2002, 344
Healthy Start Initiative, 21–22
Heaven's Gate cult, 390
heredity v. environment debate, 89,
    91–92, 176
heritage camps, 340
Hetch Hetchy Valley, 19
heterosexuality, 67, *68*
hidden curriculum, 362
hierarchical societies, 215
hierarchy of authority, 132, 133*t*, 134,
    367, 368
higher education. *See* colleges and
    universities
high school, 117, 369
hijab, 293, *293*
Hinduism, 384*t*, 385, 389, 390
caste system and, 199
partitioning of India and, 392, 395
role of women in, 383
worship of zebu, 15–16, *16,* 62
Hispanics/Latinos, 253*f*, 254, 273*f*,
    273, 273–274, 278. *See also*
    ethnic minorities
Central and South Americans, 274
Cuban Americans, 274
extended families of, *307*
family lives of, 338*f, 338,* 338–339
gender roles among, 290–291
income inequality and, 211
inequality in health care for,
    440–441
interactionist perspective on,
    262–263
interracial marriage among, 336
living near toxic waste sites,
    449, *449*
median incomes of, 257*f*
Mexican Americans, 273
percentages of, in college, 370*f*
poverty among older adults, 318
Puerto Ricans, 273–274
Roman Catholicism among, *380*
single-parent families, 338, 338*f*
social mobility of, 218–219
voter turnout among, 410

history, 6
HIV/AIDS, 50, 145
    incidence and prevalence of, 438,
        439f
    medical sociology and, 22
    physician-assisted suicide and,
        321, 322
HMIS (Homeless Management
    Information System), 48
Ho Chi Minh City Stock
    Exchange, 417
holistic medicine, 444, 447
Holocaust, 171, 263, 275, 381
Homeless Management Information
    System (HMIS), 48
homeschooling, 371, 373
homogamy, 336–337, 342
homophobia, 285–286
homosexuality
    adoption and, 341
    among older adults, 320
    considered a mental disorder, 346
    gay liberation movement, 286
    gay-straight alliances, 369
    hate crimes, 185, 185f
    labeling of, 346, 351, 437
    prejudice against, 285–286
    same-sex relationships, 348, 348f
    vulnerability of gay and lesbian
        students, 369–370
Honduras, 4, 188, 229f
honeymoon phase of retirement, 313
Hong Kong, 74, 229f
honor codes, academic, 70
Hopi tribe, 315, 404
horizontal mobility, 216
horticultural societies, 125, 125t
hospice care, 316–317
Hotel Rwanda (film), 247
housework, 293, 294f, 301
Hull House, 13, 21
human behavior, 8, 62, 63
    acceptable, defining, 177
    standards of. *See* norms
human ecology, 447–448, 455
humanistic approach, 444
human relations approach, 135, 137
Human Service Planning Alliance, 48
human services careers, 367, *367*
human sexuality, 329, 346–351
    adolescent social networks, 347, *347*
    gender and, 288, *288*
    labeling and, *346*, 346–348
    media's role in, 146, *146*
    pedophilia, 347–348
    pornography, 154, 176, 183
    prostitution, 48, 183
    same-sex relationships. *See*
        homosexuality
    sexual norms, 332
    sexual orientation, 185, 185f,
        290, 290f

social policy: same-sex marriage,
    349–350, 350f
study of, social policy and, 49, 50f,
    50–51, *51*
surveys on sexual behavior, 39, 40t
Human Terrain Team (U.S. Army),
    41, 42, 45
human trafficking, 199, 200t, 348
Human Trafficking Report, 200t
Hungary, 229f
hunting-and-gathering societies,
    124–125, 125t, 206–207
Hurricane Katrina (2005), 7–8, 23,
    151, 215
Hutterites, 390
Hyde Amendment (1976), 299
hypotheses
    conclusions supporting, 36–37, 37f
    formulating, 33f, 34, 36f

i

IBM, 259
Iceland, 344, 349, 405, 407f
Ice Road Truckers (TV series), *206*
ICTs (information and
    communications technologies),
    145, 146t
ID (intelligent design), 394, *394*
ideal body image, *286*
ideal minorities, 270, *270,* 278
ideal types, 11, 131, 417
identity(s)
    collective, development of, 463
    development of self-identity, 93
    multiple, race and, 253
    new, creation of, 117
    sexual identity, 285
    "spoiled identity," 175
identity theft, 161, 163, 184, 475
Ikebukuro Honcho, 312
*I Live in the Future and Here's How
    It Works: Why Your World, Work,
    and Brain are Being Creatively
    Disrupted* (Bilton), 460
illegal immigration, 242f, 479
Illinois. *See* Chicago, Illinois
illness. *See also* health; health care;
    specific disorders
    as deviance, 436–437, 437t
    as dysfunction, 433–434
    higher rates of, in men, 292
    sociological perspectives of,
        433–437, 437t
IMAX, 135
immigrants, 14, 184, 213
    Asian, 269, 270–271
    feminist perspective on, 48
    integrative function of religion for,
        380–381
    Japanese policy toward, 312

laborers in Dubai, treatment of,
    472–473
not seen as "White," 252
protests by, 278
in sweatshops, 270
transnationals, 276, 278, 477–479,
    478f, 480
immigration, 237, 435
    global, social policy on, 276–278,
        277f
    illegal, 242f, 479
    sociological perspectives of,
        276–277
Immigration Act of 1965, 271
Immigration and Naturalization
    Service, 271, 371
Immigration Reform and Control Act
    of 1986, 277
impersonality, 132, 133t, 134, 367, *368*
impression management, 94, 95, *95,*
    96t, 98, 103
incest taboo, 336
incidence of disease, 438
inclusion, 468
income, 17, 155f, 157. *See also*
    wealth
    "bipolar income distribution,"
        201–202
    dual-income families, 341, *341*
    education and. *See* education-
        income correlation
    financial aid for college and, 217
    gross national income, 229f
    intergenerational mobility based on,
        216, 218f
    social class and, 209–211, 210f
income inequality, 237, 237f, 240, 318
    global, 211, 231
    by race, ethnicity, and gender, 256,
        257f
    in U.S., 198f, 231, 237f, 238f
income tax rates, 202–203
Inconvenient Truth, An (documentary
    film), 57
independent variables, 34, 36f
index crimes, 186, 187t
India, 63f, 200t, 229f, 336f, 361f
    Arumugam Knowledge Centre, 153
    assimilation in, 264
    bilingualism in, 79
    British colonial domination of, 228
    call centers in, 78, *78*
    caste system in, 199
    concern for environment, 454
    Dongria Kondh tribe, *458, 459*
    female infanticide in, 239
    Hinduism and Buddhism in, 385, 392
    human sexuality in, 50f
    immigrants from, 269f, *269,*
        270–271, 472
    income inequality in, 239
    infant mortality rates in, 435f

media penetration in, 160f
Nayar people of, 339
partitioning of (1947), 263, 264f,
    392–393, 395
poverty in, 232f
religion in, *392,* 392–393, 395
religious warfare in, 381
at semiperiphery of world systems,
    230f
size of economy, 418f
social inequality in, *233*
value of ethnicity in, 71, 71f
virtual societies in, 121
voter turnout in, 410f
women in national legislature
    of, 412f
women's social movements in,
    463, 464
worship of zebu in, 15–16, *16,* 62
Indian Gambling Regulatory Act of
    1988, 268
individual(s), 9, 12, 345, 390, 454
individual adaptation, 177, 177t, 178
Indonesia, 23, 229f, 230f, 479
industrialization, 310
industrialized nations
    aid to developing nations, 232–233
    concern for environment, 454
    developing nations compared,
        227, 228f
    inequality of women in, 293, 294f
    labor unions discouraged in, 234
    proportion of older adults, 311, 311f
    responsibility for consumption, 448
    social mobility in, 237, 239
    spirituality weak in, 387
Industrial Revolution, 125, 227, 415,
    417, 470
industrial societies, 125, 415, 420
infant mortality, 21–22
infant mortality rates, 435, 435f, 440
influence, 401–402, 408
informal economy, 420
informal norms, 68, 69t, 73
information and communications
    technologies (ICTs), 145, 146t
in-groups, 129, 130, 251
Inheritors, The (documentary
    film), 247
innovation, 73, 233
    in individual adaptation, 177,
        177t, 178
    technological, 176, 184, 451
innovators, 14
institutional discrimination
    against Blacks, 259, 267
    boards of directors, 259, 274
    sexism, 292, 301
    social institutions, 121
    voter ID requirements as, 259,
        260, 260f
in-store health clinics, 443, *443*

instrumentality, 289
integrative function, 358, 380–381
intellectual technologies, 359
intelligence, 92
intelligent design (ID), 394, *394*
interactionist perspective, 18, 20, 20*t*
  on adoption, 339–340
  on aging, 309, *309,* 310*t*
  on charismatic authority, 402
  on child care, 105
  on class differentiation, 204, *205,*
    206*t,* 207
  on coalitions, 130
  on culture and society, 72*t*
  on deviance, 178–179, 181*t,* 182
  on education, 365, 365*t*
  on environment, 451
  on executive compensation, 220
  on family, 332, 333, *333,* 334, 334*t*
  on gender, 291, 291*t*
  on Gulf Coast oil spill (2010),
    19, *19*
  on health and illness, 435–436, 437*t*
  on language, 77
  on mass media, 154*f,* 154–156,
    155*f,* 156*t*
  on media concentration, 136
  on microfinancing, 424–425
  on physicians, 444, 445
  on racial and ethnic inequality,
    262–263, 263*t*
  on same-sex marriage, 349
  on school prayer, 395
  on social institutions, 121, 122*t*
  on transnationals, 479
interconnectedness, 447–448
interdependence, 233–234
interethnic marriage, 275, 336
intergenerational mobility, 216–217,
  218, 218*f,* 237
"intergenerational sex," 347–348
intermarriage, 264
  interethnic, 275, 336
  interracial, 68, 264, 336, *336*
international adoption, 91, 340
international crime rates, 187–188
International Criminal Police
  Organization (Interpol), 185
international death penalty rates, 190*f*
International Monetary Fund, 230
international trade, 405
International Women Count
  Network, 208
Internet, 136, 137, 155*f,* 157, 474, 474*f*
  access to, restricted, 419, 476
  availability of education on, 368
  cautions in using for research, 53
  communication facilitated by,
    159–160, *160*
  conflict perspective on, 162
  connection with peers, 101
  cultural transmission by, 358, 359

cyberattacks, 408
  development of, 473, 475
  in development of charismatic
    authority, 402
  functionalist perspective on,
    162, 476
  gatekeeping on, 149
  growth of online networking, 103,
    103*f, 103*
  health care information from, 444
  news of terrorist attacks, 146
  online dating, 335, 337
  online gaming, 153, 154
  political participation on,
    409–410, 411
  pornography on, 154
  religion on, 393
  restrictions on, 401
  "shadow" systems, 150
  social activism and, 464, *466*
  socialization of children by, 101,
    102, 102*f*
  U.S. dominance of, 76
  use by older adults, *98,* 155, 308
  use by transnationals, 478–479
  used by extremists, 155, 465
Internet communities, 32
Internet hosts, 475
Internet search filters, 150, *150*
internships, 25
interracial marriage, 68, 264,
  336, *336*
interview(s), 39, 44
interviewers, 39
intragenerational mobility, 217
Inuit tribes, 77
invention, 73, 233
Invisible Man (Ellison), 266–267
involuntary retirement, 313
Iowa, 48, 317, 318*f,* 350
Iowa Institute for Community
  Alliances, 48
iPhones, 144
Iran, 200*t,* 230*f,* 412*f*
  death penalty common in, 190
  value of ethnicity in, 71, 71*f*
Iraq, 229*f,* 232*f,* 405, 407*f*
  control of media in, 136
  invasion of Kuwait, 404
  norms in, 68
  overthrow of Hussein, 101
Iraq War, 145, 476
Ireland, 229*f,* 230, 357*f*
  aid to developing nations, 234*f*
  division of housework in, 294*f*
  religious participation in, 387*f*
Iron Chef (TV series), 152
iron law of oligarchy, 133–134
"Isabelle," 89–90, 91
Islam, 384*t,* 384–385, 389, 392.
  See also Muslims
Islamic extremism, 465

Islamic fundamentalism, 62,
  385, 472
Israel, 229*f,* 230, 381
Issei, 271
Italian Americans, 184, 272
Italy, 229*f,* 311*f,* 361*f,* 454*f*
  brand names from, 149*f*
  online networking in, 103
  property crimes in, 188
  size of economy, 418*f*
  voter turnout in, 410*f*

j

jail. *See* prisons
Jainism, 392
Jamaica, 229*f,* 237*f*
Japan, 200*t,* 229*f,* 357*f,* 361*f,* 454*f*
  aging in, 311, 311*f,* 312
  aid to developing nations, 234*f*
  attack on Pearl Harbor, 271
  brand names from, 149*f*
  concern for environment, 454
  at core of world systems, 228,
    230, 230*f*
  "cram schools" in, 71
  diffusion of culture, 74
  education in, 362
  gender issues in, *288,* 312
  immigrants from, 269*f,* 271–272
  infant mortality rates in, 435*f*
  marriage in, 113–114
  networked readiness of, 153*t*
  size of economy, 418*f*
  sterilization of disabled persons
    in, 116
  traditional authority in, 402
  TV series from, 152
  Universal Studios Osaka, *125*
Japanese Americans, 252*t,* 262, 269*f,*
  271–272
Jehovah's Witnesses, 390
Jewish Americans, *274,* 274–275
Jewish toys, 378
Jews, 252*t. See also* Israel
  anti-Semitism, 274, 275
  attempts of Nazis to exterminate,
    171, 263, 275, 381
Jim Crow laws, 267
Joan Rivers: A Piece of Work
  (documentary film), 325
John F. Kennedy School of
  Government (Harvard), 200
Johns Hopkins University, 80
Jordan, 229*f,* 412*f*
Judaism, 384*t,* 385, 390
Jumping The Broom (film), 223
Junior Girl Scout Handbook
  (Girl Scouts of the USA), 42
juries, 128
Justice Department, 416

k

Kaliai people, 316
kava kava, 446
Kazakhstan, 229*f,* 235*f*
Kentucky, 190
Kenya, 71, 71*f,* 229*f,* 239
Kinsey (film), 57
Kinsey Report (Kinsey et al), 50
kinship, 330–331, 334
kinship groups, 330, 343
*Kitzmiller v. Dove Area School
  District* (2005), 394
Knowledge Center (India), 153
Koran (Qur'an), 272, *412*
Korea
  North Korea, 136, 200*t,* 229*f,*
    232*f,* 417*t*
  South Korea. *See* South Korea
Korean Americans, 252*t,* 269*f,* 271
Korean War, 271
Korean Women's Association United
  (KWAU), 464
Kota people, 96
Kraft Foods, 155
Ku Klux Klan, 72, 254, 267, 465
Kuwait, 404, 412*f*
KWAU (Korean Women's Association
  United), 464
Kyoto Protocol (1997), 451
Kyrgyzstan, 229*f*

l

labeling, 179–180, *346,* 346–348
labeling perspective
  on aging, 309, 310, 310*t*
  in classroom, 365
  of deviance, 179–180, 181*t,* 182
  on health and illness, 436–437, 437*t*
  on racial and ethnic inequality,
    262, 263*t*
labor force participation. *See*
  workforce
labor unions, 135, 204, 234, 372
laissez-faire capitalism, 415–416
Lakota tribes, 315
La Mission (film), 303
language(s), 64–66, 73, 77
  Arabic, 65, 272
  bilingualism, 79–81, 80*f,* 82, 273
  of Central and South America, 274
  English-only issue, 66, 81, 259
  Internet's most-used languages, 474*f*
  linguistic isolation, 66
  nonverbal communication, 18,
    66, *475*
  Sapir-Whorf hypothesis, 65–66
  symbolism and, 67, *67*
  written and spoken, 65–66

Laos, 229*f*
Las Vegas, Nev., 9
latent functions, 16, 358, 380, 476
Latin America. *See also specific
    countries*
  abortion issue in, 299, 300*f*, 301
  concern for environment, 454
  immigration from, 276, 277*f*
  impact of globalization on, 231
  Internet usage patterns in, 474*f*
  liberation theology in, 382
  slavery in, 199
"Latin Americanization" of U.S., 253
Latinos. *See* Hispanics/Latinos
Latvia, 229*f*
law(s), 68, 220, 300, 344. *See also
    specific laws*
  against affirmative action, 422
  antitrust legislation, 416
  English-only legislation, 81
  against homeschooling
      (Germany), 372
  against human trafficking, 199, 200*t*
  immigration laws, 278
  Jim Crow laws, 267
  justifications for violating, 178
  minimum-wage laws, 206
  as social control, 173, *173*, 174
law enforcement, 168, 187
LDs (learning disorders), 371
leadership, 462
League of Arab States, 272
learning disorders (LDs), 371
Lebanon, 229*f*, 272, 381
leniency for white-collar crime, 185
leprosy, congenital, 436
lesbian relationships, 348, 348*f*
Lesotho, 153*t*, 229*f*
lethal injection, 190
liberal-labor coalition, 414
liberation theology, 382, 384
Liberia, 229*f*
Libya, 149, 229*f*
life chances, 215–216, 221, 230, 267
life course, 96–97, 97*t*, 311–316
life course approach, 97
life expectancy, 309, 435, 439, 441
Life in a Day (film), 482
lifestyles, diverse, 329, 344–345
linguistic isolation, 66
LinkedIn, 150
literature review, 33*f*, 34, 35*f*
Lithuania, 229*f*
"living wills," 316
London Business School, 477
looking-glass self, 93, 96*t*, 98
Los Angeles, Calif. *See also*
    California
  Arab American centers in, 272
  Olympics held in (1984), 450
  Watts riots of 1992, 158–159
Los Angeles Times, 146

Lou Gehrig's disease, 321
Louisiana, 7–8, 23, 151, 215
Louisiana State University, 102*t*
love relationship, 337
lower class, 201, 337
lower-middle class, 201
Lucifer Effect, The (Zimbardo), 112,
    112, 113
Luddites, 470
Lutheran Church, 389
Luther College, 286
Luxembourg, 232–233
lynchings, 17, 267

m

Macedonia, 229*f*
machismo, 338–339
macro-level research
  Asian-American stereotypes, 270
  Durkheim's suicide study, 8–9, 12*f*,
      14, 22, 46
  international crime rates, 187
macrosociological perspective
  of audience, 157
  ecological modernization, 449
  of socialization, 89
  of sociocultural evolution, 126
macrosociology, 14, 15, 17
Madagascar, 229*f*, 329
Magnolia Project, *21*, 21–22
Maid in Manhattan (film), 216
Maine, *304*, 305
"majority minority" counties, 266*f*
Malawi, 63*f*, 229*f*
Malaysia, 50*f*, 200*t*, 229*f*, 231, *239*
male-headed households, 330*f*
Mali, 63*f*, 229*f*
manifest functions, 16, 357–358,
    380, 476
maquiladoras, 241, 242*f*
Margin Call (film), 429
marijuana, 52*f*
  government campaigns against,
      180, *180*
  medical marijuana, *166, 167*, 173,
      174*f*
marital rape, 181, 347
marriage, 68, 69, 335–342
  arranged, 335, 337
  child-free, 345
  child marriage, 62–63, 63*f*
  couples living apart, 341, *341*
  courtship and mate selection,
      335–337, 336*f*
  delay in, 336, 336*f*
  divorce and. *See* divorce
  effects of female employment
      on, 296
  gay or lesbian. *See* same-sex
      marriage

impact of global recession on, 6
interethnic, 264, 275
interracial, 68, 264, 336, *336*
  in Japan, 113–114
marital rape, 181, 347
  within minority groups, 251
remarriage, 343
married couples, 330*f*
Martineau, Harriet, 10, *10*, 15
Marx, Karl, 16–17, *17*, 20*t*, 22, 23
  Communist Manifesto, The (with
      Engels), 12*f*, 22, 468
  conflict perspective on, 205–206,
      461, 468
  Das Kapital, 12*f*, 468
  development of sociology and, 12,
      12, 14, 15
  false consciousness concept, 203,
      297, 383, 462
  on health in capitalist societies, 439
  perspective on religion, 382–383,
      383*t*
  on power elite, 412–413
  socialist theory of, 417, 461, 462,
      468–469, *469*
  view of class differentiation, *203*,
      203–204, 262
Marxism
  in conflict perspective, 16, *17*
  dominant ideology concept, 72
  Marxist class theory, 261–262
  on origins of capitalism, 381–382
Maryland, 168, 350
masculinity, 287
Massachusetts, 349, 350, 372, *423*
Massmart, 75
mass media, 142–163
  audience, 157–159
  consumption promoted by, 147–148,
      149*f*, 154–155
  control of, *135*, 135–136
  in development of charismatic
      authority, 402
  differential coverage of female
      politicians, 410, 412
  global reach of, 159–163, 160*f*
  global spread of arts and, *75*
  health care information from, 444
  inaccurate views of family, 329
  socialization of children by, 101–
      102, 102*f*
  social policy: media concentration,
      135, 135–136
  social policy: right to privacy,
      161–163, *162*
  sociological perspectives on,
      145–156, 146*t*, 156*t*
mass migrations, 276
master status, 122
  "being old" as, 307, 310
  disability as, 115, 116, *116*
Match.com, 49

material culture, 76, *76*, 162, 470, 476
Mato Grosso (Brazil), 76
matriarchy, 332
matrilineal descent, 331, 334, 338
matrix of domination, 290, 290*f*, 291
Mauritania, 153*t*, 200*t*, 229*f*
Mauritius, 229*f*
McDonaldization of society, 74
  biotechnology, 476
  bureaucratization, 133, 134, *134*
  health care, *134*, 443, *443*
McDonald's, 74–75, 131, 133, 461
Meals on Wheels, 308
mean, 52
"meaningful adjacencies," 67
mechanical solidarity, 123
media monitoring, 150–151, 153
median, 52
median incomes, 257*f*
Medicaid, 315–316, 417, 446
medicalization of society, 434,
    434, 437
medical marijuana, *166, 167*, 173,
    174*f*
medical model, 116, 434
medical sociology, 22
Medicare, 315–316, 417, 446
Medium (TV series), 152
men, 210, 257*f*, 296, *296*
  in "female" occupations, 116, 287,
      287, 295
  gender roles, *287*, 287–288
  higher rates of illness in, 292
  life expectancies of, 439
  multiple masculinities, 288, 291
  occupational mobility of, 217
  single-parent families, 341–342
  support of feminist movement, 287
Merton, Robert, 20*t*
  anomie theory of deviance, 177*t*,
      177–178, 181*t*
  development of sociology and,
      14, 15
mestizos, 240
metrosexuals, 288
Mexican Americans, 252*t*, 273, 273*f*
  curanderismo, 440
  familismo and *machismo*, 338–339
  rites of passage, 96
Mexican American War of 1848, 273
Mexican Indians, 240, 241
Mexico, 200*t*, 229*f*, 230*f*, 357*f*, 454*f*
  age at first marriage, 336*f*
  brand names from, 149*f*
  as capitalist country, 417*t*
  distribution of income in, 237*f*
  foreign students from, 361*f*
  homicide rates in, 188
  human sexuality in, 50*f*
  immigration from, 273, 273*f*, 277
  income inequality in, 231
  infant mortality rates in, 435*f*

sociological imagination, 5, 9,
    22–23, 24
sociological research, 22, 26, 30–53
    on abortion, 50–51
    on adolescent social networks,
        347, *347*
    on affirmative action, 422, *422*
    on ageism, 320, *320*
    on Amish society, 100, *100*
    basic research on Blacks, 13, 20
    on campus crime, 183, *183*
    careers in, 48, *48,* 200, *200,*
        436, *436*
    on charter schools, 372–373
    complicated by cell phone usage, 40
    on computer-mediated
        communication, 465, *465*
    on cross-sex conversations, 291
    on deviance, 178
    on disability as master status,
        116, *116*
    on discrimination in hiring, 256
    Durkheim's suicide study, 8–9, 12*f,*
        14, 22, 46
    "Elmtown" study, 369
    ethics of, 40, 45–47, *46*
    on formal organizations, 135
    on gender images, 284–285
    on gender messages in scouting,
        42, *42*
    on gender preference in bosses,
        296, *296*
    global issues, 48
    graphs used in, 48, 52, 52*f*
    on Gulf Coast oil spill of 2010,
        19, *19*
    Hawthorne effect, 44
    on intellectual technologies, 359
    Internet search filters in, 150, *150*
    on jury decision making, 128
    on lying in online dating, 49, *49*
    macro-level. *See* macro-level
        research
    on McDonaldization of health care,
        443, *443*
    on microfinancing, 424–425
    micro-level, 14, 291, 333, 435
    mock prison experiment, 112,
        114, 404
    on pluralist model, 414
    on popularity, 101, 102*t*
    on poverty, 212–215, 214*f,* 226–227
    primate studies of socialization, 91
    quantitative and qualitative, 39–40
    report writing, 53
    research designs. *See* research
        designs
    research methodology, 47–51,
        50*f, 51*
    scientific method in. *See* scientific
        method
    on social institutions, 121

on socializing online, 103, 103*f, 103*
on social networks and obesity,
    118, *118*
social policy and, 50–51
statistics used in, 48, 52, 52*f*
technological advances and, 48–49
on toxic waste sites, 449, *449*
on transracial adoption, 340, *340*
twin studies, 91–92
value neutrality in, 33, 46–47
on violation of gender norms, 286,
    286*t*
on welfare reform, 200
on women leaving work, 297, 297*f*
sociological theory(ies), 8–9, 22
    activity theory of aging, 308, 309,
        309, 310, 310*t*
    anomie theory of deviance, 177*t,*
        177–178, 181*t*
    "chaos theory" of change, 472–473
    classical theory of organizations,
        134–135
    cognitive theory of development, 96,
        96*t,* 98
    control theory, 173–174
    dependency theory, 230, 236, 236*t*
    disengagement theory, 308, 309,
        310, 310*t*
    evolutionary theory of change,
        467–468, 469*t,* 471
    exploitation theory, 261–262, 265
    feminist theory, 289–290
    Marx: class theory, 261–262
    Marx: socialist theory, 417, 461,
        462, 468–469, *469*
    modernization theory, 235, 236, 236*t*
    social disorganization theory,
        179, 182
sociology, 5–9, *6,* 21–24
    applied v. clinical, 21–22, 24
    careers in. *See* careers in sociology
    common sense and, 8, 9
    macrosociology, 14, 15, 17
    microsociology, 13, 14, 15
    nature of, 5–9
    origin of term, 10
    social sciences and, 6–8, 7*t*
    sociological imagination, 5, 9,
        22–23, 24
sociology, development of, 10–15
    early thinkers, 10–13, 12*f*
    during 20th century, 13–14
Somalia, 63*f,* 229*f,* 405, 407*f*
Sonora, Mexico, 242*f*
Sony of Japan, 135
Souls of Black Folk (DuBois), 12*f*
South Africa, Republic of, 200*t,* 229*f*
    apartheid in, 200, 264
    binge drinking in, 172
    cell phone use in, 477
    distribution of income in, 237
    regulation of sexuality in, 346

same-sex marriage in, 346, 349
    voter turnout in, 410*f*
South America, 478*f. See also specific
    countries*
South Americans, 273*f,* 274
Southeast Asia, 77
Southeastern Louisiana University,
    102*t*
Southern Baptist Church, 388
Southern Christian Leadership
    Conference (SCLC), 267
Southern Sociological Society, 373
Southern U.S., 200, 267
South Korea, 200*t,* 229*f,* 230, 454*f*
    brand names from, 149*f*
    "cram schools" in, 71
    divorce in, 344
    foreign students from, 361*f*
    immigrants from, 269*f,* 271
    transracial adoption from, 340
    voter turnout in, 410*f*
    Walmart's failure in, 75
    women's social movements in, 463,
        464
sovereignty movement, 405, *405*
Soviet Union. *See also* Russia
    breakup of (1991), 404
    during Cold War era, 65
    collapse of, 472
    as communist economic
        system, 417
Space and Missile Defense Command
    (SMDC), 408
Spain, 149*f,* 200*t,* 229*f,* 361*f*
    informal economy in, 420
    same-sex marriage in, 349
    size of economy, 418*f*
    unemployment in, 243
    welfare cutback protests, *244*
Spanish-American War (1899), 271
special interest groups, 319
Spectrum of Intergroup Relations,
    263–265, 264*f*
Spencer, Herbert, 10–11, 13, 15
SPM (Supplemental Poverty
    Measure), 212
"spoiled identity," 175
sports, 17, 154
    effects of Title IX on, 364, *364*
    McDonaldization of, 134
    roller derby, 284
    teacher-expectancy effect
        in, 365
    televised coverage of, 43
"spyware," 162
Sri Lanka, 229*f*
*SSKKMS (Shoshit, Shetkari,
    Kashtakari, Kamgar, Mukti
    Sangharsh),* 464
SS St. Louis, 276
stability, 468
stability phase of retirement, 313

stages of self, 96*t*
    game stage, 94, 94*t*
    play stage, 93–94, 94*t*
    preparatory stage, 93, 94*t*
"stained glass ceiling," 382
Stanford University, 359, 372–373
Starbucks, 24, 74, 134, 234
"Star-Spangled Banner," 81
starvation, 227
State Department, 199
State University of New York at
    Albany, 102*t*
State University of New York at Stony
    Brook, 102*t*
statistics
    in completing census, 37
    on crime. *See* crime statistics
    divorce statistics, 343, 343*f*
    population statistics, 36, 266*f,* 273,
        318*f,* 467*f*
    use in sociological research, 48,
        52, 52*f*
status(es), 114–115, 122
    achieved. *See* achieved status
    ascribed. *See* ascribed status
    bestowed by education, 358,
        362–363, 363*f*
    conferred by mass media, 147, 147*t*
    master status. *See* master status
    social behavior conditioned
        by, 121
    socioeconomic status, 208,
        211, 333
    of women, inequality in, 46, 241,
        292–293, 294*f*
status groups, 204, 207
STDs (sexually transmitted
    diseases), 347
stem cell research, 392, *414*
stepfamilies, 342
stepparents, 333
stereotypes
    of Asian Americans, 270, *270*
    created through social
        meanings, 255
    of older adults, negative, 114
    of "poor people," 213
    racism rooted in, 255, 260
    unreliability of, 151
    of unwed mothers, 341
    of women, in TV and books,
        286–287
stereotyping
    in antidrug initiatives, 262
    by gender, 154, 286–287
    negative, 114, 173, 262
stigma. *See* social stigma
"Stolen Generations," 268
"stone soup," 227
stratification, 197–207
    by age. *See* aging
    along racial lines, 254

violence (violent crime)—*Cont.*
  Oklahoma City bombing of 1995, 188
  rape, 128, 181, 183, 347
  Virginia Tech shootings, 150, 172, 183
  Watts riots of 1992, 158–159
Virginia, *248, 249*
Virginia Tech shootings, 150, 172, 183
virtual worlds, *119,* 119–120, 122, 475
vocational subculture, 370
Volkswagen, 235*f*
volunteering, 309
Voter News Service, 348
voting
  eligibility issues, 479
  by older adults, 317
  voter ID requirements, 259, 260, 260*f*
  voter turnout, 409–410, 410*f*
  by young people, 411, 411*f*

W

wages. *See* compensation
Waiting for Superman (documentary film), 375
Walgreens, 443
"wallet biopsies," 446
"Wall Street greed," 185
Wall Street Journal, The, 129, 144
Walmart, 235*f,* 432, 443
  culture of (case study), 75
  sociological perspectives of, 72, 72*t*
war, 406*f. See also specific wars*
  decision to engage in, 414
  deterrents to, 405, 406
  public opinion on, 404, 408
  terrorism, 406–408, *407*
  treatment of traumatic injury, 476–477
  virtual networks used in, 120
Washington, D.C., 256, 272, *463*
Washington State, 350, 422
water pollution, 450, *450*
Watts riots of 1992, 158–159
wealth. *See also* income; income inequality
  in Dubai, 472
  of elderly, in U.S., 318
  inequality in distribution of, 237, 237*f*
  in preindustrial societies, 415
  quality of child care and, 105
  social class and, 211, 211*f*
Webelos Handbook (Boy Scouts of America), 42
Weber, Max, 46, 47, 50
  on bureaucracy, 131–133, 134, 135, 137, 366–367
  classification of authority, 401, 402, *402,* 406, 462

development of sociology and, 11–12, *12,* 13, 14, 15
  on religion and social change, 381–382, *383,* 384
  on of stratification, 203, 204
weblining, 163
web logs (blogs), 120, 154
welfare, 200, 243–245, *244,* 312
"welfare scapegoating," 243
We Live in Public (documentary film), 165
wellness clinics, 445
West Bank, 229*f*
Western Electric Company, 44
West Virginia, 317, 318*f*
We Were Here (film), 29
"What Is Occupy?" (Foroohar), 196
When the Levees Broke (documentary film), 29
Where Am I Wearing? A Global Tour to the Countries, Factories, and People that Make Our Clothes (Timmerman), 4, *4,* 24
white-collar crime, *184,* 184–185
White ethnics, 275, *275*
White privilege, 257–258
Whites, 252*t,* 253*f*
  life expectancies of, 439
  median incomes of, 257*f*
  percentages of, in college, 370*f*
  single-parent families, 338*f*
  trends in college enrollment, 361
white supremacist organizations, 254
WHO (World Health Organization), 446
Whole Foods Market, 432
Who Wants to Be a Millionaire? (TV series), 152
"Why Do Drug Dealers Still Live with Their Moms?" (Levitt), 178
Wicca, 390, 391, *391*
WikiLeaks, 161
Wisconsin, 256
witchcraft, 177
"womb lynchings," 300
women, 10, 441
  bias against, 294
  at disadvantage in networking, 119
  discrimination against, 239, 292, 295, 364
  effects of stereotyping on, 286–287
  excluded from power, 131
  executed for witchcraft, 177
  exploitation of, 293
  feminization of poverty, 213–214, 215*t,* 337
  gender roles, 286–287
  inequality in status of, 46, 241, 292–293, 294*f*
  life expectancies of, 439
  matrix of domination, 290, 290*f*

median incomes of, 257*f*
  in military, *282, 283,* 404
  missing from positions of power, 131
  new HIV/AIDS cases in, 438
  online media and, 154
  opportunities for, divorce and, 344
  as oppressed majority, 292–301
  oppression of, 290, 290*f,* 291, 364–365
  in politics, 292, 410, 412, 412*f*
  rape of, 128, 181, 183, 347
  roles in religion, 382, *382,* 383, 383*t*
  social mobility of, 219, *219*
  success with microfinancing, 425
  superior academic achievement of, 364
  value of unpaid work by, 205, 208
  violence against, 128, 181, 183, 288, 347
!Women Art Revolution (film), 303
women in workforce, 210, 213, 294–297, 337, 419
  on boards of directors, 294–295
  child care policy and, 104–105, *105*
  as child care workers, 105
  compensation issues, 295
  excluded from academic careers, 290
  female physicians, 444, 445, *445*
  feminist perspective on, 333–334
  gender inequality in housework and, 293, 294*f,* 301
  increased numbers of, 421
  labor force participation, 294*f,* 294–295, 295*t*
  in "male" occupations, 116, 294
  men outnumbered by, 210
  preference for male bosses, 296, *296*
  reasons for leaving work, 297, 297*f*
  "second shift," 294*f,* 296, 334
  self-employment difficult for, 219
  social consequences of, 294*f,* 295–297, 297*f*
  women's trade unions, 14
  working mothers, 297
  during World War II, 210, 421
women's liberation movement, 462
women's social movements, 239, 242, 298, 462, 463, 464
Women's Sports Foundation, 364
work, anomie and, 11
work environment, 121, 345
workers
  child care workers, 105
  foreign, 4, 24
  garment workers, 4, *236*
  in informal economy, 420
  occupational mobility of, in China, 419
  preference for male bosses, 296, *296*
workforce
  changes in participation, 467*t*

changing face of, 421, 422, *422*
  exit of minority groups from, 314
  gender stratification in, 294–297
  temporary, dependence on, 202
  women in. *See* women in workforce
working class, 202, 310
working conditions, 4, 419
working mothers, 297
workplace, 102–104, 106
World Bank, 230, 240
World Economic Forum, 153, 153*t*
World Health Organization (WHO), 446
world music, 159–160, *160*
world systems analysis
  of economic systems, 228, 230, 230*f,* 236, 236*t*
  on environmental refugees, 452
  of global warming, 451
  of microfinancing, 425
World Trade Center, 66, 67, *67,* 132, 149
World Trade Organization, 461
World War II, 358
  annihilation of Jews during, 171, 263, 275, 381
  women in workforce, 210, 421
World Wide Web, 76, 136. *See also* Internet
Wrestler, The (film), 109
written rules and regulations, 132, 133*t,* 134, 367

Y

Yahoo!, 49, 337
Yale University, 170–171, *171*
Yanomami people, 329
"yellow peril," 271
Yemen, *93,* 153, 153*t,* 229*f*
Y-ME National Breast Cancer Organization, 298
Young Adult (film), 325
young people
  economic independence of, 345
  socialization to workplace, 102–104, 106
  voting by, 411, 411*f*
YouTube, 151

Z

Zambia, 63*f,* 229*f,* 232
Zapatistas, 464
zebu, 15–16, *16,* 62
Zhu Zhu pet hamsters, 144
Zimbabwe, 200*t,* 229*f,* 232*f*
Zuni tribe, 315